Performing with

Projects for the Entrepreneur:
Microsoft® Office 2007

Iris Blanc
New York City Department of Education

Cathy Vento
Computer Education Consultant

COURSE TECHNOLOGY
CENGAGE Learning™

Australia • Brazil • Japan • Korea • Mexico • Singapore • Spain • United Kingdom • United States

COURSE TECHNOLOGY
CENGAGE Learning™

**Performing with Projects for the Entrepreneur:
Microsoft® Office 2007**
Iris Blanc, Cathy Vento

Contributing Author: Jaime Blanc
Executive Editor: Donna Gridley
Product Manager: Allison O'Meara
Development Editors: Carol Ruhl and Karen Porter
Associate Product Manager: Amanda Lyons
Editorial Assistant: Michelle Camisa
Senior Content Project Manager: Jill Braiewa
Marketing Manager: Valerie Lauer
Marketing Coordinator: Kelley Gilreath
Art Director: Kun-Tee Chang
Director of Manufacturing: Denise Powers
Production Service: Newgen, Chennai
Text Designer: Ann Small
Photo Researcher: Abby Reip
Manuscript Quality Assurance Lead: Jeff Schwartz
Manuscript Quality Assurance Reviewers: John Freitas,
    Serge Palladino, Danielle Shaw, Marianne Snow,
    Teresa Storch, Green Pen QA
Copyeditors: Christine Clark and Jeri Freeman
Proofreaders: Harry Johnson and Vicki Zimmer
Indexer: Rich Carlson
Cover Designer: Nancy Goulet
Cover Image: Ferruccio Sardella
Compositor: Newgen, Chennai

For product information and technology assistance, contact us at,
Cengage Learning Customer & Sales Support, 1-800-354-9706

For permission to use material from this text or product,
submit all requests online at **cengage.com/permissions**
Further permissions questions can be emailed to
permissionrequest@cengage.com

ISBN-13: 978-1-4239-0422-9
ISBN-10: 1-4239-0422-2

Course Technology
25 Thomson Place
Boston, MA 02210
USA

Cengage Learning is a leading provider of customized learning solutions with office locations around the globe, including Singapore, the United Kingdom, Australia, Mexico, Brazil and Japan. Locate your local office at:
international.cengage.com/region

Cengage Learning products are represented in Canada by Nelson Education, Ltd.

For your lifelong learning solutions, visit **course.cengage.com**

Visit our corporate website at **cengage.com**

Printed in the United States of America
1 2 3 4 5 6 7 14 13 12 11 10 09 08

PREFACE

Performing with Projects for the Entrepreneur: Microsoft Office 2007, is part of the *Performing Series* and provides mastery activities that are built around a business theme. The projects apply the skills developed in Word, Excel®, PowerPoint®, and Access™ and have been written to be used with Microsoft® Office 2007. Students complete practical, realistic applications and create materials suitable for portfolio evaluation.

Each tool-specific unit is organized by a series of outcome-based project categories, as follows:

Word
- Correspondence
- Reports and Long Documents
- Meeting Documents and Schedules
- Sales and Marketing Documents

Excel
- Business Forms
- Accounting Records
- Data Analysis
- Financial Reports

PowerPoint
- Informative Presentations
- Sales Presentations
- Persuasive Presentations

Access
- Access Tables and Datasheets
- Access Forms
- Getting Information-Queries
- Access Reports

This text is an innovative approach to applying software skills through a project-based, applied learning process. This approach is unique because it applies Microsoft Office Specialist skills in various work-based contexts. In addition, students apply software and business competencies needed to succeed in the workplace, including critical thinking, analysis, problem solving, and information and resource management. Internet activities are included wherever they are relevant so that students develop research and communication skills. The opportunity to use the skills independently and creatively will enable students to survive and thrive in a high-performance workplace.

OBJECTIVES

Performing with Projects for the Entrepreneur: Microsoft Office 2007 is intended for use as application material after Office skills are developed. The objectives of this book are:

- To apply tool software skills to business projects. (It should be noted that "desktop publishing" skills are applied within the context of the application and Web-related projects are covered within each tool.)
- To use projects to develop SCANS competencies:

  - ✴ Acquire and evaluate data.
  - ✴ Organize and maintain files.
  - ✴ Interpret and communicate information.
  - ✴ Apply technology to specific tasks.
  - ✴ Apply critical thinking and problem solving.
  - ✴ Work with members of a team.

- To provide a text that may be used in conjunction with the Performing Series or that may be used to supplement any instructional text on Microsoft Office.

When students complete a computer applications course using this text, they will develop Microsoft Office Specialist skills and workplace competencies.

ORGANIZATION OF THE TEXT

Projects for the Entrepreneur contains two parts:

Part I is divided into sections by Office tool (Word, Excel, PowerPoint, and Access). The following chart outlines the organization and numbering system for Part I.

Office Tool Section	Chapter Number	Project Number	Total Number of Applications
Sections are indicated by tool-specific color tabs on the right edge of the page.	Chapters are organized by project categories: Correspondence, Data Analysis, etc.	Projects are organized by skill sets covered.	Each project contains numerous applications (see Table of Contents).
Word	Chapters 1–6	Projects 1–16	74
Excel	Chapters 1–6	Projects 1–24	62
PowerPoint	Chapters 1–6	Projects 1–8	27
Access	Chapters 1–6	Projects 1–18	44

Each section contains:

- Numerous projects that apply tool-specific concepts.
- A final integration chapter that integrates the tool with those learned previously.

Each project contains:

- The Office skill sets applied in the project.
- Numerous applications that apply the project skills.
- A business scenario that provides a rationale for the application.
- "What You Need to Know" information related to the software and to the overall project.
- Clear directions to complete the project.
- Illustrations and model solutions.

Each project produces tangible results that represent actual professional documents within the chapter category. These documents provide a framework and a reference for students as they complete Part II.

A total of 207 projects are included in Part I.

Part II provides integrated simulation projects built around a business theme. In this part of the text, students will apply all the tool-specific and document skills they have learned in Part I to authentic business situations.

- Each project starts with a project description page, which will explain the business problem and list the documents that students must produce to achieve the project objectives. These projects may be used as portfolio work samples.
- The following integrated simulation projects are included in Part II:

  - ✳ Organizing a Business Trip
  - ✳ New Employee Orientation
  - ✳ Starting a New Business

HOW TO USE THIS BOOK

This book is correlated to *Performing with Microsoft Office 2007*; however it may be used with any computer applications text, or as a stand-alone text. If you are using *Performing with Microsoft Office 2007*, you may assign the projects in Part I after teaching the related lesson. If you are using another text for Office 2007, you may assign the projects in Part I after teaching the basic skill sets outlined below each project title. The capstone projects contained in Part II may be assigned after teaching all the Office tools. This text goes beyond teaching the mechanics of the software. It allows students to critically think and develop literacy skills as they apply technology to tasks. It also enables them to understand how technology is used in college and in the workplace.

Note: At the time of publication, the URLs noted in this book were functional and accurate based on thorough editing and testing. If, during the course of life of this text, the URLs referenced in these pages change, it is beyond the control of the publisher, and the instructor will have to make allowances within the exercises.

SPECIAL FEATURES

- **Data files** (found on the Instructor's Resource Kit CD-ROM and on the Review Pack CD) allow learners to complete many of the activities without keyboarding lengthy text.
- **An Exercise Log** lists filenames alphabetically with corresponding lesson numbers.
- **Portfolio-building projects**
- **Appendices** that include the following:
  - ✶ Portfolio Checklist
  - ✶ Proofreader's Marks
  - ✶ Ways to Cite from Source Material
  - ✶ Rubric for an Oral Report and PowerPoint Presentation Developed from Scratch
- **Instructor's Resource Kit CD-ROM** includes lesson plans, data files, and solution files.

ACKNOWLEDGEMENTS

Many people play a role in the production of a quality book, and we owe them our gratitude and appreciation. First and foremost among them are Donna Gridley, Executive Editor; Allison O'Meara, Product Manager; Amanda Lyons, Associate Product Manger; and especially to Carol Ruhl and Karen Porter, Development Editors, for their professionalism, guidance, and support through this project.

Our heartfelt thanks go to those who have made significant contributions and assisted us with the production of this book:

- To the production team at Newgen Imaging and to Arunesh Shukla.
- To the Manufacturing Quality Assurance team and to Jeff Schwartz.
- To our contributing writer: Jaime Blanc, thank you for your creative input and assistance.
- To our families for their love, their encouragement, their inspiration, and above all for their patience.

Iris Blanc
Cathy Vento

ABOUT THE AUTHORS

Iris Blanc is the founding Director of Virtual Enterprises, International, a program of the New York City Department of Education that has drawn national attention as an applied learning instructional model for business, economics, finance, and career education. Formerly, Ms. Blanc was assistant principal/department chair of Business Education at Tottenville High School, a New York City public high school. Ms. Blanc has taught business education and computer applications at the high school and college levels for over 30 years. Ms. Blanc conducts seminars, workshops, and short courses in applied learning strategies and methods of teaching and integrating technology at conferences nationwide.

Catherine Vento is currently working as a computer trainer for the New Jersey Human Resources Development Division. She was formerly the assistant principal/department chair of Business Education at Susan Wagner High School, a New York City public high school, and worked as a consultant for the Board of Education. Ms. Vento has taught business education, accounting, and computer applications at the high school level. She has presented seminars, workshops, and mini-courses at conferences, colleges, and business schools nationwide on Office applications and on integrating business, critical thinking, and software skills.

Ms. Blanc and Ms. Vento have co-authored numerous computer application texts and reference guides for over 20 years. The Performing series represents their combined pedagogical talents in an innovative approach to develop workplace skills and competencies. Over their many years as educators and authors, they have discovered that students learn best what they need to know!

EXCEL

CHAPTER 6

Create Charts and Graphics/Integration

Lesson Outcome

Indicates the workplace-related goal

In this chapter, you will complete the following projects:

PROJECT 21
Chart Sales Data
PROJECT 21.1 Chart Sales Data
PROJECT 21.2 Chart and Analyze Sales Data

PROJECT 22
Chart Expense Data
PROJECT 22.1 Chart Expense Data
PROJECT 22.2 Chart and Analyze Expense Data

PROJECT 23
Chart Investment Data
PROJECT 23.1 Chart Mutual Fund Data
PROJECT 23.2 Add Graphics to a Mutual Fund Report
PROJECT 23.3 Chart Stock Prices

PROJECT 24
Integrate Charts and Worksheets into Documents
PROJECT 24.1 Paste a Worksheet into a Memorandum
PROJECT 24.2 Embed Worksheets into a Business Plan
PROJECT 24.3 Embed a Chart and a Worksheet into a Bulletin
PROJECT 24.4 Link Charts and Worksheets into an Annual Report

Lesson Skills Sets

Lists the goal-related projects to be accomplished

Part I: Tool-Specific Projects

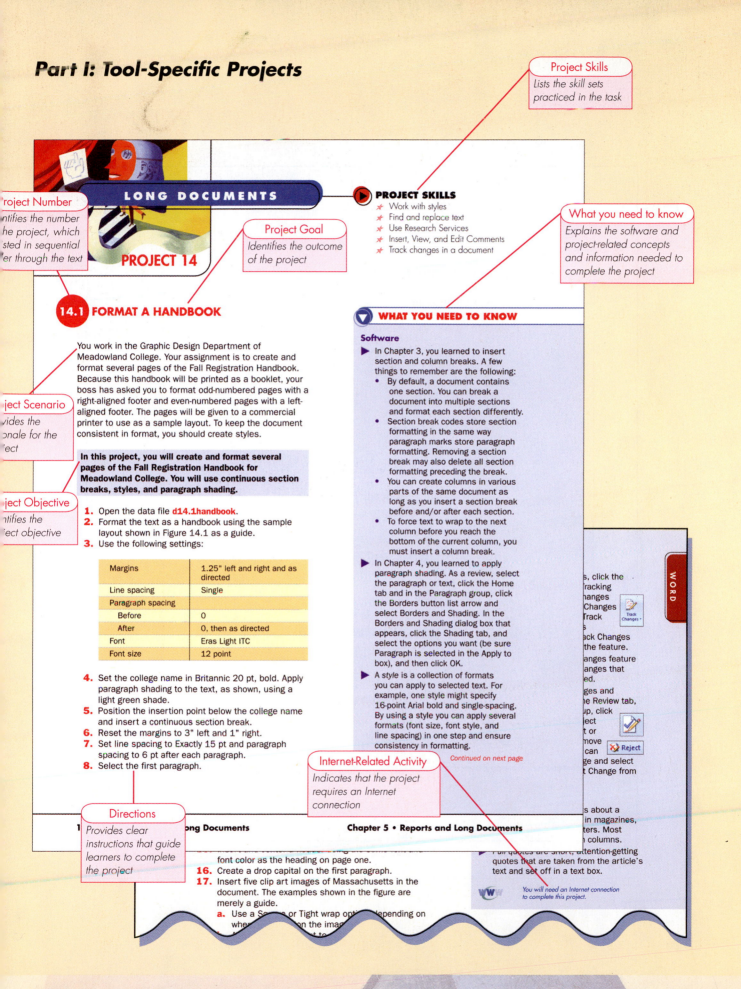

LONG DOCUMENTS

PROJECT 14

14.1 FORMAT A HANDBOOK

You work in the Graphic Design Department of Meadowland College. Your assignment is to create and format several pages of the Fall Registration Handbook. Because this handbook will be printed as a booklet, your boss has asked you to format odd-numbered pages with a right-aligned footer and even-numbered pages with a left-aligned footer. The pages will be given to a commercial printer to use as a sample layout. To keep the document consistent in format, you should create styles.

In this project, you will create and format several pages of the Fall Registration Handbook for Meadowland College. You will use continuous section breaks, styles, and paragraph shading.

1. Open the data file **d14.1handbook**.
2. Format the text as a handbook using the sample layout shown in Figure 14.1 as a guide.
3. Use the following settings:

Margins	1.25" left and right and as directed
Line spacing	Single
Paragraph spacing	
Before	0
After	0, then as directed
Font	Eras Light ITC
Font size	12 point

4. Set the college name in Britannic 20 pt, bold. Apply paragraph shading to the text, as shown, using a light green shade.
5. Position the insertion point below the college name and insert a continuous section break.
6. Reset the margins to 3" left and 1" right.
7. Set line spacing to Exactly 15 pt and paragraph spacing to 6 pt after each paragraph.
8. Select the first paragraph.

Callouts

Project Skills
Lists the skill sets practiced in the task

Project Number
Identifies the number of the project, which is listed in sequential order through the text

Project Goal
Identifies the outcome of the project

What you need to know
Explains the software and project-related concepts and information needed to complete the project

Project Scenario
Provides the rationale for the project

Project Objective
Identifies the project objective

Directions
Provides clear instructions that guide learners to complete the project

Internet-Related Activity
Indicates that the project requires an Internet connection

PROJECT SKILLS
- Work with styles
- Find and replace text
- Use Research Services
- Insert, View, and Edit Comments
- Track changes in a document

WHAT YOU NEED TO KNOW

Software

▶ In Chapter 3, you learned to insert section and column breaks. A few things to remember are the following:
- By default, a document contains one section. You can break a document into multiple sections and format each section differently.
- Section break codes store section formatting in the same way paragraph marks store paragraph formatting. Removing a section break may also delete all section formatting preceding the break.
- You can create columns in various parts of the same document as long as you insert a section break before and/or after each section.
- To force text to wrap to the next column before you reach the bottom of the current column, you must insert a column break.

▶ In Chapter 4, you learned to apply paragraph shading. As a review, select the paragraph or text, click the Home tab and in the Paragraph group, click the Borders button list arrow and select Borders and Shading. In the Borders and Shading dialog box that appears, click the Shading tab, and select the options you want (be sure Paragraph is selected in the Apply to box), and then click OK.

▶ A *style* is a collection of formats you can apply to selected text. For example, one style might specify 16-point Arial bold and single-spacing. By using a style you can apply several formats (font size, font style, and line spacing) in one step and ensure consistency in formatting.

Continued on next page

WORD

...s, click the ...Tracking ...Changes ...Changes ...Track

...ack Changes ...the feature.

...anges feature ...anges that ...ed.

...ges and ...e Review tab, ...up, click ...ject ...t or ...move ...can ...ge and select ...t Change from

...s about a ...in magazines, ...ers. Most ...columns.

▶ Pull quotes are short, attention-getting quotes that are taken from the article's text and set off in a text box.

You will need an Internet connection to complete this project.

...ong Documents   **Chapter 5 • Reports and Long Documents**

...font color as the heading on page one.
16. Create a drop capital on the first paragraph.
17. Insert five clip art images of Massachusetts in the document. The examples shown in the figure are merely a guide.
   a. Use a Square or Tight wrap option, depending on where...on the image.

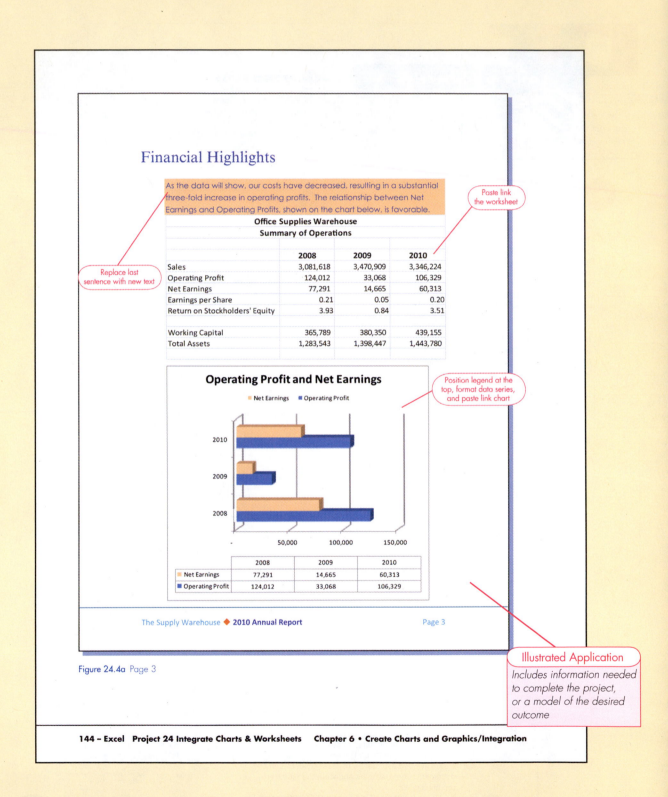

Financial Highlights

As the data will show, our costs have decreased, resulting in a substantial three-fold increase in operating profits. The relationship between Net Earnings and Operating Profits, shown on the chart below, is favorable.

Replace last sentence with new text

Paste link the worksheet

Office Supplies Warehouse
Summary of Operations

	2008	2009	2010
Sales	3,081,618	3,470,909	3,346,224
Operating Profit	124,012	33,068	106,329
Net Earnings	77,291	14,665	60,313
Earnings per Share	0.21	0.05	0.20
Return on Stockholders' Equity	3.93	0.84	3.51
Working Capital	365,789	380,350	439,155
Total Assets	1,283,543	1,398,447	1,443,780

Operating Profit and Net Earnings

■ Net Earnings   ■ Operating Profit

Position legend at the top, format data series, and paste link chart

	2008	2009	2010
■ Net Earnings	77,291	14,665	60,313
■ Operating Profit	124,012	33,068	106,329

The Supply Warehouse ◆ 2010 Annual Report   Page 3

Figure 24.4a Page 3

Illustrated Application

Includes information needed to complete the project, or a model of the desired outcome

144 – Excel   Project 24 Integrate Charts & Worksheets   Chapter 6 • Create Charts and Graphics/Integration

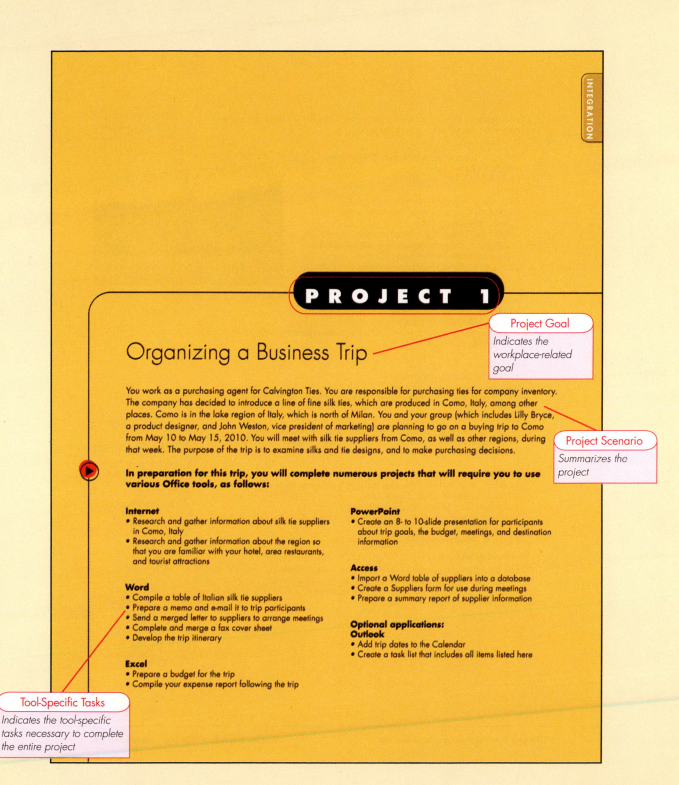

INTEGRATION

PROJECT 1

Organizing a Business Trip

Project Goal
Indicates the workplace-related goal

You work as a purchasing agent for Calvington Ties. You are responsible for purchasing ties for company inventory. The company has decided to introduce a line of fine silk ties, which are produced in Como, Italy, among other places. Como is in the lake region of Italy, which is north of Milan. You and your group (which includes Lilly Bryce, a product designer, and John Weston, vice president of marketing) are planning to go on a buying trip to Como from May 10 to May 15, 2010. You will meet with silk tie suppliers from Como, as well as other regions, during that week. The purpose of the trip is to examine silks and tie designs, and to make purchasing decisions.

Project Scenario
Summarizes the project

In preparation for this trip, you will complete numerous projects that will require you to use various Office tools, as follows:

Internet
- Research and gather information about silk tie suppliers in Como, Italy
- Research and gather information about the region so that you are familiar with your hotel, area restaurants, and tourist attractions

Word
- Compile a table of Italian silk tie suppliers
- Prepare a memo and e-mail it to trip participants
- Send a merged letter to suppliers to arrange meetings
- Complete and merge a fax cover sheet
- Develop the trip itinerary

Excel
- Prepare a budget for the trip
- Compile your expense report following the trip

PowerPoint
- Create an 8- to 10-slide presentation for participants about trip goals, the budget, meetings, and destination information

Access
- Import a Word table of suppliers into a database
- Create a Suppliers form for use during meetings
- Prepare a summary report of supplier information

Optional applications:
Outlook
- Add trip dates to the Calendar
- Create a task list that includes all items listed here

Tool-Specific Tasks
Indicates the tool-specific tasks necessary to complete the entire project

VI. ITINERARY

You must create an itinerary so that all parties will know the schedule of the trip. The information you will need is noted below.

Scenario

Introduces the business problem

- May 10
  8:00 p.m. Depart Kennedy Airport, Alitalia Airlines, Flight #222 to Milan

- May 11
  8:30 a.m. Arrive Milan International Airport
  10:00 a.m. Train from Milan International Airport to Milano Centrale in Milan
  12:00 noon. Leave from Milano Centrale, Train #2020, to Como S. Giovanni station. Take taxi to Barchetta Excelsior Hotel, Piazza Cavour 1, Como
  8:00 p.m. Dinner at Ristorante Barchetta with Carlo Bertolucci, sales representative

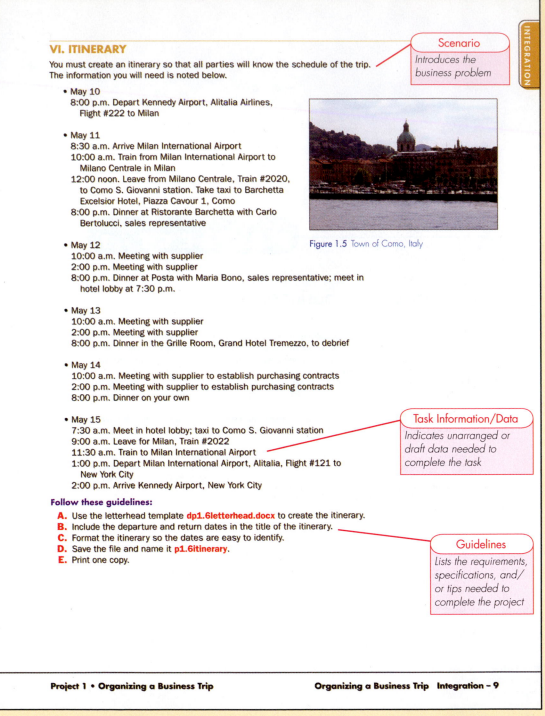

Figure 1.5 Town of Como, Italy

- May 12
  10:00 a.m. Meeting with supplier
  2:00 p.m. Meeting with supplier
  8:00 p.m. Dinner at Posta with Maria Bono, sales representative; meet in hotel lobby at 7:30 p.m.

- May 13
  10:00 a.m. Meeting with supplier
  2:00 p.m. Meeting with supplier
  8:00 p.m. Dinner in the Grille Room, Grand Hotel Tremezzo, to debrief

- May 14
  10:00 a.m. Meeting with supplier to establish purchasing contracts
  2:00 p.m. Meeting with supplier to establish purchasing contracts
  8:00 p.m. Dinner on your own

- May 15
  7:30 a.m. Meet in hotel lobby; taxi to Como S. Giovanni station
  9:00 a.m. Leave for Milan, Train #2022
  11:30 a.m. Train to Milan International Airport
  1:00 p.m. Depart Milan International Airport, Alitalia, Flight #121 to New York City
  2:00 p.m. Arrive Kennedy Airport, New York City

Task Information/Data

Indicates unarranged or draft data needed to complete the task

Follow these guidelines:

A. Use the letterhead template **dp1.6letterhead.docx** to create the itinerary.
B. Include the departure and return dates in the title of the itinerary.
C. Format the itinerary so the dates are easy to identify.
D. Save the file and name it **p1.6itinerary**.
E. Print one copy.

Guidelines

Lists the requirements, specifications, and/ or tips needed to complete the project

START-UP CHECKLIST

Minimum Hardware Configuration

- PC with Pentium processor
- Hard disk with 400 MB free for typical installation
- CD-ROM drive, or access to network drive for downloading and saving Data and Solution Files
- Monitor set at 800 × 600 or higher resolution. If your resolution differs, you will see differences in the Ribbon, and may have to scroll up or down to view the information on your screen.
- Printer
- Internet connection. If you are not connected to the Internet, see your instructor.

Software Installation

This book was written and tested using the following settings:

- A typical installation of Microsoft Office 2007
- Microsoft Windows Vista running with Aero off
- Microsoft Internet Explorer 7 browser

TABLE OF CONTENTS

PART I: TOOL-SPECIFIC PROJECTS

WORD

CHAPTER 1 Word Basics 3
PROJECT 1 Basic Editing Review 4
PROJECT 2 Basic Formatting Review 12

CHAPTER 2 Correspondence 23
PROJECT 3 Format Business and Personal Documents....................................24
PROJECT 4 Use Templates................................36
PROJECT 5 Compose and E-Mail Documents; Use Basic Mail Merge 44

CHAPTER 3 Lists, Meeting Documents, Schedules, and Forms 55
PROJECT 6 Documents for a Meeting................56
PROJECT 7 Schedules, Programs, and Forms.......70

CHAPTER 4 Sales and Marketing Documents....................... 89
PROJECT 8 Flyers and Advertisements...............90
PROJECT 9 Invitations and Menus 108
PROJECT 10 Newsletters 120
PROJECT 11 Brochures and Catalogs...............130

CHAPTER 5 Reports and Long Documents....................... 143
PROJECT 12 Multiple-page Letters 144
PROJECT 13 Reports.....................................154
PROJECT 14 Long Documents.........................166

CHAPTER 6 Integration/Word and the Web 181
PROJECT 15 Work with Integrated Files 182
PROJECT 16 Work with the Web 188

EXCEL

CHAPTER 1 Learn Excel Basics 3
PROJECT 1 Enter, Proof, and Print Data 4
PROJECT 2 Enter and Edit Formulas 10
PROJECT 3 Enhance and Edit Worksheet
Data 16

CHAPTER 2 Create Business Forms/
Work with Templates.......... 21
PROJECT 4 Purchase Orders 22
PROJECT 5 Sales Invoices 28
PROJECT 6 Work with Templates 32

CHAPTER 3 Create Accounting
Records........................... 41
PROJECT 7 Ledger Accounts and
Statements.....................42
PROJECT 8 Payroll....................................48
PROJECT 9 Journals 52
PROJECT 10 Asset Records..............................58

CHAPTER 4 Create Data Analysis
Worksheets....................... 65
PROJECT 11 Budgets 66
PROJECT 12 Billings and Listings Tables 70
PROJECT 13 Income Statements 74
PROJECT 14 Sales, Revenue, and Investment
Analyses 80

CHAPTER 5 Create Financial Reports 89
PROJECT 15 Trial Balance 90
PROJECT 16 Salary Analyses...............................94
PROJECT 17 Accounting Worksheets 98
PROJECT 18 Income Statement 102
PROJECT 19 Balance Sheet 106
PROJECT 20 Financial Report Analysis 110

CHAPTER 6 Create Charts and
Graphics/Integration 115
PROJECT 21 Chart Sales Data 116
PROJECT 22 Chart Expense Data.....................120
PROJECT 23 Chart Investment Data................128
PROJECT 24 Integrate Charts and Worksheets
into Documents 134

POWERPOINT

CHAPTER 1 PowerPoint Basics................ 3
PROJECT 1 Navigation, Views, Page Setup Options,
and Creating a Presentation 4

CHAPTER 2 Informative Presentations 13
PROJECT 2 Create and Enhance Informative
Presentations 14

CHAPTER 3 Sales and Marketing
Presentations..................... 29
PROJECT 3 Create and Enhance Sales
Presentations 30

CHAPTER 4 Persuasive Presentations 51
PROJECT 4 Create Persuasive Presentations........52

CHAPTER 5 Collaborating on and
Delivering Presentations 71
PROJECT 5 Collaborating on and Delivering
Presentations 72

CHAPTER 6 Integration/PowerPoint
and the Web 83
PROJECT 6 Integration/Powerpoint
and the Web 84

ACCESS

CHAPTER 1 Access Basics.....................3
PROJECT 1 Explore a Database 4
PROJECT 2 Understand Database Design
and Views 10

CHAPTER 2 Access Tables and
Datasheets.......................15
PROJECT 3 Create a Table with Table
Templates 16
PROJECT 4 Create Tables and Enter Data 22
PROJECT 5 Enhance Tables and Create
Relationships...............................26

CHAPTER 3 Access Forms 37
PROJECT 6 Create and Use Forms 38
PROJECT 7 Edit and Enhance Forms 44
PROJECT 8 Create a Database Table and Form
Using Calculated Controls..............48

CHAPTER 4 Getting Information............53
PROJECT 9 Find, Replace, and Filter Data..........54
PROJECT 10 Query a Database Using Wizards ...60
PROJECT 11 Query a Database in
Design View 66
PROJECT 12 Review Relationships and
Create Multi-Table Queries...........70

CHAPTER 5 Access Reports 77
PROJECT 13 Create Reports with Wizards 78
PROJECT 14 Modify Reports............................84
PROJECT 15 Create Database Objects and
Reports 90

CHAPTER 6 Integration 95
PROJECT 16 Import Data 96
PROJECT 17 Export Data................................102
PROJECT 18 Maintain the Database 106

PART II: INTEGRATED SIMULATION PROJECTS

PROJECT 1 Organizing a
Business Trip......................3

PROJECT 2 New Employee
Orientation........................15

PROJECT 3 Starting a New
Business............................27

APPENDICES

APPENDIX A Portfolio Basics 2

APPENDIX B Proofreader's Marks...........5

APPENDIX C Way to Cite from
Source Material.................7

APPENDIX D Rubric for an Oral
Report and PowerPoint
Presentation Developed
from Scratch 8

EXERCISE LOG

WORD CHAPTERS 1–6

Project Number	Title	Skill Level	Page Reference
1.1	Open a Document, Insert and Correct Text	B	WD4
1.2	Insert and Delete Text; Show/Hide Codes; Use Zoom	B	WD6
1.3	Move and Copy Text; Collect and Paste Multiple Items	B	WD8
1.4	Compose Your Autobiography	I	WD10
1.5	Compose a Thank You Communication	B	WD11
2.1	Change Font Attributes; Set Text Alignments; Use Symbols	B	WD12
2.2	Copy Formatting	B	WD14
2.3	Edit Formatting	B	WD16
2.4	Edit Formatting	B	WD18
2.5	Edit Formatting	B	WD20
3.1	Format a Business Letter and Envelope	B	WD24
3.2	Format a Business Letter with Special Notations	B	WD27
3.3	Format and Edit a Business Letter; Prepare Mailing Labels; Use Quick Parts	B	WD29
3.4	Finalize a Business Letter	B	WD31
3.5	Format a Personal Business Letter	B	WD33
4.1	Create a Memorandum	B	WD36
4.2	Create a Business Letter	B	WD38
4.3	Create a Résumé	B	WD40
4.4	Create a Custom Fax Cover and Letterhead Template	B	WD42
5.1	Compose and Format Your Own Résumé	B	WD44
5.2	Compose and E-Mail a Business Letter	B	WD45
5.3	Compose and E-Mail a Personal Business Letter with an Attachment	B	WD47
5.4	Create a Mass Mailing	I	WD49
5.5	Create a Mass Mailing and Labels to Selected Recipients	A	WD51
6.1	Create an Agenda	B	WD56
6.2	Create an Agenda; Create and Sort a List	B	WD59
6.3	Create an Agenda Using a Table Format	B	WD61
6.4	Format Minutes of a Meeting	I	WD64
6.5	Create a Memo with an Inserted Outline	I	WD67
7.1	Create an Itinerary	I	WD70
7.2	Create an Activities Schedule	I	WD72
7.3	Create a Rate Schedule	I	WD74
7.4	Create a Records List	I	WD76
7.5	Format a Project Schedule	I	WD78

7.6	Create a Program	I	WD79
7.7	Format a Program	I	WD81
7.8	Create a Calendar	I	WD83
7.9	Create a Table of Contents	I	WD85
7.10	Create a Form	I	WD87
8.1	Create a Simple Flyer	B	WD90
8.2	Design a Flyer with Special Effects	I	WD92
8.3	Create a Flyer with a Tear-Off	I	WD94
8.4	Format a Flyer	I	WD97
8.5	Create an Advertisement	I	WD99
8.6	Create a Direct-Mail Advertisement	A	WD102
8.7	Format an Advertisement	A	WD105
9.1	Create a Corporate Dining Menu	I	WD108
9.2	Create a Restaurant Menu	I	WD110
9.3	Design a Menu	A	WD114
9.4	Create an Invitation	A	WD116
9.5	Design an Invitation	I	WD118
10.1	Create a Newsletter	A	WD120
10.2	Create a Newsletter with a Mailer	A	WD123
10.3	Format a Newsletter	A	WD127
11.1	Create a Brochure for an Event	A	WD130
11.2	Create a Product Brochure	A	WD134
11.3	Create a Brochure Using a Template	A	WD137
11.4	Create a Catalog	A	WD139
12.1	Format a Two-Page Business Letter	I	WD144
12.2	Format a Multiple-Page Business Letter with Indented Paragraphs	I	WD147
12.3	Edit and Format a Multiple-Page Business Letter	I	WD151
13.1	Format a Report with Internal Citations	I	WD154
13.2	Format a Report with Citations; Prepare a Cover Page and Bibliography	A	WD157
13.3	Format a Report with Footnotes and Endnotes; Prepare a Cover Page	A	WD162
13.4	Research, Write, and Format a Report	A	WD165
14.1	Format a Handbook	I	WD166
14.2	Create an Article, Use Comments, and Track Changes	I	WD170
14.3	Format a Business Plan	I	WD174
14.4	Format an Annual Report	I	WD176
15.1	Create a Report with an Embedded Table	A	WD182
15.2	Create a Memo with a Linked Table; Use Document Properties	A	WD185
16.1	Save a Document as a Web Page	A	WD188
16.2	Create a Web Page Using a Template	A	WD192
16.3	Create a Website	A	WD194

EXCEL CHAPTERS 1–6

Project Number	Title	Skill Level	Page Reference
1.1	Create an Invoice for Professional Services	B	EX4
1.2	Preview and Print an Invoice for Professional Services	B	EX6
1.3	Create and Proof an Invoice from an Existing File	B	EX8
2.1	Create a Personnel Plan	B	EX10
2.2	Format a Personnel Plan	B	EX12
2.3	Arrange and Format a Personnel Plan	B	EX14
3.1	Create a Projected Cash Flow Statement	B	EX16

3.2	Format a Projected Cash Flow Statement	B	EX18
4.1	Create a Purchase Order	B	EX22
4.2	Modify and Enhance a Purchase Order	B	EX24
4.3	Create and Format a Purchase Order	B	EX26
5.1	Create a Sales Invoice	B	EX28
5.2	Create and Format a Sales Invoice	B	EX30
6.1	Create and Use a Sales Invoice Template	B	EX32
6.2	Use a Time Card Template	B	EX34
6.3	Use a Sales Invoice Template	B	EX36
6.4	Use a Price Quotation Template	B	EX38
7.1	Create an Accounts Receivable Ledger Account	I	EX42
7.2	Create an Accounts Payable Ledger Account	I	EX44
7.3	Create a Statement of Account	I	EX46
8.1	Create a Payroll	I	EX48
8.2	Use a Payroll Template and Internet Tax Calculators	I	EX50
9.1	Create a Sales Journal	I	EX52
9.2	Create a Purchase Journal	I	EX54
9.3	Create a Check Register and Payments Journal	I	EX56
10.1	Create a Petty Cash Register	I	EX58
10.2	Create an Asset Record	I	EX60
10.3	Create an Aging Report	I	EX62
11.1	Create a Budget	I	EX66
11.2	Format a Budget	I	EX68
12.1	Create a Billings Analysis Table	I	EX70
12.2	Create a Listings Analysis Table	I	EX72
13.1	Create and Analyze an Income Statement	A	EX74
13.2	Save a Workbook as a Web Page	I	EX76
13.3	Create and Publish an Income Statement Analysis	A	EX78
14.1	Create a Sales Analysis	A	EX80
14.2	Create a Billings and Revenue Analysis	A	EX82
14.3	Create a Revenue Forecast and Analysis	A	EX84
14.4	Create an Investment Analysis	A	EX86
15.1	Complete a Trial Balance and Schedules	I	EX90
15.2	Create a Trial Balance and Schedules with Hyperlinks	A	EX92
16.1	Create a Sales and Commissions Report	A	EX94
16.2	Create an Analysis of Salary Increases	A	EX96
17.1	Complete an Accounting Worksheet	A	EX98
17.2	Complete an Accounting Worksheet with Hyperlinks	A	EX100
18.1	Create an Income Statement Analysis	A	EX102
18.2	Create a Quarterly Income Statement Analysis	A	EX104
19.1	Create a Balance Sheet	I	EX106
19.2	Format a Balance Sheet	I	EX108
20.1	Analyze Income Statement Data	A	EX110
20.2	Analyze Balance Sheet Data	A	EX112
21.1	Chart Sales Data	I	EX116
21.2	Chart and Analyze Sales Data	A	EX118
22.1	Chart Expense Data	I	EX120
22.2	Chart and Analyze Expense Data	A	EX123
23.1	Chart Mutual Fund Data	I	EX128
23.2	Add Graphics to a Mutual Fund Report	I	EX130
23.3	Chart Stock Prices	I	EX132

24.1	Paste a Worksheet into a Memorandum	I	EX134
24.2	Embed Worksheets into a Business Plan	I	EX136
24.3	Embed a Chart and a Worksheet into a Bulletin	A	EX139
24.4	Link Charts and Worksheets into an Annual Report	A	EX141

POWERPOINT CHAPTERS 1–6

Project Number	Title	Skill Level	Page Reference
1.1	Open a Presentation; Navigate a Presentation; Change Views	B	PP4
1.2	Change Orientation and Page Setup Options; Move, Copy, Duplicate, and Delete Slides	B	PP7
1.3	Evaluate a Slide Show	B	PP8
1.4	Create a Presentation	B	PP9
2.1	Create and Print a Presentation	B	PP14
2.2	Enhance a Presentation	I	PP18
2.3	Edit and Enhance a Presentation	I	PP21
2.4	Create and Print a Presentation as an Outline	I	PP23
2.5	Develop a Presentation from Scratch	I	PP27
3.1	Enhance a Presentation	I	PP30
3.2	Create and Enhance a Presentation That Sells a Product	I	PP35
3.3	Create a Presentation That Sells a Service	I	PP39
3.4	Create and Enhance a Presentation Using Tables and Charts	A	PP43
3.5	Create a Presentation from Scratch	A	PP48
4.1	Create and Enhance a Presentation Using Charts, SmartArt, and Media	A	PP52
4.2	Use a Template to Create a Presentation from Scratch	A	PP56
4.3	Create and Enhance a Presentation Using Charts, SmartArt, and Media	A	PP62
4.4	Enhance Presentations with Animated Charts and SmartArt	A	PP66
4.5	Create a Photo Album	A	PP68
5.1	Prepare and Enhance Audience Materials	A	PP72
5.2	Prepare a Presentation for a Kiosk	A	PP76
5.3	Add, Edit, Delete, and Print Comments	A	PP79
5.4	Prepare a Presentation to Travel	A	PP81
6.1	Insert a Slide from Another Presentation	A	PP84
6.2	Export a Slide and a Presentation to Word	A	PP87
6.3	Insert an Excel Chart, an Excel Worksheet, and a Word Table	A	PP89
6.4	E-Mail a Presentation; Save and Preview a Presentation as a Web Page	A	PP92

ACCESS CHAPTERS 1–6

Project Number	Title	Skill Level	Page Reference
1.1	Explore Tables and Forms	B	AC4
1.2	Explore Queries and Reports	B	AC7
2.1	Explore Table and Form Views	B	AC10
2.2	Explore Query and Report Views	B	AC13
3.1	Create a Tasks Table	B	AC16
3.2	Create a Contacts Table for Customers	B	AC19
4.1	Create a Student Table in Datasheet View	B	AC22
4.2	Create an Inventory Table in Design View	B	AC24
5.1	Create a Member Table with a Lookup Field	I	AC26
5.2	Add Input Masks to a Students Table	I	AC28
5.3	Add Input Masks to a Customers Table	I	AC30

5.4	Create and Format a Property Listings Table with an Input Mask and Lookup Fields	I	AC32
5.5	Create and Print Relationships Between Inventory and Vendor Tables		AC34
6.1	Create a Movie Collection Form	I	AC38
6.2	Create a Customer Form Using a Split Form and the Form Wizard	I	AC40
6.3	Enter, Edit, and Delete Records in Student Forms	I	AC42
7.1	Edit an Inventory Form Design	I	AC44
7.2	Create a Members Form Using Design and Layout Views	I	AC46
8.1	Create a Property Listing Form with a Calculated Control	I	AC48
8.2	Create Forms and Add a Calculated Control		AC51
9.1	Find and Replace Student Data	I	AC54
9.2	Sort Movie Collection Data	I	AC56
9.3	Apply and Remove Filters on Inventory Data	I	AC58
10.1	Query Customer Data Using Wizards	I	AC60
10.2	Query Movie Data with Calculations	I	AC62
10.3	Create Duplicate and Unmatched Queries on Inventory Data	A	AC64
11.1	Query Student Data in Query Design View	I	AC66
11.2	Add a Calculated Field to an Inventory Query	A	AC68
12.1	Create a New Table, Relationship, and Queries for Students	I	AC70
12.2	Edit Relationships and Create Queries in an Inventory Database	I	AC73
13.1	Use the Report and Report Wizard Buttons: Customer Database	A	AC78
13.2	Use the Label Wizard: Members Database	A	AC80
13.3	Use the Report Wizard: Student Database	A	AC82
14.1	Use Report Sections and Modify a Listings Report	A	AC84
14.2	Add Calculated Controls and New Objects: Members Database	A	AC86
14.3	Create and Modify Inventory Reports	A	AC88
15.1	Add Objects to the Members Database	A	AC90
16.1	Import a Movie Collection Table	A	AC96
16.2	Import a Customer Spreadsheet	A	AC98
16.3	Import a Word Contact List	A	AC100
17.1	Export the Classes Table to Excel	A	AC102
17.2	Export a Memorabilia Query to Word	A	AC104
18.1	Back Up and Compact and Repair a Database	A	AC106
18.2	Update and Modify the Listings Database	A	AC108

DIRECTORY OF DOCUMENTS
and
PORTFOLIO WORK SAMPLES

DIRECTORY OF DOCUMENTS

The document types indicated on the left can be found on the pages noted on the right.

Document Type .... Page Number

Activities schedule .... WD, p. 72
Advertisement ....WD, p. 12, 16, 18, 89–91,
.... 99, 100, 102, 105, 114
Agenda ....WD, p. 55–57, 59, 61, 62,
.... 64, 67, 79, 185, 186
Aging report... EX, p. 41, 62
Analyses .... EX, p. 65, 80, 89, 94, 110, 112
Annual report .... WD, p. 143, 176
....EX, p. 115, 141–143
Asset record .... EX, p. 41, 58, 60
Audience materials...................................PP. p. 71, 72
Autobiography .... WD, p. 3, 10
Balance sheet .... EX, p. 89, 98, 100, 106, 108,
....112, 136, 142, 143
Brochure ....WD, p. 89, 130, 132–138
Budget................................ EX, p. 65, 66, 68, 69, 74
Bulletin..................................... EX, p. 115, 139
Business letter .... WD, p. 23, 24, 27, 29, 31, 33,
.... 38, 45, 47, 74, 143, 144, 147, 151
Business plan...................................... WD, p. 143, 174
Calendar .... WD, p. 38, 55, 83, 87
Catalog ....WD, p. 51, 52, 89, 130, 139–142, 167
Chart...............................EX, p. 115, 120, 22–126,
....128–134, 139–144
E-mail ....WD, p. 23, 25, 27, 33, 44–47, 49, 51, 67,
....................74, 75, 118, 185, 188, 189, 192, 194
Fax cover sheet............................... WD, p. 23, 42, 162
Filter.................... AC, p. 4, 53, 54, 56, 58, 59, 71, 84
Flyer..WD, p. 89–92, 94, 95, 97
Forecast.. EX, p. 65, 84
Form.................... AC, p. 3–6, 10, 22, 37–42, 44–52,
.... 56, 58, 70, 71, 90, 92, 93, 96, 100

Document Type .... Page Number

Handbook.................. WD, p. 85, 143, 166, 167, 188
Income statement ....EX, p. 65, 66, 68, 74–79,
.... 89, 98–100, 102–104, 110, 123, 136
Invitation .... WD, p. 89, 116, 118, 130
Invoice.......................EX, p. 3, 4, 6, 8, 21, 28–32, 36,
.... 42, 46, 52–56, 71
Itinerary .... WD, p. 55, 64, 70
Journal............................ EX, p. 41–45, 52–54, 56, 59
Ledgers .... EX, p. 41, 42, 44, 46, 90
Linked presentation.....................................PP, p. 92, 93
Mass mailing................................. WD, p. 23, 49, 51
Meeting minutes.................................... WD, p. 55, 64
Memorandum .... WD, p. 23, 36, 37, 67
.... EX, p. 14, 115, 134
Menu........................ WD, p. 89, 108, 109, 110, 114
Newsletter..........WD, p. 4, 72, 89, 99, 120, 121, 123,
........127, 154, 157, 165, 170, 171, 188, 192, 194
Payroll .... EX, p. 41, 48, 49, 50
Personnel plan .... EX, p. 3, 10, 12, 14, 71, 78
Presentation
   Informative.. PP, p. 13–27
   Persuasive... PP, p. 51–69
   Sales .... PP, p. 29–49
   Self-running .... PP, p. 76
Program.................................... WD, p. 55, 70, 79, 81
Projects schedule... WD, p. 78
Publication ....WD, p. 110–112
Purchase order .... EX, p. 21, 22, 24, 26,
.... 29, 30–33, 36, 54
Query.....................AC, p. 3, 7, 8, 13, 14, 53, 60–69
Rate schedule .... WD, p. 55, 74
Records list...WD, p. 55, 76

Document Type	Page Number
Register	EX, p. 41, 48, 50, 56, 58, 59
Report	AC, p. 3, 6–8, 10, 13, 14, 16–18, 34, 35, 70, 77–94, 96, 97, 99–102, 106, 108, 110
	EX, p. 10, 12, 16, 18, 41, 62, 66, 72, 75, 77, 78, 89–113, 115, 118, 121, 130, 136, 141, 142, 143
Résumé	WD, p. 23, 40, 44, 47, 67
Schedule	EX, p. 89, 90–93, 100, 101
Statement of account	EX, p. 41, 46
Table	AC, p. 7, 10–19, 22–24, 26, 28, 30–32, 34–40, 42, 44–46, 48, 51, 53–62, 64–73, 78, 82, 86, 88, 90–92, 95, 96, 98–100, 102, 104, 106, 108

Document Type	Page Number
Table of contents	WD, p. 55, 85, 86, 158, 174
Templates	WD, p. 23, 36, 38, 40, 42, 83, 137, 192, 194
Trial balance	EX, p. 89, 90, 91, 92, 98, 99, 100
Web page	WD, p. 181, 188–190, 192, 194
	PP, p. 83, 84, 92, 93
Web query	
Website	WD, p. 44, 45, 103, 134, 137, 165, 176, 181, 188–190, 192, 194
Worksheet	EX, p. 3, 4, 6, 8, 14, 16, 24, 26, 28, 30, 32, 46, 50, 52, 55, 56, 58, 59, 65, 68, 70, 74–80, 82, 84, 87, 89, 90, 92, 96, 98, 100–102, 104, 106, 108, 112, 134–142, 144–146

PORTFOLIO WORK SAMPLES

You may use the documents that you produce in Parts I and II as your portfolio work samples. Include all rough (draft) copies along with the final document.

DIRECTORIES OF DATA/SOLUTION FILES

Directory of Files, Word Chapters 1–6

Project	Data	Solution
1.1	d1.1cityguide	s1.1cityguide
1.2	d1.2auction	s1.2auction
1.3	d1.3cooking tips	s1.3cooking tips
1.4		s1.4my story*
1.5		s1.5thankyou*
2.1	d2.1book	s2.1book
2.2	d2.2committee	s2.2committee
2.3	d2.3backpack	s2.3backpack
2.4	d2.4coffee	s2.4coffee
2.5	d2.5cooking tips	s2.5cooking tips final
3.1		s3.1welcome
3.2	d3.2image	s3.2imageletter
3.3	d3.3change	s3.3change
		s3.3change labels
3.4	d3.4auction	s3.4auction
	d3.4tri-statelet	
3.5		s3.5myownlet*
		s3.5thankyou
4.1	d4.1anounce.docx	s4.1announce
4.2		s4.2interior
4.3	d4.3resume photo.tif	s4.3resume
4.4	d4.4fax	s4.4fax.dotx
		s4.4health-lethead.dotx
5.1		s5-1myresume*
5.2	d5.2csny-lethead template.dotx	s5.2reminder
	d5.2welcome	
5.3		s5.3jobposition*
		s5.3mylet-template.dotx*
5.4	d5.4health-lethead	s5.4collection letters final
		s5.4collection list.accdb
5.5	d5.5coffee-lethead	s5.5labels
	d5.5customer list.accdb	s5.5sorry final
6.1	d6.1tri-statelettemp	s6.1agenda
		s6.1agenda final
6.2	d6.2star lethead	s6.2mtgpoints
		s6.2mtgpoints final
		s6.2star agenda
6.3	d6.3ppstationery	s6.3ppagenda
		s6.3ppagenda final
6.4	d6.4ppstationery	s6.4minutes
		s6.4minutes1
		s6.4minutes2
6.5	d6.5csi-template.dotx	s6.5meetingoutline
7.1	d7.1tri-statelettemp	s7.1itinerary
7.2		s7.2schedule
7.3	d7.3cclethead	s7.3ccletter
7.4		s7.4aid
7.5		s7.5book
7.6		s7.6program
7.7	d7.7women	s7.7women
7.8		s7.8calendar
7.9		s7.9contents
7.10	d7.10calendar	s7.10timesheet
8.1		s8.1coffeead
8.2	d8.2nevada	s8.2nevada
8.3		s8.3move

Directory of Files, Word Chapters 1–6

Project	Data	Solution
8.4		s8.4flower
8.5		s8.5cruise
8.6		s8.6directmail
8.7	d8.7pet text	s8.7pet
9.1	d9.1menu text	s9.1upton dining
9.2	d9.2antipasti	s9.2symphony cafe
	d9.2pasta	s9.2symphony cafe2
	d9.2salad	
	d9.2second course	
9.3	d9.3cafemenu text	s9.3cafemenu
9.4		s9.4invitation
9.5		s9.5petseminar
10.1	d10.1cclethead	s10.1ccnewsletter
10.2	d10.2greenthumb text	s10.2greenthumb
10.3	d10.3college news text	s10.3college news
10.4		
11.1	d11.1brochure text1	s11.1brochure
	d11.1brochure text2	
11.2	d11.2coffee table	s11.2coffeebrochure
	d11.2coffee text1	
	d11.2coffee text2	
11.3		s11.3brochure template
11.4	d11.4catalog text	s11.4catalog
	d11.4order form	
	d11.4product desc	
12.1	d12.1earth	s12.1earthone
12.2	d12.2committee	s12.2ccc
12.3	d12.3cartext	s12.3car
	d12.3tri-statelethead.dotx	
13.1	d13.1japan	s13.1japan
13.2	d13.2japancities	s13.2japancities
13.3	d13.3manual	s13.3manual
		s13.3manual final
		s13.3manualcover
13.4		s13.4italy final*
	s13.4report*	
14.1	d14.1handbook	s14.1handbook
14.2	d14.2mass	s14.2article
14.3	d14.3busplan	s14.3busplan final
	d14.3tcbusplan	
14.4	d14.4annualreport	s14.4annualreport
15.1	d15.1compensation table	s15.1summit report
	d15.1summit template.dotx	
15.2	d15.2ppagenda final	s15.2ppmeeting update
	d15.2ppmeeting text	
	d15.2ppmemostationery.dotx	
16.1	d16.1aid	s16.1aid web.mht
	d16.1college news	s16.1college news web.mht
	d16.1college picture.jpg	s16.1meadowland home page
	d16.1handbook.mht	s16.1meadowland home web.mht
	d16.1schedule	s16.1schedule web.mht
16.2		s16.2kayak.mht
16.3		s16.3upton financial web.mht
		s16.3upton home web.mht
		s16.3upton investment web.mht

* Indicates student-specific files not included in the Instructor's Resource Kit CD-ROM.

Directory of Files, Excel Chapters 1–6

Project	Data	Solution
1.1		s1.1profinv
1.2		s1.2 profinv
1.3		s1.3profinv
2.1	d2.1personnel	s2.1personnel
2.2	d2.2personnel	s2.2personnel
2.3		s2.3personnel
3.1	d3.1cash	s3.1cash
3.2	d3.2cash	s3.2.dcash
4.1		s4.1purorder
4.2	d4.2purorder	s4.2Apurorder
		s4.2Bpurorder
4.3		s4.3purorder
5.1		s5.1salesinv
5.2		s5.2salesinv.pdf
		s5.2salesinv
6.1	d6.1purorder	s6.1BSKGreysons
	d6.1salesinv	s6.1BSKinv.xltx
6.2		s6.2timecard.xltx
		s6.2time7-9
6.3		s6.3OSWinv.xltx
		s6.3OSWsportsshoes
6.4		s6.4quotation.xltx
		s6.4quoteHughes
7.1		s7.1ar
7.2		s7.2ap
7.3	d7.3ar	s7.3statement
	d7.3BSKGreysons	
8.1	d8.1payroll	s8.1payroll
8.2	d8.2payroll	s8.2pay8.22
		s8.2paytemp.xltx
9.1	d9.1sales	s9.1sales
9.2	d9.2purch	s9.2purch
9.3	d9.3cashpmt	s9.3cashpmt
10.1	d10.1petty	s10.1petty
10.2	d10.2asset	s10.2asset
10.3	d10.3aging	s10.3aging
11.1	d11.1budget	s11.1budget
11.2	d11.2budget	s11.2budget
12.1	d12.1billings	s12.1billings
12.2	d12.2listings	s12.2listings
13.1	d13.1income	s13.1income
13.2	d13.2income	s13.2income
	musiclogo.tif	s13.1incweb.mht
13.3	d13.3income	s13.3income
	dunesbackground.jpg	s13.3incweb.mht
14.1	d14.1sales	s14.1sales
14.2	d14.2revenue	s14.2revenue
14.3	d14.3forecast	s14.3forecast
14.4	d14.4invest	s14.4invest
15.1	d15.1sched	s15.1sched
	d15.1tb	s15.1tb
15.2	d15.2sched	s15.2sched
	d15.2tb	s15.2tb
16.1	d16.1sales	s16.1sales
16.2	d16.2salary	s16.2salary
17.1	d17.1ws	s17.1ws
17.2	d17.2sched	s17.2sched
	d17.2ws	s17.2ws
18.1	d18.1income	s18.1income
18.2	d18.2quarter	s18.2quarter
19.1	d19.1balsheet	s19.1balsheet
	classiclogo.tif	
19.2	d19.2balsheet	s19.2balsheet
	wheelslogo.tif	
20.1	d20.1isanalysis	s20.1isanalysis
20.2	d20.2bsanalysis	s20.2bsanalysis
21.1	d21.1sales	s21.1sales
21.2	d21.2sales	s21.2sales
22.1	d22.1expenses	s22.1expenses
	classiclogo.tif	
22.2	d22.2analysis	s22.2analysis
23.1	d23.1fund	s23.1fund

Directory of Files, Excel Chapters 1–6

Project	Data	Solution
23.2	d23.2fund	s23.2fund
23.3	d23.3stock	s23.3stock
24.1	d24.1salary	s24.1memo.docx
	d24.1memo.docx	
24.2	d24.2busplan.docx	s24.2busplan.docx
	d24.2bs	
	d24.2cf	
	d24.2is	
24.3	d24.3bulletin.docx	s24.3bulletin.docx
	d24.3retirees	s24.3retirees
24.4	d24.4annreport.docx	s24.4annreport.docx
	d24.4annrpt	s24.4annrpt

Directory of Files, PowerPoint Chapters 1–6

Project	Data	Solution
1.1	d1.1pointclick	
1.2	d1.2newyork	s1.2nyc
1.3	d1.3wed	
1.4		s1.4copyme
2.1		s2.1meadowland
2.2	d2.2copyme	s2.2copyme1
	d2.2daisy.jpg	
2.3	d2.3collegepic.jpg	s2.3meadowland orientation
	d2.3meadowland	
2.4		s2.4sunstar
2.5	d2.5bridge.jpg	s2.5japan
	d2.5japan.docx	
	d2.5japan.jpg	
	d2.5japancities.docx	
3.1	d3.1meeting1.jpg	s3.1sunstar
	d3.1meeting2.jpg	
	d3.1meeting3.jpg	
	d3.1meeting4.jpg	
	d3.1sunstar	
3.2	d3.2atsign.jpg	s3.2wireless final
	d3.2wireless	
3.3	d3.3hand.jpg	s3.3testprep
3.4	d3.4air.jpg	s3.4breathe
3.5	d3.5mass.docx	s3.5masstemplate.potx
		s3.5massvacation
4.1	d4.1money	s4.1fourseasons
4.2	d4.2busplan.docx	s4.2hsbusplan
4.3	d4.3finpic.jpg	s4.3finland
4.4	d4.4breathe	s4.4breathe
		s4.4fourseasons
4.5	d4.5finpics [folder]	s4.5finland
		s4.5photoalbum
5.1	d5.1finland	s5.1finland
5.2	d5.2money	s5.2money
5.3	d5.3wireless final	s5.3wireless final1
5.4	d5.4testprep	s5.4testprep final
6.1	d6.1paris	s6.1paris
	d6.1parisphotos [folder]	
	d6.1ski	
6.2	d6.2lethead.docx	
6.2	d6.2paris	s6.2parishandouts.docx
		s6.2parisletter.docx
6.3	d6.3balancesheet.xlsx	s6.3hcbusplan
	d6.3cashflow.xlsx	
	d6.3hcbusplan	
	d6.3incomestatement.xlsx	
	d6.3mgmtteam.docx	
6.4	d6.4meadowland orientation	s6.4meadowland orientation
		s6.4meadowland orientation web.mhtml

Directory of Files, Access Chapters 1–6

Project	Data	Solution
1.1	d1.1cs	
1.2	d1.2cs	
2.1	d2.1cs	
2.2	d2.2cs	

Directory of Files, Access Chapters 1–6

Project	Data	Solution
3.1		s3.1tasks
3.2		s3.2presto
4.1		s4.1students
4.2		s4.2mdse
5.1		s5.1club
5.2	d5.2students	s5.2students
5.3	d5.3presto	s5.3presto
5.4		s5.4listings
5.5	d5.5mdse	s5.5mdse
6.1	d6.1movie	s6.1movie
6.2	d6.2presto	s6.2presto
6.3	d6.3students	s6.3students
7.1	d7.1mdse	s7.1mdse
	d7.1ollielogo.bmp	
7.2	d7.2club	s7.2club
	d7.2powerlogo.bmp	
8.1	d8.1listings	s8.1listings
	d8.1jameslogo.bmp	
8.2	d8.2mdse	s8.2mdse
	d8.2ollielogo.bmp	
9.1	d9.1students	s9.1students
	d9.1questions.docx	s9.1questions.docx
9.2	d9.2movie	s9.2movie
	d9.2questions.docx	s9.2questions.docx
9.3	d9.3mdse	s9.3mdse
	d9.3questions.docx	s9.3questions.docx
10.1	d10.1presto	s10.1presto
10.2	d10.2movie	s10.2movie
	d10.2questions.docx	s10.2questions.docx
10.3	d10.3mdse	s10.3mdse
11.1	d11.1students	s11.1students
11.2	d11.2mdse	s11.2mdse
12.1	d12.1students	s12.1students
12.2	d12.2mdse	s12.2mdse
13.1	d13.1presto	s13.1presto
13.2	d13.2club	s13.2club
13.3	d13.3students	s13.3students
14.1	d14.1listings	s14.1listings
	d14.1jameslogo.bmp	s14.1questions.docx
	d14.1questions.docx	
14.2	d14.2club	s14.2club
	d14.2powerlogo.bmp	
14.3	d14.3mdse	s14.3mdse
	d14.3ollielogo.bmp	
15.1	d15.1club	s15.1club
	d15.1powerlogo.bmp	
16.1	d16.1filmmem	s16.1movie
	d16.1movie	
16.2	d16.2creditors.xlsx	s16.2presto
	d16.2customers.xlsx	
	d16.2presto	
16.3	d16.3contact.docx	
	d16.3jameslogo.bmp	
	d16.3listings	s16.3listings
	163contact.txt	
17.1	d17.1club	s17.1classes.xlsx
	d17.1powerlogo.bmp	s17.1club
17.2	d17.2memotmp.docx	172temp.rtf
	d17.2movie	172temp2.rtf
		s17.2memo.docx
		s17.2memo2.docx
		s17.2movie
18.1	d18.1presto	s18.1presto
		s18.2presto_2008-01-14
18.2	d18.2listings	s18.2listings
		s18.2listings.mdb

Project I Task List

Project	Data	Solution
IA	dp1.1suppliers.docx	sp1.1suppliers.docx
IB		
II	dp1.2memotemp.docx	sp1.2memo.docx
III	dp1tielogo.gif	sp1.3imports.accdb
		spsuppliers.txt
IV	dp1.4letterhead.docx	sp1.4mergeletter.docx
	dp1.4imports.accdb	sp1.4mergeletterall.docx
V	dp1.5fax.docx	sp1.5mergefax.docx
	dp1.5imports.accdb	sp1.5mergefaxall.docx
VI	dp1.6letterhead.docx	sp1.6itinerary.docx
VII	dp1tielogo.gif	sp1.7budget.xlsx
VIII	dp1.8photos folder	spl.8presentation.pptx
IX		sp1.9expense.xlsx

Project II Task List

Project	Data	Solution
I		
II	dp2.2employees.xlsx	sp2.2employees.accdb
	dp2happylogo.bmp	
III	dp2.3lethead.docx	sp2.3invitemerge.docx
	dp2.3employees.accdb	sp2.3invitemergeall.docx
	dp2.3directionsmap.bmp	sp2.3directionspage.docx
IV	dp2.4benefits.xlsx	sp2.4benefits.xlsx
	dp2happylogo.bmp	
V	dp2.5upperfloorplan.bmp	sp2.5program.docx
	dp2happylogo.bmp	
	dp2.5amprogram.docx	
	dp2.5pmprogram.docx	
	dp2.5conferencecenter.tif	
VI	dp2.6newstext.docx	sp2.6newsletter.docx
	dp2happylogo.bmp	
VII	dp2.7template.docx	sp2.7web.docx
	dp2.7webtext.docx	sp2.7web.mht
	dp2happylogo.bmp	
VIII	dp2.8profile.docx	sp2.8presentation.pptx
	dp2.8eotemplate.pptx	
	dp2happylogo.bmp	
IX	dp2.9payrolldata.xlsx	sp2.9payroll.xlsx

Project III Task List

Project	Data	Solution
I		sp3.1faxcover.dotx
	sp3.1gearycard.docx	
	sp3.1hillcard.docx	
	sp3.1letterhead.docx	
	sp3.1ollielogo	
II		sp3.2vista.xlsx
III	dp3.3personnel.xlsx	sp3.3personnel.xlsx
	dp3.3fin.xlsx	sp3.3fin.xlsx
	dp3.3cashflow.xlsx	sp3.3cashflow.xlsx
	dp3.3is.xlsx	sp3.3is.xlsx
	dp3.3balsheet.xlsx	sp3.3balsheet.xlsx
IV	dp3.4busplantext.docx	sp3.4busplan.docx
	dp3.4busplandata folder	
V	dp3.5prtext.docx	sp3.5pr.docx
VI		sp3.6ad.docx
VII	dp3.7brochuretext.docx	sp3.7brochure.docx
VIII	dp3.8ollies.accdb	sp3.8ollies.accdb
	dp3.8clubs.xlsx	
	dp3.8cyclists.accdb	
	dp3ollielogo.bmp	
IX		sp3.9invite.docx
X	dp3.10bpoutline.pptx	sp3.10bppresentation.pptx
	dp3.10busplan.docx	
XI	dp3.11template.docx	sp3.11web.mht
		sp3.11web.docx

PART I:
TOOL-SPECIFIC PROJECTS

Introduction

Each project in each tool-specific section applies the software skills listed at the start of the project. By completing the applications in each project, you will produce tangible results that represent actual professional documents within the lesson category.

WHAT YOU NEED TO KNOW BEFORE YOU BEGIN

- Read information related to Part I in the Preface, page v, to review the organization of the text and the project numbering system.

- Create a folder on your local drive using the tool name, followed by your initials. This will be used for your electronic solution files.

- Keep all printouts in a folder or submit them to your teacher as you are instructed.

- Read each application's "What You Need to Know" section, which provides software and project-related information necessary to complete the application.

- Identify your work as instructed by your teacher.

Word Basics

CHAPTER 2
Correspondence

CHAPTER 3
Lists, Meeting
Documents,
Schedules, and
Forms

CHAPTER 4
Sales and Marketing
Documents

CHAPTER 5
Reports and Long
Documents

CHAPTER 6
Integration/Word
and the Web

Word Basics

In this chapter, you will complete the following projects:

PROJECT 1
Basic Editing Review
PROJECT 1.1 Open a Document; Insert and Correct Text
PROJECT 1.2 Insert and Delete Text; Show/Hide Codes; Use Zoom
PROJECT 1.3 Move and Copy Text; Collect and Paste Multiple Items
PROJECT 1.4 Compose Your Autobiography
PROJECT 1.5 Compose a Thank You Communication

PROJECT 2
Basic Formatting Review
PROJECT 2.1 Change Font Attributes; Set Text Alignments; Use Symbols
PROJECT 2.2 Copy Formatting
PROJECT 2.3 Edit Formatting
PROJECT 2.4 Edit Formatting
PROJECT 2.5 Edit Formatting

BASIC EDITING REVIEW

PROJECT 1

PROJECT SKILLS
- ✷ Navigate a document
- ✷ Insert and delete text
- ✷ Correct text using AutoCorrect and Spell and Grammar Check
- ✷ Move and copy text
- ✷ Use Save and Save As
- ✷ Use Undo
- ✷ Use Print Preview/Print
- ✷ Show/Hide codes
- ✷ Change case
- ✷ Use AutoFormat As You Type
- ✷ Compose at the computer

1.1 OPEN A DOCUMENT; INSERT AND CORRECT TEXT

You have just been hired as an assistant to Rita Bratton, travel consultant at Destinations, a travel agency located in Colorado. One of your responsibilities is to edit articles to be included in Destinations' monthly newsletter.

In this project, you will open a document and correct spelling and grammatical errors. You also will use the AutoCorrect feature when inserting new text in an article to be included in next month's newsletter.

1. Open the data file **d1.1cityguide**.
2. Open the AutoCorrect dialog box. Enter the initials **cg** in the Replace text box. Enter **CITYGuide** in the With text box, and click Add.
3. Make the insertions shown in Figure 1.1.
4. Use the quick-correct method to correct spelling and grammatical errors, which are circled in red.
5. Preview the document.
6. Print one copy.
7. Save the file as **1.1cityguide**.
8. Close the file.

WHAT YOU NEED TO KNOW

Software

▶ Use the AutoCorrect feature to correct common capitalization, spelling, and grammatical errors as you enter text. You can also use this feature to insert specific words by entering an abbreviation.

▶ The AutoCorrect feature is on by default. Click the Office Button, click Word Options, select Proofing, and then click AutoCorrect Options. In the AutoCorrect dialog box, click the AutoCorrect tab, and make the changes you want. Click OK. Click OK again to close Word Options.

▶ Correct individual spelling and grammatical errors using the quick-correct method (right-click the flagged error and select the correct spelling or grammatical correction from the shortcut menu).

▶ To check your entire document or parts of the document at one time, use the Spelling and Grammar feature. Click the Review tab, and in the Proofing group, click the Spelling & Grammar button. In the Spelling and Grammar dialog box, choose a correction option.

Project

▶ Proofreader's marks are symbols used to indicate revisions that need to be made to a document.

▶ The proofreader's mark for insertion is ^. The proofreader's mark for a new paragraph is ¶. The proofreader's mark to insert a space is #.

▶ See Appendix B, which lists common proofreader's marks.

Continued on next page

▶ Some of the projects in this chapter are shown double-spaced so that edits are clearly visible. Print all final copies using the spacing noted in the activity.

▶ Use the Save As option to save a file under a different filename on your local drive.

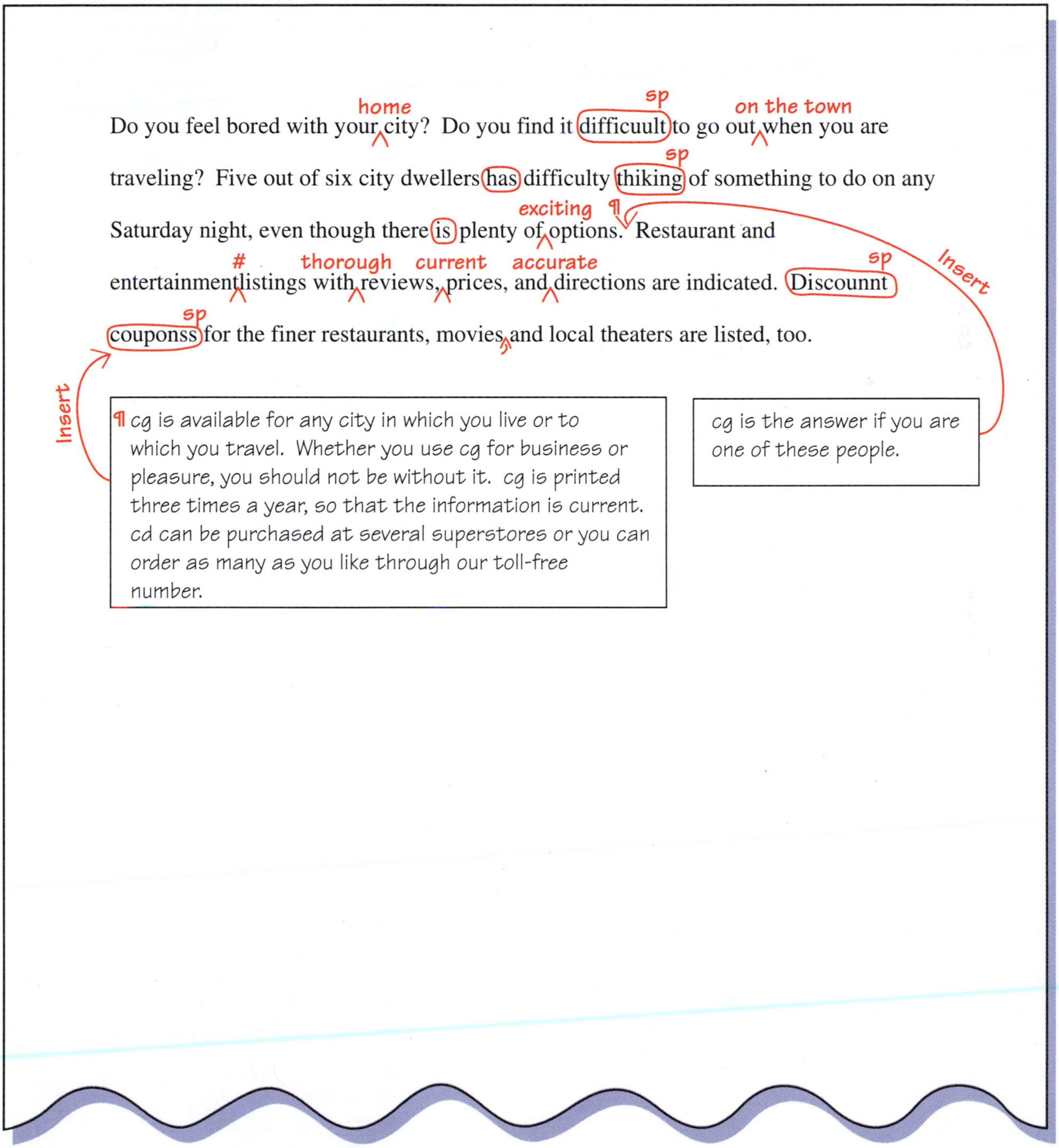

Do you feel bored with your ^home^ city? Do you find it (difficuult) [sp] to go out ^on the town^ when you are traveling? Five out of six city dwellers (has) difficulty (thiking) [sp] of something to do on any Saturday night, even though there (is) plenty of ^exciting^ options. ¶ Restaurant and entertainment[#]listings with ^thorough^ reviews, ^current^ prices, and ^accurate^ directions are indicated. (Discounnt) [sp] [Insert] ^couponss^ [sp] for the finer restaurants, movies, and local theaters are listed, too.

[Insert]

¶ cg is available for any city in which you live or to which you travel. Whether you use cg for business or pleasure, you should not be without it. cg is printed three times a year, so that the information is current. cd can be purchased at several superstores or you can order as many as you like through our toll-free number.

cg is the answer if you are one of these people.

Figure 1.1

1.2 INSERT AND DELETE TEXT; SHOW/HIDE CODES; USE ZOOM

You work for the Tri-State Auto Group, which is preparing for the annual auto auction. Your boss has asked you to edit text she has drafted.

In this project, you will open a document and navigate it to insert and delete text.

1. Open the data file **d1.2auction**.
2. Set the page magnification (Zoom) to 120%.
3. Click the Show/Hide button to display codes. ¶
4. Open the AutoCorrect dialog box. Enter the letters **au** in the Replace text box. Enter `auction` in the With text box, and click Add.
5. Make the insertions and deletions shown in Figure 1.2. Insert a nonbreaking space between names and dates for the newly inserted text.
6. Use the Change Case feature to change Tri-State Auto Group to uppercase.
7. Correct spelling and grammatical errors.
8. Press [Ctrl] + [Home] to return to the top of the document. Enter the word **DRAFT** at the left margin, and press [Enter] twice.
9. Hide the codes. Return the page magnification to 100%.
10. Preview and print the document.
11. Save the file as **1.2auction**.
12. Close the file.

WHAT YOU NEED TO KNOW

Software

▶ Use express movement keys to move the insertion point around a document quickly: Press [Ctrl] + [Home] to move the insertion point to the beginning of a document. Press [Ctrl] + [End] to move the insertion point to the end of a document. Pressing [End] moves the insertion point to the end of a line. Pressing [Home] moves the insertion point to the beginning of a line.

▶ Rotate the center wheel of an IntelliMouse forward or backward to move through a document.

▶ If you are using an IntelliMouse, you can zoom in or out by 10% increments by pressing [Ctrl] while rotating the center wheel.

▶ When you insert text, existing text moves to the right.

▶ As you create a new document, Word inserts nonprinting codes. You can choose to display these codes at any time. The codes represent paragraph marks (¶), tabs (→), and spaces (·). To display codes, click the Home tab and in the Paragraph group, click the Show/Hide button. ¶

▶ To change the case of letters quickly, select the text and press [Shift] + [F3] once to change to sentence case (capitalize each word); press twice for uppercase and three times for lowercase.

▶ The AutoFormat As You Type feature automatically changes two hyphens to a dash, fractions such as 1/2 to ½, and ordinals (2nd) to superscript 2nd. You can set options by clicking the Office Button, Word Options, Proofing, AutoCorrect Options. In the AutoCorrect dialog box, click the AutoFormat As You Type tab, and make the changes you want.

▶ To prevent two or more words from splitting during wordwrap, insert a nonbreaking space between words by pressing [Ctrl] + [Shift] + [Spacebar].

Project

▶ The proofreader's mark for capitalization is ≡.

▶ The proofreader's mark for deletion is ℓ.

▶ It is helpful to display codes when editing a document.

We are writing to inform you that ~~the~~ the Tri-State Auto Group will hold its ~~first~~ annual [be ing] auto auction on Sunday. [September 25.] Hundreds of makes and models (has) been overstocked.

~~Since you are~~ [As] a valued customer, ~~we would like to invite~~ [are invited] you to preview our stock before we open our doors to the general public. ~~We will be holding~~ [will be held] a special preview and bidding session at 8:00 a.m. before the public auction begins at 10:00 a.m. Simply bring this letter with you on the morning of the 25th, and it ~~will admit you~~ [admit you to] to the special preview session.

This au is one of the ~~biggest~~ [largest] events of the year. ~~People come from all over the state to be a part of this event.~~ [entire]

insert

¶

The au will take place at the Continental Arena, which is located on Route 95. For directions to the arena, please call 800-555-6740. We hope to see you on Sunday, the 25th of September.

This means we are able to ~~over~~ [offer] discounted prices to the public.

insert

Figure 1.2

1.3 MOVE AND COPY TEXT; COLLECT AND PASTE MULTIPLE ITEMS

Martha Halpin, your boss at *Tastings Magazine*, thinks it would be a good idea to include basic cooking tips in next month's edition of the magazine. She has drafted an article that she wants you to edit.

In this project, you will open a document and then insert, delete, move, and copy text.

1. Open the data file **d1.3cooking tips**.
2. Set the page magnification to 120%.
3. Display codes.
4. Make the revisions shown in Figure 1.3a.
5. Correct spelling and grammatical errors.
6. Move the tips into numerical order.
7. Copy each number and tip (uppercase text) in each line to the Clipboard. Paste the copied items in numerical order at the bottom of the page, at the left margin, two lines below the last sentence.
8. Restore the deleted sentence in tip 5, as shown in Figure 1.3b.
9. Save the file as **1.3cooking tips**.
10. Close the file.

WHAT YOU NEED TO KNOW

Software

▶ Most software allows you to undo a series of actions. Click the Undo button on the Quick Access toolbar to reverse an action.

▶ The Clipboard is a temporary storage area. The Clipboard can hold up to 24 items. Click the Home tab and in the Clipboard group, click the dialog box launcher. The Clipboard task pane lists each copied or cut item. Click in the document where you want to insert the cut/copied item, and then click the item in the Clipboard task pane. A list box next to each item gives you a delete option.

▶ To move text, you can use either the "cut and paste" or "drag-and-drop" methods.

Project

▶ The proofreader's mark for "let the original stand" is "...." or "stet."

▶ Sometimes it may be necessary to insert or delete spaces after moving text.

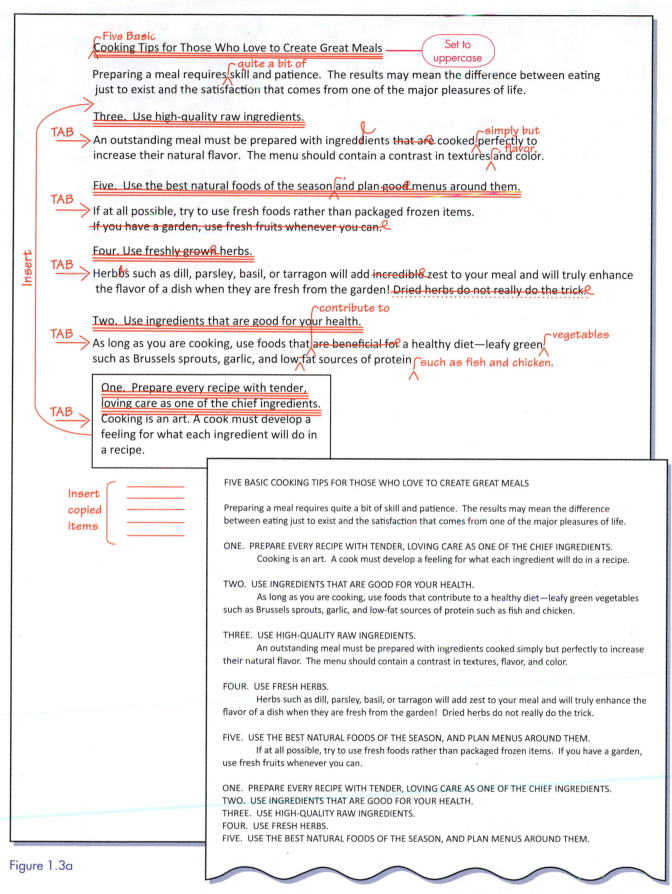

Five Basic

Cooking Tips for Those Who Love to Create Great Meals — *Set to uppercase*

quite a bit of

Preparing a meal requires skill and patience. The results may mean the difference between eating just to exist and the satisfaction that comes from one of the major pleasures of life.

Three. Use high-quality raw ingredients.

TAB

An outstanding meal must be prepared with ingredients ~~that are~~ cooked perfectly to **simply but** increase their natural flavor. The menu should contain a contrast in textures and color. **flavor,**

Five. Use the best natural foods of the season and plan ~~good~~ menus around them.

TAB

If at all possible, try to use fresh foods rather than packaged frozen items. ~~If you have a garden, use fresh fruits whenever you can.~~

Four. Use ~~freshly grown~~ herbs.

TAB

Herbs such as dill, parsley, basil, or tarragon will add ~~incredible~~ zest to your meal and will truly enhance the flavor of a dish when they are fresh from the garden! ~~Dried herbs do not really do the trick.~~

contribute to

Two. Use ingredients that are good for your health.

TAB

As long as you are cooking, use foods that ~~are beneficial for~~ a healthy diet—leafy green **vegetables** such as Brussels sprouts, garlic, and low-fat sources of protein **such as fish and chicken.**

One. Prepare every recipe with tender, loving care as one of the chief ingredients.

TAB

Cooking is an art. A cook must develop a feeling for what each ingredient will do in a recipe.

Insert

Insert copied items

FIVE BASIC COOKING TIPS FOR THOSE WHO LOVE TO CREATE GREAT MEALS

Preparing a meal requires quite a bit of skill and patience. The results may mean the difference between eating just to exist and the satisfaction that comes from one of the major pleasures of life.

ONE. PREPARE EVERY RECIPE WITH TENDER, LOVING CARE AS ONE OF THE CHIEF INGREDIENTS.
Cooking is an art. A cook must develop a feeling for what each ingredient will do in a recipe.

TWO. USE INGREDIENTS THAT ARE GOOD FOR YOUR HEALTH.
As long as you are cooking, use foods that contribute to a healthy diet—leafy green vegetables such as Brussels sprouts, garlic, and low-fat sources of protein such as fish and chicken.

THREE. USE HIGH-QUALITY RAW INGREDIENTS.
An outstanding meal must be prepared with ingredients cooked simply but perfectly to increase their natural flavor. The menu should contain a contrast in textures, flavor, and color.

FOUR. USE FRESH HERBS.
Herbs such as dill, parsley, basil, or tarragon will add zest to your meal and will truly enhance the flavor of a dish when they are fresh from the garden! Dried herbs do not really do the trick.

FIVE. USE THE BEST NATURAL FOODS OF THE SEASON, AND PLAN MENUS AROUND THEM.
If at all possible, try to use fresh foods rather than packaged frozen items. If you have a garden, use fresh fruits whenever you can.

ONE. PREPARE EVERY RECIPE WITH TENDER, LOVING CARE AS ONE OF THE CHIEF INGREDIENTS.
TWO. USE INGREDIENTS THAT ARE GOOD FOR YOUR HEALTH.
THREE. USE HIGH-QUALITY RAW INGREDIENTS.
FOUR. USE FRESH HERBS.
FIVE. USE THE BEST NATURAL FOODS OF THE SEASON, AND PLAN MENUS AROUND THEM.

Figure 1.3a

Figure 1.3b

1.4 COMPOSE YOUR AUTOBIOGRAPHY

In most jobs, you are expected to compose at the computer. The best way to train for this is by composing a document about yourself.

In this project, you will compose your autobiography. An autobiography is a written account of a person's life, narrated by that person.

1. Create a new document.
2. Use the default settings.
3. Compose a draft of your autobiography. Organize it as follows:
   a. *Your ancestry*: Describe your grandparents, where they were born, and how their experiences shaped your parents' lives. Explain, too, how your parents' experiences have shaped your life.
   b. *Early years*: Describe where you were born and raised and the schools you attended.
   c. *Family*: Explain the relationship you have with your family members.
   d. *School years*: Describe your favorite subjects and why you enjoy them.
   e. *Your hobbies and goals*: Explain what motivates you and what you like to do after school, on weekends, and on holidays.
   f. *Career goals*: Explain what career you think you might pursue and why.
4. Save the file as **1.4my story.xx** (xx = your initials).
5. Print one copy.
6. Read and edit the printout, and then transfer the handwritten edits to the file.
7. Preview and print a second copy.
8. Save the changes.
9. Close the file.

WHAT YOU NEED TO KNOW

Project

▶ It is important to be able to compose communications at the computer. As you think of what you want to say, enter it.

▶ Anything you compose at the computer is considered a draft. It remains a draft until it is proofread, edited, and printed. This may take several attempts. It is not considered a final document until it is ready for distribution.

▶ When drafting a communication, let your ideas flow—do not stop to correct errors. You can do this later in the editing stage.

1.5 COMPOSE A THANK YOU COMMUNICATION

It is a good practice to follow up a job interview with a brief thank you letter. Doing so reinforces your interest in the position and demonstrates your ability to follow through on a job.

In this project, you will assume that you were interviewed for a summer job of your choice. You will compose a note of thanks to the interviewer. In a later project, you will create a formal letter from the text you are now drafting.

1. Open a new blank document.
2. Use the following settings:

Margins	1.25" left and right
Line spacing	1.5
Paragraph spacing	
Before	0
After	0
Font	default
Font size	default

3. Compose a draft "thank you" letter to Ms. Marion Jones, the person who interviewed you for a summer job.
4. Organize the communication as follows:
   a. Explain why you are thanking Ms. Jones. Mention the date you saw her and identify the job for which you are applying.
   b. Make a convincing case for why the firm should hire you.
   c. Close by saying that you hope to hear positively from her soon. Thank her again for her time.
5. Save the file. Name it **1.5thank you.xx** (xx = your initials).
6. Preview and print one copy.
7. Read and edit the printout and then make your handwritten edits in the file.
8. Preview and print another copy. *Note: This is not the final copy. You will create a letter from this text at a later time.*
9. Save the changes.
10. Close the file.

▼ WHAT YOU NEED TO KNOW

Project

▶ Communications of thanks can be in the form of a letter or handwritten on note cards. After a job interview, it is recommended that you send a formal letter thanking the individual for taking the time to see you.

▶ In the first paragraph of a thank you letter, clearly state what you are thanking the reader for. Be sincere in your tone.

PROJECT 2

PROJECT SKILLS

✴ Work with fonts
✴ Set text alignments
✴ Use symbols
✴ Copy formatting (Format Painter)
✴ Highlight text
✴ Edit formats

2.1 CHANGE FONT ATTRIBUTES; SET TEXT ALIGNMENTS; USE SYMBOLS

The American Literacy Campaign is a not-for-profit organization that works with libraries to encourage reading. You have been hired for the summer to work on its campaign.

In this project, you will change font attributes, set text alignments, and use symbols to create an advertisement for the American Literacy Campaign.

1. Open the data file **d2.1book**.
2. Display the codes.
3. Make the changes shown in Figure 2.1a.
4. Delete any paragraph symbols so that the text begins at the top of the page.
5. Center the page vertically.
6. Change the text alignment, font face, font size, font style, and font color, as shown in Figure 2.1b.
7. Insert symbols where shown.
8. Insert number symbols (do not use the numbering feature) before each item.
9. Preview and then print one copy.
10. Save the file as **2.1book**.
11. Close the file.

WHAT YOU NEED TO KNOW

Software

▶ Formatting allows you to change the appearance of a paragraph or characters including letters, numbers, and symbols. By formatting characters, you can emphasize individual letters, words, or a block of text and/or improve the readability of text in a document.

▶ There are three basic types of font faces—serif, sans serif, and script. A serif face has lines, curves, or edges extending from the ends of the letters (serif), whereas a sans serif face is straight-edged (sans serif), and script looks like handwriting (script).

▶ You can change font faces, font styles (bold, italic), font sizes, and font colors before or after entering text by clicking an appropriate button on the Home tab, Font group, on the Ribbon or on the Mini toolbar. The Mini toolbar is displayed automatically when you select text.

▶ To change fonts, styles, sizes, and colors simultaneously, click the dialog box launcher in the Font group. In the Font dialog box that is displayed, choose the options you want, and click OK.

▶ Font size refers to the height of the font, measured in points. There are 72 points to an inch. In Word 2007, the default font is Calibri, and the default font size is 11 point.

▶ Symbols are ornamental font collections or special characters that you can use to separate items on a page, emphasize items in a list, or enhance a document. Symbols behave like fonts; that is, you can change the point size, color, or emphasis style.

Continued on next page

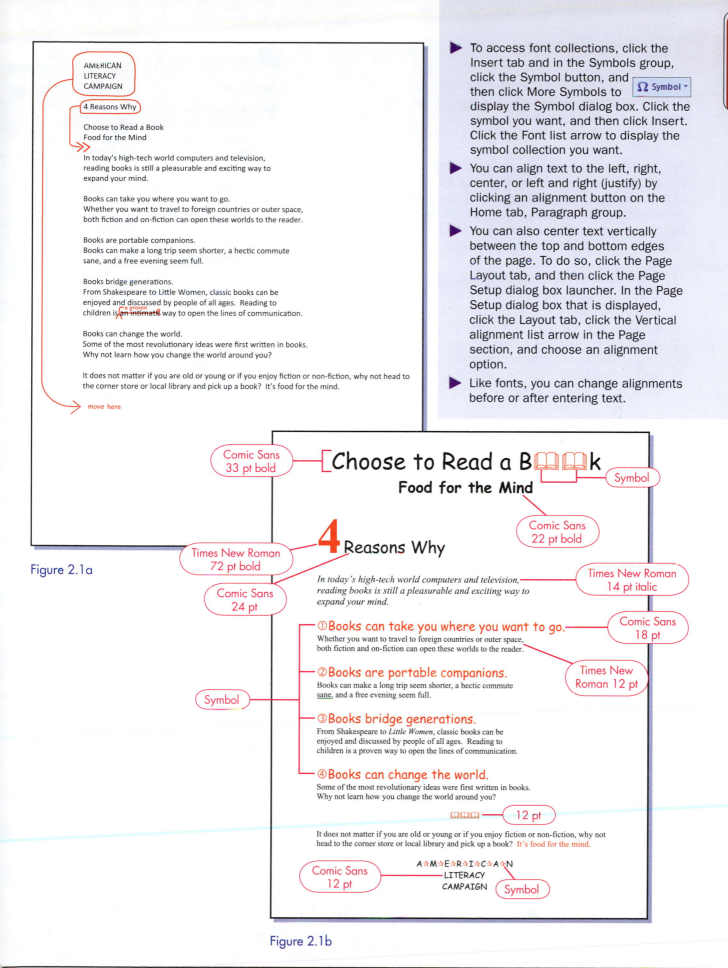

To access font collections, click the Insert tab and in the Symbols group, click the Symbol button, and then click More Symbols to display the Symbol dialog box. Click the symbol you want, and then click Insert. Click the Font list arrow to display the symbol collection you want.

You can align text to the left, right, center, or left and right (justify) by clicking an alignment button on the Home tab, Paragraph group.

You can also center text vertically between the top and bottom edges of the page. To do so, click the Page Layout tab, and then click the Page Setup dialog box launcher. In the Page Setup dialog box that is displayed, click the Layout tab, click the Vertical alignment list arrow in the Page section, and choose an alignment option.

Like fonts, you can change alignments before or after entering text.

Figure 2.1a

Figure 2.1b

2.2 COPY FORMATTING

The Children's Community Center runs many fund-raising events. Your boss at the Center has drafted text for a letter urging local businesses to participate in this year's event. You have been asked to edit this document.

> **In this project, you will use various editing features to correct a draft document, including insert, delete, move, copy, and paste techniques. To keep document paragraphs consistent in format, you will use Format Painter to copy formatting from one block of text to another.**

1. Open the data file **d2.2committee**.
2. Open the AutoCorrect dialog box. Enter the initials **ccc** in the Replace text box. Enter **Children's Community Center** in the With text box.
3. Make the corrections shown in Figure 2.2a.
4. To change the formatting to look like Figure 2.2b, do the following:
   a. Set the side heading text to Capitalize Each Word.
   b. Change the font to sans serif, 11 pt for the first three paragraphs, and then copy the formatting to the last paragraph, as shown.
   c. Change the font for the first side heading to a decorative or script, 12-pt font, and color it dark blue. Then copy the formatting from the first side heading to the other side headings.
   d. Change the font for the text below the first side heading to sans serif, 11 pt, italic, and color the font a lighter shade of blue. Copy the formatting from the first subtext to the other subtext paragraphs. *Note: Notice that the tab is also copied.*
   e. Press [Enter] before the phone number to move it to the next line (phone number text should be kept together). Apply a Bright Green highlight to Sheila Porter and a Yellow highlight to the phone number.
5. Copy each line of side heading text to the Clipboard. Paste the copied items where shown, and then center them.
6. Preview and print one copy.
7. Save the file as **2.2committee**.
8. Close the file.

WHAT YOU NEED TO KNOW

Software

▶ The Text Highlight Color feature allows you to emphasize a word, several words, a paragraph, parts of a document, symbols, or graphics using color.

▶ To highlight text, click the Home tab and in the Font group, click the Text Highlight Color button list arrow to display a palette of colors. Click to select a highlight color, and then select the text you want to highlight. After clicking the Text Highlight Color button, the insertion point changes to a highlighter pen. The color displayed on the highlight button is applied.

▶ The Format Painter feature allows you to copy formatting such as font face, style, and size from one block of text to another.

▶ To copy formatting, select the text or data that contains the formatting you want to copy, click the Format Painter button on the Mini toolbar (the insertion point becomes a paintbrush), and select the text to receive the formatting.

▶ To copy formatting from one location to several, select the text with the formatting you want to copy, and then double-click the Format Painter button. You can now "paint" the formatting on several blocks of text or data.

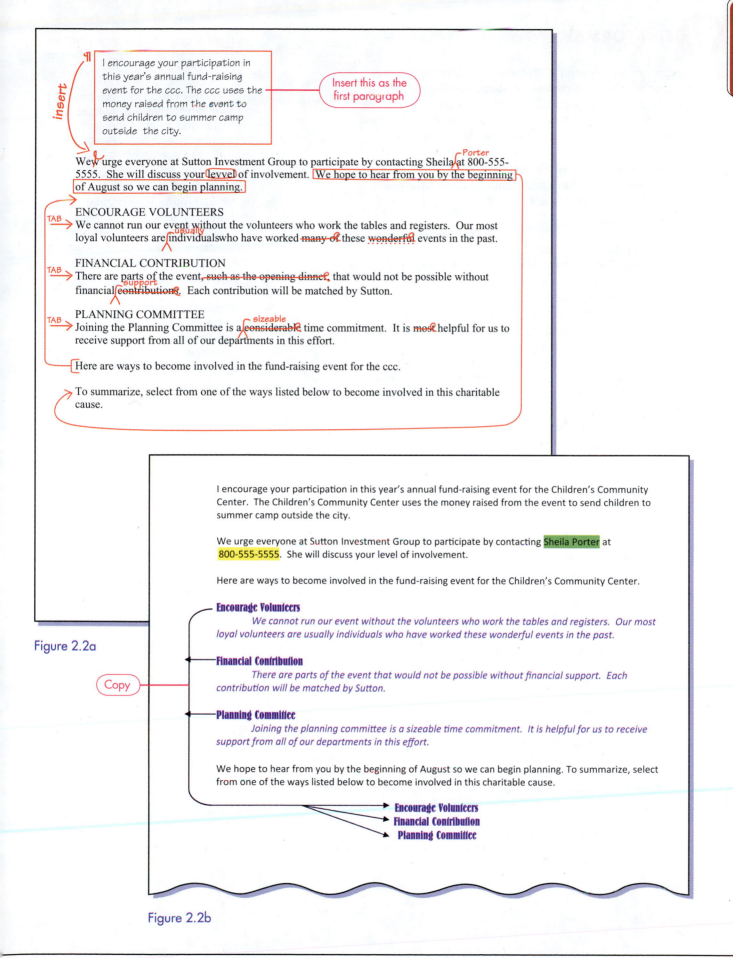

insert

I encourage your participation in this year's annual fund-raising event for the ccc. The ccc uses the money raised from the event to send children to summer camp outside the city.

Insert this as the first paragraph

Wew urge everyone at Sutton Investment Group to participate by contacting Sheila Porter at 800-555-5555. She will discuss your levvel of involvement. We hope to hear from you by the beginning of August so we can begin planning.

TAB → ENCOURAGE VOLUNTEERS
We cannot run our event without the volunteers who work the tables and registers. Our most loyal volunteers are individualswho have worked many of these wonderful events in the past. *usually*

TAB → FINANCIAL CONTRIBUTION
There are parts of the event, such as the opening dinner, that would not be possible without financial contributions. Each contribution will be matched by Sutton. *support*

TAB → PLANNING COMMITTEE
Joining the Planning Committee is a considerable time commitment. It is most helpful for us to receive support from all of our departments in this effort. *sizeable*

Here are ways to become involved in the fund-raising event for the ccc.

To summarize, select from one of the ways listed below to become involved in this charitable cause.

Figure 2.2a

I encourage your participation in this year's annual fund-raising event for the Children's Community Center. The Children's Community Center uses the money raised from the event to send children to summer camp outside the city.

We urge everyone at Sutton Investment Group to participate by contacting Sheila Porter at 800-555-5555. She will discuss your level of involvement.

Here are ways to become involved in the fund-raising event for the Children's Community Center.

Encourage Volunteers
We cannot run our event without the volunteers who work the tables and registers. Our most loyal volunteers are usually individuals who have worked these wonderful events in the past.

Financial Contribution
There are parts of the event that would not be possible without financial support. Each contribution will be matched by Sutton.

Planning Committee
Joining the planning committee is a sizeable time commitment. It is helpful for us to receive support from all of our departments in this effort.

We hope to hear from you by the beginning of August so we can begin planning. To summarize, select from one of the ways listed below to become involved in this charitable cause.

Encourage Volunteers
Financial Contribution
Planning Committee

Copy

Figure 2.2b

2.3 EDIT FORMATTING

Destinations has several affiliate companies that focus on specialized travel packages. Backpack Buddies is an affiliate that creates travel itineraries for people who like to backpack. You have been asked to format text that will be used in a Backpack Buddies advertisement.

In this project, you will format text for an advertisement for Backpack Buddies, and then use the Symbols feature to enhance lists.

1. Open the data file **d2.3backpack**.
2. Insert the text shown in Figure 2.3a.
3. Format and align the text, as shown in Figure 2.3b.
   a. Insert a symbol before each question as shown.
   b. Insert any relevant symbol that relates to each sentence in the list, as shown in Figure 2.3b. *Note: The symbols shown are merely a guide.* Size each symbol to 16 points.
   c. Use any color combinations to create the advertisement. Use the Format Painter feature to copy the same formatting from one block of text to another.
4. Center the page vertically.
5. Preview and print one copy.
6. Save the file as **2.3backpack**.
7. Close the file.

Are You Ready to Travel Abroad?
See the World and Change Your Life

Backpack Buddies, Inc.

Plan a backpacking vacation that will
maximize your fun without breaking the bank!

6 questions to ask yourself:

What is my overall budget?
How do I want to spend my budget?
For how long will I be able to travel?
Do I need a passport?
Will I need visas to enter certain countries?
How can Backpack Buddies help make my trip one to remember?

Insert Text

Backpack Buddies can help you with:
Information on the most popular and interesting places to travel
Low-cost airfare

Figure 2.3a

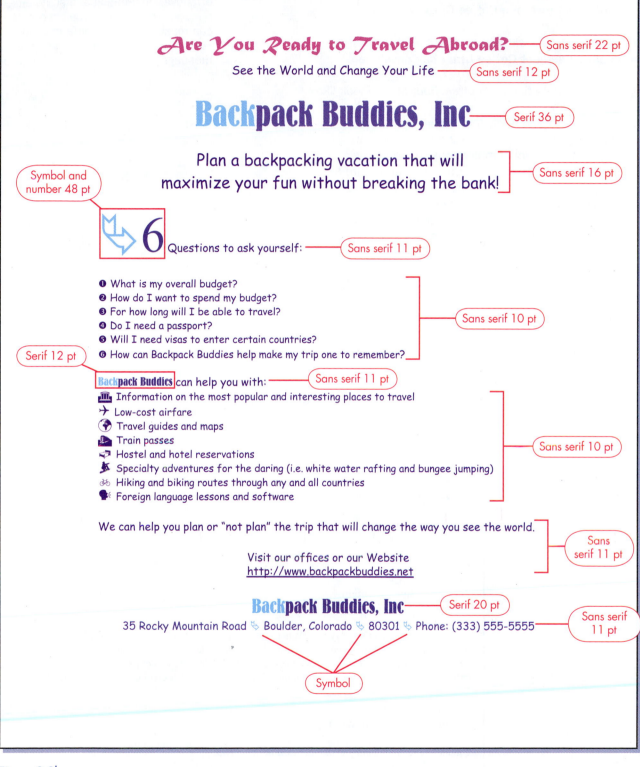

Are You Ready to Travel Abroad? — Sans serif 22 pt

See the World and Change Your Life — Sans serif 12 pt

Backpack Buddies, Inc — Serif 36 pt

Plan a backpacking vacation that will
maximize your fun without breaking the bank! — Sans serif 16 pt

Symbol and number 48 pt

6 Questions to ask yourself: — Sans serif 11 pt

❶ What is my overall budget?
❷ How do I want to spend my budget?
❸ For how long will I be able to travel?
❹ Do I need a passport?
❺ Will I need visas to enter certain countries?
❻ How can Backpack Buddies help make my trip one to remember?

— Sans serif 10 pt

Serif 12 pt

Backpack Buddies can help you with: — Sans serif 11 pt

Information on the most popular and interesting places to travel
Low-cost airfare
Travel guides and maps
Train passes
Hostel and hotel reservations
Specialty adventures for the daring (i.e. white water rafting and bungee jumping)
Hiking and biking routes through any and all countries
Foreign language lessons and software

— Sans serif 10 pt

We can help you plan or "not plan" the trip that will change the way you see the world. — Sans serif 11 pt

Visit our offices or our Website
http://www.backpackbuddies.net

Backpack Buddies, Inc — Serif 20 pt

35 Rocky Mountain Road ✎ Boulder, Colorado ✎ 80301 ✎ Phone: (333) 555-5555 — Sans serif 11 pt

Symbol

Figure 2.3b

2.4 EDIT FORMATTING

Coffee Crazy is a chain of coffee shops located in Seattle, San Francisco, and New York. It is developing a series of advertisements to promote the company. You have been asked to format text for a Coffee Crazy advertisement.

In this project, you will edit text and apply formatting for an advertisement Coffee Crazy has developed.

1. Open the data file **d2.4coffee**. Your file will look like Figure 2.4a.
2. Edit the text and apply formatting so that the document looks like Figure 2.4b. You may use any font and color combinations to create the advertisement. Use the Format Painter feature to copy the same formatting from one block of text to another. *Note: The font sizes are suggested.*
3. Insert number symbols for numbered lists and before the coffee bean varieties.
4. Center the page vertically.
5. Preview and print one copy.
6. Save the file as **2.4coffee**.
7. Close the file.

Coffee Crazy

How Many Ways Can You Make Your Coffee?

Drip Coffee
Café Latte
Cappuccino
Café au Lait
Espresso
Crazy Cold Coffee Mash

You Can Use a Variety of Coffee Beans

Kenyan
Costa Rican
Ethiopian Mocha
Jamaican Blue Mountain
Java Kona

The four questions of the day are: Where do you get your first cup of the day? Where do you meet your friends in the evening for a soothing café au lait? Are you a caffeine addict? Do you simply love the taste of rich and aromatic espresso? Whether you enjoy your drink in a local café or in the comfort of your own home, Coffee Crazy can meet all of your coffee needs.

Coffee Crazy
Seattle San Francisco New York

Check the yellow pages for the location nearest you.

Figure 2.4a

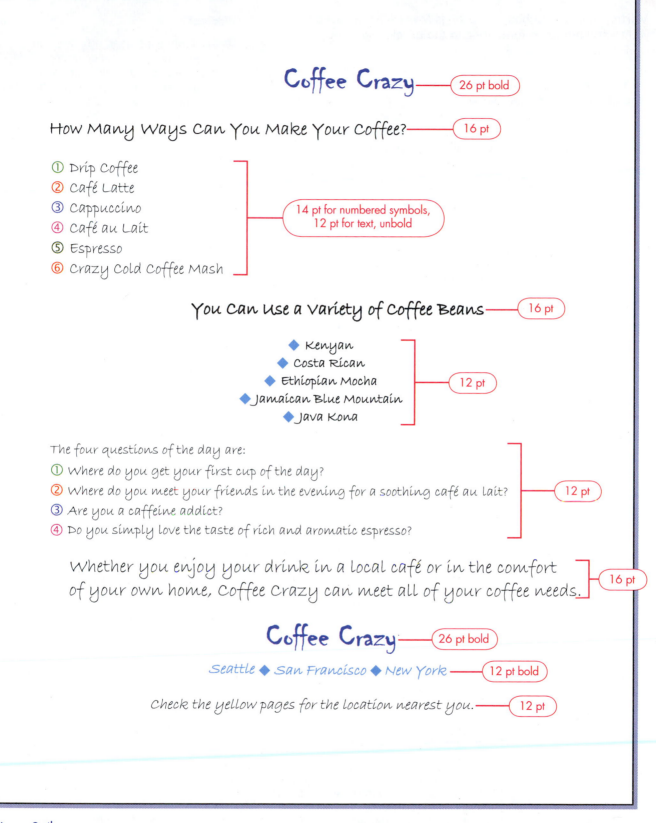

Coffee Crazy — 26 pt bold

How Many Ways Can You Make Your Coffee? — 16 pt

① Drip Coffee
② Café Latte
③ Cappuccino
④ Café au Lait
⑤ Espresso
⑥ Crazy Cold Coffee Mash

14 pt for numbered symbols, 12 pt for text, unbold

You Can Use a Variety of Coffee Beans — 16 pt

◆ Kenyan
◆ Costa Rican
◆ Ethiopian Mocha
◆ Jamaican Blue Mountain
◆ Java Kona

12 pt

The four questions of the day are:
① Where do you get your first cup of the day?
② Where do you meet your friends in the evening for a soothing café au lait?
③ Are you a caffeine addict?
④ Do you simply love the taste of rich and aromatic espresso?

12 pt

Whether you enjoy your drink in a local café or in the comfort of your own home, Coffee Crazy can meet all of your coffee needs. — 16 pt

Coffee Crazy — 26 pt bold

Seattle ◆ San Francisco ◆ New York — 12 pt bold

Check the yellow pages for the location nearest you. — 12 pt

Figure 2.4b

2.5 EDIT FORMATTING

Martha Halpin, your boss at *Tastings Magazine*, has asked you to add attractive formatting to the article you were working on in Project 1.3.

In this project, you will make further edits to enhance the article for *Tastings Magazine*.

1. Open the **1.3cooking tips** file that you created earlier. If this file is not available to you, open the data file **d2.5cooking tips**. Your file will look like the one shown in Figure 2.5a.
2. Delete the words shown in Figure 2.5a.
3. Set the left and right margins to 1.25".
4. Set the line spacing to 1.5 for the first paragraph.
5. Edit the remainder of the document so that the text looks like Figure 2.5b.
   a. Display codes and then delete the tabs before each paragraph.
   b. Use any font and color combinations to enhance the document. Use the Format Painter feature to copy the same formatting from one block of text to another. The font sizes are suggested and will depend on the font you choose.
6. Preview and print one copy.
7. Save the file as **2.5cooking tips final**.
8. Close the file.

FIVE BASIC COOKING TIPS FOR THOSE WHO LOVE TO CREATE GREAT MEALS

Preparing a meal requires quite a bit of skill and patience. The results may mean the difference between eating just to exist and the satisfaction that comes from one of the major pleasures of life.

ONE. PREPARE EVERY RECIPE WITH TENDER, LOVING CARE AS ONE OF THE CHIEF INGREDIENTS.
          Cooking is an art. A cook must develop a feeling for what each ingredient will do in a recipe.

TWO. USE INGREDIENTS THAT ARE GOOD FOR YOUR HEALTH.
          As long as you are cooking, use foods that contribute to a healthy diet—leafy green vegetables such as Brussels sprouts, garlic, and low-fat sources of protein such as fish and chicken.

THREE. USE HIGH-QUALITY RAW INGREDIENTS.
          An outstanding meal must be prepared with ingredients cooked simply but perfectly to increase their natural flavor. The menu should contain a contrast in textures, flavor, and color.

FOUR. USE FRESH HERBS.
          Herbs such as dill, parsley, basil, or tarragon will add zest to your meal and will truly enhance the flavor of a dish when they are fresh from the garden! Dried herbs do not really do the trick.

FIVE. USE THE BEST NATURAL FOODS OF THE SEASON, AND PLAN MENUS AROUND THEM.
          If at all possible, try to use fresh foods rather than packaged frozen items. If you have a garden, use fresh fruits whenever you can.

ONE. PREPARE EVERY RECIPE WITH TENDER, LOVING CARE AS ONE OF THE CHIEF INGREDIENTS.
TWO. USE INGREDIENTS THAT ARE GOOD FOR YOUR HEALTH.
THREE. USE HIGH-QUALITY RAW INGREDIENTS.
FOUR. USE FRESH HERBS.
FIVE. USE THE BEST NATURAL FOODS OF THE SEASON, AND PLAN MENUS AROUND THEM.

Figure 2.5a

FIVE BASIC COOKING TIPS FOR THOSE WHO LOVE TO CREATE GREAT MEALS

(18 pt)

Preparing a meal requires quite a bit of skill and patience. The results may mean the difference between eating just to exist and the satisfaction that comes from one of the major pleasures of life.

(11 pt)

ONE. PREPARE EVERY RECIPE WITH TENDER, LOVING CARE.

(12 pt)

Cooking is an art. A cook must develop a feeling for what each ingredient will do in a recipe.

(12 pt italic)

TWO. USE INGREDIENTS THAT ARE GOOD FOR YOUR HEALTH.

As long as you are cooking, use foods that contribute to a healthy diet—leafy green vegetables such as Brussels sprouts, garlic, and low-fat sources of protein such as fish and chicken.

THREE. USE HIGH-QUALITY RAW INGREDIENTS.

An outstanding meal must be prepared with ingredients cooked simply but perfectly to increase their natural flavor. The menu should contain a contrast in textures, flavor, and color.

FOUR. USE FRESH HERBS.

Herbs such as dill, parsley, basil, or tarragon will add zest to your meal and will truly enhance the flavor of a dish when they are fresh from the garden! Dried herbs do not really do the trick.

FIVE. USE THE BEST NATURAL FOODS OF THE SEASON.

If at all possible, try to use fresh foods rather than packaged frozen items. If you have a garden, use fresh fruits whenever you can.

ONE. PREPARE EVERY RECIPE WITH TENDER, LOVING CARE.
TWO. USE INGREDIENTS THAT ARE GOOD FOR YOUR HEALTH.
THREE. USE HIGH-QUALITY RAW INGREDIENTS.
FOUR. USE FRESH HERBS.
FIVE. USE THE BEST NATURAL FOODS OF THE SEASON.

(12 pt)

Figure 2.5b

Correspondence

In this chapter, you will complete the following projects:

PROJECT 3
Format Business and Personal Documents

PROJECT 3.1 Format a Business Letter and Envelope
PROJECT 3.2 Format a Business Letter with Special Notations
PROJECT 3.3 Format and Edit a Business Letter; Prepare Mailing Labels; Use Quick Parts
PROJECT 3.4 Finalize a Business Letter
PROJECT 3.5 Format a Personal Business Letter

PROJECT 4
Use Templates

PROJECT 4.1 Create a Memorandum
PROJECT 4.2 Create a Business Letter
PROJECT 4.3 Create a Résumé
PROJECT 4.4 Create a Custom Fax Cover and Letterhead Template

PROJECT 5
Compose and E-Mail Documents; Use Basic Mail Merge

PROJECT 5.1 Compose and Format Your Own Résumé
PROJECT 5.2 Compose and E-Mail a Business Letter
PROJECT 5.3 Compose and E-Mail a Personal Business Letter with an Attachment
PROJECT 5.4 Create a Mass Mailing
PROJECT 5.5 Create a Mass Mailing and Labels to Selected Recipients

PROJECT SKILLS

✱ Set margins
✱ Insert the date and time
✱ Create envelopes and labels
✱ Use QuickParts

PROJECT 3

3.1 FORMAT A BUSINESS LETTER AND ENVELOPE

You work for Hailey Rubino, Human Resources manager at Creative Services New York, an advertising agency. You have been asked to write an acceptance letter to an individual who has just been hired by your firm. Rather than use letterhead paper, you have been asked to create the company's letterhead directly on this letter.

In this project, you will create a block business letter and envelope.

1. Create a new document.
2. Use the following settings:

Margins	1.3" left and right
Line spacing	1.0
Paragraph spacing	
Before	0
After	0
Font	Default
Font size	Default

3. Begin the letterhead at 1". Enter the text as shown in Figure 3.1.
4. Prepare the block business letter exactly as shown. The numbers between letter parts indicate the number of times to press [Enter] between parts.
   a. Begin the date approximately 2.5" from the top of the page. Use the Date and Time feature to insert today's date.
   b. Insert a symbol of your choice before the three paragraphs as shown, and apply a green color to them.
5. Correct spelling.
6. Prepare an envelope, as shown in Figure 3.1, and append it to the letter.
7. Print one copy of the letter and envelope. *Note: If you do not have an actual envelope, print the envelope file on plain paper.*
8. Save the file as **3.1welcome**.
9. Close the file.

WHAT YOU NEED TO KNOW

Software

▶ The default left and right margins in Microsoft Word 2007 are 1"; the default top and bottom margins are 1". These margins may be changed, depending on the length of your document. To set margins, click the Page Layout tab and in the Page Setup group, click the Margins button. You can also set margins by dragging the margin markers on the ruler. To display the ruler, click the View tab and in the Show/ Hide group, click the Ruler check box.

▶ The default line spacing is 1.15 lines. To change line spacing, click the Home tab and in the paragraph group, click the Line spacing button, and choose a line spacing amount.

▶ The default paragraph spacing is 0 points before a paragraph and 10 points after a paragraph. To set paragraph spacing, click the Home tab and in the Paragraph group, click the Paragraph dialog box launcher. In the Paragraph dialog box, Indents and Spacing tab, enter a spacing amount in the Before and After text boxes.

▶ Use the Date and Time feature to insert the current date and/or time into a document. To insert a date, type the current month followed by a space. A ScreenTip showing today's date will be displayed. Press [Enter] to insert it. To change the date format or to insert or change the time format, click the Insert tab and in the Text group, click the Date & Time button. In the Date and Time dialog box, select the format you want, and click OK. To update the date each time you open the document, click the Update automatically check box.

Continued on next page

▶ The default envelope size for a No. 10 envelope (legal-size), is 4.13" x 9.5". The delivery address on an envelope is the same as the inside address in a letter. To create an envelope, click the Mailings tab and in the Create group, click the Envelopes button. On the Envelopes tab, enter the address of the person to whom the letter is being sent in the Delivery address window. If a letter is on screen, Word automatically places the inside address into the Delivery address window. Insert the envelope into your printer as shown in the Feed window, and click Print in the Envelopes and Labels dialog box. Click the Add to Document button in the Envelopes and Labels dialog box to append the envelope file to the beginning of the document. This saves you from having to re-create the envelope the next time you print the document.

Project

▶ *Correspondence* is considered any document that communicates a message, including letters, memos, and e-mail.

▶ Most letters have the following parts: date, inside address, salutation, body, closing, name and title of the writer, and reference initials of the writer and the individual who prepares the document.

▶ The layout of a letter is called a *format*. Letter formats include:

- Block—all parts begin at the left margin.

- Modified block—date and closing begin at the middle of the page or 3.5" from the left edge of the page while all other parts begin at the left margin.

- Semi-block—date and closing begin at the middle of the page or 3.5" from the left edge of the page, and each paragraph begins .5" from the left margin. The indentation of the first line of each paragraph is the only difference between the semi-block and the modified block formats.

Creative Services New York 〔16 pt〕

485 Madison Avenue ■ New York, NY 10017 〔11 pt〕
Phone: 212-555-5555 ■ Fax: 212-555-6666

Today's date ——〔Date〕

4x

Ms. Sandy Sanchez
710 Linden Boulevard ——〔Inside Address〕
Brooklyn, NY 11221
2x

Dear Ms. Sanchez: ——〔Salutation〕
2x

Congratulations and welcome to CSNY!
2x

We are excited that you have decided to further your career with us.
2x

❖ The Benefits orientation will be from 9:00 a.m. to approximately 10:30 a.m. on Monday, August 24 at 485 Madison Avenue in the 8th floor conference room. A light breakfast will be served.
2x

❖ Your supervisor or someone from your team will spend some time with you between 10:30 a.m. and 1:00 p.m.
2x

❖ Please join us in the 8th floor conference room at 1:00 p.m. for a general Human Resources orientation.
2x

To ensure that you are set up on the payroll system and that you are able to enroll in the CSNY Benefits Plan, we will need documentation establishing your U.S. citizenship. You will need to bring your Social Security card in addition to another form of identification.
2x

We look forward to seeing you on Monday. If you have any questions, or if I can be of additional assistance, please feel free to call me at the above phone number.
2x

Sincerely, ——〔Closing〕

4x

Hailey Rubino
Human Resources Manager ——〔Name and title of writer〕
2x

hr/yo ——〔Initials of writer and preparer〕

〔Body〕

Ms. Sandy Sanchez
710 Linden Boulevard
Brooklyn, NY 11221

Figure 3.1

3.2 FORMAT A BUSINESS LETTER WITH SPECIAL NOTATIONS

You work in the Marketing Department of VisionImage, a new graphic design company that has just relocated to the Chicago area. You have been asked to send a letter to the art directors of various magazines, informing them about the design services VisionImage offers.

In this project, you will create a modified-block business letter for VisionImage that contains special notations.

1. Open the data file **d3.2image**. (This file contains the letterhead.)
2. Use the following settings:

Margins	1" left and right
Line spacing	1.0
Paragraph spacing	
Before	0
After	0
Font	Default
Font size	Default

3. Prepare the modified-block business letter exactly as shown in Figure 3.2.
   a. Use the Date and Time feature to insert today's date.
   b. Begin the date at 2.0" from the top of the page.
   c. Tab once to create the bulleted summary of services, as shown. Use a symbol of your choice.
4. Correct spelling.
5. Prepare an envelope and append it to the letter.
6. Print one copy of the letter and envelope.
7. Save the file as **3.2imageletter**.
8. Close the file.

WHAT YOU NEED TO KNOW

Project

► A letter often contains special notations such as an attention line, subject line, enclosure/attachment or copy notation, and special mailing notations such as VIA E-MAIL, VIA MESSENGER, VIA FAX, and VIA FEDERAL EXPRESS. These notations are placed in a letter in specific places to alert the receiver. Special notations and their formatting are described as follows:

- Mailing notation—indicates how the document will be delivered. Sometimes documents are sent via fax, messenger, and/or e-mail, but they are also mailed in an envelope. If you are sending a document by any other means than traditional mail, the delivery type should be noted two lines below the date.

- Attention line—directs a letter to a person whose name you do not know (Office Manager, for example) or to a specific department (Marketing Department, for example). The attention line is the first line of both the inside address on the letter and the delivery address on the envelope. Use the salutation "Ladies and Gentlemen:" when you include an attention line.

- Subject line—states the subject of the letter. It appears two lines below the salutation. The word "Subject:" or "RE:" precedes the actual subject.

- Enclosure/Attachment notation—indicates when something in addition to the letter is included in the envelope. Use "Attachment" if additional pages are attached to the letter. Use "Enclosure" if they are not.

- Copy notation—shows that a copy of the letter is being sent to someone other than the addressee. Use "c:" (copy) or "cc:" (courtesy copy) followed by the name(s) of the person(s) who will receive the copy. Each name appears on a separate line and flush with the preceding name. The copy notation appears one or two lines below the last line of the enclosure/attachment notation or the reference initials if there is no enclosure/attachment.

► In a modified-block business letter, the date and closing start at the horizontal center of the page.

VISION IMAGE

245 Lamberts Lane Chicago, IL 60630-1215 (312) 555-5555

Today's date

VIA FAX —— (Special sending instructions)

2x

Attention Art Director —— (Attention line)
Departures Today Magazine
345 West Higgins
Chicago, IL 60630-1215

2x

Ladies and Gentlemen:

2x

RE: Services of VisionImage —— (Subject line)

2x

VisionImage has just opened on Lake Shore Drive in the Chicago area. We would like to introduce our services. The enclosed brochure details the graphic design and desktop expertise we offer our clients. Below is a summary of some of our services.

2x

◆ VisionImage creates state-of-the-art computer graphics and page layouts for businesses.
◆ VisionImage will find a solution to any design problem.
◆ VisionImage will consult with a company representative to create corporate designs.

2x

Zachary Westgate, our Chicago representative, will phone you sometime next week. Mr. Westgate would like to set up an appointment to show you our award-winning designs.

2x
Cordially,

4x

Martin Pilsner
President

2x
mp/yo

2x
Enclosure —— (Encloure notation)

2x
c: Zachary Westgate —— (Copy notation)

Attention Art Director
Departures Today Magazine
345 West Higgins
Chicago, IL 60630-1215

Figure 3.2

3.3 FORMAT AND EDIT A BUSINESS LETTER; PREPARE MAILING LABELS; USE QUICK PARTS

You work for Frank Malekoff, account director for Upton Investment Group. You have been asked to send a letter to one of his clients to inform him that Ms. Casavettes will now manage his account. Mr. Malekoff has already drafted the letter, but has asked you to format it properly and then send it via Federal Express. Upton Investment Group uses block format letters for business correspondence.

In this project, you will format a block business letter from unformatted copy.

1. Open a new blank document.
2. Use the following settings:

Margins	Default
Line spacing	1.0
Paragraph spacing	
Before	0
After	0
Font	Times New Roman
Font size	12 pt

3. Type the following at the top of the page:

   Sincerely,
   4x
   Frank Malekoff
   Account Director
   2x
   fm/yo (your own initials)

4. Create a Quick Parts entry for the closing, and name it **close**. Then close the file without saving.
5. Open the data file **d3.3change**, which is shown in Figure 3.3. *Note: The figure is shown double-spaced so corrections are easy to read. The data file is single-spaced.*
6. Make the revisions shown in the figure.
7. Format the text into a block letter.
   a. Use today's date.
   b. Include a mailing notation, enclosure notation, and copy notation to **S. Martin**.
   c. Include an appropriate subject line.
   d. Insert the Quick Parts entry named **close** for the closing.
8. Correct spelling.
9. Save the letter as **3.3change**.
10. Create an entire page of the same label. Select Avery US Letter as the Label vendor and 5388 as the product number. Save the label file as **3.3change labels**.

WHAT YOU NEED TO KNOW

Software

▶ The Labels feature allows you to create labels for mailings, file folders, business cards, or name badges. Once address labels are printed, they can be affixed to an envelope for mailing.

▶ To create labels, click the Mailings tab and in the Create group, click the Labels button. On the Labels tab, click Options to specify the label type you want to use. Select the label vendor and product number in the Label Options dialog box, and click OK. Click New Document in the Envelope and Labels dialog box. Blank labels appear, ready for you to begin entering text.

▶ The Quick Parts feature allows you to save and quickly insert frequently used text (such as a letter closing) and graphics (such as a letterhead with graphic elements), which are considered building blocks because they help you build your document.

▶ To create a new Quick Part, select the text or graphic you want to save as a building block entry. Include the paragraph mark in your selection if you want to save paragraph formatting with the entry. Click the Insert tab and in the Text group, click the Quick Parts button. Select Save Selection to Quick Part Gallery on the menu that appears. Enter a name for the new Quick Part in the Name box, and click OK to save it.

▶ To insert a Quick Part into a document, click to position the insertion point where you want to insert the entry, and click the Quick Parts button. Select the desired entry that was added to the Quick Parts menu.

Project

▶ "Sincerely" is generally used to close a letter. You can also use "Cordially," "Yours truly," and "Very truly yours."

11. Print one copy of the letter, and then print one sheet of labels. *Note: For the purpose of this activity, print the labels on a sheet of plain paper.*
12. Close all files.

~~Mr. Arthur Caruso, 67 Spring Street New York, NY,~~ Mr. Arthur Caruso, 67 Spring Street, New York, NY 10019 Dear Mr. Caruso: We are happy to inform you that your investment has yielded a hansome ~~annual~~ profit. ¶Our staff has recently undergone some major changes and your account is now being managed by Ms. Jill Casavettes, one of our senior account managers. Ms. Casavettes is one of our top investers and has over 15 years of experience in the field. ¶Ms. Casavettes would like to meet with you at your earliest convenience to discuss your investtment, as well as any future investments. Please call our offices between the hours of 9:00 a.m. and 6:00 p.m., Monday through Friday, to set up a time with Ms. Casavettes. In the meantime, we are enclosing some papers for you to sign, indicating the transfer of your account to Ms. Casavettes. ¶We look forward to hearing from you.

Figure 3.3

3.4 FINALIZE A BUSINESS LETTER

You work for Pamela Carson, manager of the Tri-State Auto Group. She has asked you to finalize the letter she drafted and send it to Mr. Angelo Ernesto, Angel's Used Cars, 444 Wheelwright Avenue, Bronx, NY 10467. The Tri-State Auto Group prefers the modified-block letter format for their correspondence. You have also been asked to delete the last paragraph of the letter, and compose a new one. This letter will be sent via fax, as well as via regular mail.

In this project, you will create a modified-block business letter and compose a new last paragraph.

1. Open the data file **d3.4tri-statelet**.
2. Open the data file **d3.4auction**. Copy the text from this file, and paste it in the letterhead file.
3. Use the following settings:

Margins	1.25" left and 1.5" right
Line spacing	1.0
Paragraph spacing	
Before	0
After	0
Font	Arial
Font size	11 pt

4. Make the corrections shown in Figure 3.4. *Note: The figure is shown double-spaced, so corrections are easy to read; the data file is single-spaced.*
5. Compose a new last paragraph that makes the following points:
   a. You appreciate Angel's Used Cars' past patronage.
   b. Representatives will be on hand to address any questions from specially invited guests.
   c. You look forward to doing business with Angel's Used Cars once again.
6. Format the document as a modified-block letter. Include the following:
   a. Today's date.
   b. Special mailing instructions as noted earlier.
   c. Inside address.
   d. Appropriate salutation.
   e. Closing.
   f. Enclosure notation (if necessary).
7. Preview the file. Make whatever adjustments are necessary to keep the letter on one page. *Note: You may have to adjust the start line for the date.*
8. Print one copy.
9. Save the file as **3.4auction**.
10. Close the file.

DRAFT ~~e~~

~~We are writing to inform you that~~ the TRI-STATE AUTO GROUP will be holding its annual auto auction on Sunday, September 25. Hundreds of makes and models have been overstocked. This means we are able to offer discounted prices to the public.

As a valued customer, you are invited to preview our stock before we open our doors to the general public. A special preview and bidding session will be held at 8:00 a.m. before the public auction begins at 10:00 a.m.

(along with the enclosed raffle ticket)

Bring this letter with you on the morning of the 25th to admit you to the special preview session. This auction is one of the largest events of the entire year.

The auction will take place at the Continental Arena, which is located on Route 95. For directions to the arena, please call 1-800-555-4444. ~~We hope to see you on Sunday, the 25th of September.~~

(Compose a new last paragraph)

Figure 3.4

3.5 FORMAT A PERSONAL BUSINESS LETTER

You have just returned from an interview for a summer internship at Upton Investment Group. You know that writing a follow-up letter to your interviewer is a good way to make a favorable impression.

In this project, you will format a personal business letter to Gina Jamal, Human Resources Assistant at Upton Investment Group, the person who interviewed you. Since this is the first of many interviews, you will also create your own letterhead so that you can use it on future letters.

1. Open a new document.
2. Use the following settings:

Margins	1.5" left and right
Line spacing	1.0
Paragraph spacing	
Before	0
After	0
Font	Arial
Font size	12 pt

3. Create your own letterhead; include your name, address, and phone and/or fax information. Use Figure 3.5 as a guide.
4. Save the file as **3.5myownlet**.
5. Format the personal letter as shown in Figure 3.5 using block letter format.
6. Correct spelling errors.
7. Save the file as **3.5thankyou**. Prepare an envelope and append it to the file.
8. Preview and print one copy.
9. Save the file again.
10. Close the file.

WHAT YOU NEED TO KNOW

Project

▶ Individuals, representing themselves rather than a business firm, write personal business letters.

▶ Personal business letters usually contain a personal letterhead that includes the writer's name and contact information (address, phone, fax, and e-mail address).

▶ Personal business letters use the same format as business letters and may include your title, but do not include reference initials.

Your Name
Your Address, City, State Zip
Phone number and/or Fax number and/or E-mail address

Create your
own letterhead

Today's date

Ms. Gina Jamal
Human Resources Assistant
Upton Investment Group
34562 Corona Street
Los Angeles, CA 90001

Dear Ms. Jamal:

It was a pleasure meeting you last week and discussing my summer internship prospects in Global Markets at Upton Investment Group.

I found our talk to be insightful and it has given me a new focus on a possible career in sales. The chance to work on a trading floor for the summer would, therefore, be invaluable.

Once again, thank you for your time and the opportunity to meet with you. I look forward to hearing from you soon.

Sincerely,

Your name

Ms. Gina Jamal
Human Resources Assistant
Upton Investment Group
34562 Corona Street
Los Angeles, CA 90001

Figure 3.5

PROJECT SKILLS
✷ Use existing templates
✷ Modify a template
✷ Create a template

PROJECT 4

4.1 CREATE A MEMORANDUM

You are special assistant to Janice Smith, manager of new product development for Upton Investment Group. One of your responsibilities is to prepare all correspondence, which includes memos. You have been asked to prepare a memo to Jamal Haari, with a copy to Mark Preston, about an upcoming meeting.

In this project, you will create a memo from a template.

1. Open a new document.
2. Use the Memo (Elegant design) template to create the memo shown in Figure 4.1. *Note: Memo templates are not among the Installed Templates. You must download Memo templates from Microsoft Office Online. Click the Office Button, New Button, Memos category (below Microsoft Office Online). If you do not have an Internet connection, open the data file* **d4.1announce**.
3. Highlight the bracketed text in the memo heading and enter the following:
   a. TO: **JAMAL HAARI**
   b. FROM: **YOUR NAME**
   c. SUBJECT: **NEW PRODUCT ANNOUNCEMENT**
   d. DATE: TODAY'S (automatically entered)
   e. CC: **MARK PRESTON**
   f. Select the sample text in the body and replace it with the text shown in Figure 4.1.
4. Print one copy.
5. Save the file as **4.1announce**.
6. Close the file.

WHAT YOU NEED TO KNOW

Software

▶ A *template* is a document that contains a predefined page layout, fonts, formatting, pictures, or text which may be reused as the structure for a new document.

▶ Word is installed with numerous predesigned templates that you can use to create a variety of different documents. Other Word templates can be found on Microsoft Office Online (www.microsoft.com).

▶ Templates are typically designed with a theme and a style. For each template type, there are usually several themes and styles from which to choose. A *theme* is a collection of overall colors, fonts, and effects. A *style* combines different colors, formats, fonts, and effects and determines which effect is dominant.

▶ Templates contain *placeholders*, which are boxes that identify the placement and location of text and contain preset text formats. Click the placeholder and enter new text, which will replace the sample text.

▶ To access templates, click the Office Button, and then click New. Click Installed Templates in the New Document dialog box. Thumbnails of each template installed on your computer are displayed in the middle pane. Click a template to select it. The selected template will be shown in the preview window in the right pane. Click Create to open the template.

▶ Pressing [Enter] at the end of a paragraph automatically inserts one blank line, thus creating a new paragraph.

▶ The date is automatically pulled from the computer's memory and inserted into the date location.

Continued on next page

Project

▶ A memorandum, or memo, is a written communication within a company.

▶ "Re:" in the memo heading means "in reference to" or "subject."

▶ Just as with letters, "cc:" in the memo heading refers to "courtesy copy" or "copies."

▶ Companies often include the department name and/or company logo in their memo format.

INTEROFFICE MEMORANDUM

TO:	JAMAL HAARI
FROM:	YOUR NAME
SUBJECT:	NEW PRODUCT ANNOUNCEMENT
DATE:	TODAY'S DATE
CC:	MARK PRESTON

The new Product Development Committee will meet on Thursday, January 16, 2010 at 10 a.m. to discuss the details of the Pension Plan Fund announcement.

We will need to prepare a press release later this mo nth and a plan for the promotion of this product. Please bring all relevant information with you.

Figure 4.1

4.2 CREATE A BUSINESS LETTER

You have been hired to work for Robin Viand, design consultant at SpaceWorks Interiors, a New York firm that designs office interiors. Although your career goal is to be a designer, this entry-level job enables you to "learn the business" as you assist with general office tasks. Because you are not yet comfortable formatting a letter from scratch, Robin has suggested that you use a letter template in Word to help you. You will adjust paragraph spacing in the template to conform to the company's memo format. You will also enter the company's letterhead in this template.

In this project, you will use a letter template to create a letter to a prospective client.

1. Open the Equity Letter template from Installed Templates.
2. Set 1.25" left and right margins.
3. Make the following modifications to the top part of the template:
   a. Delete the sender's name (which displays automatically), as well as the [Type the sender company name] and [Type the sender company address] placeholders.
   b. Select the [Pick a date] placeholder. Change the paragraph spacing After to 36 pt.
   c. Select the [Type the recipient address] placeholder. Change the paragraph spacing After to 12 pt.
   d. Select the [Type the salutation] placeholder. Change the paragraph spacing Before to 0 pt and After to 12 pt.
   e. Select the [Type the closing] placeholder. Change the paragraph spacing Before to 12 pt and After to 36 pt.
   f. Select the [Type the sender company name] and delete it.
   g. Double-click the footer area and enter the company's letterhead. Use the Alba font for the company information; set the company name to 14 point; and set the address and phone information to 10 pt. Apply shades of orange to the text as shown.
4. Start the dateline at approximately 2.5" from the top of the page.
5. Select the [Pick a date] placeholder and insert today's date.
6. Enter the letter text as shown in Figure 4.2.
7. Check spelling and grammar in the document.
8. Unbold the salutation.
9. Save the file as **4.2interior**.
10. Preview and print one copy.
11. Close the file.

WHAT YOU NEED TO KNOW

Software

▶ The line and paragraph spacing on letter templates will vary, and there might not be traditional spacing between the parts of the letter. You can adjust this, however. Check the line spacing setting when you use a template.

▶ Some placeholders, once selected, will provide a drop-down list of options. The [Pick a date] placeholder will display a drop-down calendar for you to choose the date to be inserted. Other placeholders automatically insert information from the computer's memory, such as your name or your school or company name.

▶ Many templates use 10 pt as the default font size, which you can change if you prefer.

Project

▶ A formal business salutation generally includes a colon after the name (Dear Mr. Miller:).

▶ An informal salutation includes a comma after the name. The name can be a first name (Dear Joan,) or a courtesy title and last name (Dear Ms. Delisi,).

Today's date

Mr. Robert Green
555 Madison Avenue
New York, NY 10016

Dear Mr. Green:

Thank you for your interest in SpaceWorks Interiors. We understand you will be opening an office in New York City sometime next year.

Our company has been designing office interiors in the New York area for the past 15 years. Our goal is to design spaces that are productive work environments, satisfying the needs of all workers, from upper-level management to support staff.

I have enclosed a catalog that highlights some of our most recent work. I can also arrange site visits for you so that you can walk through some of these spaces. If you have any questions or would like to set up a meeting, please do not hesitate to contact me at 212-555-3601. I look forward to speaking with you.

Sincerely,

Robin Viand
Design Consultant

rv
Enclosure

SpaceWorks Interiors 240 Park AvenueNew York, NY 10022 Phone 212·555·3601 Fax 212·555··3602

Figure 4.2

4.3 CREATE A RÉSUMÉ

You just interviewed a high school senior for a summer internship with your firm, Trilogy Productions. The interview went well; you thought the candidate made an excellent appearance and was very articulate. Her résumé, however, was poorly done. To help her obtain this position, you have offered to redo her résumé.

In this project, you will create a résumé using a Resume template.

1. Open the Urban Resume template from Installed Templates.
2. Create the résumé shown in Figure 4.3.
   a. Click the Name and address placeholder to display the Resume Name option. Click the list arrow and select Name with Photo. Right-click the photo, select Change Picture, and insert the photo (data file **d4.3resume photo.tif**) in the photo placeholder.
   b. Use the four side headings included in the template.
   c. Include **Hobbies** and **References** as additional side headings. To include additional rows for new side headings, position your insertion point in the last box of the last row and press [Tab] twice, which will enter two blank rows. Enter text in the second newly created row, as shown in the figure.
3. Preview the document, make any adjustments necessary, and print one copy.
4. Save the file as **4.3resume**.
5. Close the file.

WHAT YOU NEED TO KNOW

Software
▶ Word contains several Résumé template designs. Several designs give you the option of including a photo.
▶ Use the same technique to open the résumé template that you used for the letter template.

Project
▶ A résumé conveys an image to the reader about the sender. The design of a résumé should be conservative and somewhat formal. The résumé should look professional and should be appropriate for its audience.
▶ When citing your work experience, list your most recent employment position first. If you do not have a great deal of experience, list your education first.
▶ When citing your education, list the last school you attended first.

Jaime L. Blane

201 Sunset Boulevard
Beverly Hills, CA 90210
Phone: 310-555-0000
Fax: 310-555-6666
E-mail: ptblane@net.net

Objective	To obtain a summer internship that will utilize my skills and will enable me to learn about career opportunities
Skills	**Fluent in Spanish, MOS Certified in Word, Excel, and PowerPoint**
Education	**Beverly Hills High School** June 2010 • Honor Society (Upper 10% of class) • Yearbook Staff • Westinghouse Scholarship Participant, national third-place winner
Experience	**Office Assistant** July 2009– August 2009 Managed appointments, correspondence, and special assignments for ten brokers
	Sales Assistant July 2008-August 2008 Sold apparel, worked cash register, and set up displays
Hobbies	**Reading, Ice Skating**
References	**Mr. Thomas Rose, Senior Manager, G & G Investments, 55 Melrose Place, Beverly Hills, CA 90210 310-555-5555.** **Ms. Anita Carlson, College Advisor, Beverly Hills High School, 310-555-6666**

Figure 4.3

4.4 CREATE A CUSTOM FAX COVER AND LETTERHEAD TEMPLATE

You are starting your own health foods business and need to create template documents for your office. Your first two tasks are to create a fax cover sheet and a letterhead to be saved and used at a later time. The name of your company is HEALTH CONNECTIONS.

In this project, you will create two custom templates—a fax cover and a letterhead.

1. Open the Origin Fax template from Installed Templates. If this template is not available to you, open the data file **d4.4fax**.
2. Center the company name between the Fax and information tables, as shown in Figure 4.4b.
   a. Set the company name to 36 pt bold, the word Fax to 48 pt, and the text at the bottom of the document to 16 pt using the Chiller font. (Substitute another font if you do not have this one available to you).
   b. Click the [Type the sender phone number] placeholder, and enter **212–555–5555**.
   c. Click the [Type the sender fax number] placeholder, and enter **212–555–6666**.
   d. Delete the words "Company Name:" and the [Type the sender company name] placeholder from the information table.
3. Save the file as a Word template. Name it **4.4fax**.
4. Print one copy.
5. Close the file.
6. Open a new blank document.
7. Center the letterhead text, as shown in Figure 4.4a.
   a. Use the same font and font size for the company name that you used on the fax cover sheet. Apply a green font color.
   b. Enter the contact information using a 9 pt Arial font. Insert any desired symbol between address and phone information as shown. Apply a blue font color.
8. Save the file as a template. Name it **4.4health-lethead**.
9. Print one copy.
10. Close the file.

WHAT YOU NEED TO KNOW

Software

▶ You can modify a template or create a template from scratch with your company's logo and other standard information, and save it for use at a later time. You can save a custom template so that it appears in the New Document dialog box among the other template thumbnails, or you can save it to your desktop for easy access.

▶ To save a document as a template, click the Office Button and point to Save As. Select Word Template from the Save a copy of the document list. The Templates folder is automatically selected as the save location. You can save in this location or any other that you choose. Enter a filename and click Save. Since you are saving the file in the Templates folder, Word automatically enters "Word Template" as the Save as type. The file extension for a Word template is dotx.

Project

▶ A fax cover sheet is used as the first page of several to be faxed. Its purpose is to identify the recipient and the sender of the faxed pages. You can also use the fax cover sheet to include a message.

HEALTH CONNECTIONS

265 Park Avenue South ⅄ New York, NY 10003 ⅄ P: (212) 555-5555 ⅄ F: (212) 555-6666 ⅄ E-mail: hc@net.net

▶Fax

[Pick a date]

Center Company name here

HEALTH CONNECTIONS

From:	Iris Blanc
Phone:	[Type the sender phone number]
Fax:	[Type the sender fax number]
To:	[Type the recipient name]
Phone:	[Type the recipient phone number]
Fax:	[Type the recipient fax number]
Company Name:	[Type the recipient company name]

Comments:

[Type comments]

☐ Urgent	☐ For Review	☐ Please Comment	☐ Please Reply	☐ Please Recycle

Figure 4.4a
Letterhead

Figure 4.4b Fax

PROJECT 5

PROJECT SKILLS

* Compose a new document and e-mail message
* Send a Word document as an e-mail and attach another file
* Use mail merge to mass-produce letters
* Merge labels with a data source document
* Filter records during the mail merge process

5.1 COMPOSE AND FORMAT YOUR OWN RÉSUMÉ

In this project, you will create a résumé for yourself using a Word template. Be sure to include any computer skills you possess. Later, you will send the résumé as an attachment to an e-mail message.

1. Create a new document.
2. Access a résumé template that is different from the one used in Project 4.3.
3. Set 1" left and right margins.
4. Create your own résumé, using Project 4.3 as a guide.
5. Correct spelling.
6. Preview and print one copy.
7. Save the file as **5.1myresume**.
8. Close the document window.

WHAT YOU NEED TO KNOW

Project

▶ You may use any résumé template to create your own résumé.

▶ If you want, apply color or any résumé element(s) to personalize your document. You may also include your photo, if you want.

▶ Applicants may submit résumés electronically by posting to corporate Websites or attaching them to an e-mail message.

5.2 COMPOSE AND E-MAIL A BUSINESS LETTER

Your boss, Hailey Rubino, Human Resources Manager of Creative Services New York, always sends a reminder to newly hired employees to attend the next Benefits Orientation. (The next orientation is scheduled for Monday, August 24.) You have been asked to prepare a letter for your boss and send it to Ms. Sandy Sanchez to remind her of this important orientation session. You can cut and paste the inside address, salutation, and some of the details from a previous letter you sent to her (in the file named 3.1welcome).

In this project, you will compose a letter to Ms. Sanchez, and e-mail it to her on behalf of your boss, Ms. Rubino.

1. Open the data file **d5.2csny-lethead template**.
2. Save the file as **5.2reminder**.
3. Use the following settings:

Margins	default
Line spacing	1.0
Paragraph spacing	
Before	0
After	0
Font	default
Font size	default

4. Insert today's date approximately 2.5" from the top of the page.
5. Open **3.1welcome** (the document you completed in Project 3.1). If this file is not available to you, open the data file **d5.2welcome**.
6. Copy the inside address and salutation from **d5.2welcome** (or from **3.1welcome**) and paste the information into the appropriate location in the letter you are composing (**5.2reminder**).
7. Compose the body of the letter to Ms. Sanchez as follows:
   a. For the first paragraph, explain that this letter is a reminder to all newly hired employees to attend the Benefits Orientation.
   b. For the next three paragraphs, copy the paragraphs that contain the green symbols from **d5.2welcome** (or from **3.1welcome**) and paste them into this letter.
   c. For the last paragraph, tell Ms. Sanchez that you look forward to seeing her on August 24.
8. Copy the closing lines from **d5.2welcome** (or from **3.1welcome**) into this letter.
9. Preview the document, make any adjustments necessary, and print one copy.

WHAT YOU NEED TO KNOW

Software

▶ *E-mail*, an abbreviation for "electronic mail," refers to the transmission of messages over communication networks.

▶ You can quickly send a Word document that is on screen to a single person or to an entire group simultaneously without starting your e-mail program. When you send an on-screen document as an e-mail, it is sent as an attachment. You must have an e-mail program installed on your computer and an e-mail account set up to actually send a message.

▶ To e-mail a Word document that is on screen, click the Office Button, point to Send, and then click E-mail. An e-mail message window opens with the document name automatically entered in the subject line (you can change the subject name, if you want), and the document attached to the message. In the To box, enter the e-mail address of the person or persons to whom you are sending the message and attachment. In the message window, enter your message, and then click the Send button. *Note: If you do not have an e-mail program installed, the Send button will not be visible.*

Project

▶ Always provide a meaningful subject line in your e-mail message.
▶ Use business language in office communications.
▶ Keep messages short and to the point.
▶ Use proper spelling, grammar, and punctuation.
▶ Include paragraphs as you would in other correspondence.
▶ Include a salutation (Dear Ms. Hanson: if it is a formal business contact or Dear Janice, if it is a less formal contact).
▶ Always use a "signature" in your message. (A *signature* is a small block of text that contains your contact information, such as your name, a mailing address, a phone/fax number, and/or a Website address. Think of a signature as an electronic business card.)
▶ Many e-mail systems allow you to add a signature to your messages automatically.

10. Save the file.

11. Send this online document to Ms. Sanchez.

    a. Enter her e-mail address: ssan@net.net.

    b. Enter a relevant subject in the Subject box (change the one that is entered automatically).

    c. Print a copy of the e-mail, but do not send it. *Note: For this project activity, you will not actually send the message since the e-mail address is not authentic.*

    d. Close the e-mail window.

12. Close all Word files.

5.3 COMPOSE AND E-MAIL A PERSONAL BUSINESS LETTER WITH AN ATTACHMENT

Your friend, Martin Cho, who works as a desktop designer for Baxter Publishing Company, has informed you that Baxter Publishing has a summer intern position available. He has suggested that you apply for the job.

In this project, you will compose a personal business letter to apply for the position. You will e-mail the on-screen letter and also attach your résumé.

1. Open **3.5myownlet** (your personal letterhead created earlier).
2. Save the file as a template. Name it **5.3mylet-template**.
3. Use the following settings:

Margins	default
Line spacing	1.0
Paragraph spacing	
Before	0
After	0
Font	default
Font size	default

4. Compose a job application letter, using the proper format for a personal business letter (refer to Project 3.5 for the proper format) and today's date. *Note: Sample text for this type of letter is shown in Figure 5.3. Use it as a guide for developing your document. Read the project information for further guidelines. Provide appropriate closing lines.*
   a. Address the letter to **Ms. Marlene McMann, Personnel Director, Baxter Publishing Company, 52 Beacon Street, Boston, MA 02111-3384.**
   b. Indicate on the letter that the document will be sent via e-mail.
   c. Correct spelling errors.
   d. Save the file as **5.3jobposition**.
   e. Preview and print one copy.
5. E-mail the on-screen letter.
   a. Enter Marlene McMann's e-mail address: mmm@baxpubco.com.
   b. Enter an appropriate subject line.
   c. Attach the résumé you created in the previous project (**5.1myresume**) to this e-mail. *Note: Your teacher might want you to send the letter (along with the attached résumé) to his/her e-mail address.*
   d. Close the e-mail message window.
6. Close all files. *Note: For this project activity, you will not actually send the message because the e-mail address is not authentic.*

WHAT YOU NEED TO KNOW

Software

▶ As indicated in Project 5.2, an on-screen document is sent as an attachment. You can also attach other files.

▶ To attach a file, click the Office Button, point to Send, and click E-mail. In the e-mail message window, enter the recipient's address in the To line, click the Insert tab and in the Include group, click the Attach File button. In the Insert file dialog box that is displayed, navigate to the file you want to attach, and click Insert. In the E-mail message window, the Attached box displays the files that are attached to the message.

Attach File

Project

▶ When you are applying for a job, you will send a job application letter (sometimes called a cover letter) along with a résumé. A cover letter for a résumé should be structured as follows:

- The first paragraph should state the position for which you are applying. It should mention how you learned of the position. You might want to say something positive that you know about the company or someone who works for the company.

- In the next one or two paragraphs, make sure the reader knows that you understand the requirements for the position. Explain how your background qualifies you for the position. You can elaborate on some of the information in your résumé, such as courses taken or skills achieved, that is particularly relevant to the position for which you are applying. At the end of the last paragraph in this section, refer the reader to your résumé for additional information.

- In the last paragraph, request an interview. Provide the reader with an easy way to contact you to schedule the interview.

Chris Peterson, a senior production editor, has informed me of the production editor position that will be available at Haas Publishing on August 20. I have always been impressed by the award-winning magazines and catalogs produced by your company. Please consider me as an applicant for the production editor position.

I received my associate s degree in graphic design from the School of Visual Arts in June. My course work included two advanced classes in desktop publishing, one entirely on PhotoShop and QuarkXPress, which I am told is the software used by production editors at your company. In high school and college, I worked as an intern at Olympia, a small production company, designing and producing technical manuals and a sales catalog. For detailed information about my educational background and work experience, please refer to the attached resume.

I would welcome the opportunity to discuss the production editor position with you in a personal interview. Please call me at the phone number indicated above to arrange a mutually convenient time.

Figure 5.3

5.4 CREATE A MASS MAILING

HEALTH CONNECTIONS has asked you to send a letter to customers who have an outstanding account with the company.

In this project, you will use the Mail Merge feature to create a mass mailing.

1. Open the data file **d5.4health-lethead**.
2. Enter today's date approximately 2,5" from the top of the page.
3. Use the following settings:

Margins	default
Line spacing	1.0
Paragraph spacing	
Before	0
After	0
Font	default
Font size	default

4. Start the mail merge wizard.
   a. When prompted in Step 1, select Letters as the document type.
   b. When prompted in Step 2, select Use the current document.
   c. When prompted in Step 3, select Type a new list, and click Create. *Note: You will have to customize the New Address List and add two fields as noted in the following:*
   • In the New Address List dialog box, click the Customize Columns button (see Figure 5.4b). Delete the following field names: AddressLine2, Country or Region, Home Phone, Work Phone, and E-Mail Address. Add the following field names: **Amount** and **Was due**.
   • Enter the data shown in Figure 5.4b. When prompted, save the address list as **5.4collection list**.
5. Enter the text shown in Figure 5.4a.
   a. When prompted in Step 4, select the AddressBlock field code for the inside address and Greeting Line for the salutation.
   b. When prompted for a greeting line format, select a colon after the recipient's name.
   c. Click More items to insert the Amount and Was due field codes.
   d. Be sure to insert spacing between codes as if actual text were inserted.
   e. Preview your letters, make any adjustments needed, and complete the merge.

WHAT YOU NEED TO KNOW

Software

▶ The Mail Merge feature lets you mass-produce letters, envelopes, mailing labels, and other documents so they appear personalized.

▶ The merge process combines two documents: a main document and a data source document.

▶ The main document contains information that does not change as well as merge codes where variable information will be inserted. A merge field code acts as a placeholder for the variable information. All formatting, graphics, spacing (between merge codes), and paper size information should be included in the main document. Each field code is named for what will eventually be inserted into that location.

▶ The data source document contains variable information (a name and address list, for example). In Word, the data source document information is displayed in a table format with a series of columns and rows. Each column in the data source corresponds to a category of information or a data field-for example, first name, last name, and title. Each row in the table contains one data *record*, which is a complete set of related information about one person or thing. Each row in a table represents one record (information about one person or one thing).

▶ Word provides you with a help feature called a *wizard* to guide you step by step through the mail merge process. Click the Mailings tab and in the Start Mail Merge group, click the Start Mail Merge button, and select Step-by-Step Mail Merge Wizard. The Mail Merge task pane takes you step-by-step through the mail merge process.

Continued on next page

6. Save the merged letters as **5.4collection letters final**.
7. Print one copy of the merged letters.
8. Close all files.

HEALTH CONNECTIONS

265 Park Avenue South ∀ New York, NY 10003 ∀ P: (212) 555-5555 ∀ F: (212) 555-6666 ∀ E-mail: hc@net.net

Today's date

«AddressBlock»

«GreetingLine»

We must remind you, «Title» «Last_Name», that your account is now past due. As you can see from the enclosed statement, you still have an outstanding balance of $«Amount», which was due on «Was_due».

We need your cooperation so that we can continue to give you outstanding service and excellent pricing.

Please mail your remittance for $«Amount» today so we are not forced to send your account to our collection agency.

Cordially,

Brenda Nelson
Accounting Manager

bn/yo
Enclosure

Figure 5.4a Main document

▶ The AddressBlock merge code is a combination of several fields and includes Title, First Name, Last Name, Address, City, State, and Postal code (ZIP Code). (You will be prompted to choose the format for these fields during the merge process.) The Greeting Line merge code is a combination of two fields—Title and Last Name—but may include "To" or "Dear" preceding the title and the last name, as well as end-of-line punctuation (either a colon or comma), depending on your selections during the merge process.

Project

▶ In this project, the same letter is mailed to several people who have an outstanding account with HEALTH CONNECTIONS. Each letter has the same basic wording, but contains variable information (the inside address, the amount of money owed, and the date when the balance was due).

New Address List

Type recipient information in the table. To add more entries, click New Entry.

	Title ▼	First Name ▼	Last Name ▼	Company Name ▼	Address Line 1 ▼	City ▼	State ▼	ZIP Code ▼	Amount ▼	Was due ▼
	Ms.	Vanessa	Jackson	Metropolitan Foods	48 Endor Avenue	Brooklyn	NY	11221	256.98	March 1
	Mr.	Kenneth	Hall		5 Windsor Drive	West Long Branch	NJ	07764	450.70	March 15
	Mr.	Glenn	Bacco	Tribecca Sundry Shoppe	187 Beach Street	New York	NY	10001	128.86	February 28
	Ms.	Stefanie	Newman		137 Brighton Avenue	Perth Amboy	NJ	08861	612.75	February 15

Click to edit field names in columns

New Entry   Find...
Delete Entry   Customize Columns...   OK   Cancel

Figure 5.4b Source document

5.5 CREATE A MASS MAILING AND LABELS TO SELECTED RECIPIENTS

Sales at Coffee Crazy & Things have been excellent. In fact, sales are so good that it is difficult to keep some items in stock. Your boss has asked you to create a mass mailing to customers notifying them that a damaged item is no longer in stock. A customer database has already been created in Access.

In this project, you will create a mass mailing to customers, notifying them that the item they ordered is no longer in stock. You will send the letters only to those who have ordered the espresso maker.

1. Open the data file **d5.5coffee-lethead**.
2. Use the following settings:

Margins	default
Line spacing	1.0
Paragraph spacing	
Before	0
After	0
Font	default
Font size	default

3. Enter today's date approximately 2" from the top of the page.
4. Start the Mail Merge Wizard.
   a. When prompted in Step 1, select Letters as the document type.
   b. When prompted in Step 2, select Use the current document.
   c. When prompted in Step 3, select Use an existing list, and click Browse. Navigate to the data file (data source document), and open **d5.5customer list**.
5. Filter the records on Catalog Number (catno) 888 (for only those who ordered the espresso maker).
6. Enter the letter text shown in Figure 5.5.
   a. When prompted in Step 4, select the AddressBlock field code for the inside address and Greeting Line for the salutation.
   b. When prompted for a greeting line format, select a colon after the recipient's name.
   c. Click More items to insert the *item*, *catno*, *purdate*, *paymentmethod,* and *amt* fields.
   d. Be sure to insert a space between codes as though text were inserted.
7. Preview your letters, make any adjustments needed, and complete the merge.
8. Save the merged letters as **5.5sorry final**.

WHAT YOU NEED TO KNOW

Software

▶ You can use the Mail Merge feature to create labels or envelopes for mailing your new documents. The label (or envelope) is the main document, which will be merged with a data source.

▶ To create labels, use the step by step Mail Merge Wizard to create labels and envelopes in the same way you created your merged letters. Click the Mailings tab, and in the Start Mail Merge group, click the Start Mail Merge button, and select Step-by Step Mail Merge Wizard. In the Mail Merge task pane, select Labels (or Envelopes) as the document type. Select the label product or envelope size when prompted, and select the recipients that you used for your letter.

▶ You can merge a main document with all the records in the data source document, or you can set one or more conditions that the data records must meet to be included in the merge. This is referred to as "filtering" the records. For example, you may want to merge only those records within a specific ZIP Code or state.

▶ To merge selected records, display the Mail Merge Recipients dialog box. Click the list arrow next to the column heading, and choose the item in the column you want to filter. You can also use the check boxes on the left to add or remove recipients from the mail merge. After selecting the recipients you want, continue the mail merge process.

Project

▶ Companies keep a customer database that lists a customer's name, contact information, merchandise purchased, amount spent, and any other relevant customer information. If the list was created in Access or Excel, you can use that file as the data source document. Once you enter contact information such as a name, address, phone number, or e-mail address in Access or Excel, you can integrate it and use it in Word.

9. Print one copy of each letter.

10. Close the file.

11. To create the labels:

    a. Open a new blank document.

    b. Use the following settings:

Margins	default
Line spacing	1.0
Paragraph spacing	
Before	0
After	0
Font	default
Font size	default

    c. Start the Mail Merge Wizard.

- When prompted in Step 1, select Labels as the document type.
- When prompted in Step 2, select Label options. Use 5661 as the label product number.
- When prompted in Step 3, select Use an existing list, and click Browse. Navigate to the data file **d5.5customer list**, and open it.
- Filter the records on Catalog Number (catno) 888.
- When prompted in Step 4, select the AddressBlock field code for the inside address.
- Click Update all labels.

12. Preview your labels, make any adjustments needed, and complete the merge.

13. Print the labels on plain paper.

14. Save the labels file as **5.5labels**.

Today's Date

«AddressBlock»

«GreetingLine»

Thank you for placing an order with Coffee Crazy & Things for «item», «catno», on «purdate».

Unfortunately, we no longer have the item(s) you ordered in stock and do not expect another shipment for at least three months. Because we cannot fill your order at this time, we did not charge your «paymentmethod» account in the amount of «amt».

If you would like to make another purchase, please call us at the number indicated below. We will notify you when we have the item(s) back in stock, should you wish to reorder it at that time.

We are sorry for any inconvenience this might have caused you.

Sincerely,

Mary Kline
Catalog Sales

mk

P.O. Box 333 ☆ Seattle, Washington 98199
Phone: 800-555-5555 ☆ Fax: 800-666-6666
Web: www.coffeecrazynthings.com

Figure 5.5

Lists, Meeting Documents, Schedules, and Forms

In this chapter, you will complete the following projects:

PROJECT 6
Documents for a Meeting

PROJECT 6.1 Create an Agenda
PROJECT 6.2 Create an Agenda; Create and Sort a List
PROJECT 6.3 Create an Agenda Using a Table Format
PROJECT 6.4 Format Minutes of a Meeting
PROJECT 6.5 Create a Memo with an Inserted Outline

PROJECT 7
Schedules, Programs, and Forms

PROJECT 7.1 Create an Itinerary
PROJECT 7.2 Create an Activities Schedule
PROJECT 7.3 Create a Rate Schedule
PROJECT 7.4 Create a Records List
PROJECT 7.5 Format a Project Schedule
PROJECT 7.6 Create a Program
PROJECT 7.7 Format a Program
PROJECT 7.8 Create a Calendar
PROJECT 7.9 Create a Table of Contents
PROJECT 7.10 Create a Form

DOCUMENTS FOR A MEETING

PROJECT 6

PROJECT SKILLS
* Create bulleted, numbered, and multilevel lists
* Sort lists
* Create and format tables
* Insert an outline into a document

6.1 CREATE AN AGENDA

The owners of Tri-State Auto Group will hold a meeting with senior staff to discuss investments in the automotive industry. The company is considering the purchase of an automotive dealership in England. You have been asked to format an agenda for the meeting.

In this project, you will format and revise an agenda as an outline using a multilevel list.

1. Open the data file **d6.1tri-statelettemp**.
2. Use the following settings:

Margins	1.25" left and right
Line spacing	Single
Paragraph spacing	
Before	0
After	0
Font	Century Gothic
Font size	11 pt

3. Create the agenda using a multilevel list format, as shown in Figure 6.1a. Start the heading approximately 2.5" from the top of the page.
4. Format the word "Agenda" in bold.
5. Correct spelling.
6. Save the file as **6.1agenda**.
7. Preview and print one copy.
8. Edit the outline, as shown in Figure 6.1b.
9. Save the file as **6.1agenda final**.
10. Print one copy.
11. Close all files.

WHAT YOU NEED TO KNOW

Software

▶ Lists allow you to summarize information in an organized way, and they also have many different uses. You can create a numbered list to sequence information, a bulleted list to emphasize points of information that do not need a sequence, or a multilevel list to organize information in a hierarchical structure. Multilevel lists can be bulleted, numbered, or an outline.

▶ To create a bulleted list, click the Home tab and in the Paragraph group, click the Bullets button.

▶ To create a numbered list, click the Home tab and in the Paragraph group, click the Numbering button.

▶ To create a multilevel list, click the Home tab and in the Paragraph group, click the Multilevel List button, and choose a multilevel list style from the library that is displayed. Enter the first line of text, press [Enter] once to stay on the same level, or press [Enter] and then [Tab] to indent text to the next level. To move back a level, press the Decrease Indent button, or press [Enter] more than once to move back additional levels.

▶ You can restructure and edit a multilevel list (outline) by cutting and pasting text. When you insert and/or delete text from a numbered list, Word automatically adjusts the numbers.

Continued on next page

► You can change the numbering or bullet style to one of the styles that Word provides in the bullets and numbering libraries.

► To change the bullet symbol, click the Home tab and in the Paragraph group, click the Bullets button list arrow, then click to choose a bullet style from the Bullet Library. You can see a live preview of the bullet style before making your selection by placing your insertion point over each bullet style. Type your text, and then press [Enter] to start each new bullet.

► To change the numbering style, click the Home tab and in the Paragraph group, click the Numbering button list arrow, and then click to choose a style from the Numbering Library.

Project

► An *agenda* is a plan or list of things to do, events to occur, or matters to bring before a committee, council, or board.

► The format of an agenda can vary, but is usually created as an outline. Regardless of the format used, an agenda always includes the date and time, and sometimes the location of the planned activities.

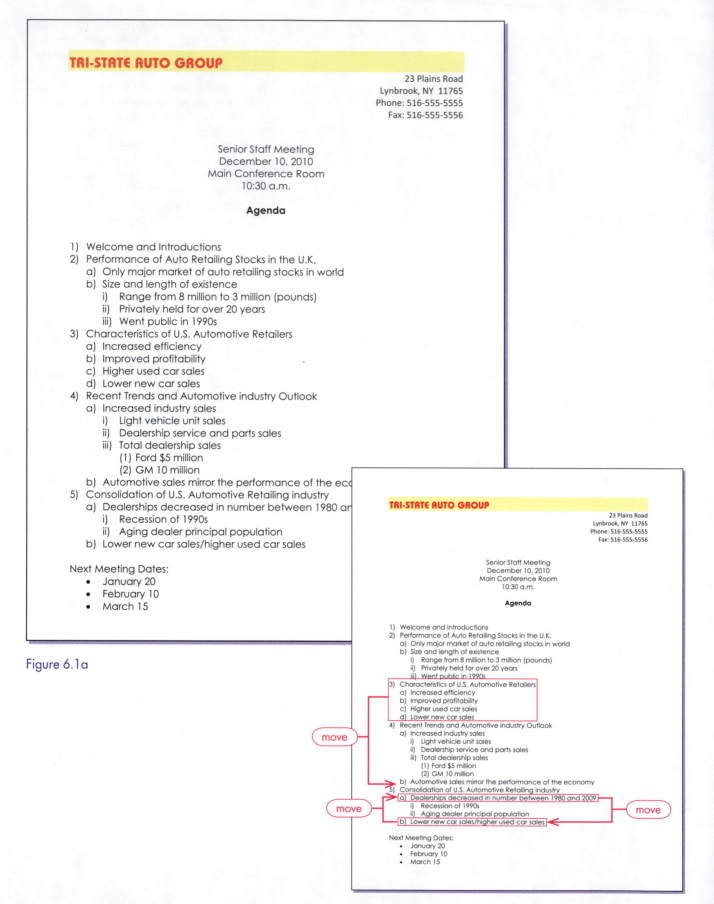

TRI-STATE AUTO GROUP

23 Plains Road
Lynbrook, NY 11765
Phone: 516-555-5555
Fax: 516-555-5556

Senior Staff Meeting
December 10, 2010
Main Conference Room
10:30 a.m.

Agenda

1) Welcome and Introductions
2) Performance of Auto Retailing Stocks in the U.K.
   a) Only major market of auto retailing stocks in world
   b) Size and length of existence
      i) Range from 8 million to 3 million (pounds)
      ii) Privately held for over 20 years
      iii) Went public in 1990s
3) Characteristics of U.S. Automotive Retailers
   a) Increased efficiency
   b) Improved profitability
   c) Higher used car sales
   d) Lower new car sales
4) Recent Trends and Automotive industry Outlook
   a) Increased industry sales
      i) Light vehicle unit sales
      ii) Dealership service and parts sales
      iii) Total dealership sales
         (1) Ford $5 million
         (2) GM 10 million
   b) Automotive sales mirror the performance of the eco
5) Consolidation of U.S. Automotive Retailing industry
   a) Dealerships decreased in number between 1980 an
      i) Recession of 1990s
      ii) Aging dealer principal population
   b) Lower new car sales/higher used car sales

Next Meeting Dates:
- January 20
- February 10
- March 15

Figure 6.1a

Figure 6.1b

6.2 CREATE AN AGENDA; CREATE AND SORT A LIST

Starr Insurance Company is planning an orientation for new employees. You have been asked to create an agenda and discussion list in preparation for the meeting.

In this project, you will format an agenda and create a discussion list.

1. Open a new blank document.
2. Use the following settings:

Margins	default
Line spacing	Single
Paragraph spacing	
Before	0
After	0
Font	default
Font size	12 pt for body

3. Create the agenda letterhead using the point sizes and font colors shown in Figure 6.2a. Start the word "agenda" at 1" from the top of the page.
4. Complete the agenda as shown in the figure.
   a. Use numbers rather than bullets for the list of attendees.
   b. Sort the list in alphabetical order.
5. Save the file as **6.2star agenda**.
6. Open the data file **d6.2star lethead**.
7. Use the following settings:

Margins	default
Line spacing	Single
Paragraph spacing	
Before	0
After	0
Font	default
Font size	12 pt

8. Create the discussion list shown in Figure 6.2b.
   a. Start the document approximately 1.7" from the top of the page.
   b. Color the primary bullets blue.
9. Save the file as **6.2mtgpoints**.
10. Change the primary bullets to numbers.
11. Sort the text below each numbered item into alphabetical order.
12. Save the file as **6.2mtgpoints final**.
13. Print one copy.
14. Close all files.

WHAT YOU NEED TO KNOW

Software

▶ It is easy to change an ordinary list of text to a bulleted or numbered one. You can change the default round bullet or number style to one of the styles available in Word. A bulleted list can be changed to a numbered list and vice versa. In addition, you can format bullets or numbers separately from text in the list so that, if desired, you could create green bullets and black text.

▶ To format bullets or numbers differently from text, select the bullets or numbers (not the text), and then format them the way you would any other text.

▶ The Sort feature allows you to rearrange a bulleted list or text in a numbered list in alphabetic (ascending) or reverse alphabetic (descending) order.

▶ To sort a list, select the text to be sorted. Then, click the Home tab and in the Paragraph group, click the Sort button. In the Sort Text dialog box that opens, click to select the Ascending or Descending option, and then click OK. By default, paragraphs should be selected as the Sort by option and Text should be selected as the Type option.

Project

▶ Some agendas include more information than just topics. Often, the meeting presenter refers to a list of reminders when speaking on agenda topics.

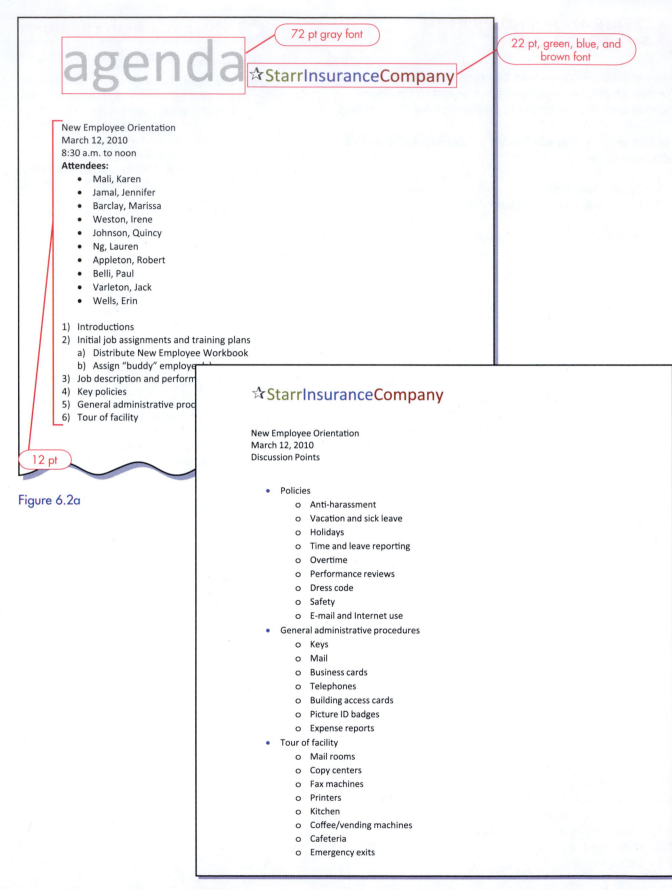

agenda

72 pt gray font

☆**Starr**Insurance**Company**

22 pt, green, blue, and brown font

New Employee Orientation
March 12, 2010
8:30 a.m. to noon
Attendees:

- Mali, Karen
- Jamal, Jennifer
- Barclay, Marissa
- Weston, Irene
- Johnson, Quincy
- Ng, Lauren
- Appleton, Robert
- Belli, Paul
- Varleton, Jack
- Wells, Erin

1) Introductions
2) Initial job assignments and training plans
    a) Distribute New Employee Workbook
    b) Assign "buddy" employee(s)
3) Job description and perform
4) Key policies
5) General administrative proc
6) Tour of facility

12 pt

Figure 6.2a

☆**Starr**Insurance**Company**

New Employee Orientation
March 12, 2010
Discussion Points

- Policies
    o Anti-harassment
    o Vacation and sick leave
    o Holidays
    o Time and leave reporting
    o Overtime
    o Performance reviews
    o Dress code
    o Safety
    o E-mail and Internet use
- General administrative procedures
    o Keys
    o Mail
    o Business cards
    o Telephones
    o Building access cards
    o Picture ID badges
    o Expense reports
- Tour of facility
    o Mail rooms
    o Copy centers
    o Fax machines
    o Printers
    o Kitchen
    o Coffee/vending machines
    o Cafeteria
    o Emergency exits

Figure 6.2b

6.3 CREATE AN AGENDA USING A TABLE FORMAT

Perfection Plus is a cosmetics company with stores located in regional malls and major cities across the country. You work in the corporate office in New York City. The company is launching an exciting new product line, and there have been a series of meetings to prepare for this launch. You have been asked to format an agenda for the next all-day meeting.

In this project, you will format an agenda using a table format.

1. Open the data file **d6.3ppstationery**.
2. Use the following settings:

Margins	1.25" left and right
Line spacing	Single
Paragraph spacing	
Before	0
After	0
Font	default
Font size	12 pt for body text; 14 pt bold for the title

3. Begin the agenda at 1" from the top of the page.
4. Create the table and enter the text shown in Figure 6.3a.
5. Save the file as **6.3ppagenda**.
6. Preview and print one copy.
7. Edit the agenda as shown in Figure 6.3b:
   a. Delete the word "Tentative" from the heading.
   b. Change the font for the column headings to 16 pt, bold.
   c. Insert one row between each agenda item.
   d. Insert a column to the right of the first column and to the right of the second column, as shown.
   e. Size the columns as follows:
      - Column 1—1"
      - Column 2—.16"
      - Column 3—2.9"
      - Column 4—.16"
      - Column 5—1.80"
   f. Apply the Medium Shading 1–Accent 4 table style.
   g. Vertically center the table on the page.
8. Save the file as **6.3ppagenda final**.
9. Preview and print one copy.
10. Close the file.

WHAT YOU NEED TO KNOW

Software

- ▶ Tables let you organize text or numeric information into columns and rows. Columns run vertically, and rows run horizontally. The rows and columns intersect to form a grid, which is made up of small boxes called cells.

- ▶ To create a table, click the Insert tab and in the Tables group, click the Table button. Point to the upper-left box and move the pointer across the number of columns and down the number of rows you want in your table. Once you create a table, the Ribbon displays the Table Tools Design and Layout contextual tabs, giving you access to table-related features to help you refine/enhance your table.

- ▶ Columns automatically adjust to fit between the left and right margins. You can, however, change the width of columns to suit your needs.

- ▶ You can edit a table by adding and/or deleting columns and rows.

- ▶ As you enter text in a table cell, the cell expands to accommodate the text. Pressing [Enter] in a cell expands the cell; it does not advance the insertion point to the next cell. Press [Tab] to move to the next cell, or click in the cell in which you want to add data. Pressing [Tab] when the insertion point is in the last row adds a new row to the bottom of the table. The new row will take on the same formatting as the previous one.

- ▶ You can format table cells by changing the alignment of text within the cell, changing the column width, row height, and/or the table borders and shading. To change column width or row height, click in the column or select the columns to affect. On the Layout tab of the Table Tools, click the Cell Size group, and enter a column width or row height in the Table Row Height or Table Column Width box or use the increment arrows to see a live preview of the change on the table cell. To adjust column width to fit cell contents, click the AutoFit button, and then select AutoFit Contents from the menu.

Continued on next page

▶ Once you insert or delete columns, the table might no longer be centered between the margins. To horizontally align the table on the page, click in a table cell, click the Layout tab and in the Table group, click the Properties button. In the Table Properties dialog box, click the Table tab, choose an alignment option, and then click OK. To vertically align the table between top and bottom margins, click the Page Layout tab, Page Setup dialog box launcher, Layout tab. Click the Vertical Alignment list box and choose Center.

[Properties]

▶ Using the Word predesigned formats called *table styles*, you can quickly change the look of a table to include a variety of borders, colors, shading, and text alignment. To apply a table style, click anywhere in the table. Then, click the Design tab and in the Table Styles group, point to each style to see a live preview, or click the More arrow to display the Table Styles gallery. Click to select a style.

Project

▶ Some agendas include more information than just topics. If an agenda includes other items, you can use a table to format the information.

Perfection Plus

Tentative Agenda
June 5, 2010
Nek Conference Center – Suite D
9 a.m. – 4 p.m.

Time	Topic	Presenter
9:00 a.m.	Review of Ageless product line	Mr. Zachary Malavo
10:00 a.m.	Review of promotions program	Ms. Wendy Carley
11:00 a.m.	Coffee beak	
11:20 a.m.	Advertising budget	Ms. Shirley DeChan
12:30 p.m.	Lunch	
1:45 p.m.	Marketing plans	Mr. Quincy Garin
3:00 p.m.	Coffee break	
3:20 p.m.	Open discussion/follow-up/action Items	Ms. Robin Jones

Insert rows

Insert columns

Figure 6.3a

Perfection Plus

Agenda
June 5, 2010
Nek Conference Center – Suite D
9 a.m. – 4 p.m.

Time	Topic	Presenter
9:00 a.m.	Review of Ageless product line	Mr. Zachary Malavo
10:00 a.m.	Review of promotions program	Ms. Wendy Carley
11:00 a.m.	Coffee break	
11:20 a.m.	Advertising budget	Ms. Shirley DeChan
12:30 p.m.	Lunch	
1:45 p.m.	Marketing plans	Mr. Quincy Garin
3:00 p.m.	Coffee break	
3:20 p.m.	Open discussion/follow-up/action Items	Ms. Robin Jones

Figure 6.3b

6.4 FORMAT MINUTES OF A MEETING

Minutes were prepared to summarize the meeting held yesterday at Perfection Plus. You have been asked to enhance the minutes before they are distributed.

In this project, you will create and format minutes of a meeting and then enhance them with table borders and shading.

1. Open the data file **d6.4ppstationery**.
2. Use the following settings:

Margins	1.25" left and right
Line spacing	Single
Paragraph spacing	
Before	0
After	0
Font	default
Font size	12 pt for date and body text; 18 pt bold for the title

3. Begin the document at 1.5".
4. Create the table and enter the text shown in Figure 6.4a.
   a. Center the heading, and set it to 18 pt bold.
   b. Set the width of column 1 to 2" and column 2 to 4".
   c. Set the headings in the left column to italic. Set the text in the right column to a serif font.
5. Correct spelling.
6. Preview and print one copy.
7. Save the file as **6.4minutes**.
8. Edit the table as shown in Figure 6.4b as follows:
   a. Insert a row between each summary item.
   b. Shade each row a light yellow and remove all table lines.
   c. Vertically center the table on the page.
9. Save the file as **6.4minutes1**.
10. Print one copy.
11. Apply any Table style that best presents the data. *Note: Figure 6.4c is shown merely as a sample.*
12. Save the file as **6.4minutes2**.
13. Preview and print one copy.
14. Close the file.

Software

▶ You may use parallel columns to create a list, script, itinerary, minutes of a meeting, or any other document in which text in the left column relates to the text in the right column.

▶ By default, tables appear with ½-pt border lines. Changing the line characteristics of cell borders and adding shading to cells are effective ways to emphasize data or add interest to a table.

▶ You can modify the line style, color, and width of borders around a table or around individual cells, and you can add shading to cells. You can also remove some or all borders.

▶ To apply table or cell borders, select the table by positioning the mouse over the table and clicking the Move box at the upper-left corner of the table, or select the cells to affect. Click the Design tab and in the Table Styles group, click the Borders button list arrow, and then click Borders and Shading to display the Borders and Shading dialog box. On the Borders tab, click a line Style and/or click the line Color list arrow and choose a color from the gallery that is displayed and/or click the line Width list arrow and choose a line width from the options that are displayed. Click one of the options below Setting to apply modifications. Select the appropriate Apply to option (Table, Text, Paragraph, Cell) depending on where you want to apply the border and shading options.

▶ To apply shading, select the cell or cells you want to shade. Click the Design tab and in the Table Styles group, click the Shading button list arrow, and choose a color from the gallery that appears.

▶ To create parallel columns, you must create a two-column table. After entering text in the left column cell, press [Tab] and then enter the necessary text in the right column cell. Remember that the cell expands to accommodate the text.

Project

▶ *Minutes* are summary points of a meeting. The summary points closely follow the agenda.

▶ You can also format minutes as a table.

Perfection Plus

Minutes of Meeting
June 5, 2010

Present	Robin Jones, Quincy Garin, Zachary Malavo, Wendy Carley, Bill McKinley, Andrew Yang, Shirley DeChan
Research	Mr. Malavo announced the development of a new product line. Several new chemical formulas were developed for a cream that will reduce skin wrinkling. The cream will be called **AgeLess**.
Publicity	To launch this new product, Ms. Carley announced that promotions would be made at all the high-end New York department stores. Samples of the product will be given away at demonstration counters. Press releases will be sent to members of the media.
Advertising	The advertising budget was estimated at $5,223,000. Several advertising agencies were asked to submit presentations, and a decision will be made by the advertising committee as to which agency will represent this new line.
Sales	Mr. Garin, National Sales Manager, projected that sales could reach $10,000,000 the first year.
Adjournment	The meeting was adjourned at 4:00 p.m. Another meeting has been scheduled for Tuesday of next week to discuss future research and marketing of this new product.

Figure 6.4a

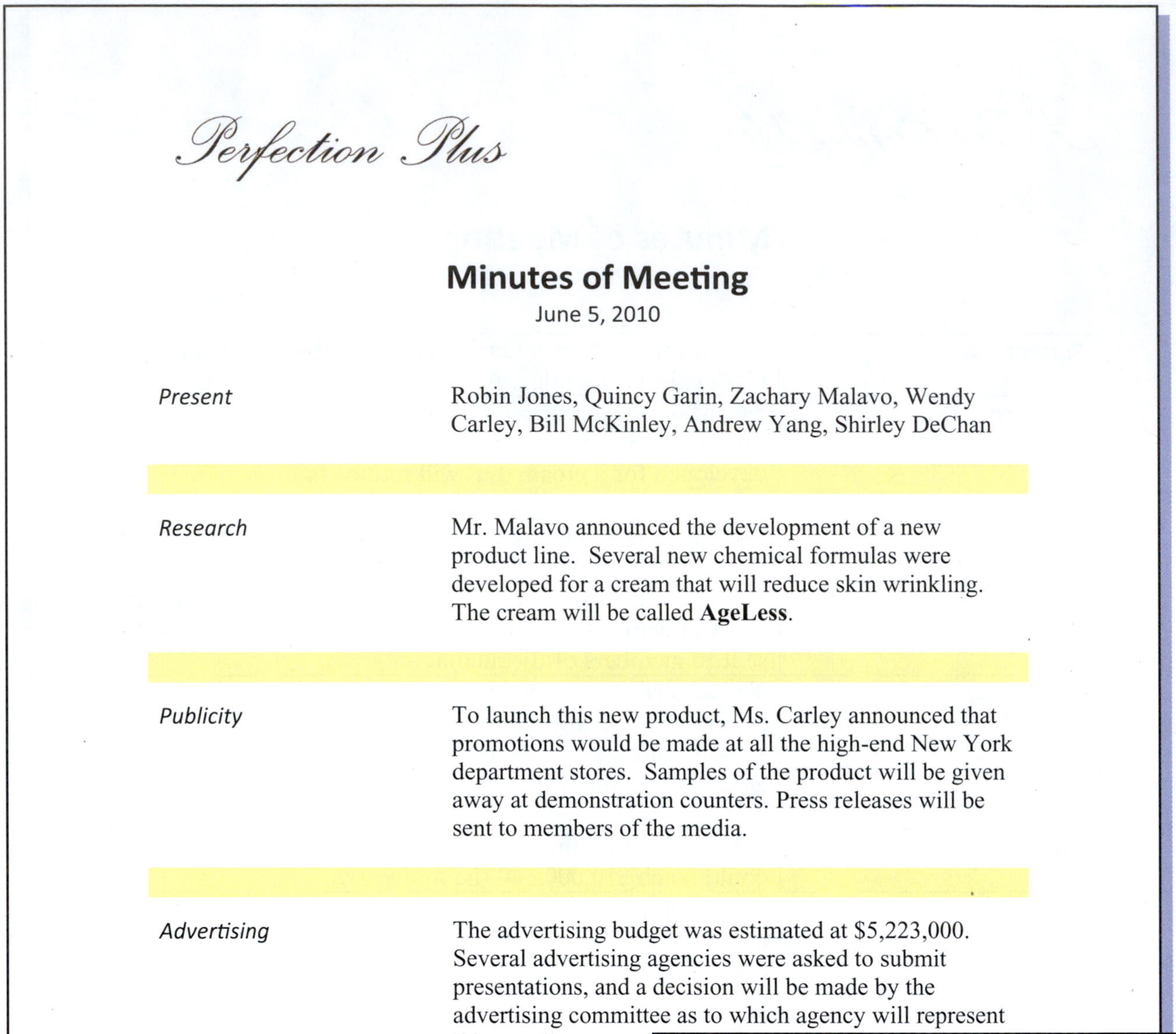

Minutes of Meeting
June 5, 2010

Present   Robin Jones, Quincy Garin, Zachary Malavo, Wendy Carley, Bill McKinley, Andrew Yang, Shirley DeChan

Research   Mr. Malavo announced the development of a new product line. Several new chemical formulas were developed for a cream that will reduce skin wrinkling. The cream will be called **AgeLess**.

Publicity   To launch this new product, Ms. Carley announced that promotions would be made at all the high-end New York department stores. Samples of the product will be given away at demonstration counters. Press releases will be sent to members of the media.

Advertising   The advertising budget was estimated at $5,223,000. Several advertising agencies were asked to submit presentations, and a decision will be made by the advertising committee as to which agency will represent this new line.

Sales   Mr. Garin, National could reach $10,000

Adjournment   The meeting was ad meeting has been sc discuss future resear

Figure 6.4b

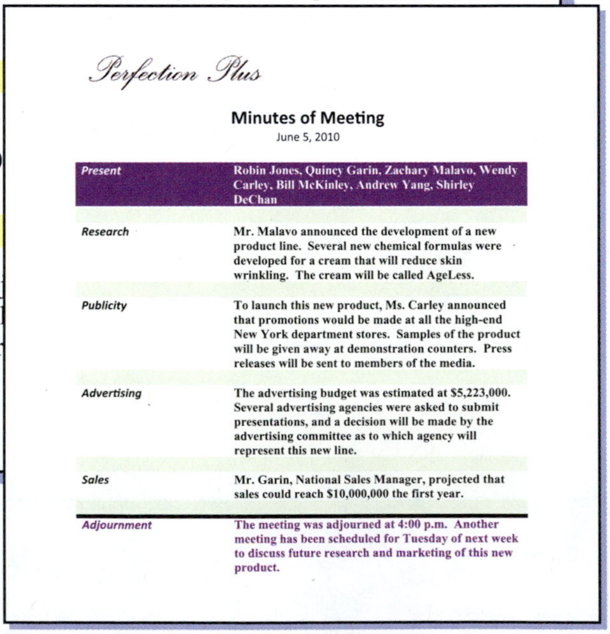

Figure 6.4c

CREATE A MEMO WITH AN INSERTED OUTLINE

Career Services Institute (CSI) is a company that specializes in helping people find meaningful employment. Career Services provides job seekers many resources: career advising, workshops, job search strategies, career fairs, a resource center, and online job and résumé postings. CSI has offices in five major cities: New York, Boston, Chicago, Atlanta, and Los Angeles. The Boston office has prepared an agenda for an upcoming career conference. Because the other offices will organize similar conferences in their cities, you have been asked to send a memo via e-mail to Janice Eyre in the California office, with copies to career counselors in the other offices. The memo outlines the agenda for the meeting.

In this project, you will format a memo that includes an agenda (created as a multilevel list), and then e-mail it to all copied individuals.

1. Open the data file **6.5csi-template**.
2. Create the memorandum shown in Figure 6.5.
   a. Insert a continuous section break after the first paragraph, and then change the left and right margins to 1.25".
   b. Create a multilevel list using an outline format for the agenda, as shown in Figure 6.5. You may use any numbering style for the outline.
   c. Insert a continuous section break after the outline, and then return the margins to the starting setting (.67" left, 1.25" right).
3. Correct spelling.
4. Preview and print one copy.
5. E-mail the memo to Janice Eyre, with copies to the other recipients:
   Janice Eyre: je@csi.com
   Rashan Williams: rash@csi.com
   William Asher: wash@csi.com
   Sara Crane: sc@csi.com
   Note: Because the e-mail addresses are not authentic, you will not actually send the e-mail. But, if instructed to do so, e-mail the message to your teacher.
6. Save the file as **6.5meetingoutline**.
7. Close the file.

WHAT YOU NEED TO KNOW

Software

▶ You must create a continuous section break before and after inserting an outline in the middle of a document. In this way, you can then change margins to better format the document.

▶ To insert a continuous section break, click the Page Layout tab and in the Page Setup group, click the Breaks button. Then, select Continuous from the options that are displayed.

Career ❖ Services ❖ Institute
Memorandum

To: Janice Eyre

From: Your name

CC: Rashan Williams, William Asher, Sara Crane

Date: January 7, 2011

Re: Presentation Outline

The following is a basic outline of the presentation that we plan to deliver at this year's conference, which is titled *Changing Careers: When and How.*

I. WHEN
    (a) Why do I want to change careers?
    (b) How do I know when it is time to leave my current position?
        (i) General Unhappiness
        (ii) Specific Complaints/Self Evaluation
           1. Limited Growth Opportunities
           2. New Interests
           3. Changing Personal Life
               a. Change of Location
               b. Birth of Child/Children
               c. Financial Considerations
           4. Poor Work Environment
           5. Education
II. HOW
    (a) Research
        (i) Network/Informational Interview
        (ii) Formal Research – Internet, Career Guides, Want-Ads
    (b) Learn how to market yourself and your skills.

If you have any additional suggestions for the topics we should discuss, e-mail them to me and I will incorporate your suggestions into the presentation. We hope to cover as much of this as time will allow.

Figure 6.5

PROJECT SKILLS

* Edit and enhance tables
* Change text direction
* Sort data in a table
* Perform simple calculations in a table
* Use custom tabs and leaders
* Use Quick Tables

7.1 CREATE AN ITINERARY

The Tri-State Auto Group holds a yearly golf outing for its managers and salespeople as a way of saying "thank you" for a job well done. Your supervisor, Karen Manning, has asked you to format an itinerary for the outing and then give it to her for approval. Once it is approved, Karen will forward it to all those who are invited.

In this project, you will format a draft itinerary.

1. Open the data file **d7.1tri-statelettemp**.
2. Use the following settings.

Margins	1.25" left and 1.5 right
Line spacing	Single
Paragraph spacing	
Before	0
After	0
Font	Arial
Font size	10 pt except where indicated in Figure 7.1

3. Save the file as **7.1itinerary**.
4. Create the itinerary as shown in Figure 7.1.
   a. Start the document at 2".
   b. Center the headings using the font sizes indicated.
   c. Set the width of the first column to 1.75" and the width of the second column to 3.75", and then center the table horizontally on the page.
5. Remove all table lines. Right-align the data in column 1.
6. Apply shading as shown.
7. Correct spelling.
8. Preview and print one copy.
9. Save the file and close it.

WHAT YOU NEED TO KNOW

Software

▶ An *itinerary* is a day-to-day travel schedule or timetable that includes times of arrival, meetings, departures, and other contact information.

▶ In an itinerary, text must be read from left to right. Use a two-column table to format parallel columns.

TRI-STATE AUTO GROUP

23 Plains Road
Lynbrook, NY 11765
Phone: 516-888-5555
Fax: 516-555-5555

2010 ANNUAL TRI-STATE GOLF OUTING ———— 12 pt
Sunday, August 10 – Thursday, August 14 ———— 10 pt

ITINERARY ———— 10 pt

Sunday, August 10
10:00 a.m. – 5:00 p.m. Arrive Reno Airport. Travel from Reno to Lake Tahoe Resort.
6:00 p.m. Meet in lobby of Lake Tahoe Resort. Introductions will be made and light snacks will be served.
7:00 p.m. Dinner
9:00 p.m. Meet in lobby. Team t-shirts will be distributed and golf teams will be discussed.
9:45 p.m. Movie or casino

Monday, August 11
8:00 a.m. – 10:00 a.m. Breakfast
10:00 a.m. Leave for Northstar-at-Tahoe golf course
12:00 noon Tee off at Northstar
Lunch at golf course (during round)
7:00 p.m. Return to resort
8:00 p.m. Dinner
9:45 p.m. Movie or casino

Tuesday, August 12
8:00 a.m. – 10:00 a.m. Breakfast
10:00 a.m. Leave for Tahoe Donner golf course
11:30 a.m. Tee off at Tahoe Donner
12:00 noon Lunch at golf course (during round)
6:00 p.m. Return to resort
7:30 p.m. Dinner at Joe's Pizza
9:30 p.m. Movie or casino

Wednesday, August 13
8:00 a.m. – 10:00 a.m. Breakfast
10:00 a.m. Leave for Incline Village golf resort
11:30 a.m. Tee off at Incline
6:30 p.m. – 8:30 p.m. Awards ce   remony and dinner at resort

Thursday, August 14
6:00 a.m. – 10:00 a.m. Leave for Reno Airport
8:00 a.m. – 11:00 a.m. Depart Reno Airport

Figure 7.1

7.2 CREATE AN ACTIVITIES SCHEDULE

Meadowland College has many interesting activities planned for the coming year. You have been asked to format its 2010 Special Events Schedule, which will be included in the next issue of the college newsletter.

In this project, you will create an activities schedule.

1. Open a new blank document.
2. Use the following settings:

Margins	1" left and right
Line spacing	Single
Paragraph spacing	
Before	0
After	0
Font	Any desired
Font size	Any desired

3. Create a table using eight columns and six rows.
4. Size columns 1, 3, 5, and 7 to .5"; size the remaining columns to 1.25".
5. Merge the first row and enter the text shown in Figure 7.2. Use any font and font size that best presents the data. *Note: The fonts and sizes shown in the figure are merely suggested*.
6. Merge the cells in columns 1, 3, 5, and 7.
7. Enter and change the text direction in the cells shown. Center the text horizontally and vertically in the cell.
8. Enter the remaining text in the cells.
    a. Apply any font and font size to the newly entered text.
    b. Center the text horizontally and vertically in the cells.
9. Save the file as **7.2schedule**.
10. Preview and print one copy.
11. Close the file.

WHAT YOU NEED TO KNOW

Software

▶ To fit information into table columns and rows, you can merge or split table cells.

▶ Merging cells lets you create a single larger cell by removing the dividing lines between cells. You can merge cells horizontally and/or vertically.

▶ Splitting cells lets you divide cells. When you split a cell into multiple cells, you divide the space of a single cell into the number of cells you specify.

▶ To merge or split cells, select the cells to merge or split. Click the Layout tab and in the Merge group, click the Merge Cells button or the Split Cells button. After clicking the Split Cells button, enter the number of columns and/or the number of rows to split in the Split Cells dialog box, and then click OK.

▶ To create an interesting effect, you can change the direction of text in a table cell. To do so, click in the cell containing the text you want to affect. Click the Layout tab and in the Alignment group, click the Text Direction button until the text is displayed in the direction you want. Each time you click the button, the text will rotate in a different direction.

▶ You can align text vertically in a cell. Text can be aligned at the top, middle, or bottom of a cell. To do so, click in any cell or select the cells to affect. Click the Layout tab, and in the Alignment group, click an alignment button.

Project

▶ A schedule lists times and some details about planned activities. A table format is the best way to organize this information.

Meadowland College
2010 Special Events Schedule

Event		Date		Location		Sponsor	
	New Student Welcome Picnic		September 2		Campus Main Library Lawn		Administration Department
	Fall Festival Carnival		October 17		Huff Pavilion		Business School
	Pilgrim Celebration Dinner		November 19		Wyndham Hall		Theatre Department
	Winter Dance		December 12		Railley Hall		Technology Club
	Summer Celebration Dinner and Dance		May 28		Wyndham Hall		Science Department

Figure 7.2

7.3 CREATE A RATE SCHEDULE

You work for Michael Richardson, Marketing Manager of Creative Cartoons, a company that manufactures cartoon-related products and has offices in New York City, England, Germany, and Japan. In September, your company will be participating in an international trade show in Milan, Italy. You have been asked to send a letter to the marketing managers in each of the foreign offices with information they need to prepare for this event.

In this project, you will send a letter via e-mail and regular mail, with copies to Pamela Savoy, London; Joerg Newmann, Germany; and Laura Ng, Japan.

1. Open the data file **d7.3cclethead**.
2. Use the following settings:

Margins	default
Line spacing	Single
Paragraph spacing	
Before	0
After	0
Font	Times New Roman
Font size	12 pt

3. Format a block business letter using the text shown in Figure 7.3a.
   a. Include an appropriate salutation and closing.
   b. Include mailing instructions.
4. Create the table shown in Figure 7.3b where indicated in the letter.
   a. Use the appropriate number of columns and rows.
   b. Size the columns and rows to fit the data.
   c. Enter foreign currency amounts into the table by doing the following:
      - Go to: www.xe.net/currency.
      - Convert each U.S. dollar amount into British pounds.
      - Copy and then paste each converted amount to the appropriate table cell in the Pound column in the table.
      - Convert each U.S. dollar amount into Euros and Yen. Copy and then paste each converted amount into the appropriate table cell in the appropriate column.
      Note: The amounts in the Pound, Euro, and Yen columns will vary depending on the rate at the time this activity is completed.
   d. Right-align the numeric data.

Software

- You can calculate numeric data in Word table cells. While you can accomplish many types of calculations in Word table cells, it is recommended that you use Excel if you regularly calculate numeric data.

- To calculate data in a column or row, position your insertion point in the cell where the answer should appear. Then click the Layout tab and in the Data group, click the Formula button. In the Formula dialog box that displays, Word automatically inserts the SUM formula and intuitively adds the direction of the calculation (LEFT or ABOVE) in the Formula box. If this is the calculation you want to perform, click OK.

Project

- A rate schedule includes numeric data, which you often must calculate.

- At present, the Euro is the official currency of 15 European Union countries: Austria, Belgium, Cyprus, Finland, France, Germany, Greece, Ireland, Italy, Luxembourg, Malta, the Netherlands, Portugal, Slovenia, and Spain. Some countries, however, still have their own currency.

- In England, the term "Ltd" in a company name means the same as "Incorporated" or "Company" in an American company's name.

- When addressing foreign mail, the USPS recommends that you capitalize the entire delivery address and avoid using punctuation. Place only the city's name and postal code (if any) on the next to last line. Place only the country's name on the last line. If possible, addresses should have no more than five lines.

You will need an Internet connection to complete this project.

    e. Enter a formula to total each column.

    f. Apply any Table style.

5. Prepare an envelope and add it to the document.

6. Send the letter via e-mail to: `jmendez@crca.net`.
Note: This is not an authentic e-mail address so you will not actually send the message. But, if instructed to do so, e-mail the message to your teacher.

7. Save the file as **7.3ccletter**.

8. Preview and print one copy.

9. Close all files.

Today's date
MS. JACQUELINE MENDEZ, VICE PRESIDENT
CREATIVE CARTOONS, LTD
21 STEPHEN STREET
WIP 2LN LONDON
ENGLAND

As you know, the 2010 International Merchandising Trade show will be held at the Grand-Milan Hotel in Milan, Italy on December 9. All five of our offices will be represented at the show. ¶As we discussed at our last meeting, we will rent a booth to display Creative Cartoon's merchandising program. A breakdown of the costs for Booth A, the booth size you suggested, is shown below. Since each office must approve the cost, I have provided the rates in several currencies so that the costs can be understood by all participants.

{insert table here}

¶If you have any questions regarding the fees, please feel free to call me.

Booth A – 600 Square Feet	Dollar	Pound	Euro	Yen
Base Rental Fee	2,500			
Assembly Charge	650			
Freight Charge	300			
Disassembly Charge	450			
Total Cost				

Figure 7.3a & b

7.4 CREATE A RECORDS LIST

Meadowland College keeps track of the amount of financial aid it gives students in certain high schools.

In this project, you will create a records list to track financial aid for Meadowland College.

1. Open a new blank document.
2. Use the following settings:

Margins	Default
Line spacing	Single
Paragraph spacing	
Before	0
After	0
Font	Times New Roman
Font size	12 pt

3. Create the records list shown in Figure 7.4 using the appropriate number of columns and rows.
4. Enter the School, City, State, Students, and Aid data in the cells, as shown. Do not merge the cells for Meadowland College and the top row at this time.
5. Sort the records in descending order by Aid.
6. Save the file as **7.4aid**.
7. Merge the cells necessary to achieve the results you want and enter the text shown.
8. Use the same font and shading for Meadowland College that you used in Project 7.2. Center the text horizontally and vertically in the cell.
9. Apply the text alignments shown in the figure.
10. Enter the totals for Students and Aid in the bottom cells provided using the Sum formula in Word.
12. Center the table vertically on the page.
13. Save the file.
14. Preview and print one copy.
15. Close the file.

WHAT YOU NEED TO KNOW

Software

▶ To adjust column width to fit the cell contents, click anywhere in the table. Click the Layout tab and in the Cell Size group, click the AutoFit button, and then choose AutoFit Contents from the menu.

▶ The Sort feature allows you to rearrange data in a table so that it is presented in alphabetic or numeric order. You cannot sort cells that are merged. Therefore, you must do the sorting before merging cells.

▶ To sort, select the data to sort, click the Layout tab, and in the Data group, click the Sort button. In the Sort dialog box that is displayed, click Header row or No header row. (This will depend on whether or not your selected text contains such a row.) Click the Sort by list box, and choose a column title to sort. Click the Type list box, choose the content type, and then click Ascending or Descending. To conduct a second- or third-level sort, enter your selections in the second- and third-tier sort options boxes, choose a sort direction, and then click OK.

▶ Use the Word Sort feature to perform simple sorts. If you require extensive sorting and/or selective data sorts, use Access.

Project

▶ A records list is a table in which each row contains related information about one person or one thing.

▶ You can use a records list that you create in Word with other applications. When a records list is integrated with other applications such as Excel and Access, the titles used in the first row are called "fields." You can, for example, use a records list as the data source document when merging documents.

Meadowland College	Freshman Class Financial Aid *Fall 2010*				
	School	City	State	Students	Aid
	Columbia HS	Orange	NJ	05	37,000.00
	Dartmouth HS	Dartmouth	MA	02	$14,000.00
	Granville HS	Granville	TX	10	75,000.00
	Long Island HS	Great Neck	NY	06	42,000.00
	Mountainville HS	Troy	NY	06	42,000.00
	New Trier HS	Newark	NJ	15	105,000.00
	Riverdale HS	Bronx	NY	04	28,000.00
	Wilson HS	Belmont	MA	05	37,000.00
	TOTALS				

Calculate totals

Figure 7.4

7.5 FORMAT A PROJECT SCHEDULE

The Baxter Publishing Company produces a project schedule for the books it plans to publish. This important document informs all those involved of who is working on the project and the deadlines they must meet. You have been asked to organize the production information provided, using a table format. You are to decide how to organize the columns.

In this activity, you will format a project schedule for the Baxter Publishing Company.

1. Open a new blank document.
2. Use the following settings:

Margins	1.25" left and right
Line spacing	Single
Paragraph spacing	
Before	0
After	0
Font	Arial
Font size	10 pt for body

3. Organize the information shown in Figure 7.5 into a table format using the number of columns and rows needed to present the data attractively.
4. Apply alignments, as necessary, to make the table attractive.
5. Save the file as **7.5book**.
6. Sort the records by title and print one copy.
7. Sort the records by sales in descending order and print one copy.
8. Sort the records by the to-printer date in ascending order and print one copy.
9. Insert a row at the bottom of the table, and include the word Total in the first cell of the leftmost column. Total the Projected lst Year Sales column.
10. Use AutoFit to size the cells to fit the contents.
11. Insert a row at the top of the table. Merge the cells and then insert the following heading and subheading:
    Baxter Publishing Company
    Non-Fiction 2010 Project Schedule
    Set the heading to 16 pt bold. Set the subheading to 10 pt italic.
12. Apply a table style of your choice.
13. Center the table horizontally and vertically on the page.
14. Save the file.
15. Print one copy.
16. Close the file.

Project

▶ A *project schedule* is a timetable for a job or jobs to be done. Many project schedules include interim deadlines so that everyone involved knows when parts of the project are due.

Title of Book and Author
The Peacemaker, Allen
September Queen, Ewing
The Fifth Dimension, Mitchell
Where There's Smoke, Kasdam
Spider's Web, Newman
Learning to Earn, Cameron
No Entry, Zaccaro
Robin's Nest, Allen

Projected 1st Year Sales
The Peacemaker – $100,000
September Queen – $105,000
The Fifth Dimension – $210,000
Where There's Smoke – $90,000
Spider's Web – $100,000
Learning to Earn – $85,000
No Entry – $250,000
Robin's Nest – $150,000

Final Manuscript to Printer
The Peacemaker – December 8
September Queen – January 4
The Fifth Dimension – March 31
Where There's Smoke – June 1
Spider's Web – August 2
Learning to Earn – September 15
No Entry – October 12
Robin's Nest – November 1

Editor
The Peacemaker – Aron Brown
September Queen – Joan Stark
The Fifth Dimension – Nelson Wayne
Where There's Smoke – Nelson Wayne
Spider's Web – Carol Vicos
Learning to Earn – Carol Vicos
No Entry – Aron Brown
Robin's Nest – Joan Stark

Figure 7.5

7.6 CREATE A PROGRAM

Meadowland College is hosting a statewide conference for business educators. You have been asked to create the program for this event.

In this project, you will create a program for a convention that Meadowland College is hosting.

1. Open a new blank document.
2. Use the following settings:

Margins	default
Line spacing	Single
Paragraph spacing	
Before	0
After	0
Font	Times New Roman
Font size	12 pt

3. Create the program shown in Figure 7.6 using four columns and 41 rows. *Note: You may use any font and font size for the body. The fonts and sizes indicated are merely suggestions. Use the same font and shading for the college name that you used in Project 7.4.*
4. Set the column widths as follows:
   a. Column one—approximately .5"
   b. Column two—approximately 1.5"
   c. Column three—approximately 1"
   d. Column four—approximately 3.85"
5. Merge the cells in column 1. Enter the text shown (Meadowland College), change the text direction, center the text, and shade the cell, as shown.
6. Merge the cells in column 2. Enter the text (Conference on Business Education—Sectional Meetings) and shade the cell, as shown.
7. Enter the text in columns 3 and 4 as shown. Merge and shade the cells as necessary to achieve the look of Figure 7.6.
8. Remove all table lines.
9. Center the table horizontally and vertically on the page.
10. Save the file as **7.6program**.
11. Preview the file. Make any necessary modifications to the document.
12. Print one copy.
13. Close the file.

Project

▶ A *program*, like an agenda and an itinerary, lists the times and details of planned activities for an event or a meeting.

▶ You should use no more than two or three font styles in a document.

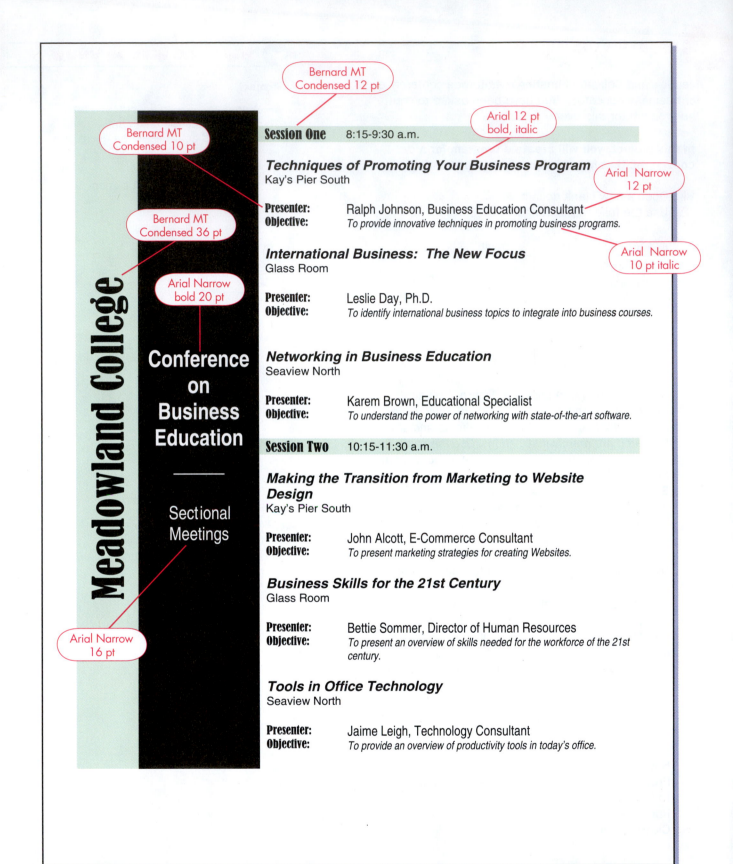

Figure 7.6

7.7 FORMAT A PROGRAM

Upton Investment Group is pleased to sponsor a conference for its employees on "Women of the 21st Century." This two-day event will feature workshops on relevant women's issues. A draft of the program has been developed. You have been asked to format the program from the draft text.

In this project, you will create a one-page program for a conference.

1. Open the data file **d7.7women**. *Note: The text is shown in Figure 7.7.*
2. Create a program as follows:
   a. Format the text so that it presents the information attractively.
   b. The program should be one page in length.
   c. Include the name of the conference as well as Upton Investment Group as the sponsor. Also include the words "Schedule at a Glance."
   d. Use any margins, line spacing, fonts, colors, or shading to enhance the text.
3. Preview and print one copy.
4. Save the file as **7.7women**.
5. Close the file.

WHAT YOU NEED TO KNOW

Project

▶ Conference programs often include a "Schedule at a Glance" section, followed by session titles.

Schedule at a Glance
Monday, May 17
5:30 p.m. Opening Reception – Horizon Tower Observation Deck
Tuesday, May 18
7:15-8:30 a.m.
Registration/Continental Breakfast/Vendor Display
8:30-9:15 a.m. Opening Plenary Session
Keynote Speaker: Mary Donahue, CEO, Perfection Plus
9:15-10:40 p.m. Multiple Breakout Sessions
10:40-12:00 noon Multiple Breakout Sessions
12:30-2:00 p.m. Luncheon
Keynote Speaker: Karen Robertson, President, Karen's Kandies
2:00-2:30 p.m. Resource Room and Vendors
2:30-3:30 p.m. Multiple Breakout Sessions
3:30-3:45 p.m. Break
3:45-4:45 p.m. Closing Plenary Session
Keynote Speaker: Linda Sherman, Anchorperson, ABC News

Sessions

Session I: 9:15-10:40
Breakout A
Insuring Your Financial Health
This session will focus on retirement strategies for healthy financial security. Long-term-care insurance – it's more than just health insurance and Social Security!
Breakout B
Entrepreneurship: Your Own Business – the Ultimate Empowerment!
Attend this workshop to hear and learn from a successful business owner and banker about the resources in your community.
Breakout C
Legal Issues
The Legal structure of your business, women and business tax issues, as well as age/gender and other legal issues will be topics of focus.

Session II: 10:40-12:00 noon
Breakout A
The Power of Women in the Workplace
Issues, questions, and needs of women in the workplace and how they are addressed by unions and corporations.
Breakout B
Communicating with Confidence and Power
This workshop will serve as a guide to being more powerful, verbally and non-verbally. This workshop will focus on the skills needed to present oneself as an assertive, professional woman.
Breakout C
Organizational Skills
Develop the attitudes, habits, and skills that will enable you to organize and simply your life.

Figure 7.7

7.8 CREATE A CALENDAR

Your boss at Perfection Plus has asked you to create a calendar for the Marketing Department for December 2010.

In this project, you will use the Calendar Wizard to customize a calendar. If you do not have access to the Internet, you can use a Quick Table to create your calendar.

1. Open the New Document dialog box to display the Templates pane.
2. Click Calendars under Microsoft Office Online and select Other calendars. Select the Calendar Wizard, and then click Download.
3. Respond to the prompts as follows:
   a. Style—Banner
   b. Direction-Landscape (if prompted to leave room for a picture, choose No)
   c. Date Range—December 2010 (for both Start and End)
   d. Complete the remaining steps of the wizard.
4. After clicking Finish, edit the calendar as follows:
   a. Insert table lines.
   b. Replace "December" with "Perfection Plus" using a 72-pt script font.
   c. Reduce the font size for "2010" to 20 pt and add the word December.
   d. Shade the boxes and enter the text below December 6, 20, 22, and 25 using a 10-pt bold font, as shown in Figure 7.8.
5. Save the file as **7.8calendar**.
6. Preview and print one copy.
7. Close the file.

WHAT YOU NEED TO KNOW

Software

▶ You can create a calendar using a table format of columns and rows, or you can create one using a Quick Table. Quick Tables are predesigned tables with sample data that you can customize. You can apply one of the table styles to a quick table.

▶ To use a Quick Table, open a new blank document. Click the Insert tab and in the Tables group, click the Table button. Then, point to Quick Tables, which will open the Quick Tables gallery. Scroll through the gallery and choose a table that best suits your needs. Replace the sample data with your own. To customize a calendar Quick Table, you must check an actual calendar to know what dates fall on what days for a particular month and year.

▶ You can also use a calendar template to create your calendar. A variety of calendar designs can be found on Microsoft Office Online. The calendar templates include a calendar wizard, which allows you to customize a calendar and insert information directly into the boxes. To access the calendar wizard template, click the Office button, and then click New. In the New document dialog box, click Calendars below Microsoft Office Online, click Other calendars, and choose Calendar Wizard from the templates that are displayed. Then, click the Download button. Follow the prompts to create the calendar.

Project

▶ A calendar is another type of agenda or schedule.

You will need an Internet connection to complete this project.

	Sun	Mon	Tue	Wed	Thu	Fri	Sat
				1	2	3	4
	5	6 Staff Meeting	7	8	9	10	11
	12	13	14	15	16	17	18
	19	20 Staff Meeting	21	22 Budgets Due	23	24	25 Happy Holiday
	26	27	28	29	30	31	
December 2010							

Perfection Plus

Figure 7.8

The English Department at Meadowland College is preparing a handbook on "College Writing" to be given to all incoming freshmen. You have been asked to format the Table of Contents for this guide.

In this project, you will create a table of contents that includes dot leaders.

1. Open a new blank document.
2. Use the following settings:

Margins	1.25" left and right
Line spacing	Single
Paragraph spacing	
Before	0
After	0
Font	Arial
Font size	14 pt for body text

3. Create a two-column table.
   a. Size the first column to 1" and the second column to 5".
   b. Merge the cells in column 1.
4. Set row heights for rows 2 and 4, as indicated.
5. Set a right-aligned tab with dot leaders at the end of the first column (at 4.55").
6. Enter the text shown using the font sizes and shading indicated in Figure 7.9. (Use the same font for Meadowland College that you used in previous projects.)
7. Center the table horizontally and vertically on the page.
8. Save the file as **7.9contents**.
9. Preview and print one copy.
10. Close all files.

WHAT YOU NEED TO KNOW

Software

▶ To change row height, click in the row or select contiguous rows you want to change. On the Layout tab of the Table Tools, and in the Cell Size group, enter a row height in the Row Height or Table Row Height box or use the increment arrows to see a live preview of the change on the table cell.

▶ In addition to organizing information into columns, you can also organize information by using tabular columns, and you can arrange text in columns that are separated by tabs.

▶ By default, tab stops are left-aligned and set every half-inch. You can, however, change the distance between settings, or you can create custom tabs. Custom tabs are tab settings that you select, and they affect the way text behaves once you begin entering text.

▶ To set a custom tab, click the Tab type selector at the left side of the ruler until it displays the button for the tab stop you want to create. Click the ruler at the position you want to be a custom tab stop. You will notice that once you set a custom tab, default tabs to the left of it are deleted. Press [Tab] to move the insertion point to a tab stop.

▶ To direct the reader's eye to text, dot leaders can be used. A leader is a series of dotted, dashed, or solid lines that connect one column to another to keep the reader's eye moving.

▶ To set a tab with leaders, click the Home tab or the Page Layout tab, and in the Paragraph group, click the Paragraph dialog box launcher. In the Paragraph dialog box that is displayed, click the Tabs button to display the Tabs dialog box. For each tab to set, enter the tab position in the Tab stop position text box, click a tab type below Alignment, and if you want to set a leader, click a leader style in the Leader section. Click Set, and then click OK. Press [Tab] to move the insertion point to each column. The leaders automatically appear preceding those columns that contain a tab setting with a leader. The default tab stops remain in place to the right of the custom tab.

Continued on next page

> ► You can set a custom tab within a table cell, but you must press [Ctrl] + [Tab] to advance to a tab stop in a table.

Project

> ► A *table of contents* is a list of topics and corresponding page numbers. It usually follows the title page of a book, magazine, or report to help guide the reader to where information can be found.

> ► A table of contents can be formatted as a table.

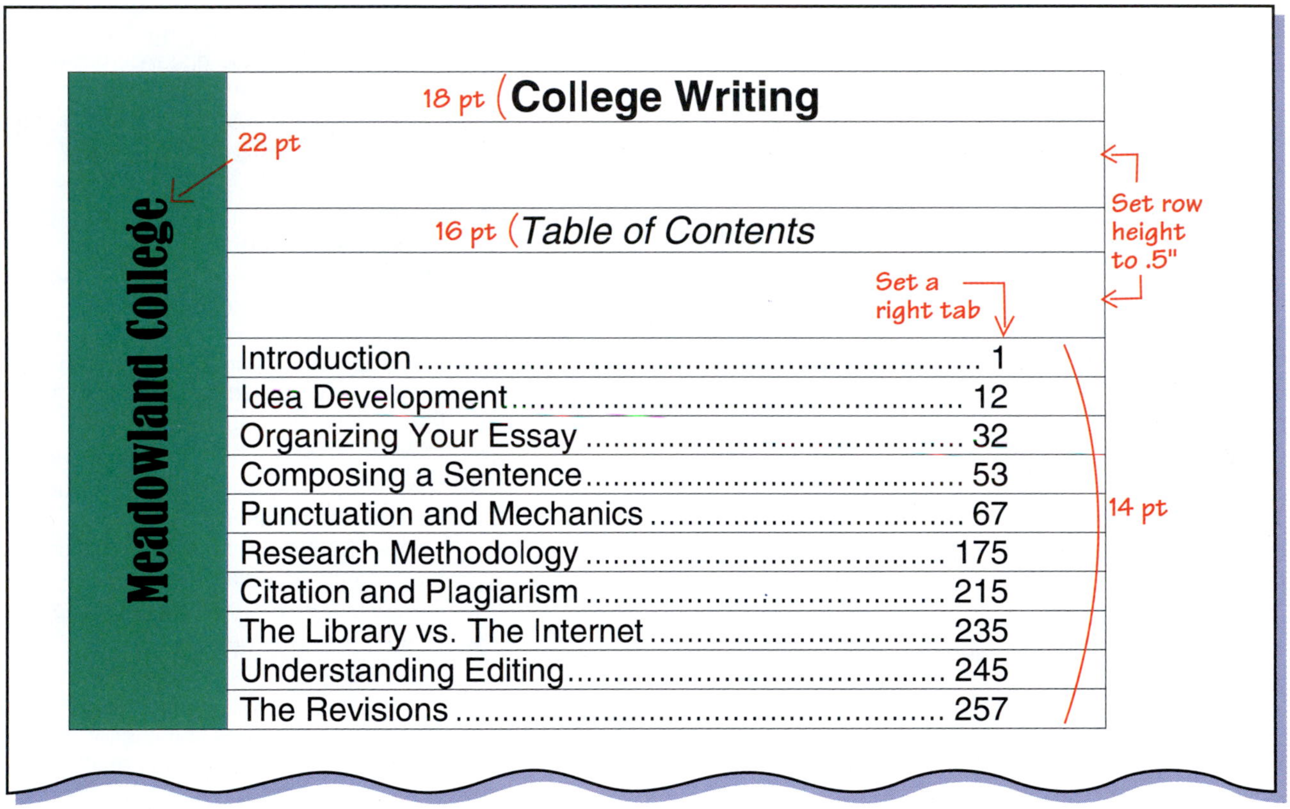

18 pt (**College Writing**

22 pt

Meadowland College

16 pt (*Table of Contents*

Set row height to .5"

Set a right tab

Introduction	1
Idea Development	12
Organizing Your Essay	32
Composing a Sentence	53
Punctuation and Mechanics	67
Research Methodology	175
Citation and Plagiarism	215
The Library vs. The Internet	235
Understanding Editing	245
The Revisions	257

14 pt

Figure 7.9

7.10 CREATE A FORM

Perfection Plus wants all its employees to fill out a time sheet to log the hours they worked each week. You have been asked to create a weekly time sheet and then save it as a template. The template will be available for use each month.

In this project, you will create a time sheet form for Perfection Plus.

1. Open a new blank document.
2. Use the following settings:

Margins	1" left and right; .3" top and bottom
Line spacing	Single
Paragraph spacing	
Before	0
After	0
Font	Arial
Font size	Various

3. Set the page orientation to landscape.
4. Create the weekly time sheet form, as shown in Figure 7.10, using the appropriate number of columns and rows.
   a. Merge the cells where appropriate.
   b. Enter the text and apply appropriate alignments, as shown in Figure 7.10.
   c. Use font sizes that you feel are appropriate. Bold text where appropriate.
5. Open **7.8calendar**, if you completed it. Otherwise, open the data file **d7.10calendar**.
   a. Copy the company name and switch to the new document.
   b. Paste the company name in the first row and center it.
   c. Use font sizes that you feel are appropriate. Bold text where appropriate.
   d. Apply shading to the cells, as shown. You may use any combination of colors.
6. Save the file as **7.10timesheet**.
7. Preview and print one copy.
8. Close all files.

▼ WHAT YOU NEED TO KNOW

Project

► Companies develop numerous forms for various aspects of their business. Most forms use tables to organize information.

► Employees are often asked to fill out a time sheet to log the hours they worked.

Perfection Plus

Weekly Time Record

Day	Morning		Afternoon		Overtime		Official Use	
	IN	OUT	IN	OUT	IN	OUT	IN	OUT
Monday								
Tuesday								
Wednesday								
Thursday								
Friday								
Saturday								
Sunday								
Employee:					TOTALS			
Department:								
Approved by:								

Figure 7.10

CHAPTER 4

Sales and Marketing Documents

In this chapter, you will complete the following projects:

PROJECT 8
Flyers and Advertisements

PROJECT 8.1 Create a Simple Flyer
PROJECT 8.2 Design a Flyer with Special Effects
PROJECT 8.3 Create a Flyer with a Tear-Off
PROJECT 8.4 Format a Flyer
PROJECT 8.5 Create an Advertisement
PROJECT 8.6 Create a Direct-Mail Advertisement
PROJECT 8.7 Format an Advertisement

PROJECT 9
Invitations and Menus

PROJECT 9.1 Create a Corporate Dining Menu
PROJECT 9.2 Create a Restaurant Menu
PROJECT 9.3 Design a Menu
PROJECT 9.4 Create an Invitation
PROJECT 9.5 Design an Invitation

PROJECT 10
Newsletters

PROJECT 10.1 Create a Newsletter
PROJECT 10.2 Create a Newsletter with a Mailer
PROJECT 10.3 Format a Newsletter

PROJECT 11
Brochures and Catalogs

PROJECT 11.1 Create a Brochure for an Event
PROJECT 11.2 Create a Product Brochure
PROJECT 11.3 Create a Brochure Using a Template
PROJECT 11.4 Create a Catalog

FLYERS AND ADVERTISEMENTS

PROJECT 8

▶ **PROJECT SKILLS**

✶ Work with clip art
✶ Work with shapes, lines, and WordArt
✶ Group and layer objects
✶ Wrap text around objects
✶ Work with text boxes
✶ Work with custom page sizes

8.1 CREATE A SIMPLE FLYER

Your boss at Coffee Crazy & Things has asked you to create a flyer to announce a coffee sale. The flyer will be inserted into the weekend edition of local newspapers.

In this project, you will use your creativity to design a flyer for Coffee Crazy & Things.

1. Open a new blank document.
2. Use the following settings:

Margins	default
Line spacing	Single
Paragraph spacing	
Before	0
After	0
Font	default
Font size	default

3. Create a flyer using WordArt and clip art. Follow these guidelines:
   a. Use the content information shown in Figure 8.1. The figure is merely a guide. Design the flyer using your creative talents.
   b. Use any WordArt design for Coffee Crazy; use any font in any size you want.
   c. Use a unique WordArt shape for the contact information.
   d. Use any image (or images) that best communicates the message.
   e. Size, position, and/or rotate the WordArt shapes and/or images, as you prefer.
4. Preview and print one copy.
5. Save the file as **8.1coffeead**.
6. Close the file.

▼ WHAT YOU NEED TO KNOW

Software

▶ Clip art includes various media types such as drawn images, photographs, movies, and sounds that are available in Word. Pictures are images that you download from a digital camera or the Internet and save on your computer.

▶ To insert clip art, click in the document where you want to insert the image. Click the Insert tab and in the Illustrations group, click the Clip Art button. In the Clip Art task pane that is displayed, enter a word or phrase in the Search for text box that describes the type of clip art you want to insert. The default is to search All media file types, which includes clip art, photographs, movies, and sounds. Then, click Go. Click the image on the task pane to insert it. If Word does not have the images you want, you can find additional images on the Web. Click the Clip art on Office Online link in the Clip art task pane to display the Microsoft Office Online home page in your Web browser.

▶ When you insert clip art or a picture, it appears in your document at the insertion point location. The image initially is displayed with sizing handles and a rotation handle, and the Ribbon displays Picture Tools to help you work with your image.

▶ To position an image at a specific location in a document, you must change its wrapping style. To do so, select the image. Click the Picture Tools Format Tab, and in the Arrange group, click the Text Wrapping button and select either Square or tight as the wrapping style. Drag the image to the desired location on the page or click the Align button, and choose an alignment option.

Continued on next page

▶ To rotate an image, click and drag the green rotation handle left or right to the appropriate angle.

▶ The WordArt feature lets you create text as art. To create WordArt, click the Insert tab and in the Text group, click the WordArt button. In the WordArt gallery that is displayed, click a WordArt style. Enter the text that you want to appear as WordArt in the Edit WordArt Text dialog box, and then choose a font, font size, and emphasis style. The new text will replace the words *"Your text here."* Click OK to insert the WordArt into your document. As with clip art, WordArt is inserted into your document as an inline graphic.

▶ To edit a WordArt image, click the WordArt shape, which displays the WordArt Tools Format tab to help you customize the WordArt shape.

Project

▶ A flyer is a communication that is often posted in public or distributed. Its purpose is to attract immediate attention to inform the reader of a special event, service, or product. A flyer is often thought of as an informal advertisement.

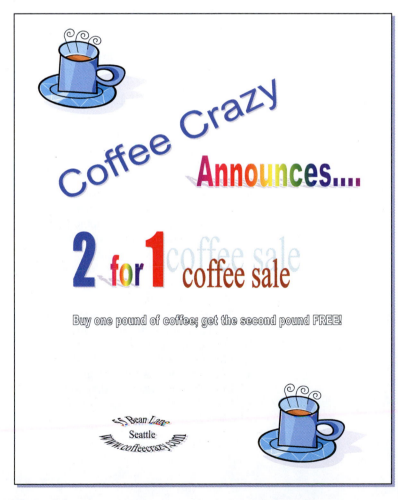

Figure 8.1

8.2 DESIGN A FLYER WITH SPECIAL EFFECTS

You work for Adventures Nevada, a company that arranges outdoor recreation activities in Nevada. You have been asked to create a flyer to be distributed to guests staying in Nevada hotels.

In this project, you will design a flyer using various special effects.

1. Open the data file **d8.2nevada** (shown in Figure 8.2a).
2. Design an eye-catching flyer for Adventures Nevada (Figure 8.2b is a guide).
   a. Set the text to any font style and color.
   b. Insert clip art photos anywhere on the page to illustrate biking, hiking, sail boating, horseback riding, canoeing, and skiing (water and snow).
   c. Apply a different picture effect to each clip art image.
   d. Create WordArt out of the words Come to Nevada. You may rotate the WordArt if you want.
   e. Size, position, and/or rotate the WordArt shapes and/or images, as you prefer.
3. Preview and print one copy.
4. Save the file as **8.2nevada**.
5. Close the file.

Software

▶ After you insert an image, you can modify it by adding special effects. You can adjust the image's brightness and contrast, change its border, and/or apply an effect or style.

▶ Picture styles offer you a combination of different picture borders, orientations, and effects. You can see a live preview of many Word effects before you actually apply them.

▶ To apply a border effect, select the image, click the Format tab and in the Picture Styles group, click the Picture Border button list arrow. Move your mouse through the gallery to see the effects of different borders, weights, or border styles (dashes). Select an effect or effects.

▶ To apply a special effect, select the image. Click the Format tab and in the Picture Styles group, click the Picture Effects button. Highlight an effect option and move your mouse through the effect gallery to see the different effects for that option. Then select an effect or effects.

▶ To apply a style, select the image, click the Format tab and in the Picture Styles group, click the More arrow to display the styles gallery. Move your mouse through the gallery to see the effects, and then select an effect.

▶ In the previous activity, you learned that you can apply a Square or Tight text wrap option to a graphic so that you could position it anywhere on the page. You can also wrap text around images using the same techniques you used for creating a floating image and for wrapping text around text boxes.

▶ To wrap text, select the graphic, click the Format tab and in the Arrange group, click the Text Wrapping button. Click to select a text-wrapping option from the menu that is displayed.

Discover Muscles You Never Knew Existed

How many muscle-toning, sweat-dripping, smile-inducing activities can you pack into a day?

Come to Nevada.

You can do any thing here – hunt, fish, hike, mountain bike, camp, ski (water/snow), or ride horses or cycles.

If you love the outdoors, Nevada is the place to be!

Call
Adventures Nevada
800-555-5555
Your Outdoor Travel Consultants in Nevada

Figure 8.2a

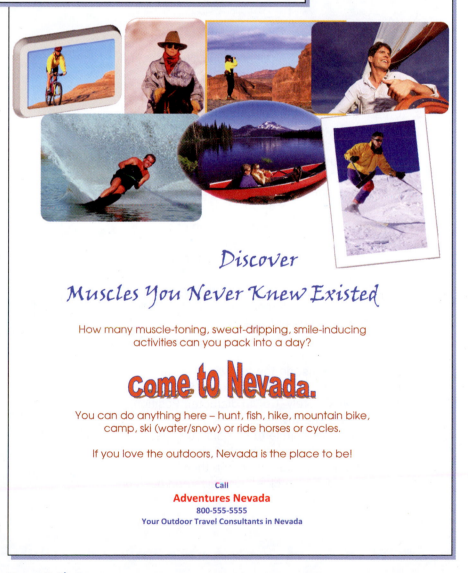

Figure 8.2b

8.3 CREATE A FLYER WITH A TEAR-OFF

The manager of Re-Lo-Cate Moving and Storage Company has asked you to create a flyer to be posted in local stores. Your boss, Carrie Smith, would like you to create a flyer similar to one that was created last year.

In this project, you will create a flyer with tear-offs for the Re-Lo-Cate Moving and Storage Company.

1. Open a new blank document.
2. Use the following settings to create the flyer shown in Figure 8.3:

Margins	Default left and right, .1" top and .5" bottom
Line spacing	Single
Paragraph spacing	
Before	0
After	0
Font	Kristen, ITC
Font size	12 pt and as directed

3. To create the truck, do the following:
   a. Create a rectangle approximately .90" high and 5.56" wide (for the base of the truck). Fill it with a dark blue shade.
   b. Create another rectangle approximately 1.5" high and 3.76" wide (for the back of the truck). Fill it with a lighter shade of blue and place it, as shown in Figure 8.3.
   c. Create a third rectangle (for the cab of the truck) approximately 1.5" high and 1" wide. Fill it with the same shade of blue as the second rectangle.
   d. Create two more rectangles for the window and door of the truck. Fill them with a white shade; size them appropriately.
   e. Using WordArt, create the "R" and position it on the truck, as shown.
4. To create the wheels, do the following:
   a. Create a perfect circle (hold down [Shift] as you drag) approximately .65" in diameter. Position the circle as shown.
   b. Create a smaller circle to fit inside the first circle. Fill it with a medium blue shade.
   c. Select the two circles and group them.
   d. Copy the grouped circles four times and position them, as shown.

Continued on next page

5. Select all parts of the truck, group them, and then position the truck as shown.
   - Select the truck. Apply a shadow style using the Shadow Style 6 Perspective Shadow option. (*Hint: Select the object, click the Drawing Tools Format tab and in the Shadow Effects group, click the Shadow Effects button.*)
6. Create the title "Re-Lo-cate" using WordArt in 60 pt, Kristen ITC. Apply a medium blue fill and a black line to the WordArt. Insert and center "Moving and Storage, Inc." using 18 pt, Kristen ITC.
7. Insert and center the remaining text using 12 pt, Kristen ITC. Color the phone information red.
8. Create the tear-offs:
   a. Create a table using nine columns and one row.
   b. Insert and center the text using the same font in 10 pt, and change the text direction as shown. (*Hint: Click inside a table cell, click the Table Tools Layout tab, and in the Alignment group, click the Text Direction button.*)
   c. Change the table line style to dashed as shown. Remove the bottom border line.
9. Save the file as **8.3move**.
10. Preview and print one copy.
11. Close the file.

▶ To layer graphics, arrange the graphics where you want to position them. (You must first apply a Square or Tight text-wrapping option to position a graphic.) Select the graphic you want to move to another level in the stack. Click the Format tab and in the Arrange group, click the Send to Back button list arrow or the Bring to Front button list arrow. Select Send to Back to move the graphic behind all other objects in the stack, Send Backward to move the graphic back one level, Bring to Front to move the graphic on top of all other objects in the stack, or Bring Forward to move the graphic up one level.

▶ To group objects, hold down [Ctrl] as you select each object. Click the Format tab and in the Arrange group, click the Group button, and then click Group. To ungroup, select the grouped object, click the Format tab, and in the Arrange group, click Ungroup, and then cllick Ungroup.

Project

▶ Flyers often include tear-offs, which contain information that can be torn off the flyer for future reference.

Figure 8.3

8.4 FORMAT A FLYER

Green Brothers Gardening is planning for its annual spring flower sale. You have been asked to create a flyer announcing the sale. Calvin Green, president of Green Brothers, would like you to create a daisy (the company's springtime logo) to use as part of the flyer design.

In this project, you will create a flyer from scratch for Green Brothers Gardening. You will create a daisy and use it as part of the flyer design.

1. Open a new blank document.
2. Use the following settings:

Margins	Default
Line spacing	Single
Paragraph spacing	
Before	0
After	0
Font	Any desired
Font size	Any desired

3. Create a daisy like the one shown in Figure 8.4a (your daisy might vary slightly).
   a. Group the parts of the daisy.
   b. Apply a Square or Tight text wrap so you can position it easily.
   c. Apply a shadow effect to the grouped object.
4. Create a flyer using the information shown in Figure 8.4b. You may use any font, font size, and design element you want, including, but not limited to, WordArt, shapes, and/or clip art to enhance the design. If you use clip art, apply an effect to each clip art image.
5. Save the file as **8.4flower**.
6. Preview the flyer. Make any modifications or adjustments necessary.
7. Print one copy.
8. Save and close the file.

WHAT YOU NEED TO KNOW

Software

▶ You can create a variety of horizontal, vertical, and curved lines in a document, in headers, or in footers using a variety of tools available in the Shapes gallery. You can use the same techniques to change a line style, color, or line size as you did when you worked with shapes.

▶ To draw a straight line (or a line with an arrowhead), click the Insert tab and in the Illustrations group, click the Shapes button. Then, click a line shape in the Lines group. Drag the insertion point (which becomes a cross symbol) to the length you want. You can angle the line in any direction or adjust the size of the line when the handles are displayed.

▶ To draw a Freeform or Scribble line, click the Freeform or Scribble line style in the Lines group. When you click to create the line, the crosshairs symbol becomes a pen. Use the mouse as a pen to draw the line and double-click to the end of line. When drawing a curve, you must click each time you create an angle, and then click again to close the shape.

▶ You can fill closed shapes with color.

Project

▶ Flyers should not be lengthy. They should catch the reader's attention and provide brief information.

Figure 8.4a

Green Brothers Gardening

Announces its annual springtime
FLOWER SALE

It's that time of year again to beautify your garden with irises, lilacs, roses, begonias, lilies, geraniums, petunias, or daisies. We have them all.
We also carry a large selection of herbs, shrubs, and small trees.
- Arrangements for Every Occasion
- Free Garden Layout Consultations
- Full Line of Baskets and Vases

All major credit cards accepted.

32 Braddock Road
Fairfax, VA 22030
Phone: 703-555-0005
Fax: 703-555-0015
E-mail: gbg@network.com
Web: www.grenbros.com

Figure 8.4b

8.5 CREATE AN ADVERTISEMENT

Universe Cruises would like to advertise in the next edition of the Destinations newsletter (which is becoming more like a magazine). Because you have experience with desktop publishing, you have been asked to create an ad about cruises to Europe.

In this project, you will create an advertisement for Universe Cruises.

1. Open a new document.
2. Use the following settings to create the advertisement shown in Figure 8.5b:

Margins	1.25" left, right, 1" top and bottom
Line spacing	Single
Paragraph spacing	
Before	0
After	0
Font	As indicated
Font size	As indicated

3. Create the headline shown in Figure 8.5b.
   a. Insert and center the headline.
   b. Set the text to a 36 pt, sans serif font.
   c. Set each occurrence of Universe Cruises to a decorative font.
4. Create a two-column table under the headline. The table is shown in Figure 8.5a.
   a. Use a 12 pt, sans serif font.
   b. Set the width of column 1 to approximately 2.80"; set the width of column 2 to approximately 1.50".
   c. Merge the cells in column 1 and enter the text shown.
   d. Apply line spacing so that the text fills the space.
   e. Apply full justification to the text in column 1.
   f. Remove all border lines.
   g. Insert and center the text, as shown in column 2.
      - Use a 12 pt, sans serif font for the first row. Apply a dark blue shade, and color the text white.
      - Set the date text to a 10 pt, serif font.

WHAT YOU NEED TO KNOW

Project

- An *advertisement* is a communication that conveys a message about a product or service and, thus, helps to market it.
- Advertisements may appear in magazines, newspapers, and billboards. The goal of a good advertisement is to have a clear, uncluttered presentation.
- Advertisements generally include a headline, which is followed by detailed information about what is for sale.

Explore Europe this year on **Universe Cruises** and enjoy magnificent savings on the only cruise line to receive the "Best Cruise Line Award" from the clients of Destinations. Special "Europe Value" fares start at just $300 a day! If you book with Destinations, you'll receive a 2-for-1 savings on a 2010 worldwide cruise with our "Universe Dividends" program.	2010 Europe Save Up to 59% **July 7 ✸ 12 days** *London to Stockholm* **August 13 ✸ 12 days** *London to Athens* **August 25 ✸ 12 days** *Athens to Venice* **September 6 ✸ 12 days** *Venice to Rome* **October 1 ✸ 12 days** *Athens to Rome* **October 25 ✸ 12 days** *Barcelona to Lisbon*

Figure 8.5a

- Set the destinations (London to Stockholm, for example) to a 10 pt, sans serif, italic font.
- Remove all border lines.

   h. Enter the remaining text. Apply a bright yellow shade.

5. Use WordArt for the second occurrence of "Universe Cruises." Set the text to a 36 pt, decorative font (use the same font that was used for the company name in the headline) in any color combination.

6. Insert and center the text below Universe Cruises.

   a. Use a boat symbol between the destinations (World Cruise, Europe, etc.).

   b. Set the text to a 10 pt, serif font.

7. Insert three relevant images (clip art or pictures) at the bottom of the advertisement. Size them so they fill the bottom of the page, as shown. Apply the same picture effect to each image.

8. Preview the ad. Make any adjustments necessary.

9. Save the file as **8.5cruise**.

10. Print one copy.

11. Close the file.

Enjoy extraordinary savings on **Universe Cruises** to Europe!

Explore Europe this year on **Universe Cruises** and enjoy magnificent savings on the only cruise line to receive the "Best Cruise Line Award" from the clients of Destinations. Special "Europe Value" fares start at just $300 a day! If you book with Destinations, you'll receive a 2-for-1 savings on a 2010 worldwide cruise with our "Universe Dividends" program.

**2010 Europe
Save Up to 59%**

July 7 ✹ 12 days
London to Stockholm
August 13 ✹ 12 days
London to Athens
August 25 ✹ 12 days
Athens to Venice
September 6 ✹ 12 days
Venice to Rome
October 1 ✹ 12 days
Athens to Rome
October 25 ✹ 12 days
Barcelona to Lisbon

Please call Jaime Ryan at Destinations at 800-555-5555 for reservations.

World Cruise · **Europe** · **Asia** · **South America** · **Alaska** · **Panama Canal**

Figure 8.5b

8.6 CREATE A DIRECT-MAIL ADVERTISEMENT

You have been asked to create a direct-mail advertisement in the form of a postcard for Perfection Plus.

In this project, you will design an advertisement on a postcard for Perfection Plus using various design elements.

Note: If you were actually going to prepare this document for mailing, you would have to insert card stock into the printer, print one page (on one side of the card), and then reinsert the page to print the other side. In this project, you will just create the design of the post card.

1. Open a new blank document.
2. Change the page size to 8" wide by 6" high and set the page to landscape.
3. Use the following settings:

Margins	1" left and right; 1.25" top and bottom
Line spacing	Single
Paragraph spacing	
Before	0
After	0
Font	As indicated
Font size	As indicated

4. Press [Ctrl] + [Enter] to insert a page break and thus create a new page.
5. To complete the main part of the card (page 2) as shown in Figure 8.6b, do the following:
   a. Insert a clip art image that measures approximately 2" x 2" and that reflects a holiday theme, and position it as shown.
   b. Enter the word **December** at approximately 1.2" down from the top of the page at the left margin using a sans serif font in 36 pt as shown.
   c. Create text boxes and insert the text shown using a serif font, as follows:
      - **6 & 13**—Use 72 pt, and apply a pink font color to the ampersand (&). Select the text box containing the ampersand (&), and click the Text Box Tools format tab, and then click the Send to Back button to place the ampersand behind the number 6.
      - **The 2 most beautiful days of the year. Join us!**—Use 20 pt. Size the number "2" to 26 pt and apply a pink font color.

Software

▶ When you position a page wider than it is tall, it is in landscape orientation.

▶ To change the page position, click the Page Layout tab, and then click the Orientation button. Choose an orientation setting from the options that are displayed.

▶ To change paper size, click the Page Layout tab, and then click the Size button. Choose a size setting from the options that are displayed.

▶ A text box allows you to set off text in a box, which you can then position anywhere on a page.

▶ You can draw your own text box or use one of Word's built-in, predesigned text boxes. Predesigned text boxes are particularly useful for pull quotes or sidebars—interesting text used to add appeal to a design.

▶ To create a text box, click the Insert tab, and in the Text group, click the Text Box button. In the menu that is displayed, click the Draw Text Box option. Drag the mouse to the required box size. The text box appears with sizing handles, small circles and squares that appear at the corners and sides of a selected box. A tab on the Ribbon provides tools to help work with text boxes. Enter text, and then click outside the box to deactivate it. Click inside the box to reactivate it.

▶ To rotate text within a text box, click inside the text box, click the Format tab and in the Text group, click the Text Direction button as many times as necessary to the direction in which you want the text to be displayed.

▶ You can also resize a text box by a specific amount. To do so, select the text box, Click the Format tab, and in the Size group, enter an amount or use the increment arrows to enter an amount in the Shape Height and Shape Width boxes.

Continued on next page

- **Perfection Plus**—Use the same font you used in Project 7.8 in 36 pt script. Apply a red font color. Set the store address to 12 pt and apply a green font color to the text.
- **Bring in this postcard....**—Use 12 pt.
- **PRE-HOLIDAY SALE**—Use 12 pt.
- Apply the Linear Up Gradient-Accent 2 text box style to the text box containing the company name and address.
- Apply a green shading to the text box containing PRE-HOLIDAY SALE and a white font color to the "PRE-HOLIDAY SALE" text. Then apply a black, 3-pt, left and right border line to the text box and add a shadow effect using the Shadow Style 6 Perspective Shadow option.
- Create WordArt using the text **$25 gift coupon** in an 18-pt font, and position it in the middle of the paragraph as shown (as an inline graphic). Apply a color that complements the current color scheme.
- Remove the default border lines and fill color of the text boxes.

6. To complete the mailing area of the card (page 1) as shown in Figure 8.6a, do the following:
   a. Press [Ctrl] + [Home] to move your insertion point to page 1.
   b. Draw a vertical line using the default width in the middle of the card, as shown.
   c. Insert WordArt using the text shown and any WordArt design you want. Position it on the left side of the card, as shown.
   d. Copy the text box containing the company name and address information created on page 2 and paste it on the bottom of page 1, as shown.
7. Save the file as **8.6directmail**.
8. Preview the file. Make any modifications or adjustments necessary.
9. Print one copy.
10. Save and close the file.

- Like other objects, you can resize, reposition, copy, or delete a text box. You can also change the outline color, weight, and style around the box. You can fill the box with a color or pattern and add a 3-D or shadow effect. You can also apply a Word text box style. A style is a collection of formats (line weight, fill color, line style, etc.).
- To change the outline around the text box, select the box, click the Format tab and in the Text Box Styles group, click the Shape Outline button list arrow. In the menu that appears, point to a line color to see a live preview and/or point to Weight, point to a line weight to see a live preview, and then click to select one.
- To apply a text box style, select the box. Click the Format tab and in the Text Box Styles group, click the More arrow to display the Text Box Styles gallery. Point to a style to see a live preview, and then click to select one.
- To fill a text box with color, select the box. Click the Format tab and in the Text Box Styles group, click the Shape Fill button list arrow and select a color or color effect from the gallery that appears.

Project

- Direct mail uses the postal service to communicate directly with customers. Direct-mail communications often include letters or postcards. If a business wants to announce a sale, they might mail a postcard that screams "Save 25% on all merchandise!" You can use a postcard to create an inexpensive monthly marketing campaign, attract people to your Website or store with a special offer, announce a private sale to selected customers, or thank customers for their business.
- When creating a direct-mail postcard, use a straightforward headline that will catch the reader's attention. Keep the message short and use a 6" x 8" or 6" x 9" card size. A postcard contains a mailing area on one side of the card and should include the organization's return address.

Figure 8.6a Mailer (Page 1)

Figure 8.6b Mailer (Page 2)

8.7 FORMAT AN ADVERTISEMENT

Knowing your skill as a desktop designer, the owner of PetParadise, a superstore for pets, has asked you to create an advertisement. This ad will run in local newspapers and will be posted to the Web as well.

In this project, you will design an advertisement for PetParadise from text that has been provided to you.

Note: Two sample solutions are shown in Figures 8.7b and 8.7c. Use these as examples as you create your own advertisement. Figure 8.7b was created using a table. Figure 8.7c was created using a predesigned text box. Use whichever format works best for you. There are so many possibilities!

1. Open a new blank document.
2. Use any appropriate settings depending on your design.
3. Create an advertisement from the text shown in Figure 8.7a or open the data file **d8.7pet text** and use the text contained in the file to create the advertisement.
4. Include any appropriate clip art to enhance the advertisement.
5. Use any font, font size, and font color.
6. Save the file as **8.7pet**.
7. Preview and print one copy.
8. Close the file.

WHAT YOU NEED TO KNOW

Software

► If you are planning to post your advertisement to the Web, you must use a table to organize the information. When viewed in a Web browser, information organized in a table stays contained; otherwise, data shifts on the page.

► Using one of Word's built-in, predesigned text boxes, you can create interesting effects. To use a predesigned text box, click the Insert tab and in the Text group, click the Text Box button. In the gallery that is displayed, select one of the predesigned boxes. Select the sample text in the box and enter your replacement text.

PETPARADISE
FOR PEOPLE WHO LOVE THEIR PETS
Upcoming Events
There's always something new and exciting happening at PetParadise. We are committed to presenting the most current, cutting edge products and information to people who love pets. Our seminars are FREE and suitable for all ages. Bring the whole family! To learn more about upcoming events, call 207-555-5556.
• Small Pet Seminar – Saturday, June 8, 10 a.m. – 12:00 noon.
Selecting your first small pet can be a tough decision. This seminar will present an overview on choosing any easy-care small pet.
• Reptiles and Amphibians – Saturday, June 16, 10:00 a.m. – 12:00 noon.
Our experts will discuss choosing a reptile or amphibian for beginners and how to care for this new pet.

24 Standish Lane, Standish, ME 04084 Phone: 207-555-5556 Fax: 207-555-5557
E-mail: pp@pet.net Web: www.petparadise.net
Products 🐾 Events 🐾 Adoption Center 🐾 Dog Obedience Classes 🐾 Junior Pet Class Program

Figure 8.7a

PetParadise

FOR PEOPLE WHO LOVE THEIR PETS
Upcoming Events
There's always something new and exciting happening at PetParadise. We are committed to presenting the most current, cutting-edge products and information to people who love pets. Our seminars are FREE and suitable for all ages. Bring the whole family! To learn more about upcoming events, call 207-555-5556.

- **Small Pet Seminar - Saturday, June 8, 10 a.m. - 12:00 noon.**

Selecting your first small pet can be a tough decision. This seminar will present an overview on choosing any easy-care small pet.

- **Reptiles and Amphibians - Saturday, June 16, 10:00 a.m. - 12 noon.**

Our experts will discuss choosing a reptile or amphibian

24 Standish Lane, Standish, ME 04084 Phone: 207-555-5556 Fax: 20
Web: www.petparadise.net

Products ✖ Events ✖ Adoption Center ✖ Dog Obedience Classes ✖

Figure 8.7b

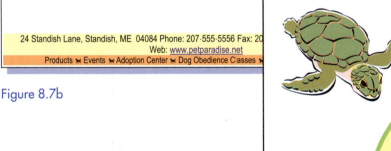

FOR PEOPLE WHO LOVE THEIR PETS
Upcoming Events
There's always something new and exciting happening at PetParadise. We are committed to presenting the most current, cutting-edge products and information to people who love pets. Our seminars are FREE and suitable for all ages. Bring the whole family! To learn more about upcoming events, call 207-555-5556.

- **Small Pet Seminar – Saturday, June 8, 10 a.m. – 12:00 noon.**

Selecting your first small pet can be a tough decision. This seminar will present an overview on choosing any easy-care small pet.

- **Reptiles and Amphibians – Saturday, June 16, 10:00 a.m. – 12 noon.**

Our experts will discuss choosing a reptile or amphibian for beginners and how to care for this new pet.

24 Standish Lane, Standish, ME 04084 Phone: 207-555-5556 Fax: 207-555-5557 E-mail: pp@pet.net
Web: www.petparadise.net

Products ✖ Events ✖ Adoption Center ✖ Dog Obedience Classes ✖ Junior Pet Class Program

Figure 8.7c

▶ **PROJECT SKILLS**

✴ Work with custom page sizes
✴ Use character spacing
✴ Use text effects
✴ Work with text boxes
✴ Work with SmartArt
✴ Insert a file

9.1 CREATE A CORPORATE DINING MENU

Upton Investment Group has an executive dining room, which is called Upton Dining. You have been asked to create a menu that has a traditional, formal tone.

In this project, you will create a menu for Upton Dining.

1. Open a new blank document.
2. Use the following settings:

Margins	default
Line spacing	Single
Paragraph spacing	
Before	0
After	0
Font	As indicated
Font size	As indicated

3. Create a table with two columns and one row.
4. Set the column widths as follows:
   a. Column 1 = 1.2"
   b. Column 2 = 5.25"
5. Insert the data file **d9.1menu text** into the second column.
6. Center the text and leave one blank line between the five menu courses, as shown in Figure 9.1.
7. Enter **Upton Dining** in the first column using a 36 pt, Old English Text MT font. Then do the following:
   a. Change the text direction, as shown in Figure 9.1.
   b. Apply a dark blue shade to the cell and color the text white.
   c. Set character spacing to Expanded by 10 pt.
8. Set "Executive Dining Room 38th Floor" to 8 pt, Times New Roman, and scale it by 200% to stretch the text.
9. Set the first course title (Appetizers) to an 18 pt, Old English Text MT font. Copy the formatting to the other course titles.

▼ **WHAT YOU NEED TO KNOW**

Software

▶ You can increase or decrease the amount of space between characters to create a special effect.

▶ Word provides three character spacing options:

1. *Expand or condense space* evenly alters the spacing between all selected letters by the same amount. Expand or condense spacing is measured in points.

2. *Scale text* changes the shapes of characters by percentages and allows you to set their width. Percentages above 100% stretch the text; percentages below 100% compress the text.

3. *Kern characters* fits letters closer together and is used to refine letter spacing, particularly when working with large or decorative letters.

▶ To set character spacing, select the text to affect. Click the Home tab and in the Font group, click the Font dialog box launcher. In the Font dialog box, click the Character Spacing tab and make the selections you want.

▶ The Insert text from File feature allows you to insert a file into the current document. The inserted file becomes part of the document. The file you insert remains intact, thus enabling you to use it again, as needed. To insert a file, click the Insert tab and in the Text group, click the Object button list arrow. Select Text from File. In the Insert File dialog box that is displayed, navigate to the file you want to insert and click Insert.

Continued on next page

10. Set the menu items to 12 pt, Times New Roman. Set the character spacing to Expanded by 2 pt. Copy the formatting to the other menu items.
11. Draw a line below the first course title, as shown. Color the line dark blue. Copy the line five times and position one line below each course title.
12. Apply a dotted, dark blue table border.
13. Save the file as **9.1upton dining**.
14. Preview and print one copy.
15. Close the file.

Project

▶ A menu not only communicates the food items available and their prices, but also creates an appeal and an image, and is thus considered a marketing document.

▶ Many companies have menus for their executive dining rooms. Generally, executive dining room menus do not contain prices.

▶ The design of a menu sets the tone for the type of restaurant. If the restaurant is contemporary, use a sans serif typeface, which tends to have a more contemporary appeal. A serif typeface conveys a more formal tone. Using Old English Text MT as the font conveys a traditional tone.

▶ Lines can be used to separate items on a page.

Figure 9.1

9.2 CREATE A RESTAURANT MENU

The Symphony Café, a new restaurant that has opened in your area, will serve Italian cuisine with classical music playing while people dine. The owners would like the menu to reflect the restaurant's musical theme. The menu will be printed as a booklet.

In this project, you will create a menu for The Symphony Café.

Note: The first page of this project is the front cover of the menu. The second page is the inside page. These two pages will ultimately be printed back-to-back and folded in half to resemble the booklet shown in Figure 9.2a.

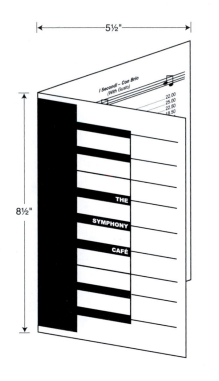

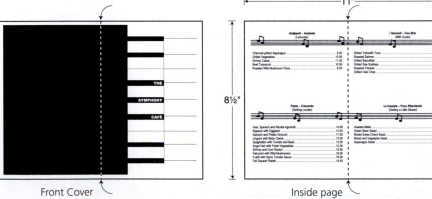

Figure 9.2a

1. Open a new blank document.
2. Use the following settings:

Margins	.5" left, right, top, and bottom
Line spacing	Single
Paragraph spacing	
Before	0
After	0
Font	As indicated
Font size	As indicated

3. Set the page orientation to landscape.
4. To create the front cover, do the following:
   a. Create a table using 3 columns and 19 rows. Set the column widths, as shown in Figure 9.2b.
   b. Set the row height for every other row to .5".
   c. Apply a black shade to the cells, as shown.
   d. Delete the rows in column 2 that do not belong.
      Note: Refer to Figure 9.2c to complete Steps e–h.
   e. Merge the cells in column 1. Fill the cell with a black shade.
   f. Merge the cells in column 3.
   g. Enter the text, as shown in Figure 9.2c, using Arial Black, 12 pt. Set the font color to white.
   h. Draw horizontal lines in column 3 to create the piano keys. Remove the right border.
5. Save the file. Name it **9.2symphony cafe**.
6. Preview and print one copy.

Figure 9.2b

7. To create the inside page, do the following:
- **a.** Open a new blank document.
- **b.** Use the same orientation and settings as the front cover.
- **c.** Create a table using two columns and six rows.

8. Set the row height for Rows 2 and 5 to .5". In the Shapes gallery, use the Line tool to draw four horizontal lines across Rows 2 and 5, as shown in Figure 9.2d.

9. Center the food category headings in Rows 1 and 4, as shown, using any font you prefer.

10. Insert the data file **d9.2antipasti** in the first column, as shown.
- **a.** Set a right tab with a dot leader at 4.5" in the first column.
- **b.** Position the insertion point in front of each dollar amount and press [Ctrl] + [Tab].

11. Insert the data file **d9.2second course** in the second column, as shown. Then do the following:
- **a.** Set a right tab with a dot leader at 9.5" in the second column.
- **b.** Position the insertion point in front of each dollar amount and press [Ctrl] + [Tab].

12. Insert the data file **d9.2pasta** in the first column, as shown. Format the text using the same settings applied to Antipasti items.

13. Insert the data file **d9.2salad** in the second column, as shown. Format the text using the same settings applied to the I Secondi items.

14. Use the shape and line tools to make the musical note. Group the parts and then copy and position the musical notes, as shown.

15. Remove all inside table border lines, as shown in Figure 9.2e.

16. Save the file as **9.2symphony cafe2**.

17. Preview and print one copy.

18. Close all files.

Figure 9.2c

Antipasti – Andante
(Leisurely)

Charcoal-grilled Asparagus	9.00
Grilled Vegetables	10.00
Shrimp Cakes	11.00
Beef Carpaccio	10.50
Roasted Wild Mushroom Pizza	8.50

Charcoal-grilled Asparagus 9.00

Grilled Vegetables 10.00

Shrimp Cakes 11.00

Beef Carpaccio 10.50

Roasted Wild Mushroom Pizza 8.50

Set a right tab and a dot leader

I Secondi – Con Brio
(With Gusto)

Grilled Yellowfin Tuna	22.00
Roasted Salmon	25.00
Grilled Swordfish	22.50
Grilled Sea Scallops	18.50
	18.50
	24.00

Grilled Yellowfin Tuna 22.00

Roasted Salmon 25.00

Grilled Swordfish 22.50

Grilled Sea Scallops 18.50

Roasted Chicken 18.50

Grilled Veal Chop 24.00

Set row heights to 5" and draw 4 horizontal lines

Pasta – Crecendo
(Getting Louder)

Veal, Spinach and Ricotta Agnolotti	14.00
Rigatoni with Eggplant	12.50
	17.00
	13.00
	12.00
	12.00
	15.50
	18.00
	19.00
	14.50

Veal, Spinach and Ricotta Agnolotti 14.00

Rigatoni with Eggplant 12.50

Spinach and Potato Gnocchi 17.00

Linguini with Baby Clams 13.00

Spaghettini with Tomato and Basil 12.00

Angel Hair with Fresh Vegetables 12.00

Shrimp and Corn Ravioli 15.50

Fetuccini with Wild Mushrooms 18.00

Fusilli with Spicy Tomato Sauce 19.00

Fall Squash Risotti 14.50

Le Insalate – Poco Ritardando
(Getting a Little Slower)

Insalata Mista	9.00
Green Bean Salad	8.50
Boiled Swiss Chard Salad	7.00
Bread and Vegetable Salad	9.50
Asparagus Salad	10.00

Insalata Mista 9.00

Green Bean Salad 8.50

Boiled Swiss-Chard Salad 7.00

Bread and Vegetable Salad 9.50

Asparagus Salad 10.00

Figure 9.2d

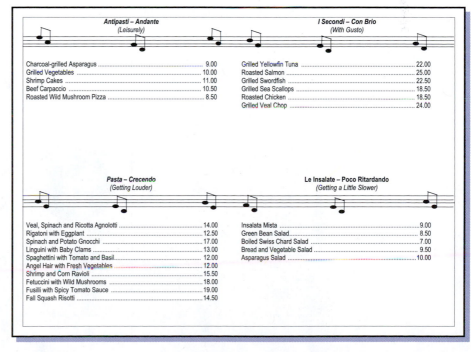

Antipasti – Andante
(Leisurely)

Charcoal-grilled Asparagus	9.00
Grilled Vegetables	10.00
Shrimp Cakes	11.00
Beef Carpaccio	10.50
Roasted Wild Mushroom Pizza	8.50

I Secondi – Con Brio
(With Gusto)

Grilled Yellowfin Tuna	22.00
Roasted Salmon	25.00
Grilled Swordfish	22.50
Grilled Sea Scallops	18.50
Roasted Chicken	18.50
Grilled Veal Chop	24.00

Pasta – Crecendo
(Getting Louder)

Veal, Spinach and Ricotta Agnolotti	14.00
Rigatoni with Eggplant	12.50
Spinach and Potato Gnocchi	17.00
Linguini with Baby Clams	13.00
Spaghettini with Tomato and Basil	12.00
Angel Hair with Fresh Vegetables	12.00
Shrimp and Corn Ravioli	15.50
Fetuccini with Wild Mushrooms	18.00
Fusilli with Spicy Tomato Sauce	19.00
Fall Squash Risotti	14.50

Le Insalate – Poco Ritardando
(Getting a Little Slower)

Insalata Mista	9.00
Green Bean Salad	8.50
Boiled Swiss Chard Salad	7.00
Bread and Vegetable Salad	9.50
Asparagus Salad	10.00

Figure 9.2e

WORD

9.3 DESIGN A MENU

Sports Fitness Center has just opened a café as part of their gym. You have been asked to design a menu that lists their regular menu items. Because they plan to offer special dishes each day, they would like for you to incorporate into your design a basic radial SmartArt graphic in which they can illustrate their special menu offerings.

In this project, you will design a menu from scratch for Sports Fitness Café.

Note: A sample solution is shown in Figure 9.3c. Use this as a guide in creating your own advertisement.

1. Open the data file **d9.3cafemenu text**, which is shown in Figure 9.3b.
2. Set margins necessary to accommodate your design.
3. Design a menu for Sports Fitness Café using the text provided in the file. Use the following design elements:
   a. Use relevant clip art or photographs that support the theme of the café.
   b. Insert a basic radial SmartArt graphic (from the Cycle category), like the one shown in Figure 9.3a that includes the daily special menu items. Color the parts to complement the colors used in the design. Apply a SmartArt style, if you want.
   c. Create a shaded text box for the title or for the menu items.
   d. Apply text spacing effects to the title and to the menu items.
4. Save the file as **9.3cafemenu**.
5. Preview and print one copy.
6. Close all files.

WHAT YOU NEED TO KNOW

Software

▶ A conceptual diagram helps you to visualize information. To create a conceptual diagram (called SmartArt in Office 2007), click the Insert tab and in the Illustrations group, click the SmartArt button. In the Choose a SmartArt Graphic gallery that is displayed, select a SmartArt graphic type (List, Process, Hierarchy, Cycle, Relationship, Matrix, or Pyramid), and then select a layout. Click in a shape to enter text directly into it, or click the first item in the text pane and enter the text for that item. If the text pane is not displayed, click the Text Pane button on the SmartArt Tools Design tab. Format the layout using the SmartArt tools found on the Design and Format tabs.

▶ You can wrap text around, position, modify the size, add special effects and styles, copy, or delete SmartArt as you did with the other graphics you learned previously.

Project

▶ Some restaurants have a standard menu and also special dishes that they prepare daily. You can use SmartArt as part of a menu design-particularly if you want to highlight daily special menu items.

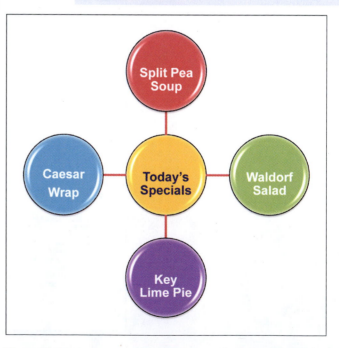

Figure 9.3a

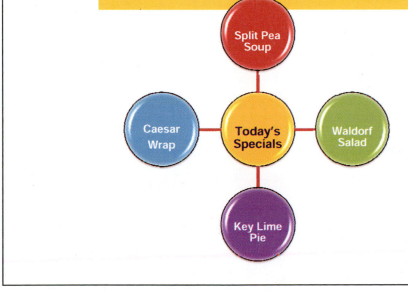

SPORTS FITNESS CAFE

APPETIZERS
Seafood Salad—$6.00

Seasonal Melon—$5.00

Cold Sorrel Soup—$5.00

Shrimp Cocktail—$7.00

Health Salad—$7.50

ENTREES
Red Snapper Baked in Parchment—$12.00

Filet of Sole Wrapped in Spinach—$14.00

Pasta with Tomato & Basil—$9.00

Mustard Chicken—$12.50

DESSERTS
Cranberry Apple Pie—$5.50

Berry Sorbet—$4.00

Seasonal Fruit Tart—$3.50

BEVERAGES
Coffee—$2.00

Herbal Tea—$1.50

Natural Spring Water—$1.00

Split Pea Soup

Caesar Wrap

Today's Specials

Waldorf Salad

Key Lime Pie

Figure 9.3c

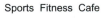

Sports Fitness Cafe

A p p e t i z e r s

Seafood Salad—$6.00

Seasonal Melon—$5.00

Cold Sorrel Soup—$5.00

Shrimp Cocktail—$7.00

Health Salad—$7.50

E n t r e e s

Red Snapper Baked in Parchment—$12.00

Filet of Sole Wrapped in Spinach—$14.00

Pasta with Tomato & Basil—$9.00

Mustard Chicken—$12.50

D e s s e r t s

Cranberry Apple Pie—$5.50

Berry Sorbet—$4.00

Seasonal Fruit Tart—$3.50

B e v e r a g e s

Coffee—$2.00

Herbal Tea—$1.50

Natural Spring Water—$1.00

Figure 9.3b

9.4 CREATE AN INVITATION

Jane Martino Interiors is sponsoring a special event and has asked you to create the invitation, which will be printed on 5" x 7" cards.

In this project, you will create an invitation for Jane Martino Interiors.

1. Open a new blank document.
2. Use the following settings:

Margins	.25" top and bottom; .5" top and bottom
Line spacing	Single
Paragraph spacing	
Before	0
After	0
Font	As indicated
Font size	As indicated

3. Set the paper size to 5" wide by 7" high.
4. Create a table using 1 column and 12 rows.
   a. Set the row height to .45".
   b. Fill every other row with red, as shown in Figure 9.4.
   c. Remove all border lines.
5. Create a text box that measures 5.25" high by 3" wide and position it, as shown.
   a. Insert and center the text shown.
   b. Set "Jane Martino Interiors" to an 18 pt, sans serif font in the colors shown.
   c. Set character spacing for Jane Martino to Expanded by 3.6 pt. Set character spacing for Interiors to Expanded by 8.8 pt.
   d. Use a sans serif font in small caps for the remaining text.
   e. Scale "The Breakers" to 200%.
   f. Use any symbol you want to separate the text, as shown.
   g. Apply a red border around the text box.
6. Save the file as **9.4invitation**.
7. Preview and print one copy.
8. Close the file.

Software

► *Small caps* are a font effect, which you can apply by clicking the Font dialog box launcher, Font tab, and then clicking the Small caps check box.

Project

► An invitation is a request to attend a special event or to celebrate an occasion.

► Invitations are printed on various paper or card sizes other than the standard 8.5" by 11" page.

► Invitations may be formal (such as a request to attend a company dinner) or informal (such as a request to attend a friend's party).

► The tone of the invitation is communicated by the typefaces and the paper used.

Jane Martino
Interiors

TAKES GREAT PLEASURE IN INVITING YOU TO ITS

SPRING/SUMMER HOME COLLECTION
∽
CONTINENTAL BREAKFAST AND
AFTERNOON TEA WILL BE SERVED DAILY
∽
OPEN TO WHOLESALE AND RETAIL
INTERIOR DESIGN CUSTOMERS
∽
THE BREAKERS
PALM BEACH, FLORIDA
∽
FEBRUARY 12, 13, AND 14
9:00 A.M. – 6:00 P.M. DAILY

FOR FURTHER INFORMATION: 305-555-5555

Figure 9.4

9.5 DESIGN AN INVITATION

PetParadise is sponsoring a free "Small Pet and Puppies, Too" seminar on Saturday, June 8 from 10:00 a.m. to 12:00 noon. The RSVP should be directed to Mary at PetParadise. PetParadise is located at 24 Standish Lane, Standish, ME, 04084, Phone: 207-555-5556, Fax: 207-555-5557, E-mail: pp@pet.net, Web: www.petparadise.net.

In this project, you will design an invitation for PetParadise.

1. Open a new blank document.
2. Design an invitation for PetParadise. Use the following guidelines:
   a. Write the wording for the invitation using the information provided.
   b. Create a layout for a 7" wide by 6" high page.
   c. Use the same logo for the company name (and the same clip art) that you used for Project 8.7.
   d. Use at least one text box. Include a photo of a puppy or puppies somewhere in the invitation (possibly in the text box) and apply a special effect to the photo.
   e. Include the address of the company on the invitation and apply letter spacing to it to create an interesting effect.
3. Save the file as **9.5petseminar**.
4. Preview and print one copy.
5. Close the file.

WHAT YOU NEED TO KNOW

Project

▶ The letters R.S.V.P. at the bottom of an invitation are an abbreviation derived from the French phrase, "Repondez, s'il vous plait." It requests that you respond to the invitation to indicate whether or not you will attend. The English translation is "Respond, if you please."

PROJECT 10

▶ **PROJECT SKILLS**

✳ Create a section break
✳ Create columns
✳ Create drop capitals
✳ Develop a newsletter
✳ Use page borders and page colors

10.1 CREATE A NEWSLETTER

The New York office of Creative Cartoons would like to develop a one-page monthly newsletter that includes information about what is happening in each department and dates for upcoming events. Michael Richardson, your boss in New York, would like you to create the first newsletter and save it as a template so the other offices can use it as a basis for creating their own.

In this project, you will create a newsletter for the New York office of Creative Cartoons.

1. Open a new blank document.
2. Use the following settings:

Margins	default
Line spacing	Single
Paragraph spacing	
Before	0
After	0
Font	As indicated
Font size	As indicated

3. Create the masthead shown in Figure 10.1 by doing the following:
   a. Create a table with two columns and six rows.
   b. Set the width of column 1 to 4.39". Set the width of column 2 to 2.19".
   c. Merge the cells in column 2.
   d. Enter the text in each row of the first column, as shown, using 12 pt, Arial Narrow with small caps.
   e. Open the data file **d10.1cclethead**. Copy the company name, and paste it into the second column. Size it to 20 pt or less.
   f. Enter the word **News** in column 2 and set it to 36 pt. Set letter spacing so that "News" spans the same space as the company name.
   g. Remove the border lines, as shown.
   h. Change the line style for column 1 to dotted.

WHAT YOU NEED TO KNOW

Software

▶ Enlarging the initial character in a paragraph creates what is often referred to as a "drop capital." Technically, a drop capital is created when the first letter is dropped below the baseline of the first line of text.

▶ To create a drop capital, select the character on which to apply the drop cap. Click the Insert tab and in the Text group, click the Drop Cap button, and select the drop cap style from the list that is displayed.

▶ By default, a document contains one section. You can use section breaks to split your document into multiple sections, which allows you to make different changes to the layout or format of each section.

▶ Position the insertion point where you want to create a new section. Click the Page Layout tab and in the Page Setup group, click the Breaks button. In the Breaks menu that appears, click the section break type that you want in the Section Breaks group. The Continuous option creates a new section at the insertion point.

▶ The Columns feature allows text to flow down one column and into the next column. Word formats columns with even widths and "gutter space" (space between columns). You can, however, create custom column widths and insert a vertical line between adjacent columns.

Continued on next page

4. Insert a continuous section break after the masthead (table).
5. Change the margins to 3.5" left and 1" right.
6. Create two columns, and enter the text shown in Figure 10.1.
   a. Set the headlines to 12 pt, Comic Sans MS. Set the body text to 10 pt, Arial Narrow.
   b. Apply paragraph shading to the headline text, as shown.
   c. Apply a dropped capital to the letter "T", as shown.
7. Create a text box. Size it to fill the blank area to the left of the first column. Enter the text shown in Figure 10.1.
   a. Fill the box with a light shade. You may apply a text box style, if you want.
   b. Remove the text box border.
8. Insert relevant images, as shown. Apply a Tight wrap option to each.
9. Save the file as **10.1ccnewsletter**.
10. Review and print one copy.
11. Close all files.

▶ To create columns, click the Page Layout tab and in the Page Setup group, click the Columns button. Click the layout you want from the list that appears. To create custom columns, click the More Columns option. In the Columns dialog box that appears, enter the column widths and spacing you want below the Width and spacing section. If you want to include a line between columns, check the Line between check box.

Project

▶ A *newsletter* is a communication that allows people who share a common interest to exchange ideas, developments, and information on a regular basis.

▶ Some newsletters are distributed within an organization; others are sent to customers.

▶ Companies produce newsletters to keep employees up to date on new products, promotions, and events.

▶ The format of a newsletter may vary. However, the following basic parts are usually found on the first page of most newsletters:

▶ The *masthead* or nameplate includes the newsletter's title, the intended audience, the division or organization publishing the document, the volume and/or issue number, and the current date of issue.

▶ The contents include the articles or topics featured in the issue.

▶ The headlines summarize the contents of the articles that follow.

▶ The body copy includes the text of the article.

Masthead

THE LATEST IN
MULTIMEDIA
CARTOONING
PRODUCTS
MAY 2010
ISSUE 5 NO 3

Creative Cartoons

N E W S

Sales Department

The Sales Department has just announced the appointment of John Vaquero to vice president of Sales. John has been an employee of Creative Cartoons for three years. He has won numerous sales contests and brings a wealth of great ideas to the company. Congratulations, John.

Human Resources

The Human Resources Department is sponsoring a company picnic to be held at Centennial Park on Saturday, May 4. John Silva and Mark Barnes from our Accounting Department will be our master BBQ Chefs. There will be games and prizes for the children. Pick up your picnic tickets from Patty Anderson at the receptionist's desk in the Human Resources Department.

Employee of the Month

Congratulations to Susan White from the Accounting Department, who has been selected as the employee of the month. Susan has just completed additional course work in managerial accounting and will receive her BS in Business Administration in June. In addition to this recognition, Susan will receive a $500 bonus and will be provided with a reserved parking spot on the first level of the parking garage. Way to go, Susan!

Technology Department

The Technology Team is currently upgrading all graphics programs, which can be accessed from the company network. All computer monitors in the Design Department will be replaced with flat-screen monitors.

Marketing Department

The Marketing Department has just completed the new spring catalog that will be mailed out to our clients by the end of the month. The new catalog will be added to our Web page with an online order form. Please e-mail any suggestions you may have for our Web page to our Webmaster, May Conners.

Accounting Department

The Accounting Department is leading the drive for community involvement. Several members of the department have volunteered to work as mentors to high school students two days a week. The "Mentorship Program at Creative Cartoons" has really taken off. The program has increased to 53 volunteers. The Board of Education is helping us to find partner schools.

Please join us for our upcoming events!

April 25
Golf Tournament

May 4
Company Picnic

May 31
Holiday

June 5
Board of Directors and Shareholders' Meeting

September 7
Mentorship Meeting

Mark Your Calendar

Figure 10.1

CREATE A NEWSLETTER WITH A MAILER

Green Brothers Gardening publishes a monthly newsletter titled GreenThumbGardens, which is sent to its customers. You have been asked to redesign the newsletter to include a mailing area.

In this project, you will create a newsletter for Green Brothers Gardening that includes a mailing area.

Note: The first page of this project is the inside page of the newsletter. The second page is the outside page. These two pages will ultimately be printed back-to-back, folded in half, and stapled. A label containing the addressee's name is then affixed to the mailer, ready for postal delivery.

1. Open a new blank document.
2. Use the following settings:

Margins	Default left and right; .5" top and bottom
Line spacing	Single
Paragraph spacing	
Before	0
After	0
Font	As indicated
Font size	As indicated

3. To create the masthead:
   a. Create a table with two columns and one row.
   b. Set the widths of the columns to approximately 1.80" for column 1 and 4.33" for column 2.
   c. Insert the newsletter name using 22 pt, Gill Sans Ultra Bold.
   d. Apply a different shade of green to each word.
   e. Create a 6 pt green line and position it below the name.
   f. Insert the company name and date information using 12 pt, Gill Sans MT Condensed, and insert a hairline below it.
   g. Insert a relevant image into the first column. Apply a Square text wrap.
   h. Remove all border lines.
4. To create the columns:
   a. Insert a continuous section break below the table.
   b. Create three columns.

WHAT YOU NEED TO KNOW

Project

▶ Some newsletters are prepared so that the back page contains space for the recipient's address and the return address. A newsletter containing a mailing area becomes a self-mailer, thus eliminating the need to insert the document into an envelope.

▶ Notice that the mailing area in this exercise also includes a prepared postmark. To include a postmark, you must go to the post office and open an account. You will be given a "Permit No." which must appear as part of the postmark. Then you will not need to affix a postage stamp to the newsletter; your account will be charged according to the number of pieces you send.

GREENTHUMBGARDENS

A Newsletter from Green Brothers Gardening   March 2010

Creating a Beautiful Backyard Fountain

It's relatively simple to build that backyard fountain you have put off as the "last thing" in your yard.  Fountains are wonderful accents to any yard. They can be dainty with minimum water movement or crash and roar with large amounts of water. No matter what type of fountain you are interested in building, they all need a basin to catch the water and a pump to re-circulate the water.

The basic equipment you will need for your fountain includes:

❑ An inexpensive submersible pump with a three-prong plug.

In This Issue

➢ Creating a Beautiful Backyard Fountain
➢ Herb of the Month
➢ Saint Patty's Clover
➢ Dandy Lions
➢ A Message from the President

❑ An electrical outlet.

❑ A reservoir that is watertight and deep enough for the submersible pump.

❑ Flexible tubing that is easy to cut.

❑ A water supply to fill the fountain and rinse it out occasionally.

Go out and look at existing water fountains, pictures in books, magazines, and the Internet for creative ideas.

Herb of the Month

You will find it in toothpaste, chewing gum, mouthwash, and breath-fresheners. Yes, it's mint!

This ancient plant is named for Minthe from Greek mythology.

Mint is easy to grow. Be careful, it will quickly spread to more space than you planned in your garden. It will grow rapidly, even in small pots.

Saint Patty's Clover

The shamrock legend goes back to the 5th century in the Emerald Isle. The three-leafed clover was used by the saint who touched down on the Isle to teach the Christian doctrine of the Trinity. The shamrock now means almost any triple-leafed plant. If you're lucky, you might just find a lucky four-leafed clover.

Dandy Lions

You see them in lawns. You spray weed killer to get rid of them. Did you ever consider that these "yard pests" could be put to good use?

My aunt would go out in the early morning and pick dandelions. That evening, these "little green gems" would appear in the dinner salad.

Dandelions have been used in "Tonic Teas" and are a rich source of Vitamins A, C, and several Bs. In fact, the Pennsylvania Dutch believed that eating dandelion greens on Thursday would keep them healthy all year.

So the next time you are out in your yard and come across a dandelion, you might think of harvesting some of those "little gems" for your dinner salad.

Figure 10.2a (News Letter) Inside Page

5. Enter the text shown in Figure 10.2a or insert the data file **d10.2greenthumb text** into the first column (which will flow into the second and third columns). Format it as shown.
   a. Use a 12 pt, sans serif font for the headlines. Use a 10 pt, serif font for the body text.
   b. Insert images to support the wording of the text. Use a Tight wrap for each image. Apply a picture style to a few of the images.
   Note: To keep the text on one page, you may have to adjust font size or spacing amounts.
6. Create a text box to fit at the bottom of the first column.
   a. Insert the text, as shown, using a 12 pt, sans serif font for the heading and a 10 pt font for the list.
   b. Apply a text box effect.
   c. Apply a Square text wrap.
7. To create the "grass," do the following:
   a. Use the Freeform line tool in the AutoShapes menu to create a series of triangles. Be sure to continue the drawing and close the bottom (you must have a closed shape to fill it).
   b. Fill the shape with a green shade.
8. To create the mailer, do the following:
   a. Insert a continuous section break at the end of the last column.
   b. Create a new page. Set columns to 1.
   c. Review the second-page information in Figure 10.2b, and determine how to format it.
   Note: You can create the design for the section "A Message from the President" as shown, or you can design it using your creative skills. Remember that the mailer will be folded in half.
   d. Copy the "grass" from the bottom of page 1 and copy it to the bottom of the mailer page.
9. Save the file as **10.2greenthumb**.
10. Preview and print one copy.
11. Close the file.

A Message from the President:

As an avid gardener, it is a pleasure to continue to provide our monthly newsletter to our customers. Whether you are an information systems engineer, a stay-at-home mom, or retired, a garden provides all of us with an opportunity to get out in the fresh air.

A garden says "Welcome" to anyone who visits your home. It provides you with an opportunity to share ideas with others and to display your "artwork." Continue to share your ideas with friends and neighbors on our Website: www.grenbros.com

Calvin Green
President

- -

GREENTHUMBGARDENS

Green Brothers Gardening
32 Braddock Road
Fairfax, VA 22030

```
BULK RATE
U.S. POSTAGE
PAID
PERMIT NO. 1111
FAIRFAX, VA
```

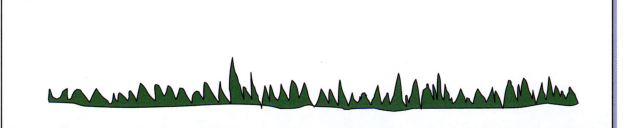

Figure 10.2b (News Letter) Outside Page

10.3 FORMAT A NEWSLETTER

You work in the Meadowland College Publications Department as a desktop publisher. Meadowland College publishes a college newspaper twice a year and has now decided to publish a quarterly newsletter, which will be available to students on campus and will also be sent to alumni. You have been asked to design the newsletter from scratch. You must create a masthead, a "Contents" section, and a "Feature Program" section (the college will feature a special departmental program or course in each issue). You have been told to include a mailer as part of the newsletter design.

In this project, you will design a two-page newsletter for Meadowland College.

1. Open a new blank document.
2. Use the following settings:

Margins	1" left; .75" right; .5" top and bottom
Line spacing	Single
Paragraph spacing	
Before	0
After	0
Font	Any desired
Font size	Any desired

3. Design a newsletter for Meadowland College. Follow these guidelines:
   a. The articles for this issue can be found in the data file **d10.3college news text**. The text is shown in Figure 10.3.
   b. Use an 8.5" x 11" page. The first page will contain the articles, and the second page will contain any overflow text (or Feature Program information) and the mailer. You may use columns if you want.
   c. Use the same font for the college name that you used in Project 7.2.
   d. Include the college address as part of the mailer:
      Meadowland College
      Farm College Road
      Princeton, New Jersey 07137
   e. You may apply letter spacing or any other design elements to create interesting effects.
   f. Insert a map of Florence, Italy, where indicated. Go to: www.florence.ala.it/map.htm. Cut and paste the map and apply a Tight text wrap.
4. Apply any desired page border.
5. Save the file as **10.3college news**.
6. Preview and print one copy.
7. Close the file.

WHAT YOU NEED TO KNOW

Software

▶ To add a final touch to your document, you can place a border around a page or apply a background color.

▶ Word provides numerous page borders styles, including interesting art borders.

▶ To apply a page border, click the Page Layout tab and in the Page Background group, click the Page Borders button. In the Borders and Shading [Page Borders] dialog box that appears, click the Page Border tab. Click Box in the Setting section. Select a line style, color, and width. To apply an Art border, click the Art box list arrow, choose an art style, and then click OK.

Project

▶ Educational institutions also use newsletters to deliver messages about schedules, events, or items of special interest.

Meadowland Happenings
A Quarterly Publication of Meadowland College
April 2010

Student Housing
Summer 2010

This summer Meadowland College is offering student housing. Space is available on a first-come, first-served basis in the Kippling Residence. Rooms are available on a weekly basis from May 28 to August 9. Your housing contract is dependent on your course registration and must run concurrently. Meadowland housing is available only for the duration of your course of Study. To apply for Meadowland housing, submit your summer housing application form (which you can pick up at the Registrar's Office) along with your payment to the Registrar's Office, 22 Pine Lane, Room 1212. You can do this by mail or hand-deliver it.

Meadowland Summer Registration – May 31.
All summer classes will be held in Conference Hall from 8:00 a.m. to 4:00 p.m. Students who have not registered in advance can do so on Registration Day. For limited enrollment classes, students must complete all forms, pay all necessary fees, and sign course lists. For open enrollment classes, students may attend the first meeting of the class.

Summer Registration Calendar
May 31 Last day to arrange for payment of summer courses and sign class lists
June 3 Classes begin
June 17 Last day to declare or drop credit/no credit option
June 28 Last day to add units
July 1 Last day to drop units
July 4-5 Holiday, no classes
July 26-30 Eight-week term exams
July 30 Eight week term ends

Art Majors Present Exhibition
An exhibit of the works of art majors will be held at the Creative Arts Center starting May 24 and lasting through the summer. A reception for senior art students will be held at the Center on May 24 at 7:00 p.m. The exhibit will feature various works by graduating students, including sculpture, oil painting, photography and installation. Refreshments will be served.

Feature Program: Art Education
Teaching art can be highly satisfying work for an artist. It is an opportunity to give your own works another dimension by drawing on your experience to help others.
The art te
process.

Figure 10.3

The Art Education Department at Meadowland College offers outstanding courses that fulfill requirements for Teacher K-12 certification. State regulations for licensing require a BA or BFA (Bachelor of Fine Arts), 36 studio credits, 15 credits in education and successful completion of teacher certification exams. Become an art teacher and change a child's vision!

International Studies--
Painting in Florence

The Meadowland College summer travel program is hosting an unforgettable four-week program in Florence, Italy. The *Painting in Florence* program will allow students to paint in a large, window-lined studio within view of the Duomo, as well as painting on location—in a piazza, along the Arno, or from a hilltop overlooking the city. Interested students should see Dr. Bruno Ruccio in the Study-Abroad Office. A map of Florence is shown below.

Insert a city map of Florence, Italy

Figure 10.3 continued

PROJECT SKILLS

✴ Use watermarks
✴ Create captions
✴ Create a tri-fold brochure
✴ Create a brochure using a template
✴ Create a catalog

PROJECT 11

11.1 CREATE A BROCHURE FOR AN EVENT

The Denver Women's Professional Organization is organizing its annual Women's Business and Leisure Traveler Fashion Show and Luncheon. It has asked Destinations Travel to sponsor the event. Destinations is launching a new line of travel gear and will feature its new travel products at the show. You have been asked to create a tri-fold brochure for the Denver Women's Professional Organization, which will also serve as an invitation to the luncheon. This brochure will be distributed to members of the organization at their next meeting.

In this project, you will create a tri-fold brochure for the Denver Women's Professional Organization.

Note: The first page of this project is the outside page of the brochure (Panels 5, 6, and cover). The second page is the inside page (Panels 2, 3, and 4). These two pages will ultimately be printed back-to-back, and folded in thirds, as shown in Figure 11.1a.

1. Open a new blank document.
2. Use the following settings:

Margins	.5" left, right, top, and bottom
Line spacing	As indicated
Paragraph spacing	
Before	As indicated
After	As indicated
Font	As indicated
Font size	As indicated

3. Set the orientation to landscape.
4. Create three columns.

WHAT YOU NEED TO KNOW

Software

▶ Remember, when working with columns, you must enter a column break to force text to the next column. To do so, click the Page Layout tab and in the Page Setup group, click the Breaks button list arrow, and click Column.

Project

▶ A brochure is a small pamphlet that provides information about a product or product line, a place, a service, an event, or a schedule. Some brochures are printed on 8.5" x 11" paper and folded into thirds like a leaflet or in half like a booklet.

▶ The quality of brochures can vary from expensively produced booklets using high-quality paper, print, and design, to inexpensive folded pamphlets created with desktop publishing software.

▶ When creating a brochure in Word (on 8.5" x 11" paper and folded in thirds), you must change the paper orientation to landscape and you must create columns.

▶ A *watermark* is any text, WordArt, image, or drawing object that appears transparent behind regular text in a document.

▶ To create a watermark, click the Page Layout tab and in the Page Background group, click the Watermark button. Select a watermark from the gallery that appears, or click Custom Watermark. In the Printed Watermark dialog box that appears, select Picture watermark or Text watermark. If you selected Picture watermark, click the Select Picture button, navigate to find the picture you want, click Insert, and then click OK. If you selected Text watermark, fill in the information in the text boxes below the option, and then click OK.

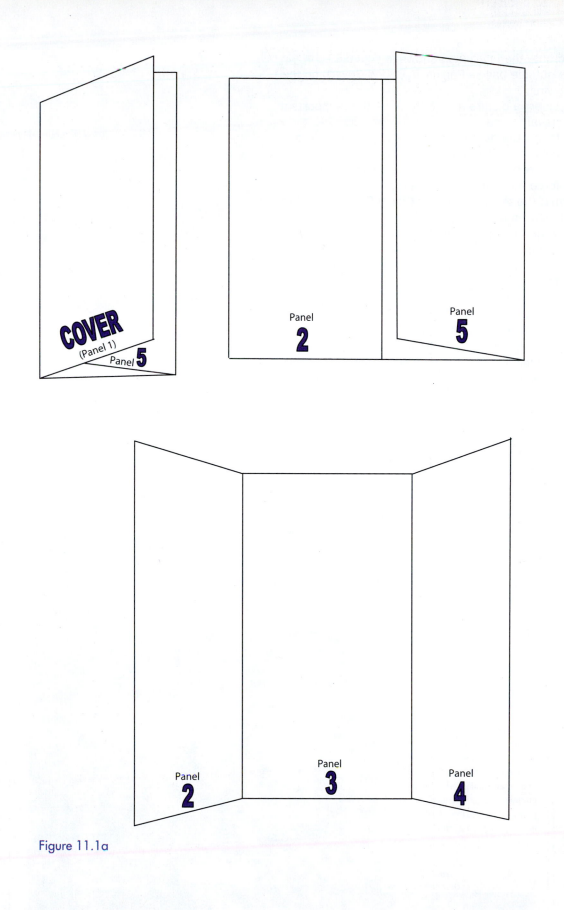

Figure 11.1a

5. To create the first page, shown in Figure 11.1b (the outside page—Panels 5, 6, and Cover), do the following:

a. Insert a picture as a watermark that supports a travel theme.

b. Insert the data file **d11.1brochure text1** into column 1 (Panel 5).

c. Insert column breaks, where appropriate, to force the text into the appropriate columns.

6. Format the text in column 1 (Panel 5) using a 14 pt, sans serif font.

a. Apply line spacing so that the text spans the column. You may apply paragraph spacing before and after each paragraph to better place the text.

b. Apply a drop capital, as shown in Figure 11.1b.

c. Apply paragraph shading to the column. Apply font colors to the text that complement the shading. Emphasize the text "5th Annual Women's Business and Leisure Traveler Fashion Show and Luncheon" by using another font color, as shown.

7. Format the text in column 2 (Panel 6) using the same font used in column 1 but set to 12 pt.

a. Center the headings.

b. Apply paragraph shading to the headings.

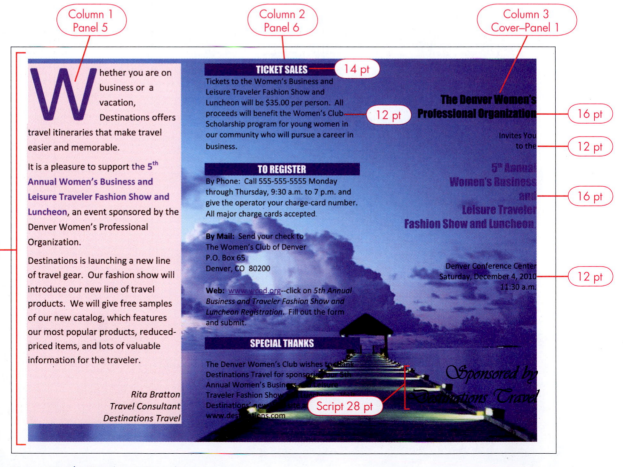

Figure 11.1b (Brochure) Outside page

8. Format the text in column 3 (cover) using similar fonts in the font sizes shown. Add spacing between the lines of text, as you prefer, so that the text spans the column.

9. Press [Ctrl] + [Enter] to create page 2 (the inside page). Notice that the watermark on the first page appears on this page as well.

10. To create the second page, shown in Figure 11.1c (the inside page), do the following:

   a. Insert the data file **d11.1brochure text2** into column 1 (Panel 2).

   b. Insert column breaks, where appropriate, to force the text into the columns, as shown.

   c. Insert a star shape and apply a shape style using a color that complements the picture you chose. Position the star as shown, and position it to appear behind the text.

   d. Apply line spacing, text alignment, and spacing, as shown. Use the illustration as a guide.

11. Preview the brochure. Make any necessary adjustments.

12. Save the file as **11.1brochure**.

13. Print one copy.

14. Close the file.

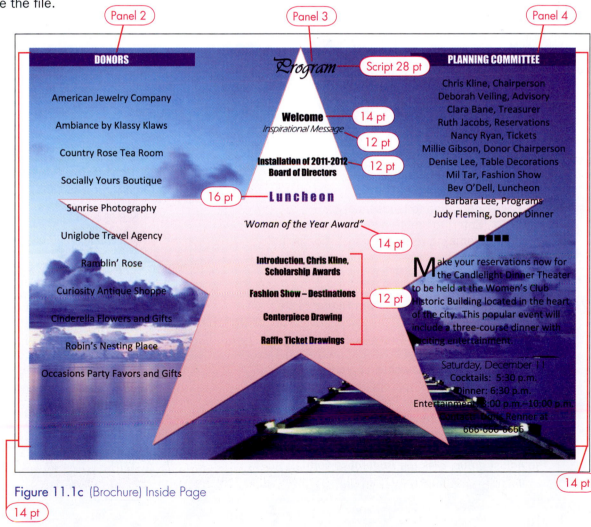

Figure 11.1c (Brochure) Inside Page

11.2 CREATE A PRODUCT BROCHURE

Coffee Crazy & Things has expanded its business to include accessories and gifts. It has also created a Website so customers can buy its delicious coffees online. One of the employees at Coffee Crazy created a brochure that everyone seemed to like. The employee left the company, and no one can find the final brochure file (they did find some of the text and table files). You have been asked to re-create the brochure that is illustrated in Figures 11.2a and 11.2b.

In this project, you will create a two-fold brochure for Coffee Crazy & Things.

Note: The first page of this project is the outside page of the brochure (Panel 4 and cover—Panel 1); the second page is the inside page (Panels 2 and 3). These two pages will ultimately be printed back-to-back, and folded in half.

1. Open a new blank document.
2. Re-create the brochure shown in Figures 11.2a and 11.2b.
3. Use the following settings:

Margins	.5" left, right, top, and bottom
Line spacing	As indicated
Paragraph spacing	
Before	As indicated
After	As indicated
Font	As indicated
Font size	As indicated

4. Set the page orientation to landscape.
5. Press [Ctrl] + [Enter] to create a second page. Then press [Ctrl] + [Home] to return your insertion point to page 1.
6. Create two columns (which will create columns on both pages).
7. To create the first page, as shown in Figure 11.2a, follow these guidelines:
   a. Insert the data file **d11.2coffee text2** into Panel 4. Size it to fill the panel.
   b. Insert a column break, where appropriate, to force the text into the appropriate columns.
   c. Insert a clip art image in Panel 4 that supports the theme. Apply a behind text wrap, size it to fill the panel, and set the Brightness to +40%. (*Hint: Click the Picture Tools Format tab, and in the Adjust group, click the Brightness button.*)

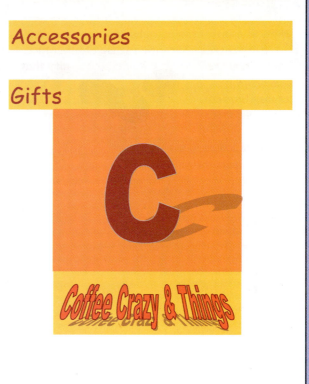

Panel 4

Cover—Panel 1

The Giving Is Easy

When we opened Coffee Crazy & Things in 2000, our goal was to make buying coffee as easy and enjoyable as drinking it.

We did so in a number of unique ways. We organized our coffees by taste. We sold only those coffees that offered great taste and great value. And we talked and wrote about our coffees in ways that were meant to be both informative and entertaining.

Over the past years, we have expanded our business to other cities, to a 24-hour store on the Internet, and to a line of more expensive coffees we call "Beyond the Best."

Coffees

Accessories

Gifts

Coffee Crazy & Things

Figure 11.2a (Brochure) Page 1

d. Format the text in column 1 (Panel 4) as you prefer so that it resembles Figure 11.2a.

e. Format the text in column 2 (Cover) as you prefer so that it resembles Figure 11.2a.

Create the design as shown. The company name and letter "C" were created with WordArt. Apply a shadow effect to the WordArt letter "C."

8. To create the second page, follow these guidelines:

a. Insert the data file **d11.2coffee text1** into Panel 2. Format the text to resemble Figure 11.2b.

b. Insert a clip art image that supports the theme. Apply a picture effect to the image.

c. Insert a caption, as shown.

d. Insert and center the file **d11.2coffee table** where shown.

e. Create Panel 3, as shown.

9. Save the file as **11.2coffeebrochure**.

10. Preview the brochure. Make any necessary adjustments.

11. Print one copy.

12. Close the file.

Panel 2
Panel 3

Monthly Coffee Clubs

Our monthly coffee clubs offer choices for any coffee lover with a sense of adventure. Truly the gift that keeps on giving, each club features themed coffees specially selected from our stores and packed with a set of detailed tasting notes and ideas for winning food pairings. All coffee club prices include shipping and handling.

Only the Finest Beans

Payment can be charged each month when your order is shipped or you can choose to prepay your coffee club order when your first order is shipped.

THE CLUBS	PRICES		
	Quantity	Monthly	Prepay
Featured Blends: All gourmet, noted for rich aroma and mild acidity	6 pounds	32.50	95.00
Simply Organic: All organic, from fresh to luscious	8 pounds	56.50	165.25
Le Club: The most sought-after varieties in the world	8 pounds	80.50	234.25

Coffees
Blended
Unblended
Flavored
Organic

Accessories
Drip Coffee Machines
Espresso Machines
Coffee Art
Demitasse cups
Books on Coffee

Gifts
Corporate gifts
Promotional Items
Twelve Coffees of Christmas
Holiday Gourmet Coffees
Home Accents

Coffee Crazy & Things
P.O. Box 333
Seattle, Washington 98199
Phone: 800-555-5555
Fax: 800-555-6666
Web: www.coffeecrazynthings.com

Figure 11.2b (Brochure) Page 2

11.3 CREATE A BROCHURE USING A TEMPLATE

Your boss at Coffee Crazy & Things would like you to re-create the brochure you designed in Project 11.2 using one of the tri-fold brochure templates.

In this project, you will re-create the brochure for Coffee Crazy & Things using a template.

1. Download and open a tri-fold brochure template of your choice. The one shown in Figure 11.3a and 11.3b is just an example. If that template is not available to you, download another tri-fold design.
2. Re-create the brochure in Project 11.2 using the template you downloaded. *Note: To use the formatting provided in the template, you can either replace the sample text with your own text (which means entering the text you want) or you can insert a file containing the text you want. An inserted file will not take on the font style of the template. You will have to use the Format Painter feature to apply the template formatting to the newly inserted text. It is recommended that you insert the data file before deleting the sample text so you can easily "pick up" formatting from the existing text using Format Painter, and then apply it to the newly inserted text.*
   a. Replace the existing image with one that is relevant to the theme.

WHAT YOU NEED TO KNOW

Software

▶ As you learned in Chapter 2, templates contain a predefined page layout, fonts, formatting, pictures, or text. In addition to those templates that are installed on your computer, Microsoft provides numerous templates, including brochure layouts, which can be downloaded from Microsoft Office Online (www.microsoft.com).

▶ To download templates from the Microsoft Website, click the Office button, and then click New. In the New Document dialog box, click the template category listed in the left pane, which will display thumbnails of each template in that category in the middle pane. Click a template to select it, and it will be displayed in the preview window. Then click the Download button to download the template to the Word window.

You will need an Internet connection to complete this project.

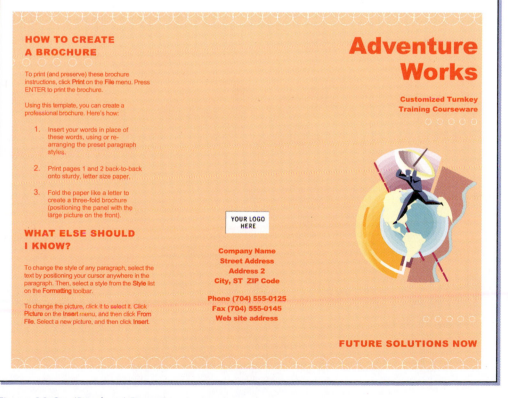

Figure 11.3a (Brochure) Page 1

b. Apply line and spacing to best present the text.

c. Delete or add any design element that you want. You may change font size and font color, if you want.

d. Use the letter "C" as the logo. You can create a WordArt image and apply a shadow effect, if you want.

e. Insert the following data files where you want to place the data: **d11.2coffee text2**, **d11.2coffee text1**, and **d11.2coffee table**.

Note: If you want to replace the sample with the text from the data files, open the data files **d11.2coffee text2** *and* **d11.2coffee text1**, *print each, and then replace the sample text with the text in these data files. You will, however, have to use the Insert File from Text feature to insert* **d11.2coffee table**.

3. Save the file as **11.3brochure template**.

4. Preview the brochure. Make any necessary adjustments.

5. Print one copy.

6. Close the file.

Figure 11.3b (Brochure) Page 2

11.4 CREATE A CATALOG

B & B Home Products sells contemporary home furnishings. Your boss has asked you to create a catalog that features lamps and chairs. She has provided you with a sample catalog and general guidelines to complete this assignment. You will apply the skills you have learned to design this catalog.

In this project, you will create an eight-page catalog for B & B Home Products. Save your work often to prevent losing data.

1. Open a new blank document.
2. Use the following settings:

Margins	.5" left, right, top, and bottom
Line spacing	Single
Paragraph spacing	
Before	0
After	0
Font	As indicated
Font size	As indicated

3. Set the orientation to landscape.
4. Create four pages, as shown in Figure 11.4a.
5. Choose two font styles you would like to use for the project (your boss suggested Impact and Papyrus, but you can use any fonts you want).
6. For page 2 (Inside Page—Panels 4 and 5) shown in Figure 11.4b, do the following:
   a. Create a four-column table.
   b. Set column widths to accommodate the text and images, as shown.
   c. Open the data file **d11.4product desc**, which contains the product descriptions. Cut each product description from the product description file and paste it into a table cell in the catalog file. Format the text as you prefer.
   d. Add images of chairs from your clip art collection or from the Web to fit the descriptions. Use a Square text wrap for the images.
7. For page 2 (Outside Page—Panel 6) shown in Figure 11.4c), do the following:
   a. Create a two-column table.
   b. Size the columns as you did for Panels 4 and 5.
   c. Cut the product descriptions from the data file **d11.4product desc** and paste them into the appropriate cells in the catalog file.
   d. Add images of lamps from your clip art collection or from the Web to fit the descriptions.

WHAT YOU NEED TO KNOW

Software

▶ Remember, you must insert a continuous section break when you change the formatting of document sections. You must insert a column break when you want to force text from one column to the next.

Project

▶ A catalog is a booklet that generally includes product photos, captions, prices, and an order form. A catalog is often sent to homes and businesses and is considered a direct-mail sales tool. Catalogs use a lot of color, which tends to increase their selling power. The inside page of a catalog usually describes the company. Sometimes, a letter from the president explaining the company's philosophy is printed on the first inside page of the catalog.

▶ To prevent images and text from shifting, use a table to format product descriptions and the images, particularly if you are going to post the catalog to the Web.

▶ To plan a catalog, use blank pieces of paper, fold them as you would the printed final copy, and mark the pages. This way, you can visualize what information belongs on what page.

WORD

8. For page 2 (Outside Page—Panel 3), do the following:

   a. Create a text box to fill the page. Insert the data file, **d11.4order form** into the text box.

9. For page 1, shown in Figures 11.4d and 11.4e (Outside and Inside pages), do the following:

   a. Create two columns.

   b. On the back cover (Panel 8), shown in Figure 11.4e, include the following information:

```
Let us Furnish Your Home
B & B Home Products
11 Hudson Street
New York, NY 10001
T (212) 555-5555 F (212) 555-6666
To Order Call 1-800-555-9999 Or
Visit Us on the Web: www.bb.com
```

   c. Create a design for the front cover (Panel 1) using the information shown in Figure 11.4e (you can re-create the illustration or design your own cover).

   d. Create the inside front cover (Panel 2) shown in Figure 11.4d using the data file d11.4catalog text. Format the text as you prefer.

   e. Insert clip art (of a chair) and the caption shown for the featured product on the inside back cover (Panel 7).

10. Save the file as **11.4catalog**.

11. Preview the catalog. Make any necessary adjustments.

12. Print one copy.

13. Close the file.

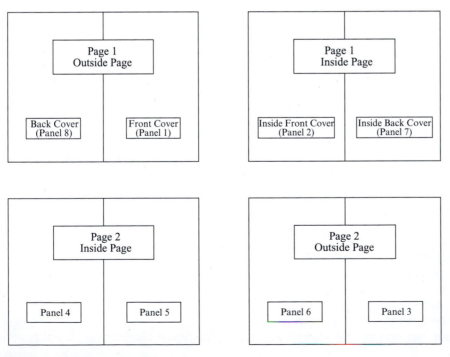

Figure 11.4a

Panel 4   Panel 5

c h a i r s

The Sleeper Chair opens up to sleep one. Comfortable, yet modern.
Sleeper Chair
Available in all fabrics
Cat.# 2334
$360.00

The Rocking Chair allows you to rock yourself or your baby to sleep.
Rocking Chair
Available in cherry or pine wood
Cat # 4444
$100.00

The Library Chair is perfect for your den or library.
Library Chair
All fabrics available
Cat # 5454
$150.00

The Italian Cab Chair is a living-room must.
Cab Chair
Available in leather
Cat # 4441
$125.00

The Elmo Chair is perfect for use as a bar or counter stool.
Elmo Chair
Available in 4 styles and 5 colors
Cat # 2222
$129.00

The Laurel Chair is a design of architectural simplicity and of graceful fluid lines.
Laurel Chair
Available in beautiful natural fabrics
Cat # 8787
$450.00

The Iris Chair has subtle detailing.
Iris Chair
Available on stainless steel glides or on black casters.
Cat # 9898
$319.00

The Lila Chair is suitable to small offices as well as large reception areas.
Lila Chair
Available with special surfaces on arm caps
Cat # 6688
$410.00

Figure 11.4b (Catalog) Page 2

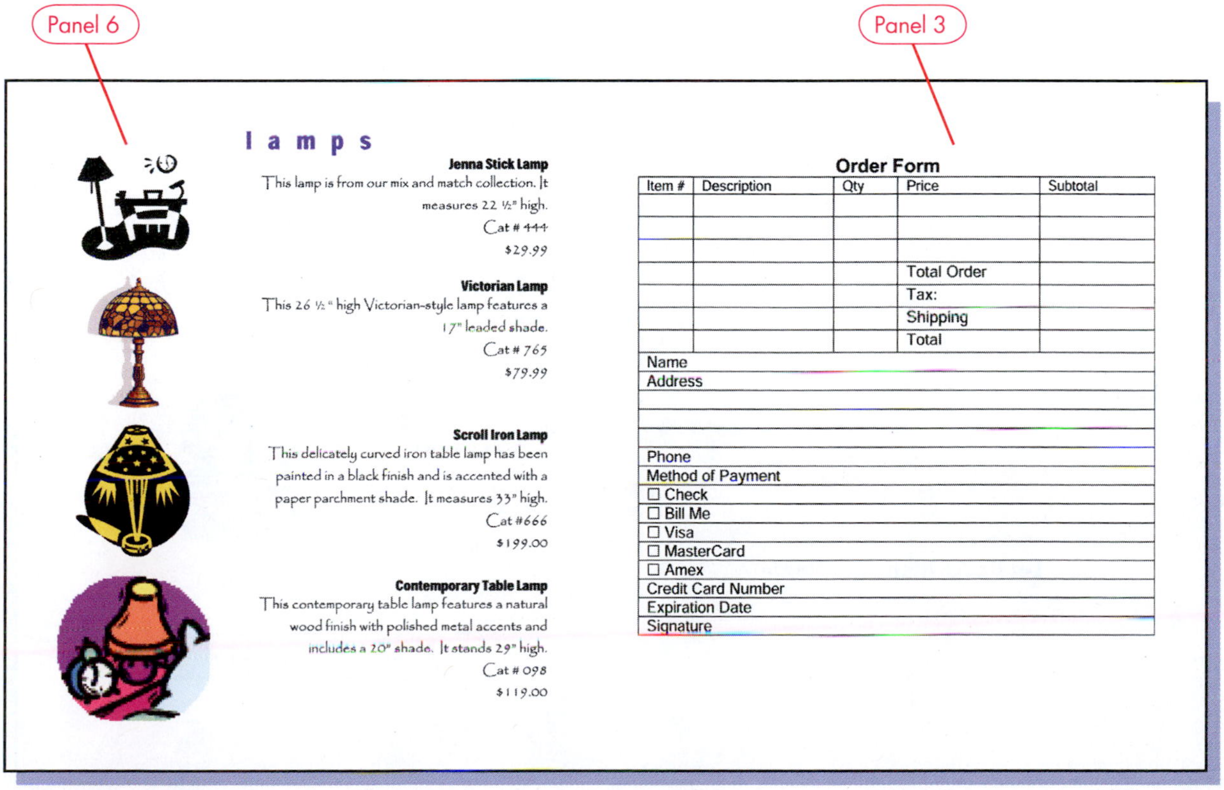

Panel 6   Panel 3

l a m p s

Jenna Stick Lamp
This lamp is from our mix and match collection. It measures 22 ½" high.
Cat # 444
$29.99

Victorian Lamp
This 26 ½" high Victorian-style lamp features a 17" leaded shade.
Cat # 765
$79.99

Scroll Iron Lamp
This delicately curved iron table lamp has been painted in a black finish and is accented with a paper parchment shade. It measures 33" high.
Cat #666
$199.00

Contemporary Table Lamp
This contemporary table lamp features a natural wood finish with polished metal accents and includes a 20" shade. It stands 29" high.
Cat # 098
$119.00

Order Form

Item #	Description	Qty	Price	Subtotal
			Total Order	
			Tax:	
			Shipping	
			Total	

Name
Address
Phone
Method of Payment
☐ Check
☐ Bill Me
☐ Visa
☐ MasterCard
☐ Amex
Credit Card Number
Expiration Date
Signature

Figure 11.4c (Catalog) Page 2

Welcome to B & B Home Products, located in the landmark Redwink Building in Tribeca, the hub of New York's gallery district. In this light and airy loft, we have transformed what was once a factory space into a lively destination filled with a mix of contemporary home furnishings – from chairs and tables, to fine accessories.

B & B Home Products represents the simplicity of natural materials with the richness of refined details. Our philosophy is pairing the sleekness of contemporary home furnishings with designs that are conscious and daring.

Jane Brennan, President

Comfy Chair
Available in green, blue and brown leather
Cat. # 2333
$560.00

Figure 11.4d (Catalog) Page 1

Let Us Furnish Your Home
B & B Home Products
14 Hudson Street
New York, NY 10001
T (212) 555-5555 F (212) 555-6666
To Order Call 1-800-555-9999
Or Visit Us on the Web: www.bb.com

B
and
B
home products

Figure 11.4e (Catalog) Page 1

CHAPTER 5

Reports and Long Documents

In this chapter, you will complete the following projects:

PROJECT 12
Multiple-page Letters
PROJECT 12.1 Format a Two-page Business Letter
PROJECT 12.2 Format a Multiple-page Business Letter with Indented Paragraphs
PROJECT 12.3 Edit and Format a Multiple-page Business Letter

PROJECT 13
Reports
PROJECT 13.1 Format a Report with Internal Citations
PROJECT 13.2 Format a Report with Citations; Prepare a Cover Page and Bibliography
PROJECT 13.3 Format a Report with Footnotes and Endnotes; Prepare a Cover Page
PROJECT 13.4 Research, Write, and Format a Report

PROJECT 14
Long Documents
PROJECT 14.1 Format a Handbook
PROJECT 14.2 Create an Article, Use Comments, and Track Changes
PROJECT 14.3 Format a Business Plan
PROJECT 14.4 Format an Annual Report

PROJECT SKILLS

✸ Insert headers and footers
✸ Indent text
✸ Set first-line Indents

PROJECT 12

12.1 FORMAT A TWO-PAGE BUSINESS LETTER

You will assume the role of J. Scott Harris, President of EarthOne Growth fund. Yesterday, you began to draft a letter to a prospective client, but you did not have an opportunity to complete the letter.

In this project, you will complete and then format the letter that you started yesterday. The letter will span two pages. The second-page heading is shown in Figure 12.1b.

1. Open the data file **d12.1earth**.
2. Set the font size for the letter to 13 pt.
3. Begin the date approximately 2.1" from the top of the page.
4. Format the text as a block business letter, single-spaced. Include an appropriate salutation and closing. Send it to:

   ```
   Mr. Curtis Capeta
   14 Church Street
   Greenfield, MA 01301-9595
   ```
5. Enter the three paragraphs shown in Figure 12.1a as the last paragraphs in the letter.
6. Insert a header for the second page that includes the name of the addressee, the page number, and the date, as shown in Figure 12.1b.
   a. Change the header font and color to match that used in the letter.
   b. Suppress the header on the first page.
7. Prepare an envelope and append it to the file.
8. Save the file as **12.1earthone**.
9. Preview and print one copy of the letter and the envelope.
10. Close the file and save the changes.

WHAT YOU NEED TO KNOW

Software

▶ As you learned previously, you can choose to end a page manually by pressing [Ctrl] + [Enter].

▶ A *header* is identical text that appears at the top of every page or specified pages. A *footer* is identical text that appears at the bottom of every page or specified pages. A header or footer might include the document title or filename, the page number, the current date or time, or any other text, graphic, or symbol.

▶ To create a header or footer, click the Insert tab and in the Header & Footer group, click the Header button or Footer button. In the gallery that appears, select the layout and content you want in the header or footer. If there are placeholders in the header design, click the placeholder, and enter your information. Click the Close Header and Footer button to return to the document.

▶ To insert a page number within a header or footer, click the Page Number button in the Header & Footer group. In the menu that appears, point to a page number position option, and then select a page number design from the gallery that is displayed.

▶ Headers, footers, and page numbers usually appear on the second and subsequent pages of a document; they generally do not appear on the first page. To suppress the header and footer on the first page, double-click the Header (or Footer) area. On the Design tab, and in the Options group, select the Different First Page check box.

Continued on next page

► The header font automatically uses the default font face and size. If you changed the font in your document and want to use the same font for the header, you must change the header font also.

Project

► For letters that are longer than one page, a standard page heading is used for subsequent pages. This typically consists of the recipient's name, the date, and the page number. Two blank lines separate the heading from the text of the letter.

► A letterhead is used only on the first page of a multiple-page letter.

► As you learned previously, draft documents are often prepared using double-spacing so corrections can be made easily.

Insert into letter

Some of the organizations in which we invest include the PathFinder Corporation, the Gorin Company, the World Energy Corporation, Renewable Resources, Inc, Northwest Recycling, and New Data, Inc. We hold 25 different issues of government bonds, primarily from the Federal National Mortgage Association, Federal Farm Credit Banks Consolidated, and the Federal Home Loan Bank System. The fund's major holdings are in information technology and healthcare. The enclosed report lists our major holdings by sectors and our performance for one, three, five, and 10 years, as compared to the S&P 500 average of similar funds.

Critics of socially responsible investing argue that screening companies for social factors must result in lower yields and lesser earnings. To such critics, our emphatic response is, "Not so!" In the past 30 years, our fund has equaled and even exceeded the rate of return of comparable funds that do not use a social investment policy.

Please look over the enclosed report and call us if we can answer any questions for you. Thank you for considering investment in EarthOne.

Enclosure

Figure 12.1a

Mr. Curtis Capeta
Page 2
Today's date

Second and subsequent page heading

issues of government bonds, primarily from the Federal National Mortgage Association, Federal Farm Credit Banks Consolidated, and the Federal Home Loan Bank System. The fund's major holdings are in information technology and healthcare. The enclosed report lists our major holdings by sectors and our performance for one, three, five, and 10 years, as compared to the S&P 500 average of similar funds.

Critics of socially responsible investing argue that screening companies for social factors must result in lower yields and lesser earnings. To such critics, our emphatic response is, "Not so!" In the past 30 years, our fund has equaled and even exceeded the rate of return of comparable funds that do not use a social investment policy.

Please look over the enclosed report and call us if we can answer any questions for you. Thank you for considering investment in EarthOne.

Sincerely,

J. Scott Harris
President

jsh

Enclosure

Figure 12.1b

12.2 FORMAT A MULTIPLE-PAGE BUSINESS LETTER WITH INDENTED PARAGRAPHS

Macon Gregory is the events coordinator for Children's Community Center. Mr. Gregory has asked you to finalize a letter using text you drafted in Project 2.2.

In this project, you will edit text and create a two-page business letter. The final letter will be printed on Children's Community Center letterhead.

1. Open **2.2committee**, the file you completed in Project 2. If that file is unavailable to you, open the data file **d12.2committee**, as shown in Figure 12.2a.
2. Use the following settings:

Margins	1" left and 1.25" right
Line spacing	Single
Paragraph spacing	
Before	0
After	0
Font	As indicated
Font size	As indicated

3. Make the insertions and deletions shown in Figure 12.2b to create the two-page block letter shown in Figure 12.2c. Insert new text (shown in script) using the same font size and style used for other paragraph text.
   a. Use the Date and Time feature to insert today's date approximately 2.1" from the top of the page.
   b. Remove the highlight from Sheila Porter and the phone number.
   c. Include an appropriate salutation and closing.
   d. Set a 1.25" left indent and a 1" right indent on the ways to become a volunteer (text set in blue).
4. Correct spelling.
5. Position your insertion point on page 1.
   a. Create a header that includes the name of the addressee (Ms. Mary Smith), the page number, and today's date in sans serif, 10 pt font.
   b. Suppress the header on the first page.
6. Create a centered footer that reads **Children's Community Center**. Use a script, 18 pt, blue font.
7. Prepare an envelope and append it to the letter.
8. Preview the document. Make any necessary adjustments to prevent awkward line breaks.
9. Print one copy of the letter and envelope.
10. Save the file as **12.2ccc**.
11. Close the file.

WHAT YOU NEED TO KNOW

Software

▶ The Indent feature allows you to set temporary left and right margins for paragraph text.

▶ To set a left and/or right indent, select the text to be indented. Then, click the Home tab and in the Paragraph group, click the Increase Indent button. Each click advances the insertion point .5". Click the Decrease Indent button to decrease the indent level of the paragraph.

▶ You can also set left and right indents by specific amounts (indentation amounts are measured from the left and/or right margins, not from the edge of the page). To do so, click the Home tab and in the Paragraph group, click the Paragraph dialog box launcher. In the Paragraph dialog box that appears, click the Indents and Spacing tab. Enter the indent amount in the left and/or right text boxes of the Indentation section.

I encourage your participation in this year's annual fund-raising event for the Children's Community Center. The Children's Community Center uses the money raised from the event to send children to summer camp outside the city.

We urge everyone at Sutton Investment Group to participate by contacting Sheila Porter at 800-555-5555. She will discuss your level of involvement.

Here are ways to become involved in the fund-raising event for the Children's Community Center.

Encourage Volunteers

We cannot run our event without the volunteers who work the tables and registers. Our most loyal volunteers are usually individuals who have worked these wonderful events in the past.

Financial Contribution

There are parts of the event that would not be possible without financial support. Each contribution will be matched by Sutton.

Planning Committee

Joining the planning committee is a sizeable time commitment. It is helpful for us to receive support from all of our departments in this effort.

We hope to hear from you by the beginning of August so we can begin planning. To summarize, select from one of the ways listed below to become involved in this charitable cause.

Encourage Volunteers
Financial Contribution
Planning Committee

Figure 12.2a

Insert)
Ms. Mary Smith, Vice President
A & C Securities
203 North Street
San Francisco, CA 94102

Insert →
salutation
I am writing once again to ~~I~~encourage your participation in this year's annual fund-raising event for the Children's Community Center. *As you know,* ~~T~~he Children's Community Center uses the money raised from the event to send children to summer camp outside the city.

If you are interested in participating in this year's event, ~~We urge everyone at Sutton Investment Group to participate by contacting~~ *call* Sheila Porter at *Sutton Investment Group at* 1-800-555-5555. She will discuss your level of involvement.

Here are ways *that you can* become involved ~~in the fund-raising event for the Children's Community Center.~~ :

Encourage Volunteers
Indent
    We cannot run our event without the volunteers who work the tables and registers. Our most loyal volunteers are usually individuals who have worked these wonderful events in the past.

Financial Contribution
Indent
    There are parts of the event such as the opening dinner that would not be possible without financial support *from individuals and corporations.* ~~Each contribution will be matched by Sutton.~~

Planning Committee
    Joining the planning committee is a sizeable time commitment. It is helpful for us to receive support from all of our departments in this effort.

"*In addition to this event, Ms. Porter is planning others. For example, the Masquerade Ball held in December is one of our biggest events of the year and attracts the largest donors. Mark your calendar with future events. I am confident that you will want to become involved in one of them.*"
¶
Masquerade Ball - December
Clothing Drive - February   *Center*
Art Sale - April
Phone-A-Thon - June

Insert
Closing
Macon Gregory
Events Coordinator

mg

We hope to hear from you by the beginning of August so we can begin planning. ~~To summarize, select from one of the ways listed below to become involved in this charitable cause.~~

~~**Encourage Volunteers**~~
~~**Financial Contribution**~~
~~**Planning Committee**~~

Figure 12.2b

Today's date

Ms. Mary Smith, Vice President
A & C Securities
203 North Street
San Francisco, CA 94102

Dear Ms. Smith:

I am writing once again to encourage your participation in this year's fund-raising event for the Children's Community Center. As you know, the Children's Community Center uses the money raised from the event to send children to summer camp outside the city.

If you are interested in participating in this year's event, call Sheila Porter at Sutton Investment Group at 1-800-555-5555. She will discuss your level of involvement.

Here are ways that you can become involved:

Encourage Volunteers
We cannot run our event without the volunteers who work the tables and registers. Our most loyal volunteers are usually individuals who have worked these wonderful events in the past.

Financial Contribution
There are parts of the event such as the opening dinner that would not be possible without financial support from individuals and corporations.

Planning Committee
Joining the planning committee is a sizeable time commitment. It is helpful for us to receive support from all of our departments in this effort.

In addition to this event, Ms. Porter is planning others. For example, the Masquerade Ball, held in December, is one of our biggest events of the year and

Children's Community Center

Figure 12.2c

Ms. Mary Smith
Page 2
Today's date

attracts the largest donors. Mark your calendar with future events. I am confident that you will want to become involved in one of them.

Masquerade Ball – December
Clothing Drive – February
Art Sale – April
Phone-A-Thon – June

We hope to hear from you by the beginning of August so we can begin planning.

Sincerely,

Macon Gregory
Events Coordinator

mg

12.3 EDIT AND FORMAT A MULTIPLE-PAGE BUSINESS LETTER

You just received another assignment from your boss, Pamela Carson, manager of the Tri-State Auto Group. She wants you to finalize another letter she has drafted and then format it for mailing. Remember that Tri-State prefers the modified-block letter style for its correspondence.

In this project, you will format a modified-block letter from an unformatted draft copy.

1. Open the data file **d12.3tri-statelethead** (this is a template file).
2. Open the data file **d12.3cartext**, which is shown in Figure 12.3a.
3. Copy the text and then paste it into the **d12.3tri-statelethead** document.
4. Close the **12.3cartext** file.
5. Use the following settings:

Margins	1.25" left and 1.5" right
Line spacing	Single
Paragraph spacing	
Before	0
After	0
Font	Serif
Font size	As indicated

6. Create a modified-block letter from the text.
   a. Use today's date.
   b. Send it to:
      Mr. Jeff Robins
      30 Belmill Avenue
      Bellemore, NY 11746
   c. Include an appropriate salutation and closing.
7. Make the revisions shown in Figure 12.3b. Format the letter as follows:
   a. Bullet each question. Indent all bulleted text .5" from the left and right margins.
   b. Indent the second set of paragraphs .5" from the left and right margins. Set a .5" first-line indent for each paragraph.
8. Correct spelling.
9. Include an appropriate header for the second page that includes a page number.
10. Preview and print one copy.
11. Save the file as **12.3car**.
12. Close the file.

WHAT YOU NEED TO KNOW

Software

▶ Use the Indent feature to create a first-line indent. A first-line indent allows you to set the distance of the first line of each paragraph indent. Each time you press [Enter] and start a new paragraph, the insertion point automatically moves to the indented setting, thus eliminating the need to press [Tab] to indent each new paragraph.

▶ To set a first-line indent, click the Home tab and in the Paragraph group, click the Paragraph dialog box launcher. In the Paragraph dialog box that is displayed, click the Indents and Spacing tab, click the Special list arrow, select First line, enter the amount in the By text box, and then click OK.

For many people, the thought of purchasing a car is stressful. Buying a car, whether new or used, is a huge investment. With new car prices at an all time high, many people are choosing to purchase used cards, but the unknowns in such a purchase are often intimidating.

You asked our advice. We are glad to give it. Before you embark upon a purchase, there are a few important questions you need to think about and some tips for the beginner who is in the early stages of buying a used car.

Ask yourself the following questions:

What is the condition of the car I currently own? Why do I want to replace it? If I don't presently own a car, what are my primary reasons for wanting to purchase one? Do I want to buy a used car from a dealership (us) or would I prefer to go through a private owner? What are the advantages and disadvantages of both? How will I finance my purchase? How will my current transportation costs compare with owning my own vehicle? What kind of car am I looking for? What functions does the car need to serve (i.e., daily transportation vs. weekend trips to the mountains or both)?

There are a few steps you need to take before actually purchasing the car. Here are a few suggested steps:

Conduct research, research, research. The most successful purchaser of a used car is one who is empowered with knowledge. Read consumer guides and books. Find the resources available to you online. Learn to speak "car talk." Look through the newspaper to get a sense of the used car market and to understand what car dealers are advertising.

Enlist the help and support of a friend or family member who knows about cars and is familiar with the process of purchasing a used card. Experience can be the best teacher.

Formulate a realistic budget so that you can arrive at a definite price range from which you will not waver when shopping and negotiating. Set up a meeting with a financial manager if necessary.

Dream a little. With knowledge, hard work, and a definite purpose, finding the used car of your dreams at the right price is possible.

We hope we have helped you to begin thinking about the purchase of a used car. Please feel free to stop our use car lot, which is next to our showroom, and we can discuss the makes and models that are for sale.

In answer to your recent inquiry as to whether Tri-State Auto Group sells used cars, the answer is YES, YES, YES!

Figure 12.3a

For many people, the thought of purchasing a car is stressful. Buying a car, whether new or used, is a huge investment. With new car prices at an all time high, many people are choosing to purchase used cars, but the unknowns in such a purchase are often intimidating.

You asked our advice. We are glad to give it. Before you embark upon a purchase, there are a few important questions you need to think about and some tips for the beginner who is in the early stages of buying a used car.

Ask yourself the following questions:

Bullet each question (on a separate line); indent all lines .5" on the left and right

What is the condition of the car I currently own? Why do I want to replace it? If I don't presently own a car, what are my ~~primary~~ main reasons for wanting to purchase one? Do I want to buy a used car from a dealership (us) or would I prefer to go through a private owner? What are the advantages and disadvantages of both? How will I finance my purchase? How will my current transportation costs compare with owning my own vehicle? What kind of car am I looking for? What functions does the car need to serve (i.e., daily transportation vs. weekend trips to the mountains or both)?

There are a few steps you need to take before actually purchasing the car. Here are a few suggested steps:

Indent .5" on the left and right; set a first-line indent

Conduct research, research, research. The most successful purchaser of a used car is one who is empowered with knowledge. Read consumer guides and books. Find the resources available to you online. Learn to speak "car talk." Look through the newspaper to get a sense of the used car market and to understand what car dealers are advertising.

Someone
~~Enlist the help and support of a friend or family member~~ who knows about cars ~~and~~ is ~~familiar with the process of purchasing a used car.~~ Experience can be the best teacher.

Then
Formulate a realistic budget ~~so that~~ you can arrive at a definite price range from which you will not waver when shopping and negotiating. Set up a meeting with a financial manager if necessary.

Dream a little. With knowledge, hard work, and a definite purpose, finding the used car of your dreams at the right price is possible.

We hope we have helped you to begin thinking about the purchase of a used car. Please
in at
feel free to stop our used car lot, which is next to our showroom, ~~and~~ we can discuss the
so that
makes and models that are for sale.

In answer to your recent inquiry as to whether Tri-State Auto Group sells used cars, the answer is YES, YES, YES!

Figure 12.3b

REPORTS

PROJECT 13

PROJECT SKILLS
* Create a multiple-page report with cover page and bibliography
* Work with quoted material
* Use Word Count
* Set hanging indents
* Insert page numbers
* Use Research Services

13.1 FORMAT A REPORT WITH INTERNAL CITATIONS

Each month, Ms. Rita Bratton, your boss at Destinations, researches a country and then writes a report about it. These reports are sent to customers who express an interest in visiting that country and are used in Destinations' monthly newsletter when a particular country is featured. This month, the featured country is Japan. Your boss has asked you to format the report using internal citations. To fit into this month's newsletter, the report cannot exceed 1200 words. Ms. Bratton has asked you to use the Word Count feature to verify final word count.

In this project, you will format a report with internal citations.

1. Open the data file **d13.1japan**.
2. Format the report, as shown in Figure 13.1. Insert an internal citation after each quote where shown in the Figure.
3. Use the following settings:

Margins	1.25" left and right
Line spacing	Single
Paragraph spacing	
Before	0
After	0
Font	Serif and as directed
Font size	Default and as directed

4. Center and set the title to Arial, 16 pt, bold. Set the font color to blue.
5. Single-space and indent the quoted text 1" from the left and right margins. Set the text to full justification.
6. Set the first side heading to Arial, 14 pt, bold. Set the font color to blue.
7. Set a 1" first-line indent. Set line spacing to Exactly 25 pt, and paragraph spacing before and after each paragraph to 6 pt.
8. Use the Format Painter feature to copy the formatting from the first side heading to the remaining side headings.

WHAT YOU NEED TO KNOW

Software
▶ The Word Count feature tells you how many words, characters, paragraphs, and/or lines a document or selected text contains. This is particularly useful if you have a page or word limit for the document. Right-click the Status bar and select Word Count, which will display the Word count indicator on the Status bar. Click the Word Count area on the Status bar to display the Word Count dialog box, which will show the statistics for the document. Then click Close. *Note: Click Word Count only if the Word Count indicator is not already shown on the Status bar (to select it and not select it).*

Project
▶ A report or manuscript communicates information about a topic. The topic may be formal or informal. Although some reports require research, others include the writer's opinion or position on a topic.
▶ The margins for a report depend on how the report is bound. The following margin amounts are suggested and may vary depending on desktop design and intended audience:
* Unbound—1" left and right, 2" top, 1" bottom
* Left-bound—1.5" left, 1" right, 2" top, 1" bottom
* Top-bound—1" left and right, 2.5" top, 1" bottom
▶ The start line for the first page of a report is generally 2.5".
▶ Line spacing of a report is generally set to 1.5 or double-spaced, but spacing may vary. The first line of each paragraph is indented .5" or 1" from the left margin.

Continued on next page

9. Include a right-aligned header (using the Stacks design, perhaps). Set the font to 12 pt script.
10. Correct spelling.
11. Check the Word count. *Reminder: The document cannot exceed 1200 words.*
12. Print one copy, and then save the file as **13.1japan**.
13. Close the file.

▶ When you include quoted or paraphrased material from another source in a report, you must identify the source of such information. Failing to cite someone else's words, ideas, statistics, artwork, or lab results constitutes plagiarism.

▶ Citations that appear at the bottom of a page are called *footnotes*; those located at the end of a report are called *endnotes*; and those that immediately follow the quoted or paraphrased sentence or paragraph are known as *internal citations*. See Appendix C for ways to write footnotes and endnotes cited from various sources.

▶ In an internal citation, just the author's name and year of publication are listed. If the author's name is not available, list the publication's title and the date.

▶ When a quote is longer than two lines, it is single-spaced and indented. Paraphrased material does not contain quotation marks.

JAPAN

I dreamed of Japan long before I went there. Moss gardens, straw-mat rooms, wooden bridges arching in the moonlight, paper lanterns with the fire glowing inside. Whenever I paged through photography books of traditional Japan, I found myself gasping with appreciation. Three rocks, a gnarled pine tree, raked white sand: awe. (*Insight Guides: Japan*, 1997).

AN INTRODUCTION

The country of Japan is an archipelago consisting of four main islands—Kyushu, Shikoku, Honshu, and Hokkaido—and about 3,900 smaller islands. Since Japan is so large with so many different landscapes, ranging from small fishing communities to large urban centers, from flat plains to towering mountain ranges, the climate varies from region to region and from season to season. The Japanese people have a "sense of uniqueness" that theirs is a culture and race distinct from any other, but "Theories regarding the racial origins of the Japanese cite both the north and the south—Manchuria and Siberia, and the South China or Indochina regions—as likely possibilities." (Davidson, 1993) And most Japanese, while identifying themselves as either Shinto or Buddhist, do not have the same strict religious boundaries as one finds in the West.

ART AND TRADITION

The Japanese have several artistic forms of expression that are well-known and considered to embody the tradition and spirit of Japan. At a most basic level, most Americans are familiar with the simplicity of origami, a method of folding paper into beautiful formations, such as birds. In addition, the Japanese practice a form of traditional calligraphy, scripting the ancient *kanji*, characters where "each single character contains a concept. Each character has many layers of meaning, giving *kanji* especially

Figure 13.1

rich connotative powers."(Kerr, 1996) In addition, the Japanese have strong
traditions in textiles, ceramics, painting, and bamboo work.

There are five forms of traditional Japanese theater—the two most
significant are *Noh* and *Kabuki.Noh* drama is considered classical and dates back to the
early fifteenth century. "As an art form, its high degree of stylization, lack of overt
action and monotonous-sounding vocal declamation makes it a distinctly acquired taste."
(*Insight Guides: Japan*, 1997) In contrast, *kabuki* is much more modern. "*Kabuki* is the
equivalent of cabaret spectacular, soap opera, morality play, religious pageant, and tear-
jerker. It is music and dance and story and color and pathos and farce and everything a
theater-lover could want." (*Insight Guides: Japan*, 1997)

LANGUAGE

The Japanese language is complex and often seems impenetrable to the
outsider. The language is based on three alphabets:*kanji,katakana* and *hiragana.Kanji*
is a hieroglyphic, character-based script that was inherited from the Chinese. There are
over eighteen hundred *kanji*, and the Japanese use them all. *Katakana* and *hiragana* are
supportive alphabets that are often used to incorporate foreign terminology or contemporary meanings into the Japanese language.

THE CHANGING ENVIRONMENT

Industrialization and modernization have brought about many changes to
the culture and natural environment that one often thinks of when visualizing Japan.
"Forget rocks and raked sand! Neon everywhere, billboards as far as the eye could see,
concrete apartment blocks dingy with pollution. Even the details radiated a sense of
urbanization run amok." (Davidson, 1993) This transformation is often dismissed as the

Internal citations

Figure 13.1 continued

necessary price to pay for economic prosperity and an increased role in the global
culture and marketplace. However, Japan is still a place like no other.
"The changes taking place in the cultural world, the rumblings of economic revolution
in the bureaucracy and in business—all of this is exciting in a way in which Japan
has not been exciting for decades." (Davidson, 1993)

13.2 FORMAT A REPORT WITH CITATIONS; PREPARE A COVER PAGE AND BIBLIOGRAPHY

As indicated in the last project, Destinations' newsletter this month will feature Japan as a travel destination. Ms. Bratton did another research report on the cities of Japan and has given you the report to format.

In this project, you will prepare a report about Japan using internal citations. You will also prepare a cover page and bibliography for this report.

1. Open the data file **d13.2japancities** and format the report, as shown in Figure 13.2.
2. Use the following settings:

Margins	1.5" left and right
Line spacing	1.5" for first, second, and last paragraphs; single for remaining text
Paragraph spacing	
Before	0
After	0
Font	Century Gothic
Font size	12 pt and as directed

3. Begin the report at 1" from the top of the page.
4. Center and set the title to 14 pt, bold. Set the font color to dark red.
5. Indent the city information .5" from the left and right margins. Set the spacing to single and apply full justification.
6. Set the font for the first city (NARA) to 14 pt, bold. Set the font color to dark red.
7. Set the font for the first city location (Southern Honshu) to sans serif, 10 pt. Set the font color to blue.
8. Use Format Painter to copy the formatting from the first city to the remaining cities and to copy the first city location to the remaining city locations.
9. Insert a symbol of your choice before the first city. Set the symbol to 14 pt, bold.
10. Copy the symbol and paste it so that it precedes each side heading.
11. Insert a footer and page number using the Tiles style, and insert the text as shown.
12. Insert a citation at the end of paragraph one where shown.
   a. Click the References tab, and in the Citations & Bibliography group, click the Style button list arrow and select MLA.
   b. Click the Insert Citation button, and select Add New Source.

WHAT YOU NEED TO KNOW

Software

▶ Word provides a gallery of predesigned cover pages. Regardless of where you insert the page, Word places the cover page at the beginning of the document. Click the Insert tab, and in the Pages group, click the Cover Page button list arrow. In the gallery that is displayed, select a design and replace the sample text with your own. Word automatically numbers the cover as page 1.

[Cover Page ▾]

▶ A *bibliography*, or references page, is a summary list of the sources used, quoted, or paraphrased within a document. A bibliography is generally the last page in a report.

▶ Each bibliographical entry includes the author's last name and first name, the name of the article and the publication, the publisher, and the date of publication. The sources are generally listed in alphabetical order by author's last name. If you use internal citations in the report, the bibliographical reference should include the page number of the quoted material.

▶ Word's Citation feature allows you to enter information about each source, which Word properly formats (based on a writing style you choose) and inserts as an internal citation at the location in your document that you specify. The Word internal citation feature generates only the author's last name (not the year of publication).

▶ The Bibliography tool automatically generates a list of sources you entered as citations and formats them based on your selected writing style. The different writing styles and by whom they are typically used are indicated in the following list:

- AMA (American Medical Association)—Used by writers in the fields of medicine, health, and biological sciences
- APA (American Psychological Association)—Used by writers in the fields of psychology, education, and other social sciences
- Chicago—Used by publishing and research communities

Continued on next page

c. Fill in the Create Source dialog box using the following information. Click the Show All Bibliography Fields check box to expand the dialog box.

Type of Source	Book
Author	Alex Kerr
Title	Lost Japan
Year	2005
Country/Region	Australia
Publisher	Lonely Planet

13. Insert a citation in the middle of paragraph three where shown.
   a. Repeat Steps 12a and 12b.
   b. Fill in the Create Source dialog box using the following information:

Type of Source	Book
Author	Brian Bell
Title	Insight Guides: Japan
Year	2008
City	Boston
Publisher	APA Publications

14. Insert a citation in the middle of paragraph five where shown.
   a. Repeat Steps 12a and 12b.
   b. Fill in the Create Source dialog box using the following information:

Type of Source	Book
Author	Joanna Grey
Title	The Wonders of Japan
Year	2009
City	Chicago
Publisher	TTX Publications

15. Create the bibliography:
   a. At the bottom of the last page, press [Ctrl] + [ENTER] to insert a page break and create a new page.
   b. Begin the bibliography approximately 2.5" from the top of the page.
   c. Click the References tab and in the Citations & Bibliography group, click the Style button list arrow and select MLA.
   d. Click the Bibliography button list arrow and select Bibliography from the gallery.
16. Create a cover page using the Tiles page design.
   a. Delete the placeholders for Company, Year, Company Address, and Subtitle.
   b. Insert your name in the Author placeholder.

- MLA (Modern Language Association)—Used by writers in the fields of literature, arts, and humanities
- Turabian—Used by college students in all subjects

▶ You learned to insert an internal citation in Project 13.1. In this Project, you learn to insert an internal citation using Word's citation feature, which will automatically generate a bibliography for you.

▶ To create an internal citation, click the References tab and in the Citations & Bibliography group, click the Style button list arrow, and then select the writing style for your citations. Click in the document where you want the citation to appear. Click the Insert Citation button list arrow. Select Add New Source. In the Create Source dialog box that is displayed, click the Type of Source list arrow, and select the type of source from which you are citing. Enter the information for the citation in the Bibliography Fields section, and then click OK.

▶ To create a bibliography, click in the document where you want the bibliography to appear (generally the last page). Click the References tab and in the Citations & Bibliography group, click the Style button list arrow, and select the same writing style you used to create the citation. Click the Bibliography button list arrow and click Bibliography. The format will vary depending on the writing style you select.

Project

▶ A report should include a cover or title page and a bibliography. It may also include a table of contents.

17. Preview the document.
18. Check spelling,
19. Save the file as **13.2japancities**.
20. Print one copy, and then close the file.

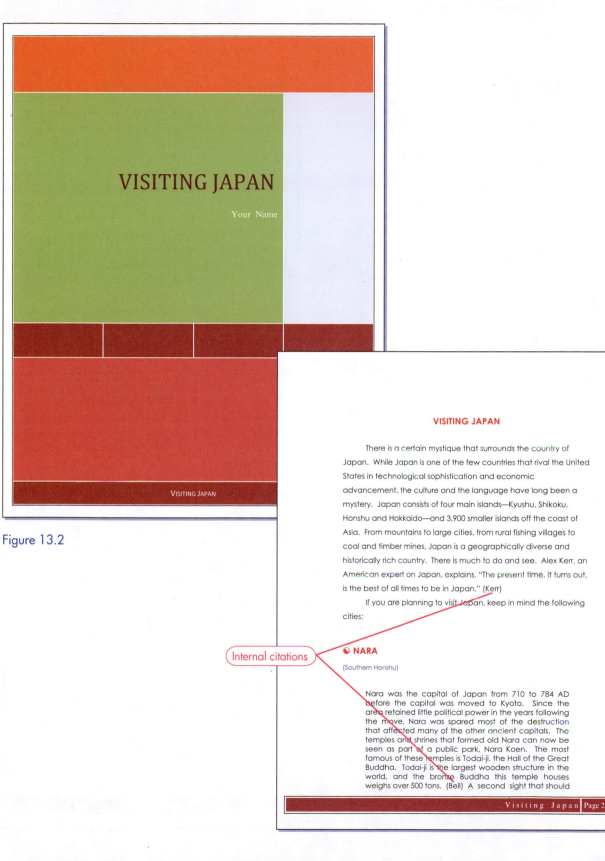

Figure 13.2

Internal citations

not be missed in Nara Koen is the Kasuga Taisha shrine. The sacred symbol of this shrine is the deer, and friendly deer are abundant around Nara Koen, existing on the goodwill and leftovers from Nara Koen's visitors.

☯ OSAKA

(Southern Honshu)

Osaka is a sprawling city that has thrived because of its port and its close proximity to Kyoto, the former capital of Japan. As a city, Osaka is not as international as Tokyo. Instead, Osaka businessmen focus on the Asian mainland. There has been speculation that Osaka will one day become the capital of Japan should an earthquake ruin Tokyo. One of the most popular sights to visit in Osaka is Osaka-jo, Osaka Castle. Osaka-jo sits in the center of Osaka in a beautiful park surrounded by moats and gardens. From the top of the castle, it is possible to look out over all of Osaka.

☯ KYOTO

(Southern Honshu)

Kyoto is the seventh largest city in Japan, but it is the first in beauty and ancient sites. Historically rich in origin, Kyoto still retains many of its original structures. One book explains that "a decision by the Americans not to bomb Kyoto during World War II—its historical heritage was considered too important—assured that these ancient structures stand today." (Grey) Although there are many, many sights worth seeing in Kyoto, one should be sure not to miss the Kinkaku-ji, the Golden Pavilion, and the Ginkaku-ji, the Silver Pavilion. Kinkaku-ji sits on the edge of a reflecting pond and is surrounded stunning gardens. The temple, covered in gold-leaf, is a bright structure and when the sun is shining, a golden glow covers the surrounding park. In

Internal citation

Figure 13.2 continued

contrast, Ginkaku-ji was never fully completed and remains without its silver cover. However, this temple is nestled on a hillside and surrounded by exquisite Zen gardens. The gardens here are green and lush, a perfect place to cool off after visiting many of Kyoto's beautiful sights.

☯ NAGASAKI

(Kyushu)

Nagasaki is often called Japan's San Francisco because of its bustling port and its booming Chinatown. However, the most important sights for any visitor to see in Nagasaki are the Atomic Bomb Museum and the Peace Park. The museum is new and it explores the origins and the effects of the atomic bomb dropped on Nagasaki during World War II, as well as the history and future of nuclear warfare in general. The nearby epicenter is marked with a stone obelisk. The Peace Park stands atop a hillside overlooking the city and is home to many beautiful statues that were donated to Nagasaki in commemoration of the destruction.

☯ TOKYO

(Central Honshu)

Tokyo is an international city, crowded and exciting. Visitors to Tokyo should keep in mind that Tokyo can easily be broken down into different districts, each with its own flavor. For example, Ueno is home to many of Tokyo's museums, including the Tokyo National Museum, a three-building structure that houses one of Japan's most extensive art collections. A second example is Asakusa, a famous shopping district, bordered by Kaminarimon, "Thunder Gate." Visitors to Tokyo find Asakusa to be one of the best places to pur-

Chapter 5 • Reports and Long Documents

chase local delicacies and traditional gift items to bring back to the United States. A third example is Shinjuku, the "Times Square and Wall Street" of Tokyo combined into one section of the city. Shinjuku is home to one of the busiest train stations in the world. This Is only a small sampling of what is available to see in Tokyo.

These are just a few of some of the exciting things that Japan has to offer. For a more extensive look at Japan, visit the travel section of your local bookstore and pick up one of the many guides that are available on this amazing country, or visit the Japan National Tourist Organization Website at: www.jnto.go.jp/eng/.

Figure 13.2 continued

Bibliography

Bell, Brian. Insight Guides: Japan. Boston: APA Publications, 1997.
Grey, Joanna. The Wonders of Japan. Chicago: TTX Publications, 2009.
Kerr, Alex. Lost Japan. Australia: Lonely Planet, 1996.

Visiting Japan | Page 6

13.3 FORMAT A REPORT WITH FOOTNOTES AND ENDNOTES; PREPARE A COVER PAGE

Health Connections, a health food business that was started several months ago, is growing by leaps and bounds. The company is now in the process of developing an employee manual. A Human Resources Practices report, which was developed by one of the partners, will be used as Chapter 3 in the manual. (In Project 4.4, you created a custom fax cover and letterhead template for this company. Use the same font for the company's name in this document so all documents complement each other.) Because the company has not yet decided whether to use footnotes or endnotes for the references, they would like you to prepare the report both ways. Also, you have been asked to create a cover page as a separate file so that the cover page does not affect the page numbers.

In this project, you will format a report that includes endnotes and footnotes, as well as create a separate cover page.

1. Open the data file **d13.3manual** shown in Figure 13.3b. Format the report using the sample layout of Page 1 (shown in Figure 13.3a) as a guide.
2. Use the following settings:

Margins	2" left and 1.5" right
Line spacing	Exactly 20 pt.
Paragraph spacing	
Before	0
After	0
Font	Chiller for company name in the header; Berlin Sans FB Demi for title in the header; Century Schoolbook for body text; Berlin Sans FB Demi for headline text
Font size	20 pt for company name in the header; 14 point title in the header; 12 pt for body text; 13 pt for headline text

3. Create a header that includes the information shown in the sample layout in Figure 13.3a (symbols were used as the graphic elements). You can design the header as you prefer.
4. Be sure to use the font faces and sizes indicated in Step 2. Apply a green font color to the headline text as shown.
5. Indent the text shown by any amount you want.
6. Insert page numbers at the bottom right, including the first page. Use the Accent bar 2 design.
7. Insert references as endnotes.
8. Correct spelling.

WHAT YOU NEED TO KNOW

Software

▶ You can insert page numbers independently of headers and footers. To insert page numbers without header/footer text, click the Insert tab and in the Header & Footer group, click the Page Number button list arrow, point to a page number position option, and then select a page number design from the gallery that is displayed.

▶ A *footnote* gives information about the source of quoted material. The information includes the author's name, the publication, the publication date, and the page number from which the quote was taken. By contrast, internal citations only provide the author's name and date of publication.

▶ Traditional footnotes are printed at the bottom of a page. A separator line distinguishes footnote text from the text on the page. A reference number appears immediately after the quote in the text and a corresponding footnote number or symbol appears at the bottom of the page.

▶ To insert a footnote, enter the footnote text, click the References tab and in the Footnotes group, click the Insert Footnote button. The first footnote number appears, ready for you to enter the first footnote. The footnote reference number automatically appears within the document after the text to be footnoted.

▶ Like footnotes, endnotes consist of two linked parts—the note reference mark and the corresponding explanatory text. Unlike footnotes, which appear at the bottom of each page on which a reference is made, endnotes appear on the last page of the document.

▶ To insert an endnote, click the References tab and in the Footnotes group, click the Insert Endnote button. Enter the endnote text and return to the document. Repeat this procedure to insert subsequent endnotes.

Project

▶ In addition to referencing quoted material, footnotes and endnotes are used to explain and/or comment on text included in a document.

9. Save the file as **13.3manual**.
10. Preview and print one copy.
11. Change the endnotes to footnotes. (*Hint: Click the References tab, Footnotes dialog box launcher. In the Footnote and Endnote dialog box, click the Convert button, choose the conversion you want, and then click OK.*)
12. Save the file as **13.3manual final** and then close the file.
13. Open a new blank document and create a cover page.
    a. Use any style cover you prefer. If necessary, change the colors and fonts to complement those used in the manual.
    b. Include the name of the report and the company name. Use the same font style as used in the report header and use a font size that you prefer. Delete all other placeholders.
    c. Delete the second blank page.
14. Save the file as **13.3manualcover** and then close the file.

3 Human Resources Practices HEALTH CONNECTIONS

■■■■■■■■■■■■■■■■■■■■■■■■□■■

Recruiting and Hiring

Hiring employees is a true investment in our business. Once a person is hired, we will invest time and money in training that individual in company practices and philosophy. We expect that we can trust that person to represent our company fairly and honestly in all business transactions. Therefore, we go to great lengths to make sure that we recruit and screen the most qualified candidates.

We use a variety of recruitment vehicles including: recommendations from managers, supervisors, and current employees; employment agencies (both private and governmental); newspaper ads; and the Internet.

We ask each candidate to provide a current résumé. Once we have reviewed the résumés, we will call qualified candidates in for a formal interview. Each candidate will fill out a company application and meet with a member of our Human Resources staff. We will conduct background checks including checking references and credentials on all candidates who have a successful interview. If all references check out, we will call the person back for a second interview with the potential supervisor. If that second interview is successful, we will then make the candidate a formal job offer. Health Connections is an equal opportunity employer and meets all of the guidelines of the Federal legislation.[i]

Employee Benefits

We offer the following benefits to all of our employees:[ii]

1|Page

Figure 13.3a

Recruiting and Hiring

Hiring employees is a true investment in our business. Once a person is hired, we will invest time and money in training that individual in company practices and philosophy. We expect that we can trust that person to represent our company fairly and honestly in all business transactions. Therefore, we go to great lengths to make sure that we recruit and screen the most qualified candidates.

We use a variety of recruitment vehicles including: recommendations from managers, supervisors, and current employees; employment agencies (both private and governmental); newspaper ads; and the Internet.

We ask each candidate to provide a current résumé. Once we have reviewed the résumés, we will call qualified candidates in for a formal interview. Each candidate will fill out a company application and meet with a member of our Human Resources staff. We will conduct background checks including checking references and credentials on all candidates who have a successful interview. If all references check out, we will call the person back for a second interview with the potential supervisor. If that second interview is successful, we will then make the candidate a formal job offer. Health Connections is an equal opportunity employer and meets all of the guidelines of the Federal legislation.

Employee Benefits

We offer the following benefits to all of our employees:

- Two weeks paid vacation
- Ten days sick leave
- Time off for jury duty
- Basic health insurance including major medical
- 401K after three years on the job
- Stock options
- Tuition reimbursement plan
- Life insurance

Our benefits package is one of the most generous in the industry. We believe that our employees at Health Connections are among the most highly paid and compensated workers in the health food industry. Our aim is to keep our workforce happy so that we can reduce employee turnover.

Employee Morale

At Health Connections, we realize that happy employees are productive employees. We know morale can affect our productivity, employee loyalty, employee turnover, and our bottom line. We, therefore, go out of our way to make the working environment a good one.

We reward our employees for work well done. Each month we recognize an employee of the month. We also have quarterly performance reviews and salary reviews every six months. We offer incentives for employees who reach our projected goals each month.

We hold weekly seminars for employee representatives to meet and discuss issues relating to working conditions. Supervisors have an open-door policy for handling complaints and we have a formal grievance procedure.

Training and Development

All newly hired employees at Health Connections are given two weeks of formal training designed to help them learn the tasks they need to perform their jobs at the very highest level of efficiency. In addition, staff is given information about our mission and philosophy of doing business. Each employee is a trusted member of the Health Connections team. All team members are expected to meet specific goals which are formulated by the entire team.

In addition to the initial training, we offer ongoing instruction in our state-of-the-art training facilities for employees who are looking to improve their skills and their lives. Employees may register for these classes during their lunch hour or after work. We offer a wide range of courses, which range from improving English and writing skills, to computer instruction and management skills. In addition, we offer self-help classes in dealing with stress or personal problems. Please check our Training Schedule for the classes we have available.

[i] Title VII of the Civil Rights Act of 1964 prohibits employment discrimination based on race, color, religion, sex, or national origin.

[ii] See Health Connections Insurance Benefits Book for full details of benefits.

[iii] Health Connections 2010 Training Schedule can be found on the Health Connections Website at: www.healthconnections.com.

Figure 13.3b

13.4 RESEARCH, WRITE, AND FORMAT A REPORT

Destinations' newsletter has become so popular that the company has decided to create an Editorial Department that is solely responsible for the development of its monthly newsletter. The newsletter began as a single page but is fast becoming a multiple-page booklet. You have been asked to work in the newly created Editorial Department. One of your first tasks is to conduct research on a country write, and then format a report for possible publication in an issue of the newsletter. Because the theme of next year's newsletters will be "Travel to Europe," you have been asked to write a report about France that is approximately 1200 words in length.

In this project, you will use translation options within Word's Research feature, the Web, and two research services to research and write a report on France. Be sure to include essential information that you feel will benefit someone traveling to France. Some topics to cover might be geography, language and culture, currency, vacation destinations, or "not to miss" tourist attractions. Once your final report is written, format it attractively. You may use footnotes, endnotes, or internal citations for your references. You may include a cover page.

1. Open a new blank document.
2. Display the Research task pane. Using MSN, search for information on Italy.
3. Create a draft report. Cite references either as footnotes, endnotes, or internal citations.
4. Save the file as **13.4report**.
5. Print one copy.
6. Edit and then format the report as follows:
   a. Use margins that you feel are appropriate.
   b. Use any font style, font color, and/or font size for the side headings and body text.
   c. Apply line and paragraph spacing for the report that you feel is appropriate.
   d. Insert a header that includes the report title. Use any header style you want.
   e. Begin the report with a centered title that reads, "Welcome to France." Use translation services to translate that title in French, and then center the French translation below the English title.
   f. Include page numbers on the bottom right of the page. Use any page numbering style that you want.
7. Save the final report as **13.4italy final**.
8. Preview and print one copy.
9. Check word count. Make any necessary adjustments.
10. Re-save the file, if necessary.
11. Close the file.

WHAT YOU NEED TO KNOW

Project

► Word's Research feature provides helpful services for you to use while you are working on your document. You can access the Dictionary, Thesaurus, Encyclopedia, Translation services, and Stock quotes and company information. Click in a word (or select a group of words about which you want information or enter what you are searching for in the Search for text box. Click the Review tab and in the Proofing group, click the Research button, which will display the Research task pane. Click the Search for list arrow, and choose a service you want to use (Encarta Dictionary, for example) and click the Start searching arrow.

► It is important to evaluate the information you find on the Internet. Some sites contain expert information, while others are amateur efforts.

► See Appendix C for ways to write footnotes and endnotes for information obtained from the Web.

► When using an internal citation for Web references, the author's last name, the Website, and the date of Web posting (if available) are indicated. Example: (Alford, www. travel.americanexpress.com, September 2009.)

You will need an Internet connection to complete this project.

● **PROJECT SKILLS**
✴ Work with styles
✴ Find and replace text
✴ Use Research Services
✴ Insert, View, and Edit Comments
✴ Track changes in a document

PROJECT 14

14.1 FORMAT A HANDBOOK

You work in the Graphic Design Department of Meadowland College. Your assignment is to create and format several pages of the Fall Registration Handbook. Because this handbook will be printed as a booklet, your boss has asked you to format odd-numbered pages with a right-aligned footer and even-numbered pages with a left-aligned footer. The pages will be given to a commercial printer to use as a sample layout. To keep the document consistent in format, you should create styles.

> In this project, you will create and format several pages of the Fall Registration Handbook for Meadowland College. You will use continuous section breaks, styles, and paragraph shading.

1. Open the data file **d14.1handbook**.
2. Format the text as a handbook using the sample layout shown in Figure 14.1 as a guide.
3. Use the following settings:

Margins	1.25" left and right and as directed
Line spacing	Single
Paragraph spacing	
Before	0
After	0, then as directed
Font	Eras Light ITC
Font size	12 point

4. Set the college name in Britannic 20 pt, bold. Apply paragraph shading to the text, as shown, using a light green shade.
5. Position the insertion point below the college name and insert a continuous section break.
6. Reset the margins to 3" left and 1" right.
7. Set line spacing to Exactly 15 pt and paragraph spacing to 6 pt after each paragraph.
8. Select the first paragraph.

▼ WHAT YOU NEED TO KNOW

Software

▶ In Chapter 3, you learned to insert section and column breaks. A few things to remember are the following:

- By default, a document contains one section. You can break a document into multiple sections and format each section differently.

- Section break codes store section formatting in the same way paragraph marks store paragraph formatting. Removing a section break may also delete all section formatting preceding the break.

- You can create columns in various parts of the same document as long as you insert a section break before and/or after each section.

- To force text to wrap to the next column before you reach the bottom of the current column, you must insert a column break.

▶ In Chapter 4, you learned to apply paragraph shading. As a review, select the paragraph or text, click the Home tab and in the Paragraph group, click the Borders button list arrow and select Borders and Shading. In the Borders and Shading dialog box that appears, click the Shading tab, and select the options you want (be sure Paragraph is selected in the Apply to box), and then click OK.

▶ A *style* is a collection of formats you can apply to selected text. For example, one style might specify 16-point Arial bold and single-spacing. By using a style you can apply several formats (font size, font style, and line spacing) in one step and ensure consistency in formatting.

Continued on next page

9. Create a style based on the first paragraph. (*Hint: Select the first paragraph, right-click the selection, point to Styles, and then click Save Selection as a New Quick Style. In the Create New Style from Formatting dialog box, enter a name for your style, and then click OK.*)
   - Name the style **College paragraph**.
10. For the first side heading, apply black paragraph shading, and color the text a light green.
11. Create a style based on the side heading; name the style **Side head**.
12. Complete the remaining sections of the document; apply the styles, where appropriate, to format the headings and paragraphs.
13. After entering the side heading "About Using the Fall Term Schedule of Courses," enter a continuous section break.
14. Set two columns and enter the text shown.
    a. Apply a light green shade to each of the four Code headings:
       - Create a style based on the first code heading. Name the style **Course code**.
    b. After completing the column text, enter another continuous section break.
15. On Page 1, insert a footer on odd-numbered pages using the Mod (Odd Page) style and enter the information shown. Format the college name using the Britannic Bold font. Format Fall Registration Information using the Eras Light ITC font.
    - Change the color of the graphic to green, as shown.
16. On Page 2, insert a footer on even-numbered pages using the Mod (Even Page) footer style. Enter and format the information using the same font face used for odd numbered pages.
    - Change the color of the graphic to green as shown.
17. Save the file as **14.1handbook**.
18. Check spelling.
19. Preview and print one copy.
20. Close the file.

▶ You can use or modify a Word Quick Style, or you can create your own. To apply an existing style, select the text to which you want to apply a style. Click the Home tab, and in the Styles group, click the style you want. To see additional styles, click the More arrow, which will display the Quick Styles gallery.

▶ To create a new style, format some text on which you want to base the style. Right-click the selection, point to Styles, and then click Save Selection as a New Quick Style on the menu. In the Create New Style from Formatting dialog box, enter a name for your new style, and then click OK. The style you created will appear in the Quick Styles gallery, ready for you to use.

Project

▶ A *handbook* is a booklet, catalog, or guidebook that provides instruction and/or information to a particular audience.

▶ The pages of a handbook should maintain a consistent format. Using headers, footers, and styles helps to accomplish this.

▶ A handbook sometimes will use paragraph shading to separate sections of text.

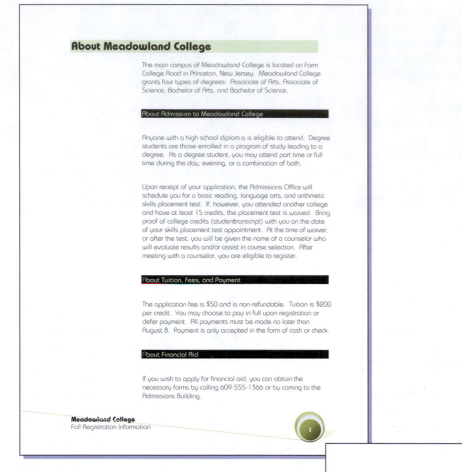

Figure 14.1

Meadowland College cancels your course and you do not register for another course in its place.

Fall Term Schedule of Courses

The schedule for the fall term will be available beginning February 18. You must come to the Registration and Records Office to pick up your schedule. We will not mail a copy to you. Any changes in scheduling will be posted in the lobby of the Conference Hall.

About Using the Fall Term Schedule of Courses

Course Code:

The course code identifies the course. It consists of three capital letters followed by three numbers (i.e., ACC101 is Principles of Accounting 1).

Section Code:

The section code designates the particular class section of the course and is followed in the schedule by the times and days that a particular class section meet. When you register for a section, you may not attend or switch to any other section unless you file a Drop/Add form in the Registration and Records Office. The section code consists of a letter and a number (i.e., T1).

Day Code:

The day code designates the day of the week the course meets:

M=Monday,
T=Tuesday,
W=Wednesday,
R=Thursday,
F=Friday,
S=Saturday, and
N=Sunday.

Room Code:

The room code refers to the building in which a class is being held:

AHI = Applied Humanities,
BUS= Business,
CFH=Conference Hall,
CRA=Creative Arts Center,
GYM=Gymnasium,
NAS=Natural and Applied Sciences,
PAC=Performing Arts,
SOS=Social Sciences, and
TEC=Technology

Calendar

Meadowland College
Fall Registration Information

3

Figure 14.1 continued

Registration begins Monday, August 15.

10-Week Evening Classes begin Monday, September 3.

How to Register

In-Person Registration

You may register in person from 9:00 a.m. to 8:00 p.m., Monday through Thursday. Please come to the Registrar's Office, 22 Pine Lane. Payment may be made by check, money order, American Express, Discover, JCB, MasterCard, Visa, or bank debit card. Checks should be made payable to: Meadowland College. Unfortunately, we cannot accept cash payments.

Fax Registration

You may register by fax, 24 hours a day, 7 days a week. Please complete the registration form and fax it to 732-555-5555.

Meadowland College
Fall Registration Information

4

14.2 CREATE AN ARTICLE, USE COMMENTS, AND TRACK CHANGES

Next month's issue of Destinations' newsletter will feature travel destinations in the United States. The Massachusetts Tourist Bureau has provided you with text about Massachusetts. You have been asked to format it in columns and enhance it with graphics. Some of the words used were not suitable. You will use the Thesaurus feature to replace them.

In this project, you will format a three-page article using columns. You will insert a file and apply styles to the newly inserted text. You will edit the document by responding to comments and tracked changes. You will also use the Thesaurus feature to substitute words and use the Find and Replace feature to replace abbreviations.

1. Open the data file **d14.2mass**.
2. Read each comment, take whatever action is needed, and then delete the comment.
3. Reject all the tracked changes.
4. Use the Thesaurus feature to replace the highlighted words and then remove the highlighting.
5. Use the Find and Replace feature to find all occurrences of "MA" and replace it with "Massachusetts."
6. Format the three pages of the document as shown in Figure 14.2. *Note: Your line breaks may not be identical to that shown in the figure.* Use the following settings:

Margins	1.25" left and right and as directed
Line spacing	Double and as directed
Paragraph spacing	
Before	0
After	0, then as directed
Font	Serif and as directed
Font size	14 point and as directed

7. Begin the document approximately 2" from the top of the page. Use any sans serif font in 14 pt for the first sentence ("Bring your family to").
8. Use the Curlz MT font in 72 pt for the heading (Massachusetts). Color the text as shown.
9. Format the first paragraph as follows:
   a. Use a 14 pt, sans serif font (the same font used for the first sentence).
   b. Create a style based on the first paragraph. Name the style **First para**.

WHAT YOU NEED TO KNOW

Software

▶ *Comments* are hidden notes or annotations that you or a reviewer can add to a document. The comments feature is useful for facilitating the only review of documents. You can read comments on screen, hide them when the document is printed, or print them with the document. You can also delete comments.

▶ To insert a comment, position the insertion point in the document where you want to insert the comment. Click the Review tab, and in the Comments group, click the New Comment button. Enter the comment in the comment balloon that opens.

▶ The Thesaurus, a feature of Research Services, lists synonyms, sometimes antonyms, and parts of speech for a selected word. Select the word you want to change and press [Shift] + [F7], which displays the Research task pane. To replace the word you looked up with one listed, position your insertion point on the word in the list, click the list arrow, and select Insert.

▶ The Find feature scans a document and searches for occurrences of specified text, symbols, or formatting. The Replace feature allows you to locate all occurrences of certain text and replace each occurrence with different text, special characters, or symbols. Click the Home tab, and in the Editing group, click the Replace button. In the Find and Replace dialog box that is displayed, click the Replace tab, if necessary, and enter text to find and/or replace in the appropriate text boxes.

▶ The Track Changes feature allows you to see where a deletion, insertion, or other formatting change has been made in a document. This feature is a useful tool when editing an online document. When you turn on Track Changes, insertions are indicated in red (or another chosen color) as underlined text; deletions are shown with a strikethrough. By default, a balloon (like the one used for comments) displays formatting changes. By positioning your insertion point on the balloon, you can see the person and the date the change was made.

Continued on next page

10. Set a continuous section break after the first paragraph.
11. Set two columns.
12. Format the text in the two columns as follows:
    a. Use a 14 pt, serif font.
    b. Set the line spacing to Exactly, 20 pt.
    c. Indent the first line of each paragraph .5".
    d. Create a style based on the first column. Name the style **Two-column text**.
    e. Set a continuous section break after the Web address.
13. Set three columns. Format the text in the three columns as follows:
    a. Use Gill Sans MT Condensed in 14 pt.
    b. Set side headings to all capitals and color the font blue. Apply a light yellow paragraph shade.
    c. Create a style based on the first side heading. Name the style **City header**.
    d. Set line spacing to Exactly, 24 pt.
    e. Set paragraph spacing to 6 pt after each paragraph.
    f. Create a style based on the paragraph text below the heading. Name the style **City text**.
14. Apply the City text and City header styles to the remaining paragraphs.
15. Insert and center a header using the same font and font color as the heading on page one.
16. Create a drop capital on the first paragraph.
17. Insert five clip art images of Massachusetts in the document. The examples shown in the figure are merely a guide.
    a. Use a Square or Tight wrap option, depending on where you position the images.
    b. Apply a picture effect to each image.
    c. Size the images as you want.
18. Create two pull quotes on pages 1 and 3 and position them as shown.
    a. Create a text box and enter the text shown.
    b. Set the text to 18 pt, Brush Script MT, and center it within the box.
    c. Remove the border around the text box.
    d. Use a Square wrap option for the first pull quote. Use a Tight wrap option for the second pull quote.
    e. Add a top and bottom border using a 2-pt line.
19. Insert a page number at the bottom right of the page using the Top Line 2 style.
20. Save the file as **14.2article**.
21. Preview and print one copy.
22. Close the file.

► To turn on track changes, click the Review tab, and in the Tracking group, click the Track Changes button. When the Track Changes feature is enabled, the Track Changes button remains highlighted. Click the Track Changes button again to turn off the feature.

► Turning off the Track Changes feature does not remove any changes that have already been tracked.

► To accept or reject changes and remove tracking, click the Review tab, and in the Changes group, click the Accept button or Reject button, which will accept or reject your change and move to the next change. You can also right-click the change and select Accept Change or Reject Change from the menu.

Project

► *Articles* are short reports about a topic and are published in magazines, newspapers, or newsletters. Most articles are formatted in columns.

► *Pull quotes* are short, attention-getting quotes that are taken from the article's text and set off in a text box.

 You will need an Internet connection to complete this project.

Bring your family to

Massachusetts

Massachusetts—the best of the past with all of the excitement of the future. Climb aboard the Mayflower; explore the USS Constitution and learn why sailors named the ship "Old Ironsides." Go to Boston harbor and throw tea into the harbor just like the colonists did in 1773.

Are you looking for the perfect place for your family to visit? Now is the time to visit Massachusetts. Massachusetts has something to amuse and interest people of all ages. A trip

Massachusetts has something to amuse and interest people of all ages.

to Massachusetts is always an educational experience as no part of the state is without historical significance.

Massachusetts is also a state for all seasons—beautiful foliage and apple-picking in the fall; majestic mountains for skiing in winter; nature trails for

Insert continuous section break

Figure 14.2

---

spring walking; and glorious beaches in the summer. And there is amazing sightseeing all year round.

Massachusetts is also filled with great places to stay during your journey, from first-class hotels

to bed and breakfasts to camping grounds. For more information, call the Massachusetts Office of Travel and Tourism at 800-555-5555 or visit our Website at www.mass-vacation.com.

BOSTON

Boston is one of the oldest cities in the nation and as such, there are many historical sights that cannot be missed, such as Old North Church and the USS Constitution, two stops along the Freedom Trail. In addition, one can visit the Museum of Fine Arts, the

Isabella Stewart Gardner Museum, the Kennedy Library and Museum, and the New England Aquarium, a surefire hit for children. And be sure not to miss the sights, sounds, and shopping in Faneuil Hall Marketplace/Quincy Hall.

CAMBRIDGE

Walk beside the majestic Charles River and within lively Harvard Square. Visit Harvard University and MIT.

SALEM

Home to the witch trials of 1690, Salem has many sights dedicated to this famous moment in history.

CAPE COD

Cape Cod is one of the most beautiful places on earth, with its endless sandy beaches nestled between desert-like sand dunes. If you choose to leave the beaches, be sure to visit the

2

Massachusetts

National Marine Fisheries Aquarium in Woods Hole, the JFK Memorial in the picturesque seaside town of Hyannis, and Provincetown, a funky artists' colony on the tip of the Cape.

THE BERKSHIRES

The Berkshires, rolling mountains and valleys in western Massachusetts, are a perfect place to visit in all seasons. Try skiing Brody Mountain and Jay Peak in the winter. Hike along the broad range of nature trails in fall and spring. Listen to the Boston Symphony Orchestra on a lazy summer evening at Tanglewood estate in Lennox. Visit historic Stockbridge, home of the elegant Norman Rockwell Museum. And watch the amazing array of Summer Theater and dance groups that come to the area each summer.

Be sure not to miss Plimoth Plantation, a living-history museum that recreates the 1627 Plymouth community

---

PLYMOUTH

Home of the Plymouth Rock, the famous sight where the pilgrims landed and founded the Massachusetts Bay Colony. Be sure not to miss Plimoth Plantation, a living-history museum that recreates the 1627 Plymouth community.

3

Figure 14.2 continued

14.3 FORMAT A BUSINESS PLAN

The owners of Health Connections are expanding their business. To obtain funding from a bank or investor for this expansion, they have developed a business plan that outlines how they plan to use the loan for which they are applying. You have been asked to format the business plan they are going to submit. Use attractive formatting techniques. *Note: The financial information and a cover page will be added to the plan in later projects.*

In this project, you will format a business plan for Health Connections.

1. Open the data file **d14.3busplan**.
2. Insert the data file **d14.3tcbusplan** (Table of Contents) into the business plan as page 1. (*Hint: Position your insertion point where you want to insert the file. Click the Insert tab and in the Text group, click the Object button list arrow, and then click Text from File. Navigate to and select the file you want to insert, and click Insert.*)
3. Use the Thesaurus feature to substitute words that are highlighted in the file. Remove the highlighting.
4. Format the data using the sample shown in Figure 14.3 as a guide.
5. Use the following settings:

Margins	As desired
Line spacing	Appropriate for a report. You may use the "At least" option for incremental spacing amounts.
Paragraph spacing	
Before	As desired
After	As desired
Font	Chiller for company name in the footer; as desired for remaining report
Font size	As desired

6. Use any desired font color for the side headings and body text.
7. Insert a footer that includes the report title.
   a. Format the footer as you prefer.
   b. Use a green font color for the company name.
8. Include page numbers at the top of the page as part of the header. Design a header using the sample as a guide or modify a page number style.
9. Save the file as **14.3busplan final**.
10. Preview the report.
11. Go to page 1 (Table of Contents). Enter the page numbers to identify on which page each part of the business plan appears.
12. Preview and print one copy.
13. Save the changes.
14. Close the file.

WHAT YOU NEED TO KNOW

Project

▶ A *business plan* is the blueprint for a business that helps the entrepreneur to develop his or her business. It outlines the goals and objectives of the business and how they will be met.

▶ A business plan demonstrates to bankers and other potential investors that the business was well planned and carefully thought out.

▶ While business plans vary in format, they all contain certain basic parts. Some business plans are more detailed than others.

1.0 EXECUTIVE SUMMARY

At Health Connections, our goal is to provide quality health food products at a competitive price. Our pricing is determined by market conditions and customer demand. Our products will fulfill the needs of health-conscious consumers.

The uniqueness of our product line and the existing untapped market ensures our success in the health foods market. The Health Connections name has become well known in New York City and the time has come to package and market our products on the Web.

Our goal is to borrow $550,000 for ten (10) years. The loan will be repaid in 120 equal payments, including interest and principal. Our present plan is to utilize the borrowed money to modify our existing warehouse to process and package foods under our own label. In addition, the capital will be used to create an e-commerce business. This funding will support packaging design, packaging equipment, Web-page design, advertising, operating costs, and salaries. We should reach our break-even point after our second year. Upon receiving our loan, we would like to incorporate, as this will protect our company, investors, lenders, products, and stockholders. We expect the savings in costs to increase our gross profit to $750,000 the first year, $900,000 the second year, and $1,200,000 the third year.

1.1 Objectives

- To develop a solid e-commerce market and to maximize our profit margin.
- To develop and repackage organic and health food products under our own brand.
- To fulfill the health foods demand with top-quality products.
- To reach gross profit of $750,000 by the end of our first year of expansion.
- To encourage our customers to live healthy lives by making health foods an integral part of their weekly shopping list.
- To begin expansion of the Health Connections store and to promote our Health Connections food line.
- To offer health-conscious individuals support through our Web page, such as interviews with health professionals to answer specific health-related issues.

HEALTH CONNECTIONS

Figure 14.3

14.4 FORMAT AN ANNUAL REPORT

You work in the Production Department of The Supply Warehouse, Philadelphia's largest supplier of office products and services. You have been asked to format the first few pages of the company's annual report. This first draft will not include graphics or financial data, which you will add in later projects.

In this project, you will format the first few pages of the annual report for The Supply Warehouse.

1. Open a new blank document.
2. Open the data file **d14.4annualreport** and format the report using Figure 14.4 as a guide.
3. Use the following settings:

Margins	1.25" left and right
Line spacing	Appropriate for a report. You may use the "At least" option for incremental spacing amounts.
Paragraph spacing	
Before	As desired
After	As desired
Font	As desired
Font size	As desired

Note: To format pages 2 and 4 as shown, set three unequal columns: column 1 = 2.2"; column 2 = 1.8"; column 3 = 1.6". Set the space between columns to .2". If you want to experiment, you may use other column widths. It is recommended that you create and use styles or copy formatting from one section to another to keep parts of the document consistent in format.

4. Include a footer and page number using any footer style and including the information shown. You may modify the footer style if you want. *Note: The Pinstripes style is shown in Figure 14.4.*
5. Insert a cover page using any cover page style you want. You may modify and enhance the cover page style as you want. *Note: The Pinstripes cover style is shown in Figure 14.4.*
6. Correct spelling.
7. Save the file as **14.4annualreport**.
8. Preview and print one copy.
9. Close the file.

WHAT YOU NEED TO KNOW

Project

▶ An *annual report* is a yearly publication that is sent to stockholders and is also often posted on the company's Website. The annual report provides information on the health of the company and generally includes the following sections:

- Company Profile
- Letter from the CEO
- Financial Highlights
- Looking Forward
- Financial Review

▶ Annual reports are often produced as booklets on high-quality paper.

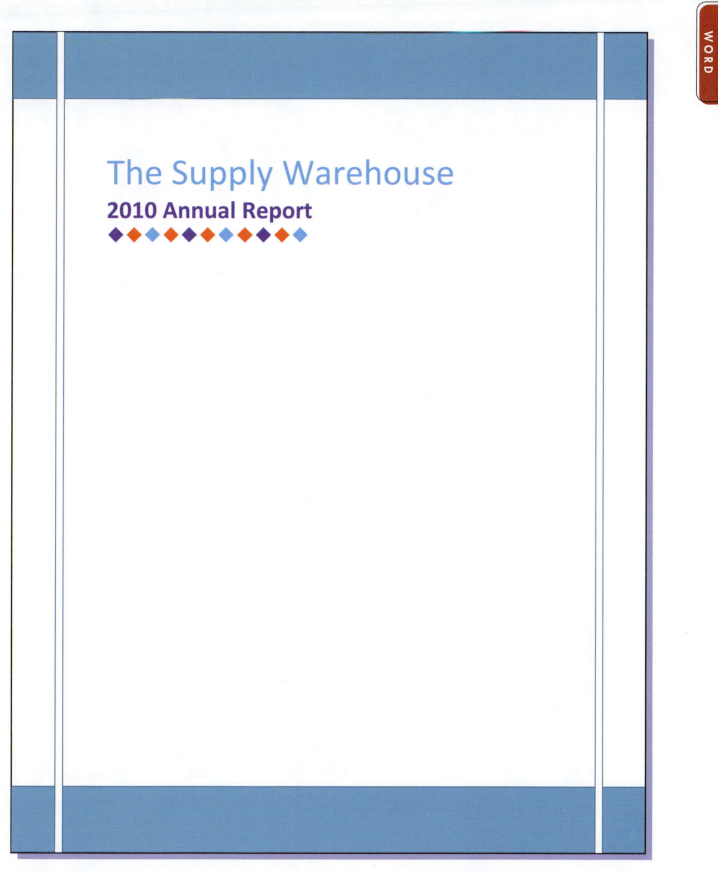

The Supply Warehouse
2010 Annual Report

Figure 14.4

Company Profile

Indent 5" Text set to 11pt, full justification and paragraph shading applied

The Supply Warehouse is Philadelphia's largest supplier of office products and services. The company sells office supplies, business machines, computers, computer software, and office furniture, as well as copy, print, reproduction, and mailing and shipping services for small office/home office and medium and large businesses in the city.

The company markets its products through catalog and telephone sales as well as through its retail outlets in Philadelphia.

Insert a continuous break

Message to Stockholders

Insert a column break

When I took the helm of The Supply Warehouse three months ago, our company faced significant challenges. We had lost sight of our core mission and competitive advances, and we had allowed parts of our business to become too complex and inefficient. The weak economy made these challenges more difficult.

In early 2010, our management team conducted a critical assessment of our company and developed a strategic plan for improvement in the areas that needed it. Our initiatives were careful and thorough. We cut staff, reduced inventory, and instituted disciplined capital spending. We also made The Supply Warehouse a more appealing place to work and shop. These collective management and operating initiatives enabled The Supply Warehouse to perform well in light of the difficult economic environment.

As we enter a new year, we are sharply focused on continuing the momentum we have created to expand our business. I look forward to our company's future with great enthusiasm, not merely because I know that we can achieve our goals, but also because I know that we will achieve those goals by working harmoniously together.

Nathan Corso,
President

Insert a continuous section break

Figure 14.4 continued

Financial Highlights

As the data will show, our costs have decreased, resulting in a substantial three-fold increase in operating profits. The return on stockholders' equity is coming back to its earlier levels and we hope to surpass that next year.

Insert a continuous section break

The Supply Warehouse ◆ 2010 Annual Report   Page 3

Figure 14.4 continued

Looking Forward

Diversity Equals Corporate Excellence

A diverse workplace is integral to our ability to make The Supply Warehouse a more appealing place to work, shop, and invest. Going forward, we are following a program to help us fulfill our commitment to foster diversity in our management and our workforce, as well as in our relationships with suppliers, vendors, and customers.

Passionate Customer Service

We realize that customers make a choice every time they walk into our store. Going forward, we dramatically improved the shipping experience in our store through a new program called "On Stage." On Stage calls for all Supply Warehouse employees, from the manager to the stock clerk, to set aside other tasks – like stocking shelves and checking inventory – to focus specifically on serving customer needs during peak business hours. This will prompt customers to spend more time and return again and again.

Lower Costs; Better Service

A fundamental goal of The Supply Warehouse is to deliver outstanding customer service. To achieve this, we instituted a new package tracking and reporting system that automates package delivery to customers, making it easier for us to manage and track shipments. Also, we have revamped our Web site to be more user-friendly, with the ultimate goal of increasing our e-commerce business.

(callout) Insert a column break

Financial Review

Figure 14.4 continued

CHAPTER 6

Integration/Word and the Web

In this chapter, you will complete the following projects:

PROJECT 15
Work with Integrated Files

PROJECT 15.1 Create a Report with an Embedded Table
PROJECT 15.2 Create a Memo with a Linked Table; Use Document Properties

PROJECT 16
Work with the Web

PROJECT 16.1 Save a Document as a Web Page
PROJECT 16.2 Create a Web Page Using a Template
PROJECT 16.3 Create a Website

WORK WITH INTEGRATED FILES

PROJECT SKILLS
* Understand integration basics
* Import an object into a document
* Use document properties

PROJECT 15

15.1 CREATE A REPORT WITH AN EMBEDDED TABLE

You work in the Human Resources Department of Summit Sports Centers, a fitness and sporting goods company with several locations throughout Chicago. Human Resources, the department responsible for monitoring employee compensation and benefits, as well as other issues related to personnel services and policies, must work with the Accounting Department and management to determine the appropriate compensation packages offered to prospective employees. You have been asked to format a report to the Accounting Department that includes salary data for one of the branches.

In this project, you will format a report using a template and insert a table as an embedded object.

1. Open the data file **15.1summit template.**
2. Enter information into the cover page, as shown in Figure 15.1a.
3. Enter the text (but not the table) on page 2, as shown in Figure 15.1b.
   a. Begin approximately 2.5" from the top of the page.
   b. Use the template's default margins, font, and line spacing.
4. Open the data file **15.1compensation table** (source file). Copy the table.
5. Switch to **15.1summit template** (destination file).
   a. Paste the table using the Paste Special/Paste command where indicated in the figure. Be sure to select Microsoft Office Word Document Object as the file type. *Note: You will have to adjust the table size so that it fits on the page.*
   b. Horizontally center the table.
   c. Make any adjustments necessary.
6. Save the file as **15.1summit report**.
7. Preview and print one copy.
8. Close all files.

WHAT YOU NEED TO KNOW

Software

▶ *Integration* is the sharing or combining of data between files in the same application or between files in different applications.

▶ When you share or combine data, it is important to know where the data is coming from and where it is going. The file where the data originates is called the *source file*. The file that receives the imported data is called the *destination file*.

▶ There are two ways to import a table (or worksheet or graph)—as an embedded object or as a linked object. As an *embedded object*, data in the destination file does not change if you modify the source file. Embedded objects become part of the destination file with no connection to the source file. As a *linked object*, when you make any changes to the source file, Word automatically updates the destination file. The source file and destination file are connected by the link.

▶ To import an object, select the table, worksheet, or graph in the source file. Click the Home tab, and in the Clipboard group, click the Copy button. Click in the document (destination file) where you want to insert the object, and then click the Paste button list arrow. Click Paste Special. In the Paste Special dialog box that opens, select Microsoft Office Word Document Object (to indicate how to paste the item), and then click Paste to create an embedded object, or click Paste link to create a linked object. Then, click OK.

▶ To edit an imported object, double-click the object. If you embedded the file, the correction does not affect the source data. If you linked the file, the correction affects both the source and destination files.

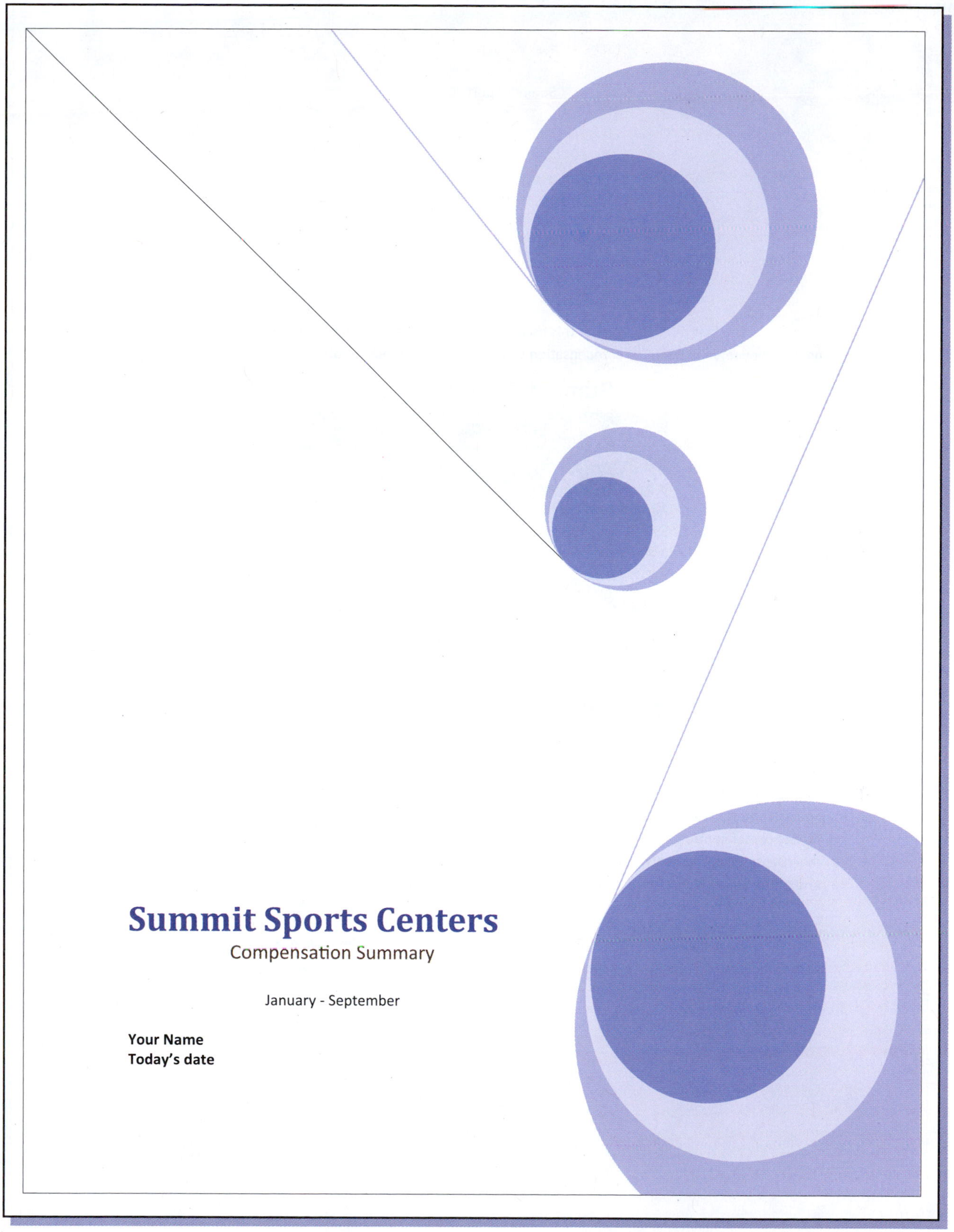

Summit Sports Centers

Compensation Summary

January - September

Your Name
Today's date

Figure 15.1a

Today's date

A review of the first three quarters of this fiscal year for the Chicago branch indicates the addition of a new employee, Jane Dante. A compensation summary for the branch is noted below.

Summit Sports Centers

Compensation Summary
January - September

Employee Name	Base Salary	Total Compensation
Adams, Jim	$ 1,800	$ 29,513
Carson, Sara	1,775	26,828
Dante, Jane	1,750	29,300
Smith, Sam	1,735	30,298
Wagoner, Terry	1,500	25,555
Wilson, Jeri	1,575	30,000
TOTALS	$10,135	$171,494
AVERAGES	1,689	48,998
HIGHEST	1,800	30,298
LOWEST	1,500	25,555

The addition of Jane Dante increases our expenses at a difficult economic turning point for Summit Sports Centers. However, it is expected that there will be an increase in sales because of numerous fitness center contracts that have just been signed. Since fitness center-based projects are now within Jane Dante's sales territory, it is expected that her total compensation will increase considerably by the end of the year which will offset the increase in salary expense.

The process of compiling expense data from all the Summit Sports Centers locations will assist in long-term planning for our organization. Early indications show that total sales have picked up in the corporate sector. A detailed data analysis report will be coming in the next quarter.

2

Figure 15.1b

15.2 CREATE A MEMO WITH A LINKED TABLE; USE DOCUMENT PROPERTIES

As you learned in Project 6.3, Perfection Plus, a cosmetics company with corporate offices located in New York City, is preparing for an all-day meeting to discuss the launch of a new product line. Your boss, Jan Hogan, Corporate Marketing Director, has asked you to finalize a memo to all U.S. marketing managers with a copy to Dan Rice, Regional Marketing Manager. The memo should include the agenda for the meeting. *Note: You created the agenda as a table in Project 6.3. Because the agenda is not yet finalized, you will insert the table as a linked file. The letter will be sent via e-mail.*

In this project, you will create a one-page memo to marketing managers and insert a linked table.

1. Open the data file **d15.2ppmemo stationery.dotx** (a memo template).
2. Insert the data file **d15.2ppmeeting text** into the **d15.2ppmemo stationery** file. *Note: The text is shown in Figure 15.2a. A sample partial solution is shown in Figure 15.2b.*
   a. Delete the paragraph marks and *Insert table here* notation.
   b. Save the file **d15.2ppmemo stationery** as **15.2ppmeeting update.docx**.
3. Use the following settings:

Margins	Default as per memo template
Line spacing	Single
Paragraph spacing	
Before	0
After	0
Font	As per memo template
Font size	As per memo template

4. Fill out the memo heading using appropriate information (refer to the scenario above) and today's date.
5. Open the data file **d15.2ppagenda final**. *Note: This is the source file and the same document you completed in Project 6.3.*
   • Copy the file (including the table heading).

WORD

6. Switch to **15.2ppmeeting update** (the destination file).

   a. Use the Paste Special command to paste the agenda (heading and table) as a linked object, where indicated by the *Insert table here* notation in Figure 15.2a. Be sure to select Microsoft Office Word Document Object as the file type. *Note: You will have to adjust the table size so that it fits on the first page*.

   b. Horizontally center the table. Preview and save the file.

   c. Right-click the table, and then select Linked Document Object, Open link (which will open the source file).

   d. Change the name of the 3:20 p.m. presenter to `Ms. Sarah Hughes`.

   e. Add the word `Final` to the heading.

7. Close and save **d15.2ppagenda final** (the source file that automatically displayed when you opened the link in Step 6c).

8. Switch to **15.2ppmeeting update**.

   • Right-click the table and select "Update Link." The date should be updated. Notice that the 3:20 p.m. presenter's name was automatically updated and "Final" was added because of the link.

9. Click the Office button, point to Prepare, and then click Properties. Enter the following information in the Document Properties Information Panel, and then close the Panel:

     Subject: `Meeting Notice`
     Keywords: `Meeting`
     Category: `Marketing`

10. Print the final memo. Close all files and save the changes.

We have scheduled an all-day meeting for Saturday, June 5, 2010 to discuss marketing strategies for our new product line. As you know, we have been planning the launch of this new product for over a year now. This meeting will focus on the details of our marketing plans. While we will have a short meeting on Wednesday in the late afternoon (we will notify you by e-mail of the exact time and location), the main meeting will be held on Thursday. The agenda is indicated below:

Insert table here. ¶We also invite you to attend the Managers' Dinner on Friday evening. We urge you to stay over Saturday night since airfares are less expensive when you do so. ¶We suggest that you make plans to arrive in New York City on Tuesday night and to depart on Sunday. We have reservations for you at the Moran Hotel, located at 275 Madison Avenue. We chose this hotel because it is located near our office as well as several New York City attractions. ¶You can e-mail me at jh@pp.net if you have any questions or concerns regarding the arrangements that we have made for you. We look forward to seeing you on June 5.

Figure 15.2a

Perfection Plus

Memo

To:

From:

CC:

Date: Today's

Re:

We have scheduled an all-day meeting for Saturday, June 5, 2010 to discuss marketing strategies for our new product line. As you know, we have been planning the launch of this new product for over a year now. This meeting will focus on the details of our marketing plans. While we will have a short meeting on Wednesday in the late afternoon (we will notify you by e-mail of the exact time and location), the main meeting will be held on Thursday. The agenda is indicated below:

Final Agenda
June 5, 2010
Nek Conference Center – Suite D
9 a.m. – 4 p.m.

Time	Topic	Presenter
9:00 a.m.	Review of Ageless product line	Mr. Zachary Malavo
10:00 a.m.	Review of promotions program	Ms. Wendy Carley
11:00 a.m.	Coffee break	
11:20 a.m.	Advertising budget	Ms. Shirley DeChan
12:30 p.m.	Lunch	
1:45 p.m.	Marketing plans	Mr. Quincy Garin
3:00 p.m.	Coffee break	
3:20 p.m.	Open discussion/follow-up/action items	Ms. Sarah Hughes

We also invite you to attend the Managers' Dinner on Friday evening. We urge you to stay over Saturday night since airfares are less expensive when you do so.

We suggest that you make plans to arrive in New York City on Tuesday night and to depart on Sunday. We have reservations for you at the Moran Hotel, located at 275 Madison Avenue. We chose this hotel because it is located near our office as well as several New York City attractions.

You can e-mail me at jh@pp.net if you have any questions or concerns regarding the arrangements that we have made for you. We look forward to seeing you on June 5.

Figure 15.2b

PROJECT SKILLS

✱ Create a Hyperlink
✱ Save a document as a Web page
✱ Create a Web page using a template
✱ Preview a Web page
✱ Link documents
✱ Apply a background

PROJECT 16

16.1 SAVE A DOCUMENT AS A WEB PAGE

Meadowland College is in the process of developing a comprehensive Website. In the meantime, they would like you to create a home page and link the handbook (that you completed in Project 14.1), the 2010 Special Events Schedule (that you completed in Project 7.2), the newsletter (that you completed in Project 10.3), and the 2010 Freshman Class Financial Aid document (that you completed in Project 7.4) to the Meadowland College home page.

> **In this project, you will create a home page document from scratch, and then save it as a Web page. You will also save several documents you created previously as Web pages and link them to the home page.**

Note: Figure 16.1 is the printed document version. Printed versions will differ from those viewed in a browser. Use Figure 16.1 as a guide.

1. Open the data file **d16.1aid** (the document you completed in Project 7.4).
2. Save the file as a Single File Web Page. Name it **16.1aid web**.
3. Close the file.
4. Open the data file **d16.1schedule** (the same document you completed in Project 7.2).
5. Save the file as a Single File Web Page. Name it **16.1schedule web**.
6. Close the file.
7. Open the data file **d16.1college news** (the same document you completed in Project 10.3).
   a. Delete the college address information found on the last page.
   b. Save the file as a Single File Web Page. Name it **16.1college news web**.
   c. Close the file.
8. Open a new blank document.
9. Create a table using 2 columns and 5 rows. Use the default column width. Remove all gridlines.

WHAT YOU NEED TO KNOW

Software

▶ You can connect a document to another document or to another location by inserting a hyperlink. If you plan to create an online document, using hyperlinks makes it easy for readers to quickly jump to other information that has been connected by the link.

▶ You can create a hyperlink on existing text or type new text on which to create the link.

▶ If you type a Web or an e-mail address in a document, you automatically create a hyperlink because the software recognizes the unique characters of these addresses.

▶ To create a hyperlink on existing text, select the word(s) or object on which you want to create the link. Click the Insert tab, and in the Links group, click the Hyperlink button. In the Insert Hyperlink dialog box that opens, click a Link to button in the left pane that describes the location to which you want to link. Enter either a filename, Web address, or e-mail address (depending on the button you clicked), and then click OK. The selected word is underlined in blue.

▶ To launch a hyperlink, position the insertion point over the underlined text, press [Ctrl], and then click the left mouse button.

▶ Pages you view on the Web must be in HTML (Hypertext Markup Language) format. HTML is the language or code used to create documents on the Web.

Continued on next page

10. Merge the first row and enter **Meadowland College**. Format the cell as follows:
  a. Center the text and set it to Arial 36 pt bold. Apply any desired font color.
  b. Shade the cell light green.
  c. Insert space before and after the heading as shown.

11. Enter the college address in the second row. Format it as follows:
  a. Center the text and set it to Arial 14 pt bold. Apply a green font color. Use any desired symbol to separate the text where shown.
  b. Shade the cell light yellow.
  c. Insert space before and after the address as shown.

12. Enter **Mission** and the text below it in the third row. Format it as follows:
  a. Set "Mission" to Arial Black and apply any desired font color.
  b. Set the paragraph text to Arial 12 pt.

13. Enter **Vision** and the text below it in the fourth row.

14. Enter **Programs** and the text below it in the fifth row.

15. Copy the formatting from "Mission" to the other two headings in the fourth and fifth rows.

16. Copy the formatting from the text below "Mission" to the paragraph text in the fourth and fifth rows.

17. Merge the cells where shown in the first column. Apply a light yellow shade to the column.

18. Insert the data file **d16.1college picture.jpg** into the first column where shown in Figure 16.1.
  a. Size the picture to approximately 3.4" high by 1.7" wide.
  b. Apply a Square wrap to the image.

19. Enter the text shown below the picture.
  a. Set it to Arial Black in 10 pt.
  b. Apply a green font color.

20. Save the file as a document. Name it **16.1meadowland home page**.

21. Save the file as a Single File Web Page. Name it **16.1meadowland home web**. *Note: Your text may shift once you convert the file to a Web page. Make any necessary adjustments to re-create the page as closely as possible to what is shown in Figure 16.1. You may need to apply an In Line with Text wrap to the image.*

22. Apply a background to the page.

▶ Word documents can be saved as Web pages. When you convert a Word document into a Web page, the file type changes to HTML or MHTML format (Multipurpose Internet Mail Extension HTML). Web pages saved in HTML format store all graphics in a separate file folder. Web pages saved in MHTML format (Single File Web Page) save all the elements of a Website—including text and graphics—in a single file.

▶ If you plan to send an entire Website as an e-mail message or attachment, or move the folder, all the elements of the site will move together.

▶ To save a document as a Web page, click the Office button, point to Save As, and click Other Formats. In the Save As dialog box that opens, enter a filename in the File name text box, click the Save as type list arrow, and then select Single File Web Page, Web Page, or Web Page, Filtered. To provide your Web page with a title other than the filename (for all the world to see), click the Change Title button, and in the Set Page Title dialog box, enter a Web page title in the Page title text box, and click OK. Then, click Save.

▶ Once you save a document as a Web page, the document automatically appears in Web Layout view. Web Layout view allows you to view a document as it will appear in a browser. In this view, you can see how Word positions backgrounds, text wraps, and graphics. You can also edit the document and/or test any links in this view.

▶ You can open your saved Web page directly in the default browser from Word. However, you cannot edit a Web document in the browser.

▶ To open a Web page in the browser, click the Office button, and then click Open. In the Open dialog box that is displayed, click the Files of type list arrow, and select All Web Pages to display only the saved Web page files. Select the file to open. Click the Open button list arrow, and select Open in Browser. Microsoft provides a warning to open files from trusted sources. Click Yes, and then click OK to acknowlegde the warning and proceed. This opens your Word Web page file in Internet Explorer, the Web browser that comes with the Microsoft Office suite.

Continued on next page

23. Insert the following links to the documents indicated:

Create hyperlink on text:	Link to:
Admission and Fall Registration Information	d16.1handbook
Special Events Schedule	16.1schedule web
Meadowland News	16.1college news web
Freshman Class Financial Aid Information	16.1aid web
Contact Us	mc@rizon.edu

24. Preview the file in your default browser.

25. Test the links. Make any necessary adjustments.

26. Save the file, and then close it.

▶ You can design your own Web page using a blank document. However, you must place graphics and text into individual cells of a table to hold those elements in position on the page when you convert the document into a Web page.

▶ Word documents generally have a white background. To add visual appeal to a document, especially Web pages, you can add a background. The Background feature allows you to apply a color, texture, pattern, or picture to the page.

▶ To add a background, click the Page Layout tab, and in the Page Background group, click the Page Color button, and then click Fill Effects from the palette that is displayed. In the Fill Effects dialog box that opens, click the tab you want (Gradient, Texture, Pattern, or Picture), choose a background effect, and then click OK.

Project

▶ Most colleges use Websites to provide information about departments, programs, schedules, and other information.

▶ A *home page* is the first page of a Website and contains general information as well as links to related pages.

Meadowland College

Farm College Road ✷ Princeton, New Jersey ✷ 07137

Mission

The mission of Meadowland College is to provide high-quality educational programs and services that are affordable and accessible to a diverse community of learners. This mission is supported by a dedicated faculty and staff and their commitment to student achievement, lifelong learning, academic excellence, and the use of current technology.

Vision

Meadowland College is a catalyst for creating collaborative relationships across the country that enhance the quality of life through excellence in education, community leadership, and economic growth.

Programs

Meadowland College offers ninety career and transfer programs of study and four types of degrees: Associate of Arts, Associate of Science, Bachelor of Arts, and Bachelor of Science.

Admission and Fall Registration Information

Special Events Schedule

Meadowland News

Freshman Class Financial Aid Information

Contact Us

Merge cells in this row

Merge cells

Merge cells

Figure 16.1

16.2 CREATE A WEB PAGE USING A TEMPLATE

You work for Kay's Kayak, a small kayak rental business, located in South Florida. Kay would like to advertise on the Web and has asked you to create a simple Web page for her business.

In this project, you will use a Web page template to create a Web page for Kay's Kayak.

Note: Figure 16.2 is a printed version. Printed versions will differ from those viewed in a browser. Use Figure 16.2 as a guide as you develop your own version. You may use any font, font sizes, font colors, and/or images you want.

1. Download a Web page template.
   a. Click the Office button, and then click New.
   b. Enter `online templates` in the search box, and click the Start searching arrow.
   c. Select a template similar to the one shown in Figure 16.2. Figure 16.2 uses the Business e-mail newsletter template.
2. Replace the sample text with the text shown and modify the template where necessary.
3. Use any font size and/or style for the heading. You may use WordArt, if you want.
4. Insert relevant images. Apply picture effects, if you want. Include one image as a watermark.
5. Apply any background.
6. Create a link on "E-mail us" to: kk@net.net.
   Create another link on "weather" to: www.wunderground.com/US/FL/Miami.html.
   Note: Your downloaded template might include links in the left column to subheadings in the right column, as shown in the template design used in Figure 16.2. If you selected a design with this feature, use the built-in links.
7. Save the file as a Single File Web Page. Name it **16.2kayak**.
8. Test the links. Make any necessary adjustments.
9. Print one copy of the page, and then close the file.
10. Preview the file in your default browser, and then close the files.

WHAT YOU NEED TO KNOW

Software

▶ You can create your own Web page design from a blank page, as you did in the previous project, or use the Web page templates that are created for Word. These templates can be found online and include font formatting, bulleted lists, and tables to align text on a page.

▶ You can apply a background color or any features previously learned to enhance the template design.

▶ Templates sometimes include text that Word formats as hyperlinks. You can remove these hyperlinks or add your own.
   Note: Word provides several basic Web page templates online; however, if you want more sophisticated template formats, it is recommended that you use Microsoft Publisher or Microsoft Expression Web to develop your Website.

▶ To access a Web page template, click the Office button, and then click New. In the New Document dialog box, enter online templates in the Search box at the top of the dialog box. Click the Start searching arrow. The results will be displayed in the center pane, and the selected template will be displayed in the preview window in the right pane. Click a Web template you want, and then click Download. The template will download to a new document window. The downloaded template will be displayed in the New Document dialog box under Recently Used Templates. You can easily download it again from this dialog box without having to search for it.

Project

▶ Small local businesses can create their own Web pages inexpensively and still have a worldwide audience as a market for their business.

KAY'S KAYAK RENTALS, SALES, & TOURS

About Kay's Rentals & Guided Tours

Tours

Introductory
Intermediate
Full-Day

Rentals & Sales

Let us organize your next kayak tour!

About Kay's Kayak's Rentals, Sales, & Tours

We are South Florida's oldest kayak rental, sales, and tour business. We offer guided kayak tours around Miami Beach and its surrounding areas.

All of our tours include an authorized guide, kayak paddle, life jacket, guidelines, and assistance. We have tours for the inexperienced as well as those who have been kayaking for years.

Come and visit us the next time you are in Miami Beach so we can organize your next Kayak Tour. E-mail us to request information of any kind. Click here to find out the weather forecast for the next five days.

4001 Collins Avenue
Miami Beach, Florida
P: (305) 555-5555
F: (305) 666-6666
E-mail: kk@net.net

Tours

Our Introductory Tour is designed especially for beginners. This three-mile tour allows participants to learn about kayaking, while having fun paddling along the channels. *Duration: 2-3 hours; Price: $40.00* Our Intermediate Tour takes you two miles to seven islands. Along the way, we beach the kayaks while you can relax and enjoy a snack. *Duration: 4-5 hours; Price: $60.00.* Our Full-Day Tour takes you 12 miles and requires that you have better paddling skills and endurance. We paddle across the bay heading towards Key West, exploring the mangroves and wildlife, and returning through the Port of Miami. *Duration: 5-6 hours; Price: $65.00.*

Rentals & Sales

You can rent all the equipment you need for a ½-day, full-day, or overnight journey. Single and double kayaks are available. A deposit is required on all rental equipment.

We sell a full-line of kayaks—both closed deck and sit-on-top varieties. We also sell a full line of accessories.

Figure 16.2

16.3 CREATE A WEBSITE

Upton Investment Group has asked you to create a Website that contains three pages—the home page and two other pages that outline the financial services Upton provides to its clients. Upton hopes to develop a more sophisticated site later this year. The site you create will contain hyperlinks to related pages. The last page will also contain links to other sites that will provide helpful investment information.

In this project, you will create a basic home page for Upton Investment Group and link it to two other pages that you will also create.

1. Create a new blank document.
2. Download the Business e-mail newsletter template from the online templates.
3. To create the home page as shown in Figure 16.3a, do the following:
   a. Replace the sample text with the text shown in Figure 16.3a, and modify the font template as necessary to create the effect shown. Delete any unnecessary text and/or text boxes.
   b. Right-align the heading, Upton Investment Group. Apply the font colors shown.
   c. Enter Upon Investment Group across the row as shown using a 10 pt sans serif font. Use any desired symbol between each occurrence.
   d. Insert a relevant graphic where shown; size it to approximately 1.75" wide by 2.50" high. Apply a picture effect, if you want.
   e. Set the font for the navigation side headings to Arial Black, 16 point.
   f. Set the before and after paragraph spacing to 0 for the navigation headings, and then press Enter three times to add the next heading.
   g. Save the file. Name it **16.3upton home web**. Do not close the file.
4. To create the two other pages, shown in Figures 16.3a and 16.3b, do the following:
   a. Save **16.3upton home web** as **16.3upton investment web**.
   b. Save **16.3upton investment web** as **16.3upton financial web**. *Note: You should now have three pages, each with the same side navigation text.*
5. Switch to **16.3upton investment web** and modify the page as follows:
   a. Replace the graphic with a different relevant graphic. Keep the same approximate size as the graphic you are replacing. Apply a picture effect, if you want.

WHAT YOU NEED TO KNOW

Software

▶ A *Website* is a collection of Web pages. You can build a Website by linking a series of Web pages. As noted earlier, if you want more sophisticated template formats, it is recommended that you use Microsoft Publisher or Microsoft Expression Web to develop your Website.

▶ Websites often contain a navigation bar, which is a set of links that appears in the same place on every page of the Website and provides the user with a consistent way to browse the Website. Creating a navigation bar is a feature of most Website programs, but this feature is not found in Word. However, you can achieve the effect of a navigation bar by using the same Web template for all the pages in the site. Each template would have the same title(s) on every page and would provide links so that the user could easily navigate the pages.

Project

▶ A Website has a specific structure.

▶ A *home page* is the first page of a Website and contains general information as well as links to related pages.

▶ Websites that are attractive and easy to navigate engage the reader.

b. Replace the text as shown in Figure 16.3b.
Note: The replacement text will change the look of the original template layout.

c. Save the file, but do not close it.

6. Switch to **16.3upton financial web** and modify the page as follows:

a. Replace the graphic with a different relevant graphic. Keep the same size as the other graphic. Apply a picture effect, if you want.

b. Replace the text, as shown in Figure 16.3c.
Note: The replacement text will change the look of the original template layout.

c. Save the file, but do not close it.

7. Switch to **16.3upton home web**.

8. Create links on "financial planning" and "investment services" to those pages. Create a hyperlink on "Contact Us" to upton@net.com.

9. Switch to each of the other pages and insert a hyperlink on all the navigation titles (except the one in red) to the appropriate pages.

10. Save each file, and then test the links.

11. Open each file in your default browser and test the links.

12. Make any necessary adjustments. Resave the files, if necessary.

13. Close all files.

Home

Investment Services

Financial Planning

Contact Us
34562 Corona Street
Los Angeles, CA 90001
Phone: 213-555-6000
Fax: 213-555-6623

Upton Investment Group □ Upton Investment Group □ Upton Investment Group □ Upton Investment Group

Upton
Investment
Group

Upton Investment Group is a full-service investment company located in Los Angeles, California. We service corporate and individual clients and provide investment, financial planning, and brokerage services.

Our financial specialists have extensive experience servicing their customers. They are each experts in their financial field and provide their clients with the most efficient and comprehensive approach to meet their needs and goals.

Figure 16.3a

Investment Services

Upton Investment Group ☐ Upton Investment Group ☐ Upton Investment Group ☐ Upton Investment Group

Home

Investment Services

Financial Planning

Contact Us
34562 Corona Street
Los Angeles, CA 90001
Phone: 213-555-6000
Fax: 213-555-6623

Upton Investment Group works with its clients to develop investment recommendations and strategies based on the personal needs of the individual or company.

Our clients have the opportunity to invest in over 8,500 mutual funds, stocks, bonds, CDs, and many other types of investments.

Our investment accounts are insured up to $100 million.

Figure 16.3b

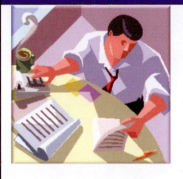

Financial Planning

Upton Investment Group ❑ Upton Investment Group ❑ Upton Investment Group ❑ Upton Investment Group

Home

Investment Services

Financial Planning

Contact Us
34562 Corona Street
Los Angeles, CA 90001
Phone: 213-555-6000
Fax: 213-555-6623

We are committed to providing comprehensive, long-term financial products to our clients.

Our financial advisors have been providing outstanding financial advice for decades. When you choose to work with us, you will get financial advice that is customized to your needs and objectives.

Our financial planners will work with you and assess your current financial situation. They will then outline an appropriate investment, income tax, retirement, and estate plan for you.

Figure 16.3c

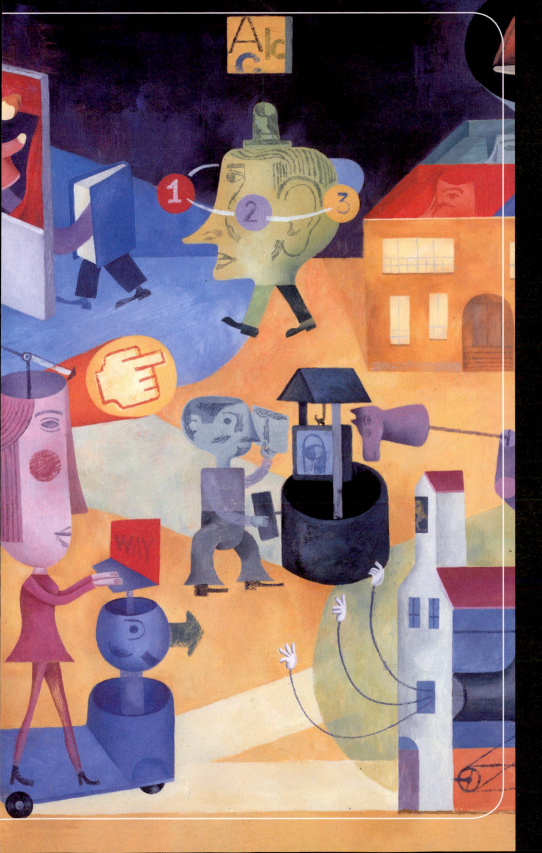

CHAPTER 1
Learn Excel Basics

CHAPTER 2
Create Business
Forms/Work with
Templates

CHAPTER 3
Create Accounting
Records

CHAPTER 4
Create Data Analysis
Worksheets

CHAPTER 5
Create Financial
Reports

CHAPTER 6
Create Charts and
Graphics/Integration

CHAPTER 1

Learn Excel Basics

In this chapter, you will complete the following projects:

PROJECT 1
Enter, Proof, and Print Data

PROJECT 1.1 Create an Invoice for Professional Services
PROJECT 1.2 Preview and Print an Invoice for Professional Services
PROJECT 1.3 Create and Proof an Invoice from an Existing File

PROJECT 2
Enter and Edit Formulas

PROJECT 2.1 Create a Personnel Plan
PROJECT 2.2 Format a Personnel Plan
PROJECT 2.3 Arrange and Format a Personnel Plan

PROJECT 3
Enhance and Edit Worksheet Data

PROJECT 3.1 Create a Projected Cash Flow Statement
PROJECT 3.2 Format a Projected Cash Flow Statement

ENTER, PROOF, AND PRINT DATA

PROJECT 1

PROJECT SKILLS

✳ Navigate the worksheet
✳ Create a folder for Excel files
✳ Enter, align, and format values, dates, and labels
✳ Save a file
✳ Use worksheet views
✳ Preview and print a document
✳ Open a file as a copy
✳ Use Save As
✳ Proof data

1.1 CREATE AN INVOICE FOR PROFESSIONAL SERVICES

Watnick & Willem Associates has created an advertising campaign for Saturn Candies, Inc. and wants you to create a bill for its services.

In this project, you will create a folder for Excel workbooks and an invoice for professional services.

1. Open a new Excel workbook.
2. Create a folder for Excel workbooks in My Documents or in your assigned area of the hard drive. Name the folder **Excel Projects**.
3. Create the invoice for professional services, as illustrated in Figure 1.1.
   a. Use directional arrow keys and/or the Go To feature to navigate to specific cells.
   b. Format the date in mm/dd/yyyy format.
   c. Format values in Accounting Number format.
   d. Right-align the Invoice # and Terms: labels.
   e. Center the Amount label.
4. Save the file and name it **1.1profinv**.
5. Close the file.

WHAT YOU NEED TO KNOW

Software

▶ To create a folder for Excel files, click the New Folder button in the Open dialog box.

▶ To move directly to a specific cell, activate the Go To feature by pressing [F5].

▶ To set date format, click the Number Format list arrow, on the Home tab in the Number group, and select Short Date or Long Date from the Number Format gallery.

▶ To format a value for two decimal places, with a comma and a dollar sign, right-click the cell containing the value and click the Accounting Number Format button on the Mini toolbar. To bold or italicize text, click the Bold or Italic buttons on the Mini toolbar.

▶ By default, labels align to the left and values and dates align to the right. To change the alignment of selected cells, use the alignment buttons on the Home tab, in the Alignment section: Align Text Left, Center, and Align Text Right.

Project

▶ A business form, such as an invoice, is a document format that is developed for an activity that occurs regularly.

▶ Business forms are generally numbered so that they can be referenced in communications.

▶ An invoice is a bill of sale.

▶ An invoice for professional services is a bill created by a company or an individual who charges fees for their services. Accountants, doctors, lawyers, consultants, and other professionals may use this type of invoice.

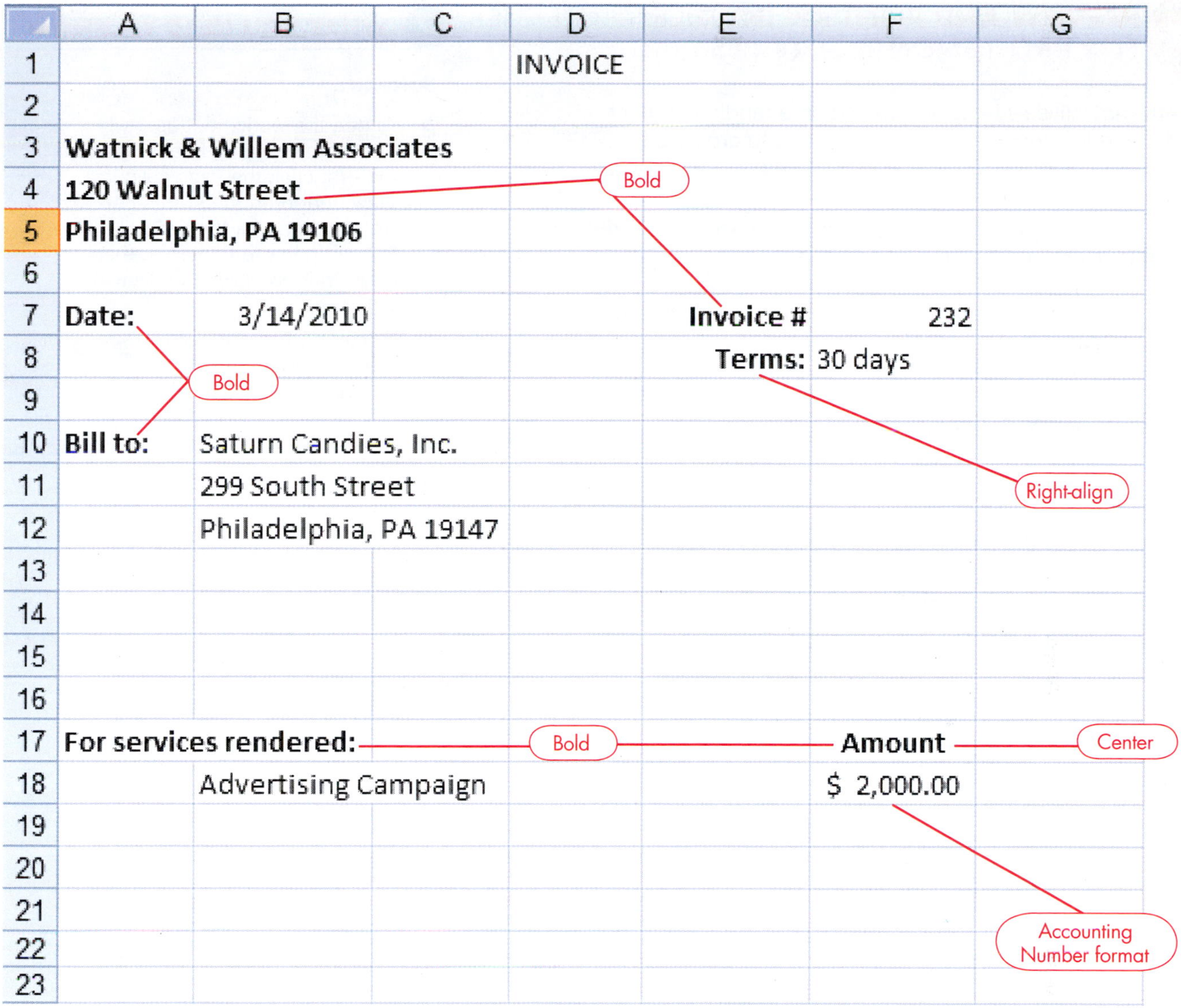

	A	B	C	D	E	F	G
1				INVOICE			
2							
3	**Watnick & Willem Associates**						
4	**120 Walnut Street**						
5	**Philadelphia, PA 19106**						
6							
7	**Date:**	3/14/2010			**Invoice #**	232	
8					**Terms:**	30 days	
9							
10	**Bill to:**	Saturn Candies, Inc.					
11		299 South Street					
12		Philadelphia, PA 19147					
13							
14							
15							
16							
17	**For services rendered:**					**Amount**	
18		Advertising Campaign				$ 2,000.00	
19							
20							
21							
22							
23							

Annotations: Bold (120 Walnut Street), Bold (Date:), Right-align (Terms:), Bold (For services rendered:), Center (Amount), Accounting Number format ($ 2,000.00)

Figure 1.1

1.2 PREVIEW AND PRINT AN INVOICE FOR PROFESSIONAL SERVICES

Attorney Alivea Justin has worked on a landlord/tenant dispute for Roberto Morales. You need to create an invoice for Ms. Justin to bill Mr. Morales for her services.

In this project, you will create, preview, view, and print an invoice for professional services.

1. Create an invoice for your employer, as shown in Figure 1.2.
   Alivea Justin, Attorney at Law
   2225 Amsterdam Avenue
   New York, NY 10040
   Invoice date: June 15, 2010
   Invoice number: 5328
   Terms: 30 days
   Client: Mr. Roberto Morales
             3243 Broadway
             New York, NY 10023
   Bill for legal services rendered: Landlord/Tenant Dispute $1,950.00
2. Format the value in Accounting Number format.
3. Bold the text as shown.
4. Use Page Layout view to check the placement of the invoice on the printed page.
5. Use the Full Page and Zoom buttons on the View tab to get a better view of the data.
6. Click the Office Button, point to Print, and then click Print Preview. Print the invoice.
7. Save the file and name it **1.2profinv**.
8. Close the file.

WHAT YOU NEED TO KNOW

Software

▶ To see the worksheet as it will print with margins, headers, and footers, click the Page Layout View button on the status bar. Or, you can click the Office Button, point to Print, and then click Print Preview to preview the worksheet.

▶ To get a better view of the data, use the Full Screen or Zoom buttons on the View tab.

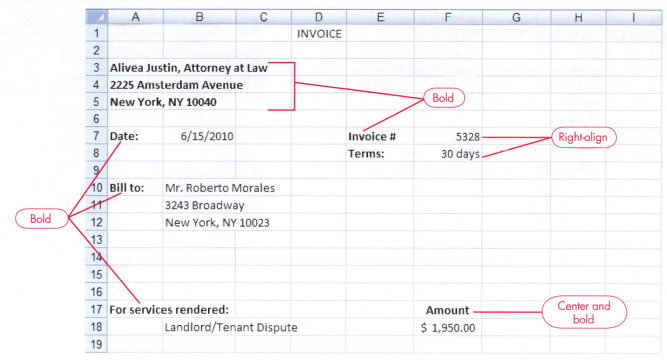

Figure 1.2

1.3 CREATE AND PROOF AN INVOICE FROM AN EXISTING FILE

Watnick & Willem Associates, an advertising company, wants to send an invoice for professional services to Greyson Tools, Inc. and needs you to create the invoice using an existing file.

In this project, you will create, proof, preview, and print an invoice for professional services using an existing file.

1. In the Open dialog box, select data file **1.1profinv**, then click Open as Copy on the Open button menu. Save the copy as **1.3profinv**.
2. Change it using the following information:
   a. Invoice date: March 15, 2010
   b. Invoice number: 233
3. Obtain other necessary information for the invoice from the letter shown in Figure 1.3.
4. Proof the spelling of the text in the invoice.
5. Preview and print the invoice.
6. Save and close the file.

WHAT YOU NEED TO KNOW

Software

▶ When you want to create a worksheet using the format from an existing file, you can select the old file in the Open dialog box, click the Open button arrow, then click Open as Copy. The old file will open as a copy, and you can edit and save it as a new file.

▶ Use the Proofing group on the Review tab to check spelling, research reference materials, refer to a thesaurus, or translate data. You can press [F7] if you just want to check the spelling.

Watnick and Willem Associates

120 Walnut Street
Philadelphia, PA 19106

February 15, 2010

Mr. Robert Greyson
Greyson Tools, Inc.
543 Reading Street
Philadelphia, PA 19147

Dear Mr. Greyson:

We are writing to summarize our meeting yesterday regarding your advertising campaign.

We will develop a radio advertisement campaign for your company and will place the commercials in the appropriate local stations for your demographic area. The campaign will consist of a series of three different ads, which will run for three weeks beginning March 15, 2010. The final version of the ads will be sent to you by March 1, 2010 for your approval.

We discussed the fee for our services and, as per our discussion, you will be billed $1300 next month.

We look forward to working with you during the weeks ahead.

Sincerely yours,

Gregory Willem
Vice President

Figure 1.3

ENTER AND EDIT FORMULAS

PROJECT 2

PROJECT SKILLS

✱ Use the Fill Color feature
✱ Use the AutoSum feature
✱ Copy and paste
✱ Enter formulas
✱ Enter formulas by selection

2.1 CREATE A PERSONNEL PLAN

As part of its business plan, Busy Bees Renovations wants you to complete a personnel plan that projects personnel costs for the next two years.

In this project, you will create a personnel plan using the AutoSum function, formulas, and number formats.

1. Open data file **d2.1personnel**.
2. Format the titles, section headings, and totals of the report, as shown in Figure 2.1. To add fill color and formats to the subtotal lines, right-click the selected area and apply formats using the Mini toolbar.
3. Calculate a subtotal in cell D11 by selecting cells D5 through D11 and clicking the AutoSum button.
4. Copy and paste the formula from cell D11 to E11.
5. Repeat this procedure to subtotal all sections of the report.
6. Format all values for commas with no decimal places by selecting and then right-clicking the range D5:E33. Click the Comma Style button, and then click the Decrease Decimal button two times to remove decimal places.
7. In cell D35, Totals, enter a formula to total the subtotal results. *Hint: =D11+D17+D33*. Format the total in Accounting Number format with no decimal places.
8. Copy the formula to cell E35.
9. Save the file and name it **2.1personnel**.
10. Close the file.

WHAT YOU NEED TO KNOW

Software

▶ To fill a row with color, right-click the row, click the Fill Color button arrow on the Mini toolbar, and select the color.

▶ Subtotal columns by clicking the cell to receive the total, selecting the range of values, and on the Home tab, and in the Editing group, click the AutoSum button.

▶ To copy and paste a formula, right-click the cell to copy, click Copy on the shortcut menu, right-click the destination cell, and click Paste.

▶ To format a cell for commas with no decimal places, right-click the cell, and on the Mini toolbar, click the Comma Style button, and then click the Decrease Decimal button two times.

▶ All formulas begin with an equal sign and include the cell addresses of the items to calculate with mathematical operators. To find the grand total, enter a formula to total the subtotal cell references.

Project

▶ A business plan is a document that a business creates to provide a road map for the company's operations over the next few years.

▶ Companies may use business plans for planning, as a strategic document, or for raising capital.

▶ Part of the business plan is the personnel plan, which projects or estimates personnel expenditures and needs going forward. This plan takes into account rising salaries, increased volume, seasonal changes, and other variables.

	A	B	C	D	E
1	**Busy Bees Renovations**				
2	**Personnel Plan Summary**				
3				**2010**	**2011**
4	*Administrative:*				
5	President			60,000	70,000
6	Finance				40,000
7	Admin. Asst.			25,000	30,000
8	Bookkeeping			25,000	30,000
9	Clerical			22,500	25,000
10	Clerical				20,000
11		**Subtotals**			
12					
13	*Sales:*				
14	Manager			33,000	38,000
15	Salesperson*			28,000	32,000
16	Salesperson*				18,000
17		**Subtotals**			
18					
19	*Construction and Repair Crew:*				
20	Foreman			33,000	37,000
21	Foreman				33,000
22	Plumbing**			30,000	34,000
23	Plumbing**				28,000
24	Carpentry**			29,000	33,000
25	Carpentry**				25,000
26	Electrical**			28,000	32,000
27	Electrical**				20,000
28	Building Trades**			28,000	32,000
29	Building Trades**				20,000
30	Laborer**			20,000	22,000
31	Laborer**				18,000
32	Other**			20,000	22,000
33		**Subtotals**			
34					
35	**Totals**				
36					
37	* Commission				
38	**Part time - as needed basis				
39					

Callouts:
- Bold, Calibri, 12 point (pointing to A1 "Busy Bees Renovations")
- Bold (pointing to "2011" in E3)
- Bold (pointing to "Subtotals")
- Enter formulas in column D and copy to column E
- Section headings bold, italics, fill color Olive Green, Accent 3, Lighter 40%

Figure 2.1

EXCEL

2.2 FORMAT A PERSONNEL PLAN

Attorney Alivea Justin needs you to prepare a personnel plan as part of her business plan. She is looking for funding to hire two attorneys and to expand her office staff in 2011.

In this project, you will prepare and format a personnel plan using formulas.

1. Open data file **d2.2personnel**, an unformatted list of staff and salaries for 2009, 2010, and 2011.
2. Enter, position, and format a title for the report. Use **Professional Staff** and **Support Staff** as the section headings, and add the **Subtotal** and **Total** labels, as shown in Figure 2.2.
3. Find subtotals for each year and each section.
4. Format numbers for commas with no decimal places.
5. Enter the formulas for the total by selection in the cells shaded in grey in Figure 2.2. *Hint: Enter the equal sign, select the first subtotal, enter the plus sign, select the second subtotal, and then press [Enter].* Format the totals in Accounting Number format with no decimal places.
6. Format section headings and total line using Aqua, Accent 5, Darker, 25% fill color, and set the font color to White. Format subtotals using Aqua, Accent 5, Lighter 60% fill color.
7. Preview and print the plan.
8. Save the file, and name it **2.2personnel**.
9. Close the file.

WHAT YOU NEED TO KNOW

Software

▶ To enter a formula by selection, enter the equal sign and select the first cell in the formula, enter the mathematical operator, select the second cell in the formula, and continue in this fashion, pressing [Enter] when the formula is complete.

	A	B	C	D	E	F
1	**Alivea Justin, Attorney**					
2	**Personnel Plan**					
3						
4				2009	2010	2011
5	*Professional Staff*					
6	Alivea Justin, Attorney			80,000	85,000	90,000
7	Attorney				50,000	60,000
8	Attorney				25,000	50,000
9		Subtotal				
10						
11	*Support Staff*					
12	Administrative Assistant			30,000	32,500	34,000
13	Administrative Assistant				30,000	32,500
14	Clerical			20,000	21,500	23,000
15	Clerical					21,500
16	Bookkeeper				30,000	32,500
17		Subtotal				
18						
19		*Total*				

Bold, Calibri, 14 point

Bold, fill color Aqua, Accent 5, Lighter 60%

Bold, italics, fill color Aqua, Accent 5, Darker 25%, font color White

Figure 2.2

ARRANGE AND FORMAT A PERSONNEL PLAN

Upon request, the bookkeeper for Watnick & Willem Associates has prepared a memorandum with a list of the company's current personnel. Bernard Watnick, the president of the company, has also added his notes to the list to estimate next year's personnel needs.

In this project, you will create and arrange a personnel plan containing formatting and formulas, using data from a memorandum.

1. Prepare a personnel plan for 2010 and 2011 using the information provided in the memorandum in Figure 2.3. Note Bernard Watnick's handwritten additions for 2011, and add the data for the additional positions in the appropriate locations. Refer to previously prepared plans for guidance.
2. Format numbers, titles, column headings, totals, and the worksheet as you prefer, using fill color.
3. Enter formulas to complete the plan.
4. Print a copy of the personnel plan.
5. Save the file, and name it **2.3personnel**.
6. Close the file.

WHAT YOU NEED TO KNOW

Project

▶ You will gather the information from the memorandum and arrange it into a worksheet formatted as a personnel plan. Be sure to leave rows for titles, subtotals, and totals.

▶ Administrative assistants, clerical help, and bookkeepers are support staff, while the other members of the firm are professional staff. Use these two categories as section headings.

Watnick and Willem

Memo

To: Bernard Watnick, President

From: Patricia Ryan, Bookkeeper

Date: 4/1/2010

Re: Current Personnel List

As you requested, I have listed below the titles and salaries of all current personnel. Let me know if you need any additional information.

		Next year
President – Creative Director	$65,000	$70,000
Vice President – Financial Director	60,000	65,000
Account Manager	48,500	54,000
Account Manager	45,000	48,500
Writer	32,500	38,500
Graphic Artist	32,500	38,500
Administrative Assistant	29,500	32,000
Bookkeeper	32,500	35,500
Clerical	24,000	27,000

Also, add the following new employees for next year:

Graphic Artist	$32,500
Administrative Assistant	29,500
Clerical	24,000

Figure 2.3

PROJECT SKILLS

✴ Drag and drop to move data
✴ Format cell borders
✴ Merge and center text

PROJECT 3

3.1 CREATE A PROJECTED CASH FLOW STATEMENT

Pressquick Printing needs to create a projected cash flow statement as part of its business plan.

In this project, you will create a projected cash flow statement using functions, formulas, and formats.

1. Open data file **d3.1cash**.
2. Select the range for the title in cells A1:A3.
3. Drag the range to cell F1:F3 and right-align the titles.
4. Format the title and section headings of the report, as shown in Figure 3.1.
5. In cell F8, use the AutoSum button to add Cash Receipts.
6. In cell F19, use the AutoSum button to add Cash Disbursements.
7. In cell F21, enter a formula to subtract disbursements from cash receipts.
8. Format all numbers for commas with no decimal places.
9. To enter single and double lines as shown, select and right-click the cells, then apply the appropriate border style using the Borders button arrow on the Mini toolbar.
10. Save the file as **3.1cash**.
11. Close the file.

WHAT YOU NEED TO KNOW

Software

▶ To move a range of cells, select the cells and move the mouse to the edge of the range. When the mouse cursor becomes a four-headed arrow, click and drag the range to the new location.

▶ To total cash increases and decreases, use the AutoSum button on the Home tab.

▶ To find the difference between cash increases and decreases enter a formula using the minus sign.

▶ To add borders, right-click the cell or range of cells, and use the Borders button arrow on the Mini toolbar. Select the appropriate cell border to apply. Typically, single line borders are used to show addition and double line borders indicate completion. For example, a single line would be used to show that a column is to be added. The grand total or final total would have a double bottom border.

Project

▶ A company uses a projected cash flow statement in a business plan to project the sources for increases and decreases in cash during a specified time period. A positive cash flow means that the increases in cash are greater than the decreases. A negative cash flow means the decreases are greater than increases.

▶ Maintaining positive cash flow is important because, although a business may have many assets, such as equipment, buildings, and accounts receivable (customers who owe the business money), it still needs cash to cover immediate expenses.

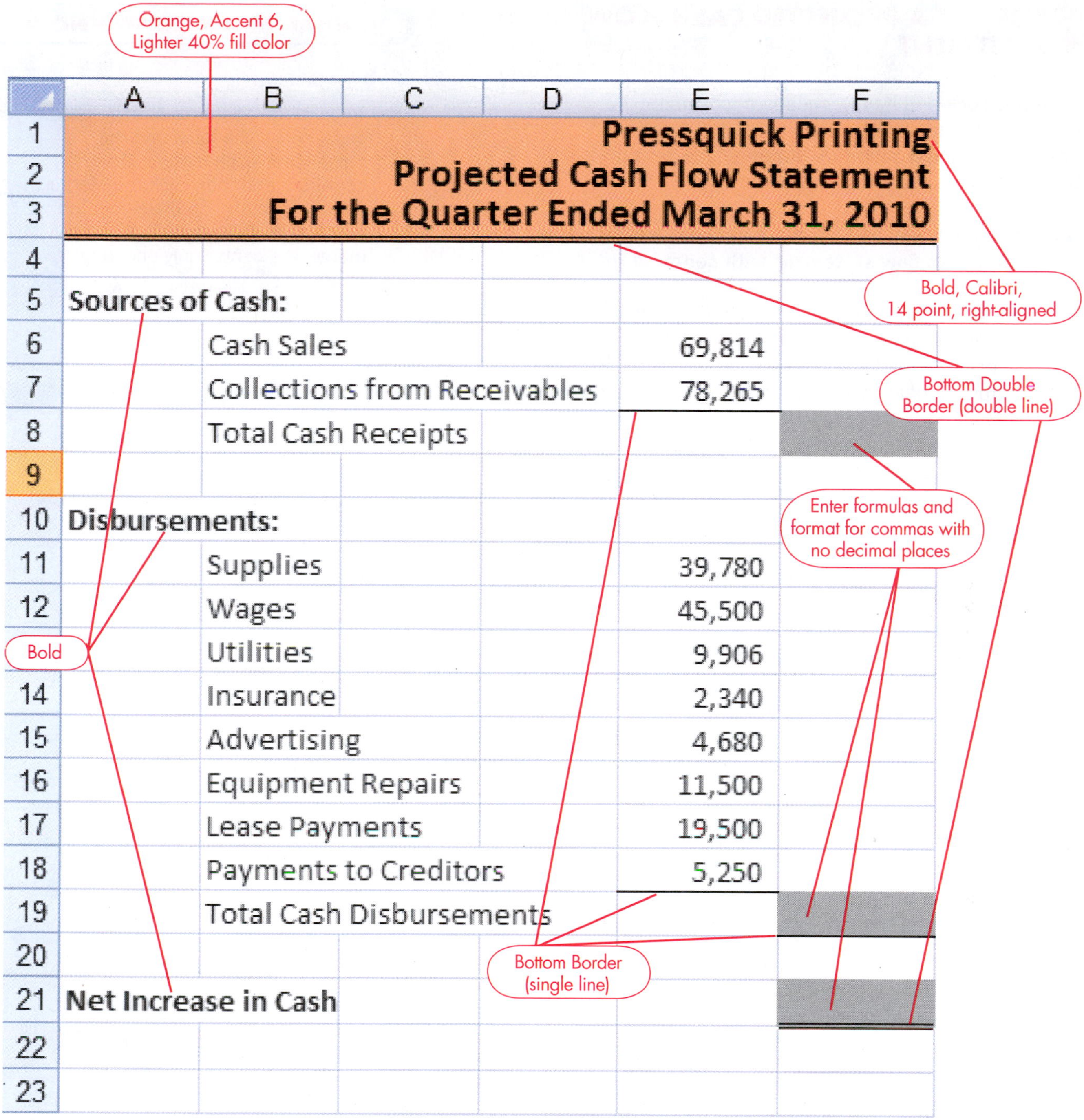

Orange, Accent 6,
Lighter 40% fill color

	A	B	C	D	E	F
1					**Pressquick Printing**	
2					**Projected Cash Flow Statement**	
3					**For the Quarter Ended March 31, 2010**	
4						
5	**Sources of Cash:**					
6		Cash Sales			69,814	
7		Collections from Receivables			78,265	
8		Total Cash Receipts				
9						
10	**Disbursements:**					
11		Supplies			39,780	
12		Wages			45,500	
13		Utilities			9,906	
14		Insurance			2,340	
15		Advertising			4,680	
16		Equipment Repairs			11,500	
17		Lease Payments			19,500	
18		Payments to Creditors			5,250	
19		Total Cash Disbursements				
20						
21	**Net Increase in Cash**					
22						
23						

Bold, Calibri,
14 point, right-aligned

Bottom Double
Border (double line)

Enter formulas and
format for commas with
no decimal places

Bold

Bottom Border
(single line)

Figure 3.1

3.2 FORMAT A PROJECTED CASH FLOW STATEMENT

Eveready Lock and Key Service is a locksmith business that is planning to expand. The business needs a projected cash flow statement as part of its business plan.

In this project, you will create, calculate, and format a projected cash flow statement with centered titles.

1. Find an unformatted list of projected cash receipts and disbursements in data file **d3.2cash**.
2. Select cells A1:F1 and then click the Merge & Center button. Repeat this step for the next two title lines.
3. Suggested formats for the title and section heading lines of the report are shown in Figure 3.2. Add a Thick Box Border to the title section A1:A3.
4. Enter formulas in Column F to calculate total cash receipts, total cash disbursements, and net change in cash flow.
5. Format numbers for commas with no decimal places.
6. Enter appropriate borders to show addition and completion of the report, as shown in Figure 3.2.
7. Save the file and name it **3.2cash**.
8. Preview the Projected Cash Flow Statement and note that the thick border appears around the title.
9. Close the file.

WHAT YOU NEED TO KNOW

Software

▶ To center a label over a range of cells, select the label and the range over which it should be centered, and then click the Merge & Center button, on the Home tab in the Alignment group. You can merge and center only one label at a time.

	A	B	C	D	E	F
1	**Eveready Lock and Key Service**					
2	**Projected Cash Flow Statement**					
3	**For the Quarter Ended September 30, 2010**					
4						
5	**Sources of Cash:**					
6		Cash Sales			55,436	
7		Collections from Receivables			15,988	
8		Total Cash Receipts				71,424
9						
10	**Disbursements:**					
11		Supplies			4,760	
12		Wages			42,356	
13		Utilities			2,987	
14		Insurance			1,700	
15		Advertising			1,900	
16		Equipment Repairs			2,000	
17		Rent			7,800	
18		Payments to Creditors			2,100	
19		Total Cash Disbursements				65,603
20						
21	**Net Increase in Cash**					5,821
22						

Bold, Calibri, 16 point

Title lines merged and centered, fill color Light Green

Thick Box Border around title section

Figure 3.2

CHAPTER 2

Create Business Forms/
Work with Templates

In this chapter, you will complete the following projects:

PROJECT 4
Purchase Orders

PROJECT 4.1 Create a Purchase Order
PROJECT 4.2 Modify and Enhance a Purchase Order
PROJECT 4.3 Create and Format a Purchase Order

PROJECT 5
Sales Invoices

PROJECT 5.1 Create a Sales Invoice
PROJECT 5.2 Create and Format a Sales Invoice

PROJECT 6
Work with Templates

PROJECT 6.1 Create and Use a Sales Invoice Template
PROJECT 6.2 Use a Time Card Template
PROJECT 6.3 Use a Sales Invoice Template
PROJECT 6.4 Use a Price Quotation Template

PROJECT SKILLS
✷ Format text and numbers
✷ Use the AutoComplete feature
✷ Edit cell data
✷ Clear cells
✷ Apply and modify cell styles
✷ Apply a theme

4.1 CREATE A PURCHASE ORDER

Sports Shoes Unlimited sells athletic shoes at retail and it is ordering merchandise from a wholesaler, BSK Shoes, Inc. to restock popular items. You will prepare the purchase order.

In this project, you will create a purchase order using formatting, formulas, AutoSum, and AutoComplete.

1. Open a new Excel workbook and create and format the purchase order illustrated in Figure 4.1.
   a. Format all bold text with Comic Sans MS in the point sizes indicated. If that font is not available, substitute another.
   b. Apply a fill color and borders, as shown. *Note: To create the fill color as illustrated, fill cells A2:H8 and A14:H14 with Light Green, and then select cells F3:H7 and select No Fill.*
   c. In cell D16 and D17, notice how AutoComplete enters the text. To accept the suggested text, press [Enter] or an arrow key.
   d. Right-align the text in cells H3:H7 and in cells G14:H14.
   e. Enter a formula in cell H15 to calculate the Amount (*Hint: Quantity*Price*) and copy the formula to cells H16:H18.
   f. Format values in cells G15:H18 in Number format using the Number Format gallery on the Home tab.
   g. In cell H20, use the AutoSum button to total the purchase order. Format the total in Accounting Number format.
2. Save the file and name it **4.1purorder**.
3. Close the file.

WHAT YOU NEED TO KNOW

Software

▶ You can format text fonts, styles, and colors by selecting and right-clicking the text and using the Font, Font Size, Bold, Italic, Font Color, and Fill Color buttons on the Mini toolbar. Or, select the text, click the Home tab, and make your settings in the Font group.

▶ Some number formats may be set using the Mini toolbar, or by using the tools in the Number group on the Home tab. The common number formats are as follows:

Accounting	two places and a $ sign aligned in the column
Currency	two places and a $ sign to the immediate left of the number
Comma	two decimal places and commas
Number	two decimal places

▶ The AutoComplete feature helps with data entry by completing subsequent entries of text previously entered. Press [Enter] to accept the AutoComplete suggestion or continue to type if there is a change.

Project

▶ A purchase order is completed by a business when supplies or merchandise are needed. The order is sent to a vendor or supplier and represents a written order to buy.

Continued on next page

▶ The Received column is left blank because it is used to check the order when it arrives.

▶ The Terms define the agreement for payment for the purchase.

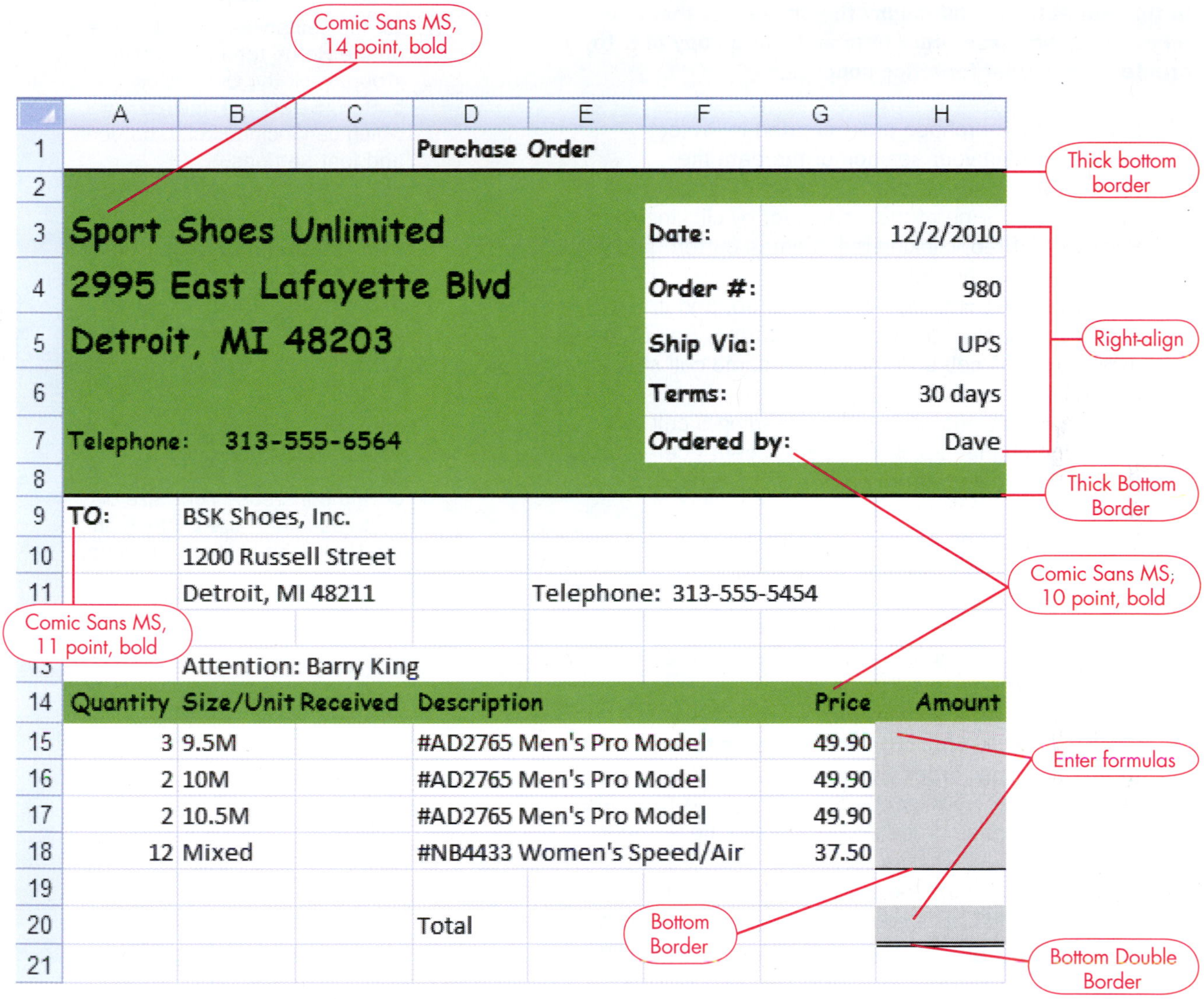

Comic Sans MS, 14 point, bold

Thick bottom border

Right-align

Thick Bottom Border

Comic Sans MS; 10 point, bold

Comic Sans MS, 11 point, bold

Enter formulas

Bottom Border

Bottom Double Border

	A	B	C	D	E	F	G	H
1				Purchase Order				
2								
3	Sport Shoes Unlimited					Date:		12/2/2010
4	2995 East Lafayette Blvd					Order #:		980
5	Detroit, MI 48203					Ship Via:		UPS
6						Terms:		30 days
7	Telephone: 313-555-6564					Ordered by:		Dave
8								
9	TO:	BSK Shoes, Inc.						
10		1200 Russell Street						
11		Detroit, MI 48211			Telephone: 313-555-5454			
13		Attention: Barry King						
14	Quantity	Size/Unit	Received		Description		Price	Amount
15	3	9.5M			#AD2765 Men's Pro Model		49.90	
16	2	10M			#AD2765 Men's Pro Model		49.90	
17	2	10.5M			#AD2765 Men's Pro Model		49.90	
18	12	Mixed			#NB4433 Women's Speed/Air		37.50	
19								
20					Total			
21								

Figure 4.1

4.2 MODIFY AND ENHANCE A PURCHASE ORDER

The owner of Sports Shoes Unlimited wants to change the design of the purchase orders they send. You will modify the previously created purchase order and use a copy of it to create an order for office supplies.

> **In this project, you will modify the styles and theme of an existing purchase order form and use a copy of it to create a new order for office supplies.**

1. Enhance the purchase order created in Project 4.1 by opening your solution or the data file **d4.2purorder**.
2. Change the theme of the worksheet by clicking the Page Layout tab, clicking the Themes button, and then selecting the Solstice theme.
3. Select cells A1:H8, click the Home tab, and in the Styles group, click the Cell Styles button. Select the 40% - Accent4 cell style. Apply the same cell style to A14:H14.
4. Change A1:H1 and A14:H14 to Heading 3 cell style, and change F3:H7 to 20% - Accent4 cell style. Delete the single bottom border in cell H18, and apply the Total cell style to H20.
5. Select the column headers in A14:H14, and click the Decrease Font Size button to reduce the font size to 10 point.
6. Select the company name and address in cells A3:A5, and click the Increase Font Size button to increase the size to 14 point.
7. Save the file as **4.2Apurorder**.
8. Dave, of Sports Shoes Unlimited, wants to use this format for a new order. Save the file as **4.2Bpurorder** and overwrite, clear, or edit the existing text to create the new purchase order. Do not change the formula cells.
   a. Dave is ordering the supplies on 12/3 with order number 981. The goods will be shipped via UPS. The terms are 30 days. He will be ordering from Maria Cortez at:
      Office Supplies Warehouse
      765 Industry Street
      Detroit, MI 48211
      Telephone 313-555-8121

WHAT YOU NEED TO KNOW

Software

- ▶ To edit cell data, select the cell and overwrite or press [F2] and make the edit.
- ▶ To clear cell data, select the cell or range and press [Delete].
- ▶ To add cell styles, select the range and on the Home tab in the Styles group, click the Cell Styles button. Select the desired style, which can include color, borders, and font settings.
- ▶ The tones of the colors in the Cell Styles gallery may be modified by applying a different theme. The default colors are those in the Office theme. Change the theme by clicking the Page Layout tab, and in the Themes group, click the Themes button and select a theme.
- ▶ To increase or decrease font size incrementally, select the text and click the Increase Font Size or Decrease Font Size buttons on the Home tab in the Font group.

b. The items ordered are as follows:

QUANTITY	SIZE/UNIT	RECEIVED	DESCRIPTION	PRICE
6	reams		Ward Copy Paper, Blue, Letter	7.90
2	reams		Index Card Stock - 90 lb white	9.80
12	each		Presentation Binders	8.22

c. Edit the description for the presentation binders to add the color: **Blue**.

9. Save and close the file.

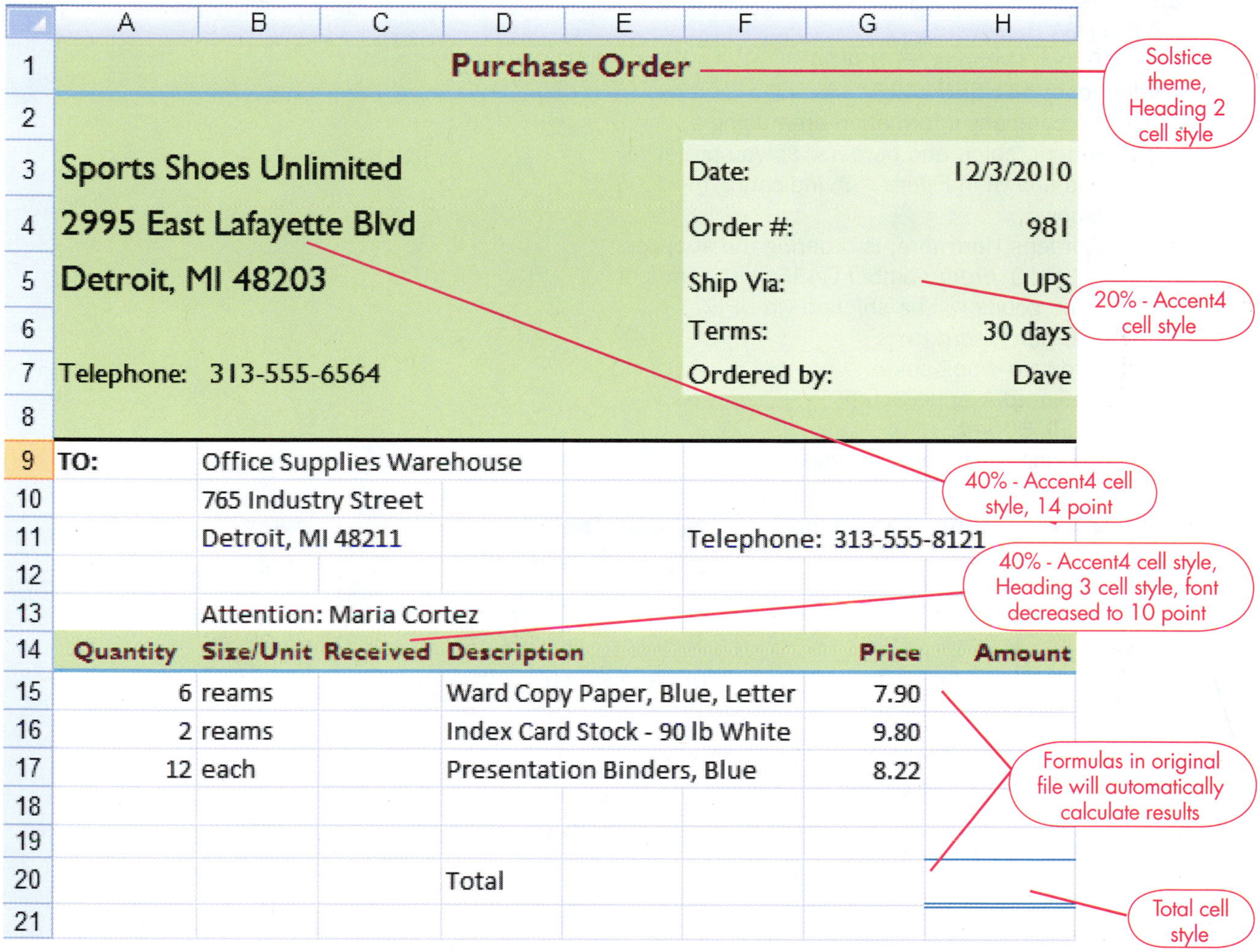

	A	B	C	D	E	F	G	H	
1				**Purchase Order**					Solstice theme, Heading 2 cell style
2									
3	Sports Shoes Unlimited					Date:		12/3/2010	
4	2995 East Lafayette Blvd					Order #:		981	
5	Detroit, MI 48203					Ship Via:		UPS	20% - Accent4 cell style
6						Terms:		30 days	
7	Telephone: 313-555-6564					Ordered by:		Dave	
8									
9	TO:		Office Supplies Warehouse						40% - Accent4 cell style, 14 point
10			765 Industry Street						
11			Detroit, MI 48211			Telephone: 313-555-8121			
12									40% - Accent4 cell style, Heading 3 cell style, font decreased to 10 point
13			Attention: Maria Cortez						
14	Quantity	Size/Unit	Received	Description			Price	Amount	
15		6	reams	Ward Copy Paper, Blue, Letter			7.90		
16		2	reams	Index Card Stock - 90 lb White			9.80		Formulas in original file will automatically calculate results
17		12	each	Presentation Binders, Blue			8.22		
18									
19									
20				Total					Total cell style
21									

Figure 4.2

4.3 CREATE AND FORMAT A PURCHASE ORDER

Gardens Hardware Shoppe has asked you to prepare a purchase order for several items that have been depleted from its inventory.

In this project, you will create a purchase order and use font, color, and border settings to enhance the form.

1. Open a new worksheet and create a purchase order form for the Gardens Hardware Shoppe. The address is:
   3350 PGA Boulevard
   Palm Beach Gardens, FL 33404
   Telephone: 561-555-3423
2. Format the company information area using a distinctive font, color, and borders, as you prefer. A sample is shown in Figure 4.3, indicating the settings shown.
3. Tony, of Gardens Hardware, is ordering the supplies on 11/21/2010, order number G435, with terms of 30 days. The goods will be shipped via UPS.
4. The order is being sent to:
   VVX Hardware Wholesalers
   1492 Railroad Avenue South
   Chicago, IL 60644
5. Tony is ordering the following items:

QUANTITY	UNIT	RECEIVED	DESCRIPTION	PRICE
24	each		Circuit Tester #T24323	7.59
12	each		Wire Stripper #B34342	8.49
3	each		ShopVac - 5 gal #R80971	45.49
5	each		Drill Bit Set 1/16"-1/2" #A60434	35.45

6. Enter formulas, format values, and add styles and themes, as shown in the example in Figure 4.3.
7. Save the file and name it **4.3purorder**.
8. Close the file.

WHAT YOU NEED TO KNOW

Project

▶ The Gardens Hardware Shoppe is a retail store that obtains its merchandise from suppliers and/or wholesalers.

▶ When merchandise is purchased for resale, there is no state sales tax collected.

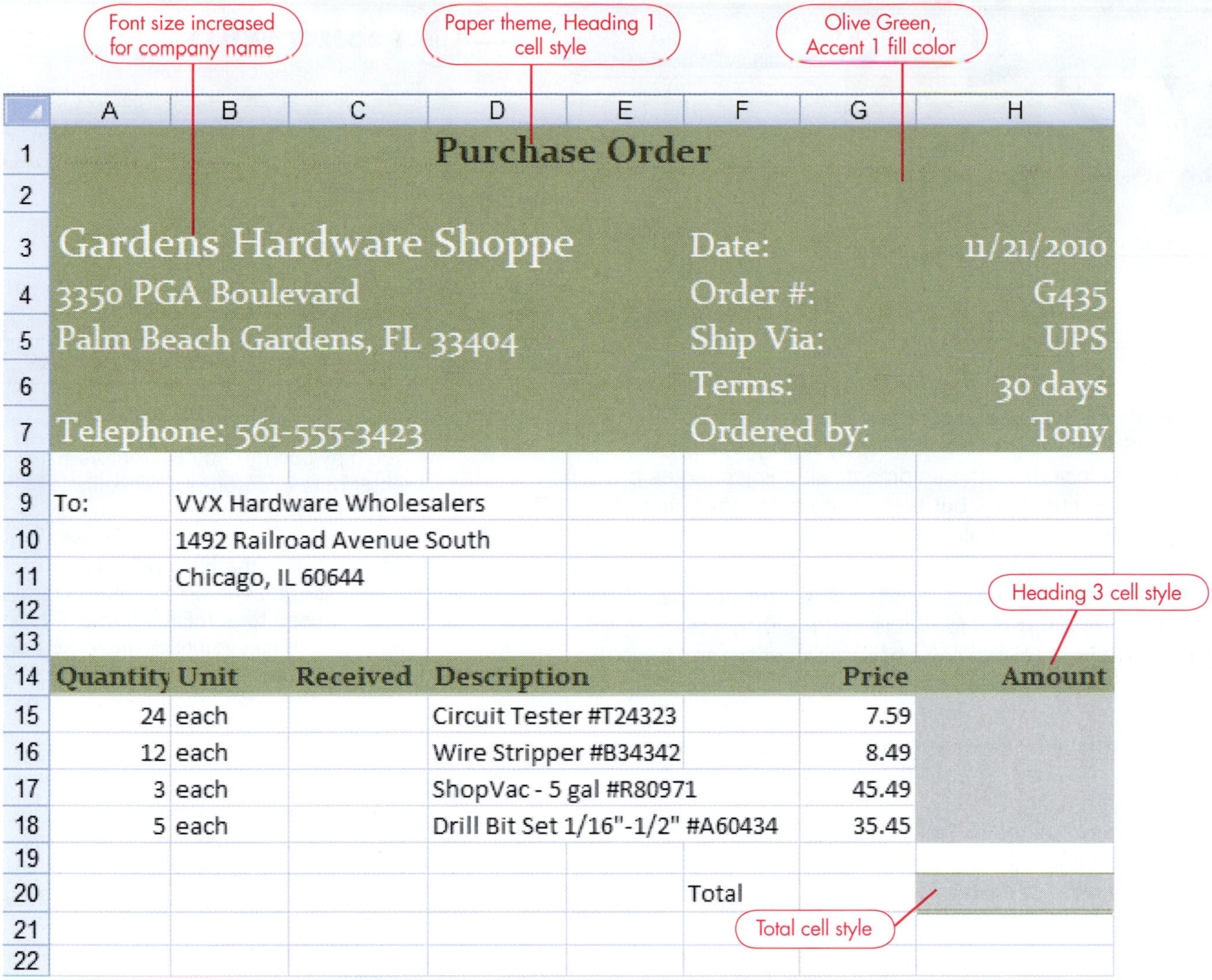

Font size increased for company name

Paper theme, Heading 1 cell style

Olive Green, Accent 1 fill color

	A	B	C	D	E	F	G	H
1				Purchase Order				
2								
3	Gardens Hardware Shoppe					Date:		11/21/2010
4	3350 PGA Boulevard					Order #:		G435
5	Palm Beach Gardens, FL 33404					Ship Via:		UPS
6						Terms:		30 days
7	Telephone: 561-555-3423					Ordered by:		Tony
8								
9	To:	VVX Hardware Wholesalers						
10		1492 Railroad Avenue South						
11		Chicago, IL 60644						
12								
13								
14	Quantity	Unit		Received	Description		Price	Amount
15	24	each			Circuit Tester #T24323		7.59	
16	12	each			Wire Stripper #B34342		8.49	
17	3	each			ShopVac - 5 gal #R80971		45.49	
18	5	each			Drill Bit Set 1/16"-1/2" #A60434		35.45	
19								
20						Total		
21								
22								

Heading 3 cell style

Total cell style

Figure 4.3

PROJECT SKILLS

✶ Use the AutoFill feature
✶ Create a custom cell style
✶ Adjust column width and row height
✶ Change print settings
✶ Save as a PDF file

5.1 CREATE A SALES INVOICE

BSK Shoes, Inc. has assembled the order placed by Sport Shoes Unlimited and needs you to prepare an invoice to include in the shipment. Shipping charges are paid by the customer, but there is no sales tax because the shoes will be resold.

> **In this project, you will create a sales invoice, use AutoFill to enter the formulas and repetitive text, create a customized cell style, then center and print it in landscape mode.**

1. Open a new Excel workbook and enter the information to create the invoice illustrated in Figure 5.1.
2. Set the theme to Trek.
3. Format row 1 as shown in Figure 5.1, and save the format as a customized cell style. Click the Home tab, and in the Styles group, click the Cell Styles button, then click New Cell Style. Name the style **Header**.
4. Format the remaining text as shown, including bold and alignment settings, and apply the new Header cell style to rows 7 and 16.
5. After entering the description for the first item, use the AutoFill feature to copy it down to the next two items.
6. Adjust column width, as necessary.
7. Enter the formula in L17 to calculate the Amount and use the AutoFill feature to copy the formula down to the next three items. Enter the Subtotal formula in L22.
8. Use the spell check feature to proof the invoice text.
9. Add shipping charges of $75.00, and enter a formula to calculate the total in L26. Apply the Total cell style and the Accounting Number format. Format all other numbers for Number format.
10. Change the print settings to center the invoice horizontally on the page and to print in landscape mode.

WHAT YOU NEED TO KNOW

Software

▶ You may use the AutoFill feature to enter data in a series. For example, if you are numbering rows, you only need to enter the first two numbers and then drag the fill handle down to complete the series. This feature may also be used to AutoFill a formula down a column. When you click and drag the fill handle in the bottom-right corner of the cell, the formula will be copied to the cells selected in the range below.

▶ You may create a custom cell style by formatting the cell with the desired fonts and colors. On the Home tab, click the Cell Styles button, then click New Cell Style in the Cell Styles gallery. When the format settings are displayed on the Style dialog box, you can name and save the style for future use. Your custom cell style will appear at the top of the Cell Styles gallery.

▶ If values are too large for a cell, number signs (###) will appear. To size a column to fit the longest entry in the column, double-click the vertical line between column headings, or select the column, right-click, then click Column Width on the shortcut menu to enter the desired width. The row height adjusts to the font size but may be modified in the same manner as the column width.

▶ To center the worksheet horizontally and/or vertically, click the Page Layout tab, and in the Page Setup group, click the Margins button. Click Custom Margins, and make the settings on the Page Setup dialog box. Use the Page Orientation button in the Page Setup group to set the landscape printing mode.

Continued on next page

11. Print a copy of the invoice.
12. Save the file and name it **5.1salesinv**.
13. Close the file.

Project

▶ A sales invoice is a bill that a seller prepares and sends to a customer for merchandise supplied. It contains a detailed description of the items sold, the terms of the sale, and the purchase order number.

▶ Sales tax and shipping may be added to the total amount of an invoice. The tax rate depends on the state and may not be charged if the goods are purchased for the purpose of resale or if the customer is tax-exempt.

Orange, Accent 6, Darker 25% fill color, Britannic Bold, 10 point, White font color

Orange, Accent 6, Lighter 40%

Britannic Bold, 24 point

Britannic Bold, 12 point

Apply custom Header style

Calibri, 11 point

Total cell style

Enter formulas and shipping charges in grey area

	A	B	C	D	E	F	G	H	I	J	K	L
1							Sales Invoice					
2												
3						BSK Shoes, Inc.						
4						1200 Russell Street						
5						Detroit, MI 48211						
6					Telephone: 315-555-5454 Fax: 315-555-5456							
7												
8												
9	Sold To:											
10												
11	Sports Shoes Unlimited					Date:		12/5/2010		Ship Via:		UPS
12	2995 East Lafayette Blvd					Invoice #:		G34235		Sales Rep:		Barry
13	Detroit, MI 48203					Terms:		30 days		Order #:		980
14												
15												
16	Quantity	Unit		Style No.	Description			Sizes		Color	Price	Amount
17	3	each		#AD2765	Men's Pro Model			9.5M		Blue/Silver	49.90	
18	2	each		#AD2765	Men's Pro Model			10M		Blue/Silver	49.90	
19	2	each		#AD2765	Men's Pro Model			10.5M		Blue/Silver	49.90	
20	1	dozen		#NB4433	Women's Speed/Air			Mixed		White	450.00	
21												
22										Subtotal		
23										Tax		
24										Shipping		
25												
26										Total		
27												

Figure 5.1

VVX Hardware Wholesalers has decided to modify and enhance its invoice form. They want you to save it in Excel and then as a PDF file so that it can be sent to their sales staff to inform them of the new layout. They have received and filled the purchase order sent by Gardens Hardware Shoppe in Florida and need you to create an invoice for that sale.

In this project, you will create a sales invoice form, save it as a PDF file, and then use the Excel file to create an invoice from the data provided on the purchase order.

1. Create an invoice using Figure 5.2a, shown on the facing page, as a guide. Set the invoice to print in landscape mode. You may develop your own formats for the form. Save it as **5.2salesinv**. Also, save the file as a PDF file.

2. Figure 5.2 provides a sample invoice format and the purchase order from Gardens Hardware Shoppe. The sale was made by Carl at VVX Hardware Wholesalers, the date of the invoice is 11/23/2010, the invoice number is 43234, the merchandise is to be shipped via UPS, and the terms are 30 days. Use this information and the details from the purchase order in Figure 5.2b, to create the invoice for VVX Hardware Wholesalers' sale to the Gardens Hardware Shoppe.

3. The shipping on the order is $98, and there is no sales tax.

4. Print a copy of the invoice in landscape mode, centered horizontally. Save the file as a PDF file.

5. Save and close the file.

WHAT YOU NEED TO KNOW

Software

▶ A file saved in PDF (Portable Document Format) cannot be changed easily. Therefore, you can use this format to e-mail a worksheet without the risk of the recipient tampering with the data. It can only be viewed if Acrobat Reader is installed on the computer. To save a file in PDF, click the Office Button, point to Save As, and then click PDF or XPS. You may have to click Other Formats in the Save As gallery to add PDF or XPS to the Save As list. If this is not possible, eliminate that part of the project.

Sales Invoice

	A	B	C	D	E	F	G	H	I	J	K
1						Sales Invoice					
2											
3					**VVX Hardware Wholesalers**						
4					1492 Railroad Avenue South						
5					Chicago, IL 60644						
6					Telephone: 321-555-4532 Fax: 312-555-4533						
7											
8											
9	Sold To:										
10											
11					Date:				Ship Via:		
12					Invoice #:				Sales Rep:		
13					Terms:				Order #:		
14											
15											
16	Quantity	Unit		Style No.	Description					Price	Amount
17											
18											
19											
20											
21										Total	
22										Tax	
23										Shipping	
24											
25										Total	
26											

Figure 5.2a Sample invoice

Purchase Order

	A	B	C	D	E	F	G	H
1				**Purchase Order**				
2								
3	Gardens Hardware Shoppe					Date:		11/21/2010
4	3350 PGA Boulevard					Order #:		G435
5	Palm Beach Gardens, FL 33404					Ship Via:		UPS
6						Terms:		30 days
7	Telephone: 561-555-3423					Ordered by:		Tony
8								
9	To:	VVX Hardware Wholesalers						
10		1492 Railroad Avenue South						
11		Chicago, IL 60644						
12								
13								
14	Quantity	Unit		Received	Description		Price	Amount
15	24	each			Circuit Tester #T24323		7.59	182.16
16	12	each			Wire Stripper #B34342		8.49	101.88
17	3	each			ShopVac - 5 gal #R80971		45.49	136.47
18	5	each			Drill Bit Set 1/16"-1/2" #A60434		35.45	177.25
19								
20						Total	$	597.76
21								

Figure 5.2b Purchase order

PROJECT SKILLS
✴ Clear cell data
✴ Work with templates
✴ Save a file as a template
✴ Work with templates from Microsoft Office Online

6.1 CREATE AND USE A SALES INVOICE TEMPLATE

BSK Shoes, Inc. would like you to use their existing invoice to create an invoice template and then use the template to bill a sale to Greyson's Sporting Goods.

In this project, you will use an existing sales invoice and customize it as a template, save it as a template, and create an invoice from the template.

1. Open your solution to **5.1salesinv** or data file **d6.1salesinv**.
2. Clear all the cells that relate to the specific sale to Sports Shoes Unlimited, including the items sold and the shipping charges. Leave the formulas in Column L.
3. Save the file as a template, as shown in Figure 6.1a, and name it **6.1BSKinv**. *The template file will be saved under My templates and will be available on the New Workbook dialog box. To save the file in your solutions folder, change the Save in location before saving the file.* Close the file.
4. Open your template using the New from existing selection in the New dialog box.
5. Modify the template with the customer and sales information detailed below, and from the customer's purchase order **d6.1purorder**, as shown in Figure 6.1b.
   a. Because the purchase order was mailed, the actual invoice date is 12/10/2010. The sales rep was Marty, and the invoice number is G34295.
   b. Use the AutoFill feature when possible to copy descriptions.
   c. Shipping on the order is $85, and there is no sales tax.
   d. You may have to adjust column width for the total to display the larger font format.
6. Save the file and name it **6.1BSKGreysons**.
7. Close the file.

WHAT YOU NEED TO KNOW

Software

▶ When you clear data from cells that are used in a formula, the answer in the formula cell will be cleared, but the formula will remain. If you are creating a template, a model worksheet design that will remain intact after each use, take care not to clear or delete entries in a formula cell.

▶ To save a file as a template, select Excel Template from the Save as type list. The new template can then be found under My templates in the New Workbook dialog box. To open a template and use it to create a new form, click the Office Button, select New, click New from existing, then select your template. The template will open with a 1 following the name so that the original template will remain as a blank form.

Figure 6.1a BSK Shoes, Inc. template

	A	B	C	D	E	F	G	H	I	J	K	L
1							Sales Invoice					
2												
3					**BSK Shoes, Inc.**							
4					1200 Russell Street							
5					Detroit, MI 48211							
6					Telephone: 315-555-5454 Fax: 315-555-5456							
7												
8												
9	Sold To:											
10												
11						Date:				Ship Via:		
12						Invoice #:				Sales Rep:		
13						Terms:				Order #:		
14												
15												
16	Quantity	Unit	Style No.	Description				Sizes		Color	Price	Amount
17												0.00
18												0.00
19												0.00
20												0.00
21												
22										Subtotal		0.00
23										Tax		0.00
24										Shipping		
25												
26										Total		$ –
27												
28												
29												

Zeros or dashes indicate that formulas are still in these cells

Figure 6.1b Customer's purchase order

	A	B	C	D	E	F	G	H	I	J	K	L
1							Purchase Order					
2					**Greyson's Sporting Goods**							
3					2125 Front Street							
4					Burlington, NC 27217							
5					336-555-5112							
6												
7												
8												
9	To:		BSK Shoes, Inc.						Date:		12/6/2010	
10			1200 Russell Street						Order #:		5499	
11			Detroit, MI 48211						Ship Via:		DHL	
12									Terms:		20 days	
13			Telephone: 315-555-5454						Ordered by:		Bob	
14												
15												
16	Quantity	Unit	Received	Style No.	Description				Sizes	Color	Price	Amount
17	1	dozen		7314545	Women's Soccer, Adonza, Volara III				Mixed	White	432.00	432.00
18	4	each		7332121	Men's Soccer, Diamora, Danza Classic				7	Black	29.50	118.00
19	4	each		7332122	Men's Soccer, Diamora, Danza Classic				7.5	Black	29.50	118.00
20	1	dozen		7332123	Men's Soccer, Diamora, Danza Classic				Mixed	Black	348.00	348.00
21												
22										Total		1016.00
23												

6.2 USE A TIME CARD TEMPLATE

Christopher Dillinger works off site as a computer network technician for Milky Way Networks, providing customer service on the networks his company has installed. He must keep a record of his hours, and you have been asked to prepare a time card of his hours.

In this project, you will create a record of the hours an employee works using an Excel time card template.

1. Click the Office Button, click New, and click Installed Templates. Select the Time Card template from the Installed Templates pane, and then click Create.
2. Customize the template by entering the information requested for the range B7:H16, excluding the date and including the salary rate information at the bottom of the form in D29:E29.
   Employee: Christopher Dillinger
   Address: 2546 Union Street
   City, ST, ZIP Code: Brooklyn, NY 11215
   Manager: Marietta Valetta
   Employee phone: 212-555-6454
   Employee e-mail: Dillinger@milkyway.net
   Rate per hour (Regular Hours): 15.00
   Rate per hour (Overtime): 22.50
3. Save the form as a template, and name it **6.2timecard**. Close the file.
4. Open the template and enter the following data for the week ending July 9, 2010. Note that July 4 is a paid holiday.
   Week ending 7/9/2010
   Monday 7/3: 8 hours
   Tuesday 7/4: Paid holiday *Note: Employee receives pay for 8 regular hours.*
   Wednesday 7/5: 12 hours (8 regular hours, 4 overtime hours)
   Thursday 7/6: 8 hours
   Friday 7/7: 11 hours (8 regular hours, 3 overtime hours)
5. Save the time card and name it **6.2time7-9**.
6. Close the file.

WHAT YOU NEED TO KNOW

Software

▶ Excel includes several templates with the software that contain formats, formulas, and font styles. Click the Office Button, click New, then click Installed Templates to view the templates provided with your software.

Project

▶ In some companies, employees keep a record of their hours using a time card. There may be a time clock that records the hour in and the hour out. In the case of professional service businesses or companies where employees work off site, employees may have to keep their own time records and submit them for payroll processing.

	A	B	C	D	E	F	G	H
1								Time Card
2								
3								
4								
5								
6								
7		Employee	Christopher Dillinger			Manager:	Marietta Valetta	
8								
9		[Street Address]	2546 Union Street			Employee phone:	212-555-6454	
10								
11		[Address 2]				Employee e-mail:	dillinger@milkyway.net	
12								
13		[City, ST ZIP Code]	Brooklyn, NY 11215					
14								
15								
16		Week ending:	7/9/2010					
17								
18								
19								

Day	Date	Regular Hours	Overtime	Sick	Vacation	Total
Monday	7/3/2010	8.00				8.00
Tuesday	7/4/2010	8.00			Paid Holiday	8.00
Wednesday	7/5/2010	8.00	4.00			12.00
Thursday	7/6/2010	8.00				8.00
Friday	7/7/2010	8.00	3.00			11.00
Saturday	7/8/2010					
Sunday	7/9/2010					
Total hours		40.00	7.00			47.00
Rate per hour		$ 15.00	$ 22.50			
Total pay		$ 600.00	$ 157.50	$ –	$ –	$ 757.50

Employee signature   Date

Manager signature   Date

Figure 6.2

6.3 USE A SALES INVOICE TEMPLATE

Office Supplies Warehouse is preparing an invoice using an Excel template. You are to customize a sales invoice template obtained from Microsoft Office Online and complete an invoice for supplies sold to Sports Shoes Unlimited per its purchase order number 981 in Project 4.2B.

In this project, you will download and customize a sales invoice template from Microsoft Office Online, save it as a template, and create an invoice from the template.

1. If necessary, establish an Internet connection. Click the Office Button, then click New.
2. In the New Workbook dialog box, click Invoices under the Microsoft Office Online list of templates. Download the Sales invoice with tax and shipping and handling calculations. Click Continue to accept software validation.
3. The contact information for Office Supplies Warehouse is:

   765 Industry Street
   Detroit, MI 48211
   313-555-8121   Fax: 313-555-8122
4. Enter the company information at the top of the invoice and the company slogan, `Just ask us, we have it!`
5. At the bottom of the invoice, change the sales tax rate to 6% and enter the following comment:
   `If you have any questions about this invoice, please contact Kevin Rannie at 313-555-8125, or Krannie@OSW.com.`
6. Save the invoice as a template, and name it **6.30SWinv**. Close the file.
7. Create an invoice for the sale to Sports Shoes Unlimited on 12/6/2010, using invoice number 2435. Use the information from the purchase order created in Project 4.2. Maria Cortez was the sales rep who handled this sale, and the merchandise will be shipped on the sale date by UPS.
8. Delete the sales tax rate since this is a wholesale transaction, and add shipping charges of $18.00.
9. Save the invoice as an Excel file, and name it **6.30SWsportsshoes**.
10. Close the file.

WHAT YOU NEED TO KNOW

Software

▶ If you need to create a business form or analysis, or a model for any application that is not available in the installed templates group, you may find a template for it in the Microsoft Office Online listings, which are on Microsoft.com. Click the Office Button, then click New, and, under Microsoft Office Online, select the type of template you need. You will be connected to the site and provided with a selection of templates within that category. When you select a template, you may download it and customize it as desired. Microsoft will validate your software before allowing a download.

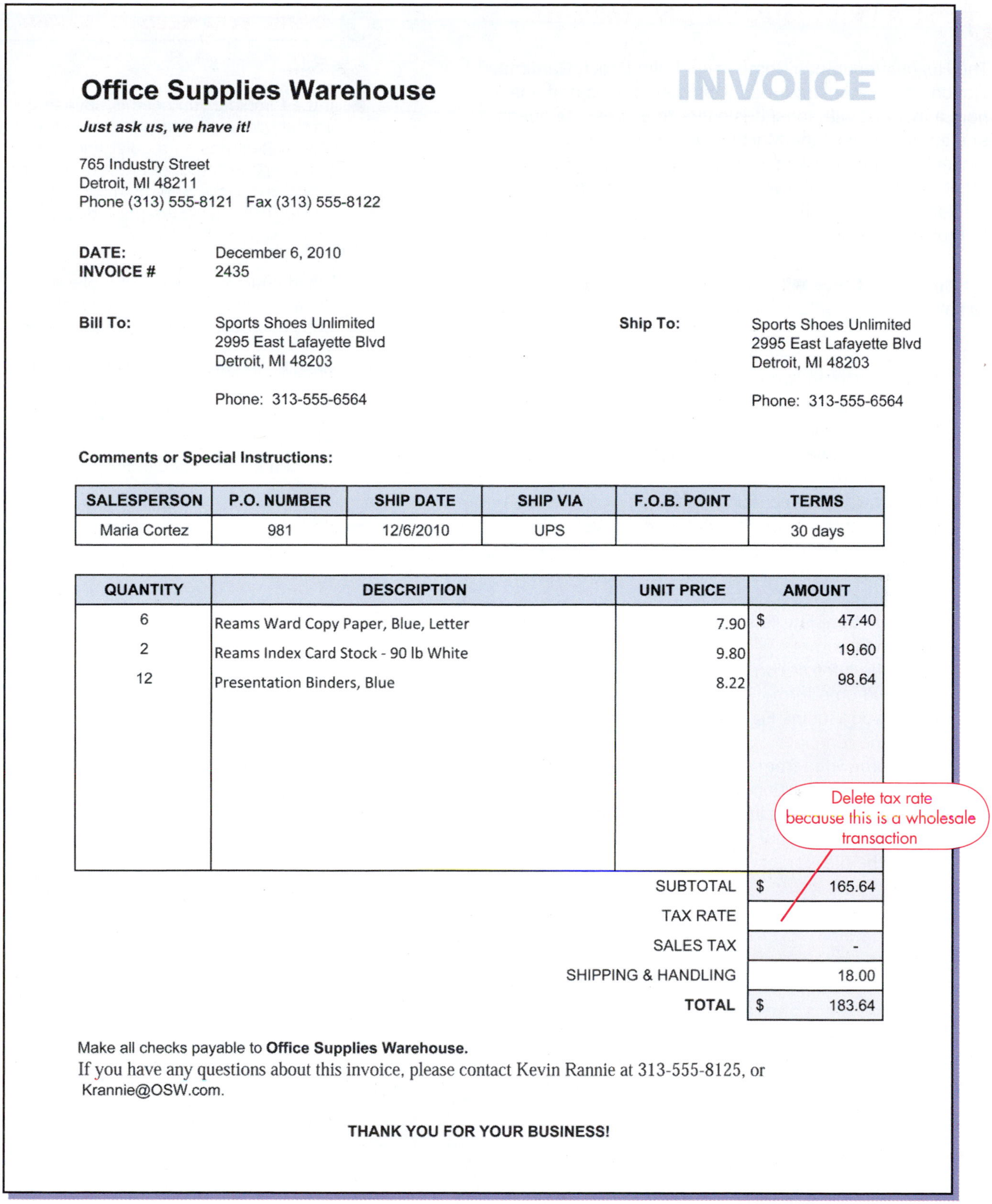

Office Supplies Warehouse

INVOICE

Just ask us, we have it!

765 Industry Street
Detroit, MI 48211
Phone (313) 555-8121   Fax (313) 555-8122

DATE: December 6, 2010
INVOICE #   2435

Bill To:	Sports Shoes Unlimited 2995 East Lafayette Blvd Detroit, MI 48203 Phone: 313-555-6564	Ship To:	Sports Shoes Unlimited 2995 East Lafayette Blvd Detroit, MI 48203 Phone: 313-555-6564

Comments or Special Instructions:

SALESPERSON	P.O. NUMBER	SHIP DATE	SHIP VIA	F.O.B. POINT	TERMS
Maria Cortez	981	12/6/2010	UPS		30 days

QUANTITY	DESCRIPTION	UNIT PRICE	AMOUNT
6	Reams Ward Copy Paper, Blue, Letter	7.90	$ 47.40
2	Reams Index Card Stock - 90 lb White	9.80	19.60
12	Presentation Binders, Blue	8.22	98.64

Delete tax rate because this is a wholesale transaction

SUBTOTAL	$ 165.64
TAX RATE	
SALES TAX	-
SHIPPING & HANDLING	18.00
TOTAL	$ 183.64

Make all checks payable to **Office Supplies Warehouse.**
If you have any questions about this invoice, please contact Kevin Rannie at 313-555-8125, or
Krannie@OSW.com.

THANK YOU FOR YOUR BUSINESS!

Figure 6.3

6.4 USE A PRICE QUOTATION TEMPLATE

The Hughes Insurance Company in Palm Beach Gardens, Florida, is updating and redesigning its offices and has held a meeting with local designers to express its needs and gather ideas. Jane Martino, who has an interior design business in West Palm Beach, attended the meeting and would like you to prepare a price quotation for decorating the offices of the Hughes Insurance Company.

In this project, you will create a price quotation using a template from Microsoft Office Online.

1. If necessary, establish an Internet connection.
2. Click the Office Button, click New, and in the New Workbook dialog box, click More categories under the Microsoft Office Online templates list. Select Quotes and then select the Price quotation without tax template.
3. Click Download and save the file as a template on your computer; name it **6.4quotation**. *Note: If the template does not display properly, click the View tab, and in the Window group, click the Arrange All button and OK.*
4. After the template is saved, you may disconnect from the Internet.
5. Enter the information that Jane Martino, Interiors will need on a form without specific customer information, using Figure 6.4 as a guide. Save and close the template.
6. Open a new file from the template and add the customer information shown in Figure 6.4. *Note: Enter comment text in cells C16 and C17.*
7. Save the file and name it **6.4quoteHughes**.
8. Close the file.

▼ WHAT YOU NEED TO KNOW

Software

▶ If the template you need is not listed on the Microsoft Office Online list, click More categories on the list and find the template there, or enter the search string text in the Search Microsoft Office Online for a template box.

Project

▶ When businesses want to make a large purchase, they may request price quotations from several vendors. The vendor or seller prepares the price quotation and sends it to the interested buyer. The buyer will compare all the quotations and decide which vendor to use for the job.

▶ You can find a template for price quotations on Microsoft Office Online under More categories.

Jane Martino, Interiors

Classic Design

4323 Graystone Street
West Palm Beach, FL 33414
Phone (561) 555-4342 Fax (561) 555-4343

Bill To:
Martin Hughes
Hughes Insurance Company
4334 Northgate Boulevard
Palm Beach Gardens, FL 33410
(561) 555-5444

Quotation

DATE	July 10, 2010
Quotation #	5342
Customer ID	1232

Quotation valid until:	August 10, 2010
Prepared by:	Jane Martino

Comments or special instructions: The estimates for furnishings and accessories are mid-range selections that fit the design concept. Your choices may change these estimates.

Description	AMOUNT
Renderings: For reception area and business offices	$850.00
Furnishings: For reception area and business offices	14,950.00
Accessories: Paintings, sculpture, etc.	5,300.00
Flooring: Tile and carpeting	12,650.00
Windows: Treatments and coverings	4,850.00
TOTAL	$ 38,600.00

If you have any questions, contact Jane Martino, 561-555-4342, jmartino@design.com

THANK YOU FOR YOUR BUSINESS!

Figure 6.4

CHAPTER 3

Create Accounting Records

In this chapter, you will complete the following projects:

PROJECT 7
Ledger Accounts and Statements
PROJECT 7.1 Create an Accounts Receivable Ledger Account
PROJECT 7.2 Create an Accounts Payable Ledger Account
PROJECT 7.3 Create a Statement of Account

PROJECT 8
Payroll
PROJECT 8.1 Create a Payroll
PROJECT 8.2 Use a Payroll Template and Internet Tax Calculators

PROJECT 9
Journals
PROJECT 9.1 Create a Sales Journal
PROJECT 9.2 Create a Purchase Journal
PROJECT 9.3 Create a Check Register and Payments Journal

PROJECT 10
Asset Records
PROJECT 10.1 Create a Petty Cash Register
PROJECT 10.2 Create an Asset Record
PROJECT 10.3 Create an Aging Report

PROJECT 7

▶ **PROJECT SKILLS**

✱ Apply and clear formulas
✱ Apply and clear number formats
✱ Cut, copy, and paste data
✱ Copy and paste between open workbooks

7.1 CREATE AN ACCOUNTS RECEIVABLE LEDGER ACCOUNT

BSK Shoes, Inc. is a shoe wholesaler. They would like you to prepare an accounts receivable ledger account for one of their customers, Greyson's Sporting Goods.

In this project, you will create an accounts receivable ledger account using formatting tools and formulas.

1. Open a new Excel workbook and create and format the account shown in Figure 7.1.
   a. Use the Merge & Center button for the top row title, and apply Accent1 cell style.
   b. Apply the 40% - Accent1 cell style to the account name section, and apply bolding as shown.
   c. Apply the Accent1 cell style to the column headings.
   d. Enter a formula in cell G8 to calculate the balance after the first charge. *Hint: =E8.*
   e. Enter a formula in cell G9 to calculate the balance, beginning with the previous balance in cell G8, adding charges and subtracting credits. *Hint: Old Balance + Charges - Credits.* You can use the selection method to enter the formula.
   f. Use the AutoFill feature to copy the formula in cell G9 to cells G10:G11.
   g. Select all number values in E8:G11 and use the Increase Decimal button to add two decimal places to each number.
   h. Clear all number formats by selecting the same range, and then selecting General format from the Number Format gallery on the Home tab.
   i. Use the Comma Style button to format all the numbers.
2. Save the file and name it **7.1ar**.
3. Close the file.

Software

▶ You can input a formula by entering the symbols and cell addresses. Or, you can enter the symbols and select the cell addresses as they appear in the formula. Selecting the cell addresses minimizes the possibility of entry errors. The answer to a formula appears in the cell, and the formula itself appears in the formula bar.

▶ You can clear formats by using the Undo button or by reformatting the cells to General format on the Number Format gallery on the Home tab.

▶ You can apply number formats for ledger accounts using the Increase Decimal, Decrease Decimal, and Comma Style buttons on the Mini toolbar, or use the tools on the Home tab in the Number group.

Project

▶ Accounts receivable ledger accounts show the increases and decreases in customers' accounts. Sales are entered as charges, and returns or payments that reduce the balance are entered as credits. Customer accounts are considered assets because the business owns the right to collect the funds.

▶ Entries in an account are based on business forms, such as invoices, credit memos, and cash receipts. Transactions are recorded first in a journal and then in the ledger accounts. Notice, as shown in Figure 7.1, that accounts receivable account data comes from the sales, sales returns, and cash receipts journals.

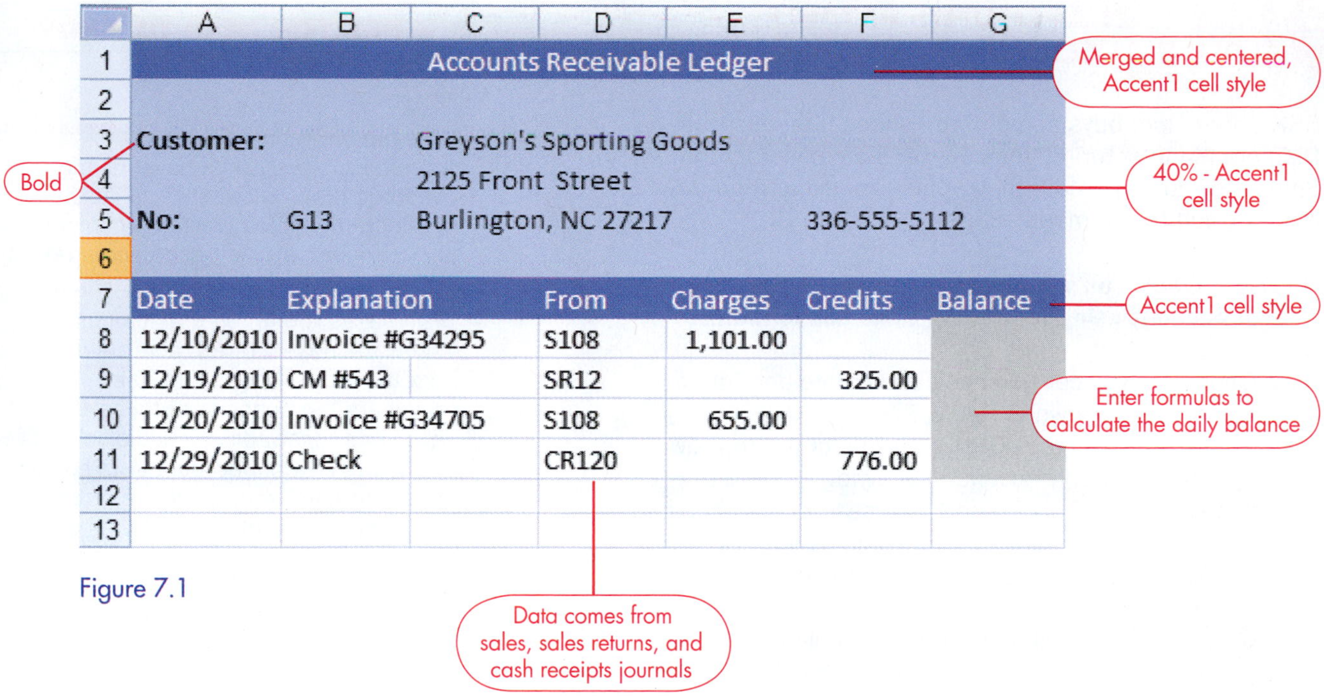

	A	B	C	D	E	F	G
1			Accounts Receivable Ledger				
2							
3	**Customer:**			Greyson's Sporting Goods			
4				2125 Front Street			
5	**No:**		G13	Burlington, NC 27217		336-555-5112	
6							
7	Date	Explanation		From	Charges	Credits	Balance
8	12/10/2010	Invoice #G34295		S108	1,101.00		
9	12/19/2010	CM #543		SR12		325.00	
10	12/20/2010	Invoice #G34705		S108	655.00		
11	12/29/2010	Check		CR120		776.00	
12							
13							

Callouts:
- Bold (pointing to Customer: and No:)
- Merged and centered, Accent1 cell style (pointing to row 1)
- 40% - Accent1 cell style (pointing to rows 3-5 area)
- Accent1 cell style (pointing to row 7 headers)
- Enter formulas to calculate the daily balance (pointing to Balance column)
- Data comes from sales, sales returns, and cash receipts journals (pointing to From column)

Figure 7.1

7.2 CREATE AN ACCOUNTS PAYABLE LEDGER ACCOUNT

BSK Shoes, Inc. buys some of the shoes it resells from Diamora Manufacturing Company, a shoe manufacturer. Since they buy on credit, they would like you to record the money owed to the manufacturer.

In this project, you will create an accounts payable ledger account using formatting tools and formulas.

1. Open a new Excel workbook and create and format the account shown in Figure 7.2.
   a. Use the Merge & Center button for the top row title and apply Accent2 cell style.
   b. Apply the 20% - Accent1 cell style to the account name section and apply bolding as shown.
   c. Apply the Accent2 cell style to the column headings.
   d. Enter a formula in cell G8 to calculate the balance after the first credit. *Hint: =F8.*
   e. Enter a formula in cell G9 to calculate the balance beginning with the previous balance in cell G8, adding credits and subtracting debits. *Hint: Old Balance + Credits – Debits.*
   f. Use the AutoFill feature to copy the formula in cell G9 to cells G10:G11.
   g. Use the Comma Style button to format all numbers.
2. Save the file and name it **7.2ap**.
3. Close the file.

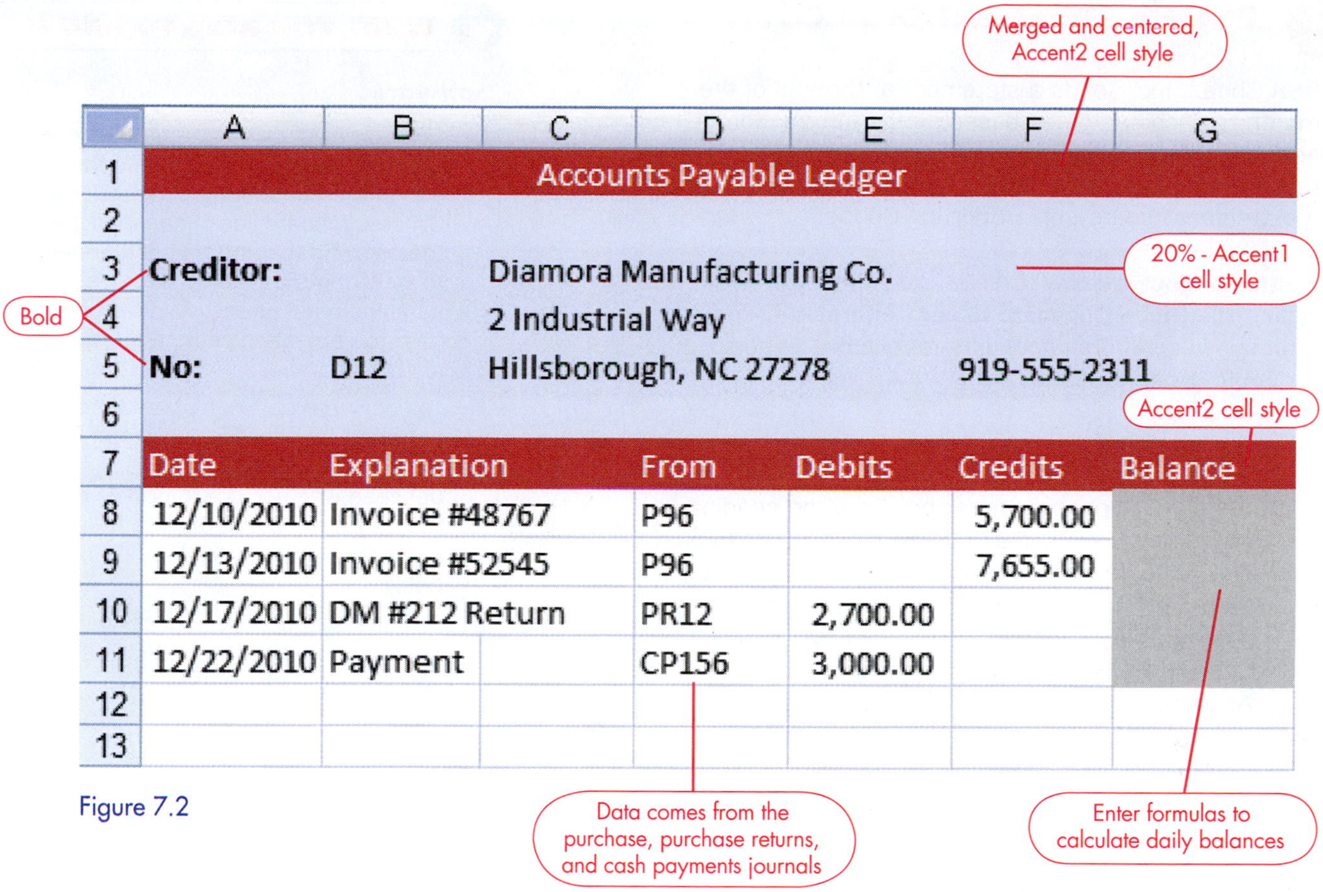

Merged and centered, Accent2 cell style

20% - Accent1 cell style

Bold

Accent2 cell style

	A	B	C	D	E	F	G
1	Accounts Payable Ledger						
2							
3	**Creditor:**		Diamora Manufacturing Co.				
4			2 Industrial Way				
5	**No:**	D12	Hillsborough, NC 27278			919-555-2311	
6							
7	Date	Explanation	From		Debits	Credits	Balance
8	12/10/2010	Invoice #48767	P96			5,700.00	
9	12/13/2010	Invoice #52545	P96			7,655.00	
10	12/17/2010	DM #212 Return	PR12		2,700.00		
11	12/22/2010	Payment	CP156		3,000.00		
12							
13							

Figure 7.2

Data comes from the purchase, purchase returns, and cash payments journals

Enter formulas to calculate daily balances

7.3 CREATE A STATEMENT OF ACCOUNT

BSK Shoes, Inc. sends a statement at the end of the month to each customer, based on the information in its accounts receivable account, to inform the customer of the balance due. The company has asked you to prepare a statement for Greyson's Sporting Goods.

In this project, you will create a statement of account, using the Office Clipboard to copy information from a sales invoice and an accounts receivable ledger account prepared earlier.

1. Open a new Excel workbook and open your solution to **6.1BSKGreysons** or open **d7.3BSKGreysons**.
2. Open the Clipboard task pane. Copy the heading from the Greysons file in the range A1:L7, and paste it into the new file. Unmerge the cells and remerge them over columns A:G. Clear the color from the range H1:L7 by setting the fill color to No Fill. Change the Sales Invoice title to **Statement of Account**, as shown in Figure 7.3.
3. Open **7.1ar**, saved earlier in Project 7.1, or open data file **d7.3ar**.
4. Copy the following: the address in the range C3:F5, the column headings in the range A7:G7, and the account information in the range A8:G11.
5. Switch to the statement of account using the Windows taskbar or the Switch Windows button on the View tab.
6. Add and format the text and use the Clipboard to select and paste the address, column headings, and account data, as shown. Close the Clipboard task pane.
7. Change the worksheet to the Trek theme.
8. Clear any unwanted color and format the column headings in the same manner as used for the title row (Orange, Accent 6, Darker 25% fill color with White font color).
9. Enter the statement date, 12/31/10, in cell B11 and any other text to complete the statement, as shown.
10. Enter **Balance Forward** in cell B19, as illustrated. Enter **0** in cell G19 and format it in Number format.
11. Adjust column width as necessary.
12. Save the file and name it **7.3statement**.
13. Close all three files.

WHAT YOU NEED TO KNOW

Software

▶ Copied data is stored temporarily on the Clipboard. Click the Home tab, and in the Clipboard group, click the Office Clipboard Task Pane launcher, the arrow in the bottom right corner, to view items as they are copied. The samples make it easy to select the data to copy when copying more than one range of cells.

▶ To copy data between open workbooks, use the worksheet file button on the Windows taskbar to switch between workbooks. Or, click the View tab, and in the Window group, click the Switch Windows button.

▶ To place all open worksheets on the screen at once, click the View tab, and in the Window group, click the Arrange All button and select the layout.

Project

▶ Account statements are bills sent to customers that show the activity in their accounts for the month and the balance due. The information for the statement comes from the customer's ledger account.

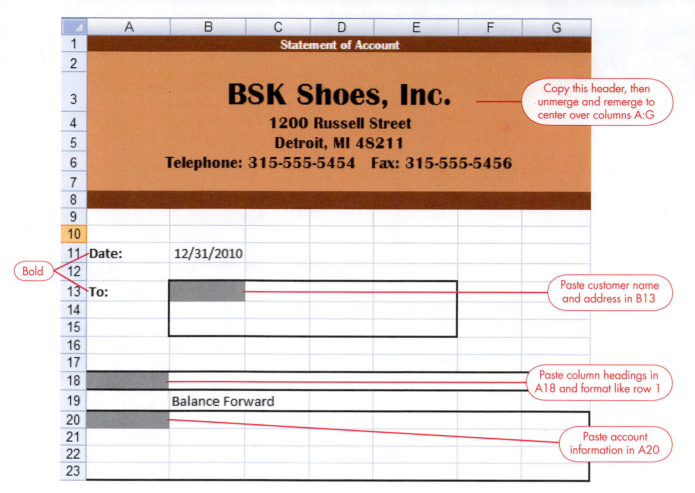

Bold

Copy this header, then unmerge and remerge to center over columns A:G

Paste customer name and address in B13

Paste column headings in A18 and format like row 1

Paste account information in A20

Figure 7.3

PROJECT 8

⏵ **PROJECT SKILLS**

✦ Summarize data using formulas
✦ Insert functions using the Insert Function button
✦ Use the Format Painter feature

8.1 CREATE A PAYROLL

Master Pavers, Inc. is an Arizona-based firm that installs walkways, patios, and pool decks. They need you to prepare a payroll register for the week of 8/9/2010-8/13/2010 with 8/15/2010 as the date of payment. Federal taxes are supplied from tax tables and there are no state payroll taxes in Arizona.

In this project, you will complete a payroll register using formulas, functions, Format Painter, and the AutoFill feature.

1. Open data file **d8.1payroll**.
2. Format the payroll register using cell styles, fill color, alignment, and border settings, as illustrated in Figure 8.1, adjusting column width as necessary.
3. Enter the Pay Period and Date of Payment labels in bold in Row 2.
4. Select the two employee numbers in A5:A6 and use the fill handle to create the series of numbers down to A11.
5. Enter the following formulas and, after each formula is created, use the fill handle to copy it to the appropriate locations:
   a. In cell G5, calculate Gross Pay by multiplying the Rate Per Hour by the number of Hours.
   b. In cell I5, calculate Social Security tax of 6.2% on Gross Pay.
   c. In cell J5, calculate Medicare tax of 1.45% on Gross Pay.
   d. In cell L5, calculate Total Deductions by adding the data in Cells H5:K5.
   e. In cell M5, calculate Net Pay by subtracting the deductions from Gross Pay.
6. Use the AutoSum function to find the Totals.
7. Format the Hours column in Number format.
8. Format G5:G11 in Comma style, and then click the Format Painter button twice. Apply the format to H5:M11. Press [Esc] to clear the Format Painter mode.

▼ WHAT YOU NEED TO KNOW

Software

⏵ To fill formulas horizontally across a row, use the AutoFill feature.

⏵ On the Home tab, in the Editing group, the AutoSum function drop-down list contains frequently used functions, such as Sum, Average, Max, Min, and Count Numbers.

⏵ You can also click the Insert Function (fx) button on the formula bar to insert functions in a formula. For example, you can insert the MEDIAN function, which finds the number that is in the middle of the list of numbers, using the Insert Function button.

⏵ Rather than making repeated formats, you can copy formats from one cell to another using the Format Painter button on the Home tab in the Clipboard group, or on the Mini toolbar that appears when you right-click a cell. When you are in Format Painter mode the cursor appears as a paintbrush. If you need to format more than one area, double-click the Format Painter button and apply the format as needed. Press [Esc] to exit Format Painter mode.

Project

⏵ A payroll register is used to calculate the salaries, taxes, and net pay for employees.

⏵ Federal and state withholding taxes vary, depending on the salary and the tax status of the employee. The tax status for each employee is shown in the Status column and combines the marital status and the number of dependents claimed. Thus, M3 means married with three dependents.

9. Apply the 40% - Accent3 cell style to the range E13:M13 and format in Total cell style. Format the totals for currency in bold.

10. Enter the functions to find the Average, Median, and Highest (Max) values in E15:E17. Use the AutoSum button arrow for the Average and Max functions. For the Median function, click the Insert Function button, and then select the Statistical category to find and enter the MEDIAN function. Copy formulas across to column M.

11. Use Format Painter to format summary totals appropriately. There should be no decimals in column F.

12. Print the payroll in landscape orientation.

13. Save the payroll and name it **8.1payroll**. Close the file.

Merged and centered, Accent3 cell style, black font, bold, 14 point, Bottom Double Border

60% - Accent3 cell style, black font, bold

Accent3 cell style, black font, Top and Bottom Border

	A	B	C	D	E	F	G	H	I	J	K	L	M
1							Payroll Register						
2	For Pay Period:		8/9/2010-8/13/2010								Date of Payment:		8/15/10
3	Employee				Rate Per		Gross	Federal	Social			Total	Net
4	Number	Status	Name		Hour	Hours	Pay	W.T.	Security	Medicare	Other	Ded.	Pay
5	107	M4	Baez, Thomas		12.75	40		16.00					
6	108	S0	Greaves, Martin		19.75	40		132.00			50.00		
7		S1	Jennings, Timothy		10.00	40		38.00					
8		S1	Ling, John		11.75	40		49.00					
9		M2	Montez, Carlos		13.33	36		25.00					
10		S2	Partridge, Grace		9.25	40		25.00					
11		M2	Warren, Denise		14.08	38		33.00			50.00		
12													
13			Totals										
14													
15			Average										
16			Median										
17			Highest										

Use fill handle to create number series

Use functions to find Average, Median, and Highest values

Use SUM function to find Totals

Calculate Gross Pay

Use tax rates to calculate taxes

Total cell style with 40% - Accent3 cell style

Calculate Total Deductions and Net Pay

Figure 8.1

8.2 USE A PAYROLL TEMPLATE AND INTERNET TAX CALCULATORS

Master Pavers, Inc. wants you to use the payroll register prepared earlier to create a template. You will then use the template to create the payroll for the week of 8/16/2010-8/20/2010. Find the federal taxes on a paycheck calculator Website.

In this project, you will create a payroll template, use it to create a payroll, and find the federal taxes on the Internet.

1. Open the **8.1payroll** file from the previous project or open data file **d8.2payroll**.
2. Prepare a payroll template by leaving all fixed information and formula cells intact and deleting variable data. You should delete the dates, and the Hours, Federal W.T., and Other deductions data, as indicated in Figure 8.2.
3. Save the file as a template, and name it **8.2paytemp**.
4. Use the template to calculate the payroll for 8/15/2010-8/19/2010, which will be paid on 8/22/2010. Enter the dates.
5. Enter the Hours, Federal W.T., and Other deductions for the week as follows:

NAME	HOURS	FEDERAL W.T.	OTHER
Baez, Thomas	38	6.91	
Greaves, Martin	40	118.21	50.00
Jennings, Timothy	38	32.37	12.50
Ling, John	36	38.82	
Montez, Carlos	40		12.50
Partridge, Grace	37		
Warren, Denise	35		50.00

6. Find the missing Federal W. T. entries on a paycheck calculator Website. You can use: www.paycheckcity.com.
   a. Select Personal Calculators, and then select Paycheck Calculator and select the tax year and the state (Arizona). Press [Tab] to move to each part of the calculation. For Montez, enter the Gross Pay, select Per Pay Period, and enter the Federal Filing Status (Married or Single) and the number of federal dependents' allowances (see Column B data). Click Calculate at the bottom of the page or press [Enter] after the last entry.
   b. Enter the Federal W.T. that appears on the Website into the payroll.
   c. Repeat this procedure for the other employees.
7. Save the payroll as an Excel Workbook and name it **8.2pay8.22**.
8. Close the file.

Software

► If you use the same worksheet often, save it as a template with the formats and formulas so that you need to change only the variable data. The worksheet created from a template should be saved with a new filename.

Project

► Federal and state taxes on gross pay must be looked up in current tables based on a taxpayer's marital status and the number of dependents claimed. You can find the taxes using paycheck calculator Websites, where you will input the state, marital status, number of dependents, and gross pay to get the correct taxes.

Delete all
variable data

	A	B	C	D	E	F	G	H	I	J	K	L	M
1							Payroll Register						
2	For Pay Period:									Date of Payment:			
3	Employee				Rate Per		Gross	Federal	Social			Total	Net
4	Number	Status	Name		Hour	Hours	Pay	W.T.	Security	Medicare	Other	Ded.	Pay
5	107	M4	Baez, Thomas		12.75		0.00		0.00	0.00		0.00	0.00
6	108	S0	Greaves, Martin		19.75		0.00		0.00	0.00		0.00	0.00
7	109	S1	Jennings, Timothy		10.00		0.00		0.00	0.00		0.00	0.00
8	110	S1	Ling, John		11.75		0.00		0.00	0.00		0.00	0.00
9	111	M2	Montez, Carlos		13.33		0.00		0.00	0.00		0.00	0.00
10	112	S2	Partridge, Grace		9.25		0.00		0.00	0.00		0.00	0.00
11	113	M2	Warren, Denise		14.08		0.00		0.00	0.00		0.00	0.00
12													
13			Totals		$90.91	0	$0.00	$0.00	$0.00	$0.00	$0.00	$0.00	$0.00
14													
15			Average		12.99	#DIV/0!	0.00	#DIV/0!	0.00	0.00	#DIV/0!	0.00	0.00
16			Median		12.75	#NUM!	0.00	#NUM!	0.00	0.00	#NUM!	0.00	0.00
17			Highest		19.75	0	0.00	0.00	0.00	0.00	0.00	0.00	0.00

Figure 8.2

Error messages
appear until data is entered
into the columns

PROJECT 9

* Understand the priority of mathematical operators
* Edit formulas on the formula bar
* Troubleshoot a formula
* Insert, view, edit, and delete cell comments
* Freeze and unfreeze rows and columns
* Print to fit page settings

9.1 CREATE A SALES JOURNAL

Sports Shoes Unlimited sells all types of sports shoes, skates, and accessories in a retail store. Most of their sales are for cash, but they do give credit terms to select customers. They would like to prepare a sales journal for the month of October. The sales tax rate in Detroit is 6% and it is collected from customers and paid later to the state. It is not collected from tax exempt organizations.

In this project, you will create a departmental sales journal, using formulas and functions, and cell borders.

1. Open data file **d9.1sales**.
2. Adjust column width as necessary, and use cell styles, cell borders, merge and center, font settings, and alignment features to match the formats in Figure 9.1. The cell styles are in the Accent3 color group.
3. Enter the remaining invoices for the month of October, per Figure 9.1. Use the fill handle for invoice numbers.
4. Enter a formula in cell E6 to find the sales tax on the total sale. The formula should use the AutoSum feature to add the sales from the departments in the range F6:H6, so that it is in parentheses, and then multiply the total by 6%. *Hint: =Sum(F6:H6)*6%.*
5. Press [F2] in the formula cell to view the formula in Edit mode. If it is correct, press [Enter] and use the fill handle to copy the formula.
6. Use the AutoSum feature to enter a formula in cell D6 that adds the taxes and all the sales values to find the Accounts Receivable Debit value, or the amount owed by each customer. Copy the formula for all items using the AutoFill feature.
7. The sales to both Central and Eastside High Schools are tax exempt. Delete the tax values for the three sales to these customers.
8. Use functions to find the totals, averages, and highest and lowest values for all columns.
9. Center the journal horizontally on the page, and print a copy.
10. Save the file and name it **9.1sales**.
11. Close the file.

WHAT YOU NEED TO KNOW

Software

▶ To enter formulas correctly, you should understand the priority of mathematical operators. The computer processes operators as follows: parenthetical items first, then exponents, then multiplication and division, and addition and subtraction last. Formulas are executed from left to right, in order of appearance, and by the priority order specified. Therefore, if you need to multiply or divide a total, put the calculation that yields the total in parentheses so that it will be done before the multiplication or division.

▶ Common formula errors are flagged by Excel, like spelling errors in Word, but errors in logic may not be picked up by the system. Excel will display a triangle in the top-left corner of a cell to indicate an error in a formula that does not follow formula rules. When you place your cursor near the triangle, a description of the error appears, and when you click the Smart Tag triangle you get possible solutions and help options.

▶ Double-click the formula or press [F2] to edit formulas. The arguments will be highlighted in color on the worksheet and on the formula bar. Once you are in Edit mode, you can backspace or drag the border of the range or cell to correct errors.

Project

▶ A sales journal is a record of the sales transactions made by a business to its customers. The business must collect sales taxes and later pay them to the state. The taxes, therefore, are debts of the business. The sale plus the tax is the amount due from the customer.

Continued on next page

▶ Some companies create a sales journal that records sales by departments to analyze the profitability of each department.

▶ In this project, formulas are used to calculate values in the journal. In practice, the figures would be calculated on the invoice and then copied to the journal.

Accent3 cell style, black font, 14 point, merged and centered as shown

40% - Accent3 cell style, borders as shown

	A	B	C	D	E	F	G	H
1				Sports Shoes Unlimited				
2	SALES JOURNAL							Page 56
3				Accounts	Sales	Sales Income, Credit		
4	Date	Invoice #	Customer	Receivable	Taxes			
5				Debit	Payable	Shoes	Skates	Accessories
6	10/1/2010	B2323	Sam Norris			545		
7	10/3/2010	B2324	Helen Keegan				210	65
8	10/6/2010	B2325	Shirley Millar			1,198	345	55
9	10/6/2010	B2326	Gloria Ross			436		145
10	10/7/2010	B2327	Central H.S.			1,032	142	85
11	10/9/2010	B2328	Sam Norris				155	55
12	10/11/2010	B2329	Eastside H.S.			1,545		230
13	10/14/2010	B2330	Helen Keegan			925		
14	10/15/2010	B2331	Arthur Wilson				335	125
15	10/17/2010	B2332	Shirley Millar			589	189	25
16	10/21/2010	B2333	Lamar Jackson				443	56
17	10/24/2010	B2334	Peter Williams			325.85		156.86
18	10/25/2010	B2335	Frank Perez				456.76	
19	10/28/2010	B2336	Central H.S.			1,087.95		
20	10/29/2010	B2337	Wendy Kingsley				325.98	125.69
21	10/31/2010	B2338	Lamar Jackson					145.99
22								
23	Totals							
24								
25	Average Sale							
26	Highest Sale							
27	Lowest Sale							

Add total departmental sales

Enter a formula to multiply the total departmental sales by 6%

Add new sales

Figure 9.1

Use SUM function to find Totals

Use function to find Average, Highest, and Lowest Sale values

9.2 CREATE A PURCHASE JOURNAL

Sports Shoes Unlimited buys on credit the merchandise it resells. Purchase orders and invoices are used as a basis for purchase journal entries. They have asked you to prepare a departmental purchase journal and complete entries for the month of December.

In this project, you will create a purchase journal using formatting, Format Painter, and the cell comment feature.

1. Open data file **d9.2purch**.
2. Use cell styles, cell borders, merge and center, font settings, and alignment features to match the formats in Figure 9.2.
3. Enter the remaining purchase invoices for the month of December, as shown in rows 14:16.
4. Enter a formula in cell D6 to find the total of all departmental purchases, including the shipping charges. Use the fill handle to copy down the formula.
5. Use functions to find the totals, averages, highest, and lowest values for all columns.
6. Format the totals in the Total cell style with an Accent 3 fill color of your choice, if necessary.
7. Select the values in the range D6:H16, and format in Comma style.
8. Right-click cell D6 and use Format Painter to copy the format from cell D6 to the range D20:H22.
9. Enter a comment in cell B8 as follows:
   This invoice can be found in our files: 5.1salesinv.
10. Save the file and name it **9.2purch**.
11. Close the file.

WHAT YOU NEED TO KNOW

Software

▶ When you want to add several formats to cells containing text or values, you can use the Format Cells dialog box to make all settings at once. Press [Ctrl]+1 to display the Format Cells dialog box.

▶ A cell comment, indicated by a red triangle in the top-right corner of the cell, provides information about the data. To add a comment, right-click the cell, and click Insert Comment. You can right-click the cell to edit, delete, or show the comment.

Project

▶ A purchase journal is a record of the purchase transactions made by a business. The business owes the money for the purchases to the vendors or creditors, who are referred to as accounts payable.

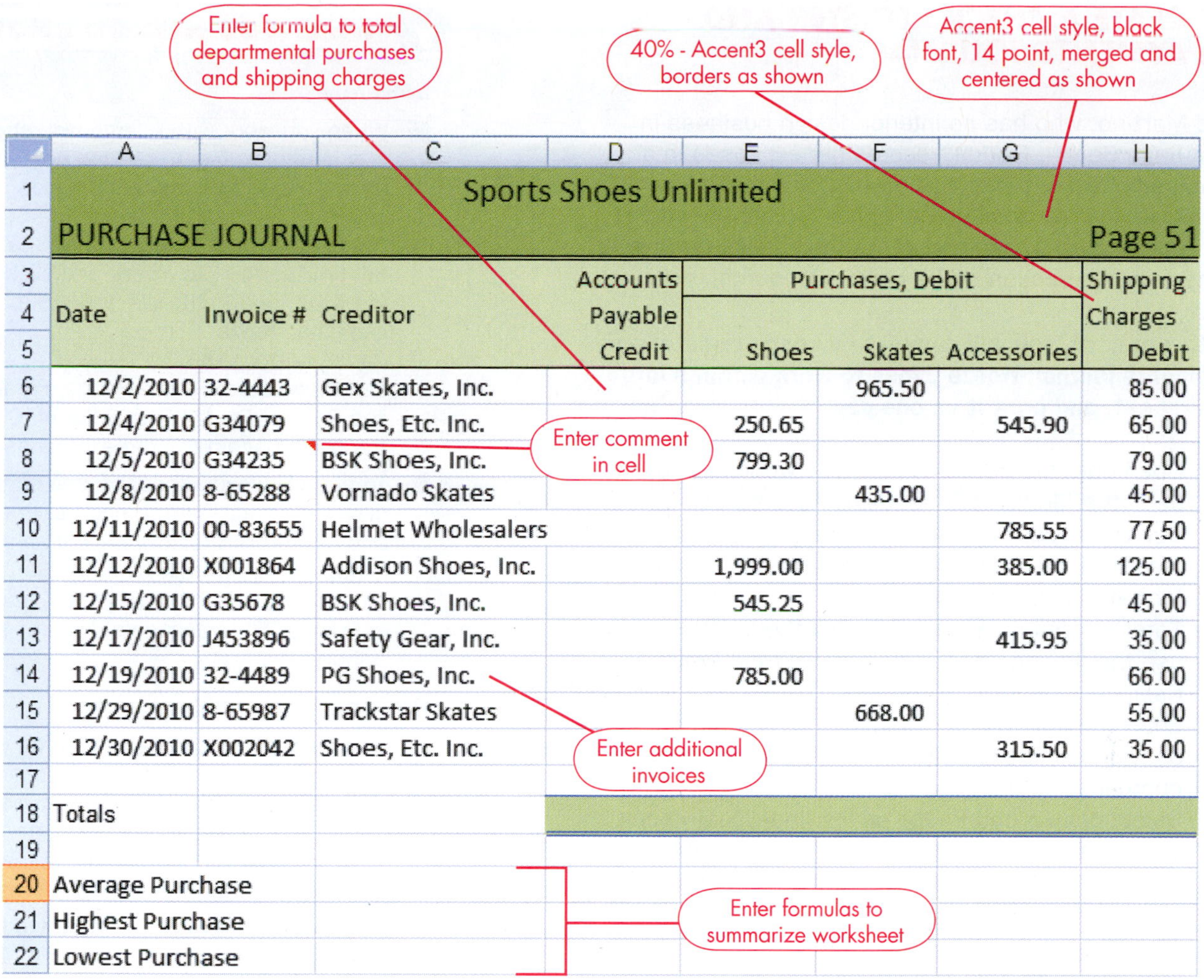

Enter formula to total departmental purchases and shipping charges

40% - Accent3 cell style, borders as shown

Accent3 cell style, black font, 14 point, merged and centered as shown

Enter comment in cell

Enter additional invoices

Enter formulas to summarize worksheet

	A	B	C	D	E	F	G	H
1	Sports Shoes Unlimited							
2	PURCHASE JOURNAL							Page 51
3				Accounts	Purchases, Debit			Shipping
4	Date	Invoice #	Creditor	Payable				Charges
5				Credit	Shoes	Skates	Accessories	Debit
6	12/2/2010	32-4443	Gex Skates, Inc.			965.50		85.00
7	12/4/2010	G34079	Shoes, Etc. Inc.		250.65		545.90	65.00
8	12/5/2010	G34235	BSK Shoes, Inc.		799.30			79.00
9	12/8/2010	8-65288	Vornado Skates			435.00		45.00
10	12/11/2010	00-83655	Helmet Wholesalers				785.55	77.50
11	12/12/2010	X001864	Addison Shoes, Inc.		1,999.00		385.00	125.00
12	12/15/2010	G35678	BSK Shoes, Inc.		545.25			45.00
13	12/17/2010	J453896	Safety Gear, Inc.				415.95	35.00
14	12/19/2010	32-4489	PG Shoes, Inc.		785.00			66.00
15	12/29/2010	8-65987	Trackstar Skates			668.00		55.00
16	12/30/2010	X002042	Shoes, Etc. Inc.				315.50	35.00
17								
18	Totals							
19								
20	Average Purchase							
21	Highest Purchase							
22	Lowest Purchase							

Figure 9.2

9.3 CREATE A CHECK REGISTER AND PAYMENTS JOURNAL

Jane Martino, who has an interior design business in West Palm Beach, Florida, records her expenses in a combined check register and payments journal. She would like you to complete her check register by adding four recent checks, and categorize the checks for August in the analysis section of the payments journal.

> **In this project, you will complete a check register and payments journal, freeze panes to work within a large worksheet, and print it on one page.**

1. Open data file **d9.3cashpmt**. The worksheet should be in the Median theme, using Accent5 cell styles.
2. Use cell styles, cell borders, merge and center, font settings, and alignment features to match the formats in Figure 9.3a.
3. Enter a formula in cell G6 to find the balance and use the fill handle to copy it down. *Hint: Previous Balance + Deposits – Checks.*
4. Enter the last four checks into the register, as shown in Figure 9.3b. Use the fill handle for check numbers and the balance calculation.
5. Select cell F5 and freeze panes. Individually copy each check amount and then scroll and paste it into the appropriate column. Use the description as a guide. Unfreeze panes.
6. Total the columns indicated with a double line in Figure 9.3a, and add the distribution columns across to check that they equal the total of the Check column.
7. View the worksheet in Print Preview, and use the Page Setup dialog box to set the worksheet to Fit on 1 page(s) wide by 1 tall. Print a copy of the file.
8. Save the file and name it **9.3cashpmt**.
9. Close the file.

WHAT YOU NEED TO KNOW

Software

- When you work with a large worksheet, it is helpful to freeze column headings or row labels to keep them in view when you scroll down or across. Select the row below or the column to the right of the area to freeze and click the View tab; and in the Window group, click the Freeze Panes button. You can then select Freeze Panes, Freeze Top Row, or Freeze First Column. Click the button again to unfreeze panes.

  Freeze Panes

- To fit a large worksheet on one page, click the Office Button, point to Print, and click Print Preview. Click the Page Setup button, and in the Page Setup dialog box, select the Page tab, and select the Fit to 1 page(s) wide by 1 tall option.

Project

- Businesses need to keep records of the money spent for various categories of expenses or payments. They can record this information in a cash payments journal or use a combined check register and payments journal.
- The source of information is the check stub. The check number identifies the transaction.
- Check descriptions are used to distribute payments to the appropriate category or accounts in the payment analysis section. Items with invoice numbers should be placed into the Accounts Payable category. Any item that cannot be placed into a category is placed in an Other column.

Median theme, Accent5 cell style, 16 point

	A	B	C	D	E	F	G	H	I	J	K	L	M	N	O	P
1	Check Register and Cash Payments Journal															
2								Payment Analysis								
3								Accounts								
4	Date	Check No.	Payee	Description	Check	Deposit	Balance	Payable	Advertising	Insurance	Rent	Salaries	Supplies	Utilities	Other	Total Pmts
5	8/1/2010		Balance forwarded				12,546.54									
6	8/4/2010	4532	Olin Properties	Rent	2,500.00						2,500.00					
7	8/5/2010	4533	Trainor Insurance	Liability insurance	625.00											
8	8/6/2010	4534	Office To Go	Supplies	189.00											
9	8/6/2010	4535	Ray's Windows	Invoice #423	1,950.00											
10	8/7/2010	4536	Palm Coast Electric	Electric bill	325.00											
11	8/8/2010		Deposit - revenues			18,500.00										
12	8/8/2010	4537	Palm Beach Post	Advertising	575.00											
13	8/11/2010	4538	Picture Depot	Invoice #5322	2,355.00											
14	8/12/2010	4539	Barton's Furniture	Invoice #23222	10,250.00											
15	8/13/2010	4540	Cincom Wireless	Mobile	185.00											
16	8/15/2010	4541	Salaries	Semi-monthly	3,500.00											
17	8/15/2010		Deposit - revenues			12,890.00										
18	8/18/2010	4542	Florida Telephone C	Telephone	278.00											
19	8/19/2010	4543	Office To Go	Supplies	210.00											
20	8/20/2010	4544	Wilson's Accessories	Invoice #5322	955.00											
21	8/21/2010	4545	Bailey's Supplies	Supplies	89.00											
22	8/21/2010		Deposit - revenues			15,500.00										
23	8/22/2010	4546	Paint and Paper Co	Invoice #T395	2,860.00											
24	8/22/2010	4547	Kingsley Paints	Invoice #211	379.00											
25	8/25/2010	4548	Paint and Paper Co	Invoice #T422	3,286.00											
26	8/26/2010	4549	American Red Cross	Donation	150.00											
27	8/27/2010	4550	Palm Beach Post	Advertising	575.00											
28	8/27/2010	4551	Yakani Rugs	Invoice #Y0984	5,500.00											
29	8/28/2010	4552	First State Insurance	Health Insurance	855.00											
30	8/29/2010	4553	Salaries	Semi-monthly	3,500.00											
31																
32																

Distribute each payment to the appropriate analysis column

Figure 9.3a

Find totals for Check and Deposit columns and confirm that total checks equal Total Pmts in P31

Total of distribution columns should match total checks in cell E31

27	8/27/2010	4550	Palm Beach Post	Advertising	575.00
28	8/27/2010	4551	Yakani Rugs	Invoice #Y0984	5,500.00
29	8/28/2010	4552	First State Insurance	Health Insurance	855.00
30	8/29/2010	4553	Salaries	Semi-monthly	3,500.00

Enter last four checks

Figure 9.3b

PROJECT SKILLS
✴ Use Wrap Text alignment
✴ Use the AutoCalc feature
✴ Format or modify text using a formula
✴ Use parentheses in a formula

PROJECT 10

10.1 CREATE A PETTY CASH REGISTER

Jane Martino, interior designer, has decided to establish a petty cash fund of $100 to pay for incidental cash expenditures. A record of all vouchers and payments from the petty cash fund will be recorded in the petty cash register. She would like you to prepare the petty cash register.

> **In this project, you will create a petty cash register that reviews formats and formulas, and use a text function to change text entries.**

1. Open data file **d10.1petty**. Jane Martino uses the Median theme and Accent5 cell style.
2. Use cell styles, cell borders, merge and center, font settings, and alignment features to match the formats in Figure 10.1. Text in cells E4, F4, and G4 should be aligned using the Wrap Text button.
3. Use the fill handle to complete the series of voucher numbers.
4. Copy the payment number into the appropriate category column, as shown for Vouchers 1 and 2 in Figure 10.1. Use the following as a guide for assigning categories:
   a. Office Supplies would include items such as pens, disks, paper, and so on.
   b. Delivery Expense would include tolls, parking, and delivery fees paid to deliver merchandise.
   c. Use the General columns to enter values and account names that are not provided in the register. For example, for the fee for an advertisement, enter Advertising in the General Account Title column.
   d. Place any small expenditure that does not fit into a specific category in Misc. Expense.
5. Add all columns. Check your distribution of all items by selecting the range of totals for all distribution columns, including the General column in the range E17:I17, and view the Sum on the status bar. It should agree with the Payments column.

WHAT YOU NEED TO KNOW

Software

▶ If you have text that is too long for the column size and wish to display it all, click the Home tab, and in the Alignment group, click the Wrap Text button, which displays the text on more than one line.

▶ The AutoCalc feature allows you to select numbers in a column or row and view the Average, Count, and Sum of those numbers on the status bar. This calculation does not appear on the worksheet but is valuable for double-checking or proving totals.

▶ In addition to arithmetic functions there are also functions that allow you to modify or edit text entries. If you want to copy text in a different way, you can use a text function to avoid retyping the entry. Some text functions are UPPER(text reference), which converts the text in the cell to upper case, or LOWER(text reference), which converts the text in the cell to lower case, and SUBSTITUTE(text, new text, old text), which replaces the text with new text.

Project

▶ Assets are items that a business owns, such as cash, equipment, and accounts receivable.

▶ Most businesses handle cash outflow by writing checks for all payments made. Because writing checks for small amounts is impractical, a business may keep a certain amount of cash on hand. This cash reserve is called a petty cash fund.

Continued on next page

6. In cell B20, enter the UPPER function to copy the Office Supplies column header into the replenishment journal entry. *Hint: =UPPER(E4).* Repeat this process to complete the list of expenses in B21, B22, and B23. Enter **CASH** in C24 and copy the totals from the columns into the areas shown in Figure 10.1. Use the Payments column total for the Cash value, which is the amount of the check to replenish the fund.

7. Format all numbers in the range D6:I24 in Comma style.

8. Set the worksheet to Fit on 1 page(s) wide by 1 tall. Print a copy of the file.

9. Save the file and name it **10.1petty**. Close the file.

▶ The employee in charge of the petty cash fund prepares a voucher and obtains a receipt for all cash withdrawals. A record of the payments made is sometimes recorded in a petty cash register. When the cash in the fund is depleted, a replenishment check is cashed to bring the fund back to its original level using a journal entry.

▶ In the petty cash register, payments are divided into the appropriate account or category just as they were in the check register. Payments made for items that do not fall into the category columns should be placed in the General column with the account name. Any small expense that is not in a specific category is considered a miscellaneous expense.

Use fill handle to extend number series

Merged and centered, Median theme, Accent5 cell style, 14 point

Wrap text in E4, F4, and G4

Distribute each payment to the appropriate column

Total all columns and check that all distribution columns equal the payments column

Use UPPER text function to copy expense accounts for entry

Enter totals for these columns or expenses

	A	B	C	D	E	F	G	H	I
1			PETTY CASH REGISTER						
2						Distribution of Payments			
3								General	
4	Date	Voucher #	Description	Payments	Office Supplies	Delivery Expense	Misc. Expense	Account Title	Amount
5	9/1/2010		Petty Cash fund $100						
6	9/2/2010	1	Envelopes	5.50	5.50				
7	9/4/2010	2	Tolls	6.25		6.25			
8	9/8/2010		Pens	6.85					
9	9/9/2010		Varsity Delivery Co	12.50					
10	9/15/2010		Advertisement - local bulletin	24.00					
11	9/15/2010		CD s for computer	10.50					
12	9/19/2010		Parking	5.50					
13	9/23/2010		Newspaper	1.50					
14	9/24/2010		Folders	8.75					
15	9/25/2010		Postage	4.85					
16	9/26/2010		Tolls	2.75					
17			Total to be replenished						
18									
19	Replenishment Entry:								
20			OFFICE SUPPLIES						
21			DELIVERY EXPENSE						
22			MISC. EXPENSE						
23			ADVERTISING						
24			CASH						
25									

Figure 10.1

10.2 CREATE AN ASSET RECORD

BSK Shoes, Inc., a shoe wholesaler, owns trucks, forklifts, and other merchandise-handling equipment. It maintains an asset record for each piece of equipment to record depreciation and book value. They have asked you to prepare an asset record for a forklift.

In this project, you will create an asset record using the straight-line method to calculate annual depreciation.

1. Open data file **d10.2asset**. BSK Shoes, Inc. uses the Trek theme and shades of Accent6 cell styles.
2. Use cell styles, cell borders, merge and center, and font settings, to match the formats in Figure 10.2. Adjust column width as necessary and make font changes indicated.
3. In cell H7, calculate the annual depreciation using the straight-line method. The disposal value and years of life are shown on the record. Use parentheses in the formula to prioritize the calculation.
4. The asset was owned only six months in 2010. In cell H12, enter a formula to calculate a half year or six months depreciation, based on the annual depreciation in cell H7.
5. In cells H13:H16, enter the annual depreciation.
6. Depreciate the asset for only six months in 2015. Input the amount from H12 to H17.
7. In cell I12, enter a formula to calculate the running balance in the Accumulated Depreciation account. *Hint: Previous Balance + Credit or = I11 + H12.*
8. In cell J12, enter a formula to calculate the book value. *Hint: Book Value from Last Period [J11] – Current Depreciation [H12].*
9. Copy the formulas in I12 and J12 down to calculate accumulated depreciation and book value for each of the years.
10. Format the numbers for no decimal places in commas format except for cell H5, which should be in Accounting Number format.
11. Print a copy of the Asset Record.
12. Save the file and name it **10.2asset**.
13. Close the file.

WHAT YOU NEED TO KNOW

Software

▶ Parentheses are used to prioritize calculations that must be completed first. Although formulas are executed from left to right, the order of calculations depends on mathematical priority. When you need to calculate a result based on another answer, place that first calculation in parentheses.

Project

▶ Companies keep careful records of their fixed or long-term assets, such as equipment, vehicles, and so on. These items are depreciated each year to estimate the assets' book value and to use the annual depreciation as a deductible expense.

▶ To calculate depreciation, you need the salvage or disposal value at the end of the asset life and the years of life. There are several methods to calculate depreciation, such as straight-line, declining balance, or sum-of-the-years digits. The IRS may require a specific method for certain types of assets.

▶ The formula to calculate depreciation using the straight-line method is as follows: (cost - disposal value)/years of life. This formula calculates a level depreciation for each year of the asset's life.

▶ If the asset is owned only part of the year, the depreciation is calculated by multiplying the annual depreciation by the fraction of the year it was owned.

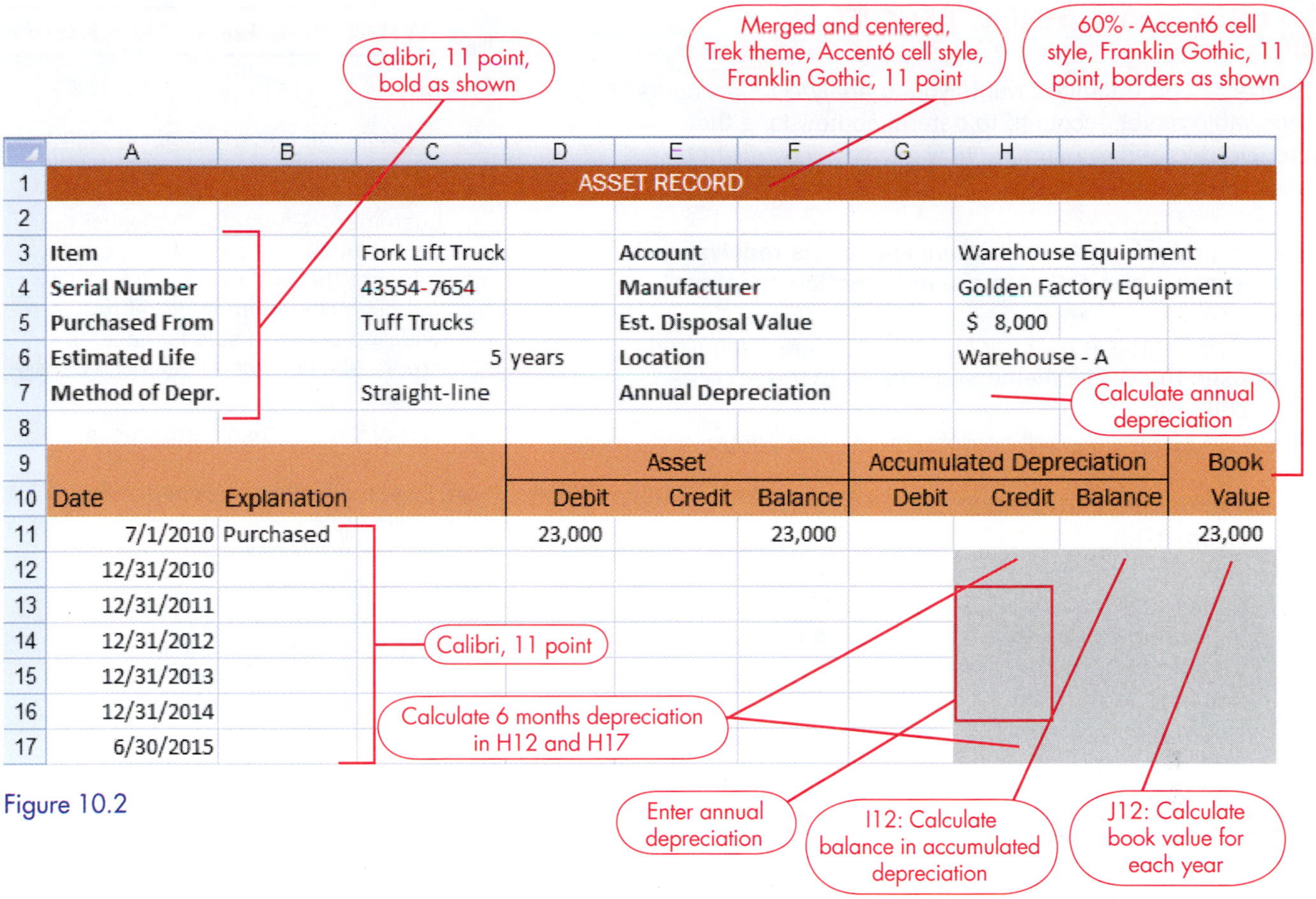

Calibri, 11 point, bold as shown

Merged and centered, Trek theme, Accent6 cell style, Franklin Gothic, 11 point

60% - Accent6 cell style, Franklin Gothic, 11 point, borders as shown

	A	B	C	D	E	F	G	H	I	J
1	ASSET RECORD									
2										
3	Item		Fork Lift Truck		Account		Warehouse Equipment			
4	Serial Number		43554-7654		Manufacturer		Golden Factory Equipment			
5	Purchased From		Tuff Trucks		Est. Disposal Value		$ 8,000			
6	Estimated Life			5 years	Location		Warehouse - A			
7	Method of Depr.		Straight-line		Annual Depreciation					
8										
9					Asset			Accumulated Depreciation		Book
10	Date	Explanation		Debit	Credit	Balance	Debit	Credit	Balance	Value
11	7/1/2010	Purchased		23,000		23,000				23,000
12	12/31/2010									
13	12/31/2011									
14	12/31/2012									
15	12/31/2013									
16	12/31/2014									
17	6/30/2015									

Calculate annual depreciation

Calibri, 11 point

Calculate 6 months depreciation in H12 and H17

Enter annual depreciation

I12: Calculate balance in accumulated depreciation

J12: Calculate book value for each year

Figure 10.2

10.3 CREATE AN AGING REPORT

Sports Shoes Unlimited wants you to analyze its accounts receivable asset accounts to determine how long they are overdue and to estimate how much money might be uncollectible.

In this project, you will create an accounts receivable aging report and estimate the uncollectible amounts.

1. Open data file **d10.3aging**. Sports Shoes Unlimited uses the Office theme and shades of the Accent3 cell style.
2. Use cell styles, cell borders, merge and center, Comma style, custom number and date formats, and font settings to match the formats in Figure 10.3.
3. The balances due from each customer have been broken down according to their due dates. Enter a formula in cell B7 that adds values in columns C:G to find the total amount due.
4. Copy the formula for all accounts.
5. Find the column totals. If necessary, add 40% - Accent3 cell style and cell borders, as shown in Figure 10.3.
6. Use the AutoCalc feature to check that the total of columns C:G is equal to the total account balances in B19.
7. Enter the Estimated Loss Percentages shown in Row 21.
8. In cell C23, multiply the column total by the Estimated Loss Percentage to find the Estimated Bad Debts.
9. Copy the formula across for all columns.
10. In cell B23, find the total of the Estimated Bad Debt amounts in columns C:G. Add the 40% - Accent3 cell style if necessary.
11. Print one copy of the aging report.
12. Save the file and name it **10.3aging**. Close the file.

▼ WHAT YOU NEED TO KNOW

Project

▶ An accounts receivable aging report analysis is necessary to determine the true value of the money due from customers. Generally, the longer the accounts are unpaid, the more likely it is that they will become bad debts. Although customer credit ratings are checked before a sale is made on credit, business conditions can change along with financial stability.

▶ The estimated loss percentages for accounts that are past due are developed by experience and are applied to estimate the amounts that might be uncollectible.

▶ The estimated true value of the accounts receivable asset is the total less the estimated amount of bad debts.

Enter formula to calculate total for each account

Merged and centered, Accent3 cell style, black font, company name in 18 point

40% - Accent3 cell style, borders as shown

40% - Accent3 cell style

Find totals

Enter formula to find loss percentages of totals in row 19

Percentage style number format to two decimal places

Comma style number format

	A	B	C	D	E	F	G
1			Sports Shoes Unlimited				
2			Accounts Receivable Aging Report				
3			October 31, 2010				
4				Past Due Accounts Receivable			
5		Account	Not Yet	1-30	31-60	61-90	Over 90
6	Customers	Balances	Due	Days	Days	Days	Days
7	Martin Abbott				665.00		
8	Central H.S.				1,389.40		
9	Eastside H.S.		2,100.00				
10	Lamar Jackson		1,423.10	533.93			
11	Helen Keegan		989.75				
12	Wendy Kingsley		904.15			425.38	
13	Sam Norris		224.70	583.15			
14	Shirley Millar		859.21	1,494.86	215.00		
15	Frank Perez		484.17			1,515.83	1,322.00
16	Gloria Ross		1,295.77	1,016.50			
17	Arthur Wilson		487.60			500.00	
18	Peter Williams		2,019.09				
19	Totals						
20							
21	Estimated Loss Percentages		0.10%	0.50%	3.00%	10.00%	80.00%
22							
23	Estimated Bad Debts						

Figure 10.3

CHAPTER 4

Create Data Analysis Worksheets

In this chapter, you will complete the following projects:

PROJECT 11
Budgets
Project 11.1 Create a Budget
Project 11.2 Format a Budget

PROJECT 12
Billings and Listings Tables
Project 12.1 Create a Billings Analysis Table
Project 12.2 Create a Listings Analysis Table

PROJECT 13
Income Statements
Project 13.1 Create and Analyze an Income Statement
Project 13.2 Save a Workbook as a Web Page
Project 13.3 Create and Publish an Income Statement Analysis

PROJECT 14
Sales, Revenue, and Investment Analyses
Project 14.1 Create a Sales Analysis
Project 14.2 Create a Billings and Revenue Analysis
Project 14.3 Create a Revenue Forecast and Analysis
Project 14.4 Create an Investment Analysis

PROJECT SKILLS
✸ Insert or delete columns and rows
✸ Indent text
✸ Apply a negative number format
✸ Use Page Break Preview mode

PROJECT 11

11.1 CREATE A BUDGET

The Accounting department of MusicMagic, Inc., an electronics retailer that specializes in MP3 players and accessories, prepared a budget in January 2010 showing income and expenses for the first quarter of the year. It is now the end of March, and they would like you to compare the budget to the actual data for the quarter.

In this project, you will create, preview, and print a comparison of budgeted amounts in the income statement with the actual data.

1. Open the data file **d11.1budget**.
2. Insert a row under the heading section (in row 4).
3. Insert a column in column A, and move the three titles (in rows 1-3) to the new column A.
4. Adjust the column width for columns B, E, and F using AutoFit. Double-click the right edge of the column to AutoFit data. Adjust the row height as necessary using AutoFit.
5. Set the formats for the titles, cell styles, and borders, as shown in Figure 11.1.
6. Bold the section headers and use the Increase Indent button to indent the text as shown.
7. Enter a formula to find the Increase/Decrease from Budget. *Hint: Actual – Budget.*
8. Format all dollar values for commas with no decimal places, and format the negative numbers in red with parentheses, commas, and no decimal places.
9. Enter a formula to find the % Increase/Decrease from Budget. *Hint: E10/Budget.* Format results for Percentage with two decimal places.
10. Use the Fill Handle to copy both formulas down for all values. Delete formula results from rows without data. Fix the borders and cell styles as necessary.
11. Save the file and name it **11.1budget**.
12. Close the file.

WHAT YOU NEED TO KNOW

Software

▶ To insert columns or rows, right-click with the insertion point in the location where the new row or column should appear. On the shortcut menu click Insert or Delete, and then select column, row, or options to shift cells. When you delete rows or columns, you delete the data in those areas as well.

▶ To indent text, select the range of cells to indent, click the Home tab, and in the Alignment group, click the Increase Indent button. Remove the indents by clicking the Undo button or by reversing the process with the Decrease Indent button.

▶ To format negative numbers, select the range and then open the Format Cells dialog box by pressing [Ctrl]+1. Click the Number tab, and in the Number category, select the red, parentheses, or minus signs to format negative numbers. Select the Percentage category to display answers that are percentages.

Project

▶ A budget is an analysis of the projected income and expenses for a future period. An income statement is the report used to show the revenues and expenses for a period and the resulting net profit. Companies project their income and expenses for stockholders and management.

▶ Data is analyzed quarterly, which is every three months, or four times a year.

▶ To be able to analyze the budgeted data compared to the actual data, you will calculate the percent increase or decrease. This shows which budgeted items are changing in an unexpected manner.

Insert column here

Insert row here

Accent2 cell style, merged and centered, 26 point

20% - Accent2 cell style, bold

Thick Bottom Border

Enter formulas

Bottom Border

Total cell style, 20% - Accent2 cell style, bold

MusicMagic, Inc.

Comparison of Budgeted Income Statement with Actual Income Statement

For Quarter Ended March 31, 2010

		Budget 1st Qtr.	Actual 1st Qtr.	Increase/ Decrease from Budget	% of Increase/ Decrease from Budget
Revenue:					
	Net Sales	535,653	540,565		
Cost of Goods Sold:					
	Cost of Goods Sold	357,876	360,876		
Gross Profit		177,777	179,689		
Expenses:					
	Advertising/Promotions	4,560	4,765		
	Depreciation	7,128	7,128		
	Insurance	5,800	5,800		
	Legal/Accounting	5,340	5,213		
	Loan Interest Payments	7,657	7,657		
	Miscellaneous Expenses	3,420	3,513		
	Payroll Expenses	4,250	4,375		
	Rent	45,780	45,780		
	Repairs/Maintenance	1,845	1,950		
	Salaries/Wages	21,560	21,880		
	Supplies	2,165	2,050		
	Utilities	2,100	2,350		
	Total Expenses	111,605	112,461		
Net Income before Taxes		66,172	67,228		
Taxes		19,852	20,168		
Net Income after Taxes		46,320	47,060		

Figure 11.1

11.2 FORMAT A BUDGET

The accountants for GameDepot prepared a budget for the third quarter, and now, at the end of the quarter, they would like you to compare the budget to the actual data.

In this project, you will create, preview, adjust the page break, and print a comparison of a budgeted income statement with the actual data.

1. Open the data file **d11.2budget**.
2. Format and complete the budget, as shown in Figure 11.2.
    a. Set the Origin theme, merge and center titles, and use the Accent6 and Accent5 cell styles or cell styles you prefer.
    b. Set the font size for the company name to 26 point, and AutoFit the row height as necessary.
    c. Use Bottom Double Line borders in the heading as shown.
    d. Use AutoFit to adjust column width as necessary.
    e. Format all numbers for commas with no decimals.
    f. Indent the data as shown.
3. Enter and copy the formulas to complete the budget.
    a. In cell B12, find Net Sales. *Hint: Sales – Sales Returns*.
    b. In cell B17, find Gross Profit. *Hint: Net Sales – Cost of Goods Sold*.
    c. In cell B29, find Total Selling Expenses. *Hint: Add Selling Expenses*.
    d. In cell B38, find Total Administrative Expenses. *Hint: Add Administrative Expenses*.
    e. In cell B40, find Total Expenses. *Hint: Add Total Selling and Total Administrative Expenses*.
    f. In cell B42, find Net Income before Taxes. *Hint: Subtract Total Expenses from Gross Profit*.
    g. In cell B44, find Net Income after Taxes and format row 44 in the Total cell style. *Hint: Subtract Taxes from Net Income before Taxes*.
    h. Copy the formulas in column B to column C, using the fill handle for each formula.
    i. In cell D10, find Increase/Decrease from Budget. *Hint: Subtract Budget from Actual data*.
    j. In cell E10, find % Increase/Decrease from Budget, and format the data with the Percent style to two decimal places. *Hint: D10/Budget*.
    k. Use a special number format for the negative numbers in column D, as you wish.
    l. Copy formulas as necessary. Delete zero or error results from cells that do not reflect data.
4. Add lines, borders, and cell styles as necessary.

▼ WHAT YOU NEED TO KNOW

Software

► If a worksheet goes beyond the page length, you may either print it on two pages or change the settings to print it all on one page. Click the View tab, and in the Workbook Views group, click the Page Break Preview button, and then you can adjust margins and page breaks to print the worksheet on one page. Click OK to enter Page Break Preview mode, and then drag the page break line to include the entire worksheet on one page. Click the Normal view button to return to the default workbook view.

5. Use the View tab and Page Break Preview to see if the budget fits on one page. If it does not, click OK to clear the message and drag the page break to fit the budget on one page.

6. Center the budget horizontally on the page, and print a copy in portrait orientation.

7. Save the file and name it **11.2budget**. Close the file.

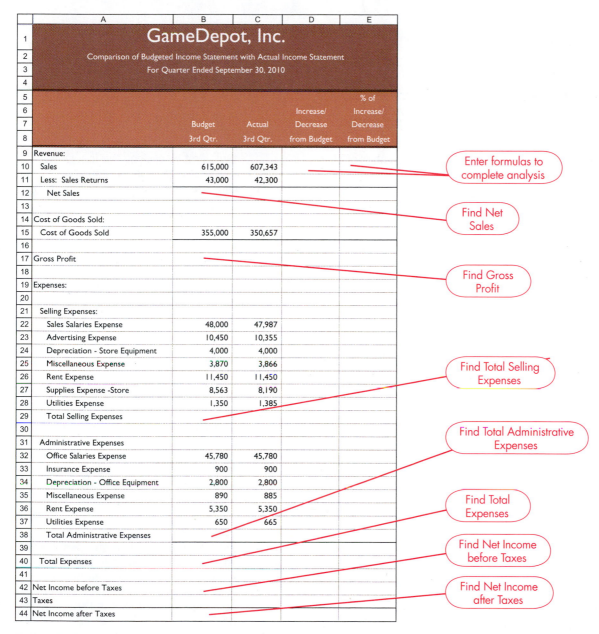

Figure 11.2

▶ **PROJECT SKILLS**
- ✷ Format data as a table
- ✷ Sort data in a table
- ✷ Use the AutoFilter feature
- ✷ Insert or delete columns or rows in a table

PROJECT 12

12.1 CREATE A BILLINGS ANALYSIS TABLE

Happenings Experts is a group of consultants that supervises and plans gatherings, conferences, and parties in Miami and Fort Lauderdale. They have asked you to compare the billings for both offices in the first six months of this year with the billings for the same period last year, and to analyze the data to answer a number of questions.

In this project, you will create a billings analysis, using Quick Styles and summary totals, and will answer questions by using filters.

1. Open data file **d12.1 billings** and adjust column width as necessary.
2. Enter and format worksheet titles as shown in Figure 12.1. Set the Origin theme and choose the cell style settings.
3. Select the range A5:F16, and format it as a table using Table Style Medium 10.
4. On the Table Tools Design tab, set table style options for Banded Columns, no Banded Rows, and Last Column.
5. Format columns E and F for commas with no decimal places.
6. Add a total line to the table, and select the Sum function for columns E and F.
7. Sort the table by Hire Date from the oldest to the newest.
   a. Which employee has the most seniority?
   b. What are the Year to Date Billings for that employee?
8. Sort by Last name in A to Z order.
9. Filter the Location column so that only Miami employees are displayed.
   a. What are the Total Year to Date billings for Miami?
   b. How do 2010 billings compare to 2009 billings? Do they increase or decrease?
   c. Change the function on the total line to Average. What is the average billing for Miami employees?

▼ WHAT YOU NEED TO KNOW

Software

▶ Data arranged in columns with headers or in a list is called a table. You can summarize, format, sort, or filter tables to arrange or find data. Create a table first by clicking the Insert tab, and in the Tables group, click the Table button and then enter the data. Or, you can create the data first, and then format it as a table by clicking the Format as Table button on the Home tab in the Styles group. Then select a predefined table style, or Quick Style, from the gallery to format the table.

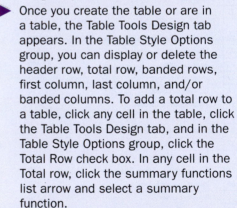

▶ Once you create the table or are in a table, the Table Tools Design tab appears. In the Table Style Options group, you can display or delete the header row, total row, banded rows, first column, last column, and/or banded columns. To add a total row to a table, click any cell in the table, click the Table Tools Design tab, and in the Table Style Options group, click the Total Row check box. In any cell in the Total row, click the summary functions list arrow and select a summary function.

▶ Sorting and filtering data is an important part of data analysis. When you apply a sort, you can order data alphabetically, from highest to lowest, or the reverse. To sort data in a non-table range, click the Data tab, and in the Sort & Filter group, click the Sort A to Z or Sort Z to A button.

Continued on next page

10. Filter the Location column so that only Fort Lauderdale employees are displayed.
    a. What is the average billing for Fort Lauderdale employees?
    b. Change the function to Sum. What are the Total Year to Date billings for Fort Lauderdale?
    c. How do 2010 billings compare to 2009 billings? Do they increase or decrease?
11. Clear the filter from the Location column.
12. Click the Data tab, and in the Sort & Filter group, click the Filter button to turn off AutoFilter arrows in the table.
13. Print a copy of the billing analysis.
14. Save the file and name it **12.1billings**. Close the file.

▶ AutoFilter is the system for sorting provided in Excel tables. To activate AutoFilter arrows in the table column headings, click the Data tab, then click the Filter button in the Sort & Filter group. To sort a table, click the AutoFilter arrow for the column by which setting you wish to sort, make the criteria settings, and then click OK. All items that do not meet the criteria you set are filtered out. To remove the filter, click Clear Filter. Filters are included on the sort/filter list for each column in a table. Turn off AutoFilter arrows by clicking the Filter button again.

Project

▶ Billings are invoices that are used to bill the clients for the services delivered. A company may wish to analyze the billings sent by their service personnel to determine staff performance and to analyze sources of revenues for future periods.

	A	B	C	D	E	F
1			Happenings Experts			
2			Analysis of Billings for Miami and Ft. Lauderdale Personnel			
3			Billings for six months ending June 30 of 2009 and 2010			
4						
5	Last	First	Hire Date	Location	Billings 2009	Billings 2010
6	Arnaz	Nicholas	8/15/2003	Miami	402,657	453,678
7	Barton	Tanya	2/10/2002	Ft. Lauderdale	652,243	654,555
8	Catalano	Ann	11/26/2005	Ft. Lauderdale	349,865	345,876
9	Forest	Peter	9/7/2007	Miami	446,342	453,678
10	Hartnet	Jennifer	5/31/2006	Miami	725,987	656,789
11	Kelly	Joseph	9/17/2009	Ft. Lauderdale	364,655	365,434
12	Martinez	Maria	6/15/2003	Miami	765,765	768,765
13	Potter	Wendy	12/3/2005	Ft. Lauderdale	485,465	488,765
14	Restivo	Mario	7/9/2008	Ft. Lauderdale	351,345	354,876
15	Sung	Rose	5/15/2006	Miami	345,323	346,543
16	Thomas	Tanisha	3/25/2002	Miami	540,887	542,554
17	Total				5,430,534	5,431,513

Origin theme, Accent2 cell style, 18 point

40% - Accent2 cell style

Banded Columns table style option

Total line with Sum function

Table Style Medium 10 with Last Column table style option

Figure 12.1

12.2 CREATE A LISTINGS ANALYSIS TABLE

Abbey Neuhaus Realtors would like you to format listings data for the month as a table so that it can be analyzed.

In this project, you will create and format a listings table, insert a row, and answer questions about the data.

1. Open the data file **d12.2listings**, and adjust the column width as necessary.
2. Format the information as follows:
   a. Title line: Use the Accent5 cell style and increase the font size as desired.
   b. Data range: Format it as a table in Table Style Light 13.
   c. Price column: Use the Accounting Number style with no decimal places. Adjust the column width as necessary.
3. In A9, insert a row into the table, as shown in Figure 12.2, and add the following data:

| Kingsley | 4/29/2010 | 654 Copperfield Drive | Paoli | Colonial | 5 | 3 | $ 575,000 |

4. Format the table using the Last Column and Total Row table style options on the Table Tools Design tab.
5. Set the report to print in landscape, centered horizontally.
6. Answer the following questions by using total functions and/or by sorting and filtering the data:
   a. What are the average, maximum, and minimum values of all listings?
   b. What are the total listings for each of the following agents: Kingsley, Neuhaus, Ramos?
   c. What are the totals and averages for the listings for Berwyn, Devon, and Paoli?
   d. Which properties are available with four or more bedrooms? Print a copy of that filtered list.
7. Print a copy of the table with all filters cleared.
8. Save the file and name it **12.2listings**. Close the file.

▼ WHAT YOU NEED TO KNOW

Software

▶ You may insert or delete columns or rows in a table by right-clicking the location for the change and using the shortcut menu. Columns may be inserted to the left or right, and rows may be inserted above or below the cell.

Project

▶ A listing is created for a property when a real estate agency has contracted with the seller to be the broker who controls the sale of the property. The listing agent and agency will share the sales commission with the selling broker when the property is sold.

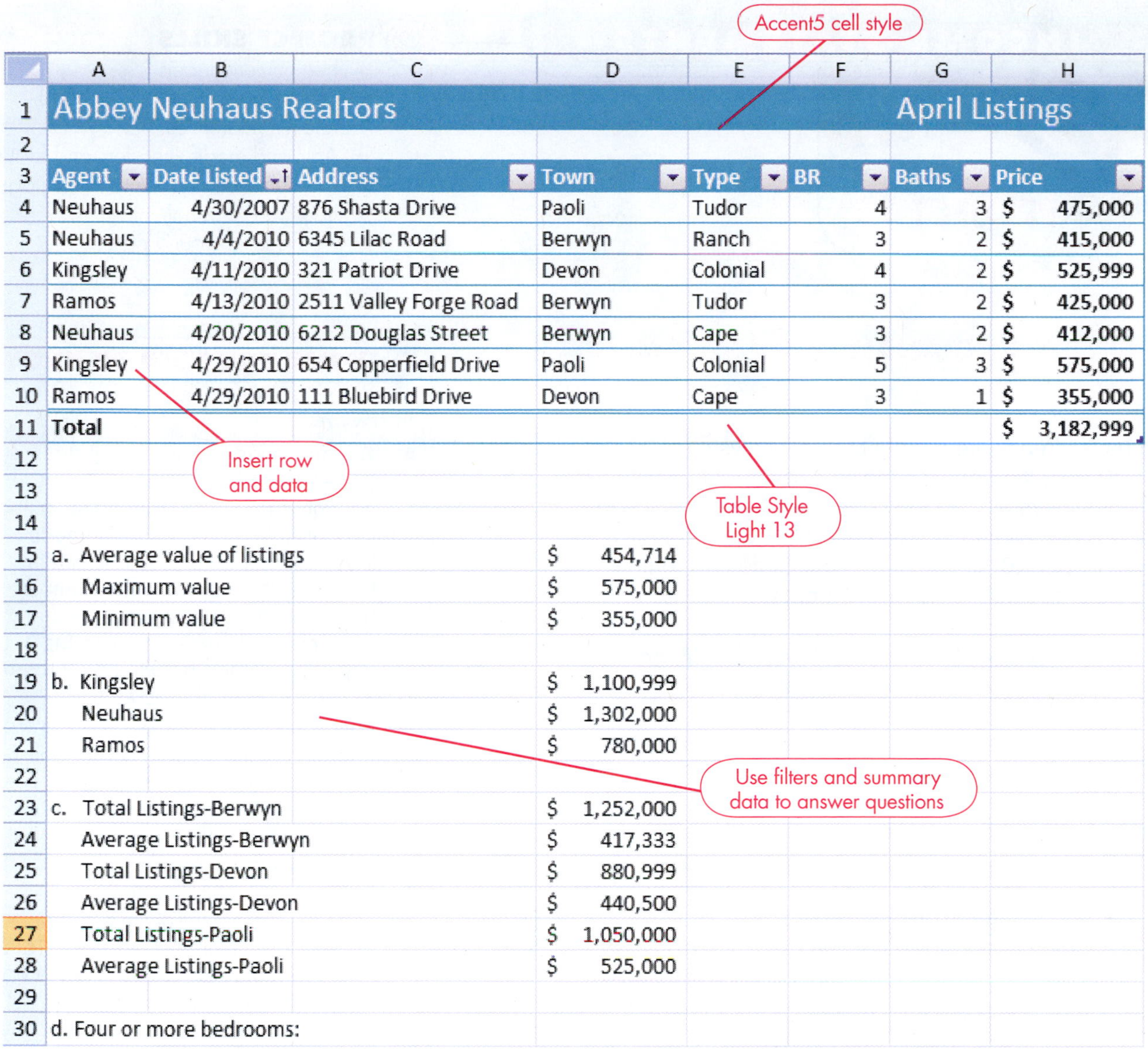

Accent5 cell style

	A	B	C	D	E	F	G	H
1	Abbey Neuhaus Realtors						April Listings	
2								
3	Agent ▼	Date Listed ▼	Address ▼	Town ▼	Type ▼	BR ▼	Baths ▼	Price ▼
4	Neuhaus	4/30/2007	876 Shasta Drive	Paoli	Tudor	4	3	$ 475,000
5	Neuhaus	4/4/2010	6345 Lilac Road	Berwyn	Ranch	3	2	$ 415,000
6	Kingsley	4/11/2010	321 Patriot Drive	Devon	Colonial	4	2	$ 525,999
7	Ramos	4/13/2010	2511 Valley Forge Road	Berwyn	Tudor	3	2	$ 425,000
8	Neuhaus	4/20/2010	6212 Douglas Street	Berwyn	Cape	3	2	$ 412,000
9	Kingsley	4/29/2010	654 Copperfield Drive	Paoli	Colonial	5	3	$ 575,000
10	Ramos	4/29/2010	111 Bluebird Drive	Devon	Cape	3	1	$ 355,000
11	Total							$ 3,182,999
12								
13								
14								
15	a. Average value of listings			$ 454,714				
16	Maximum value			$ 575,000				
17	Minimum value			$ 355,000				
18								
19	b. Kingsley			$ 1,100,999				
20	Neuhaus			$ 1,302,000				
21	Ramos			$ 780,000				
22								
23	c. Total Listings-Berwyn			$ 1,252,000				
24	Average Listings-Berwyn			$ 417,333				
25	Total Listings-Devon			$ 880,999				
26	Average Listings-Devon			$ 440,500				
27	Total Listings-Paoli			$ 1,050,000				
28	Average Listings-Paoli			$ 525,000				
29								
30	d. Four or more bedrooms:							

Insert row and data

Table Style Light 13

Use filters and summary data to answer questions

Figure 12.2

INCOME STATEMENTS

PROJECT 13

PROJECT SKILLS

* Use numeric labels
* Use formulas with absolute and relative references
* Add and modify headers and footers
* Convert workbooks into Web pages
* Use Paste Special
* Add a background pattern

13.1 CREATE AND ANALYZE AN INCOME STATEMENT

You have already prepared a budget analysis for MusicMagic, Inc., an electronics retailer that specializes in MP3 players and accessories. Now they want you to simplify their income statement for the quarter ending March 31, 2010, to compare the income for the first quarter of this year to last year's data.

In this project, you will create a simplified income statement to compare quarterly data.

1. Open data file **d13.1income**. Adjust the column width, as necessary.
2. Enter the appropriate formulas in column B in rows 11, 28, and 30, and copy the formulas to column C. Format numbers for commas with no decimals.
3. Insert a column at column C, and add the headings **% of Sales** in columns C and E.
4. Format the titles and column headings using cell styles, alignment settings, indentation, font size settings, and borders, as shown in Figure 13.1. Reenter the year column headings as numeric labels, entering an apostrophe before the year.
5. Note that the total expenses in row 26 are not formulas. Then simplify the statement:
   a. Select and delete rows 14 to 25. This deletes the details for Expenses and leaves only the total value.
   b. Move the Total Expenses numbers from row 14 to row 13. Delete row 14.

WHAT YOU NEED TO KNOW

Software

► You may need to use a number such as a year in column headings. To prevent a number in a label from being included in a formula, enter it as a numeric label. Enter a label prefix, which is the apostrophe, before the number to identify it as a label. Notice that numeric labels have a Smart Tag in the upper-left corner that identifies them as a number formatted as text.

► When you copy formulas, the cell references change relative to their new location. However, when a value in a formula must remain constant when copied, an absolute reference formula is necessary.

► To identify a value in a formula as absolute, you must place a $ before the row and column references. Thus, in the formula =B5/$B$17, $B$17 is an absolute reference and will not change as the formula is copied. You can add the dollars sign after entering the cell address by pressing [F4].

► Headers and footers allow you to repeat the same information at the top (header) or bottom (footer) of every page, such as a company name, date, filename, sheet name, or any other identifying information. There are three text boxes that make up both headers and footers. To select from the built-in headers, click the Page Layout view button on the status bar and click in the header box at the top of the worksheet. The Header & Footer Tools Design tab appears. Click the Header button to display built-in headers, and click your selection.

Continued on next page

6. In cell C8, enter a formula to calculate the percent the value in column B is of sales, making the sales value an absolute reference. *Hint: =B8/$B$8*.

   a. Format the result as a percent with one decimal place, or 100.0%.

   b. Copy the formula for all values in that column. Notice that by using an absolute reference, you are dividing by the value in B8, or the sales, in every case.

   c. Delete the formula results from cells for which there are no values to calculate.

7. In cell E8, enter a formula to calculate the percent the value is of sales, format for Percent style with one decimal place, copy the formula for all values, and then delete results where necessary.

8. Apply the Total cell style.

9. Add a built-in header to the report.

   a. Click the Page Layout view button on the status bar, and then select the Click to add header box at the top of the report.

   b. Click the Header button to view the selection of built-in headers.

   c. Select the header with the filename and page number.

   d. Click the Normal view button.

10. Print Preview the worksheet and center it horizontally. Do not print it.

11. Save the income statement analysis, and name it **13.1income**. Close the file.

Project

▶ An income statement presents a summary of all the income, costs, and expenses for the period. As a review, the formulas to calculate income are:

- Sales – Cost of Goods Sold = Gross Profit
- Gross Profit – Expenses = Net Income before Taxes
- Net Income before Taxes – Taxes = Net Income after Taxes

▶ Companies can compare the items on an income statement by finding the percentage that each value is of sales. By using percentages, a company can compare data from different periods using the same basis to judge performance and note trends.

40% - Accent2 cell style

Accent2 cell style, 20 point

Numeric labels

Section headings bold, 12 point

Summarize expenses

	A	B	C	D	E
1		MusicMagic, Inc.			
2		Income Statement Comparison			
3		For Quarters Ended March 31, 2009 and 2010			
4					
5		2009	%	2010	%
6		Amount	of Sales	Amount	of Sales
7	Revenue:				
8	Net Sales	472,543		540,565	
9	Less : Cost of Goods Sold	320,567		360,876	
10					
11	Gross Profit				
12					
13	Expenses:	100,119		112,461	
14					
15	Net Income before Taxes				
16	Taxes	-		-	
17	Net Income after Taxes				
18					
19					
20					

Figure 13.1

Enter formulas with absolute references

Enter formulas in columns B and D to complete Income Statement

13.2 SAVE A WORKBOOK AS A WEB PAGE

You have completed an income statement comparison for MusicMagic, Inc. and now the company wants you to convert the workbook into a Web page and customize the header for printing purposes. The page will be made available to the store managers throughout the city.

In this project, you will customize a worksheet header, including a company logo, and publish the worksheet as a Web page.

1. Open the solution from the previous project, **13.1income**, or open data file **d13.2income**.
2. Modify and customize the header and footer for printing purposes.
   a. In Page Layout view, select and then delete the current header data.
   b. In the left header section, click the Picture button on the Header & Footer Tools Design tab, and then insert the data file **musiclogo.tif**.
   c. Scroll down to the footer area, enter the page number in the left section and custom text in the center section, as shown in Figure 13.2a, and then click the File Name button to enter the name of the file in the right footer section.
   d. Print Preview the worksheet and compare it to Figure 13.2a. Remove the gridlines and row and column headings from the Page Layout, if necessary. Print a copy.
3. Save the file and name it **13.2income**.
4. Save the file as a Single File Web page, and name it **13.2incweb**. *Note: The file will have an .mht extension.*
   a. Change the title to: **Comparative Income Statement – 1st Qtr.**
   b. Publish the page and then view the page in your browser.
5. Close your browser and return to the **13.2income** file and Normal view.
6. Modify the worksheet as shown in Figure 13.2b.
   a. Add column headers for columns F, G, and H, and adjust the titles so that they are centered over A:H. Be sure to use numeric labels for the years.
   b. Copy the 2009 and 2010 data columns to columns F and G.
   c. In H8, enter a formula to calculate the % Increase or Decrease between the years. *Hint: =(2010 data - 2009 data)/2009 data.*
   d. Copy the formula down the column, and format for Percent style with one decimal place.

WHAT YOU NEED TO KNOW

Software

▶ To enter a customized header or footer, click in the section you wish to modify, and then select the header or footer element from the Header & Footer Tools Design tab. The elements enter a code that displays the desired result when you deselect the section. You can click the Picture button to insert a logo or graphic, and then use the Format Picture button to customize settings once the picture is in place.

▶ Gridlines and row and column headings may be added to the printed copy, or removed by clicking the Page Layout tab and selecting or deselecting the Print box for each setting in the Sheet Options group.

▶ A Web page is a location on an Internet server, part of the World Wide Web, which can be reached and identified by a Web address. You can make workbooks available to employees or stockholders by saving all or part of a workbook as a Web page, so that users can view the worksheet without Excel.

▶ To save a workbook as a Web page in one folder, save the page as a Single File Web page with the .mht or .mhtml extension. You can create a title for your Web page by clicking Change Title in the Save As dialog box. The title you enter will appear centered over your worksheet on the Web page.

▶ When you click Publish in the Save As dialog box, the published page is saved to your local drive, and the Web page opens in Internet Explorer or your Web browser for you to preview. If you later revise the worksheet, you can republish the worksheet with the corrections. To publish it directly to the Internet, your company or school needs to have an account with a Website hosting company.

Project

▶ The income statement will be published with a title and will have a customized header, including a logo, for printing purposes.

7. Resave the **13.2income** file and republish the Web page using the same **13.2incweb** filename with the same title.
8. Print a copy of the worksheet from the browser.
9. Close the browser and close the file.

Insert Picture using logo file in left header section

Remove gridlines and row and column headings, if necessary

MusicMagic, Inc.
Income Statement Comparison
For Quarters Ended March 31, 2009 and 2010

	2009 Amount	% of Sales	2010 Amount	% of Sales	2009 Amount	2010 Amount	% Increase or Decrease
Revenue:							
Net Sales	472,543	100.0%	540,565	100.0%	472,543	540,565	14.4%
Less : Cost of Goods Sold	320,567	67.8%	360,876	66.8%	320,567	360,876	12.6%
Gross Profit	151,976	32.2%	179,689	33.2%	151,976	179,689	18.2%
Expenses:	100,119	21.2%	112,461	20.8%	100,119	112,461	12.3%
Net Income before Taxes	51,857	11.0%	67,228	12.4%	51,857	67,228	29.6%
Taxes	15,557	3.3%	20,168	3.7%	15,557	20,168	29.6%
Net Income after Taxes	$ 36,300	7.7%	$ 47,060	8.7%	$ 36,300	$ 47,060	29.6%

Enter text in center section of footer and insert filename in right section

Income Statement Comparison   exfig13.2a_sourcefile.xls

Figure 13.2a Report with header and footer

Web Page title as it will be seen in browser

Comparative Income Statement - 1st Qtr.

Copy comparative data columns and add % Increase or Decrease column and formula

MusicMagic, Inc.
Income Statement Comparison
For Quarters Ended March 31, 2009 and 2010

	2009 Amount	% of Sales	2010 Amount	% of Sales	2009 Amount	2010 Amount	% Increase or Decrease
Revenue:							
Net Sales	472,543	100.0%	540,565	100.0%	472,543	540,565	14.4%
Less : Cost of Goods Sold	320,567	67.8%	360,876	66.8%	320,567	360,876	12.6%
Gross Profit	151,976	32.2%	179,689	33.2%	151,976	179,689	18.2%
Expenses:	100,119	21.2%	112,461	20.8%	100,119	112,461	12.3%
Net Income before Taxes	51,857	11.0%	67,228	12.4%	51,857	67,228	29.6%
Taxes	15,557	3.3%	20,168	3.7%	15,557	20,168	29.6%
Net Income after Taxes	$ 36,300	7.7%	$ 47,060	8.7%	$ 36,300	$ 47,060	29.6%

Figure 13.2b Published Web page

13.3 CREATE AND PUBLISH AN INCOME STATEMENT ANALYSIS

GameDepot is a retailer of small electronics and game software with stores located in several malls in Atlanta, Georgia. You are to analyze income statements for the third quarter of this year and last year, and to develop a report for a presentation to a managers' meeting. You will need to add a footer and background pattern on the analysis, and to make the workbook available as a Web page for personnel who cannot attend.

In this project, you will prepare an income statement analysis, add a footer and background pattern, and then publish it as a Web page.

1. Open the data file **d13.3income**.
2. Using Figure 13.3a as a guide, do the following:
   a. Unmerge the titles in rows 1:3 so that you can select and delete columns in the worksheet. Change the title in row 3.
   b. Delete the contents of the number data columns except for Actual 3rd Qtr. data.
   c. Right-click and copy the Actual 3rd Qtr. column, and then use Paste Special, Values, and number formats to copy it into the next column without formulas. Delete the original column. Rename the new column **2010 3rd Quarter**, using a numeric label.
   d. Delete row 6, and then insert columns and new headings, using numeric labels where necessary.
   e. Delete rows necessary to create the summary income statement shown.
   f. Retain the title cell styles and formats, and extend the merge and centered titles over the new worksheet.
   g. Use the Indent feature to correct any misalignments.
   h. Add the 2009 data as shown. Format the data for commas with no decimals.
3. Enter the following formulas and format:
   a. In cell B12, find the Gross Profit.
      Hint: Sales – Cost of Goods Sold.
   b. In cell B17, find the Total Expenses.
   c. In cell B19, find Net Income before Taxes.
      Hint: Gross Profit – Total Expenses.
   d. In cell B21, find the Net Income after Taxes.
      Hint: Net Income before Taxes – Taxes.
   e. In cell C9, find the % that each item is of Sales, and format for Percent style with one decimal place. *Hint: B9/$B$9*.
   f. In cell E9, find the % that each item is of Sales, and format for Percent style with one decimal place. *Hint: D9/$D$9*.

WHAT YOU NEED TO KNOW

Software

▶ If you wish to use data that contains formulas and you are deleting the data that the formula needs, you need to convert the formula answers to values. You can copy and paste the numbers using the Paste Special, Values commands so that the numbers are pasted as values, not text or formulas. Right-click the selected cells to copy, click Copy on the shortcut menu, move to the new location, and then right-click and select Paste Special. Click Values on the dialog box that appears, and then click OK.

▶ A background is a pattern that is added, using a picture file, to a worksheet to enhance the way it's displayed for a visual presentation. The background pattern does not print, will fill the sheet, and will be retained in the saved file. To add a background, click the Page Layout tab, and in the Page Setup group, click the Background button. To further enhance the display, you may want to remove the gridlines and headings and use the full screen setting. Remove the background by clicking the Page Layout tab, and in the Page Setup group, click the Delete Background button.

4. Copy the formulas to the appropriate locations, and then clear unwanted results.
5. Check all values and formats, including the borders.
6. Add the text **`Income Statement Analysis - 3rd Quarter`** in the center footer area, and set the filename in the right footer section.
7. Add a background using **dunesbackground.jpg**, as in Figure 13.3b. Remove gridlines, if necessary.
8. Save the file as **13.3income**, and then save it as a Web page with the name **13.3incweb**.
9. Publish the page and change the title to read: **`Income Statement Analysis - 3rd Quarter`**
10. Print a copy of the page from the browser. Close the browser, and close the file.

	A	B	C	D	E
1	GameDepot, Inc.				
2	Comparison of Budgeted Income Statement with Actual Income Statement				
3	For Quarters Ended September 30, 2009 and 2010				
4					
5					
6		2009	% of Sales	2010	% of Sales
7		3rd Quarter		3rd Quarter	
8	Revenue:				
9	Net Sales	491,650		565,043	
10	Cost of Goods Sold	307,588		350,657	
11					
12	Gross Profit			214,386	
13					
14	Expenses:				
15	Total Selling Expenses	76,962		87,233	
16	Total Administrative Expenses	51,398		56,380	
17	Total Expenses			143,613	
18					
19	Net Income before Taxes			70,773	
20	Taxes	16,711		21,232	
21	Net Income after Taxes			**49,541**	

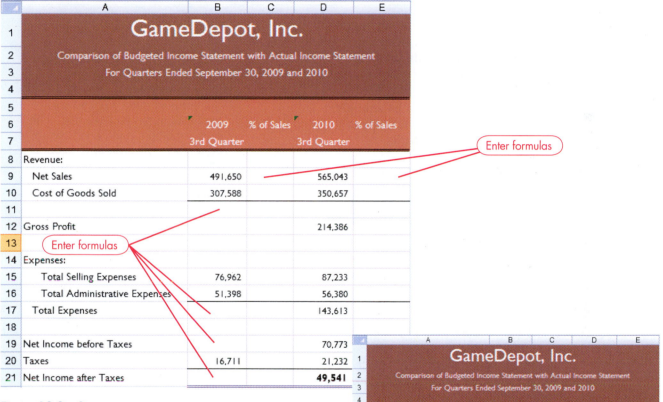

Figure 13.3a Summary income statement comparison

	A	B	C	D	E
1	GameDepot, Inc.				
2	Comparison of Budgeted Income Statement with Actual Income Statement				
3	For Quarters Ended September 30, 2009 and 2010				
4					
5					
6		2009	% of Sales	2010	% of Sales
7		3rd Quarter		3rd Quarter	
8	Revenue:				
9	Net Sales	491,650	100.0%	565,043	100.0%
10	Cost of Goods Sold	307,588	62.6%	350,657	62.1%
11					
12	Gross Profit	184,062	37.4%	214,386	37.9%
13					
14	Expenses:				
15	Total Selling Expenses	76,962	15.7%	87,233	15.4%
16	Total Administrative Expenses	51,398	10.5%	56,380	10.0%
17	Total Expenses	128,360	26.1%	143,613	25.4%
18					
19	Net Income before Taxes	55,702	11.3%	70,773	12.5%
20	Taxes	16,711	3.4%	21,232	3.8%
21	Net Income after Taxes	**38,991**	7.9%	**49,541**	8.8%

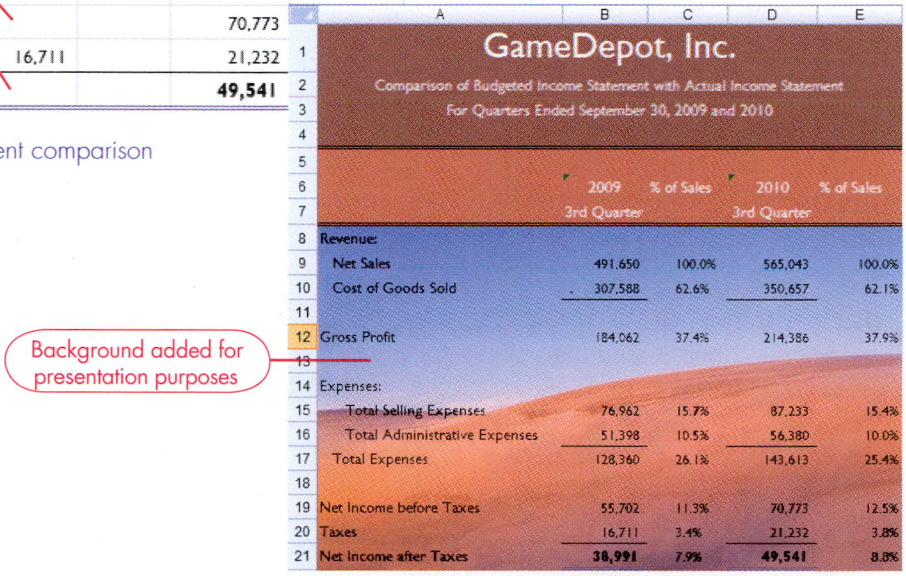

Figure 13.3b Worksheet with a background

PROJECT 14

▶ **PROJECT SKILLS**
- ✴ Group worksheets
- ✴ Rename and format worksheet tabs
- ✴ Print workbooks with multiple worksheets
- ✴ Format borders
- ✴ Insert and delete worksheets
- ✴ Move worksheets
- ✴ Hide and unhide columns
- ✴ Enter date format and functions
- ✴ Use the Fraction format

14.1 CREATE A SALES ANALYSIS

Barlow's Department Store has seven personal shoppers. You have been asked to analyze the sales, commissions, and salaries for these employees for January, February, and March.

In this project, you will create and format an analysis of sales and the earnings of each personal shopper, using a separate worksheet for each month.

1. Open data file **d14.1sales**, and note that it includes January, February, and March sales data.
2. Use the fill handle to create the employee number data, as shown in Figure 14.1. Format the numbers for commas.
3. Enter the formulas to complete the January analysis.
   a. In cell G7, find Net Sales. *Hint: Sales – Returns*.
   b. In cell H7, find the Commission. *Hint: Net Sales*10%*.
   c. In cell I7, find the January salary for Mindi Hochman. *Hint: Base Salary + Commission*.
   d. Format all the answers for commas, and then use the fill handle to bring the formulas down to each employee.
   e. In cell D14, find the total of the column, and then format it for commas.
   f. In cell D15, find the average base salary, and then format it for commas.
   g. Copy the formulas across to all columns.
4. Copy the worksheet, range A1:I15, then group Sheets 2 and 3, and then paste the worksheet into the grouped sheets. Double-click the columns that need to be widened.
5. Ungroup the sheets by clicking the Sheet1 tab, and then select Sheet2. Change January in cells A3 and I5 to **February** and rename the sheet **February**.
6. Select Sheet3. Change January to **March** in cells A3 and I5, and rename the sheet **March**.

▼ **WHAT YOU NEED TO KNOW**

Software

▶ When working with multiple worksheets in a workbook, you can expedite formatting and data entry by grouping the sheets. To group sheets and make the entries on the grouped sheets simultaneously, click the first sheet, press and hold [Ctrl], and then select all the other sheets. Or, if the sheets you want to select are next to one another, you can click the first sheet, press and hold [Shift] and then click the last sheet of the group.

▶ You can rename a sheet by right-clicking the sheet name, clicking Rename, and entering the name.

▶ When you wish to print all the pages in a workbook, either group the sheets and print them, or select Entire workbook in the Print dialog box. With multiple-page workbooks it is important to add footers so that pages can be kept in order and/or to identify the file.

Project

▶ A personal shopper is someone who helps customers shop for the things they need. A personal shopper will often know what the customer is looking for and will call when the item comes in to the store. Their customers are people who are busy, who do not like to shop, or who need help making decisions. There is usually no charge to the customer for this service.

▶ Personal shoppers are store employees, and they are given a base salary per month, which is the least amount that they will be paid monthly. In addition, they receive a 10% commission on net sales. Net sales are the sales they make less the returns on those sales.

7. Rename Sheet1 **January**.

8. Copy the February data from the January sheet in cells E18:F23, select the February sheet, and then paste it into cell E7. Notice that the formula values change with the new data. Delete the February data from the January sheet.

9. Repeat Step 8, using the March data and March sheet.

10. Delete row 17 on the January sheet.

11. Group all the sheets and then change the theme to Median. Format the analysis as shown in Figure 14.1. Use the Accent4 cell style, but change the font color to Black. Use borders, merge and center, and a lighter color cell style as indicated.

12. With the sheets still grouped, insert a footer containing the sheet name, filename, and current date.

13. Print a copy of all sheets in landscape orientation.

14. Save the workbook and name it **14.1sales**. Close the file.

	A	B	C	D	E	F	G	H	I
1				**Barlow's Department Store**					
2				Personal Shopper Sales Analysis					
3				January					
4									
5									January
6	Emp. No.	Name	Store	Base Salary	Sales	Returns	Net Sales	Commission	Salary
7	235	Hochman, Mindi	Raleigh	1,300.00	11,235.65	1,087.87			
8	236	Burns, Wendy	Raleigh	1,200.00	10,976.56	1,234.65			
9		Burkett, Grace	Raleigh	1,100.00	9,807.54	876.98			
10		Powers, Anne	Durham	1,250.00	11,657.56	879.65			
11		Nunez, Carlos	Durham	1,150.00	10,765.65	959.02			
12		Thompson, Walter	Durham	1,250.00	12,656.65	1,087.09			
13									
14		Total							
15		Averages							

Callouts: Median theme, Accent4 cell style, Black font, 20 point · 40% - Accent4 cell style · Enter formulas · Use fill handle to create number series · Cut and paste February and March data to appropriate locations · Rename sheets

Sheet tabs: January / February / March

Figure 14.1

14.2 CREATE A BILLINGS AND REVENUE ANALYSIS

Jane Martino Interiors has compiled all billing and revenue information for the last two quarters. The firm wants you to create a quarterly analysis on separate worksheets in a workbook and then compare the results of the first two quarters of the year.

In this project, you will create, calculate, and format a billings and revenue analysis workbook.

1. Open data file **d14.2revenue** and note the contents of sheets 1–3.
2. Group all sheets and format them as shown in Figure 14.2a.
   a. Change the theme to Median.
   b. Use the Accent5 cell style for the title and the 40% - Accent5 cell style for the banded rows.
   c. Merge and center the first three rows across columns A:E. Increase the font size for the company name to 20 point, and then adjust the row height if necessary.
   d. Set a bottom border in row 3 and row 19 using More Borders in the Borders gallery. Select a thick bottom border, and then set the color to Green, Accent 5, Darker 50%.
   e. Format all values for commas with no decimal places. Double-click the columns that need to be widened.
   f. Apply bold and italics to the text as shown in Figure 14.2a.
3. Group Sheet1 and Sheet2, and then enter formulas as listed below and extend them for all values. Widen the columns, if necessary, and then delete zero or error results from cells that do not reflect data. Adjust cell styles and borders as necessary.
   a. In cell E7 enter a formula to find the quarterly total, and then copy it down for cells E7:E12.
   b. Total the billings for each month.
   c. Calculate Fees on Vendor Billings, which are 15% of total vendor billings.
   d. Add all revenue items to calculate Total revenue.
4. Rename Sheet1: **1st Qtr**. Rename Sheet2: **2nd Qtr**. Rename Sheet3: **Comparison**.
5. Copy the 1st Qtr. totals in E7:E19 from the first sheet and use Paste Special, set to Values and number formats to place the numbers on the Comparison sheet. Repeat this step with the 2nd Qtr. totals. Widen the columns, if necessary.
6. Add column headers to the Comparison sheet to calculate the increase and decrease amounts and percentages, as shown in Figure 14.2b.
7. Enter formulas for comparison data. Format column D for commas with no decimal places and column E for Percent style with one decimal place.

▼ **WHAT YOU NEED TO KNOW**

Software

► You have added borders using the Borders button on the Mini toolbar and on the Home tab. You can change the type or color of the border lines by selecting More Borders from the Borders button drop-down menu.

Project

► Jane Martino Interiors is an interior design studio that offers design services to clients in West Palm Beach, Florida. They receive retainers for design services and fees for renderings or drawings of room designs. Customers also pay 15% over the wholesale decorator prices on all billings for purchases.

► The analysis of revenues and billings for the first quarter will be placed on Sheet1, the second quarter will be placed on Sheet2, and the quarterly results will be compared on the third sheet.

8. On the Comparison sheet, correct any borders and fill colors that need modification, complete any total lines that need formulas, and delete any zero or error results that do not reflect data.

9. Save the workbook and name it **14.2revenue**. Close the file.

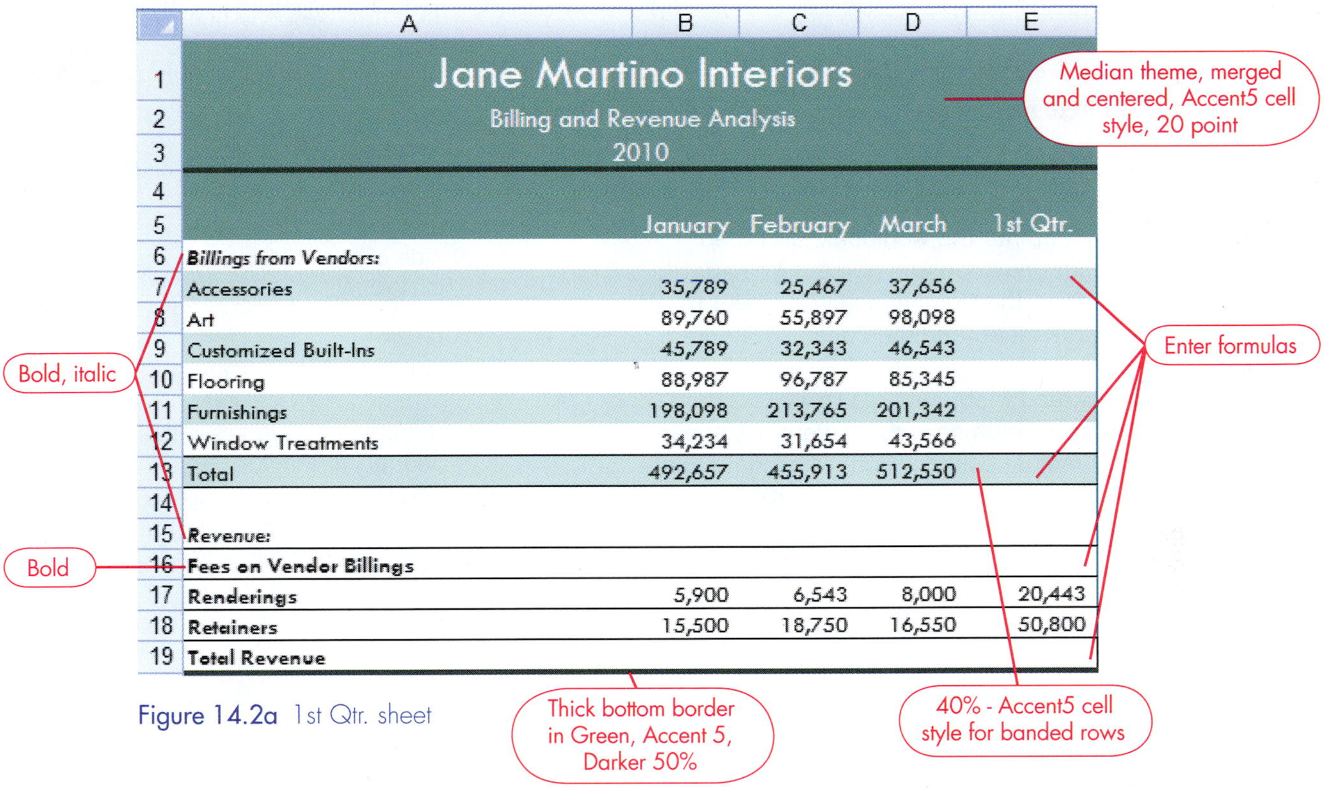

Median theme, merged and centered, Accent5 cell style, 20 point

Enter formulas

Bold, italic

Bold

	A	B	C	D	E
1	**Jane Martino Interiors**				
2	Billing and Revenue Analysis				
3	2010				
4					
5		January	February	March	1st Qtr.
6	*Billings from Vendors:*				
7	Accessories	35,789	25,467	37,656	
8	Art	89,760	55,897	98,098	
9	Customized Built-Ins	45,789	32,343	46,543	
10	Flooring	88,987	96,787	85,345	
11	Furnishings	198,098	213,765	201,342	
12	Window Treatments	34,234	31,654	43,566	
13	Total	492,657	455,913	512,550	
14					
15	*Revenue:*				
16	**Fees on Vendor Billings**				
17	Renderings	5,900	6,543	8,000	20,443
18	Retainers	15,500	18,750	16,550	50,800
19	**Total Revenue**				

Figure 14.2a 1st Qtr. sheet

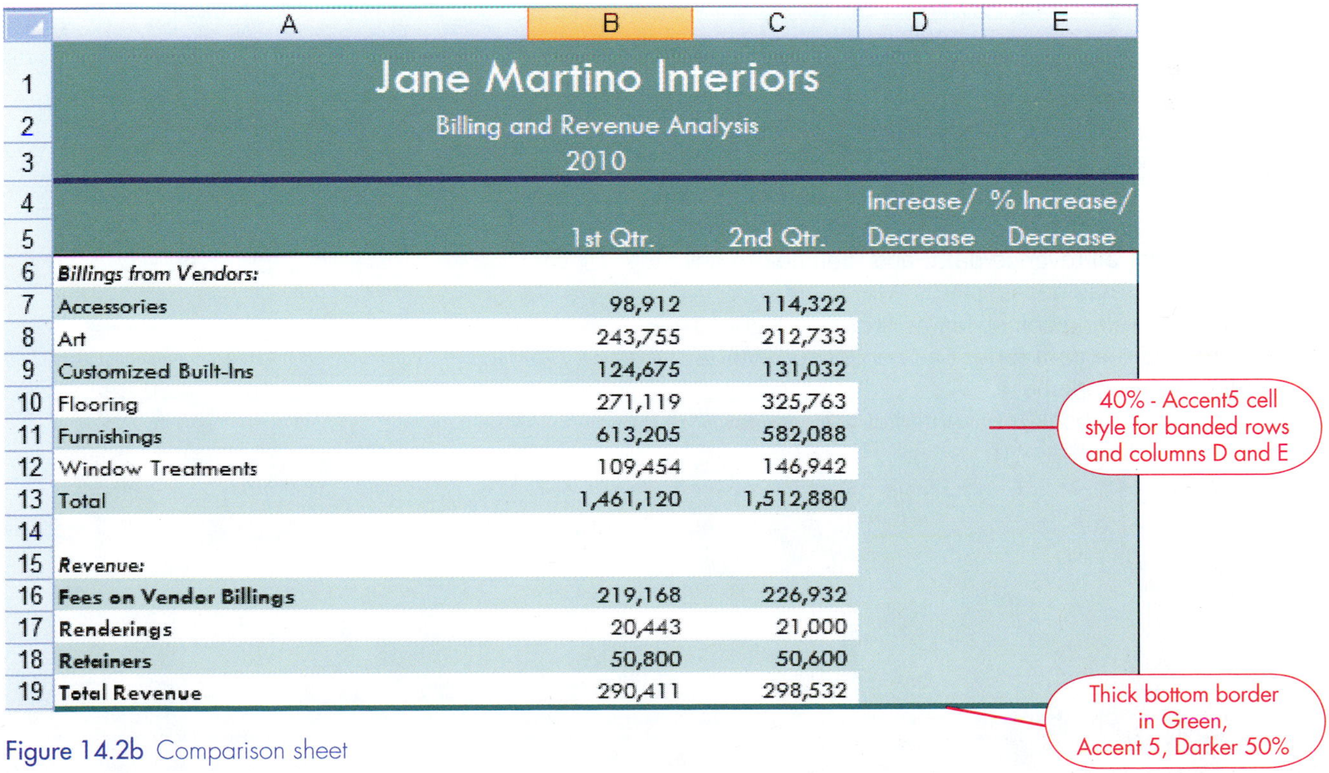

Thick bottom border in Green, Accent 5, Darker 50%

40% - Accent5 cell style for banded rows

	A	B	C	D	E
1	**Jane Martino Interiors**				
2	Billing and Revenue Analysis				
3	2010				
4				Increase/	% Increase/
5		1st Qtr.	2nd Qtr.	Decrease	Decrease
6	*Billings from Vendors:*				
7	Accessories	98,912	114,322		
8	Art	243,755	212,733		
9	Customized Built-Ins	124,675	131,032		
10	Flooring	271,119	325,763		
11	Furnishings	613,205	582,088		
12	Window Treatments	109,454	146,942		
13	Total	1,461,120	1,512,880		
14					
15	*Revenue:*				
16	**Fees on Vendor Billings**	219,168	226,932		
17	Renderings	20,443	21,000		
18	Retainers	50,800	50,600		
19	**Total Revenue**	290,411	298,532		

Figure 14.2b Comparison sheet

40% - Accent5 cell style for banded rows and columns D and E

Thick bottom border in Green, Accent 5, Darker 50%

14.3 CREATE A REVENUE FORECAST AND ANALYSIS

Jane Martino Interiors would like you to estimate its annual revenues by forecasting the revenues for the third and fourth quarters, based on the trend established this year.

In this project, you will forecast sales and calculate the estimated change for the year.

1. Open **14.2revenue**, your solution from the last project, or open data file **d14.3forecast**.
2. Insert a new sheet into the workbook, and then move it to the last position and name it **Forecast**.
3. Copy the data from the Comparison worksheet to the Forecast worksheet, and then adjust column width.
4. Hide Column D, and then unmerge rows 1, 2, and 3.
5. Add the three new columns with headers, as shown in Figure 14.3. Adjust column width to accommodate column headers. Merge and center the 2010 label over columns A:E. Add a new header, **Sales Forecast**, in cell F3, and then merge and center it over columns F:H.
6. Enter the following formulas and format the results for commas with no decimal places.
   a. Enter a formula in cell F13 to forecast 3rd Qtr. revenue. *Hint: =2nd Qtr*% Increase or Decrease+2ndQtr*.
   b. Enter a formula in cell G13 to forecast 4th Qtr. revenue by applying the percentage increase in Column E to 3rd Qtr. revenues.
   c. Copy the formulas down from row 13 to row 19 for all revenue data.
   d. Delete formulas from cells with no data.
7. Enter a formula in cell H13 to calculate the annual increase. *Hint: =(4th Qtr-1st Qtr)/1st Qtr*. Format the data for percent with one decimal place. Copy the formula for all revenue data, and then delete any error results as necessary.
8. Add borders and cell styles as shown in Figure 14.3, correcting the data format as necessary. Print a copy of the worksheet.
9. Save the workbook and name it **14.3forecast**. Close the file.

WHAT YOU NEED TO KNOW

Software
▶ To add a sheet to a workbook, right-click a sheet tab, click Insert, select Worksheet, and then click OK.
▶ To rearrange worksheets in a workbook, click the sheet tab and then drag and drop it into the desired location.
▶ To hide a column, select and right-click the column, and then click Hide on the shortcut menu. To restore it, select and right-click the columns on either side of the hidden column(s), and then click Unhide.

Project
▶ Although revenues cannot be predicted with absolute accuracy, companies try to estimate or forecast them, based on past performance.
▶ In this project, you will use the percent change between the first and second quarters as the basis for forecasting the change in revenues for the third and fourth quarters. Usually, however, data from several quarters of the previous year should be used as a basis for a forecast, and in that case, you can use the Forecast function in Excel that uses regression analysis.
▶ To find the new value after a percent increase is calculated and added, multiply the value by the percent increase and then add the original value. For example, to find what $500 is after a 10% increase, use this formula: =500*10%+500.

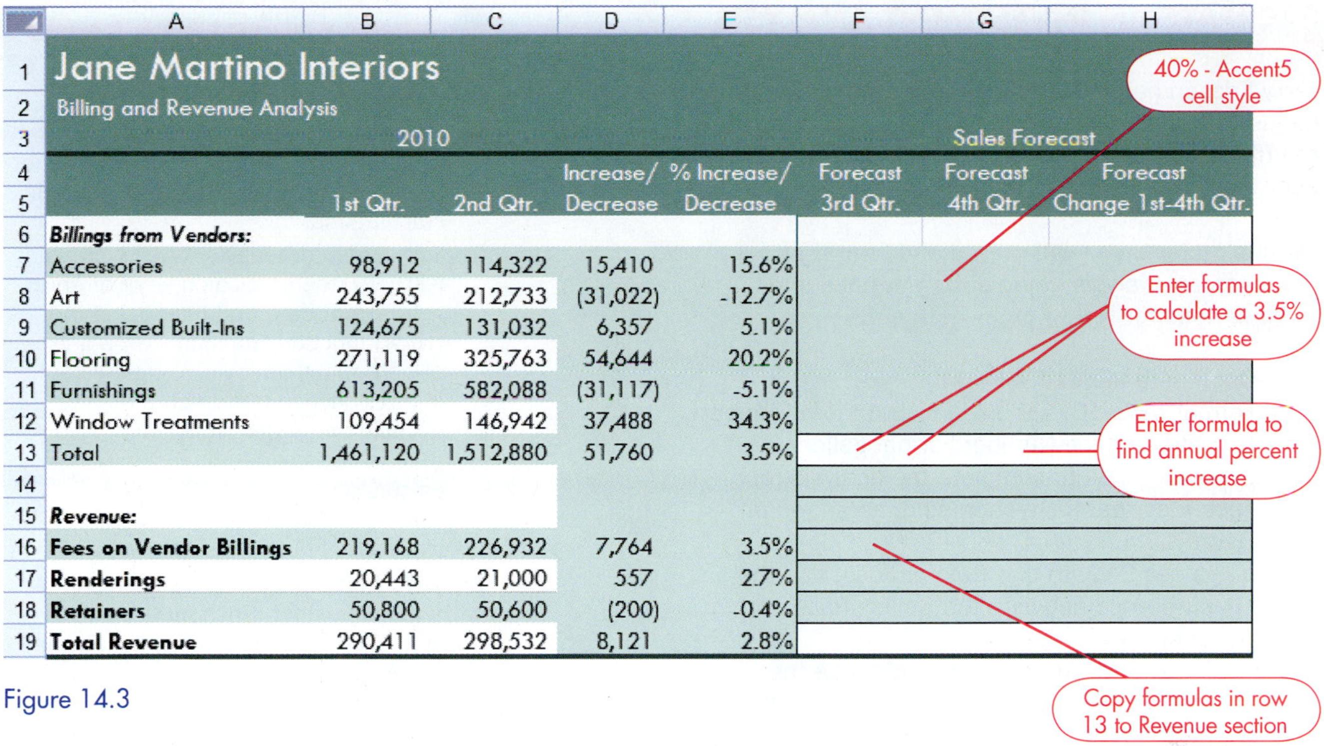

	A	B	C	D	E	F	G	H
1	**Jane Martino Interiors**							
2	Billing and Revenue Analysis							
3			2010				Sales Forecast	
4				Increase/	% Increase/	Forecast	Forecast	Forecast
5		1st Qtr.	2nd Qtr.	Decrease	Decrease	3rd Qtr.	4th Qtr.	Change 1st–4th Qtr.
6	*Billings from Vendors:*							
7	Accessories	98,912	114,322	15,410	15.6%			
8	Art	243,755	212,733	(31,022)	-12.7%			
9	Customized Built-Ins	124,675	131,032	6,357	5.1%			
10	Flooring	271,119	325,763	54,644	20.2%			
11	Furnishings	613,205	582,088	(31,117)	-5.1%			
12	Window Treatments	109,454	146,942	37,488	34.3%			
13	Total	1,461,120	1,512,880	51,760	3.5%			
14								
15	*Revenue:*							
16	**Fees on Vendor Billings**	219,168	226,932	7,764	3.5%			
17	**Renderings**	20,443	21,000	557	2.7%			
18	**Retainers**	50,800	50,600	(200)	-0.4%			
19	**Total Revenue**	290,411	298,532	8,121	2.8%			

Annotations:
- 40% - Accent5 cell style
- Enter formulas to calculate a 3.5% increase
- Enter formula to find annual percent increase
- Copy formulas in row 13 to Revenue section

Figure 14.3

EXCEL

14.4 CREATE AN INVESTMENT ANALYSIS

Terry Ericson has a portfolio of investments that she needs to check regularly. She wants you to find her return on investment, to help her with buying and selling decisions.

In this project, you will create and format an investment analysis using date functions and calculations for return on investment.

1. Open data file **d14.4invest**.
2. Format rows 10, 11, 17, 18, and 19 in Number format using the Number Format gallery.
3. Enter formulas to complete the analysis for securities that have been sold, as shown in Figure 14.4.
   a. In cell B12, to find Gain or Loss, find the difference between the Selling Price and the Cost.
   b. In cell B13, to find Time Held, use the =YEARFRAC function to calculate the time between the start and end dates. Format the answer for fractions. *Hint: =YEARFRAC(B7,B8).*
   c. In cell B14, find the Annualized Return by finding the percentage that the gain or loss is of the cost and dividing it by the time held. Format it for Percent style with one decimal place. *Hint: =Gain or Loss/Cost/Time Held.*
   d. Copy the formulas to columns C and D.
   e. Shade columns B:D as shown to indicate that these stocks were sold.
4. In cell E16, in a bordered box, press [Ctrl]+[;] to enter today's date.
5. Use the sample prices in the data file in E17:J17 or replace them with the current market prices of the securities. Use the stock symbols to obtain the current price of each security from the Internet or from the financial section of your newspaper.
6. In cell E9, change 100 shares to 200 shares. Enter a comment as follows: **Bought 100 shares. In 8/2000, split 2 for 1.**
7. Enter the formulas to complete the analysis for current holdings.
   a. In cell E18, calculate Total Market Value by multiplying the number of shares by the current market price per share.
   b. In cell E19, find the current Gain or Loss, using the market price less the cost of the investment.
   c. In cell E20, find the Time Held from the date purchased to today's date. Use an absolute reference for today's date in the YEARFRAC function. Format the result for fractions.

WHAT YOU NEED TO KNOW

Software

▶ When you enter a date, Excel automatically creates a serial value for the date, which allows you to use it in calculations.

▶ You can enter today's date by pressing [Ctrl]+[;] (the semicolon key), or enter the current date and time using the NOW() function. You can view a list of date functions by clicking the Insert Function button on the formula bar. A date function that can be used in financial calculations is =YEARFRAC, which returns the time between two dates in fractions of a year.

▶ To format a mixed number, which is a number with a fraction, use the Fraction format in the Number Format gallery on the Home tab.

Project

▶ For tax purposes, records must be kept of the purchase and sales dates of investments. The return on your investment is calculated by finding the percentage of gain or loss from the cost or purchase price. The percent gain or loss must be divided by the years held to find the annualized return on investment.

▶ In this project, dividends are not included in the calculations. Only the gain or loss on the value of the investment is calculated.

▶ For investments that are not sold, calculate the return on each investment as if it were sold today. There is no actual gain or loss until the investment is sold. The current market price may be found on the Internet or in the financial section of your newspaper. If you use current prices, overwrite the data provided in the data file.

d. In cell E21, find the Annualized Return using the gain or loss, cost price, and time held, as you did in B14. Format the result for percent with one decimal place.

e. Copy the formulas for all stocks.

8. Format the worksheet with cell styles and borders.

9. Hide the columns for sold securities, and then print a copy of the worksheet.

10. Save the workbook and name it **14.4invest**. Close the file.

	A	B	C	D	E	F	G	H	I	J
1	Terry Ericson									
2	Portfolio									
3	Investment Analysis									
4										
5	Description:	IBM	Nike, Inc	Ford Motors	Intel, Inc	Genl Elec	Microsoft	Apple	Pepsi	Coca Cola
6	Symbol:	IBM	NKE	F	INTC	GE	MSFT	AAPL	PBG	COKE
7	Date Bought	10/21/2002	9/4/2001	10/5/2002	9/8/1999	5/15/2003	6/7/2004	12/7/2005	10/8/2006	1/7/2007
8	Date Sold	12/20/2006	8/22/2007	2/1/2008						
9	Number of Shares	100	100	100	200	100	100	100	100	100
10	Cost	7825.75	2895.00	1050.56	4325.65	2958.50	2895.45	7235.45	3654.50	6225.25
11	Selling Price	9125.50	5764.25	935.00						
12	Gain or Loss									
13	Time Held -Sold									
14	Annualized Return - Sold									
15										
16	Today:									
17	Market Value Per Share									
18	Total Market Value									
19	Gain or Loss									
20	Time Held - Current									
21	Annualized Return - Current									

Enter today's date

Use market value in data file or replace with current data

Enter formulas for sold investments and copy them to columns C and D

Enter formulas in E18: E21 and copy across

Figure 14.4

CHAPTER 5

Create Financial Reports

In this chapter, you will complete the following projects:

PROJECT 15
Trial Balance

PROJECT 15.1 Complete a Trial Balance and Schedules
PROJECT 15.2 Create a Trial Balance and Schedules with Hyperlinks

PROJECT 16
Salary Analyses

PROJECT 16.1 Create a Sales and Commissions Report
PROJECT 16.2 Create an Analysis of Salary Increases

PROJECT 17
Accounting Worksheets

PROJECT 17.1 Complete an Accounting Worksheet
PROJECT 17.2 Complete an Accounting Worksheet with Hyperlinks

PROJECT 18
Income Statement

PROJECT 18.1 Create an Income Statement Analysis
PROJECT 18.2 Create a Quarterly Income Statement Analysis

PROJECT 19
Balance Sheet

PROJECT 19.1 Create a Balance Sheet
PROJECT 19.2 Format a Balance Sheet

PROJECT 20
Financial Report Analysis

PROJECT 20.1 Analyze Income Statement Data
PROJECT 20.2 Analyze Balance Sheet Data

TRIAL BALANCE

PROJECT 15

PROJECT SKILLS

* Work with multiple workbooks and links
* Create formulas that reference data from other worksheets or workbooks
* Work with hyperlinks

15.1 COMPLETE A TRIAL BALANCE AND SCHEDULES

Voyagers Travel Mart has prepared schedules of accounts receivable and accounts payable. They want you to link the schedule totals to the trial balance. Trial balance totals should be equal to prove the validity of account balances.

In this project, you will total and link schedule data to a trial balance, so that if the schedule changes, the trial balance will be updated.

1. Open data file **d15.1sched**.
2. Group the schedules on Sheet1 and Sheet2 and format the titles, as shown in Figure 15.1a. Name the sheets: **Accounts Receivable** and **Accounts Payable**.
3. Ungroup the sheets, total each sheet, add borders, and add the word **Total**.
4. Open data file **d15.1tb** and format the titles, as shown in Figure 15.1b.
5. Switch back to the Schedule of Accounts Receivable and copy the total. Switch to the Trial Balance, right-click in cell C7, click Paste Special, and then Paste link the total to the Debit column.
6. Switch back to the Schedule of Accounts Payable and copy the total. Paste link the Total to cell D14 in the Credit column of the Trial Balance.
7. Total the Trial Balance, enter **Totals** in cell B28, and add borders. Notice that the totals do not balance.
8. After all balances were checked, an error was found in Mario Sanchez's accounts receivable account. The balance should be $695.65, not $965.65. Make the correction. The linked total should automatically be updated on the Trial Balance.
9. Format values for commas in all workbooks. Adjust column width as necessary.
10. Save both files and name them **15.1tb** and **15.1sched**.
11. Close the file.

WHAT YOU NEED TO KNOW

Software

► To toggle between open workbooks when working with several workbooks at once, use the file buttons on the Windows taskbar or click the View tab, and in the Window group, click the Switch Windows button. To arrange all the workbooks on one screen, use the Arrange All button on the View tab and select the arrangement you prefer.

► To reference data from another workbook, paste link a cell from one workbook to another by copying the cell data and then, in the other workbook location, right-click, click Paste Special, and then select Paste Link. When you link summary totals between worksheets, the data in the linked location is updated when the source data changes.

Project

► Schedules of accounts receivable, accounts payable, and the trial balance are accounting forms prepared to check the accuracy of business accounts in the company's ledgers.

► The schedule of accounts receivable lists customers' balances, while the schedule of accounts payable lists balances owed to creditors. The total value of accounts receivable and accounts payable is listed on the trial balance and the numbers come from the linked total of each schedule.

► The trial balance summarizes the balances of all the ledger accounts. Some accounts have debit (left-side) balances, and the rest have credit (right-side) balances. To prove the accuracy of the ledger accounts, the debit and credit balances should be equal.

Voyagers Travel Mart
Schedule of Accounts Receivable
December 31, 2010

Calibri, 18 point, Dark Blue fill color, Yellow font color

12 point

	A	B	C
5		Avalon, Dave	765.09
6		Barton, Roger	165.98
7		Boessler, Grace	303.44
8		Carina, Tracey	1,155.34
9		Friedman, Carol	345.43
10		Harrigan, Jack	653.76
11		Jackson, Laticia	896.54
12		Martinson, William	1,546.54
13		Noto, Christina	745.54
14		Overlook, Thomas	598.76
15		Porter, Selma	1,298.65
16		Sanchez, Mario	695.65
17		Vincentian, Peter	823.43
18		Total	9,994.15

Top and Double Bottom Border

Figure 15.1a Accounts Receivable Schedule

Calibri, 18 point, Dark Blue fill color, Yellow font color

Voyagers Travel Mart
Trial Balance
December 31, 2010

12 point

11 point

Bold headings, Yellow fill color, Thick Bottom Border

	A	B	C	D
4	Account		Debit	Credit
5	Number	Account	Balances	Balances
6	100	Cash	5,875.85	
7	110	Accounts Receivable		
8	115	Allowance for Bad Debts		187.40
9	120	Merchandise Inventory	40,509.00	
10	130	Supplies	646.54	
11	140	Prepaid Insurance	410.91	
12	150	Equipment	5,280.00	
13	155	Accumulated Depreciation		1,269.00
14	200	Accounts Payable		
15	210	Payroll Taxes Payable		490.00
16	220	Sales Tax Payable		644.17
17	300	Roberto Rivera, Capital		47,987.00
18	310	Roberto Rivera, Personal	1,250.00	
19	400	Sales		38,413.07
20	405	Sales Returns	636.33	
21	500	Purchase	31,500.43	
22	610	Advertising Expense	281.38	
23	620	Insurance Expense	120.35	
24	630	Miscellaneous Expense	207.14	
25	640	Payroll Expense	163.56	
26	650	Rent Expense	600.00	
27	660	Supplies Expense	1,738.00	
28		Totals		

Paste link Accounts Receivable total here

Paste link Accounts Payable total here

Totals should balance

Figure 15.1b Trial Balance

Wheels Onboard sells skates, skateboards, snowboards, and accessories at discounted prices. The bookkeepers have prepared schedules of accounts receivable and payable and a trial balance. They would like you to link the trial balance directly to the supporting schedule.

In this project, you will total and link schedule data to a trial balance and create hyperlinks to the schedules from the trial balance.

1. Open data file **d15.2sched**.
2. Group the schedules on Sheet1 and Sheet2, and format the workbook in the Civic theme. Apply the Accent6 cell style, using the trial balance in Figure 15.2 as a guide. Adjust column width as necessary.
3. Ungroup the sheets, total each sheet, apply the Total cell style, and add the word **Total**.
4. Name the sheets **Accounts Receivable** and **Accounts Payable**.
5. Open data file **d15.2tb**, apply the Civic theme, adjust column width as necessary, and format the titles as shown.
6. Switch back to the schedules file, and copy and paste link the Accounts Receivable and Accounts Payable totals to the Trial Balance.
7. Total the Trial Balance and apply the Total cell style. Notice that the Totals do not balance.
8. After all account balances were checked, an error was found in HiStyle Boards, Inc., an accounts payable account. The balance should be $1299.78, not $1799.78. Make the correction. The linked Totals should automatically be updated on the Trial Balance. Adjust column width as necessary.
9. Format values for commas in all workbooks.
10. Create hyperlinks for the following:
    a. Save both files and name them **15.2tb** and **15.2sched**.
    b. Enter the hyperlink text **(See Schedule)** on **15.2tb** in cells C8 and C15, as shown in Figure 15.2.
    c. Right-click the text for the Accounts Receivable link, and click Hyperlink on the Shortcut menu.
    d. Select the **15.2sched** file, and click Bookmark to set the link to the appropriate sheet in the file.
    e. Repeat Steps b through d for the Accounts Payable hyperlink.
11. Save both files and test the links.
12. Close both files.

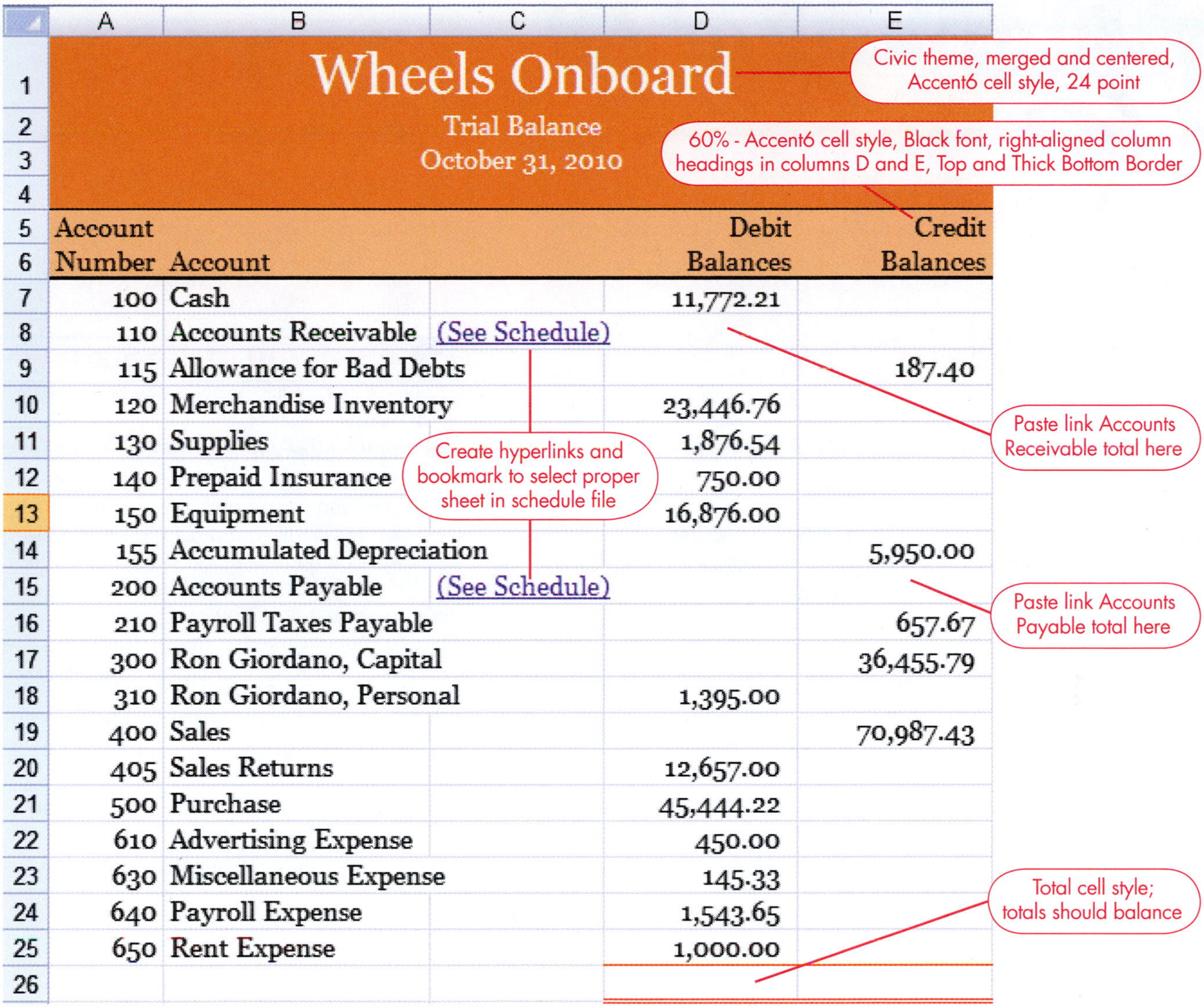

	A	B	C	D	E
1			**Wheels Onboard**		
2			Trial Balance		
3			October 31, 2010		
4					
5	Account			Debit	Credit
6	Number	Account		Balances	Balances
7	100	Cash		11,772.21	
8	110	Accounts Receivable	(See Schedule)		
9	115	Allowance for Bad Debts			187.40
10	120	Merchandise Inventory		23,446.76	
11	130	Supplies		1,876.54	
12	140	Prepaid Insurance		750.00	
13	150	Equipment		16,876.00	
14	155	Accumulated Depreciation			5,950.00
15	200	Accounts Payable	(See Schedule)		
16	210	Payroll Taxes Payable			657.67
17	300	Ron Giordano, Capital			36,455.79
18	310	Ron Giordano, Personal		1,395.00	
19	400	Sales			70,987.43
20	405	Sales Returns		12,657.00	
21	500	Purchase		45,444.22	
22	610	Advertising Expense		450.00	
23	630	Miscellaneous Expense		145.33	
24	640	Payroll Expense		1,543.65	
25	650	Rent Expense		1,000.00	
26					

Annotations:
- Civic theme, merged and centered, Accent6 cell style, 24 point
- 60% - Accent6 cell style, Black font, right-aligned column headings in columns D and E, Top and Thick Bottom Border
- Paste link Accounts Receivable total here
- Create hyperlinks and bookmark to select proper sheet in schedule file
- Paste link Accounts Payable total here
- Total cell style; totals should balance

Figure 15.2

EXCEL

PROJECT SKILLS
✶ Use conditional logic functions in formulas
✶ Review using AutoFilter on Excel tables
✶ Round numbers up or down

16.1 CREATE A SALES AND COMMISSIONS REPORT

Abbey Neuhaus Realtors has a staff of agents who receive commissions for listing and selling homes and apartments. You have been asked to complete the monthly sales and commissions report to calculate commissions on the sales that have been closed during the month. This report is also used to respond to inquiries.

> In this project, you will complete a sales and commissions report for May and June and use AutoFilter to answer questions about the report.

1. Open data file **d16.1sales**.
2. Format the title area in the Accent5 cell style, merge and center it, and use appropriate font sizes, as shown in Figure 16.1.
3. Format A5:F28 as a table using Table Style Light 13. Center the data in the Type of Agency column.
4. Enter an IF statement in cell F6 in proper format to calculate commission. *Hint: IF the agent code in cell D6 = "LS," then multiply the price in cell E6 by 3%; otherwise, multiply the price in cell E6 by 1.5%.*
5. Copy the formula down for all properties. Check that the formula is working correctly, and format columns E and F for commas with no decimal places. Adjust column width as necessary.
6. Add a total row to the table, and set the summary option for columns E and F to SUM.
7. Use the filter, sort, and summary features in the table on the appropriate columns to answer the following questions. To show all records between questions, click Clear Filter on the drop-down list.
   a. How many homes did Nancy Millar sell and what are her total commissions?
   b. How many homes did Abbey Neuhaus sell and what are her total commissions?
   c. How many homes did Mary Dolci sell and what are her total commissions?
   d. How many sales were made where the agents were both listing and selling agents (LS sales)?

WHAT YOU NEED TO KNOW

Software

▶ An IF statement in a formula tests a condition and determines a course of action based on the outcome of the test. The format of the function is =IF(Condition,X,Y); or, if the condition is true, then the result is X; otherwise, the result is Y. You can type in the formula or use the Insert Function button on the formula bar and then locate the IF function in the Logical category in the Insert Function dialog box to enter the formula arguments.

▶ If you include text in an IF statement, it should be in quotation marks.

▶ To use the AutoFilter feature on Excel tables, click the arrow on the column header to display the filter and sort options for the column, as shown in Figure 16.1. If the Filter is not active in the table, click the Filter button on the Data tab. Click the Select All box to deselect the data, and then select the item(s) you wish to see. The filter removes items that do not meet the criteria. To remove the filter, click Select All or Clear Filter.

▶ When data is formatted as an Excel table, there is a summary feature that can be used to find Sum, Average, Max, and Min values for each number field. Use the list arrow at the right of the summary cell to select the appropriate summary function for each summary value.

Project

▶ Real estate agencies have various arrangements with the agents that work with them. This project offers one such scenario.

Continued on next page

e. What were the total sales for all homes sold where our agents were only listing agents (L)?

f. What were the total sales for all homes sold where our agents were only selling agents (S)?

g. Velma Ramos is our newest agent. What were her total sales this month?

8. Clear all filters and remove filter arrows by clicking the Data tab and then deselecting the Filter button.

9. Save the file and name it **16.1sales**.

10. Close the file.

▶ When a property is sold, usually the total commission paid by the seller for brokerage costs is 6% of the sales price. Of these funds, 3% goes to the listing agent and 3% goes to the selling agent. Half of the 3% for each agent goes to the agency where the agents work. Thus, the agents get 1.5% for listing and 1.5% for selling a property.

▶ The Type of Agency code is as follows: L=Listing Agent, S=Selling Agent, and LS=Listing and Selling Agent.

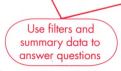

Figure 16.1

Figure showing the Abbey Neuhaus Realtors Property Sales and Commissions Report spreadsheet with callouts: "Merged and centered, Accent5 cell style, 22 point", "Center column data", "Use an IF statement to calculate the commission", "Table Style Light 13", and "Use filters and summary data to answer questions".

	Date	Property	Agent Name	Type of Agency	Price	Commission
6	4/2/2010	56 Kin...		L	459,232	
7	4/8/2010	905 Ca...		S	389,600	
8	4/12/2010	156-46...		L	345,250	
9	4/15/2010	90 Wil...		L	610,000	
10	4/18/2010	176-44...		S	299,500	
11	4/25/2010	945 Ce...		S	475,700	
12	4/26/2010	695 Cl...		S	350,500	
13	4/29/2010	699 W...		S	376,900	
14	5/2/2010	1456 J...		S	356,450	
15	5/9/2010	9815 L...		S	551,000	
16	5/11/2010	1458 J...		S	355,600	
17	5/15/2010	707 Ce...		S	410,000	
18	5/21/2010	464 Ro...		S	655,500	
19	5/25/2010	8414 L...		S	518,000	
20	5/30/2010	876 Sh...		LS	470,500	
21	5/30/2010	65 Nau...		S	292,500	
22	6/15/2010	514 Pa...		S	425,200	
23	6/16/2010	541 M...		S	567,000	
24	6/17/2010	654 Copperfield Drive	Kingsley, Helen	LS	569,900	
25	6/21/2010	15 Elm Street	Neuhaus, Abbey	S	435,200	
26	6/25/2010	65 Nautical Circle, Unit 6	Millar, Nancy	S	296,200	
27	6/25/2010	2511 Valley Forge Road	Ramos, Velma	L	468,500	
28	6/28/2010	6212 Douglas Street	Neuhaus, Abbey	LS	406,000	
29	Total				10,084,232	

Filter dropdown (on Agent Name):
- Sort A to Z
- Sort Z to A
- Sort by Color ▶
- Clear Filter From "Agent Name"
- Filter by Color ▶
- Text Filters ▶
  - ☑ (Select All)
  - ☑ Acaria, Bob
  - ☑ Dolci, Mary
  - ☑ Joyce, Linda
  - ☑ Kingsley, Helen
  - ☑ Lopez, John
  - ☑ Millar, Nancy
  - ☑ Neuhaus, Abbey
  - ☑ Ramos, Velma
  - ☑ Sullivan, Patti
- OK Cancel

16.2 CREATE AN ANALYSIS OF SALARY INCREASES

BestFriend Animal Hospital has, in the past, given raises without adhering to a set percentage of increase. This policy caused problems with the employees, and the company has now requested that you create an analysis to use seniority to determine raises.

In this project, you will calculate the percentage raise given in the previous year and then apply an IF statement to give raises this year based on seniority.

1. Open data file **d16.2salary**.
2. Format the worksheet using the Origin theme and the Accent5 cell style, as shown in Figure 16.2. Align the column headings in columns C:I to the right. Format columns C:D for commas with no decimals.
3. Enter the following formulas:
   a. In cell E6, calculate the dollar amount of the 2010 raise that was given between 2009 and 2010. Format the result for commas with no decimal places.
   b. In cell F6, calculate the percent that the raise is of the 2009 salary. Format the result as a percent with two decimal places.
   c. In cell G6, enter an IF statement that states the following: If the seniority is less than 5, then multiply the 2010 salary by 3.5%, otherwise multiply the 2010 salary by 5.5%. Format the answer for commas with two decimal places.
   d. In cell H6, calculate the 2011 salary adding the raise and 2010 salary. Format the result for commas with two decimal places.
   e. In cell I6, calculate the Final Salary. Enter the =ROUNDDOWN function to round the salary in H6 down to no decimal places. Format for commas with no decimal places since the values are rounded to that level.
4. Copy all formulas down for all employees.
5. Find the totals for all money columns, widen columns if necessary, and use the Total cell style to format the totals. Fix the formatting in G19:H19 to commas with two decimal places.
6. Print the file in landscape mode centered horizontally.
7. Save the file and name it **16.2salary**.
8. Close the file.

WHAT YOU NEED TO KNOW

Software

▶ When you format money values for commas with no decimal places, the number is rounded up to the nearest dollar for display purposes, but the actual value is still in the cell. Thus, if the value is 1125.75 and you format it for commas with no decimal places, it will appear as 1,126 but it will be used in calculations as 1125.75.

▶ If you actually want to round the values in a column, which will eliminate the decimal places from the calculations as well, you need to apply the =ROUNDUP or =ROUNDDOWN function. The formula to round down a value to zero decimal places is: =ROUNDDOWN(H6,0). In this case, the value 1125.75, located in cell H6, would be rounded down to 1125.

Project

▶ BestFriend Animal Hospital has decided to give a 3.5% raise to those employees who have worked there for less than 5 years, and a 5.5% raise to those who have five years or more seniority.

▶ When the salary increases are calculated and added to the previous year's salary, the amount is rounded to no decimal places using the =ROUNDDOWN function.

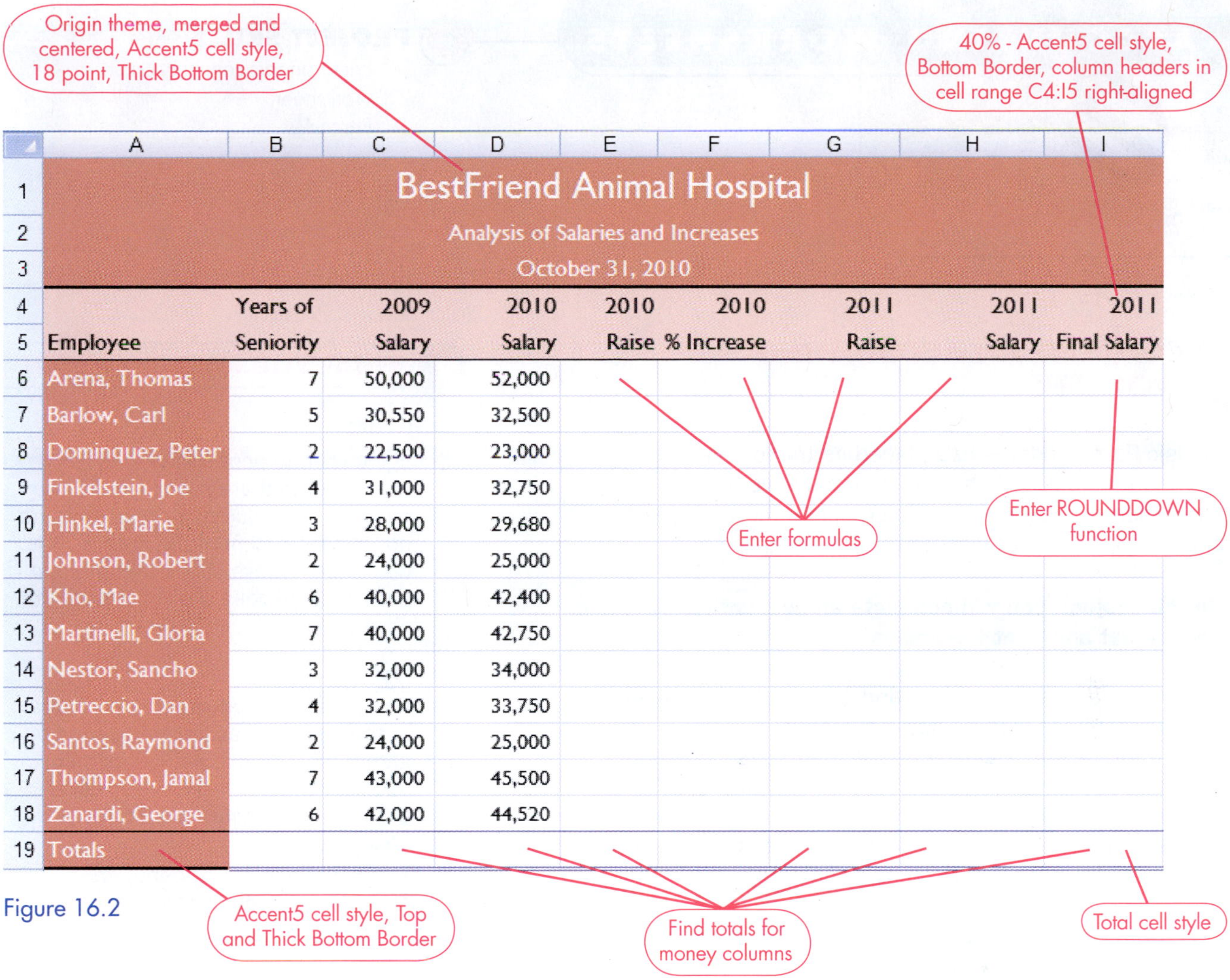

Origin theme, merged and centered, Accent5 cell style, 18 point, Thick Bottom Border

40% - Accent5 cell style, Bottom Border, column headers in cell range C4:I5 right-aligned

	A	B	C	D	E	F	G	H	I
1			BestFriend Animal Hospital						
2			Analysis of Salaries and Increases						
3			October 31, 2010						
4		Years of	2009	2010	2010	2010	2011	2011	2011
5	Employee	Seniority	Salary	Salary	Raise	% Increase	Raise	Salary	Final Salary
6	Arena, Thomas	7	50,000	52,000					
7	Barlow, Carl	5	30,550	32,500					
8	Dominquez, Peter	2	22,500	23,000					
9	Finkelstein, Joe	4	31,000	32,750					
10	Hinkel, Marie	3	28,000	29,680					
11	Johnson, Robert	2	24,000	25,000					
12	Kho, Mae	6	40,000	42,400					
13	Martinelli, Gloria	7	40,000	42,750					
14	Nestor, Sancho	3	32,000	34,000					
15	Petreccio, Dan	4	32,000	33,750					
16	Santos, Raymond	2	24,000	25,000					
17	Thompson, Jamal	7	43,000	45,500					
18	Zanardi, George	6	42,000	44,520					
19	Totals								

Enter formulas

Enter ROUNDDOWN function

Figure 16.2

Accent5 cell style, Top and Thick Bottom Border

Find totals for money columns

Total cell style

PROJECT 17

17.1 COMPLETE AN ACCOUNTING WORKSHEET

Classic Party Planners has placed its trial balance information on a worksheet and added several adjustments. They want you to complete the worksheet and calculate the net income for the month.

In this project, you will complete an accounting worksheet and print the analysis.

1. Open data file **d17.1ws** and format all number cells for commas with no decimal places.
2. Total the Trial Balance and Adjustments Debit and Credit columns on row 27. The Debit and Credit balances should balance in each pair of columns.
3. In cell F7, enter a formula to calculate the new debit balance. *Hint: Trial Balance Debit + Adjustments Debit – Adjustments Credit.*
4. Copy the formula down the debit column to cell F26. Delete all zero balances.
5. In cell G12, enter a formula to calculate the new credit balance. *Hint: Trial Balance Credit – Adjustments Debit + Adjustments Credit.*
6. Copy the formula to cells G13:G17. Delete the zero balance.
7. Copy the account balances from the adjusted trial balance to the appropriate columns, as shown in Figure 17.1, using Paste Special, with the Values command.
8. Total all remaining columns.
9. In a blank area of the worksheet, calculate the difference between the Income Statement Debit and Credit column totals in cells H27 and I27, which is the Net Income.
10. Enter the Net Income from your calculation in Step 9 in cells H28 and K28, as indicated, and add the income to the totals. All pairs of columns should balance. Delete your calculation in the blank area of the worksheet.
11. Merge and center the worksheet headings, and format titles and column headings as you prefer.
12. Hide the Trial Balance and Adjustments columns and print the worksheet in landscape to fit to one page.

▼ WHAT YOU NEED TO KNOW

Software

▶ If you want to print sections of a worksheet that are not adjacent, you can hide the columns or rows that are not needed and print the data as it is displayed. Always check that merged and centered cells are not hidden from view.

Project

▶ An accounting worksheet is prepared at the end of an accounting period to gather trial balance and adjustment information to plan the preparation of the income statement and balance sheet.

▶ The worksheet adjustments are corrections made by the accountant to reflect the true balances of accounts, such as inventory or prepaid items.

▶ The fill color added to this project is used to differentiate the columnar data. Usually, this worksheet is for planning purposes and not necessarily formatted in color.

▶ When all the totals are entered on a worksheet, you can calculate the Net Income by subtracting the Income Statement debits from the Income Statement credits. You are essentially finding the profit by subtracting expenses from revenue. The Net Income is then added to the credit side of the Balance Sheet section to show that it increases the owner's net worth, and to the debit side of the Income Statement to balance the columns.

13. Unhide the columns, save the workbook, and name it **17.1ws**.

14. Close the file.

Enter formulas to calculate the adjusted trial balance data

	A	B	C	D	E	F	G	H	I	J	K
1				CLASSIC PARTY PLANNERS							
2				Worksheet							
3				For the month ended May 31, 2010							
4											
5		Trial Balance		Adjustments		Adjusted Trial Balance		Income Statement		Balance Sheet	
6		Debit	Credit	Debit	Credit	Debit	Credit	Debit	Credit	Debit	Credit
7	Cash	23,920				23,920				23,920	
8	Accounts Receivable	23,546				23,546				23,546	
9	Equipment	14,410				14,410				14,410	
10	Office Supplies Inventory	985			450	535				535	
11	Prepaid Insurance	1,000			500	500				500	
12	Accounts Payable		15,365				15,365				15,365
13	Payroll Taxes Payable		1,450				1,450				1,450
14	Byron Brandt, Capital		40,482				40,482				40,482
15	Byron Brandt, Personal	1,850				1,850				1,850	
16	Vendor Fees Income		17,899				17,899		17,899		
17	Consultant Fees Income		18,765				18,765		18,765		
18	Advertising Expense	3,500				3,500		3,500			
19	Insurance Expense			500		500		500			
20	Miscellaneous Expense	650				650		650			
21	Office Supplies Expense			450		450		450			
22	Payroll Tax Expenses	1,450				1,450		1,450			
23	Rent Expense	5,000				5,000		5,000			
24	Travel Expense	4,000				4,000		4,000			
25	Utilities Expense	1,400				1,400		1,400			
26	Salaries Expense	12,250				12,250		12,250			
27	Totals										
28	Net Income										
29	Totals										

Figure 17.1

Complete totals in B27:K27

Calculate the difference between income statement totals in cells H27 and I27 and place on Net Income line in the two highlighted locations

Complete totals in H29:K29

17.2 COMPLETE AN ACCOUNTING WORKSHEET WITH HYPERLINKS

In Project 15.2, you created a trial balance for Wheels Onboard. This information is now part of the worksheet and adjustments have been made by the accountant. You have been asked to complete the worksheet and print it out.

> **In this project, you will complete the worksheet, add hyperlinks to the supporting schedules, and print the worksheet on multiple pages.**

1. Open data file **d17.2sched**, or your solution **15.2sched**, and data file **d17.2ws**.
2. Change the theme of the worksheet file to Civic and use the Accent6 cell style to format the titles, as shown in Figure 17.2. Adjust column width as necessary.
3. Enter a formula in column G to complete the Adjusted Trial Balance Debit column and copy the formula down to row 27. *Hint: In G7: =C7+E7–F7.* Delete any zero entries.
4. Enter a formula in H9 to complete the Adjusted Trial Balance Credit column and copy the formula to range H14:H17. *Hint: In H9: =D9–E9+F9.* Delete any zero entries.
5. The Income Summary debit and credit set to values, should be copied from columns E:F in row 28 to columns G:H. *Hint: Refer to Figure 17.2.*
6. Copy and use Paste Special, set to Values, to place the Income Statement account balances from the Adjusted Trial Balance in G19:H28 into Columns I and J.
7. Copy and use Paste Special, set to Values, to place the Balance Sheet account balances in G7:H18 into Columns K and L.
8. Calculate all totals in row 29.
9. Calculate the Net Income by subtracting the Income Statement Debits from the Credits. Do this calculation in a blank area.
10. Enter the Net Income into the locations indicated in the income statement and balance sheet, as shown in Figure 17.2. Delete your calculation.
11. In Row 31, total the values from Rows 29 and 30 for columns I:L. All pairs of columns should balance.
12. All numbers should be formatted for commas with two decimal places. Adjust column width and fix borders as necessary.
13. Save the worksheet and name it **17.2ws**. Save the schedule file and name it **17.2sched**.
14. Enter hyperlink text in cells B8 and B15, and establish hyperlinks to the schedules using the Bookmark feature to link to the appropriate sheet in the schedules file.

▼ WHAT YOU NEED TO KNOW

Software

▶ If you want to print a large worksheet on several pages, it is recommended that you print the labels for the values on each page so that you can identify the numbers. To set the feature to print column or row titles, click the Page Layout tab, and in the Page Setup group, click the Print Titles button. On the Sheet tab, select the rows or columns to repeat on each page.

▶ If cells are merged for headings you should split them before printing titles.

Project

▶ You will complete the worksheet through the Adjusted Trial Balance columns and then use the figure as a guide to separate the account balances into the two financial report columns.

15. Print a copy of the worksheet in portrait mode on several pages using the Page Layout tab and Print Titles to set titles for Column A. *Note: If you have merged title cells, remove the merge before printing with titles. If printing multiple pages is not feasible, set the titles and use print preview to view each page.*

16. Remerge the headings in rows 1:3. Clear the titles setting and print a copy to fit on one page in landscape mode.

17. Save both files.

18. Close the files.

Enter hyperlinks to schedules

Civic theme, merged and centered, Accent6 cell style, 16 point

Use Outside Borders and merge and center title for each pair of columns

	A	B	C	D	E	F	G	H	I	J	K	L
1						Wheels Onboard						
2						Worksheet						
3						October 31, 2010						
4												
5	Account		Trial Balance		Adjustments		Adjusted Trial Balance		Income Statement		Balance Sheet	
6			Debit	Credit	Debits	Credits	Debit	Credit	Debit	Credit	Debit	Credit
7	Cash		11,772.21				11,772.21				11,772.21	
8	Accounts Receivable	(See Schedule)	8,645.45				8,645.45				8,645.45	
9	Allowance for Bad Debts			187.40				187.40				187.40
10	Merchandise Inventory		23,446.76		22,343.54	23,446.76	22,343.54				22,343.54	
11	Supplies		1,876.54			1,200.00	676.54				676.54	
12	Prepaid Insurance		750.00			250.00	500.00				500.00	
13	Equipment		16,876.00				16,876.00				16,876.00	
14	Accumulated Depreciation			5,950.00				5,950.00				5,950.00
15	Accounts Payable	(See Schedule)		11,763.87				11,763.87				11,763.87
16	Payroll Taxes Payable			657.67				657.67				657.67
17	Ron Giordano, Capital			36,455.79				36,455.79				36,455.79
18	Ron Giordano, Personal		1,395.00				1,395.00				1,395.00	
19	Sales			70,987.43				70,987.43		70,987.43		
20	Sales Returns		12,657.00				12,657.00		12,657.00			
21	Purchase		45,444.22				45,444.22		45,444.22			
22	Advertising Expense		450.00				450.00		450.00			
23	Insurance Expense				250.00		250.00		250.00			
24	Miscellaneous Expense		145.33				145.33		145.33			
25	Payroll Expense		1,543.65				1,543.65		1,543.65			
26	Rent Expense		1,000.00				1,000.00		1,000.00			
27	Supplies Expense				1,200.00		1,200.00		1,200.00			
28	Income Summary				23,446.76	22,343.54	23,446.76	22,343.54	23,446.76	22,343.54		
29	Totals											
30	Net Income											
31	Totals											

Figure 17.2

Calculate totals for C29:L29

Calculate Net Income and place in I30 and L30

Calculate totals for I31:L31

INCOME STATEMENT

▶ **PROJECT SKILLS**
✦ Format sheet tab color
✦ Enter 3-D references
✦ Add headers and footers to worksheets

PROJECT 18

18.1 CREATE AN INCOME STATEMENT ANALYSIS

Wheels Onboard has a second store in the suburbs. They want you to prepare income statements for each store and a consolidated report showing the totals for both stores.

> In this project, you will complete two income statements, and then consolidate the reports into one statement using 3-D references and report headers and footers.

1. Open data file **d18.1income**.
2. Look at and then group Sheet1 and Sheet2 and do the following:
   a. Change the workbook theme to Civic and use the Accent6 cell style. Format the titles and sections of the Income Statement, as shown in Figure 18.1. Notice that certain items are indented or have bold applied for emphasis.
   b. Enter the formulas as indicated on Figure 18.1 to calculate the income statement data.
   c. Place borders and format all numbers for commas with no decimal places.
3. Ungroup the sheets and check all data.
4. Rename Sheet1 **Town Store** and rename Sheet2 **Suburb Store**. Format the sheet tabs in color.
5. Copy the Income Statement from one of the store sheets to Sheet3.
6. Rename Sheet3 **Consolidated Income Statement**, and change the second title line in row 2 to read the same. Format the sheet tab in color.
7. On the Consolidated Income Statement:
   a. Delete all the values in column C.
   b. Enter a formula with 3-D references to add the values in cell C6 on the Town Store and Suburb Store sheets. *Hint: Enter =, select C6 on the Town Store sheet, enter +, select C6 on the Suburb Store sheet, press [Enter].*
   c. Copy the formula down column C.
   d. Delete zeros where there are no data items.
   e. Add borders.
   f. Check that the formulas correctly found combined Net Income.

▼ WHAT YOU NEED TO KNOW

Software

▶ To color a sheet tab, right-click the tab, click Tab Color, and select the color from the palette.

▶ You can summarize data from several worksheets on a summary worksheet by using a formula with a 3-D reference style.

▶ To enter a 3-D reference, you begin with the equal sign and then select the sheets and cells in the worksheets. Sheet names and formula punctuation marks are entered automatically if you use the selection method. Or, you can enter the formula using this sample as a guide: ='Town Store'A1 + 'Suburb Store'A1. This formula adds the values in cell A1 from the Town Store and Suburb Store sheets. The exclamation point separates the sheet name from the cell address.

▶ When producing a multi-page report, it is recommended that you print page headers or footers to identify the report, date, and page number or name.

Project

▶ The town and suburb stores for Wheels Onboard are owned by the same proprietor, and thus the income statements may be consolidated to obtain the total earnings for the period. However, the owner wants you to prepare the income statements for each store separately, so that he can monitor the profitability of each store as well.

▶ The income statement information for the town store comes from the worksheet prepared in Project 17.2.

Continued on next page

8. Enter a custom footer on the three-page report that includes the sheet name, the report name **Consolidated Income Statement**, and the page number.

9. Print a copy of the three-page report centered horizontally.

10. Save the workbook and name it **18.1income**.

11. Close the file.

▶ The formulas for the income statement are as follows:
- Income – Sales Returns = Net Sales
- Net Sales – Cost of Goods Sold = Gross Profit
- Gross Profit – Total Expenses = Net Income before Taxes
- Net Income before Taxes – Taxes = Net Income after Taxes

	A	B	C	D	E
1		Wheels Onboard			
2		Income Statement-Town Store			
3		For the month ended October 31, 2010			
4					
5		Income:			
6		Sales Income	70,987		
7		Less: Sales Returns	12,657		
8		Net Sales			
9					
10		Less: Cost of Goods Sold	46,547	46,547	
11					
12		Gross Profit			
13					
14		Expenses:			
15		Advertising Expense	450.00		
16		Insurance Expense	250.00		
17		Miscellaneous Expense	145.33		
18		Payroll Expense	1,543.65		
19		Rent Expense	1,000.00		
20		Supplies Expense	1,200.00		
21		Total Expenses			
22					
23		Net Income before Taxes			
24		Less: Taxes		1,799	
25		Net Income after Taxes			
26					

Civic theme, Accent6 cell style 20 point

Calculate Net Sales

Indent

Calculate Gross Profit

Calculate Total Expenses

Calculate Net Income before Taxes

Calculate Net Income after Taxes

Town Store | Suburb Store | Consolidated Income Statement | Sheet

Figure 18.1

Rename sheets and color the tabs

18.2 CREATE A QUARTERLY INCOME STATEMENT ANALYSIS

The accountants for Jane Martino Interiors have gathered the data for the income statements for the first and second quarters and want you to complete the analysis.

In this project, you will complete the income statements and include analysis columns that calculate the percent each item is of total revenues.

1. Open data file **d18.2quarter**.
2. Enter the following formulas and copy the formulas to Column D:
   a. In cell C10, calculate the Total Revenue.
   b. In cell C24, calculate the Total Expenses.
   c. In cell C26, calculate Net Income before Taxes.
   d. In cell C28, calculate Net Income after Taxes.
3. Insert a column and add column headings to create the analysis shown in Figure 18.2. Format numbers for commas with no decimals.
4. Enter a formula to find ½ Yr. Totals, adding the first and second quarter values. Copy the formula for all items.
5. In the 1st Qtr. % column, find what percent each value is of the Total Revenue. Enter the formula in cell D7. *Hint: =C7/$C$10*. Format the result for Percent style with two decimal places. Copy down for all values. The Total Revenue % should be 100%.
6. Enter formulas to complete the 2nd Qtr. and ½ Yr. Totals percent analysis.
7. Money values should be formatted for commas with no decimal places, and percent values should have two decimal places.
8. Delete zeros and hyphens where there are no data items.
9. Change the worksheet theme to Median and use the Accent5 cell style and the Total cell style to format the worksheet and titles area, as shown.
10. Insert a footer into the report that contains the date and filename.
11. Print one copy of the report centered horizontally.
12. Save the workbook and name it **18.2quarter**.
13. Close the file.

WHAT YOU NEED TO KNOW

Project

▶ You will add the data from the first and second quarters to find the half-year totals and then compare each value in the income statement to the total revenue value for the quarter.

▶ You will find the percent each value is of revenue to compare the quarterly and semiannual data. Use an absolute reference for the revenue value.

▶ Calculate income using the following formula: Revenues – Total Expenses = Net Income before Taxes.

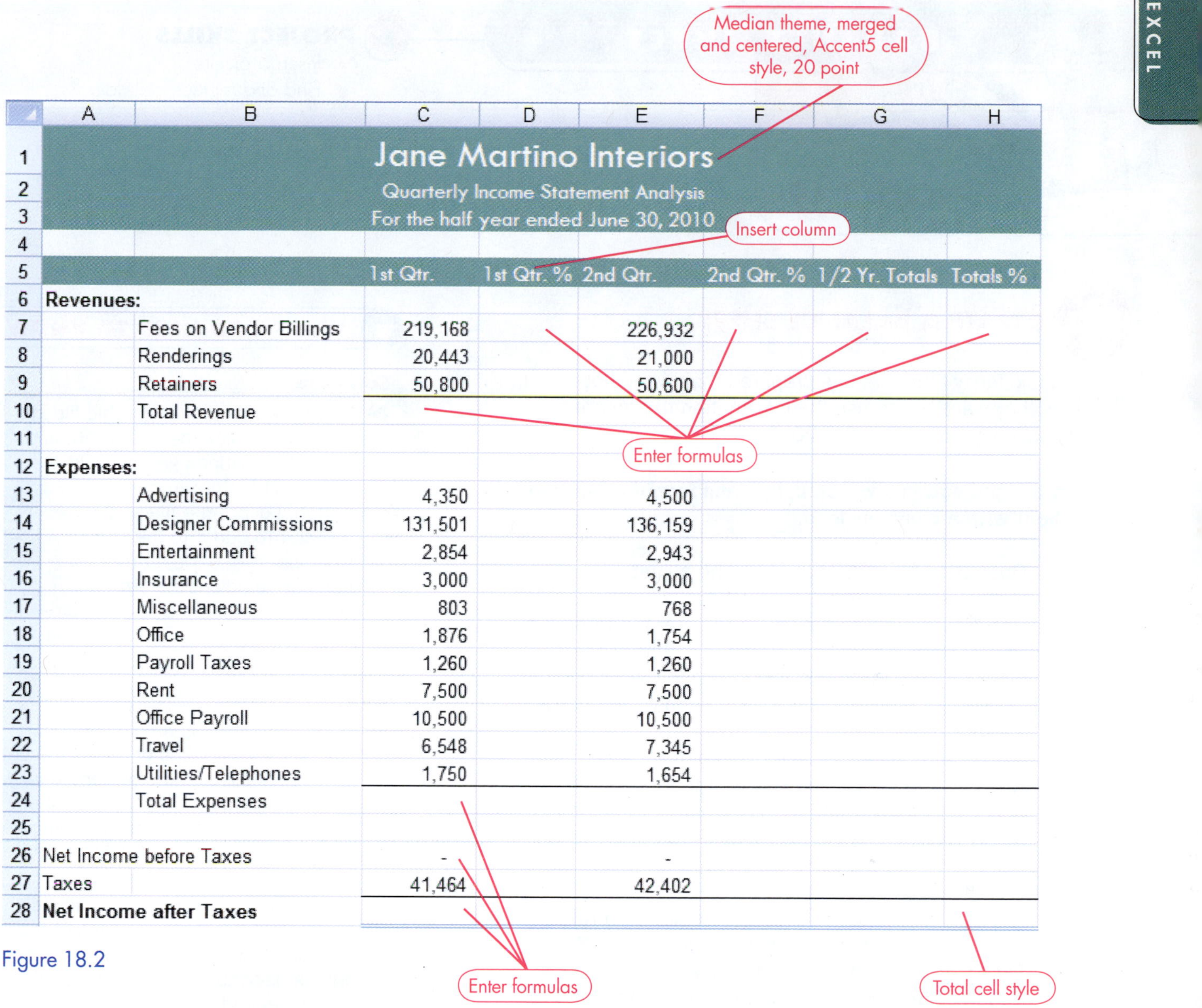

Median theme, merged and centered, Accent5 cell style, 20 point

	A	B	C	D	E	F	G	H
1			**Jane Martino Interiors**					
2			Quarterly Income Statement Analysis					
3			For the half year ended June 30, 2010		Insert column			
4								
5			1st Qtr.	1st Qtr. %	2nd Qtr.	2nd Qtr. %	1/2 Yr. Totals	Totals %
6	**Revenues:**							
7		Fees on Vendor Billings	219,168		226,932			
8		Renderings	20,443		21,000			
9		Retainers	50,800		50,600			
10		Total Revenue						
11								
12	**Expenses:**							
13		Advertising	4,350		4,500			
14		Designer Commissions	131,501		136,159			
15		Entertainment	2,854		2,943			
16		Insurance	3,000		3,000			
17		Miscellaneous	803		768			
18		Office	1,876		1,754			
19		Payroll Taxes	1,260		1,260			
20		Rent	7,500		7,500			
21		Office Payroll	10,500		10,500			
22		Travel	6,548		7,345			
23		Utilities/Telephones	1,750		1,654			
24		Total Expenses						
25								
26	Net Income before Taxes		-		-			
27	Taxes		41,464		42,402			
28	**Net Income after Taxes**							

Enter formulas

Enter formulas

Total cell style

Figure 18.2

PROJECT SKILLS

✳ Insert a picture
✳ Find and replace cell data

PROJECT 19

19.1 CREATE A BALANCE SHEET

Classic Party Planners has prepared their worksheet, and now they want you to use the information to prepare a balance sheet for May 31, 2010.

In this project, you will complete and format a balance sheet with a company logo.

1. Open data file **d19.1balsheet** and adjust column width as necessary.

2. Use Figure 19.1 as a guide, and enter the formulas to complete the Balance Sheet. The Total Assets, in cell E16, and the Total Liabilities and Owner's Equity in cell E32, should balance or be equal. Add borders as shown.

3. Merge and center the title over columns A:D to allow room for the logo. Use the Metro theme and the Accent3 cell style with the Dark Blue font color.

4. Insert the logo on the right side of the title section, using the data file **classiclogo.tif**, moving and sizing it so that it is placed correctly.

5. Use Format Painter to copy the format from row 3 to rows 5 and 18. Bold the text in rows 5 and 18.

6. Format cell B6 with the 40% - Accent3 cell style and the Dark Blue font color. Use Format Painter to copy the style to the other headings, as shown in Figure 19.1.

7. Merge and center A19:E19 and A25:E25, and format the text in bold.

8. Indent the text data as shown.

9. Format the values for commas with no decimal places. Format the totals in cells E16 and E32 in Accounting Number format with no decimal places.

10. Print a copy of the report centered horizontally.

11. Save the workbook and name it **19.1balsheet**.

12. Close the file.

WHAT YOU NEED TO KNOW

Software

▶ To insert a picture or graphic file into a worksheet, click the Insert tab, and in the Illustrations group, click the Insert Picture from File button. Locate the file and select it to add it to the worksheet. Use the sizing handles to adjust the size, and when the cursor is a four-headed arrow, you can move, or drag and drop, the graphic.

Project

▶ A balance sheet is a financial report that shows the value of a firm's assets and liabilities, and the owner's equity, on a certain date. The balance sheet is based on the following accounting equation: Assets = Liabilities + Capital (owner's equity).

▶ The information and accounts listed in the balance sheet columns of the worksheet prepared in Project 17.1 will be used to create a report called a balance sheet.

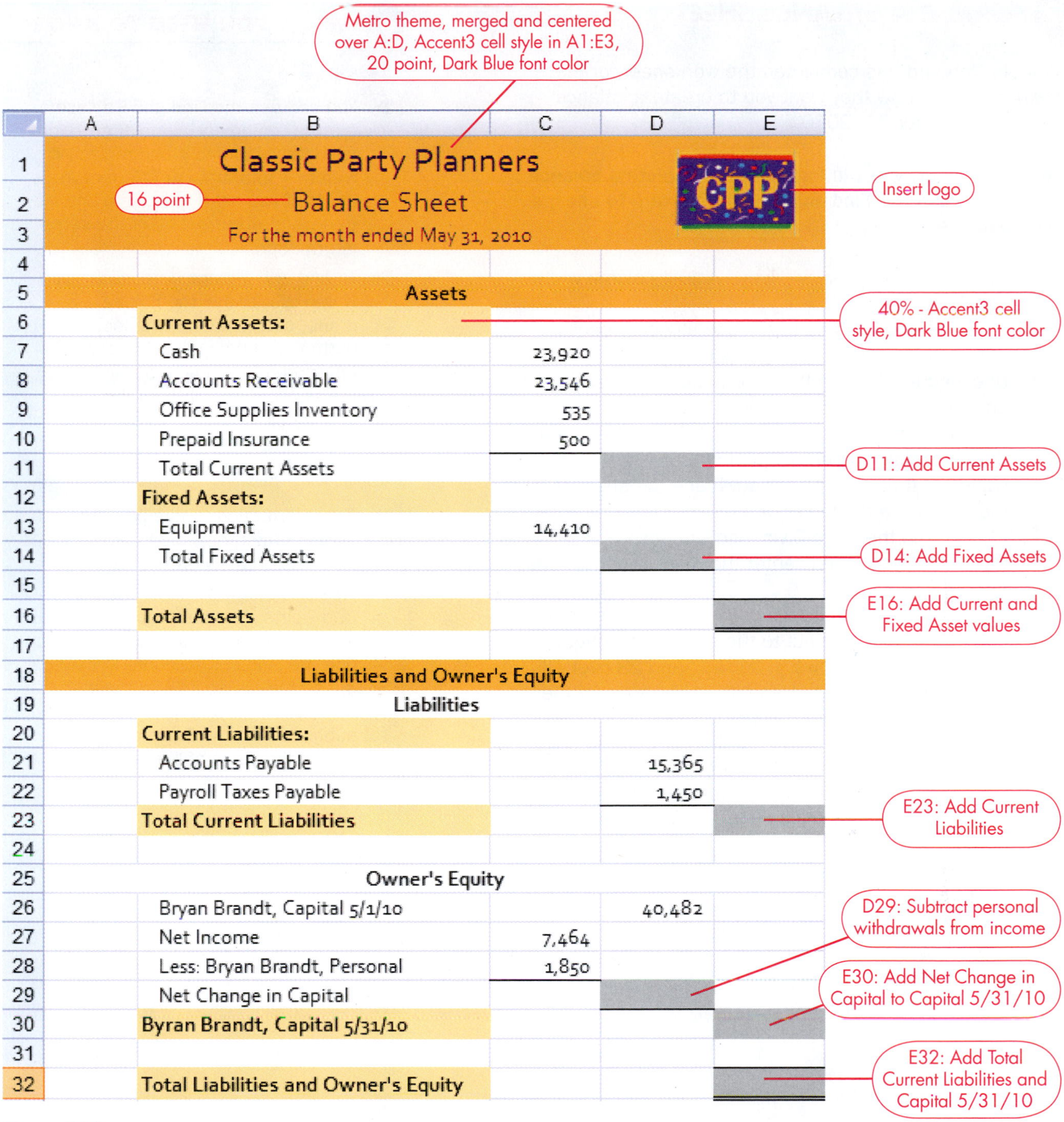

Metro theme, merged and centered over A:D, Accent3 cell style in A1:E3, 20 point, Dark Blue font color

	A	B	C	D	E
1		Classic Party Planners			CPP
2		Balance Sheet			
3		For the month ended May 31, 2010			
4					
5		Assets			
6		Current Assets:			
7		Cash	23,920		
8		Accounts Receivable	23,546		
9		Office Supplies Inventory	535		
10		Prepaid Insurance	500		
11		Total Current Assets			
12		Fixed Assets:			
13		Equipment	14,410		
14		Total Fixed Assets			
15					
16		Total Assets			
17					
18		Liabilities and Owner's Equity			
19		Liabilities			
20		Current Liabilities:			
21		Accounts Payable		15,365	
22		Payroll Taxes Payable		1,450	
23		Total Current Liabilities			
24					
25		Owner's Equity			
26		Bryan Brandt, Capital 5/1/10		40,482	
27		Net Income	7,464		
28		Less: Bryan Brandt, Personal	1,850		
29		Net Change in Capital			
30		Byran Brandt, Capital 5/31/10			
31					
32		Total Liabilities and Owner's Equity			

16 point

Insert logo

40% - Accent3 cell style, Dark Blue font color

D11: Add Current Assets

D14: Add Fixed Assets

E16: Add Current and Fixed Asset values

E23: Add Current Liabilities

D29: Subtract personal withdrawals from income

E30: Add Net Change in Capital to Capital 5/31/10

E32: Add Total Current Liabilities and Capital 5/31/10

Figure 19.1

19.2 FORMAT A BALANCE SHEET

Wheels Onboard has completed the worksheet for the town store and now they want you to create a balance sheet for October 31, 2010.

In this project, you will format and complete a balance sheet and use the Find and Replace feature to change some labels.

1. Open data file **d19.2balsheet**. Adjust column width as necessary.
2. Use Find and Replace to replace all occurrences of the word "Equity" with `Capital`.
3. Use Figure 19.2 and the information provided to enter the formulas to complete the balance sheet. Be sure to subtract the Allowance for Bad Debts and the Accumulated Depreciation amounts to find the values of the assets involved. Place the answers in the column to the right.
4. Change the theme to Civic, use the Accent6 cell style, and merge and center the titles over columns A:E.
5. Insert the logo in data file **wheelslogo.tif** and move and size it so that it fits to the right of the titles.
6. Merge and center rows 5, 21, 22, and 28 over A:F. Use the Header 1 and Header 2 cell styles for the major headings of the Balance Sheet.
7. Format the report with indentations, borders, bold, and appropriate number formats.
8. Format the numbers in cells F19 and F35 using the Total cell style and Accounting Number format with no decimal places. They should balance.
9. Print a copy of the report so it fits on one sheet, centered horizontally.
10. Save the workbook and name it **19.2balsheet**.
11. Close the file.

WHAT YOU NEED TO KNOW

Software

▶ You can use the Find and Replace feature to find certain text, data, or formats, or to find it and replace it with new information. This feature is useful if you need to make a change to several occurrences of the same information.

▶ To find and replace data, click the Home tab, and in the Editing group, click the Find & Select button, and then click Replace. Enter the data to find, as well as the replacement data on the dialog box that appears. Click Replace or Replace All.

Project

▶ The information for the balance sheet comes from the Balance Sheet columns on the worksheet.

▶ This company has an Allowance for Bad Debts account, which you should subtract from Accounts Receivable to find the value of Accounts Receivable. It also maintains an Accumulated Depreciation account, which you should subtract from the Equipment account to find the value of Equipment.

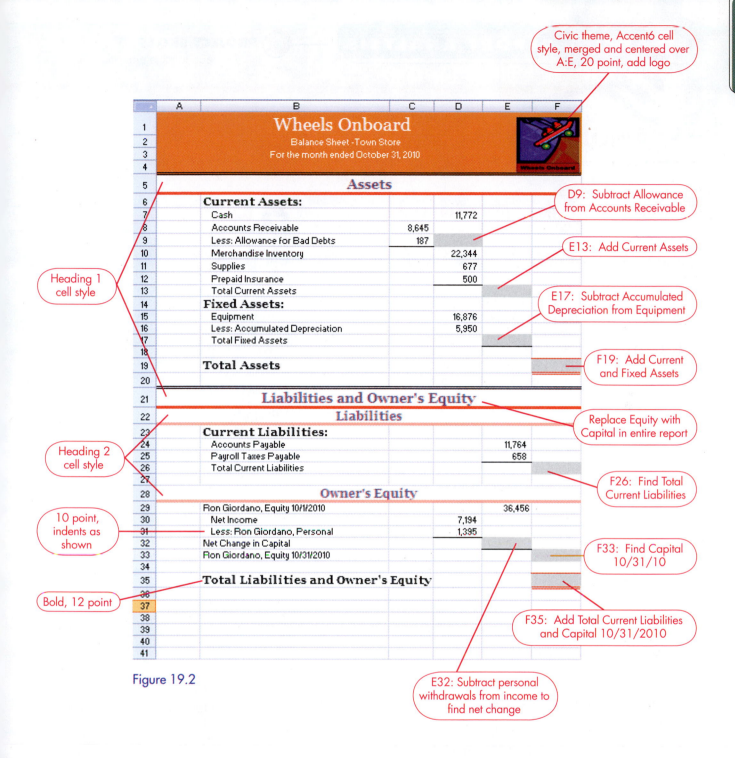

Figure 19.2

Annotations:

- Civic theme, Accent6 cell style, merged and centered over A:E, 20 point, add logo
- Heading 1 cell style
- Heading 2 cell style
- 10 point, indents as shown
- Bold, 12 point
- D9: Subtract Allowance from Accounts Receivable
- E13: Add Current Assets
- E17: Subtract Accumulated Depreciation from Equipment
- F19: Add Current and Fixed Assets
- Replace Equity with Capital in entire report
- F26: Find Total Current Liabilities
- F33: Find Capital 10/31/10
- F35: Add Total Current Liabilities and Capital 10/31/2010
- E32: Subtract personal withdrawals from income to find net change

Spreadsheet contents:

Wheels Onboard
Balance Sheet - Town Store
For the month ended October 31, 2010

Assets

Current Assets:			
Cash		11,772	
Accounts Receivable	8,645		
Less: Allowance for Bad Debts	187		
Merchandise Inventory		22,344	
Supplies		677	
Prepaid Insurance		500	
Total Current Assets			
Fixed Assets:			
Equipment		16,876	
Less: Accumulated Depreciation		5,950	
Total Fixed Assets			
Total Assets			

Liabilities and Owner's Equity
Liabilities

Current Liabilities:			
Accounts Payable		11,764	
Payroll Taxes Payable		658	
Total Current Liabilities			

Owner's Equity

Ron Giordano, Equity 10/1/2010			36,456
Net Income	7,194		
Less: Ron Giordano, Personal	1,395		
Net Change in Capital			
Ron Giordano, Equity 10/31/2010			

Total Liabilities and Owner's Equity

PROJECT 20

20.1 ANALYZE INCOME STATEMENT DATA

Health Connections would like you to use data from its income statements for two years to analyze trends.

In this project, you will complete the summary income statements and apply percentage analysis and ratios.

1. Open data file **d20.1isanalysis**.
2. Enter formulas to complete the income statement. *Note: Subtract each item until Net Income is obtained.*
3. Insert two columns for percentage analysis and add new column headings, as shown on Figure 20.1.
4. Change the theme to Origin and use the Accent4 and Accent6 cell styles for titles and column headings, as shown in Figure 20.1. Use the Brown, Accent 5, Darker 50% font color for the titles. Merge and center rows 1:3 over columns A:E. Shade the percentage analysis columns.
5. Format numbers for commas with no decimal places, as shown in Figure 20.1.
6. In cell C6, enter a formula to find the percent each 2009 item is of Net Sales. Use an absolute reference for Net Sales. Format the result for Percent style with one decimal place and copy the formula down to all items. *Hint: =B6/$B$6.*
7. Repeat Step 6 to analyze the 2010 data.
8. Check the cells with error messages and if correct, remove the error indicator, the green triangle in the top-left corner, by clicking the Smart Tag and selecting Ignore Error.
9. Add borders as shown in Figure 20.1.
10. In cell B18, find the Rate of Return on Net Sales. Format for Percent style to two decimal places, and then copy the formula to cell D18.
11. In cell B19, find the Operating Expense Ratio. Format for Number to two decimal places, and then copy the formula to cell D19.
12. Add borders to the ratio analysis results, if necessary.

▼ WHAT YOU NEED TO KNOW

Software

▶ A formula may return an error message because it is inconsistent with surrounding formulas. This may or may not be an error. If it is not, you may wish to hide the green triangle that indicates an error. To manage the error message, click the cell, click the error indicator Smart Tag, and then select Ignore Error.

Project

▶ Analyzing data from income statements can help a business make management decisions. Information obtained by comparing income statements, applying percentage analysis, and using ratios can detect trends that may require changes in operations.

▶ A ratio compares two numbers and expresses their relationship to each other. You can express the relationship as a percent or as a ratio. For example, you can say that operating expenses are 33% of net sales, or you can say that the ratio of net sales to operating expenses is 3 to 1, or that the company earned $3 in net sales for every dollar of operating expenses.

▶ Some of the financial analyses used for income statements are:
  • Rate of Return on Net Sales (percentage of net sales that represents net income) = Net Income after Taxes/Net Sales
  • Operating Expense Ratio (dollars of net sales made for every dollar of expenses) = Net Sales/Operating Expenses
  • Percentage analysis of components of income statement
  • Comparison of income statements over time

13. Answer the following questions on Sheet2 using the
data analysis statistics:
  a. What is the trend in Net Income?
  b. What is the trend in Cost of Goods Sold?
  c. What is the trend in Operating Expenses?
  d. What is the trend in the ratio of Operating
       Expenses to Sales?
  e. Why did the percent of Other Expenses go down
       while the value remained the same?
14. Save the workbook and name it **20.1isanalysis**.
15. Close the file.

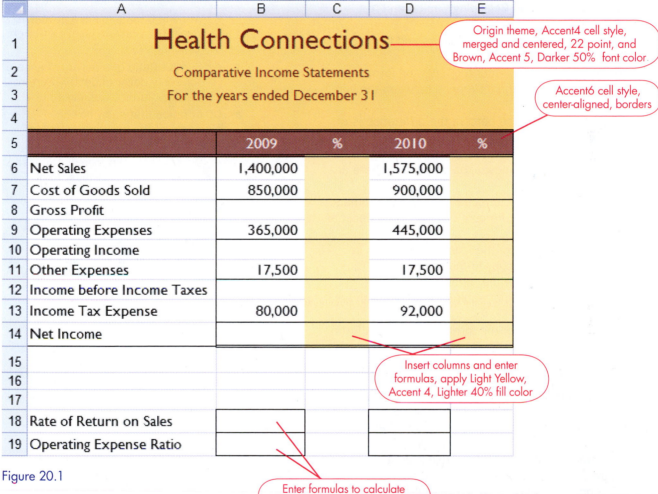

Figure 20.1

20.2 ANALYZE BALANCE SHEET DATA

Health Connections has also prepared balance sheet data for analysis. You have been asked to compare two years of data and apply ratios to the reports.

In this project, you will prepare a comparative balance sheet with ratio analyses.

1. Open data file **d20.2bsanalysis**.
2. Enter the following formulas and copy for both balance sheet columns:
   a. In cell B10, add assets.
   b. In cell B16, add liabilities.
   c. In cell B21, add Beginning Capital and Net Income.
   d. In cell B22, add Total Liabilities and Ending Capital.
3. To analyze changes, enter the following formulas:
   a. In cell D7, find the difference between the two statements.
   b. In cell E7, find the percent the difference is of the 2009 value.
   c. Copy the formulas down in both columns. Delete zeros and error messages only where there are no data items.
4. Format columns B:D for commas with no decimals. Format column E for Percent style with one decimal place.
5. To analyze data, enter the following formulas in column B and then copy formulas to column C:
   a. In cell B24, enter the formula for Working Capital. Format the result for commas with no decimal places.
   b. In Cell B25, enter the formula for Current Ratio. Format the result for Number with two decimal places.
   c. Enter formulas in cells B26, B27, and B28 to calculate analyses listed. Format all results for Percent style with one decimal place.
6. Format the worksheet, using the Origin theme, the Accent4, Accent6, and Total cell styles, and the same formats applied to Project 20.1. Use Figure 20.2 as a guide.
7. What does the analysis tell us about the ability of the company to handle its debts? You can supply your answer on Sheet2.
8. Save the workbook and name it **20.2bsanalysis**.
9. Close the file.

WHAT YOU NEED TO KNOW

Project

▶ Balance sheet data provides a picture of the assets, liabilities, and capital, or worth, of a business. To analyze comparative balance sheets, you can find the percent change in items. This analysis can detect trends in operations.

▶ One of the important strengths of a business is its ability to pay its bills and have the cash flow to conduct daily operations. This is tested by using the working capital and current ratio tests.

- Working Capital (dollars of working capital) = Current Assets – Current Liabilities

- Current Ratio (the dollars of assets for every dollar of debt) = Current Assets/Current Liabilities

▶ Other ratios that show how the elements of the business relate to each other are:

- Debt/Asset ratio (percent of assets owed) = Total Liabilities/Total Assets

- Capital/Asset ratio (percent of assets owned) = Ending Capital/Total Assets

- Liability/Capital ratio (percent debt is of ownership) = Total Liabilities/Ending Capital

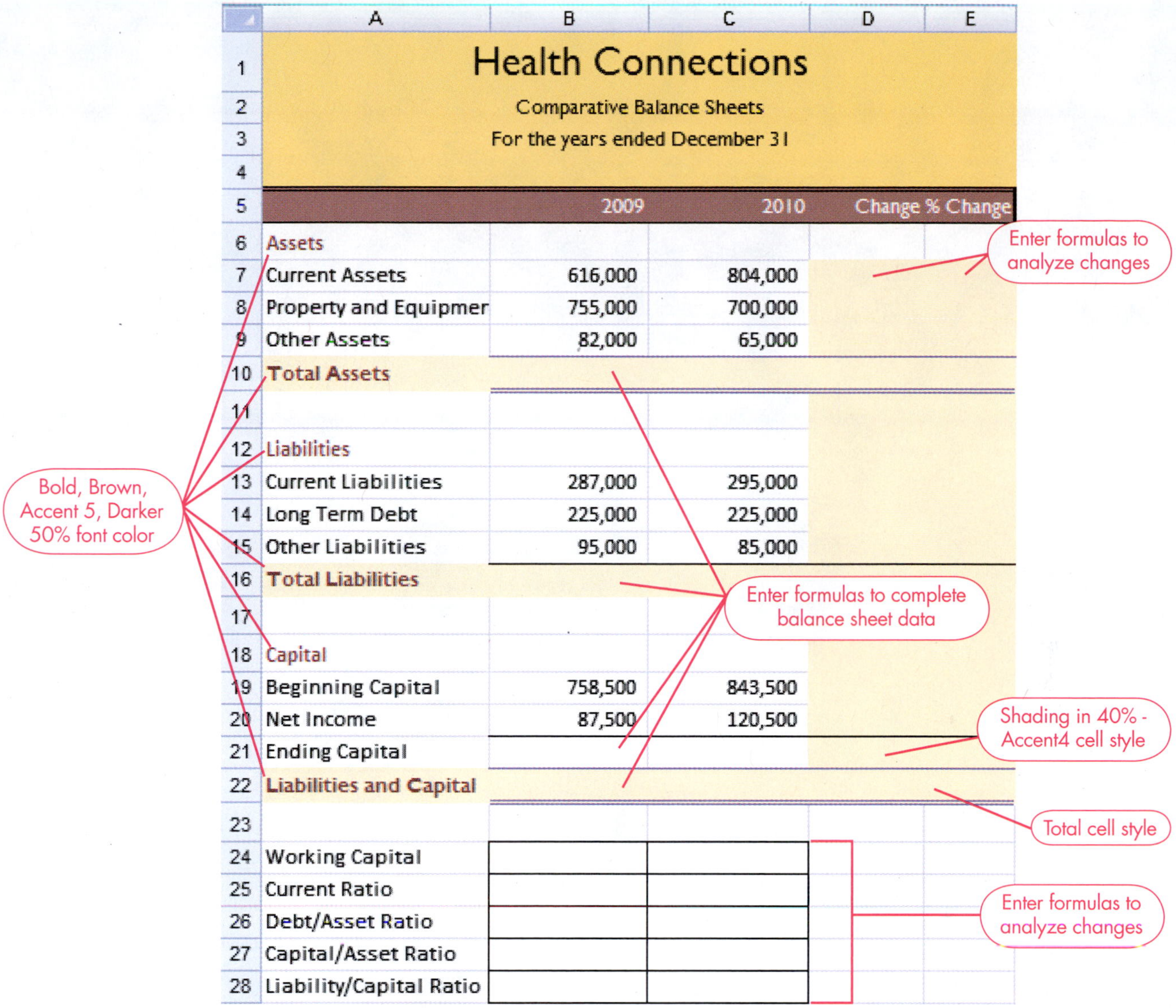

	A	B	C	D	E
1	**Health Connections**				
2	Comparative Balance Sheets				
3	For the years ended December 31				
4					
5		2009	2010	Change	% Change
6	Assets				
7	Current Assets	616,000	804,000		
8	Property and Equipmer	755,000	700,000		
9	Other Assets	82,000	65,000		
10	**Total Assets**				
11					
12	Liabilities				
13	Current Liabilities	287,000	295,000		
14	Long Term Debt	225,000	225,000		
15	Other Liabilities	95,000	85,000		
16	**Total Liabilities**				
17					
18	Capital				
19	Beginning Capital	758,500	843,500		
20	Net Income	87,500	120,500		
21	Ending Capital				
22	**Liabilities and Capital**				
23					
24	Working Capital				
25	Current Ratio				
26	Debt/Asset Ratio				
27	Capital/Asset Ratio				
28	Liability/Capital Ratio				

(Annotations:)
- Bold, Brown, Accent 5, Darker 50% font color
- Enter formulas to analyze changes
- Enter formulas to complete balance sheet data
- Shading in 40% - Accent4 cell style
- Total cell style
- Enter formulas to analyze changes

Figure 20.2

CHAPTER 6

Create Charts and Graphics/Integration

In this chapter, you will complete the following projects:

PROJECT 21
Chart Sales Data
PROJECT 21.1 Chart Sales Data
PROJECT 21.2 Chart and Analyze Sales Data

PROJECT 22
Chart Expense Data
PROJECT 22.1 Chart Expense Data
PROJECT 22.2 Chart and Analyze Expense Data

PROJECT 23
Chart Investment Data
PROJECT 23.1 Chart Mutual Fund Data
PROJECT 23.2 Add Graphics to a Mutual Fund Report
PROJECT 23.3 Chart Stock Prices

PROJECT 24
Integrate Charts and Worksheets into Documents
PROJECT 24.1 Paste a Worksheet into a Memorandum
PROJECT 24.2 Embed Worksheets into a Business Plan
PROJECT 24.3 Embed a Chart and a Worksheet into a Bulletin
PROJECT 24.4 Link Charts and Worksheets into an Annual Report

CHART SALES DATA

PROJECT 21

PROJECT SKILLS

✱ Create column, line, and pie charts
✱ Customize charts with titles, legends, and labels
✱ Size and position a chart
✱ Move chart location
✱ Copy and paste charts
✱ Change the chart type
✱ Print charts

21.1 CHART SALES DATA

Baldwin-Larson, Inc. is a wholesaler that owns divisions which specialize in food and non-food items purchased by food suppliers such as restaurants, grocery stores, hospitals, and schools. It would like you to compare its sales data using charts.

In this project, you will create and position column and pie charts embedded on a worksheet.

1. Open data file **d21.1sales**.
2. Format the title block of the worksheet as you wish, or as shown in Figure 21.1.
3. Select the range B6:D12 and click the Insert tab; and in the Charts group, click the Bar button and then select the Clustered Bar subtype.
   Note: Clustered Bar is a 2-D Bar subtype.
4. Drag the chart into the position shown and then use the handles to size the chart.
5. On the Chart Tools Layout tab, click the Chart Title button in the Labels group. Select Above Chart, and then add the title **Sales by Division**.
6. Select the range B6:C12 and then create a pie chart for 2009 data. Use the Exploded pie in 3-D subtype.
7. Size and move the chart into the position shown. Change the chart title to **2009 Sales**.
8. To add percentage labels to the chart, click the Data Labels button on the Chart Tools Layout tab and then click More Data Label Options. Set Label Contains to Percentage only, and set Label Position to Center so that labels are centered in each pie slice.
9. Hide column C, and select the nonadjacent range B6:D12, now only two columns, and then create an Exploded pie chart in 3-D for the 2010 data. Unhide column C.
10. Format, size, and position the chart as shown in Figure 21.1. Change the chart title to **2010 Sales**.
11. Save the file and name it **21.1sales**.
12. Close the file.

WHAT YOU NEED TO KNOW

Software

▶ Charts present data in a graphic format. When you create a chart from worksheet data, you select a rectangular area of data, including column and/or row labels, with a blank cell in the upper-right corner. If the data you want to chart is nonadjacent, you can hide the columns you do not need and make your selection, or you can hold down [Ctrl] while selecting the areas to chart.

▶ To create a chart, select the data, click the Insert tab, and in the Charts group, click the button for the type of chart you wish to create. There are Column, Line, Pie, Bar, Area, Scatter and Other Charts buttons. When you select one of the chart type buttons, a gallery of chart subtypes will appear. The selected chart will appear on the worksheet and the Chart Tools Design, Layout, and Format tabs will be active.

▶ To add or modify chart titles, legends, data labels, or other chart labels, select the chart and then use the Chart Tools Layout tab and click the desired label object in the Labels group. Click the Chart Title button, the Axis Titles button, the Legend button, the Data Labels button, or the Chart Data Table button to add label objects to the chart. Data labels may be added to show actual values or percentage of the total values, which is beneficial for pie charts.

Continued on next page

▶ You can embed charts in the worksheet or create a separate chart sheet. If you embed a chart in the worksheet, you will need to position and size it using the mouse. After you click the chart once to select it, handles appear around the chart's border. To size a chart, position your mouse pointer over the appropriate handle on the border of the chart and drag to expand or contract the chart. To move a chart, drag the chart when the mouse pointer changes to a four-headed arrow.

Project

▶ You will create embedded charts on the worksheet and must position and size each chart for readability.

▶ Data labels in the form of percentage values will be added to the pie charts for 2009 and 2010 so that the values can be compared.

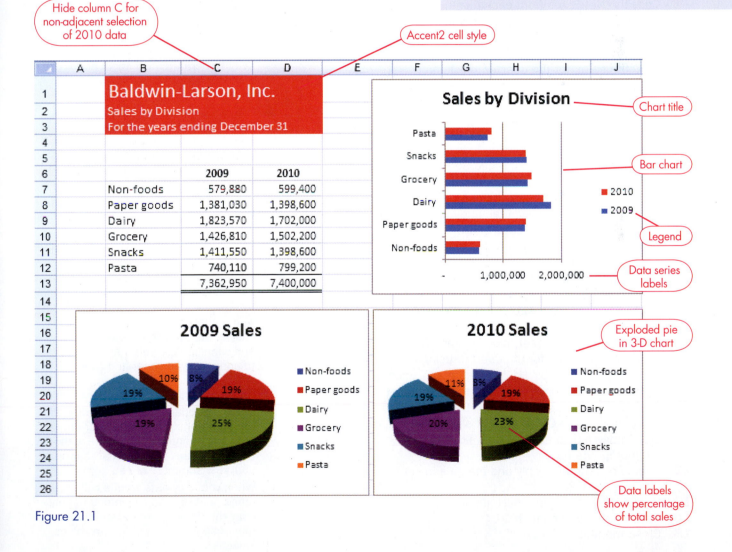

Figure 21.1

21.2 CHART AND ANALYZE SALES DATA

Barlow's Department Store would like you to create a quarterly report for personal shopper sales, as well as charts to view report data.

In this project, you will take appropriate data from a report and create a summary report with charts.

1. Open data file **d21.2sales** or **14.1sales** from your files and review the information on each sheet.
2. Copy the January worksheet so that it is placed after the March sheet, or at the end.
3. Rename the new sheet **1st Quarter**.
4. Adjust column widths so that all text and values are visible. Unmerge rows 1:3.
5. Delete the headings and data in columns D:G and then insert the new headings for columns D:I, as shown in Figure 21.2a. Change the title in row 3 to **1st Quarter 2010**.
6. Copy the Net Sales from each month and then use Paste Special, with Values and number formats selected, to place the data on the 1st Quarter sheet. Adjust the column width as necessary.
7. Total the sales for the quarter in column G. Notice that the commissions and salary columns automatically compute with the formulas that are in place.
8. Complete the totals and averages in rows 14:15.
9. To chart sales for the quarter, hide column C, and then use the nonadjacent range B6:F12 to create a Clustered Bar in 3-D chart with appropriate titles, as shown in Figure 21.2b. Click the Move Chart button on the Chart Tools Design tab and name the new chart sheet **Bar Chart**, as shown in Figure 21.2c. Move the new chart sheet to the position after the 1st Quarter sheet.
10. Copy the Bar Chart sheet and paste it at the end. Change the chart type to a 3-D Clustered Column chart. Rename the new chart sheet **Column Chart**.
11. In the 1st Quarter sheet, hide columns D:F and chart commissions for the quarter, using the nonadjacent range B7:H12 to create an Exploded pie in 3-D chart. Move the chart to a new chart sheet, name it **Pie Chart** and then move it to the position after the Column Chart sheet. Add centered percentage labels as the data values, and then add an appropriate title.
12. Unhide columns D:F only and merge and center the title in rows 1:3.
13. Print a copy of the bar chart sheet.
14. Save the file and name it **21.2sales**.
15. Close the file.

WHAT YOU NEED TO KNOW

Software

▶ To create a two-line title, enter all the text, place your cursor where you wish to have a line break, and then use [Enter] to move text to the second line. You can modify the size and position of the title text box by using the object handles.

▶ If you wish to create a chart on a chart sheet, click the Chart Tools Design tab and click the Move Chart button in the Location group. Name the chart sheet in the Move Chart dialog box, as shown in Figure 21.2c. On a chart sheet, the chart is fully expanded to fill the page. The chart title should contain the company name since it will not appear with the worksheet data.

▶ When you copy a report from one sheet to another, the formulas are copied as well. To copy a sheet, right-click the sheet tab and click Move or Copy, then select where the new sheet should be placed, click the Create a copy box, and click OK.

▶ You can copy charts or chart sheets, paste them, and then modify the copy to change the chart type while maintaining the same titles and labels. Click the Chart Tools Design tab, and in the Type group, click the Change Chart Type button and select the new chart type.

▶ To print a chart sheet, select the sheet, click the Office button, and then click Print. To print only a chart that is embedded in a worksheet, select the chart and click the Office button, and then click Print. To print the worksheet with embedded charts, deselect all charts, print preview the worksheet, and change page setup as necessary to print the worksheet and charts.

Project

▶ Barlow's Department Store prepared a monthly analysis of sales for its personal shoppers. You will take the Net Sales data and summarize it on a quarterly summary sheet.

▶ When you copy data from a cell or range of cells, and you intend to only copy the data (not the formula), you must use Paste Special, with Values selected.

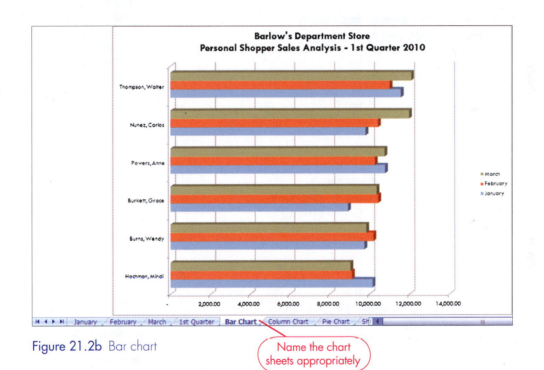

Figure 21.2a 1st Quarter Worksheet

	A	B	C	D	E	F	G	H	I
				Barlow's Department Store					
1				**Personal Shopper Sales Analysis**					
2									
3				1st Quarter 2010					
4									
5	Emp. No.	Name	Store	Net Sales for the Month				Total	Total
6				January	February	March	Total	Commission	Salary
7	235	Hochman, Mindi	Raleigh	10,147.78	9,124.91	9,046.34	28,319.03	2,831.90	12,979.68
8	236	Burns, Wendy	Raleigh	9,741.91	10,192.11	9,835.67	29,769.69	2,976.97	12,718.88
9	237	Burkett, Grace	Raleigh	8,930.56	10,436.78	10,355.44	29,722.78	2,972.28	11,902.84
10	238	Powers, Anne	Durham	10,777.91	10,267.31	10,751.22	31,796.44	3,179.64	13,957.55
11	239	Nunez, Carlos	Durham	9,806.63	10,429.89	11,973.78	32,210.30	3,221.03	13,027.66
12	240	Thompson, Walter	Durham	11,569.56	11,013.55	12,078.10	34,661.21	3,466.12	15,035.68
13									
14		Total		60,974.35	61,464.55	64,040.55	186,479.45	18,647.95	79,622.30
15		Averages		10,162.39	10,244.09	10,673.43	31,079.91	3,107.99	13,270.38

New column headings

Figure 21.2b Bar chart

Name the chart sheets appropriately

Figure 21.2c Move Chart dialog box

CHART EXPENSE DATA

PROJECT SKILLS

✷ Change orientation of data
✷ Format and modify charts
✷ Add a logo or picture to a chart
✷ Use custom chart types

PROJECT 22

22.1 CHART EXPENSE DATA

Classic Party Planners has prepared an analysis of expenses for the second quarter of 2010. This data will be presented at a meeting, and you have been asked to prepare charts to format the analysis so that the data is clear and attractive.

In this project, you will create, format, and modify charts that are on chart sheets and embedded in the worksheet.

1. Open the data file **d22.1expenses**.
2. Format the worksheet using Figure 22.1a as a guide, and complete the analysis by finding the 2nd Qtr. totals and the monthly totals.
3. To chart the expenses, select B5:E14 and create a Clustered Bar in 3-D chart, and then move it to a chart sheet named **Bar Chart-Expenses**.
4. Add the chart title shown in Figure 22.1b, and then right-click on the Chart Title object. Click Format Chart Title on the shortcut menu, and in the dialog box, click Solid fill and then select Orange. Add the company logo in data file, **classiclogo.tif**.
5. Drag and drop the Bar Chart-Expenses sheet tab after the Sheet1 tab, right-click the Bar Chart-Expenses sheet tab and make a copy of the sheet, and then place it before Sheet2.
6. On the copy of the sheet, switch the row/column orientation so that the data series is arranged by rows, which in this case is by the month, as shown in Figure 22.1c. Rename the chart sheet **Bar Chart-Month**.
7. Create an Exploded pie in 3-D chart of the 2nd Qtr. total expenses. Hide columns C:E and then make a nonadjacent selection of B6:F14 for the chart. Unhide columns C:E. Place the chart on the worksheet with the selected data, and then size and position it as shown in Figure 22.1a.
8. Add a chart title, and then select and modify the font size of legend text values to 9 point.
9. Add percentage data labels in the Best Fit position.

WHAT YOU NEED TO KNOW

Software

▶ Chart data orientation is set automatically by Excel. However, you can change the orientation of data so that the row data is shown as column data and vice versa. This changes the emphasis of the chart and may provide more information. Select the chart, click the Chart Tools Design tab, and in the Data group, click the Switch Row/Column button.

▶ You can format any chart object by right-clicking the object and opening the appropriate formatting dialog box. For example, to omit a chart border, right-click the chart area, and click Format Chart Area. In the Format Chart Area dialog box, click Border Color, and then select No line. You can also use the Chart Tools Design, Layout, or Format tabs to format or modify chart objects.

▶ You can add a company logo in a picture file to a chart to customize it. Click the Insert tab, and in the Illustrations group, click the Picture button. Locate the picture file and double-click it to insert it onto the chart. Use the sizing handles to size the picture and drag it into position.

10. Right-click the chart area and then, using the Format Chart Area dialog box, set the Border Color to No line, if necessary.

11. Click on the worksheet to deselect the chart. On the View tab, in the Show/Hide group, deselect Gridlines.

12. Print a copy of the three-page report.

13. Save the file and name it **22.1expenses**.

14. Close the file.

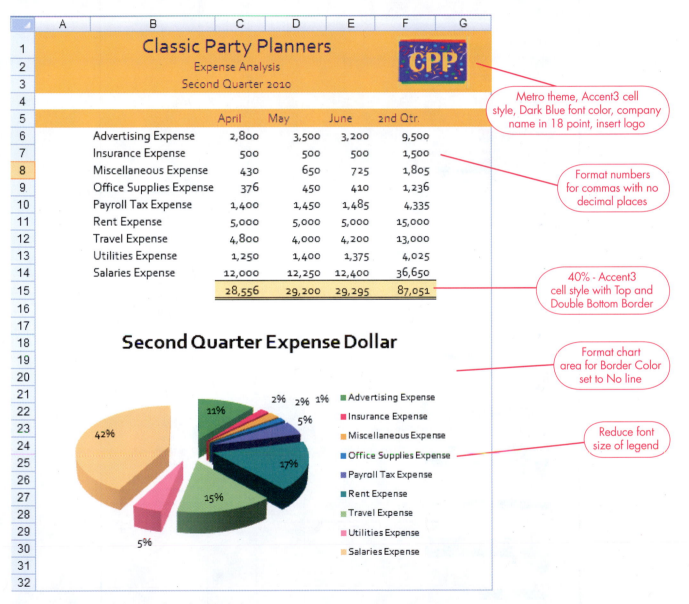

Figure 22.1a Worksheet with embedded chart

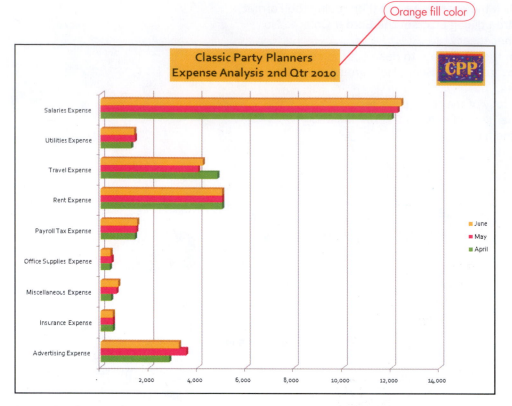

Figure 22.1b Bar Chart-Expenses

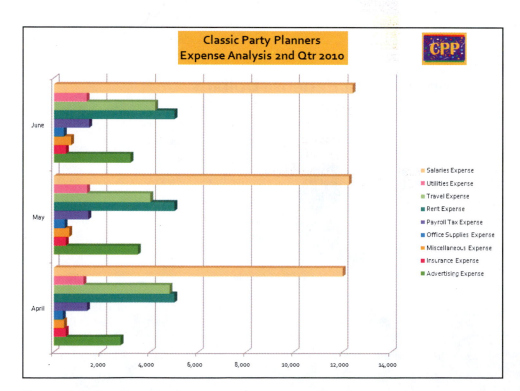

Figure 22.1c Bar Chart-Month

22.2 CHART AND ANALYZE EXPENSE DATA

Health Connections has prepared monthly income statements that divide expenses into three categories: Financial Expenses, Fixed Expenses, and Variable Expenses. You have been asked to obtain quarterly values and use charts to analyze the changes in variable expenses.

In this project, you will complete an income statement analysis and use custom chart types to analyze expenses.

1. Open data file **d22.2analysis**.
2. Format the worksheet titles as shown in Figure 22.2a and format all numbers for commas with no decimals. Health Connections uses the Origin theme with the Accent4 and Accent6 cell styles. Adjust the column width as necessary.
3. Select column E and insert a column and label it **1st Qtr**. Insert columns in appropriate locations and label them **2nd Qtr.** and **3rd Qtr.**, and then label column Q **4th Qtr**. Find the totals for each quarter.
4. Enter the following formulas and copy them across for all months and summary columns:
   a. In cell B7, calculate Gross Profit.
   b. In cell B12, calculate Total Expenses.
   c. In cell B14, calculate Net Income.
      Hint: Gross Profit – Total Expenses.
5. Add cell borders and the Total cell style as shown.
6. Hide the three monthly columns in each quarter, and then add a column for totals for the year.
7. Use the SUM function to total the quarterly totals. *Hint: Use the cell address of each quarterly total.* Extend cell borders and the Total cell style as necessary. Hide the worksheet gridlines. Change the second title to **Income Statement**.
8. Print a copy of the worksheet, without gridlines or row and column headings, and centered horizontally.
9. You need to select column headings and expense data to chart the quarterly expenses.
   a. Hide rows 5:8 and select cells A4:Q11, and then create a 3-D Clustered Column chart.
   b. Move the chart to a new chart sheet, and name it **Column Chart**. Move the Column Chart sheet to the position after the Data sheet, if necessary.
   c. Modify the placement of the legend so that it appears at the bottom of the chart, as shown in Figure 22.2b.
   d. Right-click on one of the Variable Expense columns, and then click Format Data Series. Change the Fill option to Solid fill, and then select the Light Yellow, Accent 4 fill color.
   e. Add a chart title as shown in Figure 22.2b.

▼ WHAT YOU NEED TO KNOW

Software

► To modify the placement of the legend, right-click the legend, click Format Legend, and select the location for the legend. In some cases, moving the legend improves the chart.

► Depending on the type of chart you have selected, the data series, or group of values, is represented by columns, bars, lines, slices of a pie, or some other value indicator. To modify any aspect of the data series, right-click the series and then click Format Data Series. You can then change items such as the shape, fill, border color, or border style. If you have set a theme for the worksheet, the colors available in the Format Data Series dialog box will be appropriate to the theme.

Project

► Health Connections assembled income statement data for the year and divided expenses into three categories. The Financial Expenses category is for interest payments. The Fixed Expenses category is for recurring items, such as rent, that are essential for operations. The Variable Expenses category is for expenses that vary with the amount of sales or with changes in operating procedures.

► You will insert columns to find quarterly totals, and then hide the monthly data columns so that you can prepare the charts with quarterly data. Quarterly means every three months.

10. Copy the chart and paste it to the next empty sheet. Change the chart type to a Clustered Horizontal Cylinder bar chart, as shown in Figure 22.2c. Rename the chart sheet **Bar Chart**.

11. To create the pie chart, copy the range A9:A11, and then copy it to the blank area in cell W9. Copy the range R9:R11 to cell X9, and then use Paste Special, with Values selected.

    a. Select the range W9:X11, and then create an Exploded pie in 3-D chart.

    b. Place the chart on the worksheet, as shown in Figure 22.2a.

    c. Right-click in the chart area, and then format the Border Color to No line.

    d. Add Percentage data labels in the Best Fit position.

    e. Click the variable expenses data point until only that segment is selected. Right-click, and then change the fill color to match the theme.

    f. Add the chart title and format it as shown in Figure 22.2a.

12. Save the file and name it **22.2analysis**.

13. Close the file.

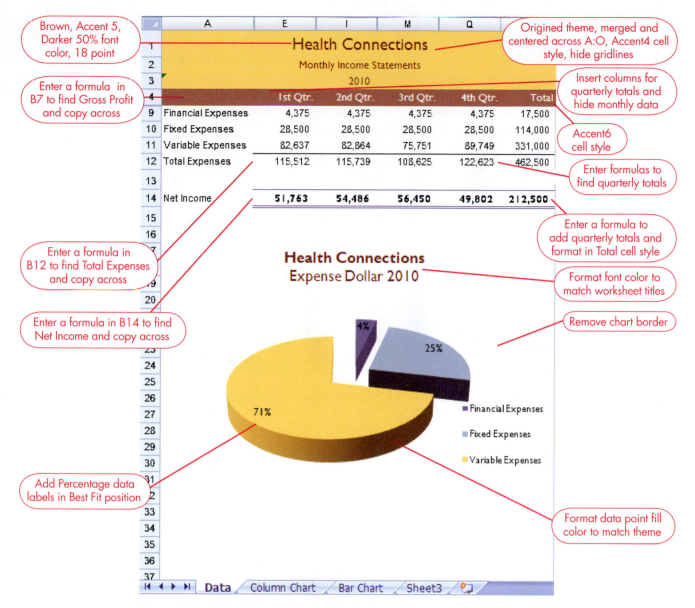

Brown, Accent 5, Darker 50% font color, 18 point

Enter a formula in B7 to find Gross Profit and copy across

Origined theme, merged and centered across A:O, Accent4 cell style, hide gridlines

Insert columns for quarterly totals and hide monthly data

Accent6 cell style

Enter formulas to find quarterly totals

Enter a formula in B12 to find Total Expenses and copy across

Enter a formula in B14 to find Net Income and copy across

Enter a formula to add quarterly totals and format in Total cell style

Format font color to match worksheet titles

Remove chart border

Add Percentage data labels in Best Fit position

Format data point fill color to match theme

	A	E	I	M	Q
1	Health Connections				
2	Monthly Income Statements				
3	2010				
4		1st Qtr.	2nd Qtr.	3rd Qtr.	4th Qtr.	Total
9	Financial Expenses	4,375	4,375	4,375	4,375	17,500
10	Fixed Expenses	28,500	28,500	28,500	28,500	114,000
11	Variable Expenses	82,637	82,864	75,751	89,749	331,000
12	Total Expenses	115,512	115,739	108,625	122,623	462,500
13						
14	Net Income	51,763	54,486	56,450	49,802	212,500

Health Connections
Expense Dollar 2010

- Financial Expenses
- Fixed Expenses
- Variable Expenses

Data / Column Chart / Bar Chart / Sheet3

Figure 22.2a Worksheet with embedded chart

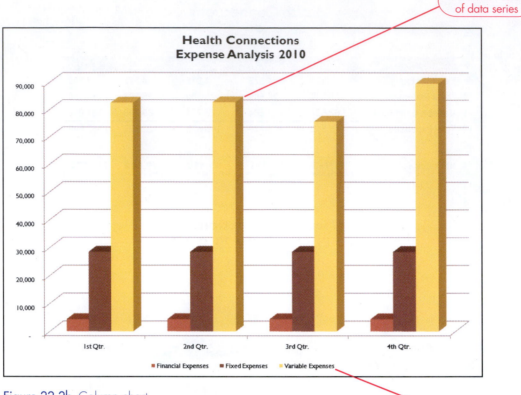

Figure 22.2b Column chart

Figure 22.2c Bar chart

CHART INVESTMENT DATA

PROJECT 23

▶ **PROJECT SKILLS**

✷ Create, position, and modify graphics
✷ Insert and download graphics and clip art
✷ Insert and modify SmartArt graphics
✷ Create stock charts
✷ Add callouts to a chart

23.1 CHART MUTUAL FUND DATA

The EarthOne Growth Fund has developed data to include in its mailings to promote the fund. You have been asked to prepare the data for the mailings.

In this project, you will format a worksheet and chart, and include graphics and clip art.

1. Open data file **d23.1fund**.
2. Format the data on the worksheet, as shown in Figure 23.1. Format the Performance data in Number format with negative numbers in black parentheses. Format the Major Holdings data in Percent style with one decimal place.
3. Insert a picture that represents "growth." Search for clip art on Office Online, and then insert, size, and position the picture.
4. Use a color from the clip art for the title fonts. For example, in Figure 23.1 the theme is Trek, the font color is Orange, Accent 6, Darker 50%, and the font for the fund name and section headings is Franklin Gothic Medium.
5. Add a Curved Right Arrow from the Shapes gallery in the position indicated and, if necessary, rotate the arrow so that it points to the 1-year Fund Return.
6. Format the arrow so that the borders and fill match are coordinated with your clip art graphic.
7. To create a chart on fund sectors, use the range B12:E23 and create a Clustered bar chart on the worksheet. Position it so that it fills the width of the worksheet, as shown.
8. Add a chart title as shown, and then format the fonts to match the worksheet.
9. Change the colors of the data series bars to match the worksheet color scheme, and then hide the worksheet gridlines.
10. Print preview and print a copy of the worksheet, centered horizontally.
11. Save the workbook and name it **23.1fund**.
12. Close the file.

▽ WHAT YOU NEED TO KNOW

Software

▶ You can add illustrations such as pictures, shapes, clip art, or SmartArt graphics to worksheets to enhance their appearance. Drawing objects, such as lines, rectangles, arrows, AutoShapes, and so on, are found on the Insert tab, in the Illustrations group, by clicking the Shapes button. You can select your object from the Shapes gallery and you can size, move, and position shapes just as you can with charts.

▶ In addition to logos, you can insert pictures into a worksheet from clip art, picture files, or image files from scanners or cameras. Click the Insert Picture from File button or the Clip Art button on the Insert tab to view and select the graphic. To search online for appropriate clip art or pictures from the Microsoft Clip Art and Media Web page, click the Clip Art button, and then click Clip Art on Office Online, at the bottom of the Clip Art task pane.

Project

▶ The EarthOne Growth Fund is a portfolio of stocks sold to investors. To encourage customers to buy a fund, advertisements or flyers are prepared to advertise the performance of the mutual fund. The performance is compared to the return on the Standard & Poor's (S&P) 500 and on an average of similar funds. The S&P 500 is a market index, made up of 500 blue-chip stocks, that is used to predict the general trend of U.S. stocks.

▶ It is informative to tell investors what types of equities are held in the portfolio. The major holdings are divided into market sectors or types of investments, such as energy, financials, or government bonds.

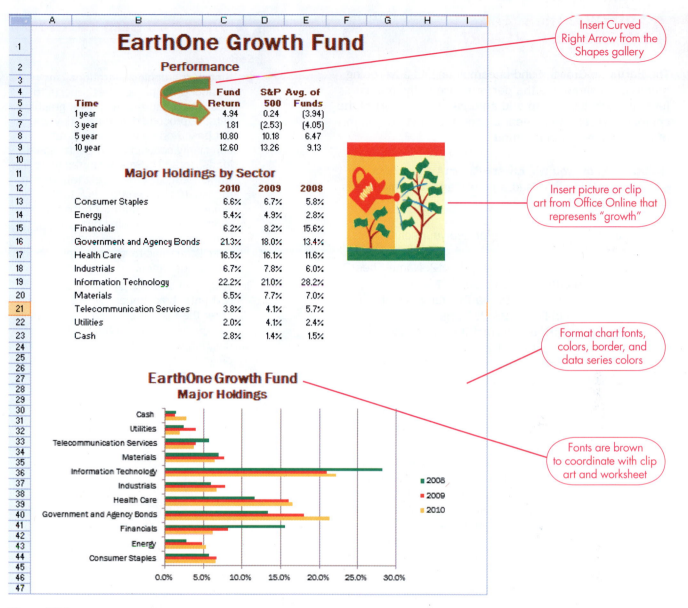

EarthOne Growth Fund

Performance

Time	Fund Return	S&P 500	Avg. of Funds
1 year	4.94	0.24	(3.94)
3 year	1.81	(2.53)	(4.05)
5 year	10.80	10.18	6.47
10 year	12.60	13.26	9.13

Major Holdings by Sector

	2010	2009	2008
Consumer Staples	6.6%	6.7%	5.8%
Energy	5.4%	4.9%	2.8%
Financials	6.2%	8.2%	15.6%
Government and Agency Bonds	21.3%	18.0%	13.4%
Health Care	16.5%	16.1%	11.6%
Industrials	6.7%	7.8%	6.0%
Information Technology	22.2%	21.0%	28.2%
Materials	6.5%	7.7%	7.0%
Telecommunication Services	3.8%	4.1%	5.7%
Utilities	2.0%	4.1%	2.4%
Cash	2.8%	1.4%	1.5%

Insert Curved Right Arrow from the Shapes gallery

Insert picture or clip art from Office Online that represents "growth"

Format chart fonts, colors, border, and data series colors

Fonts are brown to coordinate with clip art and worksheet

Figure 23.1

The EarthOne Growth Fund is completing its advertising materials to showcase the performance of the mutual fund. It would like you to add an organization chart of the company officers and a gear diagram to illustrate the mix of the investments in the fund.

In this project, you will create SmartArt graphics for an organization chart and a gear diagram to include in promotional materials.

1. Open data file **d23.2fund** or use your solution file **23.1fund**.
2. Copy the header in row 1 to Sheet2. Name Sheet2 **Diagrams** and Sheet1 **Growth Fund**.
3. Add a second header to the Diagrams sheet in row 3, as shown in Figure 23.2. Merge and center the header over A:H, and format it with the same font and font color, but at 11 point.
4. Insert a SmartArt graphic from the Process category entitled Gear. Position the graphic and add the text as shown.
5. Select the graphic and on the SmartArt Tools Design tab, change the fill and font colors to match the theme.
6. Input the additional title and text as illustrated.
7. Create an Organization Chart diagram, found in the Hierarchy category, and include the text as shown.
8. Change the fill and font colors to match your theme, and then hide worksheet gridlines.
9. Position and size the diagrams appropriately.
10. Print preview and print a copy of the diagram sheet on one page.
11. Save the workbook and name it **23.2fund**.
12. Close the file.

WHAT YOU NEED TO KNOW

Software

► SmartArt graphic illustrations can be added to spreadsheet reports to illustrate organization charts, graphical lists, or process diagrams. They are not based on number values, but can clarify concepts or organizational ideas. To add a SmartArt graphic to a worksheet, click the Insert tab, and in the Illustrations group, click the SmartArt button. In the Choose a Smart Graphic dialog box, you can select the category and the specific graphic to see an explanation of the illustration.

► When you select a graphic diagram, a text entry box appears where you can enter the text for each graphic element. You can move, size, and position the diagram using the handles. Format the diagram by right-clicking each element to open a Format dialog box, or use the Style galleries on the SmartArt Tools Design and Format tabs.

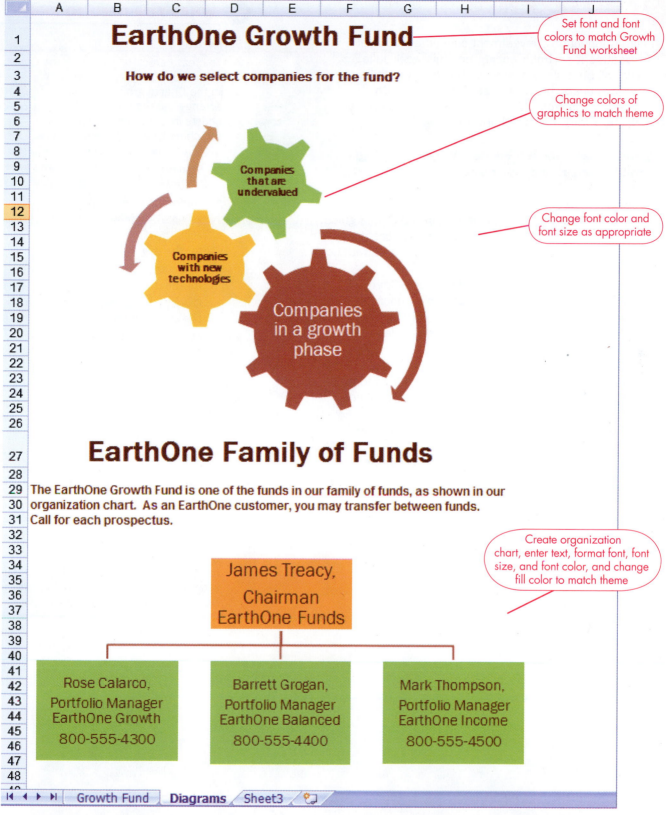

Figure 23.2

23.3 CHART STOCK PRICES

Health Connection's investment committee looks at its investment portfolio weekly, and this week Julie Pringle will be making a presentation about Excalibur Pharmaceuticals, one of the stocks in the health Connections portfolio. She has asked you to create a stock chart for Excalibur Pharmaceuticals.

In this project, you will create a Volume-Open-High-Low-Close chart and insert a callout.

1. Open data file **d23.3stock**.
2. Format the worksheet, using Figure 23.3 as a guide. Change the theme to Opulent and use Accent1 cell styles. Format the volume data for commas with no decimals.
3. Create a stock chart using the Volume-Open-High-Low-Close selection. Position it under the worksheet.
4. Reduce the font size of the data series labels for both axes to 8 point.
5. Enter and then format the chart title to match the theme. Right-click the chart area, and then format the Border Color for No line. Hide the worksheet gridlines.
6. Add the Line Callout 1 graphic shape from the Shapes gallery that points to the data showing that the stock price closed down. In the callout, enter the information about the resignation of the CEO.
7. Print a copy of the worksheet.
8. Save the worksheet and name it **23.3stock**.
9. Close the file.

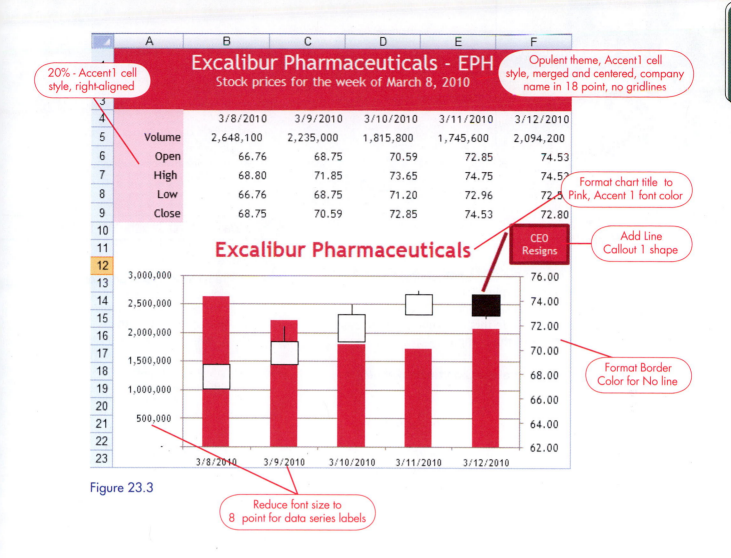

Figure 23.3

PROJECT 24

24.1 PASTE A WORKSHEET INTO A MEMORANDUM

Steve Montez is in charge of the Human Resources Department of the BestFriend Animal Hospital. He created a worksheet analyzing salary increases earlier and now would like you to include this analysis in a memo to the chief financial officer of the company.

In this project, you will integrate and edit a worksheet within a memorandum.

1. Open data file **d24.1memo.docx** in Word and data file **d24.1salary.xlsx** in Excel.
2. Right-click the taskbar and select Show Windows Side by Side, or use taskbar buttons to switch between windows.
3. Copy the entire worksheet from the source file, **d24.1salary.xlsx**, and then paste it below the first paragraph in the destination file, **d24.1memo.docx**, as shown in Figure 24.1.
4. Minimize the source file.
5. Select and delete the top three title rows in the pasted worksheet using Word table-editing methods.
6. Select the entire worksheet (table) using the selector button and change the font size to 7 point. Right-click the table and point to AutoFit on the shortcut menu, and then click AutoFit to Window.
7. Try to select a cell in the 2011 Raise column to edit the formula. Notice that you cannot do so.
8. Maximize the Excel source file and notice that there are no changes in the file.
9. Print a copy of the one-page memo.
10. Save the file and name it **24.1memo.docx**.
11. Close the file.

WHAT YOU NEED TO KNOW

Software

▶ Integration refers to sharing or combining data between Office applications. When you integrate data between applications, the data comes from a source file and is integrated into a destination file.

▶ You can integrate data between applications by pasting from, embedding, or linking to the file that contains the data. The method you select determines how you edit or make changes to the integrated object. You can edit a worksheet that you have pasted into a Word document as you would edit a Word table, but you cannot use any Excel features, such as formulas. In this project we will be pasting data from an Excel source file.

▶ To copy and paste data between applications, both the source and destination files should be open. Switch between files using the buttons on the taskbar, or right-click the taskbar and then select an option to view both files. Then use the regular procedures to copy and paste the data.

Project

▶ You will paste the worksheet into the memorandum and edit it so that the memorandum will fit on one page. To select the entire table in Word, use the selector button at the top left of the table.

▶ You will attempt to change calculated data in the worksheet and will discover that you cannot view or change the formulas.

BestFriend Animal Hospital

Memo

To: Grace Hunt, Chief Financial Officer

From: Steve Montez, Human Resources

Date: 11/2/2010

Re: Salary Increases

As per your request at our last staff meeting, we have developed an analysis of salary increases for BestFriend Animal Hospital employees for 2009 and 2010, and a proposal for 2011 increases.

Paste worksheet here and modify table to fit memo

Employee	Years of Seniority	2009 Salary	2010 Salary	2010 Raise	2010 % Increase	2011 Raise	2011 Salary	2011 Final Salary
Arena, Thomas	7	50,000	52,000	2,000	4.00%	2,860.00	54,000.00	54,000
Barlow, Carl	5	30,550	32,500	1,950	6.38%	1,787.50	34,287.50	34,287
Dominquez, Peter	2	22,500	23,000	500	2.22%	805.00	23,805.00	23,805
Finkelstein, Joe	4	31,000	32,750	1,750	5.65%	1,146.25	33,896.25	33,896
Hinkel, Marie	3	28,000	29,680	1,680	6.00%	1,038.80	30,718.80	30,718
Johnson, Robert	2	24,000	25,000	1,000	4.17%	875.00	25,875.00	25,875
Kho, Mae	6	40,000	42,400	2,400	6.00%	2,332.00	44,732.00	44,732
Martinelli, Gloria	7	40,000	42,750	2,750	6.88%	2,351.25	45,101.25	45,101
Nestor, Sancho	3	32,000	34,000	2,000	6.25%	1,190.00	35,190.00	35,190
Petreccio, Dan	4	32,000	33,750	1,750	5.47%	1,181.25	34,931.25	34,931
Santos, Raymond	2	24,000	25,000	1,000	4.17%	875.00	25,875.00	25,875
Thompson, Jamal	7	43,000	45,500	2,500	5.81%	2,502.50	48,002.50	48,002
Zanardi, George	6	42,000	44,520	2,520	6.00%	2,448.60	46,968.60	46,968
Totals		439,050	462,850	23,800	5.42%	21,393.15	483,383.15	483,380

Our proposal is to institute a system of salary increases based on seniority along with satisfactory attendance and performance reviews. We propose a 3.5% raise for employees with seniority of less than five years and a 5.5% raise for employees who have been with us for five years or more. We know that this system is in use in other facilities and it seems to encourage employees to stay.

The new plan results in a lower total cost for employee raises and the new salaries have been rounded down for purposes of payroll. Let me know if you want to change any of the suggested raise percentages or seniority levels.

Figure 24.1

24.2 EMBED WORKSHEETS INTO A BUSINESS PLAN

Health Connections, a health foods retailer, is interested in a loan to refit its warehouse in order to repackage bulk foods under its own brand. It will promote its brand in its well-respected stores and on its Website. It has created a business plan and would like you to include financial worksheets.

In this project, you will integrate financial data from several worksheets into a business plan by embedding the files.

1. Open data file **d24.2busplan.docx** in Word.
2. Review the file and place your insertion point on page 8, at the end of the explanatory text for the Comparative Income Statement, and press [Enter] to insert a line.
3. Open data file **d24.2is.xlsx** in Excel.
4. Copy the range A1:E20 of the worksheet.
5. Switch to the business plan and on the Home tab, click the Paste button arrow, and then click Paste Special. In the Paste Special dialog box, select Paste and Microsoft Office Excel Worksheet Object, and then click OK to embed the file.
6. Double-click the embedded file to make edits in Excel. Add the borders as shown in Figure 24.2a, and format the Net Income values in Accounting Number format with no decimal places.
7. If necessary, add blank lines to move the Projected Cash Flow section to page 9.
8. Place your insertion point under the explanatory text for the Projected Cash Flow and add the new text, as shown in Figure 24.2b:

   > **Therefore, we have conservatively projected that our accounts receivable collections and net income will increase as shown below:**

9. Press [Enter] to add a line, and then embed the data in the range A1:G26 from data file **d24.2cf.xlsx** file.
10. Format the Cash Ending Balance value for Accounting Number format with no decimal places, as shown in Figure 24.2b.
11. If necessary, enter blank lines to move the Balance Sheet text to the next page. Embed the data in the range A1:E28 from the data file **d24.2bs.xlsx** below the explanatory text.
12. Format the Total Assets, Total Liabilities and Capital, and Working Capital values in Accounting Number format with no decimal places. Adjust column width, if necessary.
13. Correct the page numbers for the Financial Plan section on the Table of Contents.
14. Print a copy of the business plan.
15. Save the file and name it **24.2busplan.docx**.
16. Close the file.

▼ WHAT YOU NEED TO KNOW

Software

▶ The second method of integrating data is to embed the file. An embedded file is an object that you can edit in its original source application. For example, if you embed an Excel file into a Word document, you can double-click it to select the worksheet, and then edit it within Excel. Any changes you make do not change the original source file.

▶ You can embed a selected portion of a file into a Word document by copying it in Excel, and switching to Word. Next click the Home tab, and in the Clipboard group, click the Paste button arrow, and then click Paste Special. In the Paste Special dialog box, select Paste and Microsoft Office Excel Worksheet Object. Click OK to embed the data.

▶ You can edit any embedded worksheet data by double-clicking the worksheet, and then performing edits as you would in Excel.

Project

▶ A business plan is a detailed road map of the history, operations, and future plans of a business. It should be revised annually and can be used to set and measure goals and objectives, or it can be used to obtain additional funding for new projects.

▶ You have already prepared the comparative income statement and balance sheet for Health Connections. You will use those reports, along with the cash flow statement, and incorporate all worksheets into their proper locations. They will be reformatted in the document within Excel. Be sure to paginate the report so that the explanation for the worksheet is on the same page, right above the worksheet.

5.0 FINANCIAL PLAN

At the present time, we have excellent working capital, so the debt on our loan will be manageable.

5.1 Comparative Income Statement

As the income statement shows, our profits and our rate of return on sales have increased substantially. The increase in our operating expenses has been offset by the decrease in our cost of goods sold. Packaging our own products will further lower our cost of goods sold, which will improve our profit margin. We are planning a full analysis of expenses to determine where efficiencies can be implemented to reduce our variable expenses.

Health Connections

Comparative Income Statements
For the years ended December 31

Embed worksheet, add borders, and format totals in Accounting Number format

	2009	%	2010	%
Net Sales	1,400,000	100.00%	1,575,000	100.00%
Cost of Goods Sold	850,000	60.71%	900,000	57.14%
Gross Profit	550,000	39.29%	675,000	42.86%
Operating Expenses	365,000	26.07%	445,000	28.25%
Operating Income	185,000	13.21%	230,000	14.60%
Financial Expenses	17,500	1.25%	17,500	1.11%
Income before Income Taxes	167,500	11.96%	212,500	13.49%
Income Tax Expense	80,000	5.71%	92,000	5.84%
Net Income	$ 87,500	6.25%	$ 120,500	7.65%
Rate of Return on Sales	6.25%		7.65%	
Operating Expense Ratio	3.84		3.54	

HEALTH CONNECTIONS

Figure 24.2a Page 8

5.2 Projected Cash Flow

Collections have not been a problem since we are credited in two days by American Center,

our credit card company.

Selling our products over the Internet will allow us full retail price to maximize our profit.

Therefore, we have conservatively projected our accounts receivable collections and net

income to increase as shown below:

Add new text

Health Connections

Projected Cash Flow Statement
For the year ended December 31, 2010

Cash, Beginning Balance, 1/1/2010			247,580
Sources of Cash:			
Net Income	132,500		
Collections from Receivables	475,000		
Other	50,000		
Total Cash Receipts		657,500	
Disbursements:			
Supplies	30,600		
Wages	225,000		
Utilities	25,765		
Insurance	13,098		
Advertising	25,000		
Distribution	28,500		
Interest Payments	17,500		
Payments to Creditors	223,980		
Other	25,000		
Total Cash Disbursements		614,443	
Net Increase in Cash			43,057
Cash, Ending Balance, 12/31/2010			$ 290,637

Embed worksheet and format totals in Accounting Number format with no decimal places

HEALTH CONNECTIONS

Figure 24.2b Page 9

24.3 EMBED A CHART AND A WORKSHEET INTO A BULLETIN

Abbey Neuhaus Realtors prepares an Education Bulletin for the agents on a regular basis. This bulletin covers population trends that may impact the types of housing that will be in demand in the future. You have been asked to prepare the upcoming bulletin.

In this project, you will complete preparation of a bulletin that contains a worksheet and an embedded chart.

1. Open data files **d24.3bulletin.docx** in Word and **d24.3retirees.xlsx** in Excel.
2. Within Word, on the bulletin, create a text box and format the banner for the Education Bulletin, as shown in Figure 24.3. Abby Neuhaus Realtors uses the Aqua, Accent 5 fill color for its materials.
3. Center the titles and format them, as you prefer.
4. Copy the data from the Excel worksheet and use the Paste Special feature in Word to embed it into the bulletin in the location shown.
5. In Excel, on the spreadsheet, create a Clustered Bar chart titled `Retirees per 100 Workers` to show the data in the worksheet and then place it below the data in the worksheet. Size and position it so that the chart data is readable. Format one of the data series in the Aqua, Accent 5 fill color.
6. Copy the chart and use Paste Special to embed it in the bulletin.
7. Right-click the chart and then select Format Object. In the Layout tab, select the Square Wrapping style and Right Horizontal alignment. Position the chart so that it is to the right of the worksheet in the bulletin, and make any spacing adjustments as necessary.
8. Format the worksheet data so that all numbers have one decimal place.
9. Format the chart plot area in a lighter shade of the Accent 5 fill color.
10. Print a copy of the bulletin.
11. Save the files as **24.3bulletin.docx** and **24.3retirees.xlsx**.
12. Close both files.

▼ WHAT YOU NEED TO KNOW

Software

▶ You can integrate charts into a Word document using the same methods you used with worksheets. To embed the chart so that you can make edits in Excel, copy the chart; and in the Word document, click the Paste button arrow and then click Paste Special. In the Paste Special dialog box, click Paste and Microsoft Office Excel Chart Object, and then click OK to embed the chart.

▶ When you embed chart and worksheet objects, you may have to size and position them in order to place them properly. Use the fill handles on the objects to adjust the placement and size of embedded objects.

▶ To set the alignment of a chart on the page, right-click the chart and then click Format Object. On the Layout tab, set the text-wrapping style and horizontal alignment for the chart object.

Project

▶ Abbey Neuhaus Realtors cites the source for data in the report so that credit is given and noted by the reader.

▶ To place the chart next to the worksheet, you must align the chart on the right side of the page.

▶ It is beneficial for realtors to understand the larger economic and social issues at work in their markets.

Abbey Neuhaus Realtors

Education Bulletin

Add text box in Word, format for Calibri, 18 point, Aqua, Accent 5 fill color, no border

We publish the Education Bulletin to inform you about current research that impacts on our real estate market. Today's topic is:

THE AGING WORLD

Format data series to Accent 5 fill color, embed chart, and add lighter Accent5 fill color to chart plot area

The aging of the population is a worldwide trend. There will be more retirees per workers in the future, as evidenced by the table and chart below from the World Health Organization census.

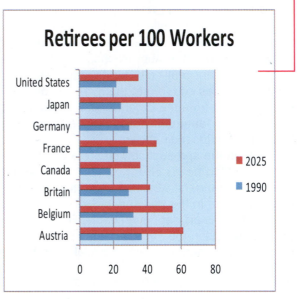

Retirees per 100 Workers

	1990	2025
Austria	36.7	61.4
Belgium	32.2	55.2
Britain	29.5	42.0
Canada	18.8	35.9
France	28.8	45.9
Germany	29.6	54.1
Japan	24.9	55.8
United States	22.3	35.1

Embed worksheet

The health and retirement systems in place for older adults will be supported by a dwindling working population. This could result in higher taxes and/or changes in the way retirement and health care are funded.

Is this trend in evidence in our real estate market? Our latest trends are:

- Older residents are trying to sell out of their large homes and are looking for a setting where home maintenance and recreation are built into the community.
- We have a demand for two bedroom, two bath apartments for singles and newlyweds in areas that are convenient for commuting to work in the city. In many cases, these are the same apartments that older residents seek to simplify their lives.
- Our young home buyers with families are looking for the larger homes but they are having difficulty selling their smaller homes in a difficult market.

Keep these trends in mind when working with clients and especially in your conversations with builders.

Figure 24.3

24.4 LINK CHARTS AND WORKSHEETS INTO AN ANNUAL REPORT

The Supply Warehouse, which sells office supplies and equipment, has prepared an annual report on operations to distribute to its stockholders. You have been asked to complete the report.

In this project, you will complete the preparation of financial worksheets and charts, and integrate them into an annual report using the paste link feature.

1. Open data files **d24.4annreport.docx** in Word and **d24.4annrpt.xlsx** in Excel. Review the contents of both files.

2. In the Excel file, on the Summary of Operations sheet, format numbers, except rows 8 and 9, for commas with no decimal places. Format rows 8 and 9 in Number format. Bold and center titles and column headings, and adjust the font size to 12 point.

3. Use the data on the Summary of Operations sheet to create two charts on the Summary of Operations worksheet.

   a. Create a Clustered Bar in 3-D chart entitled **Operating Profits and Net Earnings**. Use [Ctrl] to make a nonadjacent selection of data to select the years and the data specified. *Hint: A4:D4, A6:D7*. Add a chart title above the chart, move the legend to the top of the chart, and add a data table with legend keys under the chart. Format the chart data series bars to match the color scheme in the report. *Hint: Use Orange, Accent 6, Lighter 40% and Blue, Accent 1 fill colors*. Place the chart in A14:D36.

   b. Create a Stacked Area in 3-D chart entitled **Return on Equity and Earnings per Share**. Use a nonadjacent selection to select the years and data specified. Format the fill color to match the theme set for the other chart, and then move the legend to the top to minimize the chart width. Add a data table with legend keys under the chart. Place the chart in E14:K36.

4. On page 3 of the Word document, shown in Figure 24.4a, replace the last sentence under Financial Highlights with the sentence: **The relationship between Net Earnings and Operating Profits, shown in the chart below, is favorable.**

5. Check the line spacing format for the area where the worksheets are to be placed. If necessary, change it to single spaced.

6. Paste link the data from the Summary of Operations worksheet on page 3 under Financial Highlights, as shown. Indent the worksheet, if necessary.

WHAT YOU NEED TO KNOW

Software

▶ To review, to make a selection of data that is nonadjacent for a chart, you can hide the rows or columns you do not need and then make your selection, or you can select the first group of data and then press [Ctrl] before you select the rest of the data. The latter method is preferred if you wish to keep the worksheet intact without hidden data.

▶ You have previously embedded and pasted Excel files into a Word document, but in every case, changes made to the Excel data in either the source or destination documents did not change the other file.

▶ If you want to have the worksheet data in Excel mirror the file placed into the Word document, you should link the files. When you use the paste link feature, any change made in one file automatically updates the other file. When you open a file that contains linked files, you are prompted to update the links. If you change something in a linked file, right-click the object and click Update Link.

▶ To paste link files, copy the worksheet in Excel, and then in Word click the Paste button arrow on the Home tab. Click Paste Special and, in the Paste Special dialog box, select Paste Link and the object. Click OK to link the files.

Project

▶ The Supply Warehouse has prepared an annual report that details the activities of the company for the past fiscal year. The annual report traditionally consists of a letter from the CEO summarizing the accomplishments for the year, including financial data, comparative statements, progress toward stated objectives, and the resolution or status of problems or new operations.

▶ To embed or link charts and worksheets into this Word document, set the line spacing format to the default, which is single spaced, before linking the files.

Continued on next page

7. Below the worksheet, check that you are still in single-spaced mode, and paste link the Operating Profits and Net Earnings chart. Size and position the objects so that both the chart and worksheet fit on page 3 in line with the text above.

8. In the Excel file on the Income Statement sheet, format numbers for commas with no decimal places and format titles and column headings in 12 point bold font, centered.

9. Enter formulas for the following and then copy across the rows. Correct the number formatting as necessary.

   a. Gross Profit: Sales – Cost of Goods Sold

   b. Operating Profit: Gross Profit – All expenses in rows 8, 9, 10

   c. Income before Taxes: Add Operating Profit and rows 12, 13, 14

   d. Net Income

10. On the Balance Sheet, format the numbers for commas with no decimal places and format titles and column headings centered and in 12 point bold font.

11. Enter formulas for the following and copy them across the rows. Correct the number formatting as necessary.

   a. Total Current Assets

   b. Total Assets: Current Assets plus all other assets

   c. Total Current Liabilities

   d. Total Liabilities and Stockholders' Equity: Total Current Liabilities plus Long-term Debt and Stockholders' Equity values

12. On page 5 of the report, add new text as follows below the Financial Review heading, as shown in Figure 24.4b.

The Consolidated Income Statement shows the results of our major efforts to reduce expenses and merchandise costs. As shown on the chart, the return on stockholders' equity is returning to its earlier levels and we hope to surpass that next year.

13. Press [Enter], format the paragraph just entered in the appropriate style, and then check the line spacing below the paragraph.

14. Paste link the data from the Income Statement worksheet and the Return on Equity and Earnings per Share chart below the new text, and position it as shown.

15. On page 6, add the following new text, add a blank line, and then format appropriately, as shown in Figure 24.4c.

The Comparative Balance Sheet shows our improved cash position and reduction in long-term debt.

▶ Companies that are publicly traded or owned by stockholders must send quarterly and annual statements to all stockholders. These publications can be quite complex, with pages of financial notes made by auditors. They may also contain marketing and product information text. The report presented here is an abbreviated version of an annual report.

▶ It is important to include charts in an annual report so that stockholders who do not want to review the financial reports in detail may use the graphic format to obtain an immediate overview of the data.

16. Paste link the data from the Balance Sheet file below the new text, as shown in Figure 24.4c.

17. Adjust the size, spacing, formatting, and pagination, as necessary.

18. There is an error in the Balance Sheet. Double-click the linked Balance Sheet. Notice that you are in the Excel file. Change the Accounts Payable for 2010 to 353,323. Return to the Word document, right-click the object, and then click Update Link. The correction is made in both files.

19. Print a copy of the annual report.

20. Save the files as 24.4annreport.docx and 24.4annrpt.xlsx.

21. Close the files.

Financial Highlights

Replace last sentence with new text

Paste link the worksheet

As the data will show, our costs have decreased, resulting in a substantial three-fold increase in operating profits. The relationship between Net Earnings and Operating Profits, shown on the chart below, is favorable.

Office Supplies Warehouse
Summary of Operations

	2008	2009	2010
Sales	3,081,618	3,470,909	3,346,224
Operating Profit	124,012	33,068	106,329
Net Earnings	77,291	14,665	60,313
Earnings per Share	0.21	0.05	0.20
Return on Stockholders' Equity	3.93	0.84	3.51
Working Capital	365,789	380,350	439,155
Total Assets	1,283,543	1,398,447	1,443,780

Position legend at the top, format data series, and paste link chart

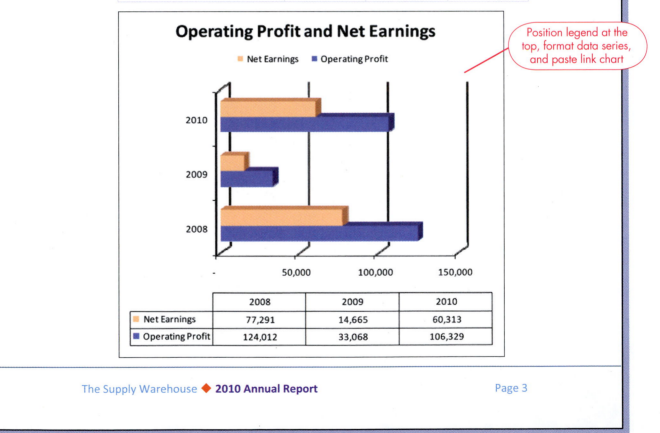

Operating Profit and Net Earnings

	2008	2009	2010
Net Earnings	77,291	14,665	60,313
Operating Profit	124,012	33,068	106,329

The Supply Warehouse ◆ **2010 Annual Report**   Page 3

Figure 24.4a Page 3

Financial Review

Add new text and format appropriately

The Consolidated Income Statement shows the results of our major efforts to reduce expenses and merchandise costs. As shown on the chart, the return on stockholders' equity is returning to its earlier levels and we hope to surpass that next year.

Paste link the worksheet

Office Supplies Warehouse Consolidated Income Statement			
	2008	2009	2010
Sales	3,081,618	3,470,909	3,346,224
Cost of Goods Sold	2,235,173	2,543,831	2,395,192
Gross Profit	846,446	927,078	951,032
Selling Expenses	606,917	722,843	703,018
General and Administrative Expenses	98,432	136,135	135,517
Other	17,085	35,031	6,168
Operating Profit	124,012	33,068	106,329
Interest Income	9,053	3,316	3,917
Interest Expense	(7,844)	(10,170)	(13,291)
Miscellaneous Income or Expense	(1,054)	1,390	(2,717)
Income before Taxes	124,166	27,603	94,239
Income Taxes	46,875	12,938	33,926
Net Income	$ 77,291	$ 14,665	$ 60,313

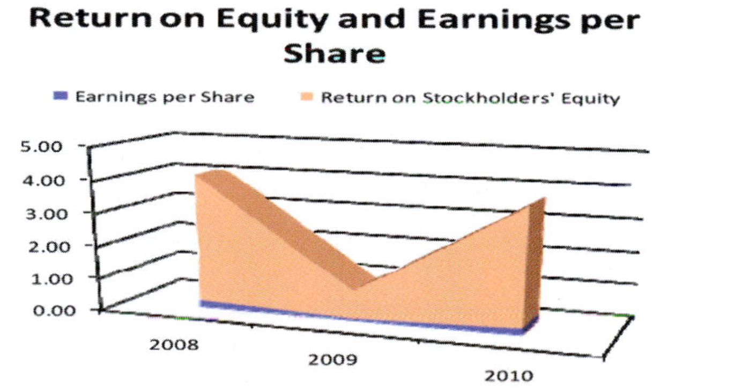

Format, paste link, and size and position the chart

Return on Equity and Earnings per Share

- Earnings per Share
- Return on Stockholders' Equity

	2008	2009	2010
Return on Stockholders' Equity	3.93	0.84	3.51
Earnings per Share	0.21	0.05	0.20

The Supply Warehouse ◆ **2010 Annual Report**   Page 5

Figure 24.4b Page 5

The Comparative Balance Sheet shows our improved cash position and reduction in long-term debt.

Office Supplies Warehouse
Balance Sheet

Add new text and format appropriately

Paste link the worksheet

	2009	2010
Assets		
Current Assets:		
Cash	50,494	187,803
Receivables	298,777	260,492
Merchandise Inventory	473,275	419,841
Prepaid Expenses	76,816	67,160
Total Current Assets	899,362	935,296
Property and Equipment	373,102	370,004
Goodwill	73,327	83,186
Other Assets	52,656	55,294
Total Assets	1,398,447	1,443,780
Liabilities and Stockholders' Equity		
Current Liabilities:		
Accounts Payable	378,998	353,323
Other Liabilities	76,576	96,576
Taxes Payable	63,458	46,342
Total Current Liabilities	519,032	496,241
Long-term Debt	210,876	198,144
Stockholders' Equity:		
Common Stock	313,071	333,614
Retained Earnings	355,468	415,781
Total Liabilities and Stockholders' Equity	1,398,447	1,443,780

Figure 24.4c Page 6

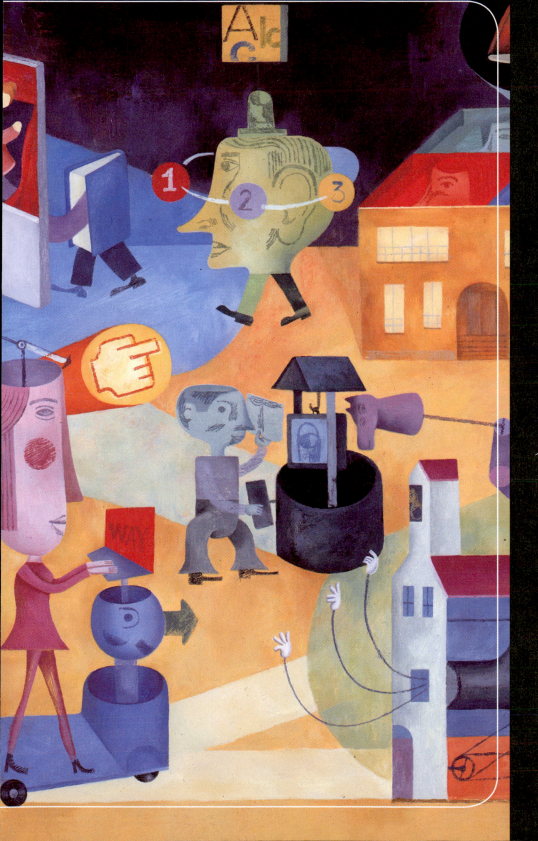

PowerPoint Basics

CHAPTER 2
Informative
Presentations

CHAPTER 3
Sales and Marketing
Presentations

CHAPTER 4
Persuasive
Presentations

CHAPTER 5
Collaborating On
and Delivering
Presentations

CHAPTER 6
Integration/
PowerPoint and
the Web

CHAPTER 1

PowerPoint Basics

In this chapter, you will complete the following projects:

PROJECT 1
Navigation, Views, Page Setup Options, and Creating a Presentation
PROJECT 1.1 Open a Presentation; Navigate a Presentation; Change Views
PROJECT 1.2 Change Orientation and Page Setup Options; Move, Copy, Duplicate, and Delete Slides
PROJECT 1.3 Evaluate a Slide Show
PROJECT 1.4 Create a Presentation

Note: You may apply the skills learned within each project to any type of presentation. This unit is organized by presentation type so that you can focus on your audience as you develop slide content. However, you can enhance any type of presentation with special effects, charts, sound, or video, providing they are relevant to the audience and to the message you want to deliver. In addition, you can save any type of presentation as a Web page and post it to the Web.

PROJECT SKILLS
- Open a presentation
- Select page setup options
- Navigate a presentation
- Change views
- Run a slide show
- Apply slide layouts
- Add slides to a presentation
- Work with placeholders
- Move, copy, duplicate, and delete slides
- Identify your audience for a presentation

1.1 OPEN A PRESENTATION; NAVIGATE A PRESENTATION; CHANGE VIEWS

Point & Click Computer Training Associates has created slides for a presentation it will present later this month at an orientation session for prospective trainees.

In this project, you will open a presentation, navigate the slides, and change views.

1. Open the data file **d1.1pointclick**. *Note: The slides are shown in Figure 1.1.* on pages 4–6.
2. Close the Outline and Slides task pane.
3. Click the Slide Sorter View button.
4. Double-click Slide 1.
5. Cycle through the slides using any method. Read the slide content.
6. Scroll back to Slide 1 and click the Slide Show View button. Click through the presentation until you reach the last slide, and then press [Esc].
7. Close the presentation. Do not save changes.

Slide 1

Figure 1.1

WHAT YOU NEED TO KNOW

Software

▶ As with other Office applications, you can start PowerPoint from the taskbar. To do so, click the Start button, point to All Programs, click Microsoft Office, and then click Microsoft Office PowerPoint 2007. Or double-click the PowerPoint program icon on the desktop.

▶ You can open presentations by clicking the Office Button and then clicking Open. When you click the Office Button, documents you have recently opened appear in the Recent Documents list on the right side of the Office menu. You can use the Recent Documents list to open one of the files listed there, or you can use the Open dialog box to find and open any file on your computer.

▶ Once a presentation is open, you can cycle through the slides in several ways:
  - Click the scroll up or scroll down arrow to scroll up or scroll down one slide.
  - Click the Next Slide button or the Previous Slide button on the vertical scroll bar.
  - Drag the vertical scroll box up or down until the slide you want appears.
  - Click above the scroll box to scroll up one slide or below the scroll box to scroll down one slide.
  - Click the slide thumbnail displayed on the Slides tab.

Continued on next page

Slide 2

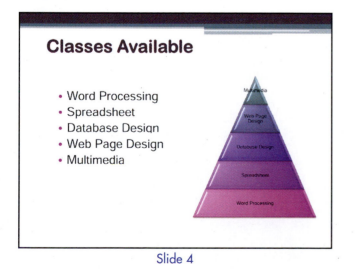

Slide 4

Figure 1.1 continued

▶ PowerPoint lets you view your presentation in several different ways:

- Normal View, the default, displays three panes: the Slide pane, the Outline and Slides tab pane, and the Notes pane.

- Slide Sorter view displays slides as thumbnails so that you can see the flow of the presentation. You can move, copy, and delete slides in this view.

▶ Slide Show view lets you see your slides as an on-screen presentation and displays each slide on the entire screen without showing the toolbars and menus. To end a presentation, press [Esc]. (You can also run a slide show by clicking the Slide Show tab and then clicking either the From Beginning or From Current Slide button.)

Project

▶ PowerPoint enables you to create visual aids in the form of slides that support an oral presentation. Visual aids are used for the following purposes:

- Increase the audience's understanding of the topic.

- Leave the audience with a lasting message, impression, or both.

- Keep the audience focused on the topic.

▶ Effective presentations require careful planning, preparation, and delivery. Visual aids only enhance a presentation. Following are four steps to guide you through the development of an effective presentation:

1. Plan your presentation.
   - Determine the purpose. Presentations inform, persuade, or sell (and sometimes have multiple purposes). Entertaining presentations keep the audience engaged while informing, persuading, or selling.
   - Know your audience. Be sure your presentation meets the needs of your audience.

2. Prepare.
   - Outline the major and minor (supporting) points.

Continued on next page

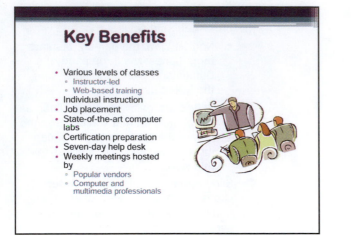

Slide 5

Slide 6

Figure 1.1 continued

- Draft a script that includes an attention-getting opening and supports key points with evidence (statistics, analogies, exhibits).
- Visualize the script (prepare the slides).
- Develop and use handout material.

3. Practice.
   - Cue the script.
   - Be sure your talking points are aligned with slide points.
   - Review slides for clarity, relevancy, eye appeal, visibility, and quality.

4. Present.
   - Speak slowly and maintain eye contact with your audience.
   - Emphasize key points.

1.2 CHANGE ORIENTATION AND PAGE SETUP OPTIONS; MOVE, COPY, DUPLICATE, AND DELETE SLIDES

Rita Bratton, your boss at Destinations, has asked you to review and make some changes to a presentation that will be presented as an on-screen slide show to new travel agents who will sell travel packages to New York City.

In this project, you will view a slide show about New York City, change setup options, and move and delete slides.

1. Open the data file **d1.2newyork**, the first slide of which is shown in Figure 1.2.
2. Switch to Slide Sorter view.
3. Click the Slide Show tab, and in the Start Slide Show group, click the From Beginning button.
4. Click through the presentation to view it entirely. Press [Esc] to end the presentation.
5. Change the orientation of the slides to landscape. Make adjustments to text and objects on slides, if necessary.
6. Switch to Slide Sorter view. Move Slide 5 (Hungry?) to become Slide 8.
7. Delete Slide 3 (Fun Facts).
8. View the presentation again. Press [Esc] to end the presentation.
9. Save the file as **1.2nyc**, and then close the file.

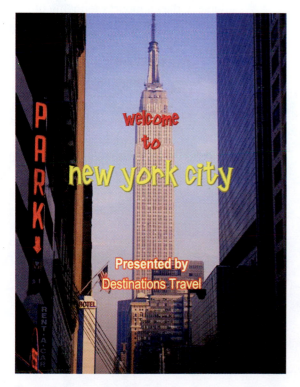

Figure 1.2

WHAT YOU NEED TO KNOW

Software

▶ You can set the orientation of slides, notes pages, handouts, and/or outlines to *portrait* (taller than wide) or *landscape* (wider than tall). To do so, click the Design tab, and then click the Page Setup button in the Page Setup group.

▶ You can move, copy, duplicate, and delete slides. The easiest way to do this is in Slide Sorter view. PowerPoint displays all the slides as thumbnails, and you can easily see the flow of the presentation as you move, copy, or delete slides.

▶ When you move a slide, a vertical bar identifies the new position of the slide. To move a slide, select it, drag it so the bar appears in the position where you want to place the slide, and release the mouse.

▶ To copy a slide, select it and press [Ctrl] as you drag it to its new location.

▶ To delete a slide, select it and press [Delete].

▶ If you move, copy, or delete a slide and then change your mind, use the Undo command to reverse the action.

Project

▶ Before creating a presentation, you must think about how you will deliver it. You can deliver a presentation as an on-screen slide show, over the Internet, or using overhead transparencies.

▶ The delivery method you choose will determine the output format. It may also require that you get additional viewing equipment.

1.3 EVALUATE A SLIDE SHOW

"Say Yes" Wedding Consultants is a wedding planning company located in Miami, Florida. To advertise the business, the company has developed a slide show that it plans to play in kiosks located in malls in Miami, West Palm Beach, and Ft. Lauderdale, Florida. You have been asked to evaluate the presentation to determine if the slides are engaging enough to sell the services of the company and whether the slides follow the basic rules for developing effective presentations.

In this project, you will review a presentation designed to play in a kiosk as an advertisement for "Say Yes" Wedding Consultants.

1. Open the data file **d1.3wed**. *Note: The first slide is shown in Figure 1.3.*
2. Go to Slide Show view to play the slide show automatically. Press [Esc] to end the presentation. *Note: After you click the Slide Show View button, the slide show will begin and the entire presentation will run automatically.*
3. Close the file.

WHAT YOU NEED TO KNOW

Project

▶ In addition to presenting slides to a live audience, you can show slides in a kiosk, a booth that provides information and usually does not have an attendant. Slide shows developed for kiosks run automatically. You will learn to create a presentation to run automatically in a later project.

▶ Keep the following basic rules in mind when reviewing and/or developing presentation slides:

- Keep the slides simple—limit the amount of text on a slide (the audience must be able to read the slide in one or two seconds).
- Use one thought per line.
- Use pictures, drawings, and diagrams, where appropriate, to support your points. Remember that "a picture is worth a thousand words."
- Use animation, where appropriate.
- Use sound and/or video only if it will enhance the effectiveness of the slide.
- Use no more than two different fonts on the same slide.
- Avoid script and decorative fonts unless they support the theme of the presentation.

Figure 1.3

1.4 CREATE A PRESENTATION

You work for CopyMe, a company that sells products for the office. You have been asked to create a presentation to be used at the National Sales Conference to inform the CopyMe sales staff about a new product.

> **In this project, you will develop the content for a presentation that informs sales staff about the DAISY 860, a new high-resolution, high-speed color printer.**

1. Open a new blank presentation.
2. Create the slide text, as shown Figure 1.4a, using the appropriate slide layouts.
3. Insert two slides at the end of the presentation as follows:
   a. Read the reviewers' comments shown in Figure 1.4b. Then create a slide titled **Reviewers' Comments**, summarizing key points into bullets and sub-bullets.
   b. Using a Title Only layout, create a final slide titled **The Daisy 840**.
      - Create a text box on the slide, and use the last reviewer's comment to summarize a final statement about the product.
      - Center-align the text in the text box.
      - Use the rotate handle to rotate the text box approximately 45°.
      - Position the text box in the center of the slide.
4. Change the layout of the Specs slide to Two Content.
   - Adjust the text so that it fits attractively in two columns.
5. Insert a title slide after Specs.
   a. Insert a title that reads **Suggested Retail Price**.
   b. Insert a subtitle that reads **$7,000**.
6. Display Slide 1, click the Slide Show View button, and view the entire presentation.
7. Save the file as **1.4copyme** and then close the presentation.

WHAT YOU NEED TO KNOW

Software

▶ The blank presentation option lets you build your own unique presentation from blank slides that contain standard default formats and layouts using the Office Theme.

▶ PowerPoint opens with a blank slide displayed, which is formatted as a title slide (generally the first slide in a presentation). There are, however, numerous other slide layouts from which to choose. A slide layout specifies how text or objects are positioned on a slide.

▶ Slides contain *placeholders*, which are empty boxes for text or objects on a slide. Each placeholder contains instructions to help you complete the slide.

▶ Clicking inside the placeholder activates it, allowing you to enter and edit text. You can move a placeholder by selecting it and then dragging the box to the appropriate location. You can also copy, delete, size, rotate, and format placeholders to create a customized look for your slides.

▶ To add text to a slide in a location other than in a given placeholder, you can create a text box. A text box serves as a text placeholder, allowing you to insert text anywhere on a slide. To add a text box to a slide, click the Insert tab and in the Text group, click the Text Box button. Click and drag the mouse diagonally on the slide to create the required box size and enter your text.

▶ You can edit a text box placeholder as you did in Word. You can add colorful border lines around the placeholder and fill the box with a color or pattern using buttons in the Shape Styles group on the Drawing Tools, Format tab. You can also add special effects, such as shadows, a glow, and a 3-D effect.

▶ To add slides to a presentation, click the Home tab and in the Slides group, click the New Slide button. The Title and Content Slide is the default layout for any slide added to a presentation. To add a slide and select a different layout, click the New Slide button list arrow to display the layout thumbnails, and then click a layout thumbnail.

Continued on next page

▶ To apply a new layout to the current slide, click the Home tab and in the Slides group, click the Layout button. Then select a layout thumbnail.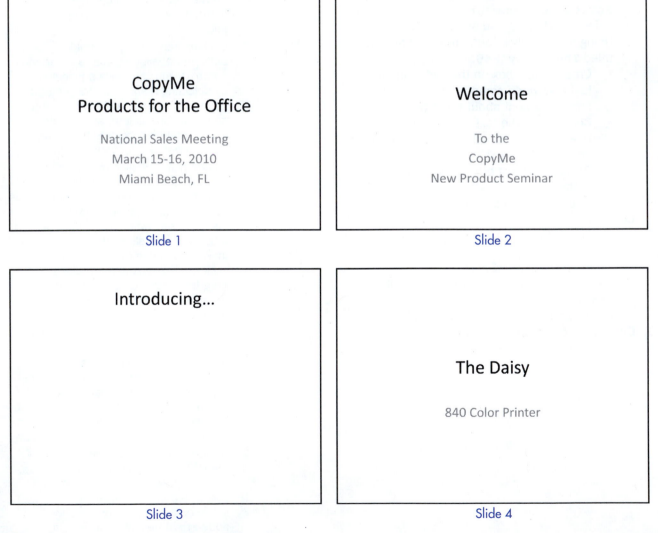

▶ When saving a presentation, the PowerPoint icon appears next to the filename, indicating that it is a presentation file. The file extension for PowerPoint files is .pptx.

Project

▶ Start with a blank presentation to organize your thoughts and develop the slide content. Color and enhancements can be distracting during the development stage.

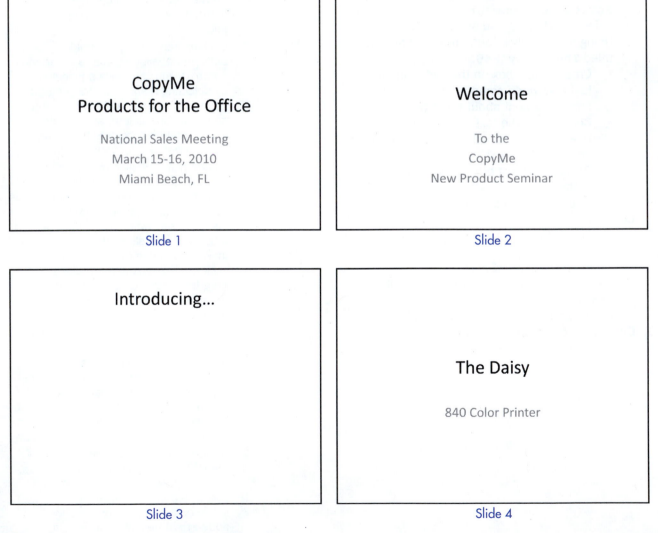

CopyMe
Products for the Office

National Sales Meeting
March 15-16, 2010
Miami Beach, FL

Slide 1

Welcome

To the
CopyMe
New Product Seminar

Slide 2

Introducing...

Slide 3

The Daisy

840 Color Printer

Slide 4

Figure 1.4a

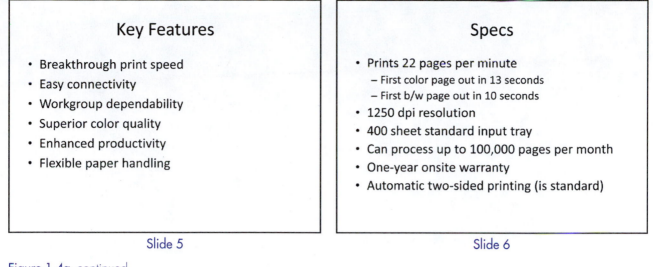

Slide 5

Slide 6

Figure 1.4a continued

- The Daisy prints color photographs quickly, taking only about 30 seconds for an 8-by-10-inch photo stored at 200 pixels per inch (ppi) and about 1 minute for a photo stored at 300 ppi.
- Just as important, output quality is excellent. The Daisy maintains that distinction. Text and lines in graphics are crisp and well formed. Color text in graphics stands out well against a color background, and photos printed on standard copier paper are as close to photo quality as we've ever seen from any laser-class printer.
- The printer also scores well on setup and network administration. Setup consists of removing the packing materials, putting four toner cartridges in the printer, inserting paper, and connecting a cable and power cord.
- As you might guess from the speed, The Daisy is designed for heavy-duty printing. The Daisy can print on paper as large as 12 by 18 inches and comes standard with a 650-page input capacity.
- Best of all, this remarkable product has a suggested retail price of $7,000.
- All of this adds up to a printer that can truly serve as an office workhorse and can, by the way, print color output at eyebrow-raising speeds.

Figure 1.4b

CHAPTER 2

Informative Presentations

In this chapter, you will complete the following projects:

PROJECT 2
Create and Enhance Informative Presentations
PROJECT 2.1 Create and Print a Presentation
PROJECT 2.2 Enhance a Presentation
PROJECT 2.3 Edit and Enhance a Presentation
PROJECT 2.4 Create and Print a Presentation as an Outline
PROJECT 2.5 Develop a Presentation from Scratch

PROJECT 2

PROJECT SKILLS

✱ Apply a slide theme
✱ Change theme colors and fonts
✱ Preview and Print a presentation
✱ Enhance slides with clip art, text boxes, transitions, and animations
✱ Change slide background
✱ Develop a presentation from scratch
✱ Work with outlines
✱ Hide a slide
✱ Link slides

2.1 CREATE AND PRINT A PRESENTATION

As a senior at Meadowland College, you have been asked to prepare a presentation, which will ultimately be shown to incoming freshmen at their freshman orientation session.

In this project, you will create and print a presentation for Meadowland College.

1. Open a new blank presentation.
2. Create the slide text, as shown in Figure 2.1a on pages 15 and 16, using appropriate slide layouts.
3. Insert two slides as the last slides of the presentation titled **Schedule of Events**.
   a. Read the schedule shown in Figure 2.1b on page 17. Then create a slide for each day, listing the day's events.
   b. Summarize the information into bulleted and sub-bulleted lists.
4. Insert a final slide titled **Welcome Freshman!** Create slide content that is encouraging to freshman students.
5. Save the file as **2.1meadowland**.
6. Change the order of the slides as follows:
   a. Meadowland College
   b. Moving In
   c. Getting Wired
   d. The Bookstore
   e. Schedule of Events, Tuesday, August 24
   f. Schedule of Events, Wednesday, August 25
   g. Dining Hours for Main Dining Room
   h. Dining Options
   i. Getting Around Campus
   j. Getting Involved
   k. Final Slide
7. Apply a design theme of your choice. Then, apply the Origin font theme. *Note: You will have to adjust text placeholders depending on the design template you choose.*

WHAT YOU NEED TO KNOW

Software

▶ Themes in PowerPoint provide you with predesigned colorful backgrounds, fonts (including font size settings), and a layout for your slides. You can choose from numerous predesigned built-in themes or find additional themes online.

▶ To apply a theme to the entire presentation, click the Design tab and in the Themes group, click More to display the Themes gallery. Then, click the theme you want to apply.

▶ To apply a theme to selected slides, select the slide(s) on which you want to apply a new design, click the Design tab and in the Themes group, click More to display the Themes gallery. Right-click a theme and click Apply to Selected Slides.

▶ You can change the color scheme and/or fonts of your applied theme. Color schemes can be changed on selected slides or all slides of a presentation, while font changes must be applied to all slides in a presentation. To change a theme color, click the Design tab, and in the Themes group, click the Colors button. Right-click a color scheme to apply it to one or all slides. To change a theme font, click the Design tab and in the Themes group click the Fonts button, and select a font style.

▶ Printed presentations are often distributed to audience participants. Because color output can be very costly, most printed presentations are in black and white. Before printing a presentation in black and white, you should view it in *grayscale*, which uses tones of gray to show the effects of color.

Continued on next page

8. View the slide show.
9. Delete the final slide.
10. View the slides in grayscale.
11. Print one copy of the slides as handouts in pure black and white with six slides per page.
12. Save and close the file.

▶ To view a presentation in grayscale, click the Office Button, highlight Print, and select Print Preview. In the Print group, click the Options button, select Color/Grayscale, and click Grayscale from the menu that appears.

▶ To print individual slides, enter each slide number separated by a comma (for example, 1,5). To print a range of slides, enter the first slide number in the range, enter a hyphen, and then enter the last slide number in the range (for example, 2–4).

▶ You can print a presentation as handouts with one, two, three, four, six, or nine slides on a page. You can give handouts to an audience so they can follow along with the on-screen presentation. You can also use handouts as a reference when editing the slide content. *Note: Handout formatting options will be detailed in PowerPoint Chapter 5.*

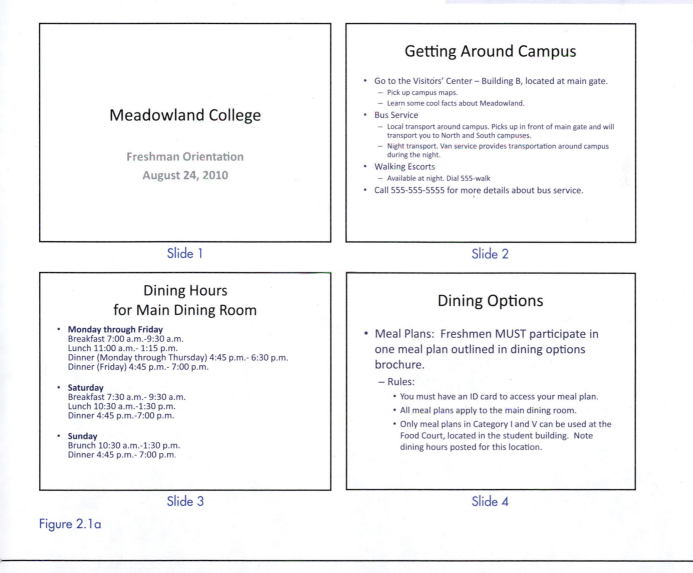

Slide 1

Slide 2

Slide 3

Slide 4

Figure 2.1a

Getting Involved

- Attend the Activities Fair
  - August 28, Administration Building, 4:00 p.m. where you will learn about Meadowland's many clubs and organizations
- Student Clubs
  - Countless clubs, intramural sports teams and volunteer organizations will enrich your mind, body and spirit.
    - Student-lead
    - Student created

Slide 5

Moving In

- **Volunteers will help freshmen move in on the morning of August 24.**
  - Drive to main gate to have a volunteer assigned to you.
  - Volunteer will accompany you to the dorm.
  - Volunteer will arrange for luggage carts.

Slide 6

Getting Wired

- After moving in, volunteer will help you set up your computer and demonstrate accessing the library and other online services.

Slide 7

The Bookstore

- Volunteer will explain how to avoid long lines at the bookstore and how to order online.
- Volunteer will accompany you to the bookstore for a firsthand look around.

Slide 8

Figure 2.1a continued

Tuesday, August 24

<u>8:30 AM – 11 AM</u>
Student check-in at Main Gate. Students will register with Volunteer Experience staff and receive room keys from Residential Services.

<u>12:00 PM-1:00 PM</u>
Student-Parent Orientation Session at South Campus Hall. After viewing a slide show about Meadowland College, a representative from the Dean of Students Office will be available to answer any questions students or parents may have about the college. The Volunteer Experience staff will also be present to talk about the Volunteer Experience program and answer any questions or concerns parents may have about the program. Participants should come to the meeting ready to leave for their volunteer site.

<u>1:00 PM</u>
Student lunch at the Main Dining Room. Students will divide into their groups and leave for sites directly from lunch. Parents are on their own for lunch and have the option of eating at the Food Court or local restaurants.

<u>5:15 PM – 7:00 PM</u>
Barbeque at North Campus. Get to know everyone with volleyball, cooking out, and group activities. In case of bad weather, activities will be moved indoors.

<u>7:00 PM – 9:00 PM</u>
Break to relax in rooms and unpack. There is also the option of participating in other activities such as campus tours.

<u>9:00 PM – 10:30 PM</u>
Choice of bowling or miniature golf. Get to know other students through a little friendly competition. Price included in the program fee.

Wednesday, August 25

<u>7:30 AM – 8:30 AM</u>
Breakfast at the Main Dining Room. Use the meal ticket provided by the program to sample some of the cafeteria's breakfast food.

<u>8:30 AM – 9:00 AM</u>
Groups meet to leave for volunteer sites.

<u>9:00 AM – 4:00 PM</u>
Work at Volunteer Sites. Lunches will be provided at sites and are also covered in the program fee.

<u>5:45 PM</u>
Dinner at local Princeton restaurants. Sample some of the dining around campus. Students will divide up by interest and go to different Princeton restaurants, and the college orientation program foots the bill.

<u>7:00 PM – 9:00 PM</u>
Game Night. Hang out in Southwest Hall and play some games with other first-year students who are on campus.

<u>9:00 PM</u>
Movie. Divide into groups to view favorite summer flicks.

Figure 2.1b

Now that the content of the presentation you created for CopyMe is completed, you will apply a design theme, insert clip art, and apply transitions and animations to enhance the clip art.

In this project, you will enhance the presentation you created for CopyMe.

1. Open **1.4copyme**, the presentation that you created in Chapter 1, or open the data file **d2.2copyme**.

2. Apply a design theme to the presentation, as shown in Figure 2.2, Slides 1–9. *Note: The Apex theme was used for this illustration*.

3. Enhance the slides as follows:
   a. Change the theme color as you prefer.
   b. Slide 1—Insert clip art that relates to office products. Size and position it as you prefer.
   c. Slide 2—Insert clip art that supports the slide content. Move placeholders to fit the image, if necessary.
   d. Slide 3—Insert a daisy photo as a slide background. The photo can be found in the Data files as **d2.2daisy.jpg**.
      * Create a text box in the eye of the daisy that reads THE DAISY.
      * Size and color the text so it is visible.
   e. Slide 4—Insert clip art that is a printer. Size and position it as you prefer.
   f. Slide 5—Change the slide layout to Two Content. Insert clip art that supports the content.
   g. Slide 6—Apply shading to both text boxes that complements the theme color.
   h. Slide 7—Apply a shape style to the text box containing the price that complements the theme color. Center and set the price to 40 pt, bold. Size the text box to fit the price, as shown in Figure 2.2.
   i. Slide 8—Apply a font color that complements the theme color to the first levels of bulleted text, as shown in Figure 2.2.
   j. Slide 9—Insert the same photo used in Slide 3 as a slide background. Adjust the text box size of the subtitle text, and then move it to the bottom of the slide. Set the font to italics, and apply a shadow to it. *Note: Adjust the text boxes as necessary to achieve the results you want*.

4. Apply animations to the slide titles and bulleted text throughout the presentation. Apply a slide transition to all slides in the presentation.

Software

▶ Each theme design has a predefined background style, which is automatically applied. However, you can change the background to be a solid color or to have a gradient effect, picture, or texture. To do so, click the Design tab and in the Background group, click the Background Styles button list arrow. In the Background Styles gallery that appears, click [Background Styles ▾] Format Background to create a custom background or right-click a Background style to apply it to one or all slides.

▶ Content slide layouts contain special placeholders that are used to contain bulleted lists, SmartArt graphics, tables, charts, pictures, shapes, and clip art.

▶ To insert clip art, select a layout that contains a content placeholder, click on the Clip Art icon, and in the Clip Art task pane that appears, search for and select an image. You can also place clip art on a slide without inserting it into a placeholder. To do so, click the Insert tab and in the Illustrations group, click the Clip Art button. Then, search for and select an image in the Clip Art task pane. [Clip Art]

▶ You can search for specific clip art by topic or category in the Insert Clip Art task pane.

▶ Clip art and other objects appear with sizing and rotation handles.

▶ Slide transitions control the way slides move on and off the screen during a slide show. You can apply transitions to slides in all views.

▶ To add a transition to a slide, display or select the slide to which you want to add a transition, click the Animations tab, and click the Transition to This Slide More arrow to display the entire gallery. Then click a transition to apply it. To add the same transition to all slides in the presentation, repeat the preceding steps, and then click the Apply to All button. [Apply To All]

Continued on next page

5. View the slide show.

6. Save the file as **2.2copyme1**.

7. Print one copy of the slides as handouts with three slides per page.

8. Close the file.

Slide 1

Slide 2

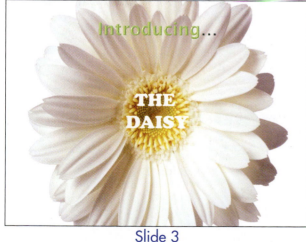

Slide 3

Figure 2.2

▶ To modify the transition speed, click the Transition Speed button list arrow and select a speed. To add a sound to a transition, click the Transition Sound

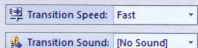

button list arrow and select a sound.

▶ *Animations* are visual or sound effects that control the way text and objects appear on a slide during a slide show. You can use a PowerPoint built-in animation effect, or you can create a custom effect.

▶ To apply a built-in animation, select the text or object to animate. Then, click the Animations tab, and in the Animations group, select the animation effect that you want from the Animate list.

▶ To create a custom animation, select the text or object to animate. Then, click the Animations tab, and in the Animations group, click the Custom Animation button. On the Custom Animation task pane that appears, click Add Effect, and select the animation effect that you want to apply.

▶ Effects appear in the Custom Animation list in the task pane with a number, timing icon, and animation effect icon. Animation numbers also appear on the slide and indicate the order in which the animations will play.

Project

▶ Use presentation themes and clip art to enhance a presentation and make it more appealing.

▶ Pictures should be used to help communicate an idea. Use visuals that are relevant to the slide's topic. Do not add pictures just to fill space.

▶ Animation effects allow you to introduce text bullet by bullet so the audience does not jump ahead of you as you deliver your presentation.

▶ Like media clips, animations should not be a distraction to your presentation. You can apply transitions and animations to any presentation regardless of its objective or audience.

THE DAISY

840 Color Printer

Slide 4

Key Features

- Breakthrough print speed
- Easy connectivity
- Workgroup dependability
- Superior color quality
- Enhanced productivity
- Flexible paper handling

Slide 5

Specs

- Prints 22 pages per minute
  - First color page out in 13 seconds
  - First b/w page out in 10 seconds
- 1250 dpi resolution
- 400-sheet standard input tray

- Can process up to 100,000 pages per month
- One-year onsite warranty
- Automatic two-sided printing (is standard)

Slide 6

SUGGESTED RETAIL PRICE

$7,000

Slide 7

Reviewers' Comments

- Color photos print quickly.
  - An 8 x 10-inch 200 pixels per inch photo printed in 30 seconds.
  - A 300 pixels per inch photo printed in 1 minute.
- Output quality is excellent.
  - Text and lines in graphics are crisp and well formed.
  - Color text in graphics stands out well against a color background.
  - Photos printed on standard copier paper are close to photo quality.
- Setup and network administration is easy.
  - Setup consists of removing the packing materials, putting four toner cartridges in the printer, inserting paper, and connecting a cable and power cord.
- Heavy-duty printing is not a problem.
  - Prints on paper as large as 12 by 18 inches and comes standard with a 650-page input capacity.

Slide 8

The Daisy 840

An office workhorse that prints color output at eyebrow-raising speeds!

Slide 9

Figure 2.2 continued

2.3 EDIT AND ENHANCE A PRESENTATION

You have been asked to enhance the presentation you created for freshman orientation at Meadowland College.

In this project, you will edit and enhance a presentation for Meadowland College that you previously created.

1. Open **2.1meadowland**, the presentation you created in project 2.1, or the date file **d2.3meadowland**.
2. Edit the slides as indicated in Steps 3–5.
3. On the title slide, do the following:
   a. Apply the Preset 2 Shape Effect to the text box that contains the college name. Rotate it left 90° and position it as shown in Figure 2.3a.
   b. Apply a light green shade to the text box.
   c. Position the subtitle to the bottom right of the slide, as shown in Figure 2.3a.
   d. Insert a picture of Meadowland College (data file **d2.3collegepic.jpg**). Apply the circle bevel effect to the picture.
4. Insert clip art to support the content of the remaining slides, as you prefer. You may use a content placeholder or you may insert clip art directly on the slide. Apply different picture effects to the images.
5. On Slide 9, do the following:
   a. Cut the last bullet (Call 555-555-5555 for more details about bus service).
   b. Create a text box and paste this sentence into it.
   c. Position it, as shown in Figure 2.3b, Slide 9, and apply a shape effect to it.
6. Apply color to any text you choose in order to enhance slide content.
7. Apply a custom animation to slide titles, bulleted text, and objects throughout the presentation, as appropriate.
8. Apply a slide transition to all slides.
9. Hide Slides 5 and 6 (Schedule of Events).
10. View the slide show.
11. Unhide Slides 5 and 6.
12. Print one copy of the slides as handouts with six slides per page.
13. Save the file as **2.3meadowland orientation**.
14. Close the file.

▼ WHAT YOU NEED TO KNOW

Software

▶ To insert a picture from a file onto a slide, click the Insert tab, and in the Illustrations group, click the Picture button.

▶ You can edit clip art and pictures (move, copy, delete, size, rotate, adjust brightness or contrast, and add special effects) using the same techniques that you used when working in Word. To add special effects to clip art or pictures, select the image, and click the Picture Tools, Format tab. Use the options on the Ribbon to make adjustments and add effects to the image.

▶ To nudge an object, select the placeholder and press the up/down/left/right arrow keys.

▶ A slide presentation created for one audience may not be suitable for another. You can use the same presentation for different audiences by hiding slides that are not relevant. Hiding slides does not delete them. Rather, doing so will hide them during the presentation.

▶ You may not want to show all the slides in a presentation. To hide a slide, select the slide(s) you want to hide in Slide Sorter view. Click the Slide Show tab and in the Set Up group, click the Hide Slide button. Repeat this procedure to unhide slides.

Project

▶ You can easily see the flow of your presentation in Slide Sorter view. It is in this view that you can change the order of slides or hide slides.

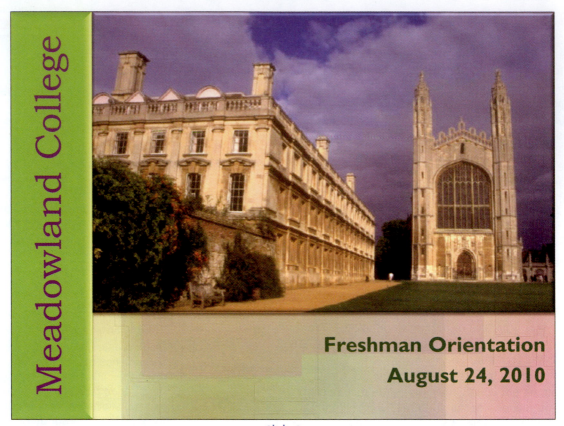

Figure 2.3a

Slide 1

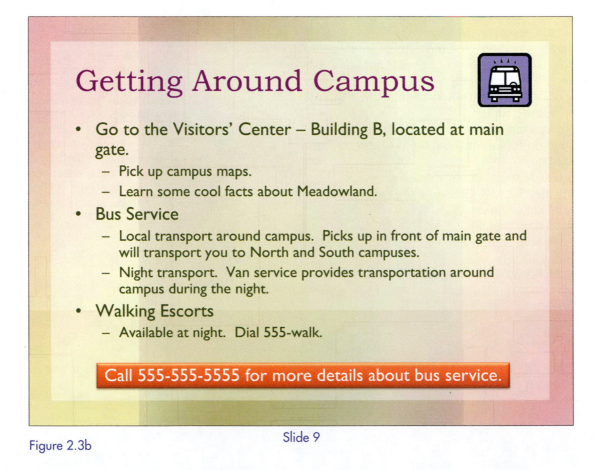

Figure 2.3b

Slide 9

2.4 CREATE AND PRINT A PRESENTATION AS AN OUTLINE

SunStar specializes in corporate meeting and special events planning. The company has offices in New York, New Jersey, Connecticut, and Massachusetts, and its main office is in New York City. SunStar has been asked to make a presentation to the corporate staff of a large bank in New York to make them aware of SunStar's services. This could be a wonderful opportunity because this bank has branches throughout the East Coast and hold numerous corporate events. You have been asked to create and print a presentation as an outline for SunStar. After it has been reviewed and edited, you will enhance it.

In this project, you will create and print a presentation as an outline for SunStar.

1. Open a new blank presentation.
2. Click the Outline tab.
3. Enter the titles for each slide, as shown in Figure 2.4a on pages 25 and 26.
4. Add the subtext, as shown in Figure 2.4b.
5. Collapse all of the subtext.
6. Move Slide 5 (Total Solutions, Imagination, & Meticulous Planning) to become Slide 9.
7. Use the following text to create a final slide (Title and Content). *Note: Set a left tab to align the phone numbers.*

   We are located in a major city in four states: New York, New York; Greenwich, Connecticut; Newark, New Jersey; and Boston, Massachusetts. Contact any one of our Sales and Marketing offices:

New York	**212-555-5555**
Connecticut	**203-555-5555**
New Jersey	**201-555-5555**
Massachusetts	**617-555-5555**

8. Insert a new slide as Slide 2. Title it **Overview**.
   a. Copy the headings of Slides 3-11 to be the bulleted text on Slide 2, as shown in Figure 2.4c on page 26.
   b. Create a hyperlink on each line of bulleted text to link to its corresponding slide.
9. Display the Outline tab and expand all of the text.
10. Display Slide 1.
11. Run the slide show.
12. Click the Outline tab.
13. Print one copy of the complete outline.
14. Save the file as **2.4sunstar**.
15. Close the file.

▼ WHAT YOU NEED TO KNOW

Software

▶ You can view slide content as an outline, which is an effective way to see the flow of your presentation.

▶ Click the Outline tab in the Outline and Slides tab pane to display slide titles and subtext in an outline format.

▶ You can add slides in Outline view the same way you did in Normal view.

▶ You can create your presentation in the Outline tab pane. To do so, select the Outline tab (be sure you are in Normal view), and click to the right of the first slide icon in the Outline pane. Enter first level text, which will become the slide's title and press [Enter]. Click the Home tab, and click the Increase List Level button or press [Tab] to promote text to the next level, and then press [Enter]. Type the same level text (a new bullet), or click the Decrease List Level button to begin a new slide.

▶ You can use an outline as a table of contents or agenda by hiding (or collapsing) the subtext on each slide. To do so, click the Outline tab to display the outline. Next, right-click the text in the outline, highlight Collapse, and select Collapse (to hide all the subheads for this slide) or Collapse All (to hide all the subheads for all slides). To expand the outline, right-click the text in the outline, highlight Expand, and select Expand or Expand All.

▶ To print an outline, use the same procedures that you use to print slides, but in the Print dialog box, select Outline View from the Print what list.

▶ You can create a hyperlink on a slide to link to another slide within a presentation, a slide in another presentation, or a document in another software program. A hyperlink can also be created to link to a Website.

▶ You can activate hyperlinks in Slide Show view.

Continued on next page

► To create a hyperlink to another slide within a presentation, select the text or object on which to create the link. Then, click the Insert tab, and in the Links group, click the Hyperlink button. In the Insert Hyperlink dialog box that appears, click Place in This Document in the Link to section. In the Select a place in this document box, click the title of the slide to which you want to link.

► You can create left, center, right, or decimal-aligned tabs using the same procedures you used in Word.

1 ☐ sun**STAR**

2 ☐ Who We Are

3 ☐ Our Mission

4 ☐ Meeting Your Objectives…Exceeding Your Expectations

5 ☐ Total Solutions, Imagination, & Meticulous Planning

6 ☐ Your Bottom Line

7 ☐ To Begin, We Will…

8 ☐ We Negotiate on Your Behalf

9 ☐ The Main Event

Figure 2.4a

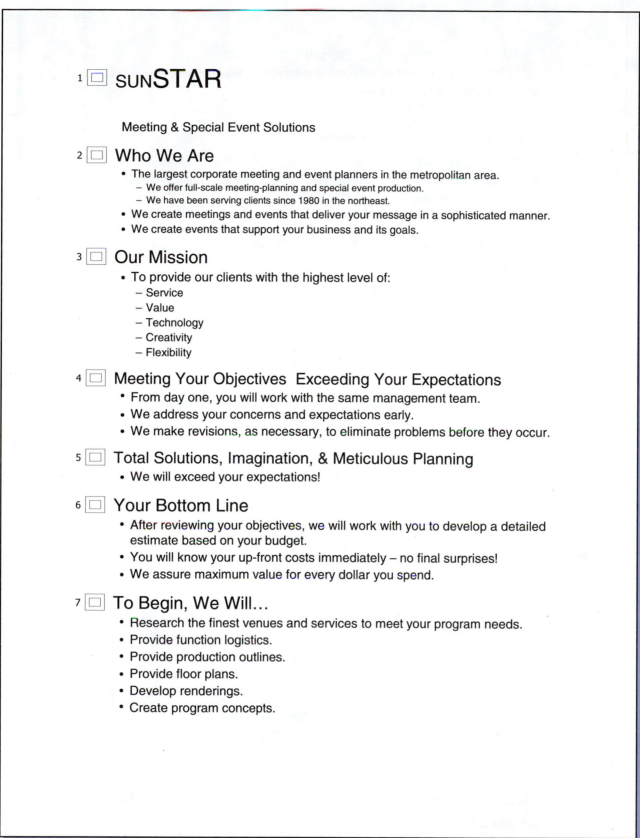

1 ☐ sun**STAR**

Meeting & Special Event Solutions

2 ☐ Who We Are
- The largest corporate meeting and event planners in the metropolitan area.
  - We offer full-scale meeting-planning and special event production.
  - We have been serving clients since 1980 in the northeast.
- We create meetings and events that deliver your message in a sophisticated manner.
- We create events that support your business and its goals.

3 ☐ Our Mission
- To provide our clients with the highest level of:
  - Service
  - Value
  - Technology
  - Creativity
  - Flexibility

4 ☐ Meeting Your Objectives Exceeding Your Expectations
- From day one, you will work with the same management team.
- We address your concerns and expectations early.
- We make revisions, as necessary, to eliminate problems before they occur.

5 ☐ Total Solutions, Imagination, & Meticulous Planning
- We will exceed your expectations!

6 ☐ Your Bottom Line
- After reviewing your objectives, we will work with you to develop a detailed estimate based on your budget.
- You will know your up-front costs immediately – no final surprises!
- We assure maximum value for every dollar you spend.

7 ☐ To Begin, We Will…
- Research the finest venues and services to meet your program needs.
- Provide function logistics.
- Provide production outlines.
- Provide floor plans.
- Develop renderings.
- Create program concepts.

Figure 2.4b

8 ☐ **We Negotiate on Your Behalf**
- We can deliver the best products and services at the best prices.
  - Hotel and off-site properties
  - Food and beverage
  - Décor and entertainment
- We can pass on all savings to you.

9 ☐ **The Main Event**
- You will find us EVERYWHERE, with our EYES OPEN during your program.
- We will eliminate problems before they occur.
- We are in constant communication with every person charged with a responsibility.

Figure 2.4b continued

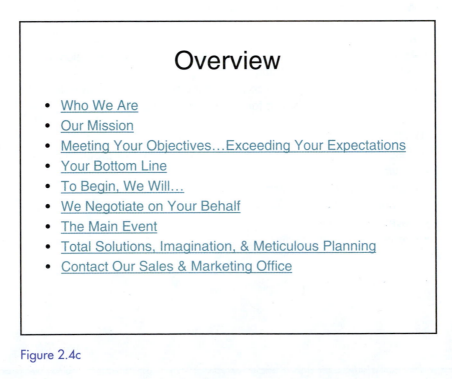

Overview

- Who We Are
- Our Mission
- Meeting Your Objectives…Exceeding Your Expectations
- Your Bottom Line
- To Begin, We Will…
- We Negotiate on Your Behalf
- The Main Event
- Total Solutions, Imagination, & Meticulous Planning
- Contact Our Sales & Marketing Office

Figure 2.4c

2.5 DEVELOP A PRESENTATION FROM SCRATCH

The International Studies Department at Meadowland College is offering a summer study-abroad program in Japan. A meeting is planned to discuss specific details about the courses students will take and the travel particulars. At this meeting, the advisor would also like to inform students about aspects of the country. You have been asked to create a presentation that informs viewers about Japan.

In this project, you will create a presentation about Japan. You will use information from two reports you created in previous projects to develop approximately ten slides.

1. Open **d2.5japan.docx** from the Data files. Print one copy.
2. Open **d2.5japancities.docx** from the Data files. Print one copy.
3. Close both data files. Do not save.
4. Open a new blank presentation.
5. Read the printed reports. Underline or highlight relevant points to include on the slides.
6. Create a title slide for the presentation.
7. Create a title for each slide that summarizes slide information.
8. Organize the slides in Slide sorter view.
9. Apply a design theme. Apply a font theme.
10. Use the photo **d2.5japan.jpg**, located on the Data files, as the slide background for the title slide. Make necessary adjustments to placeholders and font colors.
11. Insert relevant clip art throughout the presentation. If your clip art collection does not contain pictures of Japan, you can find them online at www.microsoft.com.
12. Use the photo **d2.5bridge.jpg** as the background for the last slide in the presentation. Make necessary adjustments to placeholders and font colors.
13. Enhance the slides as you prefer to create an effective presentation.
14. Apply a custom animation to slide titles and bulleted text throughout the presentation.
15. Apply a slide transition to all slides.
16. Save the file as **2.5japan**.
17. View the slide show.
18. Print one copy of the slides as handouts in pure black and white with six slides per page.
19. Close the file.

CHAPTER 3

Sales and Marketing Presentations

In this chapter, you will complete the following projects:

PROJECT 3
Create and Enhance Sales Presentations

PROJECT 3.1 Enhance a Presentation
PROJECT 3.2 Create and Enhance a Presentation That Sells a Product
PROJECT 3.3 Create a Presentation That Sells a Service
PROJECT 3.4 Create and Enhance a Presentation Using Tables and Charts
PROJECT 3.5 Create a Presentation from Scratch

PROJECT 3

PROJECT SKILLS

- Format bullets
- Insert footers
- Work with slide masters
- Create and apply multiple slide masters
- Save a design or slide master as a template
- Use action buttons
- Work with graphic objects
- Use shapes and WordArt
- Format objects
- Layer and group objects
- Rotate and flip objects
- Use the grid and guides
- Align and distribute objects
- Work with tables, charts, and SmartArt
- Create a custom show
- Link to a custom show
- Develop a presentation from scratch

3.1 ENHANCE A PRESENTATION

To finalize the SunStar presentation you created in the previous project, you will enhance it by changing the formatting and adding clip art.

In this project, you will enhance the presentation you created previously.

1. Open **2.4sunstar** (the presentation you created in Chapter 2) or open the data file **d3.1sunstar**.
2. Apply the Solstice design template.
3. Change the slide color scheme to Median. If this color scheme is not available, you may substitute another.
4. Enhance Slide 1 as follows:
   a. Insert a photo of a corporate event as the slide background (data file **d3.1meeting1.jpg**). *Note: Check the Hide background graphics check box.*
   b. Delete the title placeholder "SunStar."
   c. Reposition the subtitle placeholder to the bottom of the slide, as shown in Figure 3.1 on page 32. Set the font to Gill Sans MT, and size it to 20 pt. Apply a new font color or font style so the text is readable, if necessary.
   d. Create WordArt for the company name (SunStar) using the Fill-Accent 2, Warm Matte Bevel. Set the font to Bauhaus 93, 72 pt. Position the WordArt as shown in Figure 3.1 on page 32.

WHAT YOU NEED TO KNOW

Software

▶ You can insert slide numbers, the date or time, and other text that you want to appear as part of footer text. A *footer* is the same text that appears at the bottom of every slide. To insert a footer, click the Insert tab and in the Text group, click the Header & Footer button. In the Header and Footer dialog box that appears, click the appropriate check box to indicate whether you want to include the date and time, slide number, or footer.

▶ The Slide Master feature enables you to achieve consistency on all slides in a presentation. Use this feature to change the content or formatting (font style, font size, color, position, tabs, indents, background, and color theme) of text or object placeholders on the slide master, and then PowerPoint automatically reformats all slides throughout the active presentation with your changes.

Continued on next page

e. Use Shapes to create Rotate them slightly, as shown in Figure 3.1, and a three 5–point stars that are 1.2" x 1.2". Rotate them slightly, as shown in Figure 3.1, and apply the Intense Effect—Accent 4 style to them. (*Hint: Create one star and then copy and paste it two times.*) Position the stars behind the WordArt (Send to Back), as shown in Figure 3.1.

5. Display the slide master. Select the slide master thumbnail.

   a. Change the font for the title to Bauhaus 93.

   b. Copy the WordArt from Slide 1 and paste it in the footer area on the slide master, as shown in Figure 3.1. Size it appropriately.

   c. Copy the stars and paste them behind the company name, as you did on the title slide. Size them appropriately.

   d. Change the bullet style to any one you want.

   e. Insert the following four action buttons on the bottom left of the slide in this order: Beginning, Previous, Next, End. Use the default link option. Apply a shape style to them. *Note: Be sure not to place the action buttons over the navigational buttons, which appear in Slide Show view at the bottom-left area of the slide.*

   f. Insert today's date in the footer on all slides except the title slide.

   g. Close the slide master.

6. Further enhance Slides 2–11 as follows:

   a. Insert clip art, where appropriate, to support the slide content. *Note: The pictures on Slide 7 can be found in the data files under the filenames **d3.1meeting2.jpg** and **d3.1meeting3.jpg**. Apply a picture style of your choice to them, and then center-align them.*

   b. Display Slide 8. Insert a photo of a handshake (data file **d3.1meeting4**). Size the photo to 1.5" high (the width will adjust automatically). Apply a shadow style to the picture. Copy and paste the picture two times. Then, center-align the pictures and distribute them vertically, as shown on Slide 8 in Figure 3.1 on page 34.

   c. Display Slide 10. Remove the bullet, and create a WordArt object using the text in the placeholder. Use any style and coloring you prefer. *Note: Adjust the clip art and text box placeholders as necessary to achieve the appropriate results.*

7. Apply a custom animation to all slide titles and text in the presentation.

8. Apply a slide transition to all slides.

9. Display Slide 1 and run the slide show. On Slide 2, activate the second link (Our Mission), and then continue the slide show.

10. Save the file as **3.1sunstar**.

▶ You can make changes to any of the slide master layouts so that any time you apply one of those layouts to a slide, whatever is on that layout's master will appear automatically on the slide. If you want to apply changes to all slides regardless of the layout, you must make those changes to the Master Layout slide, which appears at the top of the layout thumbnails.

▶ Formatting changes you make to individual slides after you have applied the slide master override the slide master settings.

▶ To access the slide master, click the View tab, and in the Presentation Views group, click the Slide Master button. Click a slide master layout thumbnail to make changes to a particular layout.

▶ You can change the style, size, and color of bullets on individual slides, or you can keep the format consistent on all slides by formatting bullets on the slide master.

▶ If a slide has a graphic as part of its design, you can choose to omit it on individual slides or all slides by right-clicking the slide, selecting Format Background, and clicking Hide background graphics in the Format Background dialog box. Omitting a background will also remove a footer, if one was applied.

▶ As you learned in Word, graphic objects include clip art, photographs, shapes, lines, charts, SmartArt diagrams, tables, and media such as video and sound clips. Objects generally behave the same way in every application.

▶ WordArt lets you create text with decorative effects. It is best used to call attention to words or phrases. To create WordArt, click the Insert tab, and in the Text group, click the WordArt button. In the WordArt gallery that appears, click a WordArt style. Enter the text that you want to appear as WordArt in the placeholder that is displayed, and then click outside the placeholder to view the WordArt.

▶ You can also apply WordArt to existing text by selecting the text and using the appropriate tools in the WordArt Styles group on the Drawing Tools, Format tab.

Continued on next page

11. Print one copy of the presentation as handouts with three slides per page.

12. Close the file.

Slide 1

Slide 2

Slide 3

Figure 3.1

▶ You can format objects in PowerPoint using the same techniques you used for placeholders and clip art. You can also apply one of PowerPoint's predesigned styles. A *style* is a combination of formats such as line weight, fill color, and line style.

▶ To format an object, select the object and click the Drawing Tools, Format tab. Then, select the style option that you want to apply.

▶ The Align or Distribute feature allows you to align or distribute objects in relation to each other, or to distribute them evenly on the slide. To align or distribute objects, select the object(s) you want to align or distribute, click the appropriate Format tab and in the Arrange group, click the Align button. In the menu that appears, select Align to Slide or Align Selected Objects. Then, click the Align button again, select Distribute Horizontally, Distribute Vertically, or an alignment option.

▶ *Action buttons* are ready-made buttons found in the Shapes gallery that contain common symbols that indicate specific actions such as advancing to the next slide, returning to the first slide, and so forth. Action buttons become active when you run your presentation in Slide Show view.

▶ To insert an action button, click the Insert tab and in the Illustrations group, click the Shapes button. Click an action button from the Action Buttons group, and then click the slide where you want the action button to appear. Then, drag the mouse diagonally to draw the button. When you release the mouse button, the Action Settings dialog box opens. To have the action button activate when you click it, select activation options on the Mouse Click tab. To have the action button activate when you place the mouse pointer over it, select activation options on the Mouse Over tab.

Project

▶ Sales presentations influence an audience to buy a product, service, or an idea.

▶ While the objective of a sales presentation is to do just that—sell—it can also inform, persuade, and entertain.

▶ Use enhancements to support the content of slides and the overall objective of the presentation.

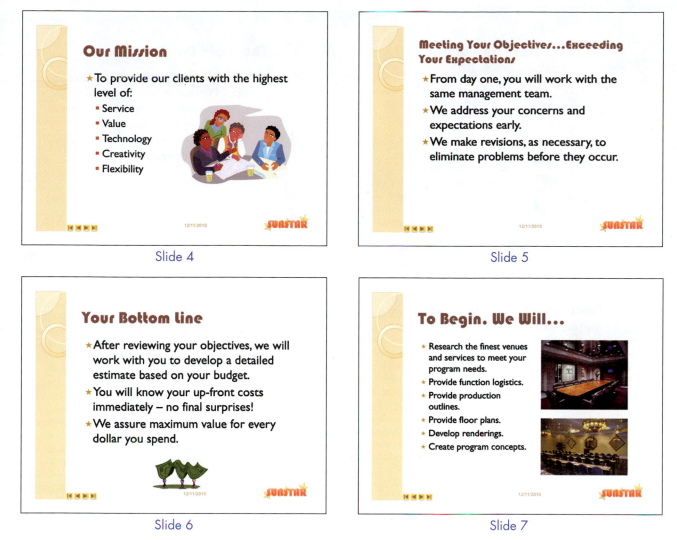

Slide 4

Slide 5

Slide 6

Slide 7

Figure 3.1continued

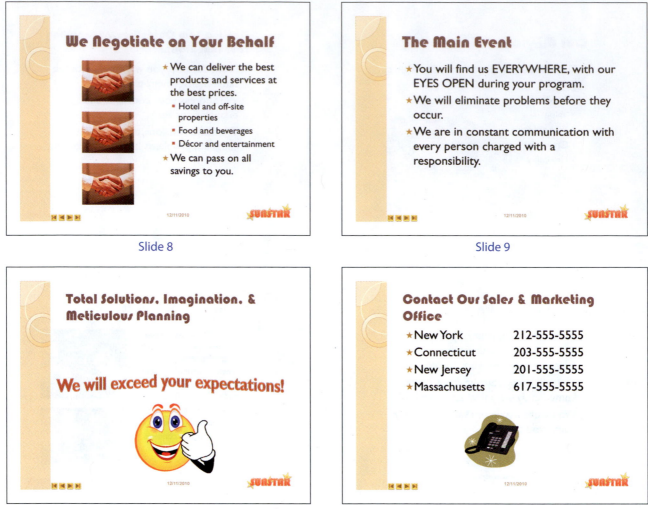

Slide 8

Slide 9

Slide 10

Slide 11

Figure 3.1 continued

3.2 CREATE AND ENHANCE A PRESENTATION THAT SELLS A PRODUCT

Uniworld Wireless sells hand-held wireless e-mail devices. The sales manager of UniWorld Wireless is making a presentation to the partners of a large law firm with the objective of selling their equipment to the attorneys in the firm. You have been asked to complete a presentation that was drafted by someone on the sales staff of Uniworld and enhance it to become an effective sales presentation.

In this project, you will finalize and enhance a presentation that sells a product.

1. Open the data file **d3.2wireless**.
2. Insert a new comparison slide, as shown in Figure 3.2a, as Slide 8. Enter the text as shown.
   a. Center-align the words "Product" and "Price" in their placeholders.
   b. Remove the bullets in the bulleted-text placeholders.
   c. Center-align the product numbers.
   d. Set a decimal tab at 2" in the text box that contains prices.
   e. Insert a text box at the bottom of the slide and enter the text, as shown in Figure 3.2a. Center-align the text box on the slide.
3. Insert a new slide as Slide 10 titled **Busy Lawyers** that reads:
   - **Need to Stay Connected**
     - **To your client**
     - **To the office**
     - **To the courts**
4. Use the Replace feature to search for each occurrence of "Wire less" and replace it with "Wireless".
5. Apply the Trek theme to all slides.
6. Apply the Paper color theme.
7. Display the slide master and click the slide master thumbnail. Make the following changes:
   a. Change the title style to Lucida Handwriting.
   b. Change the subtitle style to any font you want.
   c. Insert slide numbers on all slides except for the title slide.
   d. Create a text box that contains the company name using 14-pt, Lucida Handwriting. Position it at the bottom of the slide. Replace the "o" in "Uniworld" with a globe graphic. Size the graphic accordingly, as shown on Slides 2–10 in Figure 3.2b. Group the text box and the globe. Center-align the object on the slide.
   e. Copy the grouped object and paste it on the Section Header Layout master and the Comparison Layout master.
   f. Close the slide master.

WHAT YOU NEED TO KNOW

Software

▶ As in Word, you can find and replace words throughout a PowerPoint presentation. To do so, click the Home tab and in the Editing group, click the Replace button. Enter the [ab/ac Replace ▾] word you want to find in the Find what box, and enter the word you want to replace it with in the Replace with box.

▶ When you group objects, you create one object out of individual objects, which you can then format, size, or move as a single item. You can ungroup grouped objects to edit the objects individually, and then regroup them if you want.

▶ To group objects, select the objects you want to group. Click the appropriate Format tab, and in the Arrange group, click the Group button, and then click Group. [🔲 Group ▾]

▶ To ungroup objects, select the grouped object, click the Format tab, if necessary, and in the Arrange group, click the Group button, and then click Ungroup.

▶ The Rotate feature allows you to turn an object to a certain angle along a 360-degree axis. The Flip feature allows you to change the direction of an object horizontally (left-to-right) or vertically (top-to-bottom).

▶ To rotate an object by 90° increments, select the object and click the appropriate Format tab. In the Arrange group, click the Rotate button and select Rotate [🔄 Rotate ▾] Right 90° or Rotate Left 90°. To flip an object, click the Rotate button and select Flip Vertical or Flip Horizontal.

Project

▶ A sales presentation is more effective if you include a picture (or pictures) of the product you are selling or if you link to a Website that contains pictures of the product.

8. Display Slide 1. Replace the "o" in "Uniworld" with a globe graphic. Size the graphic accordingly, as shown on Slide 1 in Figure 3.2b.

9. Insert relevant clip art on Slides 2, 3, 4, 6, 7, and 10. Flip the clip art, if necessary, to appear appropriately on the slide.

10. On the Products & Pricing slide, adjust the placeholders to fit appropriately on the slide, as shown on Slide 8 in Figure 3.2b.

11. Change the background of the last slide to include a picture. You may use the picture shown (data file **d3.2atsign.jpg**) or any other relevant picture.
    a. Change the color of the title so that it is readable.
    b. Apply a WordArt style to the text on the slide.
    c. Make any necessary adjustments to the text.

12. Delete Slide 9.

13. Display the slide master, and apply a custom animation to slide titles and text.

14. Add slide transitions to all slides in the presentation.

15. Save the file as **3.2wireless final**.

16. Print one copy as handouts with four slides per page.

17. Close the file.
    Note: A sample solution is shown in Figure 3.2b.

Products & Pricing

Product	Price
UW555	$499.99
UW828	$659.79
UW999	$1,099.00
UW282	$550.00

Prices vary depending on the service you choose. The more expensive models come with more comprehensive desktop software. Prices do not include shipping and handling.

Figure 3.2a New Slide 8

Slide 1

Slide 2

Slide 3

Slide 4

THE BEST IN WIRELESS TECHNOLOGY

× Completely wireless handheld
× Integrates with existing e-mail
× No dial-up—always connected
× Simple to use
× Advanced security
× IT compatible

UNIWORLD

Slide 5

FEATURES

× Easy access to:
  + E-mail
  + Contacts
  + Calendar
  + Task list
  + Desktop tools
  + Server software

UNIWORLD

Slide 6

Figure 3.2b

Slide 7   Slide 8

Slide 9   Slide 10

Figure 3.2b continued

3.3 CREATE A PRESENTATION THAT SELLS A SERVICE

You work for A+ Test Prep, a company that provides test preparation instruction to help candidates pass school entrance exams. You have been asked to create a presentation to deliver to seniors at Meadowland College, who may be potential buyers of this service if they plan to attend graduate school, business school, medical school, or law school. You have also been asked to create a custom show for students planning to attend business school. At a later time, you will create a custom show for students attending medical school and another custom show for students attending law school.

In this project, you will create and enhance a presentation that sells a service. You will use multiple slide masters and create a custom show for students attending business school. *Note: A sample solution is provided in Figure 3.3 to use as a guide in developing your own version.*

1. Open a new blank presentation.
2. Apply any design theme.
3. On Slide 1, create an A+ logo and position it as shown in Figure 3.3.
   a. Use WordArt to create the letter "A", and use an AutoShape for the plus sign. Apply any text effect or shape style to get your desired result.
   b. Use WordArt to create the words "Test Prep."
   c. Use the grid and guides to position the objects as shown on Slide 1 in Figure 3.3, and then group the three objects.
   d. Copy the grouped object.
4. Display the slide master.
   a. Paste the grouped object as part of the footer, as shown on Slides 2–8 in Figure 3.3. Resize and reposition the individual objects within the grouped object to get the desired result, as shown.
   b. If necessary, change the bullet style so that it complements the theme of the presentation.
   c. Duplicate the original slide master.
   d. Rename the new slide master **courses**.
   e. Apply a blue color scheme to the new slide master.
   f. Close the slide master.
5. Enter the text for Slides 2–9 as shown using the appropriate slide master layouts. (If you choose not to apply the "courses" slide master now, you can do it later by right-clicking the slide, highlighting layout, and selecting the appropriate "courses" slide master layout.)
6. Insert relevant clip art.
7. On Slide 3, group each clip art object and its corresponding text box.

WHAT YOU NEED TO KNOW

Software

▶ PowerPoint 2007 allows you to apply multiple slide designs within the same presentation. This is particularly useful if you want to differentiate or color-code certain sections of the presentation, or create a custom show.

▶ Additional slide masters you create will appear as thumbnails (with corresponding slide layouts) to the left of the slide pane.

▶ To easily identify each slide master you create, rename the master after you customize it.

▶ To create additional slide masters, click the View tab, and in the Presentation Views group, click the Slide Master button. On the Slide Master tab and in the Edit Master group, click the Insert Slide Master button to insert a blank slide master, or in the Edit Theme group, click the Themes button to insert a slide master with a predefined theme. Make any edits to the master.

▶ To change elements of the current slide master, right-click the master slide thumbnail and select Duplicate Slide Master. Make any changes you want on the new slide master.

▶ A *custom show* is a group of related slides within a presentation that you can deliver independently of the entire presentation. Think of a custom show as a presentation within a presentation.

▶ To create a custom show, open the presentation from which you want to create a custom show. Click the Slide Show tab, click the Custom Slide Show button, and then click Custom Shows. In the Custom Shows dialog box that appears, click the New button to specify a new custom show. In the Define Custom Show dialog box, click each slide you want to include in the custom show, and click the Add button. Enter a name in the Slide show name box to name the custom show.

Continued on next page

8. On Slide 9, use the picture of a hand (data file **d3.3hand.jpg**), as the background for the slide. If the design theme has a graphic that overlays the picture, select Hide background graphics for this slide.

9. View the slide master and apply a custom animation to the slide titles and bulleted text on both slide masters.

10. Apply a slide transition to all slides in the presentation.

11. Display Slide 3. Apply a custom animation to each of the three grouped objects so that they appear on the slide one at a time during the slide show.

12. Create a custom show for Slides 4, 5, 6, and 7. Name it **Business School**.

13. Display Slide 2.
  a. Create a hyperlink on the words "Business School" to link to the Business School custom show.
  b. Choose to show the custom show and return to the linked slide.

14. Display Slide 1 and run the slide show. Click the Business School link on Slide 2 to view the custom show.

15. Save the file as **3.3testprep**.

16. Print one copy as handouts with four slides per page.

17. Close the file.

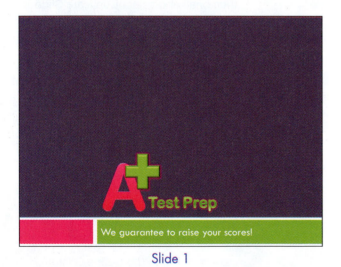

Slide 1

Figure 3.3

▶ You can set up a slide show to run only the slides in a custom show rather than all the slides in a presentation. You can also run a custom show at any time during a slide show.

▶ To run a custom show, click the Slide Show tab, and in the Start Slide Show group, click the Custom Slide Show button list arrow, and then choose a show from the list that is displayed. This begins a slide show of only the slides in the specified custom show.

▶ To link to a custom show from within the current show, click the Insert tab, and in the Links group, click the Hyperlink button. In the Insert Hyperlink dialog box, click the Place in This Document button, and select the custom show from the Select a place in this document box. Select the Show and return check box to return automatically to the slide that contained the link after viewing the custom show.

▶ The Grid and Guides feature allows you to position an object on a slide with more precision. A *grid* contains evenly spaced horizontal and vertical lines, which are hidden when you print a presentation but appear on screen to help align objects. *Guides* are invisible vertical and horizontal lines that you can also use to align objects.

▶ To display the grid and/or guides, right-click the slide and select Grid and Guides from the shortcut menu. In the Grid and Guides dialog box, click the appropriate check boxes to display the grid or drawing guides on screen. To display the gridlines and/or ruler, click the View tab and in the Show/Hide group, click the Gridlines and/or Ruler boxes.

▶ The Snap objects to grid option allows you to position an object on the grid, regardless of whether or not you have chosen to display the grid. When you turn on the Snap objects to grid option and move an object, the object snaps to the nearest point on the grid. You can also choose to snap objects to other objects. This option aligns an object with another object as you move or draw it.

Project

▶ Be sure you design your slides so that they are appropriate for your audience.

We Prepare You For...

✓ Graduate School
  ➤ GRE
✓ Business School
  ➤ GMAT
✓ Medical School
  ➤ MCAT
✓ Law School
  ➤ LSAT

A+ Test Prep

Slide 2

What We Offer

Classroom Courses

Interactive Online Courses

Private Tutoring

A+ Test Prep

Slide 3

Business School

✓ We will:
  ➤ help you find the right business school for you.
  ➤ provide you with the B-School Reality Quiz.
  ➤ help you fill out your application.
  ➤ help you connect with student-loan providers.
  ➤ provide MBA networking opportunities.

A+ Test Prep

Slide 4

Classroom Courses

✓ Small classes
  ➤ 8-10 students per class
✓ Energetic, knowledgeable instructors
✓ Free extra help
✓ Online lessons to complement each class

A+ Test Prep

Slide 5

Interactive Online Courses

✓ Test prep in a multimedia format
✓ Engaging, interactive lessons
  ➤ Animation
  ➤ Audio/video
✓ Strengths and weaknesses assessed
  ➤ Lessons focus on weaknesses
✓ Chat with or e-mail an A+ teacher anytime

A+ Test Prep

Slide 6

Private Tutoring

✓ Best way to maximize your score
✓ Learn at your own pace
✓ Master every concept
✓ Convenient scheduling
✓ Online lessons and resources

A+ Test Prep

Slide 7

Figure 3.3 continued

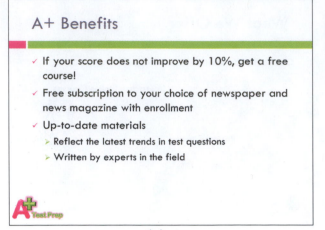

A+ Benefits

- ✓ If your score does not improve by 10%, get a free course!
- ✓ Free subscription to your choice of newspaper and news magazine with enrollment
- ✓ Up-to-date materials
  - ➢ Reflect the latest trends in test questions
  - ➢ Written by experts in the field

Slide 8

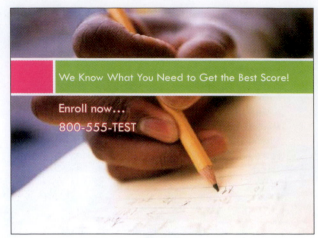

Slide 9

Figure 3.3 continued

3.4 CREATE AND ENHANCE A PRESENTATION USING TABLES AND CHARTS

You work for The National Health Institute, an organization that is committed to creating awareness of and raising money for a variety of health-related issues. NHI's latest initiative is to create a breathe-easy environment for children by reducing indoor and outdoor pollution. A special taskforce has been developed to reduce secondhand smoke, one of the greatest causes of indoor pollution that adversely affects children and adults. In an effort to promote this initiative and help fund the program to make even greater progress, they have created special "Breathe-Easy" buttons, which are for sale on their Website.

In this project, you will create and enhance a sales presentation and use a table, a chart, and SmartArt to support your points.

1. Open a new blank presentation.
2. Apply any design theme.
3. Display the slide master.
   a. Select the slide master thumbnail and make the following changes, as shown in Figure 3.4a:
      • Change the bullet style and color for levels 1 and 2.
      • Insert the slide number and today's date in the footer.
      • Use WordArt to create a logo for NHI. Apply a shape style to it, and center it at the bottom of the slide.
      • Apply custom animations to slide titles and text.
   b. Select the Title Master thumbnail.
      • Italicize the subtitle text.
   c. Close the slide master.
4. Use appropriate slide layouts to create the slides shown in Figure 3.4b on pages 45–47. Use these slides as a guide.
   a. Insert relevant clip art where you think it will enhance the slide.
   b. Adjust placeholders as necessary.
5. Display Slide 1.
   a. Use the picture **d3.4air.jpg**, which can be found in the data files, as the slide background. Select the Hide background graphics option.
   b. Change the font color to complement the background, if necessary.
6. Display Slide 6.
   a. Insert a chart and enter the data into the data sheet, as shown in Figure 3.4c on page 47. (If the data does not appear correctly on the slide, click the Switch Row/Column button in the Data group on the Chart Tools, Design Tab.)

WHAT YOU NEED TO KNOW

Software

▶ Tables, charts, and SmartArt are visual elements you can use to organize and analyze data in your presentation. As you learned in Word, SmartArt includes conceptual diagrams that help you visualize data. SmartArt is used to show a process, cycle, or hierarchy.

▶ Content slides, which you used when working with clip art, contain placeholders to work with one or more of these visual elements.

▶ To insert a table, apply a slide layout that contains a content placeholder, and click the Insert Table icon on the slide. In the Insert Table dialog box that opens, enter the number of columns and rows you want in the appropriate text boxes, and click OK.

▶ To create a table on a slide that does not contain a content placeholder, click the Insert tab, and in the Tables group, click the Table button. On the Insert Table menu, click and drag across the squares to select the number of rows and columns you want. Release your mouse and the table will appear on your slide, filling the slide area.

▶ To format a table, select the table, and then click the Table Tools, Design tab and use the appropriate buttons to change border style, add shading, apply a style, or make other changes.

▶ Charts in PowerPoint are based on the Chart feature in Excel. To insert a chart, apply a slide layout that contains a content placeholder and click the Insert Chart icon on the slide, or click the Insert tab, and then in the Illustrations group, click the Chart button. In the Insert Chart dialog box that is displayed, click a chart type in the left pane, click a chart style in the right pane, and then click OK. In the Excel datasheet window that appears, replace the sample data with your own. Click the Close button in the Excel window to return to PowerPoint and view the chart on your slide.

Continued on next page

b. Position the legend to the right of the chart, if necessary.

c. Include data labels and position them inside the chart at the end of the data points.

7. Display Slide 7.

a. Insert a table using four columns and four rows and enter the text as shown on Slide 7 of Figure 3.4b.

b. Apply appropriate styles and shading, so the table appears as it does in the figure.

8. Display Slide 11.

a. Insert the Continuous Block Process SmartArt graphic.

b. Enter text as shown in Figure 3.4d.

c. Change the colors of the SmartArt graphic and apply the Powder SmartArt style to it.

9. Display Slide 12.

a. Apply a shape style to the subtitle placeholder.

b. Size and position the placeholder, as shown in Figure 3.4b.

10. Use your creativity to design Slide 13. Use and layer shapes and text boxes, as shown in Figure 3.4b. *Note: Slide 13 was created using a callout shape, a text box, and WordArt. The text box was layered on top of the shape.*

11. Use the Replace feature to search for each occurrence of "second-hand" and replace it with secondhand.

12. Apply a slide transition to all slides.

13. Run the slide show from the beginning.

14. Save the file as **3.4breathe**.

15. Print one copy as handouts with six slides per page.

16. Close the file.

▶ You can change a chart's style and layout, as well as edit it to include a title, axes titles, a legend, and/or data labels using the tools found on the Chart Tools, Design, Layout and Format tabs.

▶ To create a SmartArt graphic, click the Insert tab and in the Illustrations group, click the SmartArt button. In the Choose a SmartArt Graphic dialog box that opens, select a SmartArt graphic type (List, Process, Hierarchy, Cycle, Relationship, Matrix, or Pyramid), Select a SmartArt thumbnail, and then click OK. Click in a shape or text placeholder to enter text.

▶ After SmartArt is inserted on your slide or selected, a frame appears around the graphic, and the SmartArt Tools, Design and Format tabs also appear with the Design tab selected by default to help you customize the SmartArt graphic.

▶ You can format a SmartArt graphic with preset styles, or format portions of it as you would format shapes by adding fill color and text, and change the line weight and style.

Figure 3.4a Slide master

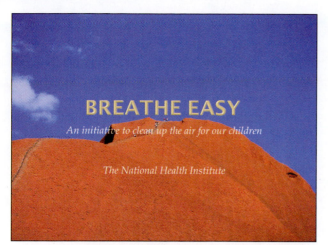

BREATHE EASY

An initiative to clean up the air for our children

The National Health Institute

Slide 1

NHI's Breath-Easy Initiative

- An outgrowth of NHII's commitment to health and wellness
- Spearheaded by parents, who want cleaner air for their children
- Encourage people to reduce air pollution indoors and outdoors
  - Newsletters
  - Conferences
  - Seminars
  - Promotional materials
- Special task force targets smokers because of the harmful effects of secondhand smoke

12/12/2010   NHI   2

Slide 2

What is Secondhand Smoke?

- Smoke exhaled by a smoker
- Smoke from the burning end of cigarettes, cigars, and pipes
- Composed of nearly 4,000 different chemicals and chemical components
- Often called involuntary smoking or passive smoking

12/12/2010   NHI   3

Slide 3

Why Should Parents Be Concerned?

- Effect on lungs
  - Children who breathe secondhand smoke are more likely to suffer from pneumonia, bronchitis, and other lung diseases.
- Ear infections
  - Children who breathe secondhand smoke can have more ear infections.
- Asthma
  - Children who breathe secondhand smoke have more asthma attacks and the episodes can be more severe.
  - Secondhand smoke causes healthy children to develop asthma each year.

12/12/2010   NHI   4

Slide 4

Secondhand Smoke is a Health Risk to the Unborn Child

- Miscarriage
- Premature birth
- Low birth weight
- Sudden infant death syndrome

12/12/2010   NHI   5

Slide 5

Living With a Smoker Makes a Child More Likely to Smoke

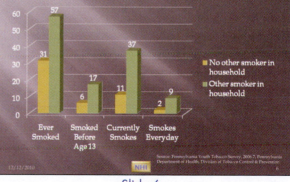

12/12/2010   NHI   6

Slide 6

Figure 3.4b

Slide 7

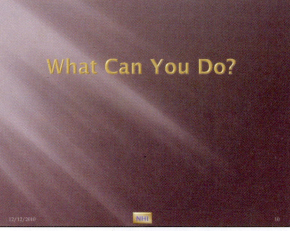
Slide 8

Slide 9

Slide 10

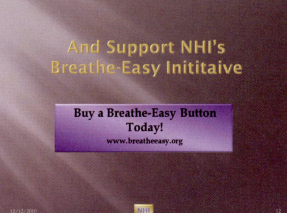
Slide 11

Slide 12

Figure 3.4b continued

Slide 13

Figure 3.4b continued

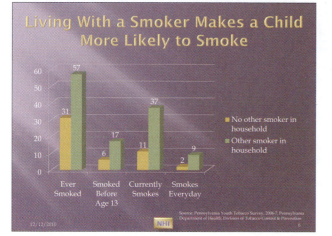

	A	B	C
1		No other smoker in household	Other smoker in household
2	Ever Smoked	31	57
3	Smoked Before Age 13	6	17
4	Currently Smokes	11	37
5	Smokes Everyday	2	9

Figure 3.4c

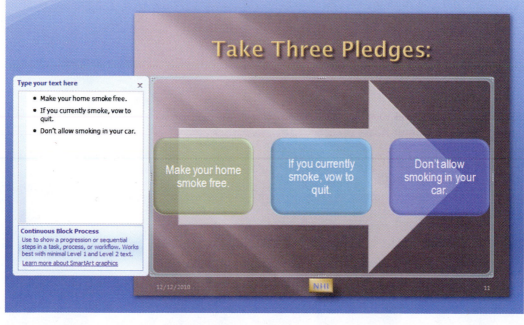

Figure 3.4d

3.5 CREATE A PRESENTATION FROM SCRATCH

The Massachusetts Tourist Bureau (MTB) is actively seeking ways to draw tourists to visit sites within the state. The MTB recently developed an article about Massachusetts as a travel destination. The article was printed in *Destinations*, a travel magazine. Representatives from the MTB will be making a presentation about Massachusetts at the next travel agents' convention, and they have asked you to help create their presentation.

In this project, you will create a presentation consisting of 10–12 slides to promote Massachusetts as a travel destination. Use information from the article created previously, as well as information you research from the Internet, to develop the content for your slides.

1. Open **14.2mass.docx**, the article you completed in an earlier Word project. If this file is not available to you, open the data file **d3.5mass.docx**.
2. Print one copy for your review.
3. Read the article and highlight facts you want to include on the slides. You can also visit www.masshome.com/tourism.html and/or www.massvacation.com for additional information or pictures.
4. Open a new blank presentation. Use an outline to create and organize the presentation content.
5. Display the slide master.
   a. Apply a design theme.
   b. Change the title and subtitle font styles on the slide master and title master layouts.
   c. Create a WordArt object for the word "Massachusetts." Center it in the footer area of the slide.
   d. Change the bullet style and color for levels 1 and 2.
   e. Insert the slide number in the footer.
   f. Apply custom animations to slide titles and text.
   g. Rename the slide master **Mass1**.
   h. Close the slide master.
6. Create a second slide master using a different design theme but complementary theme colors.
   a. Rename the slide master **Mass2**.
   b. Format the slide as you wish.
7. Apply a custom animation to slide titles and text. *Note: Use multiple slide masters to support the flow of your presentation. For example, you might want to differentiate the slides that contain cities by applying a new slide master to them.* Display Slide 1. A sample is shown in Figure 3.5.

WHAT YOU NEED TO KNOW

Software

▶ You can save your new presentation design or a slide master as a template that you can use to create new presentations or you can apply it to existing presentations.

▶ If you create multiple slide masters within a presentation and save the presentation as a template, PowerPoint saves all of the masters along with the template.

▶ To save a presentation as a template, click the Office Button, point to Save As, and click Other Formats. Enter a filename in the File name box. Click the Save as type list arrow, click PowerPoint Template, and then click Save. *Note: It is recommended that you save your templates in the Templates folder to make them easier to locate in the future.*

Project

▶ You can develop slide content for selling a product or service from information found in sales materials (brochures, catalogs, newsletters, and advertisements) or from the Internet.

a. Use a photo depicting Massachusetts as the slide background. Select the Hide the background graphics option.

b. Title the slide `Bring Your Family to Massachusetts`.

c. Apply any font style or color to the text to complement the background photo.

8. Use your creativity to design the remainder of the slides in the presentation using clip art, photos, shapes, WordArt, text alignment, SmartArt, charts, tables, or other embellishments. Be sure to include at least one SmartArt object.

9. Apply a slide transition to all slides.

10. Insert two action buttons on the bottom left of each slide (except for the title slide) in this order: Home and Next. Use the default link option.

11. Save the presentation. Name it **3.5massvacation**.

12. Run the slide show.

13. Make any adjustments to placeholders, if necessary.

14. Save the presentation as a template. Name it **3.5masstemplate**.

15. Print one copy of the slides as handouts with four slides per page.

16. Close all files.

Figure 3.5

CHAPTER 4

Persuasive Presentations

In this chapter, you will complete the following projects:

PROJECT 4
Create Persuasive Presentations

PROJECT 4.1 Create and Enhance a Presentation Using Charts, SmartArt, and Media
PROJECT 4.2 Use a Template to Create a Presentation from Scratch
PROJECT 4.3 Create and Enhance a Presentation Using Charts, SmartArt, and Media
PROJECT 4.4 Enhance Presentations with Animated Charts and SmartArt
PROJECT 4.5 Create a Photo Album

CREATE PERSUASIVE PRESENTATIONS

PROJECT 4

PROJECT SKILLS

✶ Work with media
✶ Animate charts and SmartArt
✶ Use template presentations
✶ Work with photo albums

4.1 CREATE AND ENHANCE A PRESENTATION USING CHARTS, SMARTART, AND MEDIA

Money Watch Investment Company would like to convince the residents of Four Seasons Condominiums (an over-55 community) to use Money Watch for financial advice. Kendra Garcia, President of Money Watch, has been invited to make a presentation about the company at the next meeting of the Four Seasons Investment Club.

In this project, you will create and enhance a presentation with charts, SmartArt, and media. Ms. Garcia would also like you to create a logo for the company that will be a part of the template design.

1. Open the data file **d4.1money**.
2. Change the slide orientation to portrait.
3. Apply the Section Header layout to Slides 2, 3, and 6.
4. Read through the eight slides to get a basic understanding of the subject matter. Then apply a design theme that supports the text and the content of the presentation.
5. Insert relevant clip art (including animated .gifs) where you think it will enhance the slide. Adjust placeholders as necessary.
6. Display the slide master and make the following changes to the Section Header layout master:
   a. Insert an appropriate picture as the background. Select the Hide background graphic option.
   b. Change the font color and style to complement the background. Apply a shape style to the text box, if necessary.
      Note: Any slide to which you applied the Section Header layout will appear with the elements set on the Section Header layout master.
7. Select the slide master layout thumbnail and make the following changes:
   a. Create a logo for the company and include it as part of the design theme.
   b. Include slide numbers and today's date as footer text.
   c. Change the font, font colors, and bullet style, if you want.

WHAT YOU NEED TO KNOW

Software

▶ *Media* include sound effects, music, video, or animated.gifs (clip art or pictures that have animation effects) that you can add to slides. The media are activated during a slide show.

▶ You can add media clips to slides in the same way that you add clip art images. Like clip art, media clips come preloaded with Office and are located in the Microsoft Clip Organizer. Video clips and animated .gifs are indicated by a star icon in the bottom-right corner of the thumbnail.

▶ After you select a video or sound clip, PowerPoint prompts you to choose whether to play it in the slide show automatically when the slide appears, or only when you click it.

▶ To add a media clip from clip art using a slide layout that contains a media clip icon, click the icon on the slide to open the Clip Art task pane. Enter search criteria, click the Results should be list arrow, select the Movies and Sounds check boxes, and then click Go. Click to select the clip, and if prompted, click Automated or When Clicked.

▶ To add a media clip from your files, click the Insert tab, and in the Media Clips group, click the Movie or Sound button. In the Insert Movie or Insert Sound dialog box that opens, navigate to locate an existing video, sound, or animated .gif, click the media clip to insert it, and then click OK.

▶ A media clip appears on a slide as an icon. To play a media clip, you must be in Slide Show view.

Continued on next page

8. Insert a Title and Content slide.
   a. Enter the title **Money Market vs. CDs**.
   b. Enter the data into the datasheet, as shown in Figure 4.1a, to create a column chart (you may choose any column chart style). *Note: Click the Switch Row/Column button, if necessary, so that the chart appears as shown in the figure.*
   c. Apply any chart style.
9. Insert another Title and Content slide.
   a. Enter the title **Six-Month CD Rate Trend January-June 2010**.
   b. Enter the data into the datasheet, as shown in Figure 4.1b, to create a marked line graph.
   c. Apply any chart style to it.
10. Insert a slide titled **What Is a Bear Market**?
    a. Go to www.investopedia.com/terms/b/bearmarket.asp. Research the meaning of "a bear market" and provide a definition on the slide.
    b. Use your creativity and apply any slide layout to complete the slide.
11. Insert a slide titled **Investment Options in a Bear Market**.
    a. Include the following bullet points:
       • Buy more stock to average your cost down
       • Sell short
       • Buy safer CDs and Treasury Bonds
    b. Add a sub-bullet below "Sell short" that explains the term. Go to the Website indicated in Step 10 to find the definition.
12. Insert a Title and Content slide, and create the slide shown in Figure 4.1c on page 55.
    a. Use SmartArt to create a radial diagram.
    b. Apply different fill colors to each circle and a SmartArt style to the diagram.
13. Insert a Title and Content slide, and create the slide shown in Figure 4.1d on page 55.
    a. Use SmartArt to create an organization chart.
    b. Apply a SmartArt style to the diagram.
14. Insert a last slide that will leave the audience convinced to invest with Money Watch.
15. Display Slide Sorter view.
16. Reorder the slides, as shown in Figure 4.1e on page 55.
17. Insert a sound clip on Slide 1 that provides a soothing, yet attention-getting opening.
    a. Insert the clip to play automatically.
    b. Loop it to play until stopped and choose to play the sound across slides.
18. Insert another sound clip on the last slide that supports the content you created. Insert the clip to play when you click it.
19. Save the file as **4.1fourseasons**.
20. Run the slide show and test the sounds. Make any adjustments necessary.
21. Print one copy of the presentation as handouts with six slides per page.
22. Close all files.

▶ You can loop a sound or movie so that the clip plays continuously until you advance to the next slide. To do so, click the media clip, click the Sound Tools, Options tab or the Movie Tools, Options tab, and then click the Loop Until Stopped check box.

Project

▶ The purpose of a persuasive presentation is to convince the audience to buy a product or service, to support or defend a position, or to change the audience's attitude.
▶ A presentation to persuade an audience to buy a product or service takes on similar characteristics to a sales presentation.
▶ Persuasive presentations should begin by defining the problem and providing supporting evidence of the problem. Subsequent slides should explain exactly why it is a problem and how the problem affects the audience. Slides should then show the audience how the problem can be resolved and how their actions will make a difference.
▶ Use media clips carefully. Be sure they do not overshadow the message. You can use media clips effectively at the start of a presentation to catch the audience's attention or at the end of the presentation to leave the audience with a final impression.

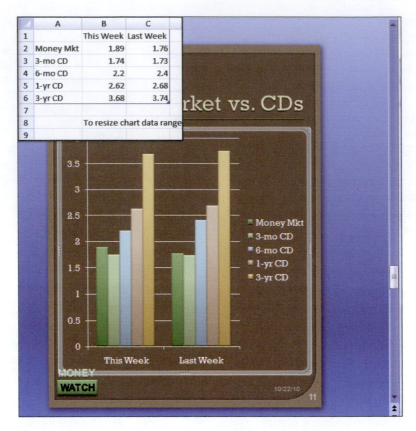

Figure 4.1a

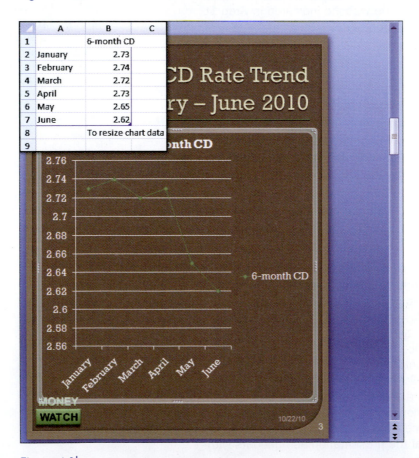

Figure 4.1b

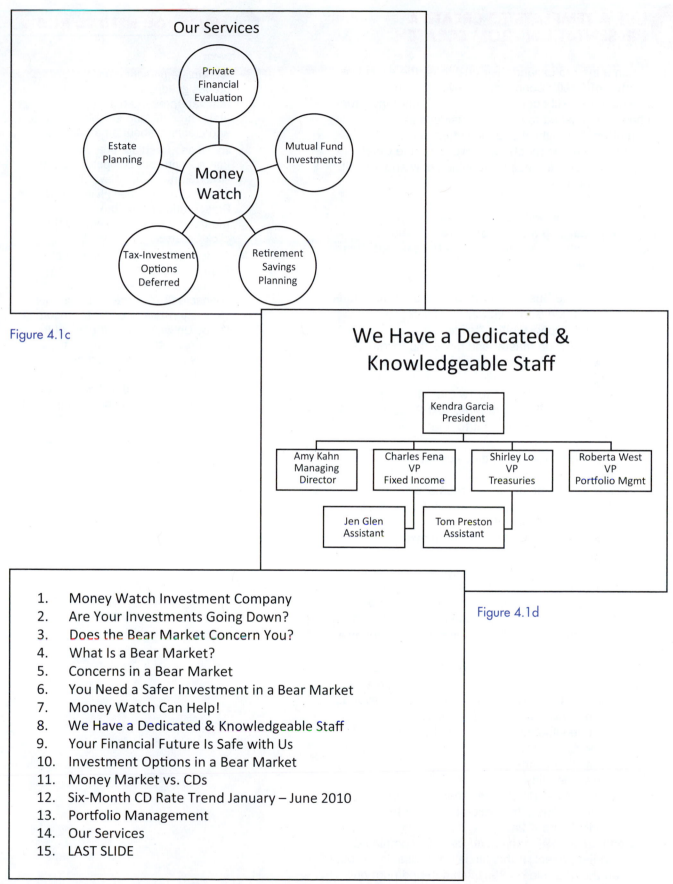

Figure 4.1c

We Have a Dedicated & Knowledgeable Staff

Figure 4.1d

1. Money Watch Investment Company
2. Are Your Investments Going Down?
3. Does the Bear Market Concern You?
4. What Is a Bear Market?
5. Concerns in a Bear Market
6. You Need a Safer Investment in a Bear Market
7. Money Watch Can Help!
8. We Have a Dedicated & Knowledgeable Staff
9. Your Financial Future Is Safe with Us
10. Investment Options in a Bear Market
11. Money Market vs. CDs
12. Six-Month CD Rate Trend January – June 2010
13. Portfolio Management
14. Our Services
15. LAST SLIDE

Figure 4.1e

USE A TEMPLATE TO CREATE A PRESENTATION FROM SCRATCH

WHAT YOU NEED TO KNOW

To obtain a loan to expand their business, the executive committee of Health Connections devised a business plan, which they will submit to banks and other investors. You have been asked to create a business plan presentation that highlights their written plan. When the executive committee meets with investors, the Chief Executive Officer will present the slide show and submit the written business plan.

In this project, you will use the Business Plan template to develop a persuasive presentation for Health Connections. You will finalize the presentation in a later project.

1. Download the Business Plan presentation template.
2. Switch to Slide Sorter view.
3. Delete the "Opportunities" slide.
4. Display the slide master and make the following changes to the title master layout, as shown in Figure 4.2a.
   a. Change the title font to Tw Cen MT, 48 pt, and the font color to Light Blue, Text 2, Darker 50%.
   b. Change the subtitle font to Arial Rounded MT Bold, 24 pt.
   c. Hide the background graphics on the title master.
5. Click the slide master layout thumbnail and make the following changes, as shown in Figure 4.2b.
   a. Change the title font to Arial Rounded MT Bold.
   b. Change the font of the bulleted text to Tw Cen MT.
   c. Insert a decorative letter H (which can be found in clip art). Position it as shown in Figure 4.2b.
   d. Use Shapes to create a thin rectangle. Position it vertically on the slide as shown in Figure 4.2b. Apply the Intense Effect—Accent 3 shape style to it.
   e. Change the bullet style for levels 1 and 2. Change the font sizes for the bulleted text as follows: Level 1, 20 pt; Level 2, 18 pt; Level 3, 16 pt; Level 3, 14 pt; Level 5, 12 pt.
   f. Include slide numbers on all slides except Slide 1.
   g. Copy the decorative letter H.
   h. Close the slide master.
6. Display Slide 1. Delete the "Your logo here" placeholder. Paste the decorative letter H as shown in Figure 4.2a.
7. Open **14.3busplan final.doc** that you completed in an earlier project. If this file is not available to you, open the data file **d4.2busplan.doc** and print one copy.

Software

▶ A *template presentation* is a predesigned set of slides. Some template presentations use themes, and others include sample layout, text, and graphics about a particular topic.

▶ To access template presentations installed on your computer, click the Office Button, click New, click the Installed Templates link in the New Presentation dialog box, click one of the template thumbnails, and then click Create.

▶ To download template presentations from Microsoft Office Online to your computer, make sure that you are connected to the Internet, and then click any category under Microsoft Office Online in the left pane of the New Presentation dialog box to display additional categories of available templates. Click a category, which will display thumbnails, click one of the template thumbnails, and then click Download.

Figure 4.2a Title master layout

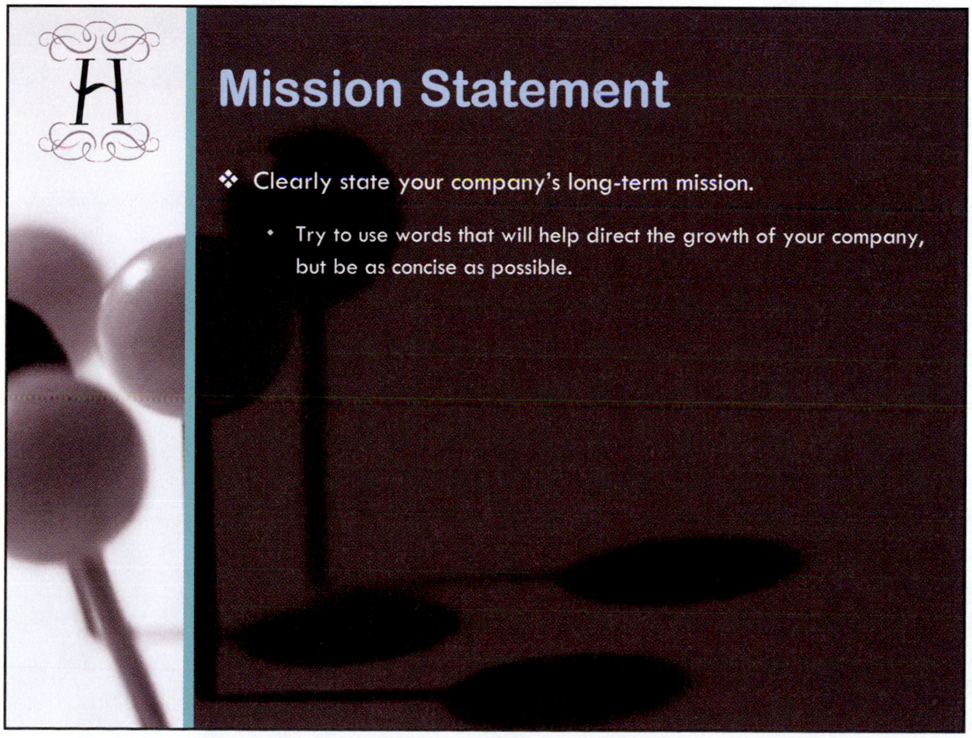

Figure 4.2b Slide master layout

8. Use the information in the written business plan to develop the slides indicated in Steps 9–11. *Note: You can copy information from the Word file and paste it into the PowerPoint slide, where it is possible to do so.*

9. On the Mission Statement slide (shown in Figure 4.2b), copy the text below "1.2 Mission" in the written plan and paste it on the slide.

10. On the Team slide:
   a. Delete the bulleted text and insert an organization chart.
   b. Include the CEO and Vice President (refer to "2.1 Company Ownership" in the written plan).
   c. Add Paul Adams as Administrative Assistant to Susan A. Samuel.

11. On the Goals and Objectives slide:
   a. Under "1.0 Executive Summary" in the written plan, copy the first sentence in paragraph three and paste it as the first bullet on the slide. Delete the words "Our goal is" and begin with "To borrow ..."
   b. Copy the text below "1.1 Objectives" in the written plan and paste it as sub-bullets on the slide. (*Hint: Decrease the font size of the bulleted text so that all of the text fits appropriately on the slide.*)

12. On the Financial Plan slide:
   a. Change the title to **Projected Cash Flow Statement**.
   b. Change the layout to Title Only. Delete the bulleted sample data. *Note: You will insert the financial data in a later project*.

13. Insert another Title Only slide after the Projected Cash Flow Statement slide.
   • Insert the title **Comparative Balance Sheet**. *Note: You will insert the financial data in a later project*.

14. Insert a Title and Chart slide after the Comparative Balance Sheet slide. Title it **See the Growth**.
   • Enter the following data to show a two-year comparison of net income:

2009	2010
$87,500	$120,500

15. Enter the text shown in Figure 4.2c for the remaining slides.
   • Insert a last slide titled **Keys to Success** using a Title and Content layout. Create a pyramid diagram and enter the text shown in Figure 4.2c on page 61. Change the font to Papyrus, and apply a SmartArt style to the diagram.

16. Add relevant clip art to Slides 12 and 13.

17. Insert a relevant sound clip on the last slide to play automatically. Run the slide show. Make any adjustments necessary.

18. Save the file as **4.2hcbusplan**.

19. Print one copy as handouts with six slides per page.

20. Close all files.

Health Connections
Business Plan

Slide 1

Mission Statement

❖ Health Connections is planning to fulfill the need for health foods, a market we have identified, based on the large volume of health-conscious consumers.

❖ Health Connections will:
- Provide reliable, fresh, organically grown foods.
- Package products under the Health Connections brand.
- Develop an e-commerce Website to sell products online.
- Encourage people to become health-conscious consumers and use the Health Connections brand of products to meet their dietary needs.

Slide 2

The Team

Steven J. Graber
Chief Executive Officer

Susan A. Samuel
Vice President

Paul Adams
Administrative Assistant

Slide 3

Market Summary

❖ Consumers come from three distinct groups:
- Commuters
- Residents
- Tourists

❖ An e-commerce site will provide the means to expand our business and satisfy our customers who wish to buy our product from home.

Slide 4

Business Concept

❖ The uniqueness of our product line and the existing untapped market ensures our success in the health foods market.

❖ The Health Connections name has become well-known in New York City and the time has come to package and market our products on the Web.

Slide 5

Competition

❖ Our competition is more expensive.

❖ Our competition does not produce its own product line.

❖ We are the first company to develop an e-commerce Website.

❖ We are the first company to develop a solid e-commerce platform.

❖ We have very experienced and knowledgeable staff.

Slide 6

Figure 4.2c

Goals and Objectives

❖ To borrow $550,000 for 10 years.

- To develop a solid e-commerce market and to maximize our profit margin.
- To develop and repackage organic and health food products under our own brand.
- To fulfill the health foods demand with top-quality products.
- To reach gross profit of $750,000 by the end of our first year of expansion.
- To encourage our customers to live healthy lives by making health foods an integral part of their weekly shopping list.
- To begin expansion of the Health Connections store and to promote our Health Connections food line.
- To offer health-conscious individuals support through our Web page, such as interviews with health professionals to answer specific health-related issues.

Slide 7

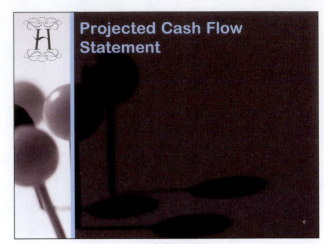

Projected Cash Flow Statement

Slide 8

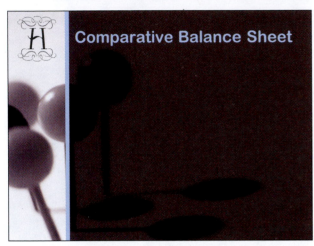

Comparative Balance Sheet

Slide 9

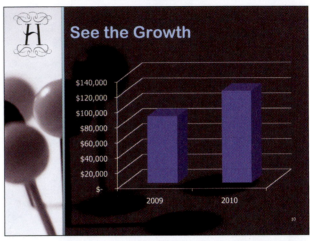

See the Growth

Slide 10

Resource Requirements

❖ Technology requirements
- Web page design

❖ Personnel requirements
- Increase staff to meet consumer needs

❖ Resource requirements
- Packaging

❖ External requirements
- Advertising
- Suppliers can meet demand
- Maximize distribution channels

Slide 11

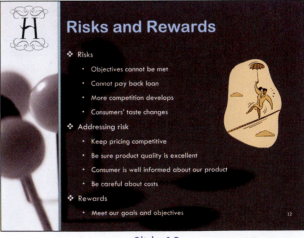

Risks and Rewards

❖ Risks
- Objectives cannot be met
- Cannot pay back loan
- More competition develops
- Consumers' taste changes

❖ Addressing risk
- Keep pricing competitive
- Be sure product quality is excellent
- Consumer is well informed about our product
- Be careful about costs

❖ Rewards
- Meet our goals and objectives

Slide 12

Figure 4.2c continued

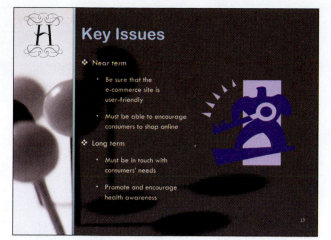

Slide 13

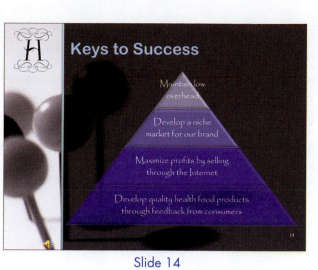

Slide 14

Figure 4.2c continued

4.3 CREATE AND ENHANCE A PRESENTATION USING CHARTS, SMARTART, AND MEDIA

The Finnish Travel Bureau wants *Destinations* to run a feature article about traveling to Helsinki, Finland. To support this article, you will make a presentation to travel agents to convince them to book travel to Helsinki, Finland. Using an information fact sheet provided to you by the Helsinki Travel Bureau, you will develop a presentation of approximately 14 slides that advertises travel to Finland.

In this project, you will create and enhance a presentation with charts, SmartArt, and media.

1. Open a new blank presentation and apply any design theme.
2. Display the slide master and select the title master layout thumbnail.
    a. Insert the picture of Helsinki (data file **d4.3finpic.jpg**) shown in Figure 4.3a as the slide background. If necessary, delete any design theme graphics that may cover the background picture.
    b. Edit the font, font color, and theme colors to complement the picture you select.
    c. Adjust text placeholder as necessary.
3. Select the slide master layout thumbnail.
    a. Edit the slide master to complement the title slide.
    b. Add a clip art image to enhance the design theme.
    c. Insert a footer that includes the date (to update automatically), **Destination: Helsinki** as the footer text, and the slide number. Apply it to all slides except for the title slide.
4. To create the remaining slide content, refer to the fact sheet shown in Figure 4.3b on pages 63–65. To find out the weather information for Helsinki noted on page 3, go online to: www.weather.com.
    a. Apply any slide layouts.
    b. Include a chart and a SmartArt graphic in the presentation. (*Hint: Your chart might refer to the growth in tourism.*)
5. Use any pictures or clip art and/or design elements to enhance the slides.
6. Include a sound clip that provides an attention-getting opening to the presentation.
7. Move the slides into an appropriate order, if necessary.
8. Run the slide show. Make any adjustments necessary.
9. Save the file as **4.3finland**.
10. Print one copy as handouts with six slides per page.
11. Close all files.

WHAT YOU NEED TO KNOW

Project

▶ Charts and SmartArt should be used to visualize information in a clear and concise way. Always choose layouts that serve a purpose and emphasize key points.

Figure 4.3a

Helsinki, Finland in the Summer

Helsinki comes to life in the summer when long hours of sunshine bring outdoor dining and arts festivals to the city. The city is in full bloom in the summer, inspiring locals to play bocce, relax on park benches, sail, or take motorboats to nearby islands. Galleries, bookstores, concert halls, and theaters offer visitors many cultural events and performances. The Helsinki Festival, from August 22 to September 7, is the city's summer highlight and culminates in the Night of the Arts, during which free performance art, readings, music, and visual and decorative arts are offered to the public.

The City

King Gustavus I of Sweden, who then ruled Finland, founded Helsinki in 1550. The city passed from Swedish to Russian rule in 1809. In 1812, Czar Alexander I made Helsinki the capital of Finland. Finland gained independence from Russia in 1917, and the Helsinki region's population and commercial importance have grown since then. Helsinki is currently home to approximately 874,953 inhabitants. The center of the city's old section is Senate Square, which has many buildings designed in the neoclassical style of the 1800s.

Everything in the center of Helsinki is within easy walking distance, but the trams provide a warm, cheap, and comfortable way of exploring the city. There is even a pub tram that makes a circuit of the city. In the summer, many people rent a bike or roller skates to enjoy the city. Sightseeing buses and boats (often serving refreshments and food) are relaxing and rewarding options.

Events

As part of the Helsinki Festival, the Helsinki Filharmonia and Finnish Philharmonic Choir will present a music program beginning at 8 P.M. on August 24 at Huvila, a waterfront space near the Helsinki Theater. Tickets are $18-$24.

The 26.7-mile Helsinki Marathon lures thousands of spectators along its course, which spans the city's waterways and streets. It starts at 3 P.M. August 16 at Olympic Stadium at the statue of Paavo Nurmi, winner of nine Olympic gold medals for running.

Sightseeing

The quickest and least expensive way to see the city is on the tram 3T, which passes through the major areas every 15 minutes. There is an English-language guidebook available on board. Fare is approximately $3.

Suomenlinna, a living historic island village surrounded by 18th-century fortifications, is a 13-minute ferry ride from downtown. The village contains numerous small museums, cafes, art galleries, and a beach. Tickets for the ferry are $3.50 round trip.

Helsinki has many outdoor markets. The most famous outdoor bazaar, Kauppatori, is made up of various stalls and boats where produce and crafts are sold. It is open Monday through Saturday morning all year, with extended hours during the summer months. It is on the South Harbor near the President's Palace.

Figure 4.3b Page 1

The Helsinki Tourist Association offers guided walking tours in English, by appointment, for $140 a person.

What to See

- Senate Square with the Lutheran Cathedral, Council of State, University
- Esplanade Park and the neighboring buildings, including the Kappei restaurant
- Main seafront Market Square, Uspensky Orthodox Cathedral
- Suomenlinna Sea Fortress
- Seurasaari Open Air Museum
- Sibelius monument
- Temppeliaukio Church (also known as the "Church in the Rock")
- Finlandia Hall and the National Museum
- Kiasma Museum of Contemporary Art
- Ateneum Art Museum
- Helsinki City Museum
- Stockmann, northern Europe's biggest department store

Where to Stay

Rates are approximately 50% lower in the summer than they are at other times of the year.

- The Lord Hotel has 48 rooms and is decorated with Art Nouveau murals and unusual architectural features. Rooms are $192 for a double.
- Grand Marina is on the harbor east of Market Square. The building dates back to 1912 and has 420 rooms. Rates are $197 for a double.
- The 200-room Strand Inter-Continental is one of the most luxurious hotels in the city. It offers a view of the city from across a channel that leads to the Gulf of Finland. Rates are $396 for a double.

Where to Eat

The following restaurants serve Finnish fare:

- Valhalla is located on Suomenlinna, a short ferry ride from town. Dinner for two with wine averages about $120.
- Kosmos serves excellent Finnish, Russian, and French dishes. Dinner for two with wine averages about $60.
- Elite serves the city's arts and theater crowd. There is outdoor seating in the summer. Dinner for two with wine averages about $55.

Growth in Tourism

Year	Number of Visitors
2005	2,082,927
2006	2,953,978
2007	3,284,783
2008	3,674,836
2009	3,827,522

Figure 4.3b Page 2

The following statistics might be helpful to the Helsinki visitor:

Population

Metro area: 874,953

Weather in August

High: ?
Low: ?
Days with rain   ?

Hotel

Room for two with tax: $285.00

Dinner for One

With tax and tip: $38.00

Taxi

Upon entry $3.98
Each additional km $1.05
From the airport: $28.30

Car Rental for a Day

Mid-sized, manual shift $148.25

Figure 4.3b Page 3

You will apply custom animations to enhance the presentation you created for the National Health Institute on creating a breathe-easy environment for children. You will then do the same for the presentation you created for the Money Watch Investment Company.

In this project, you will apply custom animations to two presentations you created previously.

National Health Institute Presentation

1. Open **3.4breathe** that you completed in a previous project, or open the data file **d4.4breathe**. (The title slide is shown in Figure 4.4a.)

2. Apply any animation effect to the clip art throughout the presentation. Set the timing for all clip art (except for clip art on Slide 13) to animate with the previous effect.

3. Display Slide 6. *Note: If you applied animation effects to the slide master, you will first have to copy the master effects to the slide in Normal view, and then delete the effect that was applied to the content placeholder. If you do not do this first, you will apply two effects to the content placeholder.*
   a. If necessary, copy the slide master effects to the slide, and delete the content placeholder effect.
   b. Apply the Wipe (From Bottom) entrance effect to the chart.
   c. Set the chart to animate by category.

4. Display Slide 7.
   a. If necessary, copy the slide master effects to the slide, and delete the content placeholder effect.
   b. Apply the Pinwheel entrance effect to the table.

5. Display Slide 11.
   a. If necessary, copy the slide master effects to the slide, and delete the content placeholder effect.
   b. Select the SmartArt graphic, and apply the Fly In (From Left) entrance effect to it.
   c. Set the SmartArt graphic to animate one by one.

6. Display Slide 13.
   a. Apply any animation effects to the clip art, shape(s), and text on the slide.

7. Insert a sound clip on Slide 1 to play when clicked.

8. Insert a sound clip on Slide 12 to play automatically. Format the sound to stop playing after two slides. *Note: If you applied animation effects to the slide master, you will have to copy the effects to the slide in Normal view, and reorder the sound clip to play as the first animation on the slide.*

9. Run the slide show. Make any adjustment necessary.

10. Save the file as **4.4breathe**.

11. Close the file.

WHAT YOU NEED TO KNOW

Software

▶ As you learned previously, animations are visual or sound effects that you can add to text or objects.

▶ You can animate charts and SmartArt (diagrams) with the same techniques used to animate text and objects. You can also animate individual sections of a chart or diagram and/or add sound effects, which can add interest when emphasizing data during your slide show. When an animation is added to a slide or object, it appears in the Custom Animation task pane with a descriptive name for the animation.

▶ To animate a chart, select the chart, click the Animations tab, and in the Animations group, click the Custom Animation button. In the Custom Animation task pane, [Custom Animation] click Add Effect, and then select the animation effect to apply.

▶ To animate a section of a chart, you must first apply an animation to the chart as indicated above. Then, in the Custom Animation task pane, click the animation list arrow for this animation, and click Effect Options. In the Effect Options dialog box, click the Chart Animation tab, and then select As One Object or By Category from the Group chart list to indicate how you want the chart animated.

▶ To add a sound effect to a chart animation, in the Custom Animation task pane, click the animation list arrow for the animation, and then click Effect Options. In the Effect Options dialog box, click the Effect tab, and then select a sound from the Sound list arrow in the Enhancements group.

▶ To animate SmartArt, select the SmartArt graphic or SmartArt section you want to animate. Click the Animations tab, and in the Animations group, click the Custom Animation button. In the [Custom Animation] Custom Animation task pane, click Add Effect and select an effect to apply. Then, click the animation list arrow for this animation, and then click Effect Options. In the Effect Options dialog box, click the SmartArt Animation tab, and then select an element from the Group graphic list.

Continued on next page

Money Watch Investment Company Presentation

1. Open **4.1fourseasons**, which you completed previously in this chapter. (The title slide is shown in Figure 4.4b.)

2. Display the slide master and select the slide master layout thumbnail.

   a. Apply a custom animation to the titles and bulleted text, which will appear on all slides in the presentation. *Note: On the slides where music clips have been set to play automatically, you will have to copy the slide master effects to the slide in Normal view, and reorder the sound clip to play as the first animation on the slide.*

3. Display Slide 8.

   a. Copy the slide master effects to the slide, and delete the content placeholder effect.

   b. Apply a custom animation to the organization chart that displays one box at a time.

4. For Slides 11 and 12:

   a. Copy the slide master effects to the slides, and delete the content placeholder effect.

   b. Apply a custom animation to each chart that displays the data by series.

5. Display Slide 14.

   a. Copy the slide master effects to the slide, and delete the content placeholder effect.

   b. Apply the Spinner entrance effect to the SmartArt graphic.

   c. Set the animation effect to introduce the radial diagram from the center, one by one.

6. Run the slide show. Make any necessary adjustments.

7. Save the file as **4.4fourseasons**.

8. Close the file.

▶ To add a sound effect to SmartArt animations, follow the same procedures provided for adding sound to charts.

▶ The animations play in the order in which they are numbered and the numbers appear on the slide. You can change the animation order by clicking the up/down reorder buttons.

▶ As you learned previously, you can use the slide master to apply the same animation effect to all titles and bulleted text throughout a presentation. However, if you are in Normal view and try to reorder an animation effect that you created in Slide Master view, you must first click the Master Animation list arrow in the Custom Animation list and click the Copy Effects to Slide option.

▶ Remember, if you added an animation to a placeholder on the slide master, applying an animation to the same placeholder in Normal view will mean that two animations have been applied to that placeholder.

Project

▶ Too many animations in a presentation can be distracting to your audience. Therefore, you should use animations consistently and sparingly.

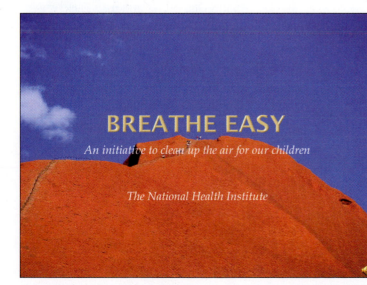

Figure 4.4a

Figure 4.4b

Money Watch
Investment
Company

Financial Investment
Advisors Work to Make
Your Money Grow

4.5 CREATE A PHOTO ALBUM

Soon you are going to present your presentation on Helsinki, Finland to a group of travel agents. To finalize the presentation, you will add a photo album and enhance it with custom animations.

In this project, you will create a photo album that contains pictures of Helsinki and Finland. You will then add the photo album to the presentation on Helsinki that you created in Project 4.3 and enhance the presentation with custom animations.

1. Create a photo album that contains photos of Finland, including Helsinki.
   a. Use the four photographs found in the data files in the subfolder **d4.4finpics**.
   b. Place two pictures on a slide, each with a title. Order them as indicated by their filenames.
   c. Apply any frame shape and include a caption.
2. Insert slide titles, as shown in Figure 4.5.
3. Replace the current filename captions below each photograph with the captions shown in Figure 4.5.
4. Save the file as **4.5photoalbum**.
5. Close the file.
6. Finalize the presentation on Helsinki, Finland.
   a. Open **4.3finland** that you completed earlier in this chapter.
   b. Apply a custom animation to slide text and objects on each slide. (*Hint: You can use the slide master, if you prefer.*)
   c. Apply a custom animation to the SmartArt graphic and chart. *Note: If you applied a custom animation to the slide master, you will have to copy the master effects to the slide and delete the content placeholder effect before you apply an animation effect to the SmartArt graphic and chart. Otherwise, you will have multiple effects on these objects.*
   d. Insert the three slides from **4.5photoalbum** as the last three slides in the presentation. Make any adjustments necessary to placeholders, photos, or captions.
   e. Save the newly created presentation as **4.5finland**.
7. Run the slide show.
8. Print one copy of the presentation as handouts with six slides per page.
9. Close all files.

Software

▶ A *photo album* is a collection of pictures that you can create from a file or from a device such as a scanner or digital camera. You can customize the photo album with special layout options, including oval frames and captions.

▶ A photo album is an independent presentation that you can add to an existing presentation, publish to the Web, e-mail, or print. The pages of your photo album are slides. You can customize the layout of the photo album pages to include frame options, captions, and/or text boxes. The layout you create applies to the entire photo album.

▶ To create a photo album, click the Insert tab, and in the Illustrations group, click the Photo Album button list arrow, and then click New Photo Album. In the Photo Album dialog box, click the File/Disk button to indicate the source of your photos. Navigate to the folder, disk, or device drive, and click the desired picture. To select additional pictures, press and hold [Ctrl] while you click them. Click Insert, select options, and then click Create, which will open a new presentation with a custom title slide. Change the title and subtitle on the slide, as desired.

▶ To insert a photo album into another presentation, click the Home tab, and in the Slides group, click the New Slide button list arrow, and then click Reuse Slides from the menu. In the Reuse Slides task pane, click Open a PowerPoint File, double-click the photo album file, and then in the Reuse Slides task pane, click a thumbnail.

Project

▶ The special layout options you choose to add to your photo album, such as frames and captions, should enhance your overall presentation message.

Photos of Finland

Things to See and Do

Flower Market

Traditional Dancers

Summer in Helsinki

Helsinki

Fishing in Finland

Figure 4.5 Photo album slides

CHAPTER 5

Collaborating on and Delivering Presentations

In this chapter, you will complete the following projects:

PROJECT 5
Collaborating on and Delivering Presentations
PROJECT 5.1 Prepare and Enhance Audience Materials
PROJECT 5.2 Prepare a Presentation for a Kiosk
PROJECT 5.3 Add, Edit, Delete, and Print Comments
PROJECT 5.4 Prepare a Presentation to Travel

PROJECT SKILLS

✸ Use handouts
✸ Use notes pages
✸ Work with handout master and notes master
✸ Work with the pen and annotations
✸ Rehearse timings
✸ Use slide show set-up options
✸ Add, edit, delete, cycle through, and print comments
✸ Save a presentation to a CD
✸ Prepare a presentation as read-only

5.1 PREPARE AND ENHANCE AUDIENCE MATERIALS

In Chapter 4, you developed a presentation on Helsinki, Finland to present to travel agents. You are now ready to prepare handouts to provide the travel agents with information about Finland that they can share with their clients. You will also prepare speaker notes with cue marks and add annotations, which you will use when you deliver the presentation.

In this project, you will create and enhance handouts and speaker notes, and cue your speaker notes in preparation for delivering the final presentation.

1. Open **4.5finland**, which you completed in a previous project. If this file is not available to you, open the data file **d5.1finland**.
2. Display the notes master.
   a. Set the font size in the notes box to 14 pt.
   b. Enter **Presentation to Travel Agents** in the footer area. Set the font to blue. Apply a light gray fill to the footer text box.
   c. Insert a page number.
3. Display the handout master.
   a. Set the page to display four slides per page.
      Note: The software will automatically default to six slides per page when the presentation is closed.
   b. Apply any preset background style. Enter the same text in the footer area that was used on the notes master, and set the font to blue.
   c. Insert a page number.
4. Display Slide 1, and switch to Notes Page view.
   a. Click in the text placeholder, and enter the notes for Slide 1, as shown in Figure 5.1a.
   b. Click the Next Slide button to advance to the next slide. Enter the notes for Slide 2, as shown in Figure 5.1a on page 74.
   c. Use the fact sheet shown in Project 4.3 (Figure 4.3b, pages 63–65), and enter speaking points for the remaining slides.

WHAT YOU NEED TO KNOW

Software

▶ At the start of this unit, you learned to print your presentation as handouts with 1, 2, 3, 4, 6, or 9 slides on a page. You can distribute these handouts to the audience so they can follow along with your on-screen presentation and have material to which they can refer at a later time.

▶ Notes pages, often referred to as *speaker notes*, are used to assist the speaker in delivering a presentation. You can also distribute speaker notes to the audience, providing them with detailed information about each slide.

▶ You can enter and format speaker notes in the notes pane in Normal view or in Notes Page view.

▶ To enter text in the notes pane, click the notes pane and enter notes. To display more or less of the notes pane, drag the top border of the pane up or down.

▶ To enter text directly in the notes placeholder, click the View tab, and in the Presentation Views group, click the Notes Page button. A notes page, which contains a slide and a text placeholder, appears. Click in the text placeholder to enter and/or format your notes.

▶ In an earlier project, you used the slide master to customize all slides of a presentation by adding text, objects, headers and footers, and/or color themes to a master slide. Similarly, the handout master and the notes master allow you to customize your handouts and notes pages.

Continued on next page

Note: Use the notes shown in Figure 5.1a on page 74 as a guide to help you develop your own speaking points to coordinate with your slide content.

d. Add cue marks (text indicated with a bright font color or highlighted) to indicate when the speaker should click the mouse or keyboard to activate the next on-screen action.
Note: An asterisk can be the last cue on the page to prompt you to advance to the next slide.

5. Save the file as **5.1finland**.

6. Print one copy of the notes pages.

7. Print one copy of the handouts with four slides per page.

8. Run the slide show and test the sound clip.

9. Using the notes pages with the cue marks, deliver the presentation and slide show.

   a. Use the annotation pen to highlight important sights or items of distinction as you go through the presentation. (*Hint: Place the insertion point in the lower-left corner of the slide to display and activate the hidden toolbar that contains the annotation pen.*)
   - On Slide 5, highlight the words "Suomenlinna" and "Kauppatori," as shown in Figure 5.1b on page 75.
   - On the chart slide, use the annotation pen to circle the last bar.

   b. Do not save the annotations.

10. Close all files.

▶ To view and format the handout master, click the View tab, and in the Presentation Views group, click the Handout Master button. On the Handout Master tab and in the Placeholders group, click to deselect any or all of the four placeholders from the handout as you prefer. In the Page Setup group, click the Slide Orientation button or Handout Orientation button, and choose Portrait or Landscape. Then, click the Slides Per Page button, and choose an option. You can also use the buttons in the Edit Theme or Background groups to choose formatting options.

▶ To view and format the notes master, click the View tab, and in the Presentation Views group, click the Notes Master button. On the Notes Master tab, and in the Placeholders group, click to deselect any or all of the four placeholders from the handout as you prefer. In the Page Setup group, click the Slide Orientation button or Notes Page Orientation button, and choose Portrait or Landscape. You can also use the buttons in the Edit Theme or Background groups to chooseformatting options.

▶ You can enter a header and/or footer on the handout or notes master the same way you did on the slide master.

▶ PowerPoint provides a pen tool that allows you to use your pointer as a writing instrument. When delivering a presentation, you can "write" on the slides using the annotation pen, and later choose to erase or save the notations. You can select from three different pen types: ballpoint, felt tip, and highlighter. You can also change the ink color. All animations and animation timings are suspended when you are annotating.

▶ Annotations made on screen during a slide show do not alter the slide in any way, and they disappear when you move to another slide.

Continued on next page

[Sound clip will automatically activate.]
Good morning. My name is *(your name)*, and I am here today on behalf of the Finnish Travel Bureau, which would like Destinations to feature travel to Helsinki in its next issue of *Destinations Magazine*. During this presentation, I will attempt to persuade you to encourage your customers to visit Helsinki and the rest of Finland so they can experience a beautiful, cultural, and charming city and countryside—especially in the summer. *

Slide 1

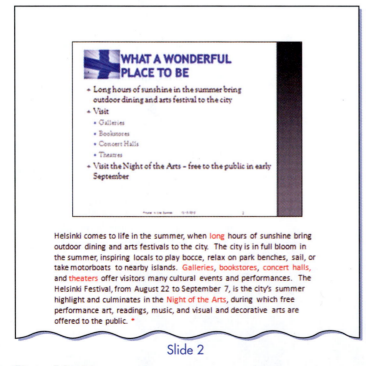

Helsinki comes to life in the summer, when long hours of sunshine bring outdoor dining and arts festivals to the city. The city is in full bloom in the summer, inspiring locals to play bocce, relax on park benches, sail, or take motorboats to nearby islands. Galleries, bookstores, concert halls, and theaters offer visitors many cultural events and performances. The Helsinki Festival, from August 22 to September 7, is the city's summer highlight and culminates in the Night of the Arts, during which free performance art, readings, music, and visual and decorative arts are offered to the public. *

Slide 2

Figure 5.1a Notes pages

▶ To add annotations, you must be in Slide Show view. On the lower-left corner of the slide, there is a hidden toolbar. Place the insertion point in the lower-left corner to display and activate the toolbar.

▶ To make an annotation on a slide, click the Slide Show view button on the status bar. Click the Pen button, and choose a pen type from the menu. Then, click on the slide and draw, write, or highlight what you want to add or emphasize on the slide. Click the Pen button again, and select Arrow to turn off the pen. When prompted at the last slide in the dialog box, click Keep to save your annotations or Discard to not save them. You can also press [E] to erase your annotation on a slide. A saved annotation is displayed on each slide in Normal view.

Project

▶ When delivering a presentation, it is important that the slide content coordinate with the oral narrative. To ensure this coordination, it is important that you "cue" your speaker notes (which serve as your script).

▶ To add cue marks, highlight the word(s) that will serve as your "cue" or prompt. (You can also print the speaker notes and insert the cue marks by placing a large handwritten dot over the word.) When you are delivering your presentation, the cue mark will prompt you to click to advance to the next slide or to display bulleted text that corresponds to the information provided in the oral narrative.

▶ You should always practice a presentation with saved annotations before giving a live presentation to make sure that the effect is what you want.

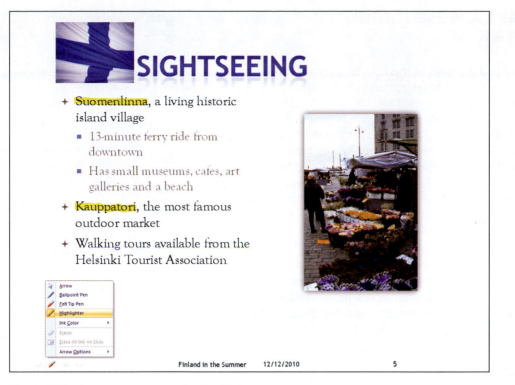

Figure 5.1b Annotation pen used to highlight text

PREPARE A PRESENTATION FOR A KIOSK

In addition to being shown at the Four Seasons Retirement Community, the presentation you created for Money Watch Investment Company will also be shown in the reception areas of all Money Watch Investment offices (at an unattended booth). To prepare for the meeting at the Four Seasons Retirement Community, you have been asked to create speaker notes and handouts and rehearse the presentation. You will have 5 minutes to deliver the presentation. For the presentation that will be shown in the Money Watch Investment offices, you have been asked to prepare the presentation to run automatically for a kiosk.

In this project, you will create audience handouts and speaker notes for the meeting at the Four Seasons Retirement Community and time the presentation. You will then set the presentation to run automatically for the kiosk in the Money Watch Investment offices.

1. Open **4.4money**, which you completed in a previous project, or open the data file **d5.2money**.
2. Display the handout master.
   a. Set the page to display nine slides per page. *Note: The software will automatically default to six slides per page when the presentation is closed.*
   b. Insert a footer that includes the title (but not the subtitle) of the presentation.
   c. Insert a header that reads "Presentation to Four Seasons Retirement Community." Set the text color to red.
   d. Insert a page number and today's date.
   e. Apply an attractive background.
   f. Include a logo at the bottom, as shown in Figure 5.2a. Use the same logo you used in the presentation.
3. Display the notes master. *Note: The header and footer that you inserted on the handout master will also appear on the notes master.*
   • Set the font size in the notes box to 14 pt.
4. Switch to Notes Page view.
   • Add notes to the pages using Slides 1 and 2 (shown in Figure 5.2b on page 78) as a guide. For each of the remaining slides, develop your own speaking points to coordinate with the slide content. Add cue marks where appropriate.
5. Print one copy of the notes pages.
6. Rehearse and time the presentation using your notes. If prompted to keep timings, click Yes.
   a. On Slide 11, use the annotation pen to show that the 3-year CD has the greatest return on investment.
   b. On Slide 12, use the annotation pen to show the rate trend on the 6-month CD.
   c. Do not save the annotations.

WHAT YOU NEED TO KNOW

Software

▶ If you need to deliver a presentation within specific time constraints, you can rehearse how long it takes to deliver the presentation. To do so, click the Slide Show tab, and in the Set Up group, click the Rehearse Timings button to start your slide show and display the Rehearsal dialog box. Leave each slide displayed for as long as necessary to present the slide content. *Note: The clock in the Rehearsal dialog box times how long the slide is displayed.* Click the Next button on the Rehearsal dialog box to activate the next animation or advance to the next slide. *Note: The clock in the Rehearsal dialog box resets (goes back to 00:00) when a new slide is displayed, while the clock measuring the presentation's total running time continues.* At the end of the show, a dialog box opens showing the total time of the show. Click Yes to save the timings, or click No to discard them.

▶ You can set a slide show to run on its own, so that slides advance automatically and the presentation restarts (or loops) when the slide show is finished.

▶ To create a self-running presentation, you must set slide transition timings to allow enough time for people to review the information presented on each slide.

▶ To set slide show options to create a self-running presentation, click the Slide Show tab, and then click the Set Up Slide Show button. The Set Up Show dialog box opens. Below Show type, select the Browsed at a kiosk option. Below Show options, select the Loop continuously until 'Esc' check box. Below Advance slides, select Using timings, if present.

▶ The Loop continuously until 'Esc' option sets the slide show to restart automatically when it ends. Clicking the Browsed at a kiosk option also sets the presentation to loop continuously.

7. Save the file as **5.2money**.
8. Print the presentation as handouts in pure black and white with nine slides per page.
9. Click the Slide Show tab, and then click the Set Up Slide Show button.
   a. Under Show type, select the Browsed at a kiosk option.
   b. Under Advance slides, select Using timings, if present option.
10. Run the slide show.
    Note: The slide show will automatically restart after the last slide is shown.
11. Save the file.
12. Close all files.

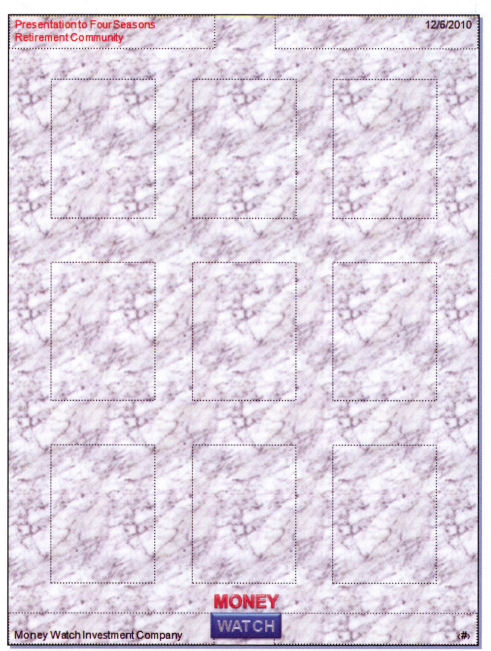

Figure 5.2a Handout master

Figure 5.2b Notes pages

Slide 1

Slide 2

5.3 ADD, EDIT, DELETE, AND PRINT COMMENTS

Several members of your department are working collaboratively to finalize the presentation you created for Uniworld Wireless in Project 3.2. Because you will be on vacation when they are working on the final review of the presentation, you will insert comments on slides that need their input. You will also add notes and format the notes master for the presenter.

In this project, you will insert comments on selected slides and add notes to the presentation.

1. Open **3.2wireless final**, the presentation you completed in Project 3. If this file is not available to you, open the data file **d5.3wireless final**.
2. Insert a sound clip on Slide 1 that plays automatically. *Note: If you applied a custom animation to the slide master, you will have to copy the effects to the slide, and reorder the sound clip to be first in the custom animation list.*
3. Display Slide 3.
   - Insert a comment on the clip art image that says: **Include other images of Uniworld Wireless devices**. Move the comment to appear next to the clip art image on the slide, as shown in Figure 5.3 on page 80.
4. Display Slide 5.
   - Insert the following comment: **You might want to add statistics as evidence of UniWorld Wireless' success**.
5. Display Slide 9.
   - Insert the following comment: **Include comments made by lawyers who have used the product**.
6. Display the notes master.
   a. Change the font size to 16 pt for all levels.
   b. Insert the following header: **Uniworld Wireless**.
   c. Insert today's date.
   d. Insert your name as the footer.
7. Switch to Notes Page view.
   a. Display Slide 1.
   b. Add the following notes.
      - **Introduce the purpose of the presentation.**
      - **Give a general overview of the product.**
   c. Display Slide 2.
   d. Add the following note.
      - **For each bullet, give an example of when this would be helpful.**

WHAT YOU NEED TO KNOW

Software

- *Comments* are notes that you or a reviewer can add to a presentation. You can read these comments on the screen, hide them when you print the presentation, print them with the presentation, or incorporate them into the presentation.
- Comments do not show in Slide Show or Slide Sorter view.
- To add a comment, you must be in Normal view. Click on the slide where you want to attach the comment (to attach a comment to an object or placeholder, click to select it). If you do not select an object or placeholder, PowerPoint will insert the comment at the top-left corner of the slide. Click the Review tab, and then click the New Comment button. Enter your comment, and then click anywhere outside the comment box to resume working on the slide. The comment box changes to a small icon showing the initials of the author and the comment number. To view the full comment, place your mouse pointer over the icon.
- To edit a comment, insert a new comment, or delete a comment, right-click the comment icon, and select an option from the shortcut menu. You can also click the appropriate button on the Review tab, in the Comments group.
- To move the comment, click and drag the icon or comment box.
- To cycle through comments, click the Next button or Previous button in the Comments group.
- Comments will appear below the slide in Slide sorter view.
- Comments print with slides unless you choose to hide them. To print comment pages, click the Office Button, and then click Print. In the Print dialog box, select the Print comments and ink markup check box. The slide will print along with the printed comments page.

Project

- Several people often collaborate on the development of a presentation.
- The Comment feature allows multiple people to have input on a presentation. A comment can include opinions, suggestions, or reminders.

8. Display Slide 1. Run the slide show.
9. Make any necessary adjustments.
10. Display Slide 1.
11. Click the Review tab, and use the Next and Previous buttons to cycle through the comments.
    a. Delete the comment on Slide 9.
    b. Edit the comment on Slide 5. Add the following sentence to the comment: `Or, instruct the audience to go to our Website to view the statistics`.
12. Print one copy of the notes pages for Slides 1 and 2.
13. Print one copy of Slides 3 and 5 in pure black and white and include the comments pages.
14. Save the file as **5.3wireless final1**.
15. Close the file.

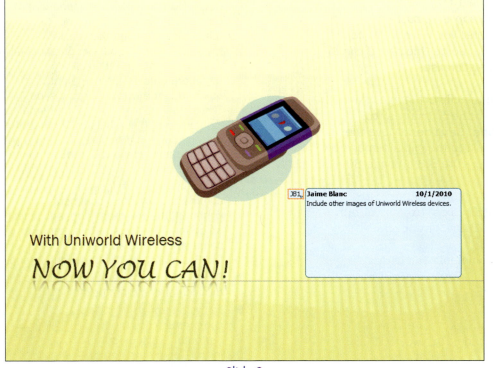

Slide 3

Figure 5.3

5.4 PREPARE A PRESENTATION TO TRAVEL

You are scheduled to deliver the A+ Test Prep presentation you completed in Project 3.3 to the seniors at Meadowland College next week. Because you will be using the computer equipment provided for you at Meadowland, you will need to prepare your presentation to travel. You have also been asked to send a copy of the presentation to the head of the career services office. You will first save the presentation as read-only so no changes can be made to it.

> **In this project, you will finalize the A+ Test Prep presentation you created earlier, copy the presentation to a CD, and then mark it as final.**

1. Open **3.3testprep**, the presentation that you completed in a previous project. If this file is not available to you, open the data file **d5.4testprep**.
2. Insert a comment on Slide 5 that reads: **Add an online link to a live connection or have Mary simulate it.**
3. Insert a comment on Slide 8 that reads: **Add a link to the newsletter page, if it is completed.**
4. Display the handout master.
   a. Insert the following header: **Presentation to Meadowland College Seniors**
   b. Include today's date.
   c. Include page numbers.
5. Edit the comment on Slide 8 to read: **Add a link to the newsletter page and news magazine page. Scan previous issue covers and link to the scanned images.** (See Figure 5.4.)
6. Delete the comment on Slide 5.
7. Copy this presentation to a CD if a CD is available to you. Otherwise, skip this step.
   • Embed TrueType fonts.
8. Print one copy of the slides as handouts with six slides per page.
9. Add a sound effect on the first slide.
10. Run the slide show and make any adjustments necessary.
11. Mark the presentation as final (read-only). *Note: A Marked as Final icon in the Status bar indicates that the presentation is read-only.*
12. Save the file as **5.4testprep final**.
13. Close the file.

▼ WHAT YOU NEED TO KNOW

Software

► If you must give your presentation on a computer other than the one you used to create it, you must take the presentation file with you. You can save your presentation to a blank recordable CD (CD-R), a blank rewritable CD (CD-RW), or a CD-RW with existing content that can be overwritten. *Note: If you use a CD-R, make sure you copy all the files you need onto the CD the first time. After the files are copied, you cannot add more files to the CD.*

► When you copy a presentation to a CD, Microsoft Office PowerPoint Viewer and any linked files (such as movies or sounds) are copied also. You can also choose to embed fonts, which ensures that the fonts you use in a presentation are available no matter what computer you use to deliver it.

► To save a presentation to a CD, display the presentation you want to save. Click the Office Button, point to Publish, and select Package for CD. In the Package for CD dialog box, enter a name for the CD in the Name the CD box. To add more presentations or other files, click Add Files and select the files you want to add. To embed fonts, click the Options button, and in the Options dialog box that appears, select the Embedded TrueType fonts check box and click OK. Then, click Copy to CD. Click Yes when prompted to include linked files.

► A *read-only* file can be viewed, but cannot be modified unless you save it with a new name or turn off read-only status. PowerPoint enables you to protect your file from further editing by using the Mark as Final command to make the document read-only and prevent inadvertent changes. When a document is marked as final, editing commands are disabled. The Mark as Final command can be removed from the document so that a reviewer who wants to make a change can do so.

► To mark a file as read-only, display the presentation you want to mark. Click the Office Button, point to Prepare, and then click Mark as Final. Click OK in any dialog boxes that open. *Note: A read-only document will display a Marked as Final icon in the status bar.*

Continued on next page

Project

► Reminder: If you plan to run your presentation on a computer other than your own, it is wise to embed fonts so that your presentation appears correctly with the fonts you used to create it. You should not assume that the fonts you used to create the presentation will be available on another computer.

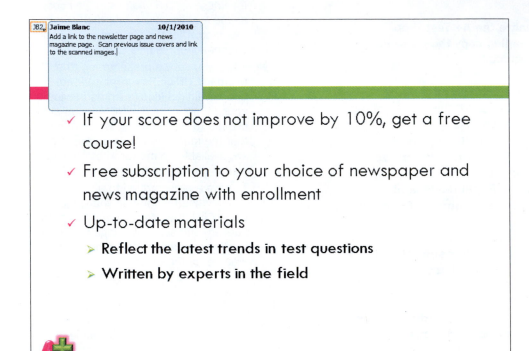

Slide 8

Figure 5.4

CHAPTER 6

Integration/PowerPoint and the Web

In this chapter, you will complete the following projects:

PROJECT 6
Integration/PowerPoint and the Web

PROJECT 6.1 Insert a Slide from Another Presentation
PROJECT 6.2 Export a Slide and a Presentation to Word
PROJECT 6.3 Insert an Excel Chart, an Excel Worksheet, and a Word Table
PROJECT 6.4 E-Mail a Presentation; Save and Preview a Presentation as a Web Page

PROJECT 6

PROJECT SKILLS

✳ Share data between Office applications
✳ Insert a slide from another presentation
✳ Export a presentation to Word
✳ Insert an Excel chart or worksheet
✳ Insert a Word table
✳ E-mail a presentation for review
✳ Save a presentation as a Web page
✳ Preview a presentation as a Web page

6.1 INSERT A SLIDE FROM ANOTHER PRESENTATION

Destinations Travel has invited your boss, Rita Bratton, to present information about travel packages to Paris, France to members of the Denver Chamber of Commerce. The chamber plans to sponsor a trip to Paris that will be open to all Denver residents. Ms. Bratton has asked you to enhance the draft presentation she has prepared.

In this project, you will use several slides from another presentation to enhance a presentation about Paris as a travel destination.

1. Open the data file **d6.1paris**.
2. Save the file as **6.1paris**.
3. Import Slides 1, 8, and 9 from the data file **d6.1ski** to become Slides 1, 8, and 9 in **6.1paris**. Keep the source file's formatting. (This will include the transitions and animations.) *Note: If necessary, switch to Slide Sorter view to move slides in the correct order.*
4. Edit Slide 1, as shown in Figure 6.1a.
   a. Insert a photo of a Paris attraction as the slide background. You can find such photos in the clip art gallery or online.
   b. Change the slide title to `Destination: Paris, France`.
   c. Change the slide subtitle to `Presentation to the Denver Chamber of Commerce`.
   d. If necessary, apply a new font color and style to the title and subtitle so that they are readable.
5. Edit Slide 8 as shown in Figure 6.1b.
   a. Change the slide layout as shown.
   b. Add the word `Services` as the last word in the title.
   c. Enter the additional services into the second column.

WHAT YOU NEED TO KNOW

Software

▶ You can insert one or more slides from another presentation (source document) into your current presentation (destination document). To do so, open the presentation in which you want to insert slides. In the Slides pane, click a slide where you want to insert your new slides (new slides will be inserted after the selected slide). Click the Home tab, and in the Slides group, click the New Slide button list arrow, and then click Reuse Slides. Enter the location and presentation filename of your source file in the Insert slide from text box, and click the right arrow button. If you do not know the location of the presentation, click Browse, and then click Browse File. Navigate to and select the file you want to insert, and click Open. Use Slide Sorter view to rearrange the slides, if necessary.

▶ The inserted slides will assume the same formatting as the destination slides, unless you select Keep source formatting in the Reuse Slides task pane.

6. Create a new slide master.
   a. Rename the master **Paris**.
   b. Apply any design theme to it.
   c. Apply the Berlin Sans FB font to the title text and Tw Cen MT to the bulleted text.
   d. Insert a footer on all slides that says **Paris, France**. Include today's date and slide number. Do not include the footer on the title slide.
   e. Apply a custom animation to the slide titles and bulleted text.
7. Apply the Paris slide master to Slides 2–7.
   Note: You may have to right-click each of these slides and select Reset Slide so that these slides take on the new slide master settings.
8. Edit Slide 4, as shown in Figure 6.1c.
   • Position the three photos (found in the data file folder **d6.1parisphotos**) appropriately on the slide. Apply the Bevel Relaxed Inset picture style to each of the photos. Position the photos horizontally on the slide, as shown on page 86.
9. Display Slide 6.
   a. Edit the slide title to read **Top Four Restaurants**.
   b. Go to: http://www.eatinparis.com.
   c. Review the restaurant listings and identify the top 10 Paris restaurants. List four of them on the slide. Link the slide title to the Website.
10. Display Slide 7.
    a. Edit the slide title to read **Top Four Hotels**.
    b. Go to: www.france.com. Click Hotels, and then click the Luxury Chain Paris Hotels link.
    c. Review the hotel listings. Select four luxury hotels and list them on the slide. Link the slide title to the Website.
11. Insert a new Title and Content slide as Slide 2. Use the Paris slide master layout.
    • Insert the title: **Overview**
    • Use the slide titles of Slides 3–10 as the bulleted text.
    • Insert a clip art image of a site in Paris.

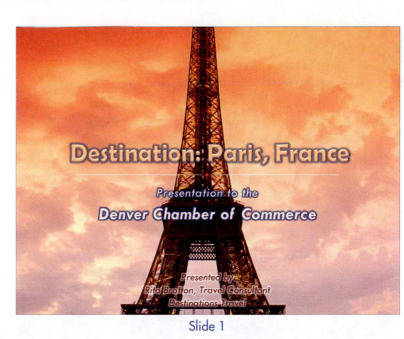

Slide 1

Figure 6.1a

Slide 8

Figure 6.1b

12. Insert photos or clip art on slides where appropriate.

13. Display the handout master.
   a. Apply an attractive background.
   b. Insert today's date and the title of the presentation as a header.

14. View the slide show.

15. Make any necessary adjustments to the transitions, animations, or other effects.

16. Save the file.

17. Print one copy of the slides as handouts with six slides per page.

18. Close all files.

Slide 4

Figure 6.1c

6.2 EXPORT A SLIDE AND A PRESENTATION TO WORD

In March, you are scheduled to show the slide presentation you enhanced in Project 6.1 to the Denver Chamber of Commerce. You now need to include the financial data and biographies of key executives, information that was not available previously. To confirm your scheduled presentation and provide information about the presentation content, you will create a letter with an overview slide inserted. You will also export the presentation as handouts to enclose with the letter.

In this project, you will insert a PowerPoint slide into a Word document. You will also include a slide with the biographies of key executives. You will then export the presentation as handouts to Word.

1. Open the data file **d6.2letterhead.docx**.
2. Create the letter, as shown in Figure 6.2.
    *   Use the margins and font settings that have already been applied to the letterhead (Times New Roman, 12 pt).
    *   Begin the date approximately 2.3" from the top of the page.
3. Open **6.1paris**, the presentation you created in the previous project.
4. Copy the Overview slide (Slide 2) and paste it into the letter where shown in Figure 6.2.
    a. Apply the In Line with Text text-wrap option, and center the slide.
    b. Size the slide so that the letter fits on one page.
5. Save the file as **6.2parisletter**.
6. Preview and print one copy.
7. Export the presentation **6.1paris** as handouts with blank lines next to slides to a new Word document.
    *   Delete the Overview slide and its corresponding blank lines. *Note: Because the handouts are in a table format, you should delete the row in the table that contains the Overview slide.*
8. Save the file as **6.2parishandouts**.
9. Preview and print one copy.
10. Close all files.

▼ WHAT YOU NEED TO KNOW

Software

► As you learned previously, Microsoft Office 2007 allows you to easily share data between applications. In PowerPoint, for example, you can insert data that has been created in Excel or Word to enhance your presentation.

► You can export slide text from a presentation to Word and format it to become notes pages or an outline. When creating an outline from slide text, each slide title translates into level 1 headings; bulleted lists translate into level 2 headings.

► To export a presentation, display the presentation. Then, click the Office Button, point to Publish, and click Create Handouts in Microsoft Office Word. In the Send To Microsoft Office Word dialog box, select an option and click OK. Word starts automatically, and the slide text exports to a new document in the format you chose.

► To export a slide to Word, copy the slide in PowerPoint (in Slide Sorter view or in the Slides pane). Then, paste it into Word using the Paste Special command. If you want to link the slide, click the Paste Link option in the Paste Special dialog box.

Destinations Travel

1276 Lindt Lane ■ Denver, CO ■ 80010 ■ Phone: 303-555-5555 ■ Fax: 303-555-6666

Today's date

Mr. David Greene, President
Denver Chamber of Commerce
455 Mountainview Lane
Denver, CO 80021

Dear Mr. Greene:

On Friday, March 12, I will be giving a presentation to the members of the Chamber of Commerce.
You indicated that the Chamber plans to sponsor a trip to Paris as part of its annual fundraising efforts.

To give you a general idea of the presentation, I'm including the overview slide, below, which lists the
slide titles from the presentation. Enclosed with this letter is a handout that includes slide miniatures
with lines next to them for notes. Please let me know if you have any comments about the presentation
or feel that I should include additional information.

[Insert slide here]

Thank you for the opportunity to present this exciting city to your members and to list the many
services our company provides.

Sincerely,

Rita Bratton
Travel Consultant

rb/
Enclosure

Figure 6.2

6.3 INSERT AN EXCEL CHART, AN EXCEL WORKSHEET, AND A WORD TABLE

In Project 4.2, you created a business plan presentation for Health Connections. You now need to include the financial data or contact information for key employees, information that was not available previously. You also need to finalize the presentation by adding transitions, animations, and clip art.

In this project, you will insert the financial data on a selected slide. You will also include a slide with the contact information of key employees. You will then finalize the presentation using the enhancements you have learned previously.

1. Open **4.2hcbusplan**, the presentation you created earlier. If this file is not available to you, open the data file **d6.3hcbusplan**. pptx

2. Save the file as **6.3hcbusplan**.

3. On Slide 8 (Projected Cash Flow Statement):
   a. Import the data file **d6.3cashflow.xlsx** as a linked file, as shown in Figure 6.3a.
   b. Size the worksheet to fill the slide.
   c. Change the background color of the worksheet object to white, so that the text is visible.
   Note: You can format the worksheet object as you would any other object.

4. On Slide 9 (Comparative Balance Sheet):
   a. Import the data file **d6.3balancesheet.xlsx** as a linked file, as shown in Figure 6.3b.
   b. Size the table to fill the slide.
   c. Change the background color of the worksheet object to white so that the text is visible.

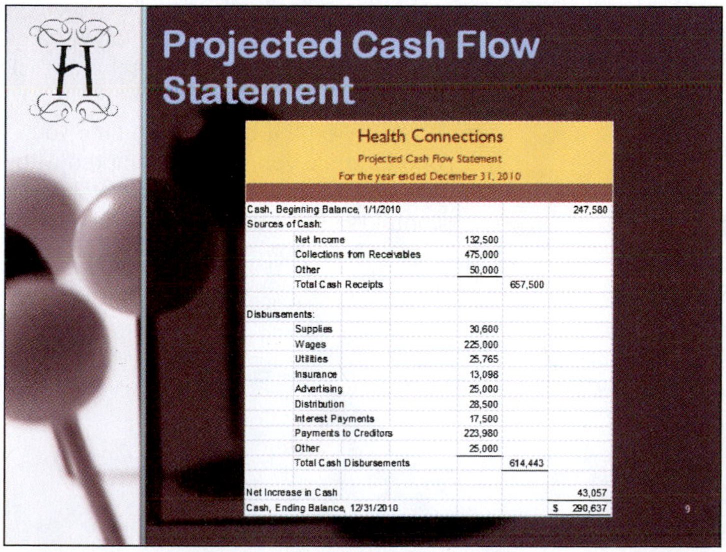

Slide 8

Figure 6.3a

WHAT YOU NEED TO KNOW

Software

▶ Imported charts and worksheets function like other objects—that is, you can size, copy, move, edit, or delete them.

▶ There are two ways to import an object—as an embedded object or as a linked object. Each method has a different effect on data. For example, if you import a chart by copying it from the source file and pasting it in the destination file, you embed the object. With an embedded object, data in the destination file does not change if you modify the source file.

▶ You can also import data as a linked object. With a linked object, any change made to the source file is automatically updated in the destination file. The source and destination files are connected by the link.

▶ To import a chart or worksheet as a linked object, display the slide on which you want to add the object. Click the Insert tab and in the Text group, click the Object button. In the Insert Object dialog box, click Create from file, and then click Browse. Select the folder and filename that contains the Excel chart or worksheet you want to insert, and click OK. If you want to create a linked file, click the Link check box, and then click OK. The imported chart or worksheet appears in a placeholder (if the slide contains one).

▶ Another way to import a chart or worksheet is to copy the worksheet or chart. To do so, open the Excel file from which you want to copy the chart or worksheet. Right-click the chart or selected cells on the worksheet, and select Copy. Switch to PowerPoint, and select the slide on which you want to paste the chart or worksheet. Click the Home tab, and in the Clipboard group, click the Paste button list arrow and choose Paste Special. In the Paste Special dialog box, select Microsoft Office Excel Worksheet Object (or Microsoft Office Excel 2003 Worksheet Object if you are using an .xls file, or Microsoft Office Graphic Object if you are selecting a chart), and choose the Paste or Paste link options, and then click OK.

Continued on next page

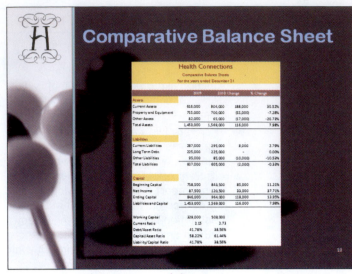

Slide 9

Figure 6.3b

As with charts and worksheets, you can insert tables you created in Word onto a slide. Once inserted, tables also function like other objects. The procedure for inserting a Word table as an embedded or linked object into PowerPoint is the same as for charts and worksheets.

To insert a table as a linked object, display the slide on which you want to insert the object (Word table). Click the Insert tab and in the Text group, then click the Object button. In the Insert Object dialog box, click Create from file. In the Insert Object dialog box that now opens, enter the location and filename that contains the Word table or click Browse to navigate and select the file, and then click OK. If you want to create a linked file, click the Link check box, and then click OK.

5. Insert a new Title Only slide as Slide 4.
   a. Include the title: **Senior Management Team Biographies**.
   b. Copy the table from the data file **d6.3mgmtteam.docx** and paste it on the slide.
6. Insert a new slide as Slide 11.
   a. Apply a Title and Content slide layout.
   b. Insert the title **See the Overall Picture for Two Years**.
   c. Import the chart on the Chart1 tab of the data file **d6.3incomestatement.xlsx** as a linked file, as shown in Figure 6.3c.
   d. Size the chart to fill the slide. Adjust the placeholder, if necessary.
7. Display Slide 12 (See the Growth).
   • Edit the title to read **See the Growth in Net Income**.
8. Apply transitions and animations to all slides.
9. Run the slide show.
   • Use the annotation pen to point out the growth areas on the data slides.
10. Display the handout master.
    a. Apply an attractive background.
    b. Insert **Health Connections** and today's date as a header.
11. Switch to the Excel file **d6.3cashflow.xlsx**. Change the Cash, Beginning Balance to **$250,000**.
12. Switch to the presentation file, Slide 9 (Projected Cash Flow). Notice that the file has been updated with new data for Cash Beginning Balance.
13. Repeat Steps 11 and 12 to return the Cash, Beginning Balance to **$247,580**.
14. Print one copy of the slides as handouts with six slides per page.
15. Save the presentation file.
16. Close all files.

To insert a table using the copy and paste commands, open the Word file that contains the table you want to copy. Select the table, right-click, and select Copy. Switch to PowerPoint and select the slide on which you want to paste the table. Click the Home tab, and in the Clipboard group, click the Paste button list arrow, and choose Paste Special. In the Paste Special dialog box, select Microsoft Office Word Document Object, if it is not already selected, choose the Paste or Paste link option, and then click OK.

If you make changes to the source file, you must update the slide containing the destination file. To do this, right-click the slide containing the destination file's linked object and click Update Link.

If you linked the chart, each time you open the file you will be prompted with a reminder that the file you are opening contains linked data. Respond to the prompt appropriately.

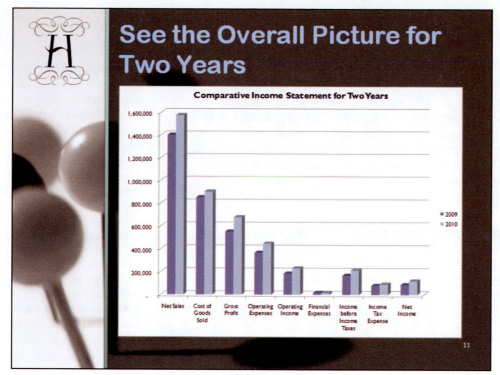

Slide 11

Figure 6.3c

6.4 E-MAIL A PRESENTATION; SAVE AND PREVIEW A PRESENTATION AS A WEB PAGE

Meadowland College has asked you to finalize the Freshman Orientation presentation that was created in a previous project and post it to the Web for those students who cannot attend the orientation session. However, before the presentation is posted to the Web, the Dean of Admissions would like to review it. Therefore, you will e-mail a copy of the presentation to the Dean for his review before it is considered truly final.

In this project, you will finalize the presentation you created in PowerPoint Project 2.3 and attach it to an e-mail. You will then save and preview the presentation as a Web page. Unless your instructor advises otherwise, you will not actually post this presentation to the Web.

1. Open **2.3meadowland orientation**. If this file is not available to you, open the data file **d6.4meadowland orientation**.
2. Insert a new slide as the last slide of the presentation.
   a. Apply the Section Header layout.
   b. Include the following:
      - `Learn more about the Princeton community`.
      - `Call or e-mail Linda Grey, Freshman Advisor, with any questions or issues`.
   c. Create a WordArt object for the words "Meadowland College." Center the WordArt at the top of the slide, as shown in Figure 6.4.
   d. Create a link on the word "Princeton" to www.princetonol.com.
   e. Create a link on the name "Linda Grey" to her e-mail address lg@mc.edu.
3. Insert an appropriate music clip on the first slide.
4. Display the handout master.
   a. Set the page to display six slides per page.
   b. Insert **Meadowland College** and **Freshman Orientation** as the header.
   c. Include today's date and page number.
   d. Apply an attractive background.
5. Save the presentation as **6.4meadowland orientation**.
6. E-mail **6.4meadowland orientation** to Dean Hubbard.
   a. Click the Office Button, point to Send, and click E-Mail.
   b. In the e-mail header window, enter `hubbard@mc.edu` in the To text box.
   c. Enter `Freshman Orientation Presentation` in the Subject text box.

WHAT YOU NEED TO KNOW

Software

▶ It is common practice to collaborate with others when developing a presentation. Doing so often requires that you e-mail the presentation to one or more people for review.

▶ When you e-mail a presentation, the presentation will be attached as a PowerPoint file and the filename automatically appears in the Subject text box, which you can change, of course. If you are sending the presentation to someone who might not have PowerPoint, you should save the presentation as a PowerPoint Show file. This format will open your presentation as a Slide Show on any computer running Microsoft Office, but it does not allow you to use PowerPoint features, such as comments.

▶ To e-mail a presentation, open the presentation you want to e-mail. Click the Office Button, point to Send, and click E-mail. In the e-mail header window that opens, enter a recipient's e-mail address in the To text box. Enter a subject in the Subject text box, and enter the text of a message you want to send in the body of the message. Then, click Send.

▶ You can save any presentation as a Web page or as a single file Web page. A *single file Web page* saves all the elements of a Website, including text and graphics, into a single file. Doing so allows you to publish your entire Website as a single encapsulated aggregate HTML document (called an MHTML file).

▶ When you view a presentation saved as a Web page or single file Web page in a browser, PowerPoint automatically displays *frames*, which are regions or sub-windows on the page that make navigating the presentation easier and more Web-friendly.

▶ To save a presentation as a Web page or single file Web page, display the presentation you want to save. Click the Office Button, point to Save As, and click Other Formats. In the Save As dialog box, enter a filename, click the Save as type list arrow, and then select Web Page or Single File Web Page.

Continued on next page

d. Enter the following in the message window:

```
Dean Hubbard:
As you requested, I am attaching
a copy of the presentation that
will be delivered at this year's
freshman orientation. Please let me
have your comments by end of the
day tomorrow.
Thank you.
```

e. Type your name below the message.

f. Close the e-mail window. *Note: Because Dean Hubbard's address is fictitious, you will not actually send the e-mail.*

7. Switch to **6.4meadowland orientation**.

8. Save the presentation as a Single File Web Page.

a. Name it **6.4meadowland orientation web**.

b. Change the title of the Web page to:
Meadowland College: Freshman Orientation.

9. Preview the presentation in your browser and test the links. Make any adjustments necessary to the text or graphics if the slide does not display the contents properly.

10. Close all files.

In the Save As dialog box that opens, you can click the Change Title button and enter a Web page title in the Page title text box.

▶ You can preview a presentation in your Web browser so that you can see how PowerPoint positions backgrounds, text wraps, and graphics on a Web page. To do so, click the Office Button, and click Open. In the Open dialog box, click the All files button list arrow, and select All Web Pages to display only the saved Web page files. Select the file to open, click the Open button list arrow, and select Open in Browser. This opens your presentation in Internet Explorer.

▶ You cannot edit a presentation in a browser if you saved it as a Single File Web Page.

▶ Saving a presentation as a Web page does not mean the page has been posted to the Web. You can easily publish your presentation to the Web, which means you are actually publishing it to a Web server, from which an audience can view it with a browser. This requires that you contact your Internet service provider or that you install Web server software.

Figure 6.4

CHAPTER 1
Access Basics

CHAPTER 2
Access Tables and
Datasheets

CHAPTER 3
Access Forms

CHAPTER 4
Getting Information

CHAPTER 5
Access Reports

CHAPTER 6
Integration

CHAPTER 1

Access Basics

In this chapter, you will complete the following projects:

PROJECT 1
Explore a Database
PROJECT 1.1 Explore Tables and Forms
PROJECT 1.2 Explore Queries and Reports

PROJECT 2
Understand Database Design and Views
PROJECT 2.1 Explore Table and Form Views
PROJECT 2.2 Explore Query and Report Views

PROJECT SKILLS
* Start Access
* Explore the Access database screen
* Explore the Navigation Pane
* Explore database objects
* Close a database

1.1 EXPLORE TABLES AND FORMS

Creative Services, Inc. is a small New York company that arranges seminars, meetings, and conferences for its clients. It has started its database with a customer list and an employee list, which you will open and review.

In this project, you will start Access, explore the Access opening and database screens, open a database, and explore tables and forms.

1. Start Access, and on the Access opening screen under the Template Categories, click Local Templates. Review the choices for templates by clicking each one to view an explanation of its purpose, as shown in Figure 1.1a.

2. Click the Office Button, click Open, and then locate and double-click on the data file **d1.1cs**. You will see the Navigation Pane on the left containing all the objects organized by tables.

3. In the Navigation Pane, click the list arrow on the menu bar to note the sorts that can be applied to the database objects in the file. The default setting is Tables and Related Views.

4. Click the Object Type setting to view the parts of the database organized by object type. Click the menu bar arrow, and then click Tables and Related Views to return to the default setting.

5. Note the table icon next to the object name Customers: Table. Double-click the name and note that the file opens in the work pane.

6. Review the customer data list, as shown in Figure 1.1b, using the scroll bar to view all the fields (columns) and records (rows). *Note: You can double-click a column border to view its full width*.

7. Press the right arrow key to move the insertion point to each field. Notice the field names at the top of each column, the data in each field, and the Customer Number field, which is the primary key. There is no indication of the primary key field here, but it is the field that provides unique identification data for the record.

WHAT YOU NEED TO KNOW

Software

▶ A database is an organized collection of facts about a particular subject that can be maintained electronically.

▶ Access is a database management system that provides functions to store, search, filter, query, link, and report on the data in a database. Database objects are the tools in the database that perform all the management activities.

▶ To open a database file, click the Office Button, click Open, locate the file, and then click Open. All the objects in a database are stored under one filename. The database objects we will use are tables, forms, queries, and reports, which can be created, maintained, organized, and viewed using the Navigation Pane on the left side of the screen and the work pane at the right. The Navigation Pane has a menu bar where you can change how the objects are listed on the pane.

▶ Each object is represented by its name and an icon. The table and form objects are used to enter, edit, and display the records in a database. In a table, the data is formatted in a spreadsheet format so that each row represents one record in the database. In a form, one record at a time is visible, which makes it easy to enter or edit data. Double-click a table or form object to open and display it in the work pane.

Continued on next page

8. Click each of the tabs on the ribbon to view the command options for the table object. Note that the Table Tools Datasheet tab is active when a table is open.

9. Close the Customers table, saving changes if asked, and double-click Employees: Table to open the Employees table. Which field is the primary key? Close the Employees table.

10. Double-click the Customers Form object, as shown in Figure 1.1c. Notice the icon for forms next to the object name.

11. Use the navigation buttons at the bottom of the form to review the records one at a time.

12. Click each of the tabs on the ribbon to review the command options for the form object.

13. Close the form and then open the Employees form object.

14. Move to Record 7 and notice the blank form to enter a new employee.

15. Close the form and close the database.

▶ When defining data in a table or form, there should be one field that is unique and can act as the identifier for each record. This may be a customer number, employee number, Social Security number, and so on. The unique field that identifies each data item is called a primary key.

▶ When a database is closed all changes are automatically saved. Click the Office Button, and then click Close Database.

Project

▶ Creative Services, Inc. employs account managers who develop and work with specific clients.

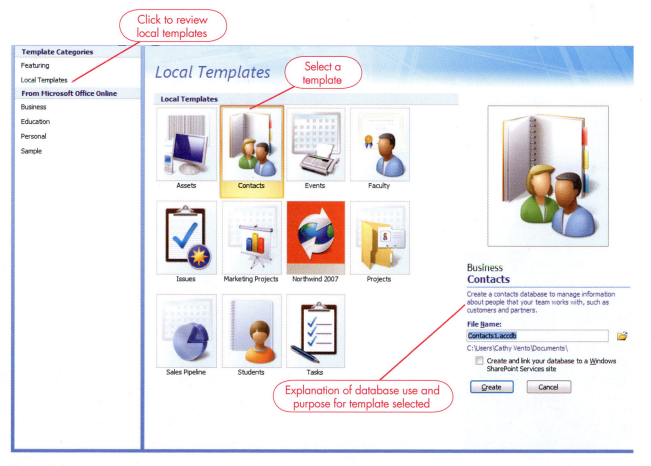

Figure 1.1a Access opening screen

Cust	Company Name	Street Address	Telephone N	Contact	Account I	Date of Initial	Preferr	Last Year Revenue	Add
0001	Park Ave Investments	122 Park Ave	(212) 555-9090	Anna Jones	Jane	12/1/2003	1	$45,000	
0014	Fifth Avenue Medical Practic	45 Fifth Avenue	(212) 555-0987	Tom Evans	Beth	2/3/2004	3	$100,000	
0022	Delaney Law Firm	23 Broadway	(212) 555-8888	Ed Tobias	Margie	5/12/2007	4	$78,000	
0034	Bradford Traders	2 42nd Street	(212) 555-9393	Jim Pon	Sam	12/2/2003	6	$54,000	
0040	Superior Consultants	122 72nd Ave	(212) 555-9999	Joan Sullivan	Tom	12/1/2004	2	$67,000	
0055	Wall Street Art Gallery	54 Wall Street	(212) 555-5454	Kristen Avery	George	12/1/2004	4	$25,000	
0060	Scott Law Firm	2 East Ave	(212) 555-3338	Niki Santos	Margie	5/12/2005	5	$78,000	
0074	Soho Tours	123 West Ave	(212) 555-0981	Evan Green	Beth	2/3/2006	4	$43,000	
0080	Monet Art Gallery	54 Walnut Street	(212) 555-5458	Liz Roth	George	3/1/2006	6	$90,000	
0090	Jewelry Exchange	122 43rd Street	(212) 555-2333	Paul White	Sam	6/9/2007	3	$120,000	
0101	East Ave Investments	12 East Ave	(212) 555-9090	Andrew Jones	Jane	12/1/2008	3	$49,000	
0114	West Avenue Legal Practice	4 West Avenue	(212) 555-0987	Evan Smith	Beth	2/3/2004	1	$58,000	
0122	O'Mara Law Firm	23 Gilbert Street	(212) 555-8888	Tobias Davis	Margie	5/12/2004	4	$98,000	
0134	Valerie Designers	2 2nd Street	(212) 555-7393	Tom Pond	Sam	12/2/2003	2	$80,000	
0140	Technical Consultants	22 2nd Ave	(212) 555-9999	Jo Moran	Tom	12/1/2003	2	$66,000	
0155	Post Art Gallery	54 Post Street	(212) 555-5454	Avery Adams	Tom	12/1/2004	1	$98,000	
0160	Engles Law Firm	2 North Ave	(212) 555-3338	Nick Jules	Margie	5/12/2007	3	$87,900	
0174	Ski Tours	123 West Ave	(212) 555-0981	Ellenor Breen	Beth	2/3/2009	6	$89,000	
0180	Togo Art Gallery	54 Maplet Street	(212) 555-5458	Lizzie Tish	George	3/1/2009	6	$58,000	
0190	Apex Jewelry	12 3rd Street	(212) 555-4443	Paula Black	Sam	8/9/2009	5	$98,000	
*								$0	

Figure 1.1b Table object

Customers Form

Customers

Customer Number:	0001
Company Name:	Park Ave Investments
Street Address:	122 Park Ave
Telephone Number:	(212) 555-9090
Contact:	Anna Jones
Account Manager:	Tom / Jane / Sam
Date of Initial Order:	12/1/2003
Preferred Caterer:	1
Last Year Revenue:	$45,000

Navigation bar

Record: 1 of 20   No Filter   Search

Num Lock

Figure 1.1c Form object

Creative Services, Inc. has created queries and reports from the data in the CS database that you will view.

> **In this project, you will explore the queries and reports created from the data in the CS database.**

1. Open data file **d1.2cs**.
2. Notice the query icons and the two queries in the database, which are Full Week Payroll and Number of Accounts.
3. The first query, Full Week Payroll, shown in Figure 1.2a, is the result of a query to calculate the payroll for a 40-hour week. The information is obtained from the Employees table and by using a mathematical expression. Double-click the query to see the answers.
4. Click the tabs on the ribbon to review the command options for queries. Close the query.
5. The second query, Number of Accounts, is the result of a query to find out how many accounts each manager controls. The information is gathered from both the Customers and Employees tables. Double-click the query to see the answers. Close the query.
6. Note the report icon and the two reports in the database.
7. Double-click the first report, Account Manager Customer Summary, shown in Figure 1.2b, to view a report on customers grouped by account manager.
8. On the Print Preview tab in the Zoom group, click the Zoom button arrow and then select Zoom 100%. Notice that the report is formatted and the data is easy to read. What was the revenue earned last year from George's clients? Close the report.
9. Double-click the Employee List report to view a report listing the information on the company's employees. Close the report.
10. Close the database.

Software

▶ Queries are objects in the database management system designed to retrieve data that meets certain criteria. The data specified in the query object appears in a table format. When you save a query, only the criteria are stored. Therefore, each time a query is opened, the database is queried and any new data will be included.

▶ Reports are objects that display or analyze formatted information retrieved from the database. You can use them to present data to interested parties, and you can create them from data in tables or queries.

Project

▶ The account managers work on an hourly rate and generally work part time. The owner created a query to see what the weekly salaries would be if the account managers worked a 40-hour week.

▶ The company is taking on some new clients and has created a query to find out the number of customers assigned to each account manager so that new customers can be assigned to those with the fewest accounts.

▶ Reports have been created to display the data from the Employees table and to summarize the customer list by account manager and revenues.

Full Week Payroll

Last Name ▾	Hourly Wage ▾	40 Hour Salary ▾
Moran	$25.30	$1,012.00
Plut	$27.50	$1,100.00
Samson	$22.00	$880.00
Smith	$22.00	$880.00
Taylor	$24.20	$968.00
Wilshire	$25.30	$1,012.00

Figure 1.2a Query object

Calculated field

Account Manager Customer Summary

Account Manager	Company Name	Customer Number	Telephone Number	Contact	Last Year
Beth	Fifth Avenue Medical Practice	0014	(212) 555-0987	Tom Evans	$100,000
	Ski Tours	0174	(212) 555-0981	Ellenor Breen	$89,000
	Soho Tours	0074	(212) 555-0981	Evan Green	$43,000
	West Avenue Legal Practice	0114	(212) 555-0987	Evan Smith	$58,000
Summary for 'Account Manager' = Beth (4 detail records)					
Sum					$290,000
George	Monet Art Gallery	0080	(212) 555-5458	Liz Roth	$90,000
	Togo Art Gallery	0180	(212) 555-5458	Lizzie Tish	$58,000
	Wall Street Art Gallery	0055	(212) 555-5454	Kristen Avery	$25,000
Summary for 'Account Manager' = George (3 detail records)					
Sum					$173,000
Jane	East Ave Investments	0101	(212) 555-9090	Andrew Jones	$49,000
	Park Ave Investments	0001	(212) 555-9090	Anna Jones	$45,000
Summary for 'Account Manager' = Jane (2 detail records)					
Sum					$94,000
Margie	Delaney Law Firm	0022	(212) 555-8888	Ed Tobias	$78,000
	Engles Law Firm	0160	(212) 555-3338	Nick Jules	$87,900
	O'Mara Law Firm	0122	(212) 555-8888	Tobias Davis	$98,000
	Scott Law Firm	0060	(212) 555-3338	Niki Santos	$78,000
Summary for 'Account Manager' = Margie (4 detail records)					
Sum					$341,900
Sam	Apex Jewelry	0190	(212) 555-4443	Paula Black	$98,000
	Bradford Traders	0034	(212) 555-9393	Jim Pon	$54,000

Page 1 of 2

Figure 1.2b Report object

PROJECT SKILLS

✱ Understand database views
✱ Understand database design
✱ View the Relationships window

PROJECT 2

2.1 EXPLORE TABLE AND FORM VIEWS

Creative Services, Inc has added a new table to its database. You will familiarize yourself with the updated database.

In this project, you will review the database objects in all views especially Design view, notice the primary field, and explore the concepts of database design.

1. Open the data file **d2.1cs**.
2. Double-click the new Caterers table. Click the View button arrow on the Home tab to see the views that are available for a table object. Click Design View.
3. Notice the primary key symbol next to the Caterer No field name. This is a primary key field, and it has an AutoNumber data type.
4. In the row for the Company field, click in the Data Type column, and then click the list arrow to review the list of data type settings, as shown in Figure 2.1a.
5. Click the Telephone Number field. Notice the Input Mask in the Field Properties pane at the bottom of the Design view window.
6. Notice the Table Tools Design tab that appears in Design view. Close the table.
7. Double-click the Customers table. Right-click the Customers tab and then click Design View. Notice the data types and the primary key. Close the table.
8. View the Employees table in Design view. Notice the Currency data type for the Hourly Wage field. Close the table.
9. Double-click the Customers form and then view it in Design, Form, and Layout views. Close the form.
10. Open the Employees form and then switch to Layout view. Notice and review the Form Layout Tools Format and Arrange tabs that appear in Layout view. Close the form.
11. Click the Database Tools tab, and then click the Relationships button to view the relationships between tables in the Relationships window, as shown in Figure 2.1b. Note how the tables are linked using fields they have in common. Close the window.
12. Close the database.

WHAT YOU NEED TO KNOW

Software

▶ Because reports, queries, and forms rely on tables, tables are created first. Each field in a table should relate to the subject of the table, and one unique field is designated as the primary key to identify the record. Data should not be duplicated in tables unless it is there to relate to another table.

▶ A database view is a way to look at the data or the structure of a database object. On the Home tab in the Views group, the View button allows you to change the view of the object, or you can right-click the title bar of the object and change views on the shortcut menu that appears.

▶ A table has four views, but generally you will use Design or Datasheet view. Design view is where you can create and modify table structures. Datasheet view is the tabular view where you can add, edit, delete, and view data. The PivotTable and PivotChart views summarize the table data. In Design view, you will see that the primary key field is identified with a key icon in the far left column. The bottom section of Design view shows the properties for each selected field.

▶ Forms have three views: Design, Layout, and Form. As with tables, you can modify and create the form in Design view. In Layout view you can add a variety of formats and change the arrangement of data.

▶ You can view any object in Design view by selecting the object, clicking the View button arrow on the Home tab, and clicking Design View, or by right-clicking the object tab in the work pane and selecting the view from the shortcut menu.

Continued on next page

► To be able to use data from different tables in forms, queries, and reports, a relationship should be established between tables by linking common field data. You can view the relationships between tables by clicking the Database Tools tab and then clicking the Relationships button in the Show/Hide group. In the Relationships window, the links between tables with common data are shown.

Relationships

Project

► Creative Services has added another table to its database. Be sure you review all the fields in each table and notice the primary key and fields that relate tables to each other.

► The tables are related through the account managers and the caterers. The first name of the account manager is in the Customers table and the Employees table. The primary key, or Caterer No, for the Caterers table is used in the Customers table as the Preferred Caterer field.

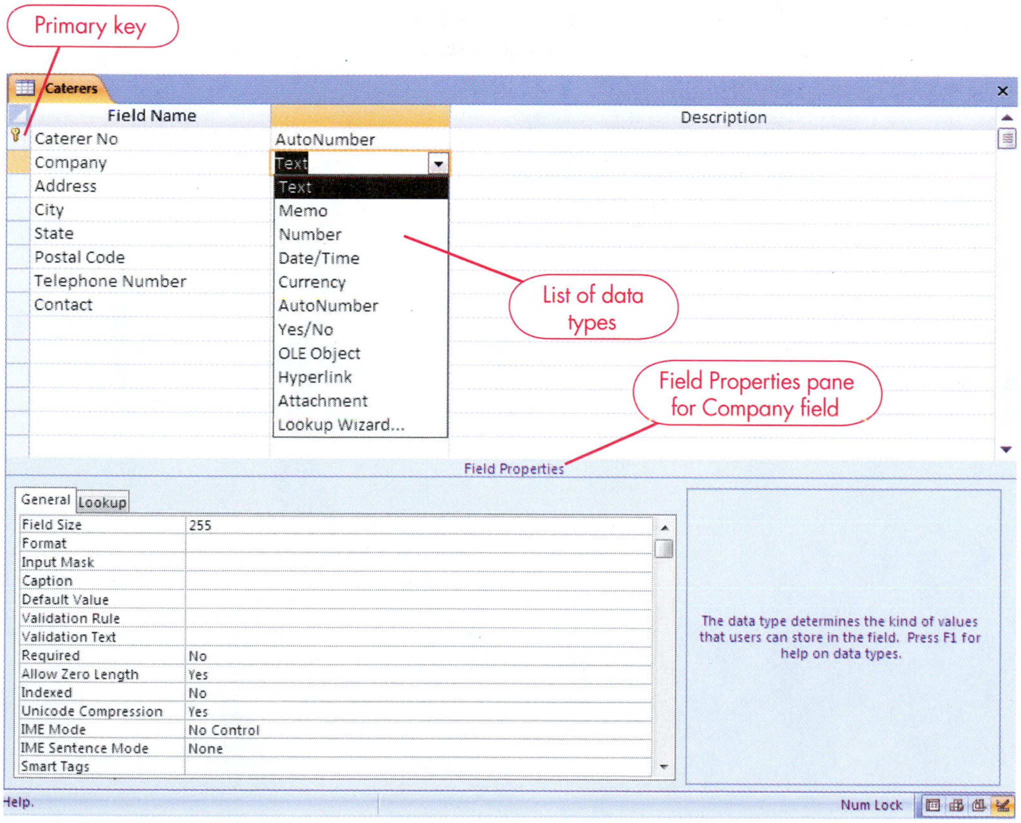

Figure 2.1a Table Design view

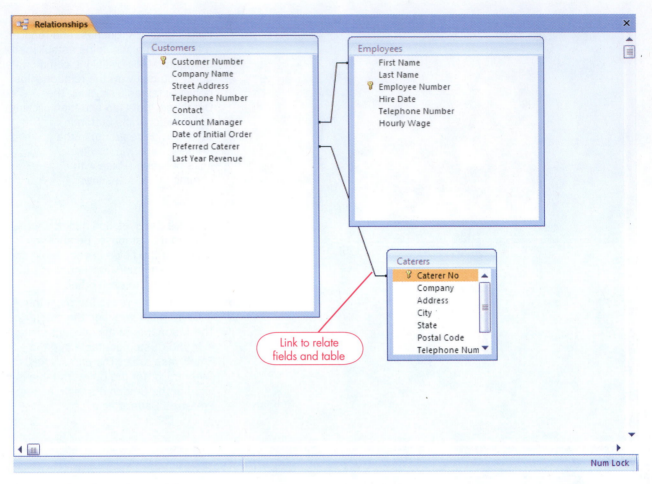

Figure 2.1b Relationships window

2.2 EXPLORE QUERY AND REPORT VIEWS

Creative Services, Inc. uses Design and Layout views to edit and enhance its queries and reports, which you are to review.

In this project, you will review Design and Layout views for queries and reports.

1. Open data file **d2.2cs**.
2. Double-click the Full Week Payroll query. Notice the fields in the query table.
3. Click the View button arrow and notice the views that are available for queries. Click Design View.
4. Notice the table in the query at the top, the fields displayed for the query at the bottom, and the expression column, as shown in Figure 2.2a. The expression column contains a formula (not visible) to calculate the salary for a 40-hour week. Drag the right edge of the column to widen it to view the formula.
5. Notice the Query Tools Design tab and the commands available to modify the query. Save and close the query.
6. View the Number of Accounts query in Design view and notice the two tables in the query. Switch to Datasheet view to see how the design is reflected in Datasheet view. Both tables can be used in one query because the tables are related. Close the query.
7. Double-click the Account Manager Customer Summary report. Notice that it opens in Print Preview with the appropriate tab and commands.
8. In the work pane, right-click the report tab and notice the views that are available for reports. Click Design View.
9. Notice the Report Header, Page Header, and Detail sections, as shown in Figure 2.2b.
10. Note the Report Design Tools Design, Arrange, and Page Setup tabs. Click each to view the commands.
11. Right-click the report tab and change to Layout view. Note the Report Layout Tools Format, Arrange, and Page Setup tabs. Click each to view the commands. Close the report.
12. Select and review the Employee List report in Print Preview, Design, and Layout views. Close the report.
13. Close the database.

WHAT YOU NEED TO KNOW

Software

▶ Queries and reports have several views that may be used to view, edit, or enhance the objects. Use the View button arrow to change views or right-click the object tab in the work pane to change views.

▶ In query Design view, the tables in the query are shown along with the fields that should be displayed in the results table. New tabs appear with tools to modify the design. Notice the result of the query after looking at the design.

▶ In report Design view, notice the header, footer, and detail sections and the Print Preview tab that appears.

Project

▶ Creative Services, Inc. used a wizard to create its reports, but it uses Design view to enhance, edit, and change the reports.

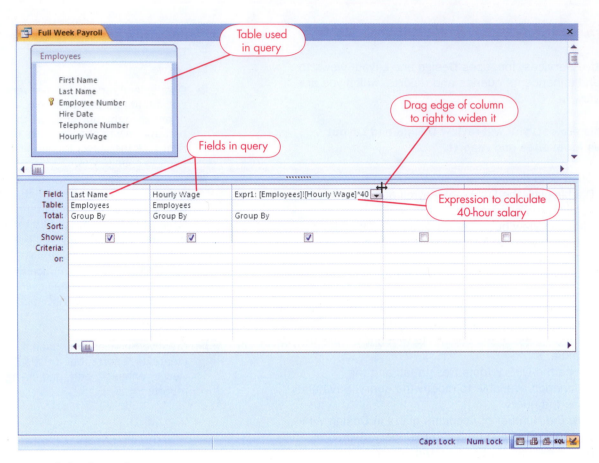

Figure 2.2a Query Design view

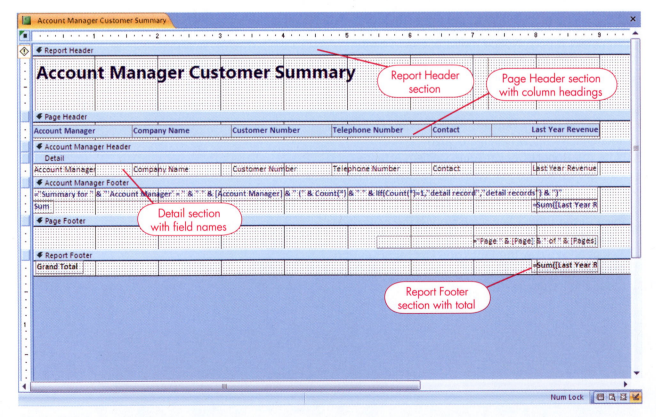

Figure 2.2b Report Design view

CHAPTER 2

Access Tables and Datasheets

In this chapter, you will complete the following projects:

PROJECT 3
Create a Table with Table Templates

PROJECT 3.1 Create a Tasks Table
PROJECT 3.2 Create a Contacts Table for Customers

PROJECT 4
Create Tables and Enter Data

PROJECT 4.1 Create a Students Table in Datasheet View
PROJECT 4.2 Create an Inventory Table in Design View

PROJECT 5
Enhance Tables and Create Relationships

PROJECT 5.1 Create a Member Table with a Lookup Field
PROJECT 5.2 Add Input Masks to a Students Table
PROJECT 5.3 Add Input Masks to a Customers Table
PROJECT 5.4 Create and Format a Property Listing Table with an Input Mask and Lookup Fields
PROJECT 5.5 Create and Print Relationships between Inventory and Vendor Tables

PROJECT 3

▶ **PROJECT SKILLS**
✶ Create a new file with a blank database
✶ Create tables from templates
✶ Add, set, change, and remove the primary key
✶ Delete fields from a table
✶ Enter data using a datasheet
✶ Use navigation controls to move through records in a datasheet
✶ Delete records from a table
✶ Modify field size settings

3.1 CREATE A TASKS TABLE

Zack Tremaine wants you to set up a database to keep a record of his projects and reports that are due this semester.

> In this project, you will use the Tasks table template to create and enter data into a datasheet and will then view the table design.

1. Open a blank database and name it **3.1tasks**. Locate the folder for your database solutions, click OK, and then click Create. Close the blank table that displays.
2. Click the Create tab, and in the Tables group, click the Table Templates button, and then select Tasks.
3. Note the fields that appear, as shown in Figure 3.1a. The field column header with the paper clip symbol is the Attachments field. Save the table and name it **Fall Semester**.
4. Switch to Design view and note the primary key field, each of the other fields and their data type, and the Attachments field, as shown in Figure 3.1b. The primary key field is an AutoNumber data type, which will automatically enter and increment the numbers as you enter data. Click the Primary Key button once to remove the primary key setting, and then click it again to restore the primary key setting. Return to Datasheet view.
5. Right-click the Attachments field column header, and then click Delete Column. Delete the Start Date column.
6. Right-click the ID field column header, click Rename Column, rename it **Task ID**, and then press [Enter].
7. Double-click the Add New Field column header, enter the field name **Professor**, and then press [Enter].
8. Switch to Design view, and note that the default data type setting for the new field is Text. Switch back to Datasheet view.

▼ WHAT YOU NEED TO KNOW

Software

▶ A database file can be created by using a database template or by using a blank database and building your own database objects. Tables are generally created first to list the records in the database. On the Getting Started with Microsoft Office Access page, click the Blank Database button, enter a filename, click the folder icon to place it in the correct folder, click OK, and then click Create.

▶ Access provides five table templates with field names and data types. You may customize the template for your purposes. Click the Create tab, and in the Tables group, click the Table Templates button and select one of the templates.

▶ Each field has a specific data type, or attribute, that determines what kind of information the field can contain. The field data type is defined in Design view.

▶ A primary key, a field that is unique and that identifies the data, should be set for the records in a table. This field is usually an ID number, set to AutoNumber data type, which Access creates automatically as you enter the records.

▶ To delete a field in Datasheet view, right-click on the field column header and then click Delete Column.

Continued on next page

9. Enter the data from Figure 3.1c, using [Tab] and the arrow keys to move between the fields. Access will enter consecutive numbers automatically in the Task ID field. The data is listed as the projects are assigned. *Note: The Priority column is a lookup field where you can select the appropriate entry using the list arrow. Also, the text will not wrap in the Access table.*

10. Use the arrow keys to go to Task ID 3. Right-click the record selector box on the left and then delete the task because Zack has decided to take an exam rather than complete the paper.

11. Close the table and the database.

12. Reopen the database and table to see that the data was automatically saved when the file was closed.

13. Close the table and the database.

▶ To enter data in a table, input the data in the appropriate field as you would in a spreadsheet, and then use [Tab] or the arrow keys to move between fields or to the next record. When you close the file, Access automatically saves all the data you entered.

▶ To delete a record in Datasheet view, select the row by right-clicking the record selector box, the small box to the left of the first field, and then click Delete Record. You must confirm the deletion.

Project

▶ The table template choices are Contacts, Tasks, Issues, Events, and Assets. The Tasks template will be used to record due dates for projects and reports for Zack Tremaine, a college student.

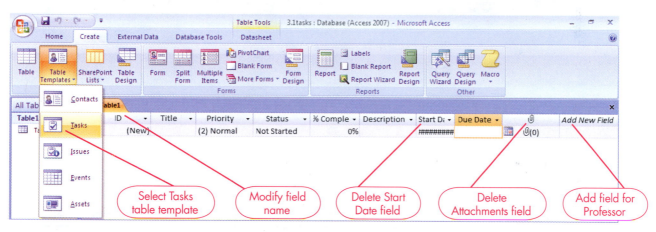

Figure 3.1a Tasks table template

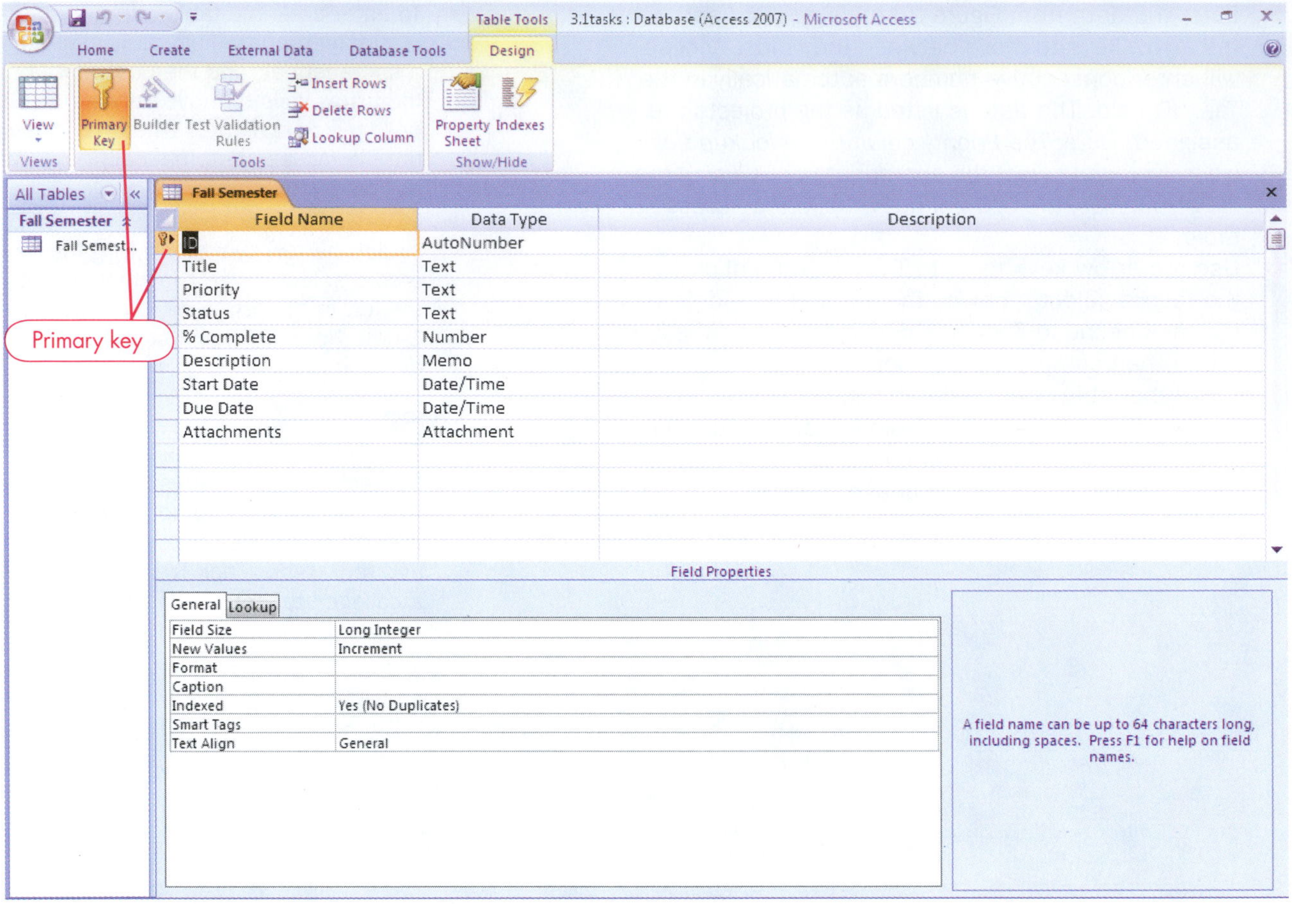

Figure 3.1b Table Design view

TASK ID	TITLE	PRIORITY	STATUS	% COMPLETE	DESCRIPTION	DUE DATE	PROFESSOR
1	Chaucer and the Middle Ages	(2) Normal	Not started	0%	Discuss cultural setting for Chaucer's works; need bibliography	11/10/2010	Cooper
2	Travel to Barcelona	(1) High	In progress	25%	Description of city and its features in Spanish	10/15/2010	Melendez
3	Renaissance Art in Spain	(3) Low	Deferred	0%	Major artists and their work	12/10/2010	Hirschman
4	Political Science Project	(1) High	Waiting for someone else	60%	Team report on the impact of political influences on the American Revolution	9/30/2010	Powell

Figure 3.1c Tasks table data

3.2 CREATE A CONTACTS TABLE FOR CUSTOMERS

Presto Printing, located in Akron, Ohio, wants you to develop a database for its business by creating a Contacts table for customers.

In this project, you will use the Contacts table templates to create a customer contacts table and then modify field properties in Design view.

1. Open a blank database and name it **3.2presto**. Close the blank table that appears.
2. Click the Create tab, click the Table Templates button, and then select the Contacts template.
3. Right-click and then delete each of the following fields: Home Phone, Mobile Phone, Country/Region, Web Page, and Attachments.
4. Select the State/Province field column header, and then rename it **State**. Change the field name for the ZIP/Postal Code field to **ZIP**.
5. Save and name the table **Customers**.
6. Switch to Design View and note that ID is the primary key field and that the data type is AutoNumber. This means that it will automatically number the records as you enter data.
7. Switch back to Datasheet view and enter the data for the three contacts listed in the table below. *Note: The data is listed vertically due to space limitations.*

WHAT YOU NEED TO KNOW

Software

► The default property setting for text field size is 255 characters. In Design view, you can modify the Field Size property to a size appropriate for the data in that field in the Field Properties pane.

► In table Design view, you may notice that some fields have input masks that create a required format for the data to prevent data entry errors and to provide a consistent format.

Project

► Presto Printing would like to enter contact information for some of its customers to the new database.

► The field sizes will be modified in the Field Properties pane of table Design view, as shown in Figure 3.2.

ID	1	2	3
Company	Bradford College	Crown Pizza	Ravenna Civic Association
Last Name	Harris	Maccarone	Parker
First Name	Margaret	Louis	Frank
E-mail Address	mharris@bradford.edu	crownpie@net.com	parkercivic@ravenna.com
Job Title	Administrative Assistant	Owner	President
Business Phone	330-555-3434	330-555-6789	330-555-9038
Fax Number	330-555-3435	330-555-6790	330-555-9039
Address	23 Main Street	15 Alben Avenue	145 First Street
City	Fairlawn	Akron	Ravenna
State	OH	OH	OH
ZIP	44333-1212	44301-1111	44266-1040

8. Switch to Design view and click each field to review the data type and field properties, as shown in Figure 3.2.
9. In the Field Properties pane, change the Field Size property for Last Name, First Name, and City to **30**. Change the Field Size property for the State field to **2**.
10. Close and save the table design and confirm the change. You have not entered any data that would be deleted by this change.
11. Close the table and the database.

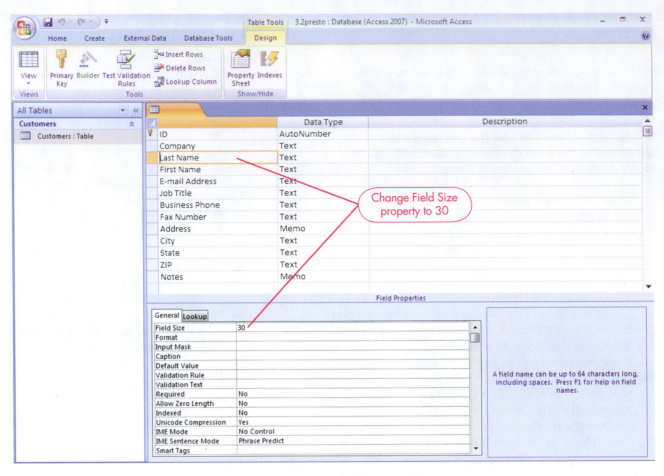

Figure 3.2

CREATE TABLES AND ENTER DATA

PROJECT 4

PROJECT SKILLS

✵ Create tables in Datasheet view
✵ Set or modify data types
✵ Set the primary key in Design view
✵ Create tables in Design view

4.1 CREATE A STUDENTS TABLE IN DATASHEET VIEW

Schuyler College, located in Peoria, IL, wants you to place its student data in a database.

In this project, you will create a Students table in Datasheet view.

1. Open a blank database and name it **4.1students**.
2. A blank table appears when the database opens. Leave the ID column, and double-click the Add New Field column heading. Create a table by entering field names and data from the first registration form as listed below.

    ID: (No entry. Access automatically enters a
    number when data is entered in second field.)
    First Name: Agnes
    Middle Name: Louisa
    Last Name: Kelly
    Address: 634 Arden Avenue
    City: Bartonville
    State: IL
    ZIP Code: 61607-1111
    Phone: (309) 555-9021
    E-mail Address: Akelly@jus.com

3. Switch to Design view. Save and name the table **Students**. Note that ID is the primary key with an AutoNumber data type.
4. Click the Primary Key button to remove the setting. Rename the first field from ID to **Student ID**. Change the data type to Number. We will be using a four-digit ID number. Set the Student ID as the primary key.
5. Select each field of Text data type, and in the Field Properties pane, modify the Field Size property to **50**. Modify the ZIP Code Field Size property to **20**. Use [Tab] to move between field names.
6. After the E-mail Address field, create a text field for the student's major, and then set the field size to **50**.
7. Save the modified table design.

WHAT YOU NEED TO KNOW

Software

▶ You can create tables in Datasheet view by entering the field names and data directly into a datasheet. A blank table appears when you create a database, or you can click the Create tab, and in the Tables group, click the Table button to create a blank table. Access will set the data type according to the data you enter.

Table

▶ You can modify field names and data types in Design view, if necessary. The properties of each field vary, depending on the field data type. Press [F6] to switch to the Field Properties pane to modify or set properties for the field, such as Field Size, Format, Caption, and so on.

▶ You can set the primary key in Design view by selecting the field you wish to be the primary key and clicking the Primary Key button on the Table Tools Design tab. A primary key should be a unique identifier for the record.

Project

▶ Colleges maintain several databases to manage their data. They may create several tables in one database that relate students, courses, teachers, transcripts, and so on, and they may use another database for items such as vendors or inventory.

▶ Data for databases comes from documents that collect data at the source of the information. For example, the source documents for student information would be student registration forms.

▶ Students will be assigned a unique four-digit number as their student identification number.

8. Switch to Datasheet view, and on the first record enter **Computer Science** in the Major field, and then enter the student ID **2314** to complete the record for Agnes Kelly.
9. Enter the data from the four registration forms in Figure 4.1 into the Students table.
10. Close the table and database.

Schuyler College Student Registration Data Form

Student ID	First Name	Middle Name	Last Name
2315	Floyd	David	Goldstein

Address	City	State
89 Oakdale Rd	Peoria	IL

ZIP Code	Phone Number	E-mail Address
61606-1001	(309) 555-8874	Gold@ent.com

Major
Accounting

Schuyler College Student Registration Data Form

Student ID	First Name	Middle Name	Last Name
2316	Anna	Maria	Falcone

Address	City	State
654 Medina Blvd	Metamora	IL

ZIP Code	Phone Number	E-mail Address
61548-2450	(309) 555-3334	AMFalcone@cos.com

Major
Computer Science

Schuyler College Student Registration Data Form

Student ID	First Name	Middle Name	Last Name
2318	Joanne		Pellegrino

Address	City	State
12 Garret Ave	Peoria	IL

ZIP Code	Phone Number	E-mail Address
61607-1200	(309) 555-6903	Garret@jus.com

Major
Marketing

Schuyler College Student Registration Data Form

Student ID	First Name	Middle Name	Last Name
2319	Juan	Pedro	Berrito

Address	City	State
298 First Ave	Peoria Heights	IL

ZIP Code	Phone Number	E-mail Address
61616-1100	(309) 555-1919	PedroB@klc.com

Major
Accounting

Figure 4.1

4.2 CREATE AN INVENTORY TABLE IN DESIGN VIEW

Ollie's Cycles sells bicycles and accessories. You have been asked to record its merchandise inventory using a database.

In this project, you will create an Inventory table in Design view.

1. Open and create a blank database and name it **4.2mdse**. Close the blank table.
2. Click the Create tab, and then click the New Object: Table button to open a blank table in Design view.
3. Create the following fields with the indicated data types:

FIELD NAME	DATA TYPE
ProductID	Number
VendorID	Text
Product Description	Text
Units in Stock	Number
Unit Price	Currency

4. Click the VendorID field, and then press [F6] to move to the Field Properties pane. Change the field size to **12**.
5. Set ProductID as the primary key.
6. Save the table and name it **Inventory**.
7. Switch to Datasheet view, and enter the data from the Inventory List in Figure 4.2 into the Inventory table.
8. Save and close the database.

Software

▶ You have created tables with templates and by entering data directly into the datasheet. To have full control over the design of the table, you can create the table in Design view.

▶ After you plan which fields you want to include, click the Create tab, and then click the New Object: Table button in the Tables group. In Design view, enter the field names, and press [Tab] to move to the Data Type field. Use the drop-down list to select the data type. You can enter a description in the next column, if necessary.

▶ Access will start every table with an ID field with an AutoNumber data type as the primary key. You can modify this field name and data type and use the Primary Key button if it is necessary to remove or change the primary key field.

Project

▶ This database will contain information about the merchandise in inventory. Later we will add a table for the vendors or the companies that sell the business its merchandise. A VendorID number, which will relate to the Vendors table, will be included along with the ProductID in the Inventory table.

Ollie's Cycles
Inventory List

ProductID	VendorID	Product Description	Units in Stock	Unit Price
451	BM0929	Finer BMX	8	$149.99
452	MCR-3409	MCR Folding Bike	2	$329.99
453	MCR-3409	MCR Junior Bike	14	$199.99
454	986-01	Roughtime Hybrid	5	$329.99
455	A41-34-512	Ace Baby Joggers	4	$139.99
456	BA-333-3	Sun Mtn Saddles	2	$ 99.99
457	BA-333-3	X-Ray Saddles	4	$34.55

Figure 4.2

ENHANCE TABLES AND CREATE RELATIONSHIPS

▶ PROJECT SKILLS

✦ Use the Lookup Wizard
✦ Use the Input Mask Wizard
✦ Print a datasheet
✦ Create, modify, and print relationships

PROJECT 5

5.1 CREATE A MEMBER TABLE WITH A LOOKUP FIELD

Power Fitness, a Phoenix-based gym and sports center, wants you to prepare a database for its members.

In this project, you will create a table in Design view with two lookup fields and enter some of the data.

1. Open and create a blank database, place it in your solutions folder and name it **5.1club**. Close the blank table.
2. Click the Create tab, and then click the New Object: Table button.
3. Look at the data in Figure 5.1b. The second telephone number is the work telephone. The Single and Family notations are the types of membership.
4. Create the table design using the data shown as the basis for your design.
   a. Use a Member ID field with an AutoNumber data type as the primary key.
   b. Create lookup fields in the City and Type of Membership fields.
   c. In the City field, use the following in the list of values for the Lookup Wizard: **Avondale**, **Gilbert**, **Glendale**, **Litchfield Park**, **Phoenix**, **Sun City**, and **Tempe**, as shown in Figure 5.1a.
   d. In the Type of Membership field, use **Family** and **Single** in the list of values for the Lookup Wizard.
   e. Save the table design as **Members**.
5. Enter the data for the 10 members in Figure 5.1b.
6. Save and close the database.

▼ WHAT YOU NEED TO KNOW

Software

▶ A lookup field is a field that pulls from a list of values and is used when there is a limited set of possible data for the field. Instead of entering the data, you can select the data from a list of values. For example, if the State field in your database only contains one of three choices, you can list the three choices and select the appropriate data instead of entering the value. A lookup field is created with the Lookup Wizard data type. Using the Lookup Wizard screens, you can get the list of values from another table, or you can enter the data for the lookup list, as shown in Figure 5.1a. The value list you create will become the list of possible data entry choices in the field.

▶ Lookup fields are useful when the data in a field is limited to several choices. By looking up and selecting the correct value, you save time and prevent errors in data entry. You may also type the first letter in a list of choices to get the full value from the list.

Project

▶ Power Fitness draws its members from seven nearby cities. It has decided to use a lookup field to enter the city in each member's address and the type of membership.

▶ When you create a design, remember to keep each field for one item. For example, City, State, and Postal Code should be separate fields even though they are on one line in an address.

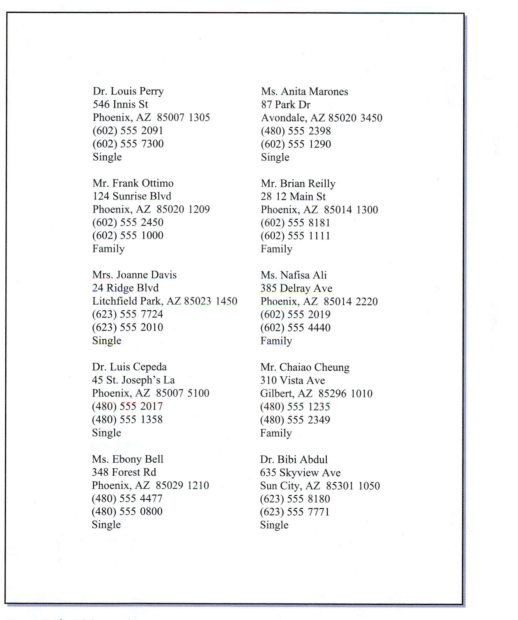

Figure 5.1a Lookup Wizard

Dr. Louis Perry
546 Innis St
Phoenix, AZ 85007 1305
(602) 555 2091
(602) 555 7300
Single

Ms. Anita Marones
87 Park Dr
Avondale, AZ 85020 3450
(480) 555 2398
(602) 555 1290
Single

Mr. Frank Ottimo
124 Sunrise Blvd
Phoenix, AZ 85020 1209
(602) 555 2450
(602) 555 1000
Family

Mr. Brian Reilly
28 12 Main St
Phoenix, AZ 85014 1300
(602) 555 8181
(602) 555 1111
Family

Mrs. Joanne Davis
24 Ridge Blvd
Litchfield Park, AZ 85023 1450
(623) 555 7724
(623) 555 2010
Single

Ms. Nafisa Ali
385 Delray Ave
Phoenix, AZ 85014 2220
(602) 555 2019
(602) 555 4440
Family

Dr. Luis Cepeda
45 St. Joseph's La
Phoenix, AZ 85007 5100
(480) 555 2017
(480) 555 1358
Single

Mr. Chaiao Cheung
310 Vista Ave
Gilbert, AZ 85296 1010
(480) 555 1235
(480) 555 2349
Family

Ms. Ebony Bell
348 Forest Rd
Phoenix, AZ 85029 1210
(480) 555 4477
(480) 555 0800
Single

Dr. Bibi Abdul
635 Skyview Ave
Sun City, AZ 85301 1050
(623) 555 8180
(623) 555 7771
Single

Figure 5.1b Club members

5.2 ADD INPUT MASKS TO A STUDENTS TABLE

Schuyler College has added more students to the database. You have been asked to improve the data entry features of the Students table by creating input masks for several fields.

In this project, you will edit the table design to include input masks and enter additional data.

1. Find data file **d5.2students**, copy it to your Solutions folder, rename it **5.2students**, and then open the file.
2. Open the Students table and notice the new data that has been added to the file. Switch to Design view.
3. Select the Phone Number field, press [F6], and then click the Build button at the right of the Input Mask property in the Field Properties pane, as shown in Figure 5.2a.
4. Select the Phone Number input mask, accept the default settings, but select the option to store the data with the symbols in the mask. Save the design.
5. Select the ZIP Code field, and then click the Build button to set an input mask. Select the Zip Code input mask and accept all the default settings for the mask, but store the data with the symbols in the mask. Save the table design.
6. Switch to Datasheet view.
7. Use the data from the four registration forms shown in Figure 5.2b to create new student records. Note the input mask feature in the Phone Number and ZIP Code fields.
8. Save and close the database.

WHAT YOU NEED TO KNOW

Software

► An input mask controls how Access enters data in a field by providing a pattern or template to which data must conform. For example, you can set a required format for dates or telephone numbers that includes the slashes or parentheses. This will ensure that data is entered in a consistent format and reduce data entry keystrokes and errors.

► Access provides an Input Mask Wizard that works with Date/Time or Text data types. In Design view, click the field for which you want to design an input mask, and then press [F6] to move to the Field Properties pane. In the Field Properties pane, click the Build button in the Input Mask property field, as shown in Figure 5.2a. Select the format from the list of input masks displayed. You can customize the mask and decide if you want to store the separators, such as parentheses or slashes, with the data or not. If the data is stored without the special characters, it will consume less space in the file but it will not be easy to read on the datasheet.

► When you input data into a field with an input mask, you are required to conform to the format set for the field.

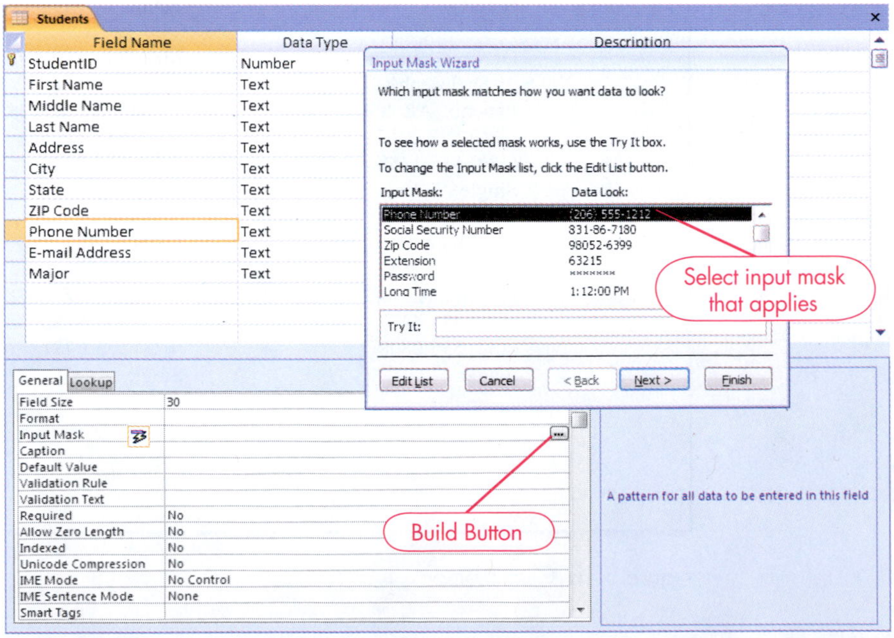

Figure 5.2a Design view - Input Mask Wizard

Schuyler College Student Registration Data Form

Student ID	First Name		Middle Name		Last Name
2392	Nathan		Joseph		Levine

Address	City		State
28 Smith St	Chillicothe		IL

ZIP Code	Phone Number		E-mail Address
61523-1001	(309) 555-7888		NathanL@cos.com

Major
Computer Science

Schuyler College Student Registration Data Form

Student ID	First Name		Middle Name		Last Name
2395	Brian		Anthony		Duffy

Address	City		State
248 Hull Ave	Eureka		IL

ZIP Code	Phone Number		E-mail Address
61530-1000	(309) 555-9911		BrainaDuff@jus.com

Major
Office Administration

Schuyler College Student Registration Data Form

Student ID	First Name		Middle Name		Last Name
2396	Carol		Ann		Edwards

Address	City		State
248 Pennbrooke Rd	Peoria		IL

ZIP Code	Phone Number		E-mail Address
61603-1007	(309) 555-7103		Cedwards@res.com

Major
Accounting

Schuyler College Student Registration Data Form

Student ID	First Name		Middle Name		Last Name
2397	Milton		John		Stevens

Address	City		State
109 Hancock St	Peoria		IL

ZIP Code	Phone Number		E-mail Address
61603-1007	(309) 555-0020		MiltonS@cos.com

Major
Computer Science

Figure 5.2b Registration forms

5.3 ADD INPUT MASKS TO A CUSTOMERS TABLE

Presto Printing wants you to improve the data entry features of the Customers table by creating input masks and a lookup field.

In this project, you will edit the table design to include input masks and a lookup field, and then enter additional data.

1. Find your solution **3.2presto** or data file **d5.3presto**, copy it into your Solutions folder, and then rename it **5.3presto**. Open the file.
2. Open the Customers table and switch to Design view.
3. Select the ZIP Code field, and then click the Build button at the right of the Input Mask property in the Field Properties pane. This will launch the Input Mask Wizard.
4. Select the Zip Code input mask, accept all the default settings for the mask, but store the data with the symbols in the mask. Save the table design.
5. Select the Business Phone field, and then click the Build button at the right of the Input Mask property in the Field Properties pane.
6. Select the Phone Number mask and store the data with the symbols in the mask. Save the table design.
7. Set the input mask for the Fax Number field using the Phone Number input mask.
8. In the City field, change the data type to Lookup Wizard. Use the following in the list of values for the Lookup Wizard: **Akron**, **Bedford**, **Fairlawn**, **Ravenna**, and **Shaker Heights**, as shown in Figure 5.3.
9. Save the table design and switch to Datasheet view.

WHAT YOU NEED TO KNOW

Software
► As you work on a database, you may decide to improve the data entry features by adding an input mask or lookup field.

Project
► When you have the cities listed in a lookup field for Presto Printing, it is faster to enter the first letter of the city and have Access enter the full value, than to select the city from the drop-down list.

10. Add the customers in the table below: *Note the data is listed vertically due to space limitations.*

ID	4	5	6	7	8
Company	Congress Church	Seemore PTA	Chen's Restaurant	Security Bank	Joe's Homemade Candy
Last Name	Valdez	Reilly	Chen	Lee	Dolcetti
First Name	Maria	Robert	Li	David	Joseph
E-mail Address	mvaldez@congress.com	reillyr@pta.net	chenli@world.net	dlee@security.net	jdolcetti@candy.com
Job Title	Office Manager	President	Owner	Vice President	Owner
Business Phone	(330) 555-0900	(330) 555-1809	(440) 555-2000	(216) 555-3000	(440) 555-6709
Fax Number	(330) 555-0990	(330) 555-1810	(440) 555-2005	(216) 555-3009	(440) 555-6710
Address	35 Main Street	1532 8th Avenue	21 Market Street	15 Artis Boulevard	2 Mark Street
City	Akron	Akron	Bedford	Shaker Heights	Bedford
State	OH	OH	OH	OH	OH
ZIP Code	44301-1211	44301-1111	44146-1200	44118-1200	44116-1100

11. Save and close the database.

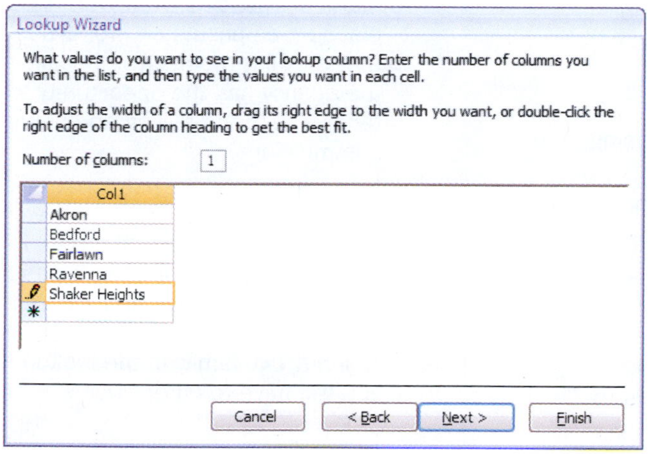

Figure 5.3 Lookup Wizard value list

5.4 CREATE AND FORMAT A PROPERTY LISTING TABLE WITH AN INPUT MASK AND LOOKUP FIELDS

Chris James has started a small real estate agency in the Philadelphia area. She wants you to create a database of the properties listed by her agency.

In this project, you will create and format a table for property listing data that includes two lookup fields and a field with an input mask.

1. Open and create a blank database, and name it **5.4listings**. Close the blank table.
2. Click the Create tab, and then click the New Object: Table button.
3. Use the data listing shown in Figure 5.4 to decide on the field names, field sizes, and field properties.
4. Create lookup fields for the Type of Property and City fields. Decide on the items that should be on the values list, and then alphabetize them for the list.
5. Set the ID number as the primary key.
6. Save the table as **Listings**.
7. Create an input mask for the Date Listed field using the Short Date input mask.
8. Format the Price field for Currency data type, and then set the Decimal Places field property to zero. Save the table.
9. In the Datasheet view, enter the data shown in Figure 5.4. Use the drop-down list of values, or enter the first few letters of the data for the Type of Property and City. Enter leading zeros in dates to correctly use the Short Date input mask.
10. Widen the Address column so that it displays the longest entry.
11. Print a copy of the Listings table.
12. Save and close the table and database.

WHAT YOU NEED TO KNOW

Software

▶ When you enter a date into a field with an input mask, you will have to enter a space or a zero if the month or day is less than two characters.

▶ To widen a datasheet column, double-click the line between two column headers to adjust the column width to the size of the longest field entry.

▶ You can print a datasheet by clicking the Office Button and then clicking Print.

Project

▶ Most real estate agencies sell properties to their clients from the Multiple Listing Service, or MLS, which is made up of listings from all the member agencies. However, agencies place an emphasis on properties that they list themselves because the agency has the opportunity to receive both the selling and listing commissions.

▶ In the table design, use lookup fields for the type of property and the city, and an input mask for the date listed. In this case, there are two types of property, Townhouse and Two-family, that begin with the letter T. Therefore, to input Two-family in the lookup field, you will have to enter **Tw**.

Chris James Realtors

Listings

	Type of Property	Bedrooms	Address	City	Price	Date Listed
1	Townhouse	2	35 Targee St.	Philadelphia	$299,900.00	7/3/2010
2	Split Level	3	89-01 Main St.	Drexel Hill	$535,000.00	8/24/2010
3	Cape Cod	4	91 Alberta Dr.	Philadelphia	$495,000.00	8/30/2010
4	Two-family	6	35 Reid Ave.	Philadelphia	$625,000.00	9/1/2010
5	Townhouse	1	890 Vargo La.	Springfield	$283,000.00	9/3/2010
6	Ranch	3	429 Hart Blvd.	Philadelphia	$385,900.00	9/5/2010
7	Apartment	1	43 Arlo Rd.	Philadelphia	$243,900.00	9/8/2010
8	Split Level	4	301 Seguine Ave.	Kellyville	$502,000.00	9/12/2010
9	Colonial	5	215 Medina Ave.	Philadelphia	$550,000.00	9/15/2010
10	Split Level	3	651 Tysens La.	Kellyville	$399,900.00	9/16/2010
11	Apartment	2	432 Mule Rd.	Drexel Hill	$258,500.00	9/18/2010
12	Ranch	2	874 Edison St.	Philadelphia	$345,800.00	10/15/2010
13	Two-family	5	721 St. Marks Pl.	Philadelphia	$699,900.00	10/29/2010
14	Townhouse	3	777 Stobe Ave.	Springfield	$309,900.00	11/10/2010
15	Townhouse	2	28 Naughton St.	Drexel Hill	$368,500.00	11/15/2010

Figure 5.4

5.5 CREATE AND PRINT RELATIONSHIPS BETWEEN INVENTORY AND VENDOR TABLES

Ollie's Cycles has added data and a new table to their database. They want you to include a field to identify the department where each item is sold in the Inventory table and to create a relationship between the Inventory and Vendors tables.

In this project, you will add a lookup field to the design of a table, enter new data, and create a relationship between the two tables.

1. Find data file **d5.5mdse**, copy it to your Solutions folder, and rename it **5.5mdse**. Open the file and note that there are two tables.
2. Open the Inventory table to view the new data. Open the Vendors table and view the data. Close the Vendors table.
3. Switch the Inventory table to Design view.
4. Insert a row before Units in Stock, and name the new field **Department**.
5. Select Lookup Wizard as the data type, and then select the option to type in the values. Enter **Bicycles** and **Accessories** as the values. Save the table.
6. Switch to Datasheet view. In the new Department field, enter the appropriate department data in the lookup field, as shown in Figure 5.5b.
7. Save and close the Inventory table.
8. Click the Database Tools tab, and then click the Relationships button. In the Show Table dialog box, select the Inventory table and click Add, and then select the Vendors table and click Add again. Close the Show Table dialog box.
9. Click the VendorID field from the Inventory table, and then drag it to the VendorID field in the Vendors table. The Edit Relationships dialog box appears. Click Create to create the relationship. A line will be drawn between the fields.
10. Print a copy of the Relationships window. Save and close the window.
11. Save and close the database.

WHAT YOU NEED TO KNOW

Software:

▶ You can modify the design of a table in Design view. To insert a new field, click the location for the new row, and then click the Insert Rows button on the Table Tools Design tab in the Tools group.

▶ If a database has several tables, you must provide a means to bring that information together for queries, forms, and reports that use data from several tables. Use relationships to create a correlation between common field data that appears in two tables. Create a relationship by using the Relationships window, shown in Figure 5.5a. The common field does not have to have the same name in both tables but it must have the same data, data type, and field size settings. Often the primary key from one table is related to the same data in another table.

▶ To create a relationship in an open database, click the Database Tools tab, and in the Show/Hide group, click the Relationships button. In the Show Table dialog box, select the tables to display, click Add for each, and then click Close. Drag a field from one table to the related field in the other table. Click Create in the Edit Relationships box to create the relationship and draw a line between the two tables. To document the relationships between tables, 🖾 Relationship Report you may print the Relationships window by clicking the Relationship Report button on the Relationship Tools Design tab, and then click Print on the Print Preview tab.

Project

▶ Additional inventory data has been added to the Inventory table in the database. Ollie's Cycles has two types of merchandise or departments: bicycles and accessories. A Department field will be added to the Inventory table, and items will be categorized as either bicycles or accessories.

Continued on next page

► A new Vendors table has been added with the contact information for the manufacturers or wholesalers that sell merchandise to Ollie's Cycles. This table needs to be related to the Inventory table to make data from both tables available for reports, forms, and queries.

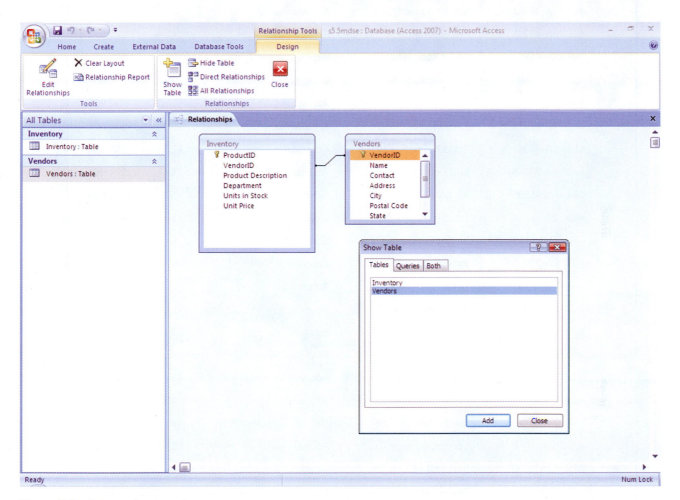

Figure 5.5a Relationships window

ProductID	VendorID	Product Description	Department	Units In Stock	Unit Price
451	BM0929	Finer BMX	Bicycles	8	$149.99
452	MCR-3409	MCR Folding Bike	Bicycles	2	$329.99
453	MCR-3409	MCR Junior Bike	Bicycles	14	$199.99
454	986-01	Roughtime Hybrid	Bicycles	5	$329.99
455	A41-34-512	Ace Baby Joggers	Bicycles	4	$139.99
456	BA-333-3	Sun Mtn Saddles	Accessories	2	$99.99
457	BA-333-3	X-Ray Saddles	Accessories	4	$34.55
458	MI-45891	Coast Road Bike	Bicycles	1	$5,099.00
459	MI-45891	Joy Mountain Bike	Bicycles	2	$1,549.00
460	TR-37371	Cross II Tires	Accessories	12	$39.99
461	TR-37371	Carbon Cross Tires	Accessories	10	$45.00
462	BA-333-3	Pride Helmets	Accessories	12	$99.99
463	BA-333-3	XXC Helmets	Accessories	3	$54.99
464	MI-45891	Aft BMX Bikes	Bicycles	5	$169.90
465	23-2222-S	Premier Road Bikes	Bicycles	1	$1,639.00
466	EL-23999	Elton Cyclometers	Accessories	5	$120.00
467	BA-333-3	Pace Air pumps	Accessories	3	$15.00
468	V-22222	Hepp Auto Rack	Accessories	4	$29.99
469	V-22222	J's Vehicle Rack	Accessories	2	$59.00
470	23-2222-S	Rugged Mountain Bikes	Bicycles	23	$250.00
471	MI-45891	Select Cruisers	Bicycles	24	$199.99
472	TR-37371	Favo Wheels	Accessories	43	$25.99
473	23-2222-S	Uris Hybrid Bike	Bicycles	4	$765.00
474	778810-QV	Lite Mountain Bike	Bicycles	3	$459.00
475	BA-333-3	Security System	Accessories	5	$59.89
476	5487-230	Indy Road Bikes	Bicycles	3	$950.00
477	778810-QV	Bay Mountain Bikes	Bicycles	2	$650.00
478	CR-526	Cole Cruiser	Bicycles	2	$900.00
479	778810-QV	State Cross Country	Bicycles	2	$875.00
480	ATF-3333-09S	Junior Bikes	Bicycles	7	$150.00
481	BM0929	BMX Bikes	Bicycles	2	$1,100.00
482	23-2222-S	Mark Cruiser	Bicycles	1	$1,250.00
483	778810-QV	Queen Hybrid	Bicycles	1	$690.00
484	5487-230	West Road Bikes	Bicycles	4	$450.00

Figure 5.5b Inventory table

CHAPTER 3

Access Forms

In this chapter, you will complete the following projects:

PROJECT 6
Create and Use Forms

PROJECT 6.1 Create a Movie Collection Form
PROJECT 6.2 Create a Customer Form Using a Split Form and the Form Wizard
PROJECT 6.3 Enter, Edit, and Delete Records in Student Forms

PROJECT 7
Edit and Enhance Forms

PROJECT 7.1 Edit an Inventory Form Design
PROJECT 7.2 Create a Members Form Using Design and Layout Views

PROJECT 8
Create a Database Table and Form Using Calculated Controls

PROJECT 8.1 Create a Property Listing Form with a Calculated Control
PROJECT 8.2 Create Forms and Add a Calculated Control

CREATE AND USE FORMS

PROJECT 6

PROJECT SKILLS
- Create forms using form tools
- Print a form
- Create a split form
- Create forms using the Form Wizard
- AutoFormat a form
- Enter, edit, and delete records using a form

6.1 CREATE A MOVIE COLLECTION FORM

Your friend with a movie collection has asked you to make it easier to enter new data into his database. He wants to be able to view only one record at a time.

In this project, you will create a form for the movie collection.

1. Find data file **d6.1movie**, copy it to your Solutions folder, rename it **6.1movie**, and open the database.
2. Open the Movie Collection table. Click the Create tab and then click the Form button. Notice the form that appears; it includes all the fields in the table and displays the first record.
3. Use the navigation bar, shown in Figure 6.1a, to view all the records.
4. Close the form but do not save it. Close the table.
5. With the Movie Collection table selected in the Navigation Pane, click the Create tab and then click the Form button. The form shown in Figure 6.1a will appear.
6. Save the form as **Movie Collection Form**. Click the Maximize button to fill the screen with the form, if necessary.
7. Use the New (blank) record button on the navigation bar to add a blank record.
8. Switch to Form view, and enter the data for Record 11, shown in Figure 6.1b, using [Tab] to move between fields and to the next blank record. The MovieID field is an AutoNumber field and will be incremented automatically.
9. Enter MovieIDs 12 through 17, using the Movie Collection form.
10. You are interested in selling MovieID 13. Move to that form and print a copy of the selected record.
11. Close the form and open the Movie Collection table. All the data entered using the form displays in the table.
12. Close the database.

WHAT YOU NEED TO KNOW

Software

▶ The Form object, which displays one record at a time, is another way to view, edit, delete, and enter data in a database. You can create a form automatically by using form tools on the Create tab, which includes various types of form design formats and a New Object: Form button to create a form in Design view.

▶ To create a form when a table is either open or closed, click the table, and click the Form button in the Forms group on the Create tab.

▶ Forms have a navigation toolbar that you can use to add a record, move to the next record, or move back to a previous record. Press [Tab] to move between fields when entering data. Any data added in a form is automatically visible in the datasheet.

▶ Forms may be printed by clicking the Office Button and selecting the Print command. You must specify if you wish to print all the forms or the selected record.

Project

▶ A movie database has been created to keep a record of a collection of classic movies. You will create a form which will make it easier to view each record in the Movie Collection table twice, once with the table open and again with the table closed. The form will be used to enter data.

Name of saved form

Movie Collection Form

Movie Collection

MovieID:	1
Movie Title:	African Queen
Actress ID:	Hepburn
Actor ID:	Bogart
Director ID:	Huston
Year Released:	1951
Subject:	Action/Adventure
Purchase Price:	$5.35

Navigation bar   New (blank) record button

Record: 1 of 16   No Filter   Search

Num Lock

Figure 6.1a Movie Collection form

MovieID	Movie Title	Actress ID	Actor ID	Director ID	Year Released	Subject	Purchase Price
1	African Queen	Hepburn	Bogart	Huston	1951	Action/Adventure	$5.35
2	Autumn in New York	Stritch	Gere	Chen	2000	Drama	$19.95
3	Best in Show	Coolidge	Hitchcock	Guest	2000	Comedy	$19.95
4	Gladiator	Nielsen	Crowe	Scott	2000	Drama	$15.50
6	Life With Mikey	Wasserstein	Fox	Lapine	1993	Comedy	$9.95
7	Midnight Run	Phillips	De Niro	Brest	1998	Comedy	$12.50
8	My Blue Heaven	Cusack	Martin	Ephron	1990	Comedy	$19.95
9	No Alibi	Doig	Cain	Pittman	2000	Mystery	$9.95
10	Pay It Forward	Hunt	Osment	Leder	2000	Drama	$19.95
11	Postcards from the Edge	Streep	Heald	Nichols	1990	Drama	$12.50
12	Traffic	Zeta-Jones	Douglas	Soderbergh	2000	Drama	$12.50
13	The X Files	Anderson	Duchovny	Bowman	1998	Science fiction	$19.95
14	Singing in the Rain	Reynolds	Kelly	Donin	1956	Musical	$9.95
15	Cape Fear	Bergen	Mitchum	Thompson	1952	Mystery	$14.95
16	Ocean's Eleven	Roberts	Clooney	Soderbergh	2002	Comedy	$18.95
17	Crash	Bullock	Howard	Haggis	2005	Drama	$19.95

Figure 6.1b Movie Collection table

6.2 CREATE A CUSTOMER FORM USING A SPLIT FORM AND THE FORM WIZARD

Presto Printing has a table for its customers, but it would like to have a form to use for data entry. You have been asked to prepare several options for them to review.

In this project, you will create forms using the Split Form button and the Form Wizard and use a form to enter additional data.

1. Find data file **d6.2presto**, copy it to your Solutions folder, rename it **6.2presto**, and open the database.
2. Click the Customers table, click the Create tab, and then click the Split Form button. Click a record in the datasheet at the bottom of the screen, and note that the record appears in the form section at the top of the screen. Close the form without saving it.
3. Click the Customers table, click the Create tab, click the More Forms button, and then click Form Wizard.
   a. On the first screen, double-click each field to move it to the form, or click the double-arrow pointer to move all fields to the form list. Click Next.
   b. On the layout screen, select each layout option and view the sample preview. Select the Justified option, and then click Next.
   c. On the Styles screen, select each style option and view the sample. Select one of the options, and then click Next.
   d. On the final screen, name the form `Customers Form`. Click Finish and notice that the form appears. Close the form.
4. Repeat Step 3 using all the fields, but with the Columnar layout and the Paper style. Name the form `Customers Form2`. Close the form.
5. The staff at Presto has reviewed both form designs and prefers the Columnar layout, shown in Figure 6.2a. Right-click the Customers Form and click Delete, and then confirm the deletion. Right-click the Customers Form2 and rename it `Customers Form`.
6. Use the columnar form to enter the additional customer data, which is shown in Figure 6.2b.
7. Switch to the Customers table and see that the additional data is now in the table.
8. Close the database.

WHAT YOU NEED TO KNOW

Software

▶ A split form is a style that shows the form for one record with the datasheet below the form. You can select a record from the datasheet and display the selected record in the form at the top of the screen. To create a split form, click the table, click the Create tab, and in the Forms group, click the Split Form button.

▶ Using the Form or Split Form button automatically creates a form using all the fields in a table. However, if you want to omit certain fields, add style and layout features, or use fields from other tables, use the Form Wizard.

▶ To use the Form Wizard, click the Create tab, and click the More Forms button, and then click Form Wizard. The first screen allows you to select the tables and fields for the form. The second screen provides layout selections.

▶ The Form Wizard provides four layout options. The Columnar and Justified options appear one record at a time. The third screen of the Form Wizard gives you predefined style options with a preview screen. On the final screen, you name the form and either display the form or go into Design view to modify the design.

Project

▶ Presto Printing has added customers to its Customers table and has modified the lookup field to contain any new cities that must be listed. Use the data file for this project.

▶ The company wants to look at a Split Form and forms using the Justified and Columnar layouts. They will select one after viewing the selection of form layouts and then you will enter new data.

Figure 6.2a Customers Form: Columnar layout

ID				
Company	Bradford College			
Last Name	Harris			
First Name	Margaret			
E-mail Address	mharris@bradford.edu			
Job Title	Administrative Assistant			
Business Phone	330-555-3434			
Fax Number	330-555-3435			
Address	23 Main Street			
City	Fairlawn			
State	OH			
ZIP Code	44333-1212			

Columnar layout and Paper style

Customers Form

Record: 1 of 33 No Filter Search

Microsoft Access - s6.2presto : Database (Access 2007)

Figure 6.2a Customers Form: Columnar layout

ID	29	30	31	32	33
Company	PTA of Ekbert HS	Acme Sporting Goods	Nunzio's Pizza	Academy Bus Tours	Manor Civic Association
Last Name	Cassidy	Kosinski	Buono	Mendelsohn	Brandoff
First Name	Nora	Walter	John	John	Kurt
E-mail address	norac@ ekbertpta.com	kosinski@ acme.com	buono@ nunzio.com	johnm@ academy.net	brandoffk@ manor.net
Job Title	President	Manager	Owner	Vice President	President
Business Phone	(330) 555-8193	(330) 555-2228	(330) 555-3676	(330) 555-6111	(330) 555-1212
Fax Number	(330) 555-8194	(330) 555-2229	(330) 555-3677	(330) 555-6112	(330) 555-1213
Address	248 Garretson Road	438 Oakdale Road	458 Avenue C	330 Market Street	4891 Delaware Street
City	Ravenna	Akron	Akron	Bedford	Shaker Heights
State	OH	OH	OH	OH	OH
ZIP Code	44266-1890	44302-1212	44305-1838	44146-1000	44118-1212

Figure 6.2b New customer data

ACCESS

6.3 ENTER, EDIT, AND DELETE RECORDS IN STUDENT FORMS

Schuyler College wants you to create a form for its Students table, change its format, and enter, edit, and delete records as necessary.

In this project, you will create a form using the Form Wizard, use AutoFormat to change the style, and enter, edit, and delete records in the form.

1. Find **5.2students** in your files or data file **d6.3students**, copy it to your Solutions folder, and rename it **6.3students**.

2. Create a form for the Students table using the Form Wizard. Include all the fields, and set the Justified layout and the Origin AutoFormat style. Name the form **Students Form**.

3. Right-click the title bar of the form, and then click Layout View. On the Form Layout Tools Format tab in the AutoFormat gallery, click the bottom of the scroll bar at the right to view more of the format choices. Change the AutoFormat style to Equity, as shown in Figure 6.3. Save the form design and switch back to Form view.

4. Find the following records using the Find feature. Click in the Last Name field to use that field to find the data, and then click the Find button. Enter the search data, and then click Find Next to be sure that there are no other students with that name. To make the changes indicated, click on the field name to be edited, and the data will be selected and can be overwritten.

   a. George Krute has a new telephone number: **(309) 555-6921**.

   b. Joseph Presto has changed his major from Marketing to **Computer Science**.

   c. Michael Johnson says that his mail is incorrectly addressed. Use **Jo*** to search for the record and correct the spelling of his last name.

   d. Kerry Burke has a new e-mail address: **kerry24@res.com**.

5. Joanne Pellegrino has dropped out of school. Delete her record.

6. Close the database.

Software

▶ You can change the format of a form in Layout view. Right-click the form title bar, and click Layout View. On the Form Layout Tools Format tab, select a format from the AutoFormat gallery.

▶ One of the features of a database is the ease of locating data for viewing or editing. You can find data in Form view by scrolling through the records using the navigation keys, if you have the record number. If there are a large number of records, you can use the Find feature to search for the record.

▶ To find records using data in a specific field, click the field, click the Home tab, and then click the Find button in the Find group. You can then input the search data. Or, you can search the whole table for the text you specify. If you only know part of the data to be found, you can use a wildcard key, the asterisk, to find items with any other characters in that location. For example, if you wish to find all text that starts with Ra, you would enter **Ra***.

▶ When you click the name of a field in a form, the contents are selected so that you can overwrite them with new data. All changes are saved when you move to the next record.

▶ To delete a record in the Forms object, click the Home tab, and click the Delete button arrow in the Records group. Click Delete Record on the menu that appears. Access always prompts you to confirm a deletion because there is no Undo feature for this operation.

Project

▶ If you do not have the file from the previous Schuyler College project, use the data file.

▶ Schuyler College has discovered some errors, has received updates on addresses, and needs to add and delete records. All these operations are to be completed in a new form.

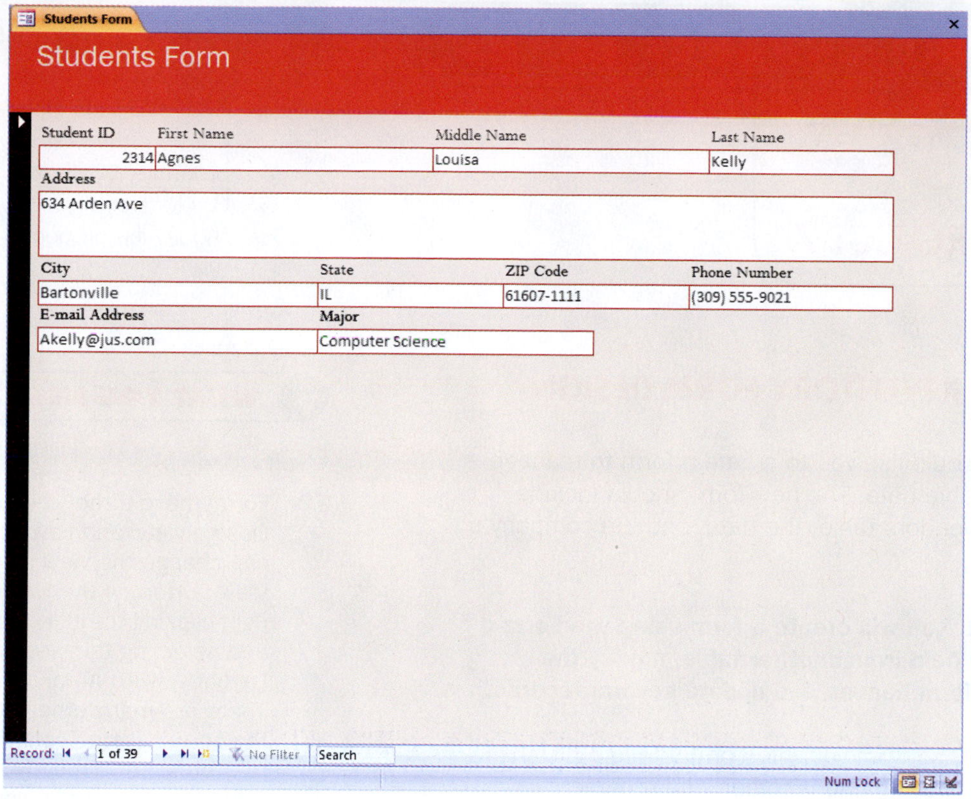

Figure 6.3

EDIT AND ENHANCE FORMS

PROJECT 7

PROJECT SKILLS
* Modify a form in Layout view
* Add, size, and move controls
* Create a form using the Blank Form button
* Use form Design view
* Modify the properties of a control

7.1 EDIT AN INVENTORY FORM DESIGN

Ollie's Cycles would like you to create a form to manage the Inventory table data. The new form should include data from the Vendors table, the date, and the company's name and logo.

In this project, you will create a form using the Form Wizard, add a field from another table, modify the layout of the form header, and update several records.

1. Find **5.5mdse** from your files or data file **d7.1mdse**, copy it to your Solutions folder, and rename it **7.1mdse**.
2. Create a form for the Inventory table using the Form Wizard and all the fields from the table. Use the Columnar layout, select the Metro AutoFormat style, name the form **Products**, and then view the form when it's completed.
3. Switch to Layout view and maximize the form. Close the Field List pane if it is open.
4. Select the text box in the form header, delete the text and enter **Ollie's Cycles Products**. Use the sizing handles to change the width and height of the text box so that the form header appears as shown in Figure 7.1. The header should be in 20 point font.
5. Click the Logo button in the Controls group of the Form Layout Tools Format tab, and add the bicycle graphic found in data file **d7.1ollielogo.bmp**.
6. Drag and size the graphic, and place it at the left side of the form header.
7. Click the Add Existing Fields button to add a field from the Vendors table to the form. On the Field List pane, double-click the Vendors table to view the fields. Double-click the Name field to add it to the form.
8. Drag the Name field to the position under the VendorID field. Double-click the field name and then edit it to read **Vendor Name:**, as shown in Figure 7.1.
9. Switch to Form view.

WHAT YOU NEED TO KNOW

Software

▶ Forms have three views: Form view, Design view, and Layout view. You can change the view by using the View button on the Home tab or by right-clicking the title bar of the form and selecting the view. We have used Layout view to AutoFormat a form. There are many other format tools on the Form Layout Tools Format tab that may be used to modify the design of a form. For example, you can add or modify the font, font color, fill colors, lines, and logos in Layout view.

▶ In Layout view, you can also add controls, which represent items such as additional fields, logos, the date and time, or lines, to a form. To add existing fields to a form, click the Add Existing Fields button on the Form Layout Tools Format tab in the Controls group to display fields from related tables. You can view the fields on the Field List pane and double-click the field to add it to the form.

Project

▶ Ollie's Cycles would like you to design a form that can be used by the personnel in the store and can be seen by customers. It would like to include the date and the company name and graphic in the form. These are all features that are set in Layout view to be added to the header or footer of the form. In addition, Ollie's Cycles would like to add data from another table as a field on the form.

▶ There are several additions and updates that you will need to make to the inventory using the new form. You can use the Find feature to search for a specific record, but you must enter the search text as it appears in the record.

44 – Access   Project 7 Edit and Enhance Forms
Chapter 3 • Access Forms

10. Find the form for the product Rugged Mountain Bikes. The count was in error; there are 24 in stock, counting the window display bicycle. Make the correction.
11. Find the Security System product, and then change the name to **BA Security System**.
12. Save and close the form and the database.

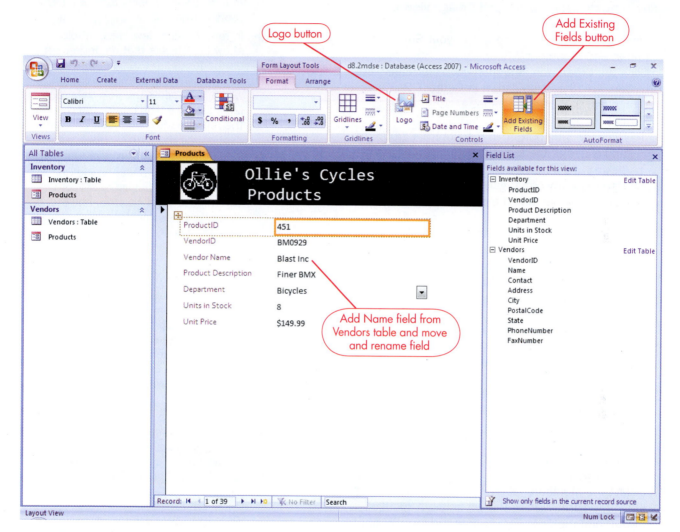

Figure 7.1 Form in Layout view

7.2 CREATE A MEMBERS FORM USING DESIGN AND LAYOUT VIEWS

Power Fitness, a Phoenix-based gym and sports center, wants you to prepare forms to be used at the reception desk and for data entry.

In this project, you will create two forms and add and modify controls using Layout and Design views.

1. Find data file **d7.2club**, copy it to your Solutions folder, and rename it **7.2club**.
2. Click the Create tab, and then click the Blank Form button. Add the fields shown in Figure 7.2a, and then close the Field List pane.
3. Format the form as follows:
   a. Click the Title button, in the Controls group, to add a title at the top of the form. Enter the text **Power Fitness Reception**.
   b. Use the AutoFormat gallery to apply the Civic style, and then add the company logo using data file **d7.2powerlogo.bmp**.
   c. Move and size the title and logo as shown in Figure 7.2a.
   d. Add a date and time control, which will appear on the right side of the form header.
   e. Switch to Design view, and note the Form Design Tools Design tab. Add a Label control and drag it to create a rectangle at the right side of the detail section. Enter the text as shown in Figure 7.2a. Right-click the control and then click Properties to open the Property Sheet pane. Change the Property Sheet to set the Back Color to Background Light Header and the Special Effect to Shadowed. Close the Property Sheet pane.
   f. Save the form and name it **Power Fitness Reception**.
4. Select the Members table, and then create a form using the Form Wizard. Use all fields, a Justified layout, and the Civic style. Name the form **Members Form**.
5. In Layout view, add the company logo and place it to the left of the Members Form title. *Note: You will need to move the title to the right.*
6. Switch to Design view, as shown in Figure 7.2b.
7. Click the Postal Code field name control, and then click the Property Sheet button.
8. On the Property Sheet pane, change the Caption property to read **ZIP Code**. Close the Property Sheet pane and save the form. Switch back to Form view.
9. Close the forms and the database.

WHAT YOU NEED TO KNOW

Software

▶ You can create a form from scratch using the Blank Form button on the Create tab. [Blank Form] You will be in Layout view and can add fields, add controls, and format the form using the Form Layout Tools Format tab.

▶ In form Design view, the controls show the objects that organize data on the form. For example, a field control contains the bound control, which represents the field data, and a label with the field name. You can see the form header and footer and the sections of the form clearly.

▶ To add today's date to the form, use the Date & Time button in the Controls group, in either Design or Layout view. You will set the date style, and the =Date() expression will allow today's date to appear whenever the form is opened.

▶ A label control may be added in Design view to display a title or caption. This is called an unbound control. Click the Label (Form Control) button in the Controls group on the Form Design Tools Design tab, and then click the location for the label, and size it appropriately. Enter the text and format it as you prefer.

▶ Every control on a form has properties that determine its appearance, format, behavior, and characteristics. In Design view, right-click any control and click Properties, or click the Property Sheet button on the Form Design Tools Design tab in the Tools group to open the Property Sheet pane. Change the desired property and close the Property Sheet pane.

Project

▶ Power Fitness would like you to create two forms. They need a form containing member notes that can be used to verify Member information for the reception desk. On this form they do not want to display all the information in the file. They also want another form for data entry purposes containing all fields.

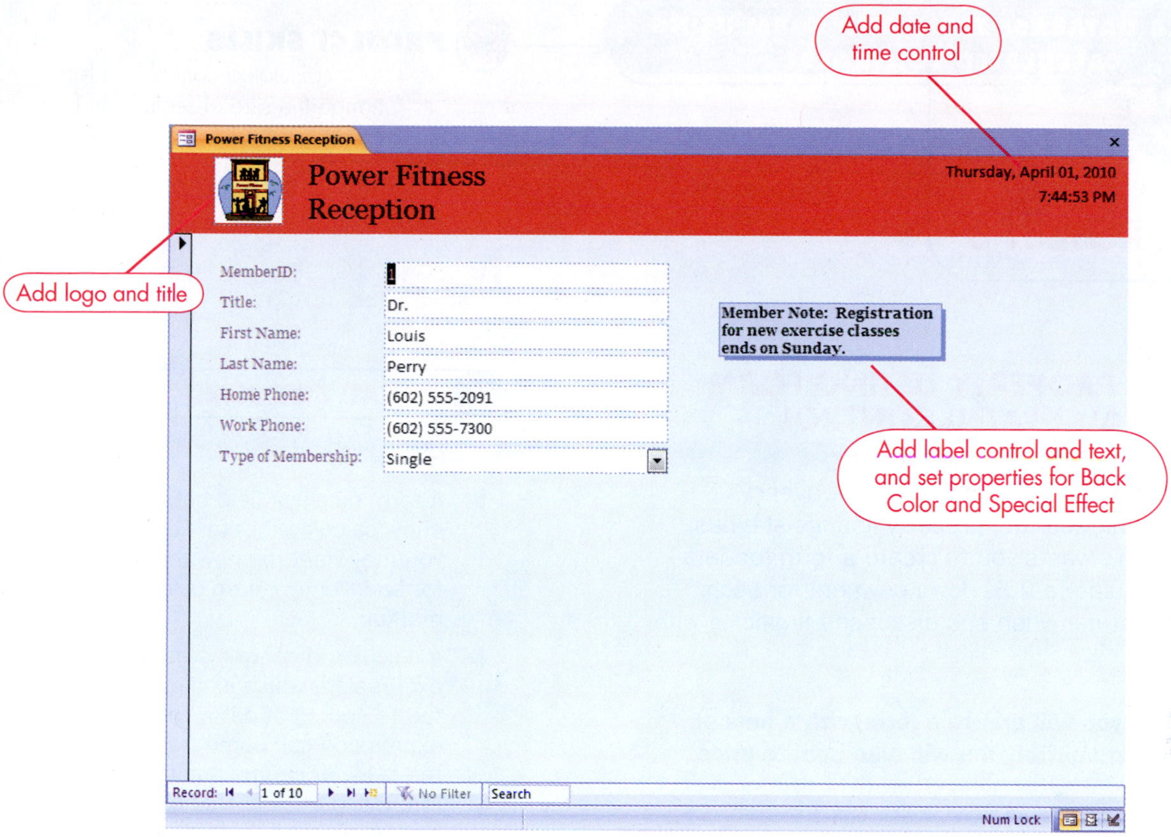

Add date and
time control

Figure 7.2a Power Fitness Reception form

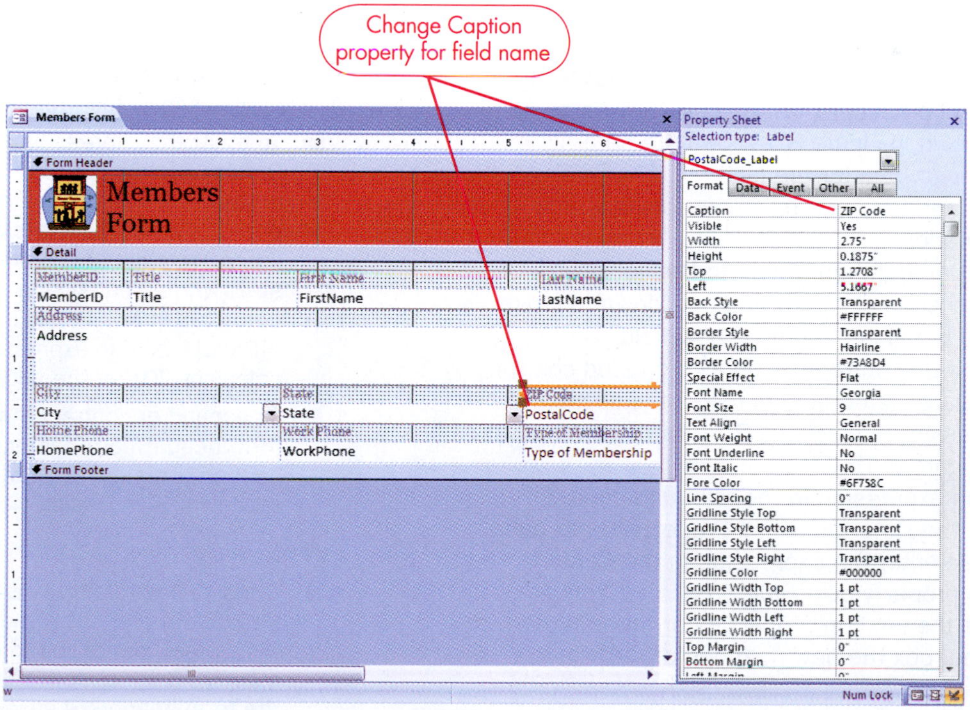

Add logo and title

Add label control and text,
and set properties for Back
Color and Special Effect

Change Caption
property for field name

Figure 7.2b Members Form in Design view

CREATE A DATABASE TABLE AND FORM USING CALCULATED CONTROLS

▶ PROJECT SKILLS
✴ Use a calculated control in a form
✴ Change the size of sections in form Design view

PROJECT 8

8.1 CREATE A PROPERTY LISTING FORM WITH A CALCULATED CONTROL

Chris James, who has her own real estate agency, has created a table with the property listings she has obtained. She now wants you to create a form for data input and to calculate a 20% down payment for each property to assist her when she discusses financing with clients.

In this project, you will create a form with a header and a calculated control. You will also update price data.

1. Find **5.4listings** from your files or data file **d8.1listings**, copy it to your Solutions folder, and rename it **8.1listings**.
2. Create a form with the wizard using all fields, a Columnar layout, and the Opulent style, and name it `Listings Form`.
3. In form Layout view, delete the form header text, and then add a header with the company name and logo, as shown in Figure 8.1a. Use the data file **d8.1jameslogo.bmp** for the logo.
4. Add a date and time control to the top-right side of the form header.
5. Save the form and then switch to Design view.
6. Drag the top edge of the form footer down to make room in the detail section for a new field.
7. Use the Text Box button to add a calculated control, under the Date Listed field in the Detail section of the form design, to display a 20% down payment, as shown in Figure 8.1b.
   a. Enter an expression in the unbound control or click the Data tab of the Property Sheet pane, and then enter the expression in the Control Source property box. *Hint: =[Price]*0.2.*
   b. Change the caption properties or enter in the text label box the new field name: `20% Down Payment`.
   c. Adjust the sizes of the boxes to fit the form.

▼ WHAT YOU NEED TO KNOW

Software

▶ A form displays field data but can also show calculated data. For example, you may want to show the retail price for an inventory item by calculating the markup.

▶ A calculated control uses an expression, which is like a formula, for its source of data. The data for the expression can come from a field in the table or can be a constant value in the expression. Use a text box to display a calculated value. In Design view, click the Text Box button in the Controls group, and then place the box where you want it on the form design. When you use a text box control, a caption is assigned to the text box. You may change the caption by changing the control's Caption property on the Format tab of the Property Sheet pane.

▶ To enter the expression, modify the Control Source property for the field on the Data tab of the Property Sheet pane, or enter the expression in the control directly. The expression should start with an equal sign and include field data in brackets. For example: =[Price]*.2 is an expression that would calculate 20% of the price.

▶ To expand or contract the size of the form header, form footer, or detail section, drag the edge of the section to its new size in Design view.

Project

▶ Chris James Realtors needs a form to make data entry and updates easier. Ms. James wants you to include the agency name, a logo, and the date in the form header. She would also like a calculated field to display 20% of the price of the home as a down payment value.

Continued on next page

8. Change to Form view and, if necessary, switch back to Design view to make modifications. Change the Format property for the calculated control value to Currency on the Property Sheet pane. Save the form design and then switch to Form view.

9. Several listing prices have been lowered, two listings have sold, and there are two new listings. Make the following updates:

   a. Delete the records for the townhouses in Philadelphia on Targee St. and in Springfield on Stobe Ave. They have both been sold.

   b. The price on the Cape Cod on Alberta Drive in Philadelphia has been reduced from $495,000 to $482,500.

   c. The price of the split level on Tysens Lane in Kellyville has been reduced from $399,900 to $385,900.

   d. New listings obtained on 11/16/2010:
- A 3-bedroom colonial on 567 Tryon Boulevard in Springfield listed at $396,500.
- A 3-bedroom townhouse on 41 Greenley Place in Drexel Hill listed at $355,500.

10. Save and close the database.

▶ Banks like to see a 20% or better down payment on a mortgage. However, there are mortgages available with lower down payments.

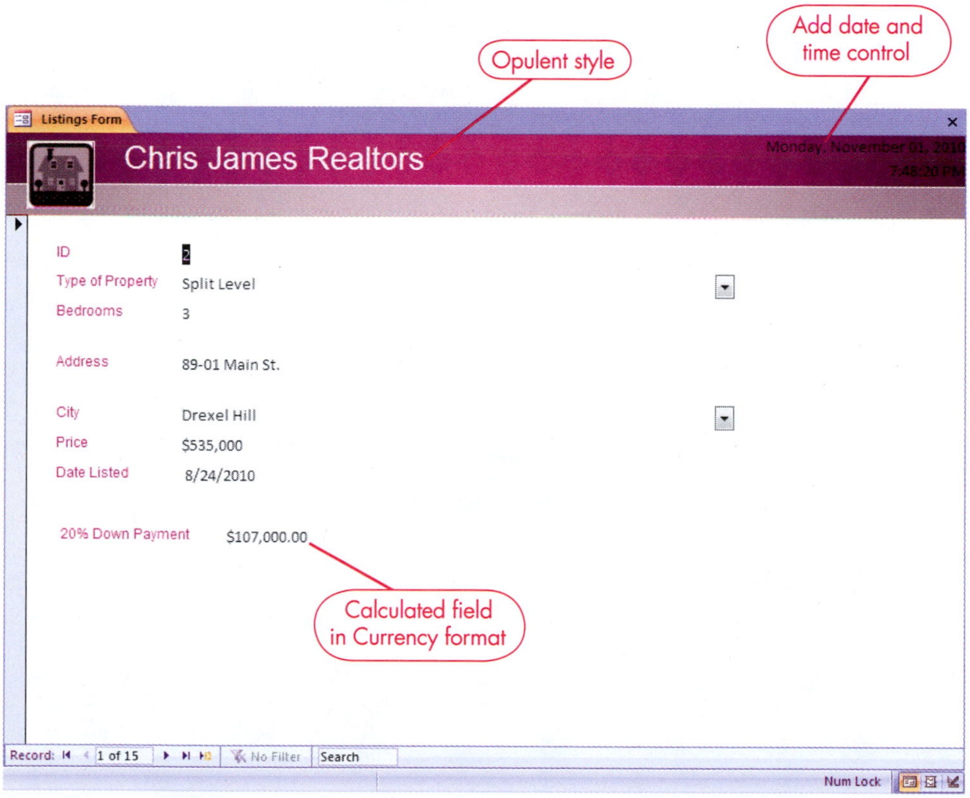

Figure 8.1a Listings form

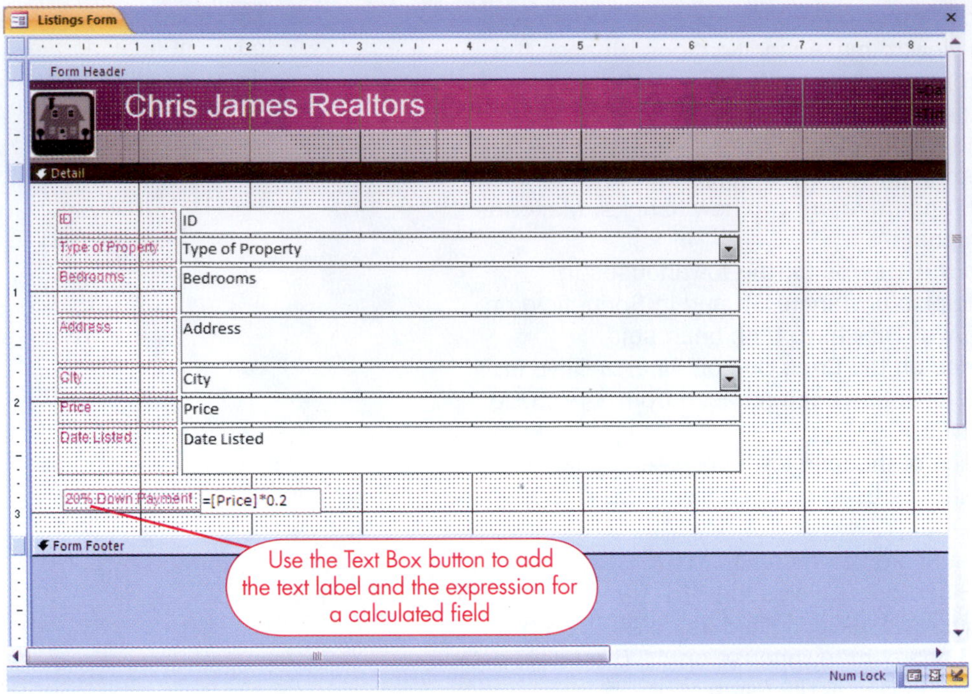

Figure 8.1b Listings Form in Design view

8.2 CREATE FORMS AND ADD A CALCULATED CONTROL

Ollie's Cycles has two tables in its database. They would like you to create forms for both tables that use the same theme, and would also like you to create a calculated field to find the value of each inventory item.

In this project, you will create a new Vendors form and modify the Products form by adding a calculated field and changing the form header.

1. Find **7.1mdse** from your files or data file **d8.2mdse**, copy it to your Solutions folder, and rename it **8.2mdse**.
2. Create a form with the Form Wizard using all the fields in the Vendors table, the Columnar layout, and the Metro style, and then name the object `Vendors Form`.
3. Switch to Layout view, and then add the header and the company logo, shown in Figure 8.2a. Use the graphics data file **d8.2ollielogo.bmp**. Save and close the form.
4. Open the Products form in Design view. Change the form header text as shown in Figure 8.2b.
5. Use the Text Box button to add a calculated control in the Detail section to display the value of the inventory, as shown in Figure 8.2b.
   a. Enter an expression in the unbound control or click the Data tab of the Property Sheet pane and then enter the expression in the Control Source property box. *Hint:* =[Unit Price]*[Units in Stock].
   b. Set the format property for the calculated control value to Currency.
   c. Change the caption properties or enter in the text label box the new field name: `Value of Inventory`.
   d. Adjust the sizes of the boxes to fit the form.
6. Save and close the form and the database.

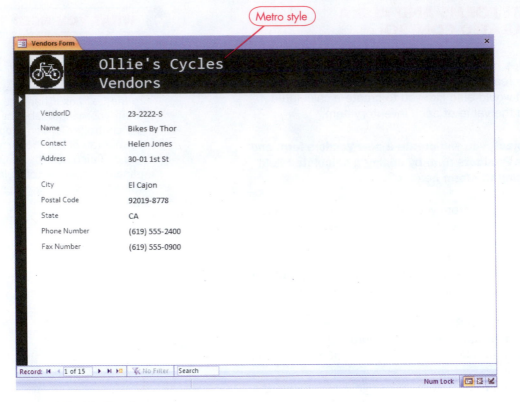

Figure 8.2a Vendors form

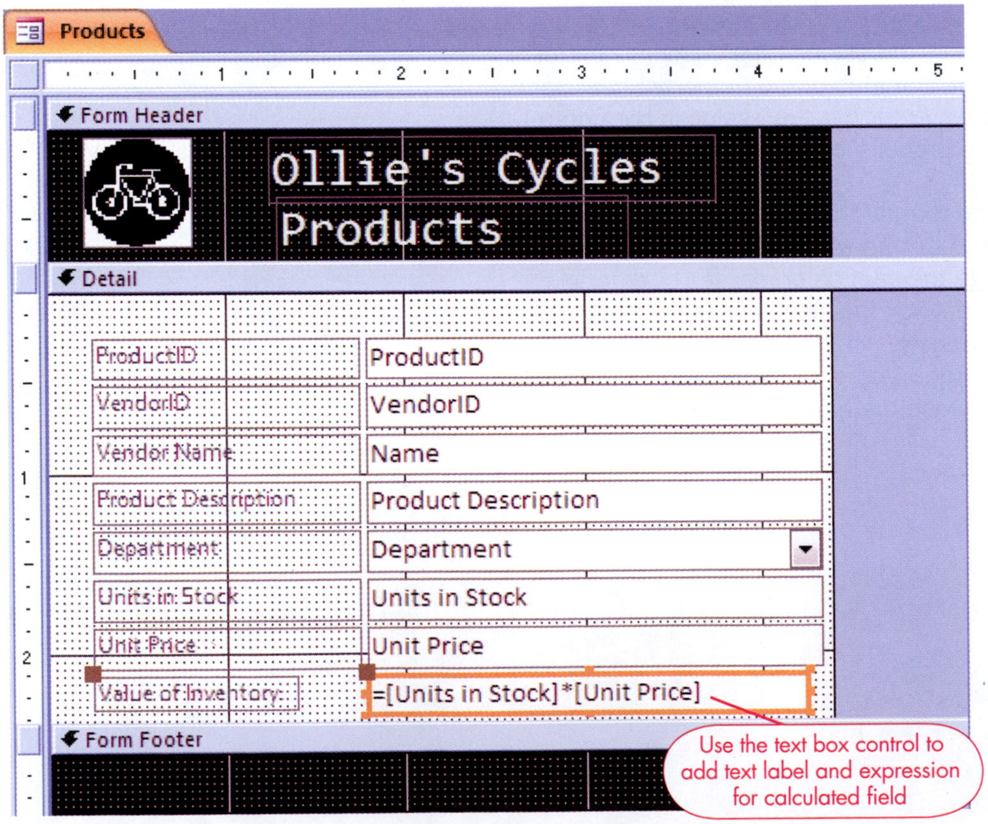

Figure 8.2b Products form in Design view

CHAPTER 4

Getting Information

In this chapter, you will complete the following projects:

PROJECT 9
Find, Replace, and Filter Data
PROJECT 9.1 Find and Replace Student Data
PROJECT 9.2 Sort Movie Collection Data
PROJECT 9.3 Apply and Remove Filters on Inventory Data

PROJECT 10
Query a Database Using Wizards
PROJECT 10.1 Query Customer Data Using Wizards
PROJECT 10.2 Query Movie Data with Calculations
PROJECT 10.3 Create Duplicate and Unmatched Queries on Inventory Data

PROJECT 11
Query a Database in Design View
PROJECT 11.1 Query Student Data in Query Design View
PROJECT 11.2 Add a Calculated Field to an Inventory Query

PROJECT 12
Review Relationships and Create Multi-Table Queries
PROJECT 12.1 Create a New Table, Relationship, and Queries for Students
PROJECT 12.2 Edit Relationships and Create Queries in an Inventory Database

FIND, REPLACE, AND FILTER DATA

PROJECT SKILLS
✳ Find a record
✳ Find and replace field data
✳ Sort records in a datasheet
✳ Apply and remove filters

PROJECT 9

9.1 FIND AND REPLACE STUDENT DATA

Schuyler College needs you to locate data from the student database and also to make some replacements to change address formats.

In this project, you will use the Find and Replace features to search and update records in the database.

1. Find **6.3students** in your files or data file **d9.1students**, copy it to your Solutions folder, and rename it **9.1students**. Open the file.

2. You are looking for a student whose last name begins with "O." With the Students table open in Datasheet view, select the Last Name column, and then click the Find button. Enter **O** and set the Match option to Start of Field. Click Find Next to see any field data that is a match. What is the student's name and major?

3. There is a student whose last name ends in "quin" but you do not know how to spell his or her name to get the record. Use the Find feature and the Any Part of Field Match option. What is the student's name and major?

4. A student whose last name is Kretova has come into the office to provide her middle name for her student record. Find her record and add the middle name, **Riesa**.

5. Use a wildcard in the last name field to find a record for a student whose last name begins with Ap. We are not sure of the spelling. What is the student's name and Student ID number?

6. Select the Major field, and then find and replace all occurrences of Computer Science with **Information Technology**.

7. Select the Address field. Use the Find and Replace operations to eliminate all the abbreviations in the addresses. Review each replacement by clicking the Find Next and/or Replace buttons as necessary, to avoid replacing the letters in street names by mistake.

WHAT YOU NEED TO KNOW

Software

▶ You used the Find and Replace feature to locate data in an entire table. You can also use this feature to search for the contents of specific fields by selecting the field before opening the Find and Replace dialog box. Click the Find button on the Home tab to open the Find and Replace dialog box.

▶ In addition, there are settings that allow you to look for an exact match, a match to the start of a field, or a match to any part of a field. This allows you to find a record when you are guessing at spelling or know only part of the information. As discussed earlier, you can use a wildcard (*) in the search to indicate any number of unknown characters.

▶ The Find feature ignores case and format unless you specify Match Case or Search Fields as Formatted. Use these restrictive features to limit results if the database is large and would ordinarily return many records.

▶ You can use the Find and Replace feature to update field contents in many records. Use the Replace button to replace one occurrence at a time, and the Replace All button to change all occurrences automatically. Use Replace All judiciously because there is no Undo feature. You can review each replacement by clicking Find Next to go to the next occurrence of the search item and then click Replace when necessary.

Continued on next page

Replace: Ave with **Avenue**
Blvd with **Boulevard**
Dr with **Drive**
La with **Lane**
Pl with **Place**
Rd with **Road**
St with **Street**

8. Close the Find and Replace dialog box.

9. Switch to table Design view, and then change the data type for the Major field to a lookup field. Enter the following majors: `Accounting`, `Information Technology`, `Marketing`, `Office Administration`. Save and close the table.

10. Add the new students shown in Figure 9.1 to the database in the Students form.

11. Close and save the database.

Project

▶ You will use the Find feature to locate several records for which you have limited information. Also, one student wants to have her middle name added to her data. In addition, the administration has decided that there should be no abbreviations in students' addresses.

▶ Write the answers to the questions as part of your solution for this project. The questions are provided in data file **d9.1questions.docx**.

New Students

#2399	#2402
Harold Ray Gordon	Patricia Ann Kelly
135 Thompson Street	7564 Ripley Road
Peoria, IL 61607-2312	Metamora, IL 61581-1209
(309) 555-8234	(309) 555-5477
hrgordie@jus.com	patkelly@ent.com
Accounting	Marketing

#2403	#2405
John Wells Trainor	Olivea Marie Vanderling
298 Arizona Avenue	654 Currier Place
Peoria Heights, IL 61616-1006	Bartonville, IL 61607-1243
(309) 555-1998	(309) 555-0097
jwtrainor@res.com	vander2@klc.com
Information Technology	Accounting

Figure 9.1

9.2 SORT MOVIE COLLECTION DATA

Your friend with the movie collection would like you to help him find data in his database by sorting the records.

In this project, you will sort the database to obtain answers to specific questions.

1. Find data file **d9.2movie**, copy it to your Solutions folder, and rename it **9.2movie**. Open the file.
2. Open the table in Design view, and then change the Subject field to a lookup field with the following list of test values: **Action**, **Classic**, **Comedy**, **Drama**, **Musical**, **Mystery**, **Science fiction**, **Thriller**.
3. Save the new table design.
4. In Datasheet view, find the African Queen record and then change the subject to Classic.
5. Add the new movies listed in Figure 9.2b, using the drop-down list to enter the Subject field data.
6. In Datasheet view, sort the Subject field in ascending order. How many movies are there in each category?
7. Switch to the Movie Collection Form, and then sort the Director ID field in ascending order.
8. Use the Find feature to find movies directed by Ridley Scott. Which movies directed by Ridley Scott are in the collection? Notice that this would be easier to view in a table in Datasheet view.
9. Switch back to the table and then sort by Director ID. Which movies directed by Steven Soderbergh are in the collection?
10. Select the Year Released field, and then sort it in ascending order. Save the table.
11. Print a copy of the datasheet, which is in sequence by year of release, as shown in Figure 9.2a. Be sure to use Page Setup to set the orientation to landscape for the table.
12. Save and close the database.

WHAT YOU NEED TO KNOW

Software

▶ Records are entered into a database in random order, but you may need to see them in alphabetical order or by category. You may sort a column of data in ascending or descending order in Form or Datasheet view. It is easier to see the results of a sort in Datasheet view.

▶ Ascending order displays data in alphabetical order or in numerical order from lowest to highest. Descending order is the reverse.

▶ If you need to keep the records in the order in which they were entered, you can always sort them by ID number.

▶ To sort a table in Datasheet view, as shown in Figure 9.2a, select the column to sort, click the Ascending or Descending button on the Home tab in the Sort & Filter group, or click the list arrow on the right of the column heading to display the sort options. You may print the sorted version of the table and/or save the table in that order. To sort a Form, click the field and then click the appropriate sort button to display the first record in that sort.

Project

▶ You will change one of the fields in the Movie database to a lookup field and then you will need to add several more records.

▶ You will sort the movie collection to find the answers to various questions. The owner of the collection would like to see the films owned in each category and the films in the collection by specific directors.

Continued on next page

Sort applied

Movie Collection

MovieID	Movie Title	Actress ID	Actor ID	Director ID	Year Released	Subject	Purchase Price	Add New
1	African Queen	Hepburn	Bogart	Huston	1951	Classic	$5.35	
15	Cape Fear	Bergen	Mitchum	Thompson	1952	Mystery	$14.95	
14	Singing in the Rain	Reynolds	Kelly	Donin	1956	Musical	$9.95	
8	My Blue Heaven	Cusack	Martin	Ephron	1990	Comedy	$19.95	
11	Postcards from the Edge	Streep	Heald	Nichols	1990	Drama	$12.50	
6	Life With Mikey	Wasserstein	Fox	Lapine	1993	Comedy	$9.95	
7	Midnight Run	Phillips	De Niro	Brest	1998	Comedy	$12.50	
13	The X Files	Anderson	Duchovny	Bowman	1998	Science fiction	$19.95	
3	Best in Show	Coolidge	Hitchcock	Guest	2000	Comedy	$19.95	
10	Pay It Forward	Hunt	Osment	Leder	2000	Drama	$19.95	
4	Gladiator	Nielsen	Crowe	Scott	2000	Drama	$15.50	
2	Autumn in New York	Stritch	Gere	Chen	2000	Drama	$19.95	
12	Traffic	Zeta-Jones	Douglas	Soderbergh	2000	Drama	$12.50	
9	No Alibi	Doig	Cain	Pittman	2000	Mystery	$9.95	
18	Spy Game		Redford	Scott	2001	Drama	$19.95	
16	Ocean's Eleven	Roberts	Clooney	Soderbergh	2002	Comedy	$18.95	
19	Mothman Prophecies	Linney	Gere	Pellington	2002	Science fiction	$18.95	
20	Sea Biscuit		Maguire	Ross	2003	Drama	$22.12	
21	Spider-Man 2	Dunst	Maguire	Raimi	2004	Action	$20.49	
17	Crash	Bullock	Howard	Haggis	2005	Drama	$19.95	
22	The Bourne Ultimatum	Allen	Damon	Greengrass	2007	Action	$22.19	
23	Hairspray	Blonsky	Travolta	Shankman	2007	Musical	$22.49	
(New)								

Figure 9.2a Movie Collection by year of release

▶ Write the answers to the following questions as part of your solution for this project. The questions can also be printed from data file **d9.2questions.docx**.

QUESTIONS	ANSWERS
• How many movies are there in each category?	Action: Classic: Comedy: Drama: Musical: Mystery: Science fiction:
• Which movies directed by Ridley Scott are in the collection?	
• Which movies directed by Steven Soberbergh are in the collection?	

Movies Added to Collection

Movie Title: Sea Biscuit
ActressID: -
ActorID: Maguire
DirectorID: Ross
Year Released: 2003
Subject: Drama
Purchase Price: 22.12

Movie Title: Spider-Man 2
ActressID: Dunst
ActorID: Maguire
DirectorID: Raimi
Year Released: 2004
Subject: Action
Purchase Price: 20.49

Movie Title: The Bourne Ultimatum
ActressID: Allen
ActorID: Damon
DirectorID: Greengrass
Year Released: 2007
Subject: Action
Purchase Price: 22.19

Movie Title: Hairspray
ActressID: Blonsky
ActorID: Travolta
DirectorID: Shankman
Year Released: 2007
Subject: Musical
Purchase Price: 22.49

Figure 9.2b New data

9.3 APPLY AND REMOVE FILTERS ON INVENTORY DATA

Ollie's Cycles needs to get answers about its inventory quickly and accurately. It would like you to filter the data to provide the information it needs.

In this project, you will apply filters by selection and by form to obtain answers and printed lists for management's questions.

1. Find **8.2mdse** in your files or data file **d9.3mdse**, copy it to your Solutions folder, and rename it **9.3mdse**. Open the file.
2. Open the Inventory table to print a list of accessories in the inventory.
   a. Click the list arrow in the Department field heading.
   b. Apply an ascending sort.
   c. Click the list arrow again, click to deselect the Select All box, and then click Accessories. Click OK.
   d. Print a list of the Accessories stock on hand.
   e. Click the Toggle Filter button to remove the filter.
3. Open the Products form. Notice that there are 39 product inventory forms.
   a. Select the Bicycles department on any form, and then click the Selection button in the Sort & Filter group. Select Equals "Bicycles".
   b. Looking at the navigation bar, how many different models of bicycles are in stock?
   c. Click the Toggle Filter button to remove the filter.
4. Switch back to the Inventory table, and then in the Units in Stock field, find records with one unit.
   a. Click the list arrow in the Units in Stock field. Deselect Select All and select 1.
   b. How many items have only one unit in stock?
   c. Remove the filter.
5. Sort the records in numeric order by ProductID.
6. Print a list of products in stock from vendors BA-333-3 and MI-45891.
   a. In Datasheet view, click the list arrow in the VendorID field. Deselect Select All and select the vendors to be filtered.
   b. Print a copy of the list and then remove the filter.
7. Use the Sort/Filter feature in the Units in Stock field to find which items have only one or two units in stock. Deselect all items and then select 1 and 2.
   a. Sort the result first alphabetically by Product Description and then from smallest to largest by Units in Stock
   b. Print a copy of the list, and then remove the filter.

WHAT YOU NEED TO KNOW

Software

▶ In the last project, you used sorting to answer questions about categories of data. A better way to get information is to use filters to view only the records that satisfy a set of conditions. The Filter feature is available in Form and Datasheet views.

▶ To filter data in a datasheet column, click the list arrow at the right of the column heading. A list of data in the field appears, which you can select or deselect to filter records. If the filter arrow does not appear on the column headings, click the Filter button on the Home tab in the Sort & Filter group. Deselect the Select All box, and then click the values you wish to see in the filtered list. Click the Toggle Filter button on the Home tab to remove the filter.

▶ To use additional filtering tools, click the Advanced button in the Sort & Filter group, and then click Filter By Form. A sample of the datasheet or form, with drop-down lists for each field, will appear in the work pane. Click on the list arrow to select criteria for the field. If you want to use more than one field, click the Or tab at the bottom of the window and then enter another criterion. Click the Toggle Filter button in the Sort & Filter group to apply the filter. Only the records that meet the selected criteria are displayed. Click the Toggle Filter button again to remove the filter. You can save the table with the filter active or clear the filter and save the table as it was.

▶ You can filter data in a form as well. Click the field to be filtered, and then click the Selection button in the Sort & Filter group. You can then select from the list of criteria related to the field.

Continued on next page

8. Use the Filter By Form function to find the bicycles produced by VendorID numbers 778810-QV or MI-45891.
   a. Click the Advanced button on the Home tab, and then select Filter By Form.
   b. On the form that appears, select 778810-QV and Bicycles from the appropriate fields.
   c. Click the Or tab and select MI-45891 and Bicycles from the appropriate fields.
   d. Click Toggle Filter.
   e. Print a copy of the list. Remove the filter.
9. Close and save the Inventory table and open the Vendors table.
10. Which vendors are in San Diego in the 92125-2987 ZIP code area?
    a. Sort the table in alphabetical order by vendor name.
    b. Use the best method to find any San Diego vendors in the 92125-2987 zone.
    c. Who are they?
    d. Remove the filter.
11. Close and save the database.

Project

▶ Ollie's Cycles would like you to generate the following lists and/or answers. You can print the list from data file **d9.3questions.docx**.

QUESTIONS	ANSWERS
Print a list of accessories in inventory.	
How many different models of bicycles are in stock?	
How many items have only one item in stock?	
Print a list of products that are in stock from Vendors BA-333-3 and MI-45891. How many items are on the list?	
Print a list of items that have only one or two units in stock.	
Print a list of bicycles produced by Vendors 778810-QV or MI-45891.	
Ollie's Cycles needs immediate delivery of an item. Which vendors are in San Diego in the 92125 ZIP code area?	

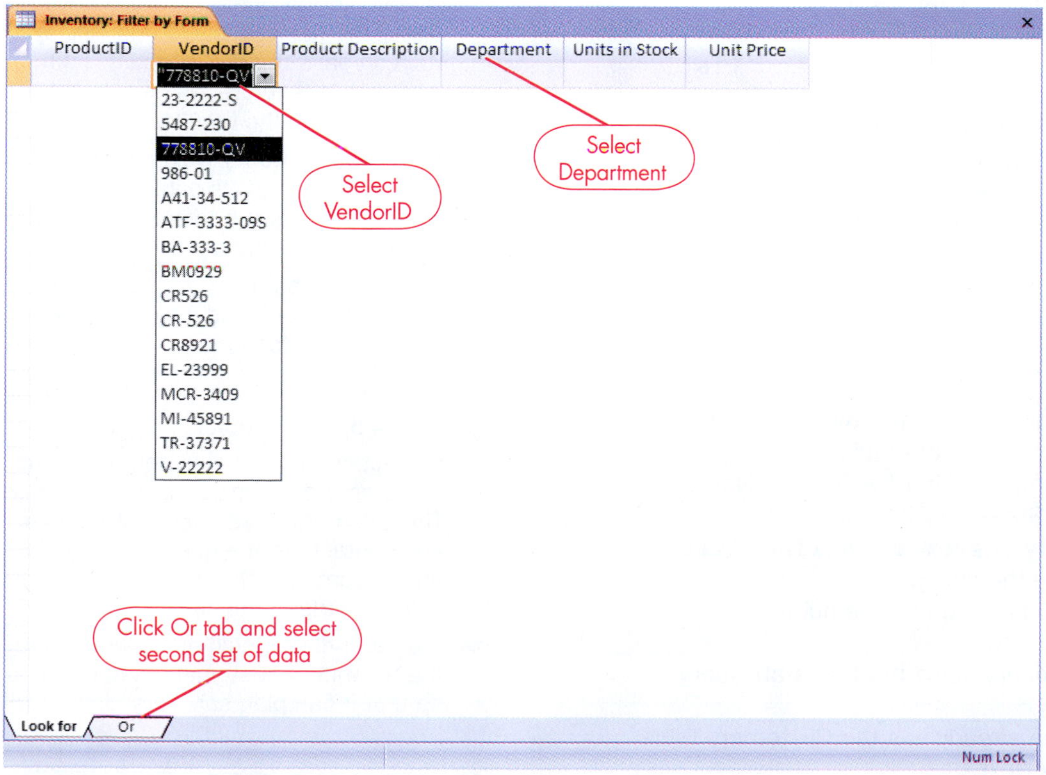

Figure 9.3

QUERY A DATABASE USING WIZARDS

PROJECT SKILLS

✴ Create queries with calculations using the Simple Query Wizard
✴ Create crosstab, duplicates, and unmatched queries

PROJECT 10

10.1 QUERY CUSTOMER DATA USING WIZARDS

Presto Printing Company would like you to use the Query feature to get information from its database of customers.

In this project, you will use the Simple and Crosstab Query Wizards to create queries and produce the lists requested by management.

1. Find **6.2presto** in your files or data file **d10.1presto**, copy it to your Solutions folder, and rename it **10.1presto**. Open the file.
2. Create a query to list customer contacts.
   a. Click the Create tab, click the Query Wizard button, and then click OK to create a Simple Query Wizard.
   b. Select the Company, First Name, Last Name, Job Title, and Business Phone fields. Click Next.
   c. Name the Query **Customer Contact List** and click Finish.
3. On the Customer Contact List query datasheet, add the following new contact made today:
   ```
   All Cruise Travel,
   Marie Buffington,
   Manager,
   (330) 555-8123
   ```
4. Save and close the query.
5. Create a new query that produces a customer mailing list.
   a. Create a new query using the Simple Query Wizard and the Customers table.
   b. Include the Company, First Name, Last Name, Address, City, State, and ZIP Code fields.
   c. Name the query **Customer Mailing List**.
   d. Save and close the query.
6. Create a crosstab query to find the number of customers in each city.
   a. Create a new query using the Crosstab Query Wizard.
   b. The first screen already has the Customers table selected. Click Next.

WHAT YOU NEED TO KNOW

Software

▶ Access provides a Query object and Query Wizards to help you develop queries. Queries retrieve and analyze data from one or more tables or queries. You can create a query in Design view or by using the Query Wizard.

▶ When you click the Query Wizard button on the Create tab in the Other group, a list of four types of Query Wizards appears. They are the Simple Query, the Crosstab Query, the Find Duplicates Query, and the Find Unmatched Query Wizards. The Simple Query Wizard is the one most commonly used. Using the screens in the Query Wizard, you can select the fields to query and display. You can save the query, and if you run it again in the future, all new data will be included in the results.

▶ The Crosstab Query Wizard creates a query that displays data in a spreadsheet format to calculate values of groups of records.

▶ You can add a record or data into a datasheet query, and it will become part of the datasheet.

Project

▶ Presto Printing needs a customer contact list for its sales personnel and a customer mailing list for the office. The sales staff has been instructed to add contacts to the query datasheet and to complete the record only if a sale is made to the client.

▶ Presto Printing would also like to know the number of customers in each city so that it can plan sales visits.

c. On the second screen, select the City field as the row headings and then move it to the Selected Fields list.

d. On the third screen, select the State field as the column headings in your query.

e. On the fourth screen, select the Count function to be calculated in each field or column/row intersection.

f. Name the query **Number of Customers by City**, and then click Finish.

g. In Figure 10.1, notice the number of customers in West Akron and that the first item has no city entry.

h. Save and close the query.

7. A sale was made to the new contact, Marie Buffington. In the Customers table, add the following to the incomplete data for ID 34 for All Cruise Travel: buffington@cruises.com, Fax Number: **(330) 555-8124**, **654 Greene Street, West Akron, Ohio, 44307-1200**. Save and close the table.

8. Open the Number of Customers by City query and notice the number of customers in West Akron. Close the query.

9. Open the Customer Contact List query datasheet, and then add the following new contact made by the Sales Department:

Southside Fitness,
William Morrison,
Office Manager,
(330) 555-7712

10. Save and close the database.

City	Total Of ID	<>	OH
	1	1	
Akron	16		16
Bedford	5		5
Fairlawn	1		1
Hudson Village	3		3
Mogadore	2		2
Ravenna	2		2
Shaker Heights	3		3
West Akron	1		1

Number of Customers by City

Figure 10.1

One City field has no entry

10.2 QUERY MOVIE DATA WITH CALCULATIONS

You would like to apply simple calculations to the movie database using the Query Wizard to get an idea of the total and average costs of the collection.

In this project, you will create a simple query with calculations and a crosstab query.

1. Find **9.2movie** in your files or data file **d10.2movie**, copy it to your Solutions folder, and rename it **10.2movie**. Open the file.

2. To create a query to summarize purchase price data:

   a. Click the Create tab, click the Query Wizard button, and then select the Simple Query Wizard.

   b. Select the PurchasePrice field and, on the next screen, select Summary query.

   c. Click Summary Options and select all the summary options, including Count records in Movie Collection, as shown in Figure 10.2. Click OK.

   d. Click Next, and on the last screen, name the query **Movie Collection Price Statistics**. Click Finish.

   e. View the query. Close the query.

3. Create a crosstab query to find how many movies are in each subject category for each year of release. Use the Year Released as the row heading field and Subject as the column heading field, and calculate the Count in the fields. Name the query **Movie Collection by Year Released**. Close the query.

4. Add one more movie, using the Movie Collection table in Datasheet view: **The Bourne Supremacy**, Actress: **Allen**, Actor: **Damon**, Director: **Greengrass**, Year: **2004**, Subject: **Action**, Purchase Price: **$22.50**. Sort again by the Year Released field in chronological order.

5. Reopen the queries created earlier and notice the changes in the statistics.

6. Use the queries to answer the questions.

7. Save and close the database.

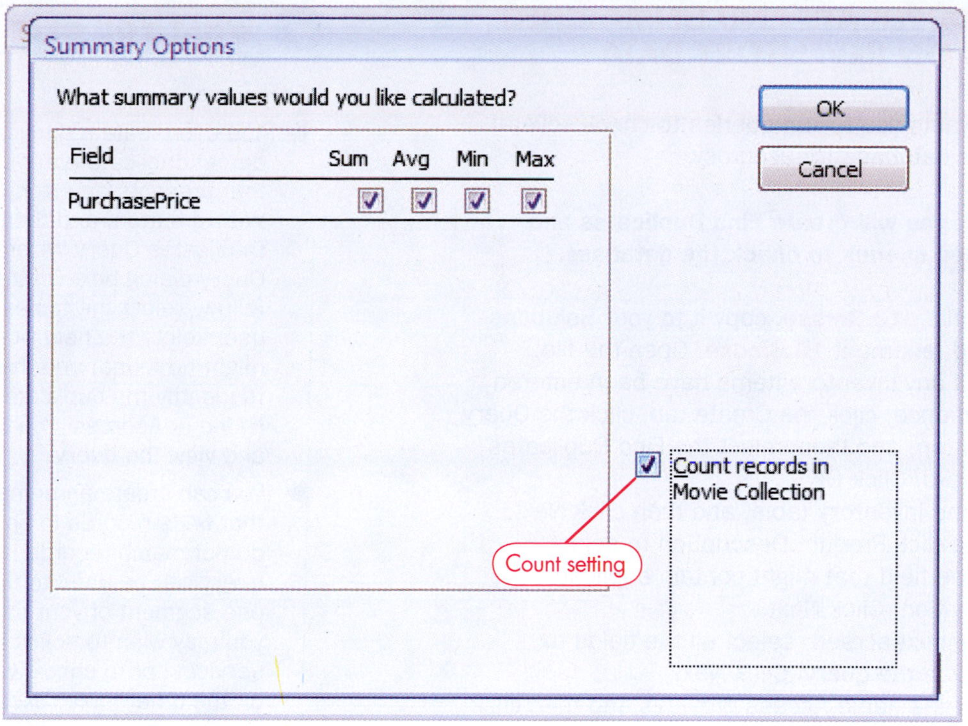

Summary Options

What summary values would you like calculated?

Field	Sum	Avg	Min	Max
PurchasePrice	☑	☑	☑	☑

OK

Cancel

☑ Count records in Movie Collection

Count setting

Figure 10.2

10.3 CREATE DUPLICATE AND UNMATCHED QUERIES ON INVENTORY DATA

Ollie's Cycles wants you to run queries to check several aspects of their database for accuracy.

In this project, you will create Find Duplicates and Find Unmatched queries to check the database.

1. Find data file **d10.3mdse**, copy it to your Solutions folder, and rename it **10.3mdse**. Open the file.
2. To check if any inventory items have been entered more than once, click the Create tab, click the Query Wizard button, and then select the Find Duplicates Query Wizard. Click OK.
   a. Click the Inventory table, and then click Next.
   b. Double-click Product Description to select it as the field that might contain duplicate information. Click Next.
   c. On the next screen, select all the fields to display in the query. Click Next.
   d. Accept the name Access provides and then click Finish.
3. The results of the query, as shown in Figure 10.3a, show that one inventory item has been entered twice. Note the two ProductID numbers. Close the query.
4. Switch to the Inventory table and delete the duplicate record, ProductID 462. Confirm the deletion and close the table.
5. Open the Find duplicates for Inventory query again. Close it.
6. To check if all inventory items have a matching Vendors table entry, click the Query Wizard button, and then select the Find Unmatched Query Wizard.
   a. Click the Inventory table, and then click Next.
   b. Click the Vendors table, and then click Next.
   c. The fields that relate between tables is VendorID which should already be selected in each table list, as shown in Figure 10.3b. Click Next.
   d. Click the double arrow to select all fields for the query results. Click Next.
   e. Accept the name Access provides for the query and click Finish.
7. Note that the query returns one record in the Inventory table that has no matching record in the Vendors table. Note the VendorID and ProductID numbers, and then close the query.
8. Open the Vendors table to check the VendorID that appeared in the query. The Vendors table has the correct number and the Inventory table needs to be corrected. Make the correction.
9. Open the Inventory Without Matching Vendors query again. It should show no values.
10. Close the database.

▼ WHAT YOU NEED TO KNOW

Software

▶ You can create a duplicates query to detect duplicate entries in a field, when that presents an error. Click the Query Wizard button, and then click Find Duplicates Query Wizard in the New Query dialog box. On the screens that follow, select the tables or queries to use; select the field where duplicates might be found; and then select fields to identify the duplicates data, such as Name or Address. You can then name and view the query.

▶ You can create an unmatched query that finds records in one table that do not match records in another. This query can be used to find records from one segment of your database that you may wish to solicit for additional services, or to check why they are not on the other table. Click the Query Wizard button, and then click Find Unmatched Query Wizard in the New Query dialog box. On the screens that follow: Select the table or query that might have unmatched records; select the table or query that contains the related records; select the field that is the same in both tables, as shown in Figure 10.3b; and then select the fields you need to see in the results table. You can then name and view the query.

Project

▶ Ollie's Cycles wants to be sure that the inventory table does not contain any duplicates. It is possible that some items were recorded more than once, and the total inventory value must be verified. In addition, every inventory item must have a related vendor entry. This will require running the Find Unmatched Query Wizard.

Find duplicates for Inventory						✕
Product Descripti ▾	ProductID ▾	VendorID ▾	Department ▾	Units in Stoc ▾	Unit Price ▾	
Pride Helmets	491	BA-333-3	Accessories	12	$99.99	
Pride Helmets	462	BA-333-3	Accessories	12	$99.99	
✳	0					

In Inventory table, delete duplicate record

Figure 10.3a Find duplicates for Inventory

Find Unmatched Query Wizard

What piece of information is in both tables?

For example, a Customers and an Orders table may both have a CustomerID field. Matching fields may have different names.

Select the matching field in each table and then click the <=> button.

Fields in 'Inventory' :

ProductID
VendorID
Product Description
Department
Units in Stock
Unit Price

Fields in 'Vendors' :

VendorID
Name
Contact
Address
City
PostalCode
State
PhoneNumber

<=>

Matching fields: VendorID <=> VendorID

Cancel   < Back   Next >   Finish

Figure 10.3b Find Unmatched Query Wizard

QUERY A DATABASE IN DESIGN VIEW

PROJECT 11

PROJECT SKILLS
- Modify queries in Design view
- Use aggregate functions
- Add a calculated field to a query in Query Design view
- Format and sort query results

11.1 QUERY STUDENT DATA IN QUERY DESIGN VIEW

Schuyler College would like you to create lists of students by college major, a mailing list arranged by ZIP code, and a mailing list of non-Information Technology majors.

In this project, you will create queries using wizards and query Design view.

1. Find **9.1students** in your files or data file **d11.1students**, copy it to your Solutions folder, and rename it **11.1students**. Open the file.

2. Create a simple query using the Query Wizard and include the following fields in the order listed: StudentID, Last Name, First Name, Phone Number, and Major. Name the query **Student Query**.

3. Switch to the Design view of the query. Change the criteria, as shown in Figure 11.1a, adding the "Accounting" criteria in the Major field and deselecting the Show box. It is not necessary to show the major, Accounting, since the list is only for these students. In the design grid, on the Sort line for the Last Name field, select Ascending.

4. Click the Office Button, point to Save As, and then click Save Object As. Name the new query design **Accounting Majors**, and then run the query, as shown in Figure 11.1b.

5. Switch to Design view for the Accounting Majors query, and modify it for Information Technology majors. Click the Office Button, point to Save As, and then click Save Object As. Name the new query **Information Technology Majors**.

6. Create queries to produce lists for "Marketing" and "Office Administration" majors. Right-click and delete the Student query.

7. Create a mailing list using a simple query.
   a. Include the following fields from the Students table: First Name, Middle Name, Last Name, Address, City, State, and ZIP Code.
   b. On the last screen, click the Modify the query design option and name the Query **Student Mailing List**.

WHAT YOU NEED TO KNOW

Software

▶ The Query Wizards help you to create queries; however, you can also create or customize a query in Query Design view. Query Design view shows the structure of a query and it allows you to set criteria for the fields to appear.

▶ You specify criteria for the fields in the design grid by using an expression. For example, you can enter a text data value to be displayed using quotation marks, include a numeric value, or use the greater than ($>$) or less than ($<$) symbols with values.

▶ In the design grid, you can also set sort options and the Show option if the field should not be displayed. If you are displaying records that will have the same entry in a field, it is best to hide the repetitive data by deselecting the Show option.

▶ You can modify a query and save it with a new query name by clicking the Office Button and then clicking the Save As command.

▶ The result of the query is not stored but is recreated each time you open the query. If the query you want to run is currently open in Design view, you can also run it by clicking the Run button on the Design tab in the Results group.

Project

▶ Schuyler College needs lists of its students in each major and would like a mailing list arranged by postal code. Once the queries are saved, they can be rerun anytime and will include all new students.

▶ The college would also like to send a mailing to non-Information Technology majors to advertise their computer courses as electives.

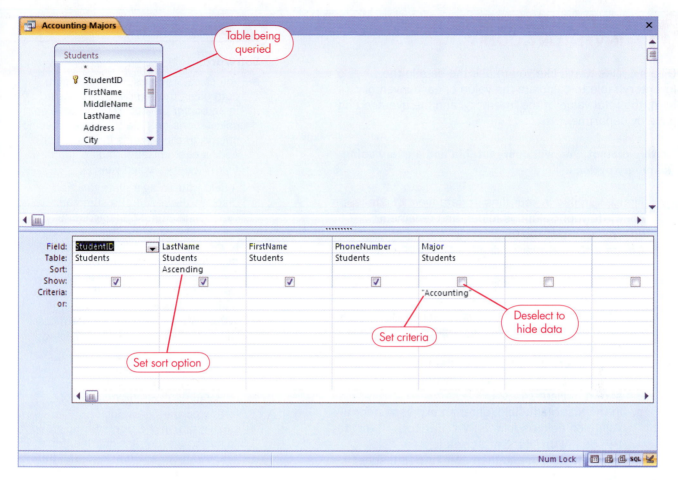

Figure 11.1a Query Design view

c. In query Design view, sort the ZIP Code field in ascending order.

d. Save the design.

e. Click the Run button on the Query Tools Design tab in the Results group.

f. Print a copy of the mailing list.

8. Use the Find Unmatched Query Wizard to compare the Students table with the Information Technology Majors query.

a. Use the StudentID field as the field to compare.

b. Use the First Name, Middle Name, Last Name, Address, City, State, and ZIP Code fields as the fields to display for the non-Information Technology mailing list.

c. Name the query **Computer Electives Mailing List**, and select the Modify the query design option.

d. In query Design view, sort the ZIP Code in ascending order.

e. Run the query.

f. Print a copy of the mailing list.

9. Close and save the database.

Student ID	Last Name	First Name	Phone Numl
2319	Berrito	Juan	(309) 555-1919
2396	Edwards	Carol	(309) 555-7103
2343	Geisler	Dorothy	(309) 555-4240
2335	Gjonbalaj	Adem	(309) 555-1052
2315	Goldstein	Floyd	(309) 555-8874
2399	Gordon	Harold	(309) 555-8234
2382	Kremer	Ilya	(309) 555-7771
2365	Kuang	Hui	(309) 555-7774
2368	Kubis	Eric	(309) 555-0908
2320	Lorenzo	Mario	(309) 555-8989
2388	Lubetrin	Tatiana	(309) 555-4433
2337	Ortiz	Ramon	(309) 555-1601
2405	Vanderling	Olivea	(309) 555-0097

Figure 11.1b Accounting Majors query

11.2 ADD A CALCULATED FIELD TO AN INVENTORY QUERY

Ollie's Cycles would like you to use the data in the Inventory table to calculate the value of each inventory item, the total value of the inventory, and the average unit price by department.

In this project, you will query a table and a query using summary options.

1. Find **10.3mdse** in your files or data file **d11.2mdse**, copy it to your Solutions folder, and rename it **11.2mdse**. Open the file.
2. Create a simple query using the Query Wizard, and edit it in Design view, as shown in Figure 11.2a.
   a. Use the Inventory table and all fields except for VendorID to create a Detail query.
   b. Name the query **Inventory Valuation**, click the Modify the query design option, and then click Finish.
   c. In the query design grid, set the Sort option to Ascending for the Product Description field, as shown in Figure 11.2a.
   d. In the first blank field, enter an expression for a Valuation field as follows: **Valuation: [Unit Price]*[Units in Stock]**.
   e. Save the design and then switch to Datasheet view.
3. Create a simple query using the Query Wizard to find the sum of the valuations and average unit price by department.
   a. Use the Inventory Valuation query and the Department, Valuation, Unit Price, and Units in Stock fields.
   b. Click the Summary option and then click Summary Options. Select Sum for the Valuation field and Average for the Unit Price and Units in Stock fields.
   c. Name the query **Inventory Summary by Department**.
   d. Finish the query and then switch to Design view.
   e. Set the Sort option to Ascending for the Department field, as shown in Figure 11.2b.
   f. Notice the Group by, Sum, and Avg settings on the Total line in the design grid.
   g. Right-click the Sum of Valuation field, click Properties, and set the Format property for Currency.
   h. Save the design and switch to Datasheet view.
4. Close the database.

Software

▶ You calculated or summarized field data using the Simple Query Wizard in an earlier project. You can develop calculations on data that meet specific criteria by using fields in a table, or by adding customized formulas in a new field in query Design view.

▶ A field with an aggregate function displays the result of a summary expression. To add an aggregate calculation, click the Totals button to display the Totals row on the design grid. You can group records for calculation in this row or select mathematical functions. If you select summary functions in the Query Wizard, these settings and formulas will be visible in Query Design view.

▶ You can also use an empty field as a calculated field and enter an expression or formula for the calculation. Click the Builder  button on the Query Tools Design tab, in the Query Setup group, to create the expression, or enter the field names in brackets with the appropriate mathematical operators, using the symbols and syntax used in Excel.

▶ Format the results of a calculation by right-clicking the field in Design view, selecting Properties, and setting the Format property on the General tab of the Property Sheet pane.

Project

▶ To find the inventory valuation, use an expression in a new field. The expression contains the name of the new field, the names of the fields to multiply, and the multiplication sign. The expression is: Valuation: [Unit Price]*[Units in Stock].

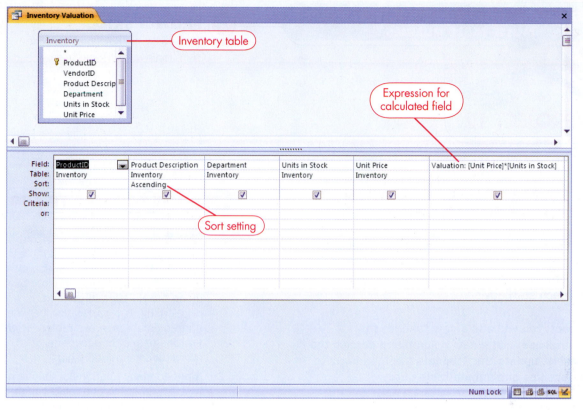

Figure 11.2a Inventory Valuation query

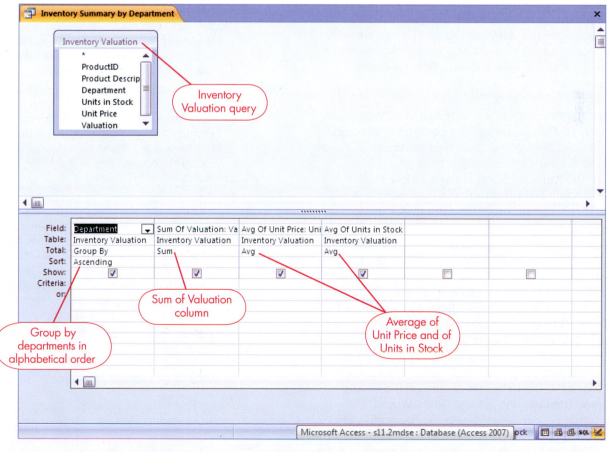

Figure 11.2b Inventory Summary by Department query

PROJECT SKILLS
✶ Review the Relationships window
✶ Create a multi-table query

PROJECT 12

12.1 CREATE A NEW TABLE, RELATIONSHIP, AND QUERIES FOR STUDENTS

Schuyler College would like you change their database so that they are able to find student advisor information when in the Students table and to see the list of students assigned to each staff advisor.

> **In this project, you will add a new table to the Students database, add a new column and data to the Students table, update the Students form, and create table relationships and a multi-table query.**

1. Find **11.1students** in your files or data file **d12.1students**, copy it to your Solutions folder, and rename it **12.1students**. Open the file.
2. Using the information shown in Figure 12.1a as a guide, create the Advisors table in Design view. Use Advisor ID as the primary key, with an AutoNumber data type, and create a lookup field for the Department.
3. Enter the advisor data.
4. Open the Students table in Design view. Add an Advisor ID field in the second position by inserting a row. Use the Number data type for the field. Save the new design and close the table.
5. Open the Students Form in Layout view. Click the Add Existing Fields button, and then add the Advisor ID field to the bottom of the form under the E-mail address. Save the form.
6. Carefully add the advisor information, as shown in Figure 12.1b, to the datasheet or the form. Check your work.
7. Create a one-to-many relationship between the tables, using the Advisor ID field, by clicking on the Advisor ID field in one table and dragging it to the same field in the other table.
8. Create a multi-table query using the Advisors and Students tables.
   a. Click the Query Wizard button on the Create tab, and then use the Simple Query Wizard.
   b. In the Students table, use the StudentID, Last Name, and First Name fields.
   c. Click the list arrow and select the Advisors table. Use the Title, Last, and Department fields.

WHAT YOU NEED TO KNOW

Software

▶ Before you can create multi-table queries, forms, or reports, you must establish how the tables relate by using the Relationships window. A relationship is a correlation between shared columns in two tables. There are one-to-one, one-to-many, or many-to-many relationships.

▶ A one-to-many relationship is one in which a record in one table can match many records in a second table. However, each record in the second table can only have one match in the first table. For example, the same VendorID can be found several times in the Inventory table. But each VendorID in the Inventory table can have only one match in the Vendors table.

▶ To create or view relationships, click the Database Tools tab, and then click the Relationships button. To create a relationship, you can drag the primary key from one table to a similar field, called the foreign key, in the other table.

▶ Once tables are related you can create a multi-table query, based on data from several tables. In the first screen of the Simple Query Wizard, click the first table to include in the query, and then double-click each field to add to the query. Next, click the list arrow in the Tables/Queries box, and then click the next table to include. Include the fields you need, and then complete the query in the usual way.

Continued on next page

d. Name the query **Advisors Query**, and select the Modify the query design option.

e. In Query Design view, set the LastName field for students to an Ascending sort.

f. Save the query and view the results.

9. In the Advisors Query, use the list arrow in the Last field for the Advisor name to find out how many students are assigned to Professor Poling. Click the Toggle Filter button to reverse the filter. Close and save the query.

10. Create a Crosstab Query using the Advisors Query as the basis for the data. Use the Advisor's last name as the row headings and the Department as the column headings. Set the Count function to calculate at each row/column intersection. Name the query **Students per Advisor Query**, and run it as shown in Figure 12.1c.

11. Close the query and the database.

Project

▶ Schuyler College has assigned advisors to each student according to their major. The Students table needs a new column, Advisor ID, and you need to enter the data that will identify the advisor assigned. When you add a new column to the table, the form associated with that table does not automatically include that new field. You must go into the form and add the new field in Layout view to update the form.

▶ You will need to create the Advisors table, add advisor data to the Students table, establish relationships between tables, and then create a query based on both tables.

Advisor ID	Title	First	Last	Department	Add New Field
1	Dr.	William	Martino	Accounting	
2	Professor	Mary	Poling	Office Administration	
3	Dr.	Edwin	Zhang	Information Technology	
4	Professor	Anthony	Willhelm	Marketing	
5	Dr.	Lois	Sheinfeld	Information Technology	
6	Dr.	Alivea	Tyler	Accounting	
(New)					

Figure 12.1a New Advisors table

Students	
Student ID	Advisor ID
2314	5
2315	1
2316	5
2319	6
2320	1
2325	3
2326	4
2328	3
2329	5
2331	4
2335	1
2336	2
2337	6
2338	4
2339	2
2340	2
2343	1
2345	4
2365	6
2367	2
2368	6
2370	5

Students	
Student ID	Advisor ID
2371	3
2372	2
2374	2
2375	2
2378	4
2380	3
2381	4
2382	1
2383	2
2384	2
2385	4
2388	6
2390	2
2392	5
2395	2
2396	6
2397	3
2399	1
2402	6
2403	5
2405	5

Figure 12.1b New Advisor ID data for Students table

Students per Advisor Query

Last	Total Of StudentID	Accounting	Information	Marketing	Office Administration
Martino	6	6			
Poling	11				11
Sheinfeld	7		7		
Tyler	7	7			
Willhelm	7			7	
Zhang	5		5		

Figure 12.1c Students per Advisor Query

12.2 EDIT RELATIONSHIPS AND CREATE QUERIES IN AN INVENTORY DATABASE

Ollie's Cycles wants you to edit the relationships of its database tables and wants queries and summaries for data using both tables.

In this project, you will edit a relationship between the tables, and create and edit a multi-table select query.

1. Find **11.2mdse** in your files or data file **d12.2mdse**, copy it to your Solutions folder, and rename it **12.2mdse**. Open the file.
2. Edit the relationship between the two tables, as shown in Figure 12.2a, to enforce referential integrity.
   a. Click the Database Tools tab, and then click the Relationships button.
   b. Right-click the join line between the tables, and then click Edit Relationship.
   c. When the Edit Relationships dialog box opens, notice that the relationship is correctly listed, including the fact that this is a one-to-many relationship.
   d. Select the Enforce Referential Integrity box. Click OK.
   e. Save and close the Relationships window.
3. Create a new multi-table query with the Simple Query Wizard.
   a. From the Inventory table, select the ProductID, Product Description, and VendorID fields.
   b. From the Vendors table, select the Name, Contact, Phone Number, and Fax Number fields.
   c. Name the query **Reorder List**.
   d. View the results and then switch to Design view.
   e. Set the sort option to Ascending for Product Description.
   f. Add the Unit Price field from the Inventory table to the query, as shown in Figure 12.2b. In query Design view, drag the field from the table list at the top to the grid, and place it after the Product Description field. You may drag and drop fields to reorder them.
   g. Save the new design.
4. To test referential integrity, add a product to the Inventory table with a new VendorID:

   ProductID: **491**,
   VendorID: **QA-122**,
   Product Description: **Miller Mountain Bike**,
   Department: **Bicycles**,
   Units in Stock: **2**,
   Unit Price: **129.59**

   You should get an error message and the record will not be saved.

▼ WHAT YOU NEED TO KNOW

Software

▶ To view relationships, click the Database Tools tab, and then click the Relationships button. To edit a relationship, right-click the join line between tables, and then click Edit Relationship. In the Edit Relationships dialog box, you can enforce referential integrity, which prevents you from adding a record to a related table if there is no related record in the primary table. For example, you could not add a new VendorID to the Inventory table unless you first defined it in the Vendors table.

Project

▶ You will edit the Vendors and Inventory tables relationship to enforce referential integrity. You will test referential integrity by making an entry in the Inventory table without defining the vendor first.

▶ You will create a multi-table query to find a list of inventory items with vendor data. You will modify the query in Design view to add a field to the query by dragging the new field to the appropriate location in the query design grid.

5. To maintain referential integrity, enter the vendor information into the Vendors table as follows:

VendorID: `QA-122`
Name: `Quality Bike Company`
Contact: `Mike Miller`
Address: `1565 Carling Lane`
City: `El Cajon`
State: `CA`
Postal Code: `92019-8778`
Phone Number: `(619) 555-6524`
Fax Number: `(619) 555-6520`

6. Reenter the Inventory information as listed in Step 4, if necessary.

7. Close and save the database.

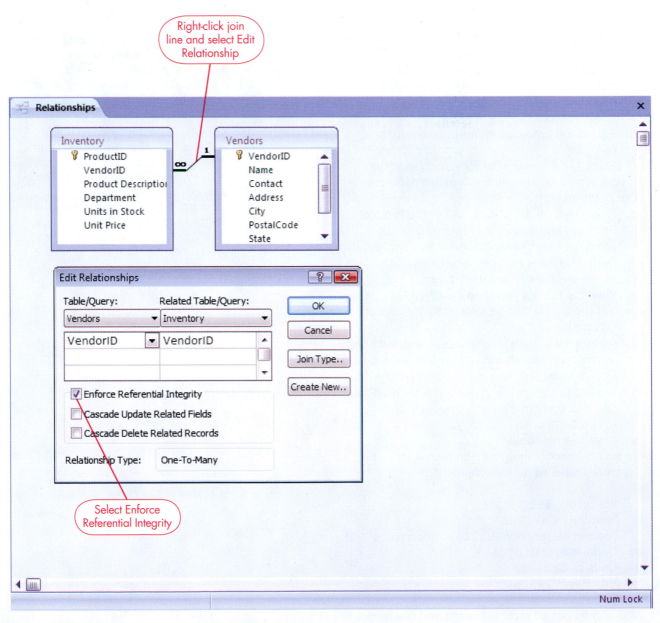

Figure 12.2a Edit Relationships dialog box

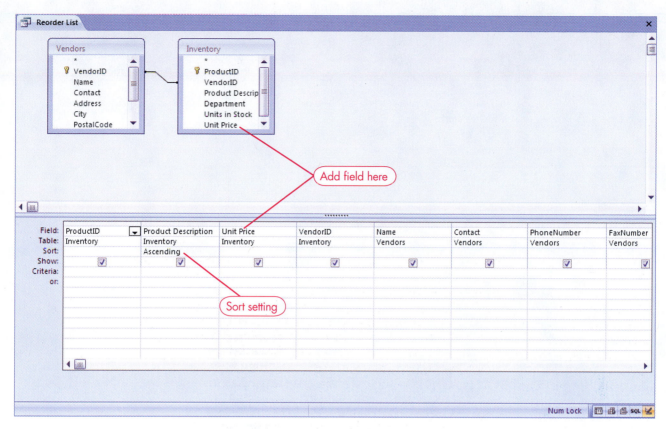

Figure 12.2b Query Design view

CHAPTER 5

Access Reports

In this chapter, you will complete the following projects:

PROJECT 13
Create Reports with Wizards
PROJECT 13.1 Use the Report and Report Wizard Buttons: Customer Database
PROJECT 13.2 Use the Label Wizard: Members Database
PROJECT 13.3 Use the Report Wizard: Student Database

PROJECT 14
Modify Reports
PROJECT 14.1 Use Report Sections and Modify a Listings Report
PROJECT 14.2 Add Calculated Controls and New Objects: Members Database
PROJECT 14.3 Create and Modify Inventory Reports

PROJECT 15
Create Database Objects and Reports
PROJECT 15.1 Add Objects to the Members Database

CREATE REPORTS WITH WIZARDS

PROJECT SKILLS
* Create a report using the Report button
* Create and format reports using the Report Wizard
* Create a report using the Label Wizard

PROJECT 13

13.1 USE THE REPORT AND REPORT WIZARD BUTTONS: CUSTOMER DATABASE

Presto Printing would like you to create a report showing its customer mailing list and other items from its database.

In this project, you will use the Report button to view and create reports from tables and queries.

1. Find **10.1presto** in your files or data file **d13.1presto**, copy it to your Solutions folder, and rename it **13.1presto**. Open the file.

2. The sales force reported a sale to Southside Fitness. Add the missing information to the customer record for Southside Fitness in the Customers table: Customer ID: **35, morrison @southside.com**, Fax: **(330) 555-7715, 450 South Street, Akron, Ohio, 44301-1211**.

3. With the Customers table open, click the Create tab and then click the Report button. View the report that appears. Notice that there are headers and footers and that data is arranged in columns.

4. Close the report without saving it and close the Customers table.

5. Open the Customer Contact List query and create a report using the Report button. Note the order in which the Company names are listed. Close the report without saving it.

6. Create a report using the Report Wizard button.
   a. Click the Create tab, and then click the Report Wizard button.
   b. Use the Query: Customer Contact List for the report and include all fields. Click Next.
   c. Skip the Grouping Level screen. Click Next.
   d. Sort the Company name in Ascending order. Click Next.
   e. Select the Tabular layout in Portrait orientation. Click Next.
   f. Select the Paper style. Click Next.
   g. Name the report **Customer Contact List**, and then click Finish.
   The report will be displayed in Print Preview. Notice that the data in the first column is not fully visible.

WHAT YOU NEED TO KNOW

Software

▶ Reports are database objects that use data from tables and queries to create a presentation-quality printout. Click the Create tab and then click the Report button to create a basic report to display all the fields in a selected table or query automatically. The report data is arranged in columnar fashion with headers and footers for the report and the page.

▶ If you wish to select the columns to appear in a report, add grouping levels or a sort order, or change layout settings, click the Create tab, click the Report Wizard button, and then follow the screens to complete the report. A report's layout or design can be modified in Design or Layout view.

7. Click the Close Print Preview button and switch to Layout view. Close the Field List pane, if necessary. Select the first column containing the Company name and drag the edge of the column to widen it to display the data fully, as shown in Figure 13.1a.

8. Print a copy of the report. Close and save the report.

9. Create a report using the Customer Mailing List query. Use all the fields, group by City, sort the Company name in ascending order, set the Stepped layout with Landscape orientation, and use the Paper style. Name the report **Customer Mailing List by City**, as shown in Figure 13.1b.

10. Switch to Layout view, and then modify the column width of the City column to fully display the data. Also, in Design view, check that the Page Number and ZIP Code controls at the bottom of the report and the edge of the report fit within 10 inches for landscape orientation. Print a copy of the report.

11. Close and save the database.

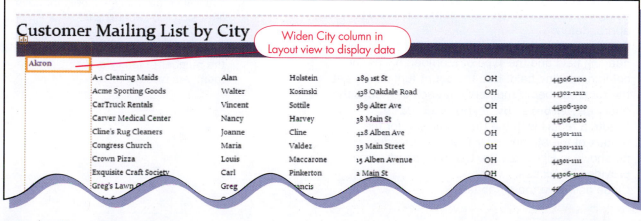

Figure 13.1a Customer Contact List

Figure 13.1b Customer Mailing List by City

USE THE LABEL WIZARD: MEMBERS DATABASE

Power Fitness, a Phoenix-based gym and sports club, wants you to update its Members database and create some queries and reports.

In this project, you will create queries and reports using the Label Wizard.

1. Find data file **d13.2club**, copy it to your Solutions folder, and rename it **13.2club**. Open the file.
2. Create two queries to produce mailing lists for family and single members.
   a. Use the Simple Query Wizard to create a mailing list for family members. Use only the fields necessary for mailings and include the Type of Membership field. Name it **Mailing List-Family Members**, and select the Modify the query design option.
   b. Modify the query design to sort the list by postal code, to set a criterion for "Family" members, and to hide the Type of Membership field. Save the query.
   c. Modify the query design again to find single members. Save it as **Mailing List-Single Members**. Close the query.
3. Create a report using the Labels button to create labels for Family members.
   a. Use the Avery Label, Product number C2242, 3 across, and the default settings for the font.
   b. Move the fields into the sample label so that the Title, First, and Last Names are on the first line; the Address is on the second line; and the City, State, and Postal Code are on the third line. Insert spaces and punctuation as shown in Figure 13.2a.
   c. Set the labels to sort by Postal Code, and name the report **Labels Mailing List-Family Members**.
4. Create the mailing labels for single members using the same settings, and name the report appropriately.
5. Create a crosstab query using the City as the row heading field and the Type of Membership as the column heading field. Use the count function to get the total number of members in each city. Save the query as **Members by Type and City**.
6. Create a report with the Report button for the results of the Members by Type and City query, as shown in Figure 13.2b. Use the report name provided by Access.
7. Close and save the database.

WHAT YOU NEED TO KNOW

Software

▶ The Label Wizard is a report tool that creates mailing labels in standard and custom sizes based on database data. To create mailing labels, select the data source table, click the Create tab, and then in the Reports group click the Labels button. On the first Label Wizard screen, you [Labels] select the label size, unit of measure, label type, and manufacturer. You will then set the font, font size, font color, and font weight. Click Next, and a dialog box opens to assist you in constructing the label, shown in Figure 13.2a. Double-click each field you want to include, in the order you want them to appear. As you complete each line in the address, press [Enter] or [Tab] to move to the next line. Add spaces, returns, other text, and punctuation between fields as necessary. Be certain that the field layout represents how you want the label to print.

▶ In addition, you can enter text that you would like to appear on every label in the Prototype label. For example, if you were doing a mailing to the membership of a club about a family event, you might want to create the label using the Last Name field followed by the word Family. You can then set sort fields, and name and preview the labels.

Project

▶ The management of Power Fitness would like to have separate mailing lists for family and single members to target mailings for special events.

▶ You will create mailing labels for each list using the Label Wizard.

▶ The company would also like to create a query and a report that summarizes the number of family and single members by city.

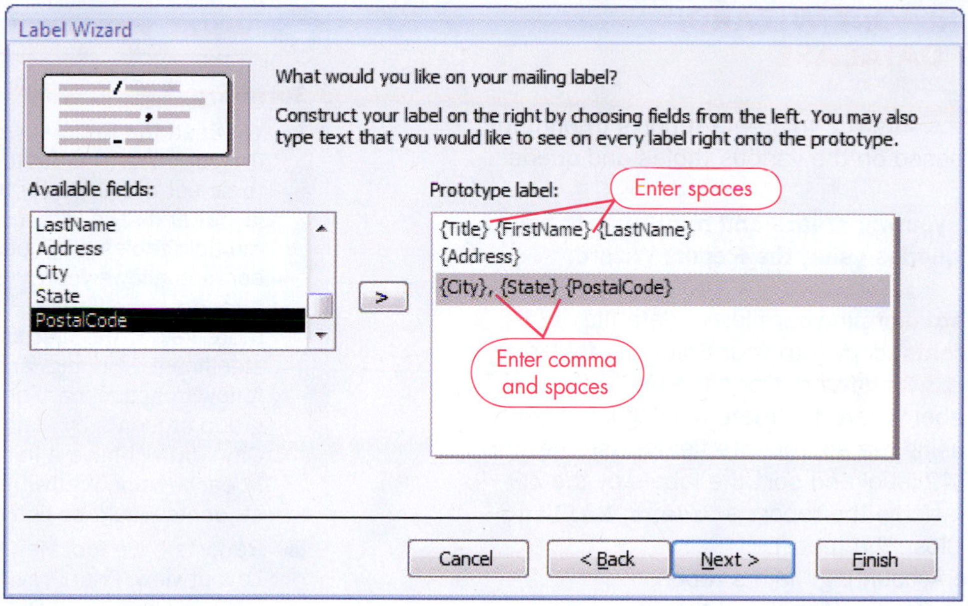

Figure 13.2a Label Wizard dialog box

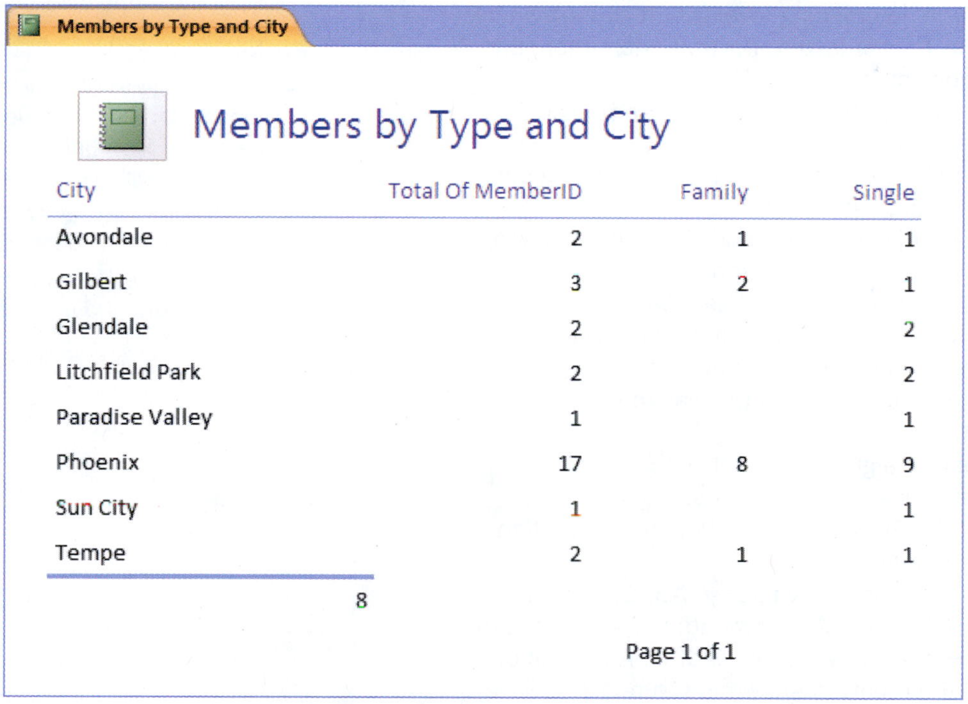
Members by Type and City

Members by Type and City

City	Total Of MemberID	Family	Single
Avondale	2	1	1
Gilbert	3	2	1
Glendale	2		2
Litchfield Park	2		2
Paradise Valley	1		1
Phoenix	17	8	9
Sun City	1		1
Tempe	2	1	1
8			

Page 1 of 1

Figure 13.2b Crosstab query

13.3 USE THE REPORT WIZARD: STUDENT DATABASE

Schuyler College wants you to create reports to print for administrators based on the various tables and queries.

In this project, you will create and print reports based on tables and queries using the Report Wizard.

1. Find **12.1students** in your files or data file **d13.3students**, copy it to your Solutions folder, and rename it **13.3students**. Open the file.
2. Use the Label Wizard to create mailing labels for students using the appropriate fields. Use the Avery C2242 label and sort the labels by the ZIP Code field. Name the report **Student Mailing Labels**. Close the report.
3. Create the Accounting Majors report.
   a. Use the Report Wizard and the Accounting Majors query.
   b. Select the fields in the following order: Last Name, First Name, Phone Number, Student ID.
   c. There are no grouping levels; sort by Last Name.
   d. Use the Tabular layout, Portrait orientation, and the Equity style.
   e. Name the report **Accounting Majors**.
   f. Print and close the report.
4. Create the Advisory Assignments report using data from two tables, as follows.
   a. Use the Report Wizard, and select the following fields from the tables listed:
      • Advisors table: Title, Last, Department
      • Students table: Last Name, First Name, Phone Number, E-mail Address
   b. Select "by Advisors" as the way to view the report.
   c. Do not add a grouping level.
   d. Sort by students' last names.
   e. Select the Stepped layout, Portrait orientation, and the Equity style.
   f. Name the report **Advisory Assignments**.
5. Preview the Advisory Assignments report. Switch to Layout view to modify column widths. A section of Page 1 of the report is shown in Figure 13.3. Save the changes and then print the report.
6. Save and close the database.

WHAT YOU NEED TO KNOW

Software

▶ We used the Report Wizard in Project 13.1. This feature allows you to select the fields for the report, set layout and style, and use fields from multiple tables and queries. One of the screens allows you to group records in a report based on the values of one or more fields. The first field is the most significant grouping, and the others follow in sequence. For example, if you group students by Major and then by City, you will have a list of students in each major, and within each major, students would be listed by city.

▶ Reports have four views: Design view, Layout view, Print Preview, and Report view. In Layout and Design view you can modify settings and formats to meet your needs. All reports for a company or an organization should have the same style.

Project

▶ The college would like you to create mailing labels for students sorted by ZIP code. In addition, they need the following reports:
   • Accounting Majors: A list of students majoring in Accounting
   • Advisory Assignments: A list of advisors and the students they advise

Advisory Assignments

Title	Last	Department	Last Name	First Name	Phone Number	E-mail Address
Dr.	Martino	Accounting				
			Geisler	Dorothy	(309) 555-4240	DCGeisler@ent.com
			Gjonbalaj	Adem	(309) 555-1052	AdamBJ@jus.com
			Goldstein	Floyd	(309) 555-8874	Gold@ent.com
			Gordon	Harold	(309) 555-8234	hrgordie@jus.com
			Kremer	Ilya	(309) 555-7771	IlyaK@jus.com
			Lorenzo	Mario	(309) 555-8989	CorvetteJim@klc.com
Professor	Poling	Office Administration				
			Andino	Ralph	(309) 555-2123	RalphV@ent.com
			Bradley	Susan	(309) 555-6992	Sbradley@jus.com
			Caban	Angelia	(309) 555-6660	ReginaA@jus.com
			Duffy	Brian	(309) 555-9911	BrainaDuff@jus.com
			Joaquin	Angela	(309) 555-2348	AngelaJ@res.com
			Johnson	Michael	(309) 555-2091	MikeJohnson@cos.com
			Kretova	Maya	(309) 555-8656	MayaK@klc.com
			Krol	Andrez	(305) 555-4949	AndrezK@cos.com
			Krute	George	(309) 555-6921	Gkrute@cos.com
			Langly	Judy	(309) 555-1301	Jlangley@jus.com
			McCarron	Austin	(309) 555-5992	AustinMac@ent.com
Dr.	Zhang	Information Technology				
			Acevedo	Karina	(309) 555-6688	RoseA@jus.com
			Haebich	Hermann	(309) 555-8778	HPHaebich@jus.com
			Ku	Hui	(309) 555-8876	ZhenKu@klc.com
			Putney	Angel	(309) 555-3884	AngelRose@cos.com
			Stevens	Milton	(309) 555-0020	MiltonS@cos.com
Professor	Willhelm	Marketing				
			Apreza	Julio	(309) 555-1010	Japreza@ent.com
			Castle	Brian	(309) 555-8104	Mcastle@cos.com

Figure 13.3 Advisory Assignments report

PROJECT 14

PROJECT SKILLS
* Modify reports in Design view
* Use report sections
* Modify report format properties
* Modify reports in Layout view
* Add aggregate functions using a calculated control

14.1 USE REPORT SECTIONS AND MODIFY A LISTINGS REPORT

Agents for Chris James Realtors have questions that you will answer using queries and reports on various types of listings.

In this project, you will query the listings database and create reports from the queries. The reports will be modified and enhanced in Design view.

1. Find data file **d14.1listings**, copy it to your Solutions folder, and rename it **14.1listings**. Open the file.
2. Using the Simple Query Wizard, create a Listings Query using all fields. Use query Design view to modify the query and switch between Design and Datasheet views to answer the following questions. The questions can also be printed from data file **d14.1questions.docx**. In some cases, you can use the Sort/Filter arrows in Datasheet view to answer the questions.
   a. How many listings does the agency have for any style home with two bedrooms? *Hint: Use 2 in the criteria line in the query design grid under Bedrooms.*
   b. In which towns does the agency have split-level homes listed? *Hint: Use "Split Level" as the criteria.*
   c. How many listings does the agency have for 5-bedroom homes?
   d. How many listings are there for townhouses for less than $350,000? *Hint: Use "Townhouse" and <350000 on the criteria line.*
3. Use the last query to create a new query showing all townhouse listings. Delete the price criteria and deselect the Show button for the Type of Property. Name the query `Townhouse Listings`.
4. Modify the Townhouse Listings query to create a query for all colonials. Name the query `Colonial Listings`.
5. Create a report using the Report Wizard and fields from the Townhouse Listings query.
   a. Select the fields in the following order: City, Price, ID, Address, Bedrooms, Date Listed.

WHAT YOU NEED TO KNOW

Software

▶ In previous projects you used a query to answer questions about data by setting various criteria in Design view. After you get the answers, you can remove the criteria or save each query using the Save As command.

▶ You can improve the usefulness and design of a report by using and customizing headers and footers for the report section, group levels, or pages. View the report in Design view to see the report sections, headers, and footers. You can expand the sections and include information for groups, pages, or the entire report.

▶ When you use the mouse to change the height of a report section by dragging the edge of the section, you are changing the format properties of the report. You can also change the height of report sections by double-clicking the section selector at the left of the section bar, and changing the height property. The placement of a field may also be changed by dragging and dropping it into a new position.

▶ You can modify label controls in Design view by selecting and changing the label or the format. To further customize the report, you can add a label using the Label (Form Control) button in the Controls group of the Report Design Tools Design tab.

Aa
Label

Project

▶ Use the data file provided because the property database has been updated with new listings, and properties that were sold have been removed.

Continued on next page

b. Group data by City and sort by Price.

c. Select a Stepped layout, Portrait orientation, and the Opulent style.

d. Name the report **Townhouse Listings**.

6. Modify the report in Layout view to widen the City column. Notice that there is no visible title.

7. Switch to Design view, and make the following changes:

a. Change the Report header height to one inch to accommodate an additional title and graphic.

b. Right-click the Report header section, and change the Fill/Back Color to Grey and the font color to Black.

c. Change the font size for the report name to 16 point.

d. Move the report name down, add a label for the company name, and then change the font size to 22 point and the font color to Black, if necessary.

e. Save the design and switch to Layout view.

8. In Layout view:

a. Insert the **d14.1jameslogo.bmp** and adjust the spacing of the titles as shown in Figure 14.1.

b. Drag the Bedrooms title and field controls to change the placement of the field to the right of the Price field as shown.

c. Format the Bedrooms data to center it in the field.

d. Save the design.

9. Create the same report for Colonial Listings. Create the report with the fields in the correct order with the same format.

10. Print copies of both listings reports.

11. Close and save the database.

▶ The agency gets requests for information from its agents by telephone. You will create queries to answer their questions. You can print the questions from data file **d14.1questions.docx**.

▶ Chris James would like to distribute reports to her agents every week with the current listings in specific popular categories. Agents would like to have reports for townhouse and colonial offerings. She would also like you to add the agency name and graphic to all reports and to arrange listings by city and price so that they are easy to use.

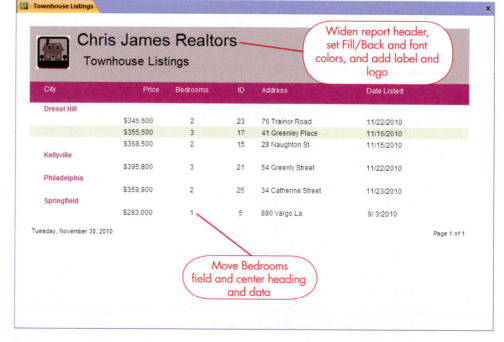

Figure 14.1 Townhouse Listings report

14.2 ADD CALCULATED CONTROLS AND NEW OBJECTS: MEMBERS DATABASE

Power Fitness would like you to create a list of members and their annual dues with a calculation of the total dues that will be collected from all members.

In this project, you will add a new table, enter data, establish relationships, create a query, and then create a report with a calculated control.

1. Find **13.2club** in your files or data file **d14.2club**, copy it to your Solutions folder, and rename it **14.2club**. Open the file.
2. Create a new table in Design view with the following fields:
   a. **Type of Membership**: Set as the primary key with text data type.
   b. **Dues**: Set the data type to Currency.
   c. **Class Fee Discount**: Set the data type to Number and the field properties as Field Size: Decimal, Format: Percent, and Scale: 2.
3. Switch to Datasheet view, save the table as **Dues and Fees**, and enter the data as follows: Family membership is $1800 with a 60% class fee discount, and Single membership is $1200 with a 50% class fee discount.
4. Create a one-to-many relationship between the Dues and Fees table and the Members tables, relating the Type of Membership fields.
5. Create a query to display a list of members and their dues.
   a. Use the following fields from the two tables:
      - Members: Title, Last Name, First Name, MemberID, Type of Membership
      - Dues and Fees: Dues
   b. Create a detail query and name it **Members Annual Dues List** and then open it in Design view.
   c. Sort the query by last name. Save the query.
6. Create a report using the Report Wizard and all the fields in the Members Annual Dues List query.
   a. View data by Members, set no grouping levels, sort by last name, use a Tabular layout, Portrait orientation, and the Civic style.
   b. Name the report **Members Annual Dues List**.
7. Modify and enhance the report in Design view as follows and as shown in Figure 14.2.
   a. Set the report header section height to one inch.
   b. Add a label control for the Power Fitness Club heading. Change font size to 22 point.
   c. Change the report title font size to 20 point.

Software

▶ As you saw with Access forms, you can calculate and display data in a report by using a calculated control containing an aggregate function. An aggregate function is used to calculate totals and includes functions such as Sum, Count, Average, or Variance. A text box is the most common type of control used to display a calculated value.

▶ To add a calculated control in Design view, click the Text Box button in the Controls group of the Report Design Tools Design tab. You can place controls in all sections of the report, but if you want to total the value of all the records in a report, you must place the control in the report footer. The text box appears with a label that Access assigns. You can display the properties of a text box or other control by selecting it and pressing [F4]. Change the properties as necessary to set the name of the text box, enter the expression in the control source property, or calculate a running total.

abl
Text
Box

Project

▶ Power Fitness wants to produce a membership list showing the annual dues for each member and the total dues from all members.

▶ Create a new table that contains the fee discounts and dues for Single and Family members. Before you design the query, you must set the relationships between the two tables. You will prepare the report from the query and calculate the total dues.

d. Double-click the report footer section selector, and then on the Property Sheet pane set the Height to `0.5"`. Close the Property Sheet pane.

e. Use the Text Box button to add a calculated control for Total Dues in the report footer.

f. Select the label control to the left of the text box and press [F4] to open the Properties dialog box.

g. Set the Caption property to `Total Dues`. Close the Property Sheet pane and resize the label control so that all text is visible.

h. Select the unbound control, press [F4], and then click the Data tab on the Property Sheet pane. Set the Control Source property to: `=Sum([Dues])`, and then set the Running Sum property to Over All.

i. Click the Format tab and set the Format property to Currency. Close the Property Sheet pane.

j. Adjust the placement of the controls under the Dues column.

k. Delete the =Now() or date function from the page footer.

l. Save the report design.

8. Switch to Layout view, modify the placement of the titles, and then add the logo in data file **d14.2powerlogo.bmp**, as shown in Figure 14.2.

a. Center the data and column heading in the MemberID field.

b. Adjust the width of column headers and columns so that the column heading and data are visible.

c. Adjust the position of the page number and Dues total fields as necessary so that the report fits on one page.

9. Print a copy of the Members Annual Dues List report.

10. Close and save the database.

Figure 14.2 Members Annual Dues List report

Ollie's Cycles wants you to produce several reports from queries it has already created.

In this project, you will create labels and a report with summary options, then modify them in Design view.

1. Find **12.2mdse** in your files or data file **d14.3mdse**, copy it to your Solutions folder, and rename it **14.3mdse**. Open the file.

2. Create mailing labels from the Vendors table using Avery C2242 labels. On the label, place the data as shown below, inserting a comma after the city. Sort by Postal Code and name the report **Vendor Mailing Labels**.
   {Name}
   Attn: {Contact}
   {Address}
   {City}, {State} {Postal Code}

3. Create a report from the Inventory Valuation query.
   a. Use all fields.
   b. Group by Department.
   c. Sort by Product Description.
   d. Set Summary Options for the Sum of Units in Stock and for the Sum of Valuation data. Show both detail and summary data.
   e. Use the Stepped layout, Portrait orientation, and the Metro style.
   f. Name the report **Inventory Valuation**.

4. In Report Design view, modify the report as follows and as shown in Figure 14.3.
   a. Increase the height of the report header section to 1".
   b. Add a label for the company name and format to the same font and font color as the report title in 22 point.
   c. Change the font size of the report title to 16 point.
   d. Move Sum of Units and Sum of Valuation controls in the Department and Report footers into position under the appropriate columns and clear any extra summary lines, if necessary. *Note: They should align with the headers in the page header section.*
   e. Change the Format property of the Sum of Valuation controls in the Department and Report footers to Currency.
   f. Save the design.

5. In Layout view, make the following modifications:
   a. Apply bold to the labels and totals for summary data.

b. Change the size and placement of column headers and summary totals, if necessary, for proper alignment. Adjust column width as necessary.

c. Insert the logo file **d14.3ollielogo.bmp** into the header, and then align the titles as shown.

d. Save the layout.

6. Print a copy of the report.

7. Close and save the database.

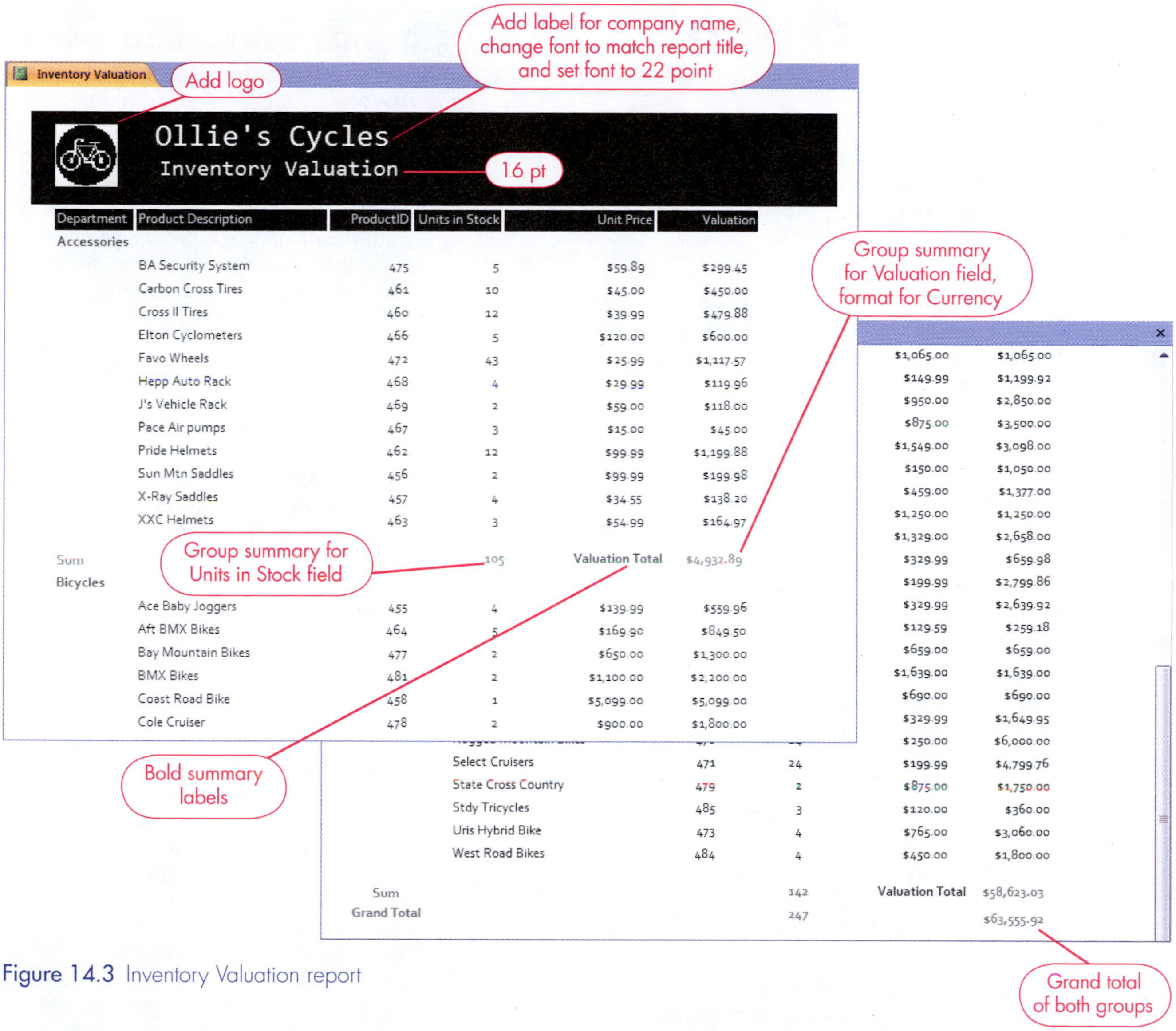

Figure 14.3 Inventory Valuation report

PROJECT 15

PROJECT SKILLS

✳ Create a subform
✳ Use the Expression Builder for a calculated field

15.1 ADD OBJECTS TO THE MEMBERS DATABASE

Power Fitness Club has begun its registration period for class offerings. Members get a discounted rate for classes, which are also open to nonmembers. You will add database objects to meet the needs of the registration process.

In this project, you will create new tables, a form with a subform, a query, and a report to prepare the database for registration and billing of members.

1. Find **14.2club** in your files or data file **d15.1club**, copy it to your Solutions folder, and rename it **15.1club**. Open the file.

2. Use Figure 15.1a as a guide to create and populate a new table named **Classes**. The first field is the primary key and should be set to the AutoNumber data type. You can use a Lookup data type for Time and Day fields.

3. Use Figure 15.1b as a guide to create a new table for Registration. The first field is the primary key and should be set to the AutoNumber data type, and the ClassID and MemberID should be the Number data types. Enter the registrations that have come in so far.

4. Open the Relationships window and add the two new tables to the window.
   a. Join the MemberID from the Members table to the MemberID in the Registration table.
   b. Join the ClassID from the Classes table to the ClassID in the Registration table.
   c. Save the Relationships window.

5. Using the Form Wizard, create a form so that registrations can easily be taken in the office. Use all the fields from the Classes table and the MemberID, Last Name, First Name, and Type of Membership from the Members tables. View the data by Classes, and use the Form with subform(s) option. Select the Tabular subform option and the Civic Style. Name the form **Class Registration Form**, as shown in Figure 15.1c. In Layout view, add the logo file **d15.1powerlogo.bmp** to the Form header, as shown.

▼ WHAT YOU NEED TO KNOW

Software

▶ As you add tables to a database, you should not repeat field data except for primary or identifying fields of related tables. You should relate tables in the Relationships window if you will use them together in queries, forms, and reports. When you open the Relationships window, click the Show Table button to display the dialog box to add new tables to the window.

▶ When you are working with relational data, you may wish to view data from two tables or queries on the same form. For example, to create a registration form, you will need class information and member data. Subforms are a convenient tool for doing this, and Microsoft Office Access 2007 will create a subform as an option in the Form Wizard. In the Datasheet view of a subform, the data from one table or query will be explained or detailed by the data in another.

▶ In the last chapter on queries, you added a calculated field to a query by entering the expression directly into the grid. You can also build the expression in query Design view by clicking the Builder button on the Query Tools Design tab. You can select the table, field, and the mathematical operators in the Expression Builder dialog box. After the expression is complete, you can change the name of the expression, which becomes the name of the field.

Project

▶ You will create a new table for class offerings, including the fees for nonmembers. You will create another table to record registration information for members.

Continued on page 92

ClassID	Class	Instructor	Sessions	Time	Day	NonMember Fee	Add New Field
1	Aerobics	Jasko	12	9 a.m.	Tuesday	$120.00	
2	Aerobics	Jasko	12	10 a.m.	Tuesday	$120.00	
3	Aerobics	Jasko	12	7 p.m.	Thursday	$120.00	
4	Aerobics	Jasko	12	8 p.m.	Thursday	$120.00	
5	Pilates	Vaughn	10	9 a.m.	Monday	$110.00	
6	Pilates	Vaughn	10	10 a.m.	Monday	$110.00	
7	Spinning	Reidel	10	9 a.m.	Wednesday	$110.00	
8	Spinning	Reidel	10	7 p.m.	Tuesday	$110.00	
9	Hatha Yoga	Souleigh	12	9 a.m.	Thursday	$125.00	
10	Hatha Yoga	Souleigh	12	10 a.m.	Thursday	$125.00	
11	Ashtanga Yoga	Greene	12	9 a.m.	Friday	$125.00	
12	Ashtanga Yoga	Greene	12	10 a.m.	Friday	$125.00	
13	Body Conditioning	Miller	10	9 a.m.	Saturday	$110.00	
14	Body Conditioning	Miller	10	10 a.m.	Saturday	$110.00	
15	Weight Training	Campbell	10	7 p.m.	Monday	$100.00	
16	Weight Training	Campbell	10	8 p.m.	Monday	$100.00	
(New)			0			$0.00	

Figure 15.1a New Classes table

RegistrationID	MemberID	ClassID	Add New Field
1	4	5	
2	8	3	
3	9	7	
4	20	8	
5	23	5	
6	13	9	
7	28	1	
8	6	2	
9	12	9	
10	17	4	
11	19	8	
12	21	10	
13	29	12	
14	24	10	
15	15	4	
16	12	6	
17	18	6	
18	1	8	
19	5	9	
20	7	7	
(New)	0	0	

Figure 15.1b New Registration table

6. Create a query using the following fields from the four tables, in the order listed:
   - RegistrationID: From the Registration Table
   - Last Name: From the Members table
   - MemberID, ClassID: From the Registration table
   - NonMember Fee: From the Classes table
   - ClassFee Discount: From the Dues and Fees table

   a. Create a detail query and name it **Billings for Classes**. Select the option to go into Design view, as shown in Figure 15.1d.

   b. Sort the query by Last Name in ascending order.

   c. Add a calculated field to the query in the next blank field by using the Builder button and the Expression Builder, or by entering the expression directly.
   - Click the Builder button, on the Query Tools Design tab.
   - To enter the expression, either use the build feature and double-click fields to select, as shown in Figure 15.1e, or enter the expression directly. *Hint: MemberFee: [NonMemberFee]–([NonMemberFee]*[Class Fee Discount])*).
   - If you use the build feature, in the query design grid, edit the expression label (Expr1:) to **Member Fee**, as the column heading.
   - Right-click on the column, click Properties, and then format the result for Currency on the Property Sheet pane.

7. Create a report, in the Civic style, using data from the new query and the class name from the Classes table in the order shown in Figure 15.1f. Name the report **Billings for Classes Report**.

8. Modify the report as shown:

   a. In Design view, increase the size of the report header and add a label control for the company name. Format the headers in the appropriate font and font sizes.

   b. Increase the size of the report footer and add a text box and an aggregate function to add the total of the Member Fee column. *Hint: =SUM([Member Fee])*. Format the result for currency and change the text box label to **Total**.

   c. In Layout view, add the company logo to the report header and adjust the placement of the titles.

   d. Center the data and headings in the RegistrationID, MemberID, and ClassID columns.

   e. Change the column heading from "Class Fee Discount" to **Discount**.

   f. Right-align the column headings for Discount and Member Fee.

▶ You will establish relationships between tables so that you can use them together in forms, queries, and reports.

▶ You will create a form to enter registration data when members call in to register for classes. You will use fields from several tables for the form.

▶ You will create a multi-table query and add a calculated field for the discounted class fees. Members get a discount on the class fees as listed in the Dues and Fees table. You can enter the expression on the first line of the grid where the Field name generally appears, or use the Expression Builder to create the calculated column.

▶ You will create a report that lists the classes and billing amounts for the members who have registered up to this point.

g. Make any other adjustments to the layout as necessary, and adjust page footers so that they are within the page width.

9. Print a copy of the report.

10. Close and save the database.

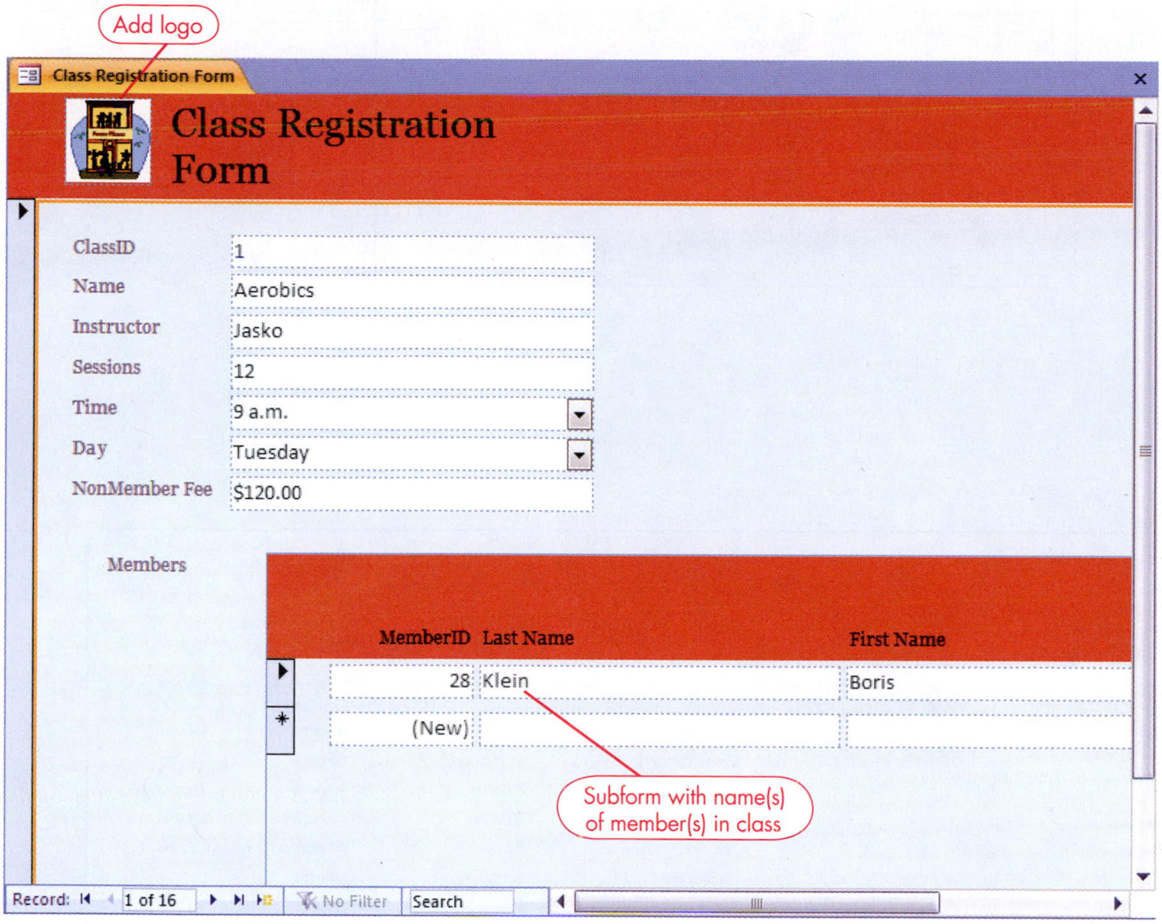

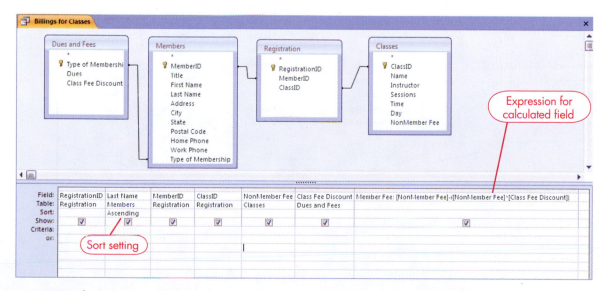

Figure 15.1c Class Registration Form

Figure 15.1d Query Design view

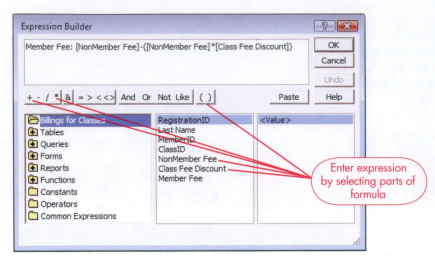

Figure 15.1e Expression Builder

Add logo

Power Fitness Club

Civic style, 22 point

Billings for Classes Report

14 point

Right-align and change heading to Discount

Last Name	RegistrationID	MemberID	ClassID	Class	NonMember Fee	Discount	Member Fee
Ali	8	6	2	Aerobics	$120.00	60.00%	$48.00
Batista	6	13	9	Hatha Yoga	$125.00	60.00%	$50.00
Bell	3	9	7	Spinning	$110.00	50.00%	$55.00
Cepeda	20	7	7	Spinning	$110.00	50.00%	$55.00
Cheung	2	8	3	Aerobics	$120.00	60.00%	$48.00
Davis	19	5	9	Hatha Yoga	$125.00	50.00%	$62.50
Gulperrez	15	15	4	Aerobics	$120.00	50.00%	$60.00
Ishmael	17	18	6	Pilates	$110.00	60.00%	$44.00
Joseph	9	12	9	Hatha Yoga	$125.00	50.00%	$62.50
Joseph	16	12	6	Pilates	$110.00	50.00%	$55.00
Klein	7	28	1	Aerobics	$120.00	50.00%	$60.00
Knight	10	17	4	Aerobics	$120.00	50.00%	$60.00
Lafontant	11	19	8	Spinning	$110.00	50.00%	$55.00
Patel	13	29	12	Ashtanga Yoga	$125.00	50.00%	$62.50
Perry	18	1	8	Spinning	$110.00	50.00%	$55.00
Raza	4	20	8	Spinning	$110.00	50.00%	$55.00
Reilly	1	4	5	Pilates	$110.00	60.00%	$44.00
Roberts	12	21	10	Hatha Yoga	$125.00	60.00%	$50.00
Smith	14	24	10	Hatha Yoga	$125.00	50.00%	$62.50
Taylor	5	23	5	Pilates	$110.00	50.00%	$55.00
						Total	$1,099.00

Center heading and data

Use Text Box button to add aggregate function and caption

Figure 15.1f Billings for Classes Report

CHAPTER 6

Integration

In this chapter, you will complete the following projects:

PROJECT 16
Import Data
PROJECT 16.1 Import a Movie Collection Table
PROJECT 16.2 Import a Customer Spreadsheet
PROJECT 16.3 Import a Word Contact List

PROJECT 17
Export Data
PROJECT 17.1 Export the Classes Table to Excel
PROJECT 17.2 Export a Memorabilia Query to Word

PROJECT 18
Maintain the Database
PROJECT 18.1 Back up and Compact and Repair a Database
PROJECT 18.2 Update and Modify the Listings Database

IMPORT DATA

PROJECT 16

PROJECT SKILLS

✴ Import structured data into Access tables
✴ Import Access table objects
✴ Import Excel spreadsheet data into a new table
✴ Create an append query
✴ Import a Word table into Access

16.1 IMPORT A MOVIE COLLECTION TABLE

Your friend has just purchased a small collection of film memorabilia to enhance his movie collection. He wants you to import the database of information on the film memorabilia into his database.

In this project, you will import objects from another database into the Movie database and then create objects using the new data.

1. Find **10.2movie** in your files or data file **d16.1movie**, copy it to your Solutions folder, and rename it **16.1movie**. Open the file.
2. Click the External Data tab, and then click the Import Access database button to import the database file **d16.1filmmem**. Specify the import option and click OK. As shown in Figure 16.1a, click the Tables tab on the Import Objects dialog box, if necessary, select all objects for import, and then click OK. Do not save the import steps.
3. View the new table of movie memorabilia.
4. Create a relationship between the Movie Title field of the Movie Collection table and the Film field of the Memorabilia table. Save and close the Relationships window.
5. Create a form for the Memorabilia table, using the same style and format that you used for the other form in the database. The Movie Collection form was created by using the Form button on the Create tab. Change its format to Equity style using the AutoFormat feature. Close, save, and name the new form **Memorabilia Form**.
6. Modify the format of the Movie Collection form in Layout view to the Equity style.
7. To determine which items of memorabilia you do not have matching movies for, create a Find Unmatched Query, titled **Memorabilia without Matching Movies Query**, using both tables and showing all fields in the Memorabilia table. The Movie Title and Film fields are the fields that are related.

WHAT YOU NEED TO KNOW

Software

▶ The Import feature copies data from a text file, spreadsheet, or database table into an Access table. You can also link data, which allows you to view and edit data in both applications.

▶ To import data from another database, open the destination Access database, click the External Data tab, and click the Import Access database button in the Import group. Browse to select the name of the database containing the data to import, specify Import, and click OK. You can then select any or all objects in that database to import.

Project

▶ The owner of the movie collection has purchased a small collection of film memorabilia. Information about the collection was kept in an Access database, but in some cases the data is incomplete.

▶ You will import the film memorabilia database into the movie database so that you can monitor both collections with one database. You will also establish relationships between the tables so that you can create queries and reports using both tables.

8. Using the Report Wizard, create the following reports. Modify the reports in Layout view so that all fields and column headings are easy to read. Use the Equity style and center the ItemID and/or the MovieID data in all reports.

a. **Movie Collection** report: Use all fields, sort by Movie Title, Tabular layout, and Landscape orientation.

b. **Movie Collection by Subject** report: Use all fields, group by Subject, sort by Movie Title, Stepped layout, and Landscape orientation.

c. **Memorabilia** report: Use all fields, sort by Item, Tabular layout, and Landscape orientation.

d. **Memorabilia without Matching Movies** report: Use all fields of the Memorabilia without Matching Movies Query, group by Actor, sort by Film, Stepped layout, and Landscape orientation.

9. Print a copy of the Memorabilia without Matching Movies report, as shown in Figure 16.1b.

10. Save and close the database.

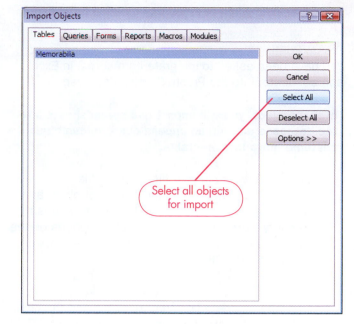

Figure 16.1a Import Objects dialog box

Memorabilia without Matching Movies

Actor	Film	ItemID	Item	Description	Size	Actress	Cost	Year
Bogart								
	Knock on Any Door	9	Lobby card	Scene card	5 X 8		$65.00	1949
Bowie								
	The Hunter	6	Poster	Full color	27 X 41	Sarandon	$30.00	0
Ford								
	Star Wars	5	Poster	Full color	27 X 41	Fisher	$120.00	1982
	Star Wars	4	Mini Poster	Special Edition Trilogy	16 X 26	Fisher	$30.00	0
Kelly								
	Living in a Big Way	1	Poster	Dancing	27 X 41		$150.00	0
Mitchum								
	River of No Return	3	Poster	Set of 3	41 X 81	Monroe	$250.00	0
	Undercurrent	2	Advertisement	Full color	Full page	Hepburn	$10.00	1946
Redford								
	Downhill Racer	8	Poster	Full color	27 X 41		$45.00	0
	The Sting	7	Poster	Full color	27 X 41		$140.00	0

Wednesday, March 19, 2010   Page 1 of 1

Figure 16.1b Memorabilia without Matching Movies report

16.2 IMPORT A CUSTOMER SPREADSHEET

Presto Printing has purchased another small print shop. You have been asked to integrate its records, in Excel spreadsheets, into the Presto Printing database.

In this project, you will import two spreadsheets into the database and run an append query to combine customer data into one table.

1. Find **13.1presto** in your files or data file **d16.2presto**, copy it to your Solutions folder, and rename it **16.2presto**. Open the file. If there is a Security Warning message bar, click Options on the message bar, click the Enable this content option, and then click OK.

2. In Excel, open **d16.2customers.xlsx** and **d16.2creditors.xlsx**, and view the spreadsheet data from the company Presto acquired. Close the files.

3. In the **16.2presto** database, click the External Data tab, and click the Import Excel spreadsheet button in the Import group. Select **d16.2creditors.xlsx**, click the Import option, and then click OK.
   a. The first row contains Column Headings. *Note: If Access does not accept the titles, they will be changed to acceptable field names.*
   b. Let Access add the Primary key since there is no ID data in this table.
   c. Name the table **New Creditors**, and click Finish. Do not save the import steps.

4. Click the External Data tab, and in the Import group, click the Import Excel spreadsheet button. Select data file **d16.2customers.xlsx**, click the Import option, and then click OK. The first row contains column headings; choose the CustID column as the primary key. Name the table **New Customers**.

5. Look at the New Customers table and the Customers table. The data is compatible but some field names are not the same and some fields are missing.

6. Run an append query to consolidate the two customer tables.
   a. Create a query using the New Customers table.
   b. Name it **New Customers Query**, and modify it in Design view.
   c. Click the Query Type: Append button, and then select the Customers table as the table to receive the new data. Click OK.
   d. In the Append To box under each field, use the list arrow to select the related field in the Customers table, as shown in Figure 16.2. Notice that some fields have the same name, but the field name should still be selected.

WHAT YOU NEED TO KNOW

Software

▶ You can import Excel data into a new Access table. When you click the Import Excel spreadsheet button on the External Data tab in the Import group, you can select the worksheet and then choose to import, append, or link the file. If you select the option to store spreadsheet data in a new table, the Import Spreadsheet Wizard will step you through naming the fields and the primary key.

▶ You can only append the data to an existing table if the data structure matches exactly. If the tables do not match, you can import the table and run an append query to correlate the fields and add the new data to an existing table.

▶ To run an append query, create a query using all the fields in the new table and view the query in Design view. Click the Query Type: Append button on the Query Tools Design tab, and then select the table to receive the appended data. An Append To: line will appear on the query design grid, as shown in Figure 16.2. You then select the name of each field in the destination table to receive the data. In this way, you can append data from fields with different names to an existing table.

Project

▶ Presto Printing has purchased the equipment and customers and has assumed the debts of a small competitor in West Akron, Ohio. It would like to consolidate the spreadsheet data from the purchased company into its database.

▶ Both spreadsheets will be brought into the database as new tables, and the customer data will be appended to the Presto Customer table.

e. Click the Run button on the toolbar to append the records. You will have to confirm the append operation.

f. Check that all the new customers have been added to the Customers list. Save and close the query.

7. View all the other query and report objects in the database, and notice that they all include the new data that has been appended to the Customers table and that some data is missing from the new customer entries.

8. Print a copy of the Customer Contact List that includes the new data.

9. Save and close the database.

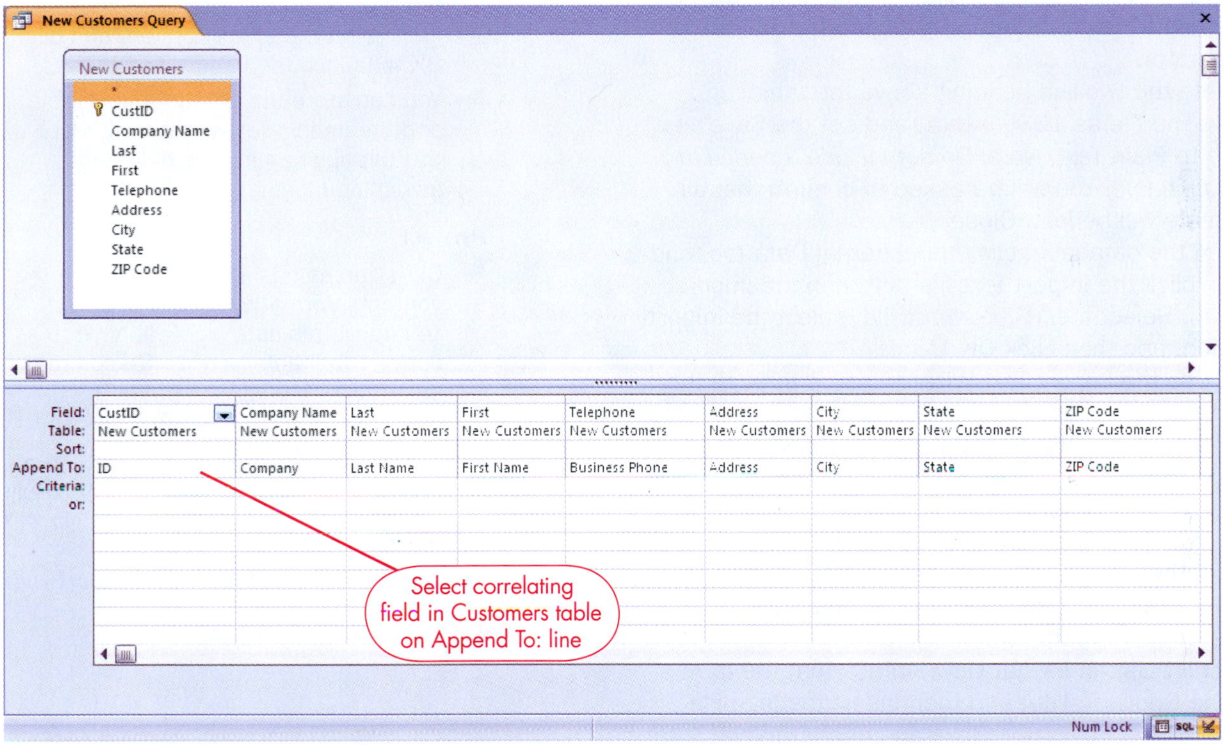

Figure 16.2

16.3 IMPORT A WORD CONTACT LIST

Chris James has a contact list for her agents in a Word table. She would like you to consolidate all her data into the Listings database.

> **In this project, you will import a Word table into an Access table and create a form and report with the new data.**

1. Find **14.1listings** in your files or data file **d16.3listings**, copy it to your Solutions folder, and rename it **16.3listings**.
2. In Word, open data file **d16.3contact.docx** and view the file.
3. Select the table and convert it to text using the Convert to Text button and set commas as the separator.
4. Delete the two-line heading above the table.
5. Save the file as **163contact**, and set the Save as type to Plain Text. *Note: Do not include a period in the filename.* You will be asked to confirm that all formats will be lost. Close the file.
6. Open the database, click the External Data tab, and then click the Import text file button in the Import group. Select the **163contact** file, select the Import option, and then click OK.
   a. Use the Import Text Wizard to step through the import process. The file is delimited text.
   b. Select the First Row Contains Field Names option, as shown in Figure 16.3a.
   c. Let Access set the primary key.
   d. Name the table **Agent Contact List**.
7. Open the Listings form. It is formatted in the Opulent style and includes the company logo.
8. Use the Form button to create a form for the Agent Contact List. In Layout view, AutoFormat the form in the Opulent style, and then insert the logo file **d16.3jameslogo.bmp**. Save and name the new form **Agent Contact List Form**.
9. View the reports.
10. Using the Report Wizard, create a report for the Agent Contact List. Use all fields except the ID number field and place the last name field first. Sort the report by last name, use Tabular layout and Landscape orientation, and apply the Opulent style, as shown in Figure 16.3b. Name it **Agent Contact List Report**.

11. In Design view, apply a grey Fill/Back Color and change the font color to black. Modify the header to add the company name and logo. In Layout view, reduce the font size of the second line of the header to 14 point, and move and expand fields so that all data is visible. Move the page footer control to the left and the edge of the report to within 10" to fit to one page wide.

12. Print a copy of the report.

13. Save and close the database.

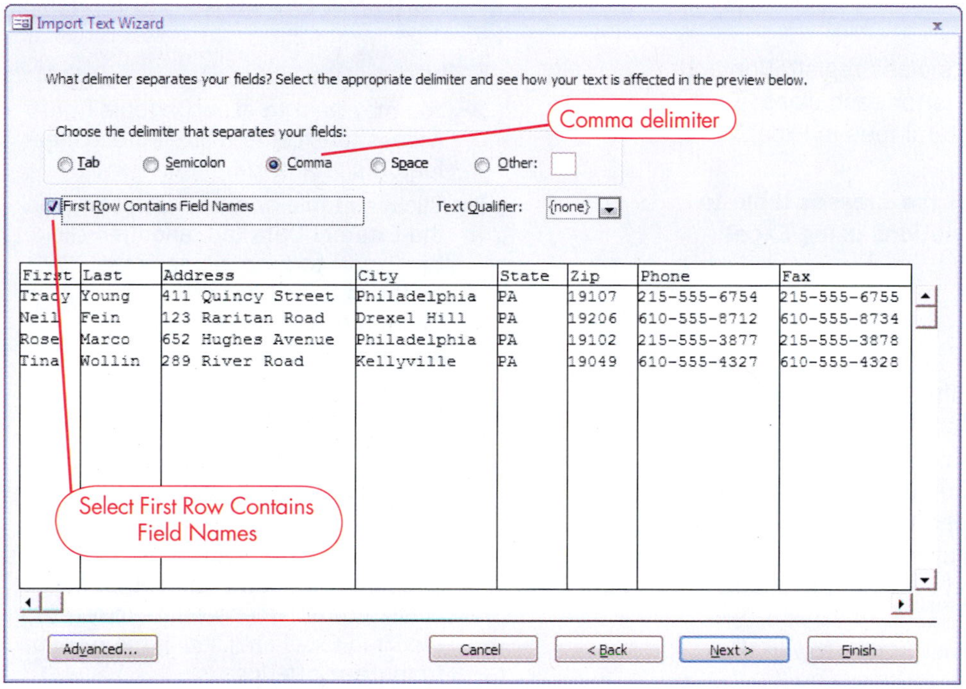

Figure 16.3a Import Text Wizard dialog box

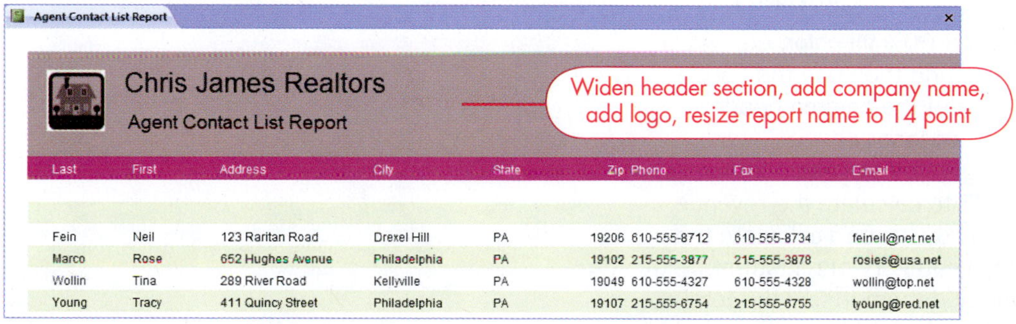

Figure 16.3b Agent Contact List Report

EXPORT DATA

PROJECT 17

PROJECT SKILLS

✶ Export data from Access tables or queries to Excel

✶ Export data from Access tables or queries to RTF format

17.1 EXPORT THE CLASSES TABLE TO EXCEL

Power Fitness has completed its class registration and has the breakdown of registrants for each class. They would like you to calculate the total fees in Excel.

> In this project, you will export the Classes table to Excel and complete the calculations using Excel formulas.

1. Find **15.1club** in your files or find data file **d17.1club**, copy it to your Solutions folder, and rename it **17.1club**. Open the file.

2. Select the Classes table on the Navigation Pane, click the External Data tab, and then click the Export to Excel spreadsheet button in the Export group. Name the new spreadsheet **17.1classes**, select the Export data with formatting and layout option, and then select the option to open the new file. Click OK.

3. Insert three rows above the header row in the Excel file you have just created, and then insert the headings and logo in data file **d17.1powerlogo.bmp**, as shown in Figure 17.1.

4. Hide columns D:F.

5. Add the new column headings in cells H4:K4. Apply the Blue, Accent 1, Lighter 60% fill color, and wrap text alignment to cell A4, and then use the Format Painter to format the rest of the column headers. Adjust column width as necessary.

6. Enter the numbers of registrants in each category.

7. Enter a formula in cell K5 to calculate the revenue collected for each class. You have to calculate the fees collected from each category of registrant, apply the discount, and add them to find the total revenue for the class. To calculate the amount paid after the discount is taken, multiply by the reciprocal; that is, for a 60% discount, multiply by 40% to find the amount paid. Format the results in Comma format and copy the formula down for all classes. *Hint: =(Fee*Number of Single Members*.5)+(Fee* Number of Family Members*.4)+(Fee*Number of Non-members), or =(G5*H5*.5)+(G5*I5*.4)+(G5*J5).*

WHAT YOU NEED TO KNOW

Software

▶ You may want to export a table from Access to Excel to utilize spreadsheet features to analyze data.

▶ Click the table or query to export, click the External Data tab, and then click the Export to Excel spreadsheet button in the Export group. Name the new file, select the appropriate export option, and then click OK.

Project

▶ Power Fitness has tallied the number of single members, family members, and nonmembers who have registered for each class. Each type of participant has paid a different amount for the class. Power Fitness wants to create a report in Excel calculating the revenue from class offerings.

8. Use AutoSum to find the total revenue in cell K22, and then format it in the Total cell style.
9. Print a copy of the Excel spreadsheet.
10. Save and close all the files.

Insert three rows, logo, and header text

Apply Blue, Accent 1, Lighter 60% fill color, and wrap text

Hide columns D:F

Calibri, 20 point

Calibri, 12 point, bold, blue font

Add new columns and enter text

Enter formulas

Add data into new columns

Power Fitness Club
Class Registration Revenue - Spring 2010

	A	B	C	G	H	I	J	K
4	ClassID	Name	Instructor	NonMember Fee	Single Members 50% Discount	Family Members 60% Discount	Non-Members	Total Revenue
5	1	Aerobics	Jasko	$120.00	6	4	5	1,152.00
6	2	Aerobics	Jasko	$120.00	3	6	5	1,068.00
7	3	Aerobics	Jasko	$120.00	4	5	6	1,200.00
8	4	Aerobics	Jasko	$120.00	8	1	4	1,008.00
9	5	Pilates	Vaughn	$110.00	3	6	4	869.00
10	6	Pilates	Vaughn	$110.00	2	4	9	1,276.00
11	7	Spinning	Reidel	$110.00	3	4	6	1,001.00
12	8	Spinning	Reidel	$110.00	5	6	2	759.00
13	9	Hatha Yoga	Souleigh	$125.00	6	3	6	1,275.00
14	10	Hatha Yoga	Souleigh	$125.00	2	5	4	875.00
15	11	Ashtanga Yoga	Greene	$125.00	8	3	3	1,025.00
16	12	Ashtanga Yoga	Greene	$125.00	5	5	5	1,187.50
17	13	Body Conditioning	Miller	$110.00	3	6	2	649.00
18	14	Body Conditioning	Miller	$110.00	5	2	8	1,243.00
19	15	Weight Training	Campbell	$100.00	2	5	4	700.00
20	16	Weight Training	Campbell	$100.00	3	3	6	870.00
21								
22		Total						16,157.50
23								

Figure 17.1

17.2 EXPORT A MEMORABILIA QUERY TO WORD

Your friend belongs to a collectors club and wants you to send a memo to another member with data from a query. He is interested in acquiring movies that relate to the memorabilia in his collection.

In this project, you will prepare a memorandum, and then export a query table to Word to include in the text.

1. Open **16.1movie** in your files or data file **d17.2movie**, copy it to your Solutions folder, and rename it **17.2movie**. Open the file.
2. In Word, use a memorandum template to create the memorandum text shown in Figure 17.2, or use **d17.2memotemp**.
3. Save the file and name it **17.2memo**.
4. Select the Memorabilia without Matching Movies Query, click the External Data tab, and then click the Export to RTF file button to export the query to Word. Name the RTF file **172temp** and select the option to open the file. Delete the ItemID and Cost columns from the RTF file and adjust column widths before copying the table to the memo. If necessary, insert a continuous break after the text and set the margins to Narrow in the memo to accommodate the wide table.
5. Select and copy the entire table, and then switch to **17.2memo**.
6. To insert the table below the memorandum text, click the Paste button arrow, and then click Paste Special. Paste the table as a Microsoft Office Word Document Object.
7. Size and position the table to fit on one page.
8. Print preview and make any other adjustments. Print a copy of the memorandum.
9. *Optional*: Write a similar memo to another collector, Kevin Thompson, who has a memorabilia collection. You would like to purchase memorabilia for movies without matching memorabilia. Change the words in the memo accordingly. Create a Movie Collection without Matching Memorabilia query, including the Movie Title, Actor ID, Actress ID, and Year Released fields. Follow the same procedures for the memo already created. Name the file **17.2memo2**.
10. Save and close all files.

WHAT YOU NEED TO KNOW

Software

▶ You can export Access tables and queries to Word, which creates a copy of the data in Microsoft Word Rich Text Format, with the .rtf file extension. Rich Text Format is a file format developed by Microsoft that is used for document interchange between applications and/or types of word processing programs. Tables and queries exported from Access to Word will appear as tables.

▶ To export data, click the name of the query or table to export, click the External Data tab, and then click the Export to RTF file button in  the Export group. After you name the new file and click OK, the object will be exported to a Rich Text Format file.

Memorandum

To: Frank Rotella

From: Your Name

Date: 7/2/2010

Re: Movie Collection

Memorandum template

I have just purchased a small memorabilia collection and have cross-referenced it with my movie collection. The table below lists the memorabilia that do not have any matching movies. I am interested in acquiring the films to match these items. Is there anything in your collection that you are interested in selling that would meet these requirements?

Paste Special Memorabilia without Matching Movies Query

Item	Description	Film	Size	Actor	Actress	Year
Poster	Dancing	Living in a Big Way	27 X 41	Kelly		0
Advertisement	Full color	Undercurrent	Full page	Mitchum	Hepburn	1946
Poster	Set of 3	River of No Return	41 X 81	Mitchum	Monroe	0
Mini Poster	Special Edition Trilogy	Star Wars	16 X 26	Ford	Fisher	0
Poster	Full color	Star Wars	27 X 41	Ford	Fisher	1982
Poster	Full color	The Hunter	27 X 41	Bowie	Sarandon	0
Poster	Full color	The Sting	27 X 41	Redford		0
Poster	Full color	Downhill Racer	27 X 41	Redford		0
Lobby card	Scene card	Knock on Any Door	5 X 8	Bogart		1949

1

Figure 17.2

MAINTAIN THE DATABASE

PROJECT 18

PROJECT SKILLS
- ✶ Back up a database
- ✶ Compact and repair a database
- ✶ Save or open previous versions of Access
- ✶ Identify object dependencies

18.1 BACK UP AND COMPACT AND REPAIR A DATABASE

Presto Printing has added sales staff that is often out of the office on calls. You have been asked to provide the sales staff with additional queries. Management would also like you to start a maintenance program to be sure that the database is secure and running efficiently.

In this project, you will add a new query, back up the database, and compact and repair the database.

1. Find **16.2presto** in your files or data file **d18.1presto**, copy it to your Solutions folder, and rename it **18.1presto**. Open the file.
2. Create a new query and name it **Customers Query by City**. Include the following fields, in the order listed, from the Customers table: City, Company, Last Name, First Name, Job Title, Business Phone, and Address.
3. In the new query, in Datasheet view, sort the Company field in alphabetical order and then sort the City field in alphabetical order. Save the query.
4. Create a report using all the data in the Customers Query by City. Group the data by City, sort by Company, apply a Stepped layout and Portrait orientation, and use the Paper style. Name it **Customers by City Report**.
5. Print a copy of the report, as shown in Figure 18.1.
6. To make the database more efficient, compact and repair the database. Click the Office Button, point to Manage, and click Compact and Repair Database.
7. To secure the database, back up the database and place it in a different folder, if possible. Click the Office Button, point to Manage, and click Back Up Database. The Save As dialog box will appear, and the file will have the database name with the current date.
8. Close and save the database.

WHAT YOU NEED TO KNOW

Software

▶ Databases contain data that is difficult to replace quickly. To prevent loss of data, it is advisable to back up, or copy, the database to another location. A daily or weekly backup protocol should be developed to ensure database safety.

▶ To back up the database, open it, click the Office Button, point to Manage, and then click Back Up Database. The Save As dialog box will appear with the database name and today's date. Save the file to another location as another measure of safety.

▶ When you use a database regularly, especially when you add or delete objects, the database may become fragmented. The result is that the database runs slowly and errors may develop in the file. To improve the performance of the database, use the Compact and Repair feature. Compacting, or defragmenting, is a process by which unnecessary space is eliminated in the database. To compact a database, click the Office Button, point to Manage, and then click Compact and Repair Database.

Paper style

Group by City and sort by Company

Customers by City Report

Akron

A-1 Cleaning Maids	Holstein	Alan	President	(330) 555-8320	289 1st St
Acme Sporting Goods	Kosinski	Walter	Manager	(330) 555-2228	438 Oakdale Road
CarTruck Rentals	Sottile	Vincent	Office Manager	(330) 555-9875	389 Alter Ave
Carver Medical Center	Harvey	Nancy	Office Manager	(330) 555-1000	38 Main St
Cline's Rug Cleaners	Cline	Joanne	Owner	(330) 555-0950	428 Alben Ave
Congress Church	Valdez	Maria	Office Manager	(330) 555-0900	35 Main Street
Crown Pizza	Maccarone	Louis	Owner	330-555-6789	15 Alben Avenue
Exquisite Craft Society	Pinkerton	Carl	President	(330) 555-1200	2 Main St
Greg's Lawn Care	Francis	Greg	President	(330) 555-3891	1900 Elm St
Help for the Needy	Aceveda	Cal	Office Manager	(330) 555-7805	78 3rd Ave
J's Ice Cream	Contera	June	Owner	(330) 555-8191	223 Main St
Junior Camp Center	Davis	Edward	Administrator	(330) 555-4010	38 Richmond Ave
Nunzio's Pizza	Buono	John	Owner	(330) 555-3676	458 Avenue C
See World Travel Agenc	Mansfield	Sylvia	President	(330) 555-8383	29 Forest Ave
Seemore PTA	Reilly	Robert	President	(330) 555-1809	1532 8th Avenue
Southside Fitness	Morrison	William	Office Manager	(330) 555-7712	450 South Street
Unique Florists	Sanchez	Carla	Owner	(330) 555-0949	125 Davis Blvd

Bedford

Academy Bus Tours	Mendelsohn	John	Vice President	(330) 555-6111	330 Market Street
AQC Carpenter's Union	Cortland	John	Office Manager	(440) 555-8900	28 Market St
Chen's Restaurant	Chen	Li	Owner	(440) 555-2000	21 Market Street
Church of Unitarians	Avino	Teresa	Office Manager	(440) 555-6220	490 Market St
Joe's Homemade Candy	Dolcetti	Joseph	Owner	(440) 555-6709	2 Mark Street

Fairlawn

Bradford College	Harris	Margaret	Administrative Assistant	330-555-3434	23 Main Street

Hudson Villag

Bundles of Joy	Cardoza	Anita	Owner	(330) 555-9614	34 Forbes St
Prize Dance School	Wilson	Phyllis	Director	(330) 555-8400	55 Anders St
RentaVehicle	Cordero	Morris	Vice President	(330) 555-8210	4890 Carter Blvd

Mogadore

JC Sports Club	Clarington	George	Office Manager	(330) 555-9817	12 Mill Rd
Playhouse Day Care	Frank	Helen	Director	(330) 555-7800	2 Hull Ave

Ravenna

PTA of Ekbert HS	Cassidy	Nora	President	(330) 555-8193	248 Garretson Road
Ravenna Civic Associatio	Parker	Frank	President	330-555-9038	145 First Street

Shaker Height

Elite Party Supplies	Benvista	Mario	President	(216) 555-1209	12 Ace Ave
Manor Civic Association	Brandoff	Kurt	President	(330) 555-1212	4891 Delaware Street

Figure 18.1

Chris James would like her agents to be able to access the current agency listings when they are away from the office, but some of their computers do not have Access 2007. In addition, she wants you to delete one of the queries, and you need to check object dependencies before the deletion.

In this project, you will save the database for Access 2003 software and then check object dependencies so that you can delete one of the queries.

1. Find **16.3listings** in your files or data file **d18.2listings**, copy it to your Solutions folder, and rename it **18.2listings**. Open the file.

2. Open the Townhouse Listings query in Design view. Change the Criteria setting for the Type of Property field from Townhouse to **Split Level**. Click the Office Button, and select Save As. Name the new query **Split Level Listings**.

3. Check Object Dependencies before deleting the Colonial Listings report.
   a. Select the Colonial Listings report, click the Database Tools tab, and in the Show/Hide group, click the Object Dependencies button. Note that no objects depend on the report.
   b. Select the Objects that I depend on option, as shown in Figure 18.2a, and note that the report depends on the Colonial Listings query. Close the Object Dependencies pane.
   c. Close the Colonial Listings report, right-click it on the Navigation Pane, and then delete it. Confirm the deletion.

4. Repeat Step 3 and delete the Townhouse Listings report.

5. Create a new report using the Listings table, named **Listings by Property Type**.
   a. Include the fields as listed: Type of Property, City, Address, Bedrooms, Price, Date Listed.
   b. Group by Type of Property, sort by City, set Summary Options to average the price field, and set the Show option to Detail and Summary. Select Stepped layout and Portrait orientation, and use the Opulent style.
   c. Modify the report as shown in Figure 18.2b. In Layout view, set the report header Fill/Back color to grey, and then add the company name and the logo from data file **d16.3jameslogo.bmp**. In Design view, delete the Summary label, and modify the Average price label to align with the Price column. Expand any labels as necessary, and then move the page footer to the left to fit all on one page wide.
   d. Print a copy of the report. Close the report.

6. Save the database in Access 2002–2003 format.

▼ **WHAT YOU NEED TO KNOW**

Software

▶ As you develop relationships between tables and queries, object dependencies are developed between database objects. If you later decide to delete a query or table that is no longer useful, it is helpful to be able to see what other objects are using the item to be deleted. You would then either modify the dependent objects to remove dependencies or delete the dependent objects before deleting the table or query.

▶ To view object dependencies, select the object, click the Database Tools tab, and then in the Show/Hide group, click the Object Dependencies button. You can then view all the connections this object has with the others in the database.

▶ Access 2007 can read files created in earlier versions but earlier versions cannot read Access 2007 files. You may have Access files created in an earlier version and wish to use them with Access 2007 or you may need to format your Access 2007 file for use by someone without the new software.

▶ To save an Access 2007 file for an earlier version, click the Office Button, point to Save As, and select the desired file format. You may get a message that the database contains features that are not supported by the earlier version.

a. Click the Office Button, point to Save As, and select the Access 2002–2003 Database format.

b. Place the new .mdb file in your solutions folder. The newly saved database will open.

7. Save and close the database.

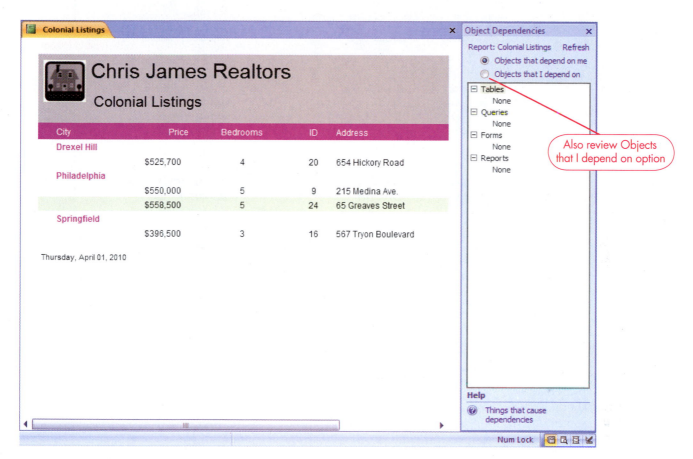

Figure 18.2a Object Dependencies pane

Chris James Realtors
Listings by Property Type

Type of Property	City	Address	Bedrooms	Price	Date Listed
Apartment					
	Philadelphia	534 Thompson Street	2	$285,500	11/18/2010
Average				$285,500	
Cape Cod					
	Springfield	745 Circle Drive	3	$393,500	11/18/2010
Average				$393,500	
Colonial					
	Drexel Hill	654 Hickory Road	4	$525,700	11/19/2010
	Philadelphia	65 Greaves Street	5	$558,500	11/23/2010
	Philadelphia	215 Medina Ave.	5	$550,000	9/15/2010
	Springfield	567 Tryon Boulevard	3	$396,500	11/16/2010
Average				$507,675	
Ranch					
	Philadelphia	874 Edison St.	2	$345,800	10/15/2010
	Philadelphia	429 Hart Blvd.	3	$385,900	9/ 5/2010
Average				$365,850	
Split Level					
	Drexel Hill	89-01 Main St.	3	$535,000	8/24/2010
	Kellyville	301 Seguine Ave.	4	$502,000	9/12/2010
	Springfield	521 Bache Avenue	4	$489,500	11/22/2010
Average				$508,833	
Townhouse					
	Drexel Hill	28 Naughton St.	2	$368,500	11/15/2010
	Drexel Hill	76 Trainor Road	2	$345,500	11/22/2010
	Drexel Hill	41 Greenley Place	3	$355,500	11/16/2010
	Kellyville	54 Greenly Street	3	$395,800	11/22/2010
	Philadelphia	34 Catherine Street	2	$359,900	11/23/2010
	Springfield	890 Vargo La.	1	$283,000	9/ 3/2010
Average				$351,367	

Group by Type of Property and sort by City

Average of Price by Type of Property

Move into position and widen fields as necessary

Figure 18.2b Report

PART II: INTEGRATED SIMULATION PROJECTS

Introduction

In this part of the text, you will apply all the tool-specific and document skills you have learned thus far to three real business situations. Each project will begin with a description of the business problem, followed by a list of documents you will need to produce in order to achieve the project objectives. You will be given guidelines for producing each document in the project.

While this text focuses on application material for Word, Excel, PowerPoint, and Access, you can also use Publisher to complete many of the assignments if you are familiar with this application. These tasks are labeled Word/Publisher on the project summary pages. In addition, optional tasks for Outlook are also included in each simulation.

You can use a completed project as a portfolio work sample. Therefore, save all copies of your work, including draft copies. Be sure all copies contain your name and the current date.

WHAT YOU NEED TO KNOW BEFORE YOU BEGIN

- Create folders on your local drive using the project number followed by your initials (**isp1.yi**, **isp2.yi**, **isp3.yi**).
- Save each file within the appropriate folder. Name each file with the project number, the file name, and your initials (**p1.1letter.yi**).
- Label a manila folder with your name. This will be used for your printed drafts, research results, and final copies.
- Print one copy of each project task list, e.g., **dp1.0tasklist.docx**, which can be found on the Data CD. Paste this sheet on the outside of your manila folder to keep track of your progress and to help you organize your printouts. *Note: The tasks for each project can be found on the first page of each project.*

INTEGRATED SIMULATION

PROJECT 1
Organizing a
Business Trip

PROJECT 2
New Employee
Orientation

PROJECT 3
Starting a New
Business

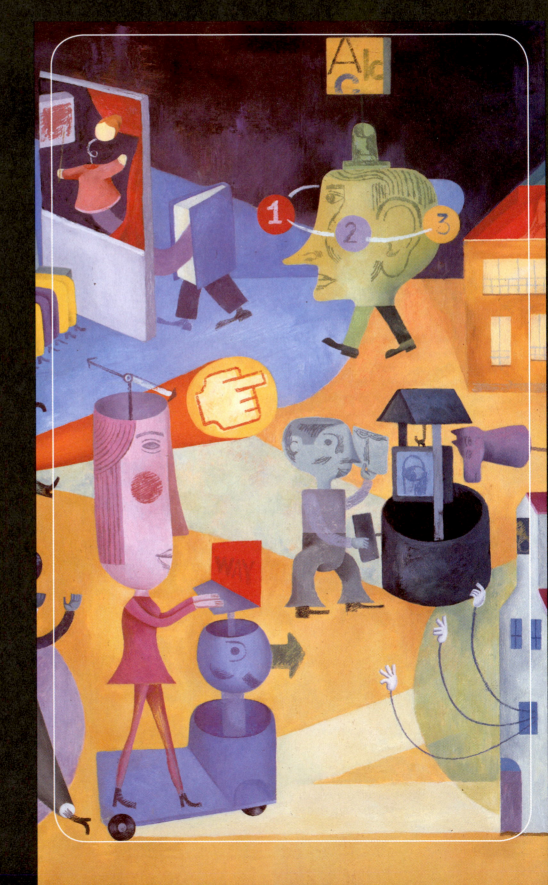

PROJECT 1

Organizing a Business Trip

You work as a purchasing agent for Calvington Ties. You are responsible for purchasing ties for company inventory. The company has decided to introduce a line of fine silk ties, which are produced in Como, Italy, among other places. Como is in the lake region of Italy, which is north of Milan. You and your group (which includes Lilly Bryce, a product designer, and John Weston, vice president of marketing) are planning to go on a buying trip to Como from May 10 to May 15, 2010. You will meet with silk tie suppliers from Como, as well as other regions, during that week. The purpose of the trip is to examine silks and tie designs, and to make purchasing decisions.

In preparation for this trip, you will complete numerous projects that will require you to use various Office tools, as follows:

Internet
- Research and gather information about silk tie suppliers in Como, Italy
- Research and gather information about the region so that you are familiar with your hotel, area restaurants, and tourist attractions

Word
- Compile a table of Italian silk tie suppliers
- Prepare a memo and e-mail it to trip participants
- Send a merged letter to suppliers to arrange meetings
- Complete and merge a fax cover sheet
- Develop the trip itinerary

Excel
- Prepare a budget for the trip
- Compile your expense report following the trip

PowerPoint
- Create an 8- to 10-slide presentation for participants about trip goals, the budget, meetings, and destination information

Access
- Import a Word table of suppliers into a database
- Create a Suppliers form for use during meetings
- Prepare a summary report of supplier information

Optional applications:
Outlook
- Add trip dates to the Calendar
- Create a task list that includes all items listed here

ORGANIZING A BUSINESS TRIP

I. INTERNET RESEARCH

To prepare for this trip, you need to research the silk tie suppliers you will visit and compile information on the travel destination.

Follow these guidelines:

A. To maximize the time spent in Como, you will create a table in Word that lists silk tie suppliers, their addresses, cities, phone numbers, and fax numbers. You will continue to add data to this table.

  1. Open data file **dp1.1suppliers.docx**, which includes some silk suppliers.

  2. Go to this Website: www.italianmoda.com.

    a. Click ENTER Now, enter **neckwear** in the Search box, and then click the SEARCH! button.

    b. Click the Visit our Showroom link for each supplier, which will display the needed information. Copy the name, address, phone, and fax information from the Storefront page of a tie supplier that you like from Como, and then paste it below the Suppliers table, using the Match Destination Formatting paste option from the SmartTag. Repeat this procedure for at least four other tie suppliers. Note that sometimes the town and province are the same.

    c. Drag the data from the pasted information under the table into the appropriate columns in the table.

    d. Save the table and name it **p1.1suppliers**. (Since Internet items change frequently, the suppliers you locate may vary from those in the solution file.)

B. Your group will stay at the Barchetta Excelsior in Como, Italy. Como is located in the Lombardy region of Italy, as shown in Figure 1.1. You will research information about the hotel and about Lake Como.

  1. To find information about Lake Como, go to the Website www.initaly.com/regions/lombardy/como.htm and print out the page. You will refer to this page later in the project.

  2. To find detailed information about the hotel, go to the www.hotels.com Website and search for Como, Italy, as the destination and for the Barchetta Excelsior. Print the description page so that you will have the address and telephone number of the hotel. You will refer to this page later in the project.

Figure 1.1 Como is located in the Lombardy region of Italy

II. MEMO TO PARTICIPANTS

WBR pg 36

You will write a memo to John Weston, vice president of marketing, and Lilly Bryce, product designer, who will accompany you on the upcoming trip to Italy.

Follow these guidelines:

A. Use the memo template found in the data file **dp1.2memotemp.docx**, as shown in Figure 1.2.

B. Write the following memo to those participating in the trip:

> Per the decisions made by the Marketing Department, the purchasing team will go to Como, Italy, to sample and ultimately purchase a line of silk ties.
>
> We will depart on May 10 and return on May 15, 2010. We are planning to schedule appointments with suppliers on May 12 and 13 and then meet for dinner on May 13 to debrief and review the samples we have collected. We will implement any buying decisions on May 14. You are free to make personal plans for the evening of May 14.
>
> We will stay at the Barchetta Excelsior in Como, Italy. The hotel is in the center of Como, and it will be convenient to meet with our suppliers.
>
> We will meet next week to review the itinerary, which you will receive in a few days. At our meeting, there will be a presentation giving you an overview of our mission and the region.

omit

C. Send the memo via e-mail to the participants, using an e-mail address provided by your teacher.

D. Save the memo and name it **p1.2memo**.

E. Print one copy for your files.

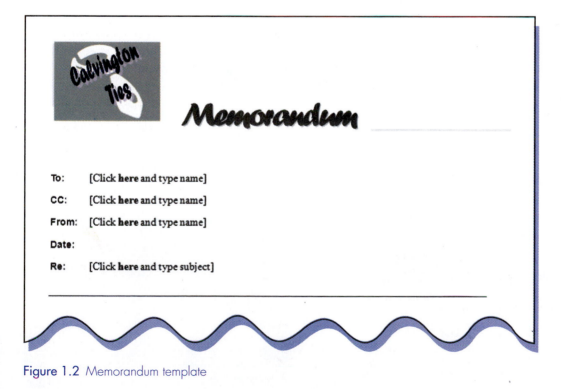

Figure 1.2 Memorandum template

III. SUPPLIERS DATABASE

It has been decided that all the supplier information should be in a database. You have already entered the information for suppliers in a Word table. You will create a new database and import the supplier data from Word.

Follow these guidelines:

A. Create a new Access database and name it **p1.3imports**. Close the blank table which opens.

B. In Word, open **p1.1suppliers.docx**, and convert the table to text with commas as the separators, using the Table Tools Layout tab. Save the file as a Plain Text or .txt file, and name it **psuppliers**. Close the file.

C. Import the information from **psuppliers.txt** into a new table. In the import screens, select commas as the separators, select First Row Contains Field Names, let Access set the primary key, and then name the table **Suppliers**.

D. Add additional fields titled **Contact First** and **Contact Last** to the table. *Note: Contact names will be added to the database as they are developed.*

E. Create a form from the table and insert the company logo, found in data file **dp1tielogo.gif**, and a form title in the form header, as shown in Figure 1.3. Format the form in the Foundry style, and name the form **Suppliers Form**.

F. Go to this Website: www.italianmoda.com and click ENTER Now.

G. Enter **neckwear** in the Search box, and then find information on three more suppliers.

H. Enter the data into the database using the form or table. You now have records for 11 suppliers.

I. Create a report listing all the suppliers that the participants might see while they are in Italy. They will fill in the contact names as they attend meetings and demonstrations. Include the name of the company, Contact First, Contact Last, the telephone and fax numbers, and the address. Sort the report by Company Name and set it for landscape orientation.

J. Enhance the report in Layout view by adding the logo and full gridlines. Apply the Foundry style, and then adjust column sizes as necessary. Name the report **Italian Tie Suppliers**.

K. Print a copy of the report.

L. Close and save the database.

Figure 1.3 Italian Tie Suppliers form

IV. LETTERS TO SUPPLIERS

To introduce your company to potential suppliers, and to schedule meetings, you will need to write letters, which you will send via fax and regular postal mail.

Follow these guidelines:

A. Use the data file **dp1.4letterhead.docx** for the letterhead, which is illustrated in Figure 1.4, to prepare a letter (main document) for a merge. You will use the table of suppliers in the **p1.3imports.accdb** database that you created as your data source document. If this table is not available to you, you can use the data file **dp1.4imports.accdb**.

B. Use the following settings:

Margins	1.25" left and right
Line spacing	Single
Paragraph spacing	
Before	0
After	0
Font	Calibri
Font size	11 point

C. At the top of the letter, include the proper mailing notation (**VIA FAX AND POSTAL MAIL**). Use today's date.

D. Address the letter to the Sales Department since you do not have a contact name for each supplier. The address in the main document should be formatted as follows. The country name should be in all caps, and so should be entered manually.

>   Sales Department
>   <<Company>>
>   <<Address>>
>   <<Postal Code>> <<Province>>
>   ITALY

E. Prepare the main document using the following text:

>   Calvington Ties, a small men's tie company, is located in New York and sells a line of classic ties produced in the United States. During the past five years, our brand name has grown along with our sales. Now, we would like to add a line of silk Italian-made ties.
>
>   We have visited your Web storefront and are interested in your products. Our group will be in Como, at the Barchetta Excelsior Hotel, and available to meet with your sales representatives on May 12 or May 13, 2010. May we schedule a morning or afternoon meeting with you on one of these dates? Please reply at your earliest convenience so that we can arrange our appointments for the short time we are in Italy.
>
>   We suggest that you e-mail or fax your reply so that we have the opportunity to consider your products for our new line. We are looking forward to meeting with your sales representatives.

F. Include an appropriate salutation and closing. Use Purchasing Agent as your title. *Note: When the name of the addressee is unknown and the letter is sent to a department, rather than an individual, the salutation should read Ladies and Gentlemen.*

G. Save the main document file as **p1.4mergeletter**.

H. Merge the main document with the data source, and print one copy of the merged letters.

I. Save the merged file as **p1.4mergeletterall**.

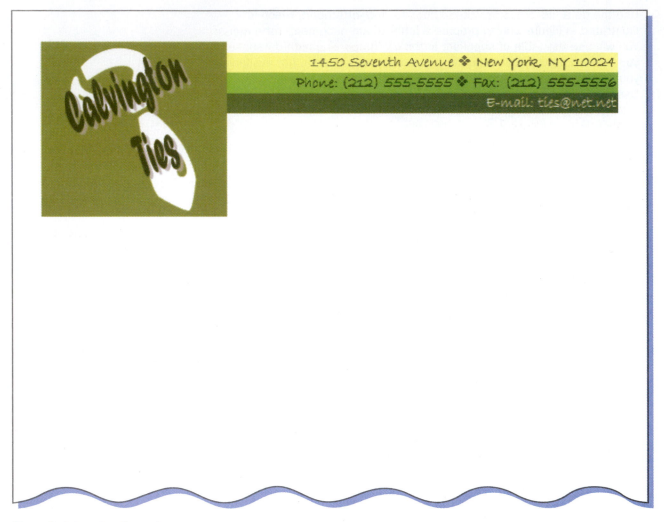

Figure 1.4 Letterhead template

V. FAX COVER SHEET

Since you will send the letters via fax, you will need to prepare a fax cover sheet for each supplier for whom you have a fax number.

Follow these guidelines:

A. Prepare a fax cover sheet for each supplier using the data file **dp1.5fax.docx**, which is a fax cover sheet template. You can create a merge file for this assignment using the table in the **dp1.5imports.accdb** database as the data source.

B. In the From line, enter your name.

C. For Number of Pages, enter **2**.

D. In the subject line, enter `Visits on May 12 or 13, 2010`.

E. Save the file and name it **p1.5mergefax**. Complete the merge and name it **p1.5mergefaxall**.

F. Print one copy of the fax cover sheet for each supplier.

VI. ITINERARY

You must create an itinerary so that all parties will know the schedule of the trip. The information you will need is noted below.

- May 10
  8:00 p.m. Depart Kennedy Airport, Alitalia Airlines, Flight #222 to Milan

- May 11
  8:30 a.m. Arrive Milan International Airport
  10:00 a.m. Train from Milan International Airport to Milano Centrale in Milan
  12:00 noon. Leave from Milano Centrale, Train #2020, to Como S. Giovanni station. Take taxi to Barchetta Excelsior Hotel, Piazza Cavour 1, Como
  8:00 p.m. Dinner at Ristorante Barchetta with Carlo Bertolucci, sales representative

Figure 1.5 Town of Como, Italy

- May 12
  10:00 a.m. Meeting with supplier
  2:00 p.m. Meeting with supplier
  8:00 p.m. Dinner at Posta with Maria Bono, sales representative; meet in hotel lobby at 7:30 p.m.

- May 13
  10:00 a.m. Meeting with supplier
  2:00 p.m. Meeting with supplier
  8:00 p.m. Dinner in the Grille Room, Grand Hotel Tremezzo, to debrief

- May 14
  10:00 a.m. Meeting with supplier to establish purchasing contracts
  2:00 p.m. Meeting with supplier to establish purchasing contracts
  8:00 p.m. Dinner on your own

- May 15
  7:30 a.m. Meet in hotel lobby; taxi to Como S. Giovanni station
  9:00 a.m. Leave for Milan, Train #2022
  11:30 a.m. Train to Milan International Airport
  1:00 p.m. Depart Milan International Airport, Alitalia, Flight #121 to New York City
  2:00 p.m. Arrive Kennedy Airport, New York City

Follow these guidelines:

A. Use the letterhead template **dp1.6letterhead.docx** to create the itinerary.
B. Include the departure and return dates in the title of the itinerary.
C. Format the itinerary so the dates are easy to identify.
D. Save the file and name it **p1.6itinerary**.
E. Print one copy.

VII. TRAVEL BUDGET

You will need to create a budget that estimates the cost of the trip. This is necessary to request a cash advance for some of the expenses.

Follow these guidelines:

A. Use an Excel spreadsheet to find the total estimated cost for this trip. Include the company logo on the sheet using data file **dp1tielogo.gif**. Format the header in a related fill color and use the font used in the logo, Forte, for the title of the report.

B. The heading on the budget should include the following:
Participants: John Weston, Lilly Bryce, Your Name
Dates: May 10–May 15, 2010
Trip: Como, Italy
Purpose: Select and buy Italian silk product line

C. Format the columns for your data as follows:

EXPENSE DETAIL	PER PERSON	TOTAL	GROUP	TOTAL
Enter categories of expenses and details about each expense	Enter individual costs	Multiply by 3 to get expense total for all participants	Enter any group costs here	Add per person total and group costs

D. The categories and estimated expenses are:
- Transportation (per person expense):
  - Airfare round trip: $850.00
  - Train fare: $70.00
  - Taxi to and from airport in US: $100.00
  - Taxis (water and land) for three days in Italy: $150.00
- Lodging (per person expense): Using the information you obtained from your Internet research on the Barchetta Excelsior, in Como, enter the lowest U.S. rate for the high season for the four-night stay (or use $250 per night). You can use Expedia.com, Hotels.com, or Travelocity.com to research the hotel rates. Include the four-night cost in the Per Person column. Notice that the hotel rates include breakfast.
- Meals (per person expense): Estimated cost for meals for five days is $500.00.
- Entertainment (group expense): Luncheon and Dinner Meetings, etc. $1000.00

E. Add all columns to find the totals.

F. Use cell styles including the Total cell style to format the worksheet to match the logo color scheme.

G. Save the budget and name it **p1.7budget**.

H. Print one copy.

Figure 1.6 View of Lake Como

VIII. PRESENTATION

There will be a meeting of the participants, at which time you will present the details of the trip. Create an 8- to 10-slide presentation that details this information.

Follow these guidelines:

A. Prepare a title slide, as shown in Figure 1.7.

B. Prepare a slide titled **Goals and Objectives** that includes the following bullet points:

- **Expand product line to include Italian silk ties**
- **The ties should have a classic look**
- **Pricing should be competitive**
- **Limit the number of manufacturers to four**
- **Seek out the best quality for the lowest price**

C. Research and prepare a slide titled **A Typical Silk Tie Supplier** summarizing company information for a silk tie supplier, such as what types of ties the supplier sells, information about the company, and the other products it carries.

1. Go to this Website: www.italianmoda.com/storefronts/antartide.
2. This is a tie supplier's site. Research the site to create bullet points for this slide. Create a link to the company's site so that you can show the group more detailed information.

D. Create a slide that is titled **Types of Neckties** and presents photos of four neckties with descriptions of each. You can create a photo album for this slide, if you wish. Use the photos found in the data file folder **dp1.8photos**.

E. Link the next slide to the itinerary.

F. In the next slide, embed the Excel budget spreadsheet. *Note: To import the budget as an embedded file, click the Insert tab and then in the Text group, click the Object button. Select Create from file, locate your budget worksheet, and then click OK. Size the worksheet to fill the slide.*

Figure 1.7 Presentation title slide

G. Provide highlights of Como, using the information you obtained from the Internet research on Lake Como to create relevant bullet points for the next slide. *Note: You might want to add another slide entitled "Don't Miss . . . " that features two or three very special places to visit in Como.*

H. Create a summary slide, beginning with Slide 2. Title the slide `Summary`, and include the titles of each slide in the presentation as bullets. Link each bulleted item on the slide to the actual slide.

I. Enhance the presentation as follows:

   1. Use any design theme. You may use a photo of Como, if you want, as the background for the first slide. *Note: Depending on the design theme you apply, you may need to adjust the background color for the budget slide so that the worksheet is visible.*

   2. Use relevant clip art or photos on slides where they would be effective. Apply a picture effect to each piece of clip art or photo you use.

   3. Insert a music clip to create an Italian mood on any slide you want. Set it to play automatically.

   4. Apply transitions and animations.

J. In the handout master, insert a header that includes today's date and the title of the presentation, and then apply an attractive background.

K. Save the file and name it **p1.8presentation**.

L. Print one copy of the presentation as handouts with six slides per page.

M. *Optional: Create speaker notes with cue marks, time your presentation, and deliver it.*

IX. EXPENSE REPORT

The group has returned from its trip and will submit expense reports. You will create a report for your expenses and will submit this report with receipts. You, as the leader of the group, have charged all group meetings to your account. The airfare was paid directly by the company. Each participant was given a $500 advance.

Follow these guidelines:

A. Use the Travel expense report template provided in Microsoft Office Online or the Expense report template in Excel.

B. Customize the template for Calvington Ties by adding the logo.

C. Group meetings are to be charged as entertainment.

D. Your title is Purchasing Agent, your employee ID is #32, you are in the Purchasing Department, and your manager is Kyle Trumble. Use 100 as the expense report or statement number. All expense items are being charged to Account number 342.

E. Use the template to enter the expenses. You have arranged your receipts by date. Enter them on the template in that order and consolidate items on one line so that all the data fits on one page. Use the Description space to list the name of any restaurant used for meals. Use two lines per date when there is a group expense item for Entertainment and enter the name of the restaurant in the Description column for that entry. *Note: Since hotel rates change frequently, the hotel rate provided below may differ from the rate you obtained from the Internet.*

Figure 1.8 Silk tie

5/10/10	Airport Food Shop	$21.50
	Taxi to airport	$50.00
5/11/10	Hotel	$250
	Breakfast	15.00
	Rosa Trattoria, Como Lunch	$28.50
	Train, taxi	$50.00
	Meeting—dinner for 4, Ristorante Barchetta	$485.00
	Phone	$23.42
	Misc.	$36.75
5/12/10	Hotel	$250.00
	Azzuro Café—lunch	$22.00
	Taxis	$36.00
	Meeting—dinner for 4, Posta	$265.00
	Phone	$29.57
	Misc.	$18.54
5/13/10	Hotel	$250.00
	Luna Trattoria—lunch	$25.00
	Taxis	$45.00
	Meeting—dinner for 3, Tremezzo Grille Room	$300.00
	Phone	$25.76
5/14/2010	Hotel	$250.00
	Casa Rotini—lunch	15.00
	Taxis	45.00
	Dinner—Ristorante Barchetta	35.00
	Phone	24.87
	Misc.	42.78
5/15/10	Lunch and Dinner in Transit	$76.00
	Trains and taxis	$75.00

F. You received a $500.00 advance.

G. Add a note that the dinner meetings, in the Entertainment category, include all trip participants.

H. Format fonts and shading on the template to match the logo color scheme.

I. Print a copy of the report.

J. Save the report and name it **p1.9expense**.

PROJECT 2

New Employee Orientation

You work in the Human Resources Department of the corporate headquarters of HappyTime Park, a theme park with locations throughout the United States. For the summer tourist season, the company hires many employees who are typically college students.

Your job is to organize a New Employee Orientation workshop for new recruits hired for the Massachusetts location. There will be approximately 400 new hires.

In preparation for the workshop, you will complete numerous projects, requiring you to use various Office tools, as follows:

Internet
- Research conference center Website to obtain the necessary details about the conference site
- Copy text and pictures from various Websites for use in documents
- Use a payroll Website to calculate federal and state taxes

Word/Publisher
- Prepare a letter for new employees, inviting them to the orientation workshop
- Create an employee newsletter to be distributed at the workshop

Word
- Format a two-sided brochure containing the workshop program
- Develop a Web page for new hires

Excel
- Prepare a Benefits worksheet, formatted for inclusion in the employee manual and presentation
- Compile Payroll spreadsheet by importing employee data from database, inputting tax formulas, and formatting worksheets for clarity

PowerPoint
- Create a 10-slide presentation to new hires, summarizing company history and policies

Access
- Import data from an Excel spreadsheet to create an employee database

Optional applications:
Outlook
- Add important dates to the Calendar
- Add new hires to contact list

NEW EMPLOYEE ORIENTATION

I. INTERNET RESEARCH

The Bayside Expo Center, in Boston, Massachusetts, will accommodate the new employee group for the orientation workshop. You will use the Internet to get information about the workshop location.

Follow these guidelines:

A. Go to the Bayside Expo Center Website at:
www.baysideexpo.com.

B. Click each of the following links, view the contents of the page, then bookmark the site (add to your Favorites folder). You will return to this site later in the project.
- Directions
- Calendar
- Floor Plans
- About Us
- Press Releases

Figure 2.1

II. DATABASE

As new employees are hired, they are listed in an Excel spreadsheet. *Note: This list is a representative sample of the 400 new employees who have been hired.* The Human Resources Department has asked you to put the data into a database, to create a form for data entry and mailing labels, and to develop several queries and reports.

Follow these guidelines:

A. Open the Excel worksheet, **dp2.2employees.xlsx**, to view the data collected on the new hires. Notice the entries in the Unit column, which is the department employing the new hire. You will need this information later to create a lookup field.

B. In Access, open a blank database and name it **p2.2employees**.
  1. Import the columns in the worksheet, except for the M/F, Status, and Unit columns.
  2. Let Access create the primary key, and then save the new table as `Employee Data`.

C. Import the worksheet again, but only import the three fields that were omitted in the last step.
  1. Let Access create the primary key, and then save the new table as `Payroll Data`.
  2. In the Payroll Data table in Design view, edit the data type of the Unit field to Lookup and then enter the names of the five units in the Lookup Wizard: `Administrative`, `Attractions`, `Entertainment`, `Food and Drink`, and `Maintenance`. Save the table.

D. Create a relationship between the tables using the ID or primary key fields.

E. Create a form titled **Employee Data** that includes all the fields from both tables. Include the ID number only once.
1. In Layout view, enhance the form design using the Module style.
2. Add the name of the form and the company logo, which can be found in the data file **dp2happylogo.bmp**, and as shown in Figure 2.2.

F. Create a query using the Simple Query Wizard, and name it **Contact List**.
1. Include the following fields: ID, Last, First, Phone, E-mail, and Unit.
2. Sort the query by Unit.

G. Create a set of payroll queries, formatted to display data for each unit.
1. In the first query, include the following fields: ID, Last, First, M/F, Status, and Unit. Name the query **Administrative Payroll**.
2. Sort by Last name, set criteria for **"Administrative"** using the quotation marks, and then deselect the Show box for the Unit field.
3. Repeat this query, changing the criteria and saving them under each unit name. You should now have five payroll queries.

H. Create mailing labels for the employees by clicking the Labels button on the Create tab in the Reports group. Use the Avery 2242 label, sort them by ZIP code, and name the report **Employee Mailing Labels**.

I. Create a report using the Employee and Payroll Data tables, and title it **Employees by Unit**.
1. Exclude the following fields: Title, M/F, and Status.
2. Group the data by Unit and sort it by Last name.
3. Use landscape orientation and the Module style.
4. Enhance the report header using the logo, which is in the data file **dp2happylogo.bmp**. Adjust the column width as necessary.
5. In Print Preview, check to be sure that the report will print one page wide. The location of the page footer may have to be adjusted. Print one copy of the report.

J. Close all files.

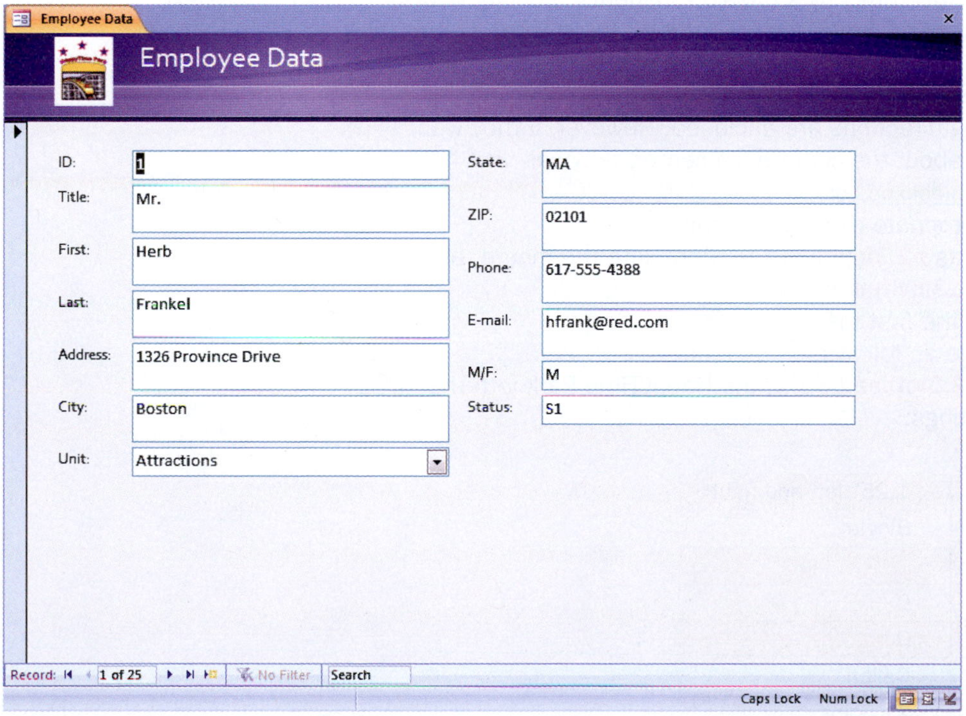

Figure 2.2

III. WRITE A LETTER TO NEW HIRES

You will send a letter of congratulations to new hires inviting them to attend the orientation workshop. You will also prepare driving directions to the Bayside Expo Center.

Follow these guidelines:

A. Prepare a merge letter to new hires from Joy Sommers, director of Human Resources.

1. Open the data file **dp2.3lethead.docx**, which is the HappyTime Park letterhead.

2. Use the following settings:

Margins	1.25" left and right
Line spacing	Single
Paragraph spacing	
Before	0
After	0
Font	Calibri
Font size	11 point

3. Use the Employee Data table in the **p2.2employees.accdb** database, which you created in Phase II, as the data source. If this file is not available, use the data file **dp2.3employees.accdb** and select the Employee Data table.

4. Include the following information in the letter:

a. Congratulate the new hire on his/her association with HappyTime Park.

b. Explain that all new employees must attend an orientation workshop before starting work. The orientation workshop will provide information about the company's mission, benefits, working hours, and housing. This year's workshop will take place on Wednesday, May 19, 2010 from 8:30 a.m. to 4:00 p.m. and will be held at the Bayside Expo Center in Boston.

c. Explain that driving directions are enclosed. However, if they want more information about the conference center, they can visit its Website: www.baysideexpo.com.

5. Conclude with an appropriate closing and name.

6. Save the merged file as **p2.3invitemerge**. Complete the merge, and save the letters as **p2.3invitemergeall**.

7. Print one copy of just the first merged letter.

B. Create the directions page as follows:

1. Open the data file **dp2.3lethead.docx**, the HappyTime Park letterhead.

2. Use the following settings:

Margins	1.25" left and right
Line spacing	Single
Paragraph spacing	
Before	0
After	0
Font	Calibri
Font size	11 point

3. Start at approximately 2" from the top of the page. Center the title, **Driving Directions to the Bayside Expo Center**, as shown in Figure 2.3. Set the text to a blue font color and bold it.

4. Go to the Directions page of the conference center Website.

5. Copy the directions for "From the South," "From the North and West," and "Transit," and paste them on the directions page.

   a. Set the text to the Calibri font, 11 point.

   b. Set the headings to a blue font color and bold them.

   c. Hyphenate the word "right hand" in the "From the South" section.

   d. Make any adjustments necessary to better display the text.

6. Insert the data file **dp2.3directionsmap.bmp** below the directions. *Hint: On the Insert tab, click on the Insert Picture from File button.*

   a. Apply the In Front of Text wrapping option, and center the map.

   b. Size the map to fill the bottom of the page, as shown in Figure 2.3.

7. Save the file as **p2.3directionspage**.

8. Print one copy.

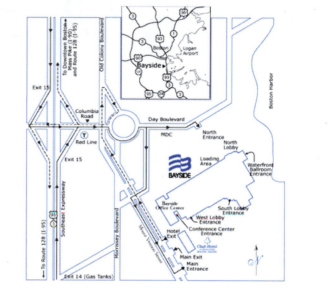

Figure 2.3

32 Hobbs Lane ☆ Harvard, MA 01451
P: (978) 555-5555 ☆ F: (978) 555-5556

Driving Directions to the Bayside Expo Center

From the South
Use Exit 14 from I-93, the Southeast Expressway. Stay in the right-hand lane and follow Morrissey Boulevard. At your 3rd set of lights take a right onto Mount Vernon Street. Follow the signs and take your 3rd left into the Bayside Expo Main Entrance.

From the North and West
From points North and/or West take the Massachusetts Turnpike, Interstate-90 East to Interstate 93 South. Take Exit 15 (Columbia Road) off of Interstate 93. Stay in the left-hand lane and take a left off of the ramp. Go ¾ of the way around the Rotary and bear right onto Day Blvd. Proceed past the Mass State Police Barracks and take your first right into the Bayside Expo North Entrance.

Transit
As a convenient alternative, take the T or Commuter Rail. The MBTA Red Line and Old Colony (Plymouth/Kingston and Middleboro/Lakeville) Branch of the commuter rail system both stop at the UMass/JFK station directly across the street from us.

IV. BENEFITS SUMMARY

In the employee manual and presentation, management would like to include information about the benefits the company offers. This information is currently contained in an Excel worksheet. You will format the data in a worksheet so that it can be included in other applications.

Follow these guidelines:

A. Open data file **dp2.4benefits.xlsx**. This is an unformatted Excel worksheet that lists the benefits for employees who have been with the company more than six months.

B. Insert the company logo, which can be found in the data file **dp2happylogo.bmp**.

C. Insert rows, apply borders, fonts, color, alignment, and other enhancement techniques to format this worksheet, using the logo's color scheme. An example is shown in Figure 2.4.

D. Be sure to include the following text, as shown: `Benefits begin after six-month probation period`.

E. Center the worksheet horizontally using Page Setup.

F. Print one copy of the benefits summary.

G. Save the file and name it **p2.4benefits**.

Figure 2.4

V. WORKSHOP PROGRAM

A workshop program will be distributed to all attendees, and you will have to design this program. Your boss has given you a sketch of what she has in mind, a sample of which is shown in Figure 2.5. Use the sketch as a guide in developing the layout. *Note: The two pages will be printed back to back to create the booklet.*

Follow these guidelines:

A. The program should be in the form of a booklet. Use an 8.5" by 11" page set to landscape orientation.

   1. Use the following settings:

Margins	.5" left, right, top, and bottom
Line spacing	Single
Paragraph spacing	
Before	0
After	0
Font	Default
Font size	Default

2. Set the page for two columns with a 1" gutter space.

3. Insert an attractive border as a header and footer.

B. Create the back cover, as shown in Figure 2.5a, on the left side of the first page, as follows:

  1. Insert the map of the upper floor of the conference center, found in data file **dp2.5upperfloorplan.bmp**.

  2. Include a text box that reads **Bayside Expo Center, Upper Level**.

    a. Apply any font color and font size to the text.

    b. Apply any color text box shading and a shadow effect to the box.

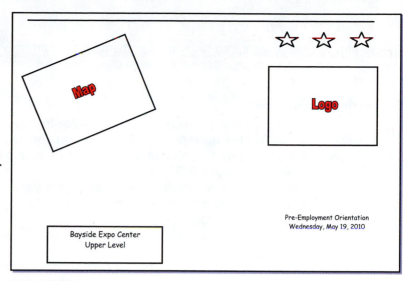

Figure 2.5a Front and back covers

C. Create the front cover, on the right side of the first page. Insert the company logo, located in data file **dp2happylogo.bmp**, the workshop's name, **Pre-Employment Orientation**, and the date of the workshop. You may use WordArt and any WordArt effect for these elements. *Hints: Press [Ctrl]+[Enter] to create a new page. Insert a column break to force the insertion point to the next column.*

D. On the second page of your document, create the inside left and inside right pages. These will be pages 2 and 3 of the program.

  1. In the left column (page 2), center the heading **Morning Program**. Insert the table from the data file **dp2.5amprogram.docx** below the heading. *Note: The text is contained in a table. You may format the table as you prefer with a table style or another attractive shading.*

  2. In the right column (page 3), center the heading **Afternoon Program**.

    a. Insert the table from the data file **dp2.5pmprogram.docx** below the heading.

    b. Insert the photo, found in data file **dp2.5conferencecenter.tif**, in the location shown in Figure 2.5b. Apply a picture effect of your choice.

E. Print the pages back to back, and fold the booklet in half.

F. Save the file and name it **p2.5program**.

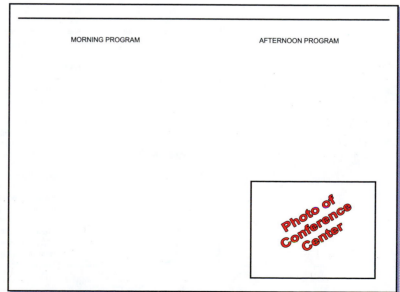

Figure 2.5b Inside pages

VI. EMPLOYEE NEWSLETTER

To give new hires an insight into the events at the park and company updates, copies of the employee newsletter will be distributed. You have been asked to create this month's issue.

Follow these guidelines:

A. Create a one-page newsletter, using any font and size that you want. Set margins that you feel are appropriate to fit the text on one page.

B. Use your creativity to plan the newsletter layout. A portion of a sample newsletter is shown in Figure 2.6.

C. Create a masthead with the company name, logo, the issue number: `Vol. 1, No. 5`, and the date: `May 2010`. Use the data file **dp2happylogo.bmp** for the logo.

D. Insert the text (cut and paste) from data file **dp2.6newstext.docx** into the newsletter.

E. Use a drop capital to enhance the first paragraph.

F. Include relevant clip art to enhance the newsletter articles, and apply any picture style or effect to them.

G. Save the file and name it **p2.6newsletter**.

H. Print one copy.

The HappyTime Park Employee Newsletter — Vol. 1 No. 5 ☐ May 2010

New Hires

On May 19, 2010, a pre-employment orientation will be held for our new employees at the Bayside Expo Center, in Boston. We know that the conference will be a success because our group of new hires is exceptional. The employee group is made up of college students from local schools, graduates of business schools, students who worked for us in previous years, as well as a small group of employees that are from six foreign countries. We are looking forward to a great season with the 2010 staff.

Eye on Tomorrow

On July 4, we will distribute American Flags to the first 100 families to enter the park.

Employee Park Specials

HappyTime Park offers many specials to its employees, including family and friend rates. You can arrange to have your next family reunion or friend's birthday at the park at bargain rates. Just ask Nina Block, park event coordinator, for the details. She can be reached at Extension 2222.

Employee Recognition Awards

While working in a theme park certainly has its attractions, it's still a job. At HappyTime Park, we understand and appreciate our employees' efforts and have instituted several different awards programs.

- *SuperStars*. This program is the foundation of HappyTime Park. It recognizes the top three employees from each department each month. Department managers select the honoree and Super Stars are honored at a monthly dinner. Honorees may invite friends and family to attend. In addition, gifts are given to the Stars, which include a watch and/or an Achievement Pin to wear while on the job.

- *HappySpot Awards*. Supervisors will reward employees on the spot if the employees are observed providing a high level of guest services. The awards are special scratch-off cards where employees can win from $10 to $25 or free lunches or movie theatre passes.

- At the end of July, the park hosts the annual HappyTime Park Competition, with five to seven teams competing in events such as a water-balloon toss and tug-of- war. The winners and participants celebrate the all-day event at a luau, which includes a barbecue and a pie-throwing booth, featuring members of the park's management team as targets.

- Each year, five college grants – ranging from $500 to $1200 – are awarded to employees who are selected by a committee that reviews the applications and interviews finalists. Submit your applications by the end of June.

Figure 2.6

VII. NEW HIRES WEB PAGE

Since many of the new hires live in different parts of the United States, your manager thought it would be a good idea to create a Web page that includes information about the workshop.

Follow these guidelines:

A. Use the data file **dp2.7template.docx**, which is a Business E-mail newsletter template. *Note: While this template is designed for an e-newsletter, it can be used to create a Web page in Word.*

B. Open the data file **dp2.7webtext.docx**, and copy each paragraph from the data file into the paragraphs of the template.

C. Format the template so that it looks like Figure 2.7.
  1. Add the title `HappyTime Park New Hires Information`, and then remove any references specific to newsletters (date, volume number).
  2. Use a sans serif font for all text. *Note: Comic Sans MS was used in Figure 2.7.*
  3. Use the Light Green font color for the main title and subheadings, since the background color will be blue on the Web page. Size the font as you wish.
  4. Use any relevant pictures and the company logo to enhance the page. Use the data file **dp2happylogo.bmp** for the logo, and apply picture effects to each graphic.

D. Insert a link to the directions page of the Bayside Expo Center Website, which you bookmarked earlier, on the words "Bayside Expo Center" in the Workshop paragraph.

E. Insert a link to the workshop program file you created earlier, **p2.5program.docx**, on the word "program" in the Workshop paragraph.

F. Insert a link to the benefits Excel file you created earlier, **p2.4benefits.xlsx**, on the words "benefits package" in the Benefits paragraph.

G. Link the titles in the left pane to the paragraph section titles in the right pane.

H. Save the file as a Word document, and name it **p2.7web**.

I. Apply a blue background to the page. Then save it as Single File Web Page using the same filename.

J. Preview the page in your browser.

K. Print one copy. *Note: This page will not actually be posted to the Web unless you have access to a local server and can post it there.*

Figure 2.7

VIII. ORIENTATION PRESENTATION

An Employee Orientation slide show will be presented to workshop participants. You have been asked to create a 10-slide presentation.

Follow these guidelines:

A. Open the data file **dp2.8profile.docx** and print the company profile information. Close the file.

B. Open the data file **dp2.8eotemplate.pptx**, which is an Employee Orientation template presentation.

C. Prepare the Title slide by adding the title `New Employee Orientation` and the company logo, located in data file **dp2happylogo.bmp**. Use the title and slide masters to change the font and font colors to complement the logo. Insert the name, the date of the presentation, and slide numbers on all slides.

D. Link each item on the Agenda/Topics to be Covered slide to the actual slide.

E. Use the History of Company template slide text to guide you in summarizing the company profile information as bulleted slide text.

F. On the Who's Who slide, insert an organization chart SmartArt graphic that indicates the key executives, as shown in Figure 2.8. Apply any SmartArt effect to the graphic.

G. Refer again to your company profile information and then complete the bulleted text for the Company Policies, Benefits Review, Performance Review, and Required Paperwork slides.

H. On the Benefits Review slide, summarize the benefits outlined on the profile into bulleted text.

    1. Add a final bullet that reads `Medical, dental, and disability`.

    2. Create a link on that text to the summary of benefits you prepared earlier, **p2.4benefits.xlsx**.

I. On the Other Resources slide, enter the following information, and create a link on the InsidetheParkNews text to the newsletter you created earlier, **p2.6newsletter.docx**.

    `After the orientation meeting, pick up:`
- `Company Handbook`
- `Company Directory`
- `InsidetheParkNews`
- `All forms`

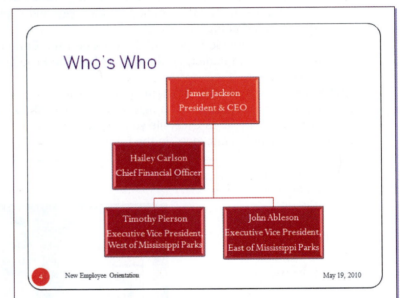

Figure 2.8

J. Prepare a summary slide that welcomes the new hires to the family and includes a reminder to submit all paperwork in a timely manner. You might also want to include clip art that creates a positive feeling.

K. Format the handout master to include an attractive background and a footer that contains the title and date of the workshop.

L. Apply animations and transitions.

M. Insert appropriate images and/or music clips to enhance the slides.

    1. Apply a picture effect to the images.

    2. Make any adjustments to text boxes to better present the bulleted text.

N. Save the file and name it **p2.8presentation**.

O. Print one copy as handouts with six slides per page.

IX. PAYROLL

The Accounting Department must prepare the first weekly payroll. It will use the database queries to create a workbook with a sheet for each unit. Payroll columns will be added and the payrolls calculated. A summary sheet will summarize all unit payrolls.

Follow these guidelines:

A. In Access, open **p2.2employees.accdb**, which you created in Phase II.

B. Select the Attractions Payroll query, and export it to an Excel file with formatting and layout named **p2.9payroll.xlsx**.

C. Export the four remaining payroll queries to separate files, named with the following unit names: **Administrative Payroll**, **Entertainment Payroll**, **Food and Drink Payroll**, and **Maintenance Payroll**.

D. Close the Access file, and then copy the worksheets in each of the files listed above onto separate sheets in the **p2.9payroll** file, leaving the Attractions Payroll as the first sheet. Rename the sheets appropriately and close the Excel files for individual unit payrolls, keeping **p2.9payroll** open.

E. In **p2.9payroll**, group the sheets and insert rows, insert headings, add columns, format headers for wrap text, and format the data, as shown on the Attractions Payroll sheet in Figure 2.9. *Note: Enter the Unit names on row 3 of each sheet after ungrouping the sheets.*

F. The hours and rates for the week of 5/17 are in the data file **dp2.9payrolldata.xlsx**. Sort the data by Last name first and then by Unit using the Sort button on the Data tab. Copy the hours and rate data carefully to the appropriate payrolls. Match destination formatting during the paste process by clicking the SmartTag and selecting that option.

G. Select the Attractions Payroll worksheet (the largest), so that you are working with that payroll on top, and then group all the payroll worksheets. Enter formulas to calculate the following data:

- Salary
- Social Security Tax: Use 6.2% in your formula
- Medicare Tax: Use 1.45% in your formula
- FWT and State Tax: Must be entered individually; see step H
- Total Deductions
- Net Pay

H. Ungroup the sheets and then calculate federal and state taxes for each employee on each payroll.

1. FWT must be entered individually. Use a payroll Website, a tax table, or the table in Step H3 to find actual federal taxes for each employee, using the status information. *Note: You can use www.paycheckcity.com. Specify that it is an hourly payroll for the state of Massachusetts.*

2. State tax must be entered individually. Use a payroll Website, a tax table, or the table in Step H3 to find actual taxes for each employee, using the status information for the state of Massachusetts.

3. If you prefer, you can enter formulas individually to approximate the federal and state taxes by using the table below. Once you enter formulas for 0, 1, or 2 exemptions in Federal and State columns, you can copy the formulas to the employees with the same number of exemptions.

EXEMPTIONS	0	1	2
FWT	10%	8%	5%
STATE TAX	5%	4%	3%

I. Regroup the sheets. Create a Totals line, and then enter formulas and borders, as shown in Figure 2.9. Fix any formatting and format numbers for commas with two decimals.

J. Print a copy of all the payroll sheets.

K. Save and close the file.

	A	B	C	D	E	F	G	H	Social	J	K	L	Total	N
1		HappyTime Park												
2		Payroll for the week of:				5/17/2010								
3		Unit:	Attractions											
4														
5	ID	Last	First	M/F	Status	Hours	Rate	Salary	Social Security	Medicare	FWT	State Tax	Total Deductions	Net Pay
6	3	Biesi	Edward	M	S1	35	8.50	297.50	18.45	4.31	23.80	11.90	58.46	239.04
7	10	Clanton	Cathy	F	S2	40	8.75	350.00	21.70	5.08	17.50	10.50	54.78	295.23
8	12	Edmonds	Diane	F	S1	25	8.50	212.50	13.18	3.08	17.00	8.50	41.76	170.74
9	5	Everson	Barbara	F	S1	32	8.50	272.00	16.86	3.94	21.76	10.88	53.45	218.55
10	1	Frankel	Herb	M	S1	36	8.50	306.00	18.97	4.44	24.48	12.24	60.13	245.87
11	16	Hon	Gina	F	S1	38	8.50	323.00	20.03	4.68	25.84	12.92	63.47	259.53
12	18	Kinsella	Edward	M	S1	40	8.75	350.00	21.70	5.08	28.00	14.00	68.78	281.23
13	19	McCoy	Ben	F	S1	28	8.50	238.00	14.76	3.45	19.04	9.52	46.77	191.23
14														
15								2,349.00	145.64	34.06	177.42	90.46	447.58	1,901.42

Sheet tabs: **Attractions Payroll** / Administrative Payroll / Entertainment Payroll / Food and Drink P...

Figure 2.9

PROJECT 3

Starting a New Business

Leigh Hill and Oliver Geary have been bicycle enthusiasts since they were young and have always wanted to own their own bicycle business. They have degrees in business, Leigh has worked for a bicycle industry publication, Oliver has worked in retail, and they both have many contacts in the industry. This year, they have finally decided to open a bicycle and accessories shop named Ollie's Cycles. The shop will be located in Vista, California, in San Diego County.

They have hired you as their administrative assistant to help complete the many tasks required to launch the business. Listed below is a summary of the documents that you will need to prepare and the tools you will need to produce them.

As administrative assistant, you will prepare numerous documents and complete projects that will require you to use various office tools, as follows:

Internet
- Research cycling in the San Diego area to determine the viability of a business in Vista, California
- Research trends in biking by viewing product Websites and cycling publications
- Compile data on the demographics of Vista, California, for inclusion in the business plan

Word/Publisher
- Design and prepare corporate identity materials, including:
  - Logo
  - Letterhead
  - Fax cover sheet
  - Business cards
- Generate a business plan
- Format the press release announcing the grand opening of Ollie's Cycles
- Create an advertisement for the grand opening
- Prepare an invitation to the grand opening
- Format a trifold brochure mailer

Word
- Develop a Website designed to market the company and its products

Excel
- Complete and format financial documents, including:
  - Personnel plan
  - Financial assumptions
  - Cash flow statement
  - Income statement
  - Balance sheet
  - Charts of demographics research

Chap 1,2
5,6

PowerPoint
- Prepare a 13-slide presentation of the business plan to obtain additional financing

Access
- Import data from an Excel spreadsheet — *AC98* *Chap 6*
- Create a customer database of local cyclists and cycling clubs *(3) AC 16+19 Chap 2*
- Generate customer mailing labels *AC80 - Chap 5*
- Prepare a formatted customer list report *AC82 - Chap 5*

Optional applications:
Outlook
- Add business and customer contact information
- Add events to a calendar

I. CORPORATE IDENTITY MATERIALS

A. Logo
Create a logo for Ollie's Cycles in Word. This logo will appear on all publications and should clearly represent the company name and what it sells.

Follow these guidelines:

1. Use any design elements (lines, shapes, text boxes, WordArt) and graphics. Apply any effect to enhance the elements. Group the elements to create a logo. The font you use in the logo should also be used in headers and other contact information as part of the corporate identity. A sample is shown in Figure 3.1a.

2. Save the file and name it **p3.1ollielogo**. *Note: You will have to copy and paste the logo from Word into other documents where the logo is needed. Or, you can use a screen capture program to save the logo in a picture format such as .bmp, .gif, or .tif, and then insert it where needed as a picture.*

Figure 3.1a

B. Letterhead
Create a letterhead for the business.

Follow these guidelines:

1. Use the logo and the following contact information to create your letterhead. *Note: If the logo you create contains the name Ollie's Cycles, you need not include the company name in your letterhead.*
Ollie's Cycles
980 Central Street
Vista, CA 92084-1234
P: (760) 555-5800
F: (760) 555-5801
E-mail: ollies@net.net

2. Save the file and name it **p3.1letterhead.docx**.

C. Fax Cover Sheet
Create a fax cover sheet for the business.

Follow these guidelines:

1. Customize an existing Fax template with the appropriate contact information. You may include the **p3.1ollielogo** file you created earlier.

2. Save the file as a template and name it **p3.1faxcover.docx**.

D. Business Cards
Ms. Leigh Hill is president of the company and Mr. Oliver Geary is vice president. In order to network and make business contacts for the new store, they need business cards that they can distribute. You have been asked to give this task your immediate attention.

Follow these guidelines:

1. Create one card for Leigh Hill, President, and one for Oliver Geary, Vice President. A sample is shown in Figure 3.1b.

2. Include the company logo and any other relevant information.
3. Save the files and name them **p3.1hillcard** and **p3.1gearycard**. *Note: If you have Publisher, you can easily create the business cards. Otherwise, use Word to create sample cards measuring 3.5" wide by 2" high, using .3" margins, which you can give to a print shop to produce professional cards.*

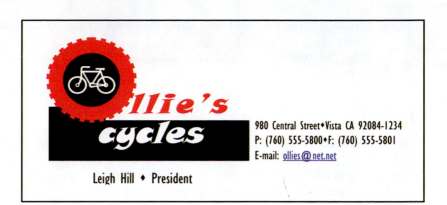

Figure 3.1b

II. INTERNET RESEARCH

Start-up companies conduct extensive market research to learn about their potential competition, customers, vendors, products, store locations, and economic conditions. You will limit your research to questions included in the guidelines below.

Follow these guidelines:

A. Go to a search engine such as Google.com and use keywords such as San Diego County, bicycle clubs, cycling, cycling publications, Vista, California, and so on, to find the required data. Some of the Websites that may be helpful are www.mybikesite.com and www.cityofvista.com.

B. Research cycling publications to familiarize yourself with the industry.

C. Obtain a list of the bicycle clubs in San Diego County.

D. How many bicycle stores are in the San Diego area? How many of these are in Vista, California?

E. Search the www.cityofvista.com site for a link to demographic information for Vista, California. Click the Doing Business link, and find demographics data for the city. Although the Federal census is taken every ten years, the data provided on the Website is estimated within the last two years and shows extensive information for the city.

1. From the Population section of the demographics data, copy the Estimated Population by Age data to an Excel worksheet. From the Income section of the demographic data, copy the Estimated Family Households by Household Income data to another sheet in the same Excel file. On both sheets, adjust row height and column width if necessary, add the title **Demographics of Vista, California**, and name the sheets **Population** and **Income**.

2. Create a pie chart on a separate sheet using the population data showing the percentage in each age group. Name the chart sheet **Pie Chart Population**. Label the pie segments with the percentage for each age group, and change the size of the legend so that it is legible. Add a chart title, and include the year for the estimated statistics. See the sample chart in Figure 3.2.

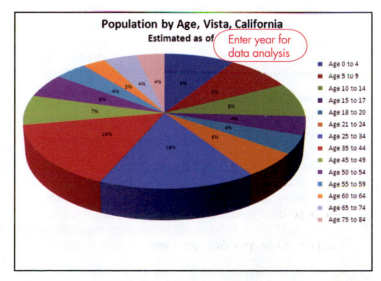

Figure 3.2

3. Create another pie chart on a separate sheet for the data on the Income sheet using the same settings.

4. Save the worksheet and name it **p3.2vista**.

F. Close the file.

III. FINANCIAL REPORTS

These reports will be used in the business plan that you will prepare. Most of these reports are projections of future revenues and expenses for the purposes of planning and funding. All of these reports will be used in the business plan and should therefore have a consistent look and format.

A. Personnel Plan

A personnel plan has been drafted that will help the owners plan for payroll expenses. They expect to hire a part-time bookkeeper and a technician in the first year and then gradually increase salaries and add sales personnel. You will need to format the plan and complete it.

Follow these guidelines:

1. In Excel, open the draft of the personnel plan in data file **dp3.3personnel.xlsx**.

2. Format the report header area using fonts, color, and the company logo. Create a color scheme that coordinates with the logo. The illustration shown in Figure 3.3a is an example of the final report. The format you use should be applied to all the financial reports.

3. Use bold to highlight personnel section headings and subtotal headings.

4. On the table below the report, calculate the salaries for technicians and salespeople using the hourly rate and number of hours. Place the answers in the correct locations in the personnel sections of the report.

5. Calculate the total salary for each position for each year by multiplying the number of positions by the salary listed.

6. Calculate the following:
- Subtotals for each section in Count and Total columns
- Row 19: Total Payroll
- Row 20: 10% of the payroll for taxes and benefits
- Row 21: Total Payroll Expenses

7. Format the subtotals and totals in Accounting Number format with no decimals.

8. Save the file and name it **p3.3personnel**.

B. Financial Assumptions: Revenues and Cost of Sales

The owners need to estimate their revenues and costs to project income and cash flow. They have prepared a draft of the financial assumptions for the next three years, which you need to format and complete.

Follow these guidelines:

1. In Excel, open the draft of the financial assumptions worksheet in data file **dp3.3fin.xlsx**.

2. Format the worksheet so that it is consistent with the personnel plan you just created, including the logo, color scheme, and text formats.

3. Calculate the Projected Cost of Sales for each category and for each year by applying the percentage to the Projected Revenue values.

4. Total the Projected Cost of Sales columns and format the values in rows 11 and 14 in Accounting Number format with no decimals. Other values should be formatted for commas with no decimals or Percent style, as appropriate.

5. Save the file and name it **p3.3fin**.

	A	B	C	D	E	F	G	H	I	J
1	**Ollie's Cycles**									
2	Personnel Plan									
3			YEAR 1			YEAR 2			YEAR 3	
4	Personnel	Count	Salary	Total	Count	Salary	Total	Count	Salary	Total
5										
6	*Gen'l & Admin. Personnel*									
7	Bookkeeper/Admin. Assist. - part time	1	7,000	7,000	1	7,000	7,000	1	7,000	7,000
8	President	2	40,000	80,000	2	50,000	100,000	2	60,000	120,000
9	Administrative Subtotal:	3		$ 87,000	3		$ 107,000	3		$ 127,000
10										
11	*Technical Support*									
12	Technicians - see below	1	26,000	26,000	1	28,000	28,000	1	30,000	30,000
13	Technical Support Subtotal:	1		$ 26,000	1		$ 28,000	1		$ 30,000
14										
15	*Sales & Marketing*									
16	Sales People - see below	-			1	12,000	12,000	2	12,000	24,000
17	Sales Support Subtotal:	-		-	1		$ 12,000	2		$ 24,000
18										
19	Total Payroll:	4		$ 113,000	5		$ 147,000	6		$ 181,000
20	Payroll Taxes and Benefits (10%) :			11,300			14,700			18,100
21	Total Payroll Expenses			$ 124,300			$ 161,700			$ 199,100
22										
23										
24										
25										
26			Wage	Total		Wage	Total		Wage	Total
27		Hours	Per Hour	Salary	Hours	Per Hour	Salary	Hours	Per Hour	Salary
28	*Technicians*									
29	Assume 40 hrs per week per technician	2,000	$ 13.00	$ 26,000	2,000	$ 14.00	$ 28,000	2,000	$ 15.00	$ 30,000
30	Assume 2000 hrs per year *									
31										
32	*Sales People*									
33	Assume small base + commission				2000	$ 6.00	$ 12,000	2000	$ 6.00	$ 12,000
34	Assume 2000 hrs per year*									
35										
36										

Sheet1　Sheet2　Sheet3

Figure 3.3a

C. Cash Flow Statement

This statement shows the projected cash flow for the next three years and is shown in Figure 3.3b. You must obtain and link some of the data needed for this statement from the personnel plan and the financial assumptions worksheets.

Follow these guidelines:

1. In Excel, open the draft of the cash flow worksheet in **dp3.3cashflow.xlsx**, and save it as **p3.3cashflow**.

2. Format the worksheet so that it is consistent with the other reports you just created, including the logo, color scheme, and text formats. A sample is shown in Figure 3.3b. Notice that several items on this worksheet refer to the financial assumptions or the personnel plan worksheets.

3. Open **p3.3fin.xlsx**. Copy the Projected Revenue from cell B14 and paste link it to cell B7, Gross Revenues, in the cash flow statement. Repeat this for the second- and third-year projected revenues.

4. Copy and paste link the Projected Cost of Sales from cell D14 of the **p3.3fin.xlsx** worksheet to cell B12, Purchases, in the cash flow statement. Repeat this for the second and third year.

5. Open **p3.3personnel.xlsx**. Copy and paste link the Total Payroll Expenses for each year to cells B28, C28, and D28 on the cash flow statement.

6. Close **p3.3personnel** and **p3.3fin**.

7. In **p3.3cashflow.xlsx**, calculate the following:
   - Row 33: Total Expenditures
   - Row 34: Net Cash Before Taxes (subtract Total Expenditures from Gross Revenues)
   - Row 36: Net Cash After Taxes (subtract Taxes)
   - Row 39: Ending Cash, Cumulative (add Rows 36:38)

8. Use the labels in cells A7, A12, and A28 as hyperlink text and create hyperlinks to the **p3.3fin.xlsx** or **p3.3personnel.xlsx** worksheet as appropriate.

9. Format the values in rows 36:39 in Accounting Number format with no decimals. Format all other values for commas with no decimals.

10. Save the file.

	A	B	C	D
1		**Ollie's Cycles**		
2		**Projected Cash Flow for Three Years**		
5		First Year 12 Months Including Startup	Second Year 12 Months	Third Year 12 Months
7	Gross Revenues - See Financial Assumptions	$ 218,500	$ 420,176	$ 581,664
9	*Expenditures*			
10	Tools/Equipment	7,500	5,000	7,500
11	Computer Equipment	3,500	-	4,000
12	Purchases - see Financial Assumptions	113,150	211,523	290,820
13	Freight In	8,000	10,000	12,000
14	Advertising	2,000	3,000	4,000
15	Auto Repairs/Gas	1,200	2,600	3,000
16	Bank/Credit Card Charges	800	1,000	1,500
17	Computer Expense	350	500	750
18	Dues & Subscriptions	200	400	500
19	Entertainment/Meals	800	1,000	1,200
20	Garbage Removal	200	300	400
21	Insurance	6,000	7,000	8,000
22	Leased Equipment	600	1,000	2,000
23	Postage	400	750	1,000
24	Professional Fees	2,400	3,000	3,500
25	Office Expense	4,000	4,000	4,000
26	Repairs & Maintenance	2,000	3,000	4,000
27	Rent	8,000	8,000	8,000
28	Salaries and Benefits - see Personnel Plan	124,300	161,700	199,100
29	Telephone	800	1,800	2,500
30	Travel	400	500	600
31	Utilities	3,000	4,000	5,000
32	Vehicle	4,800	6,000	7,000
33	**Total Expenditures**	294,400	436,073	570,370
34	**Net Cash Before Taxes**	(75,900)	(15,897)	11,295
35	Corporate Income Taxes	-	1,011	2,188
36	**Net Cash After Taxes**	$ (75,900)	$ (16,908)	$ 9,107
37	Cash Balance		$ (900)	$ (17,808)
38	Additional Paid-in Capital	$ 75,900		
39	**Ending Cash, Cumulative**	$ (900)	$ (17,808)	$ (8,701)

Sheet1 / Sheet2 / Sheet3

Figure 3.3b

D. Income Statement

This statement shows the projected income for three years. The data for Gross Revenues, Purchases, and Salaries and Benefits should be linked from the cash flow statement prepared in Step C.

Follow these guidelines:

1. In Excel, open the draft of the income statement in data file **dp3.3is.xlsx**.

2. Format the worksheet so that it is consistent with the other reports you just created, including the logo, color scheme, and text formats.

3. Copy the data for Gross Revenues, Purchases, and Salaries and Benefits from the **p3.3fin.xlsx** and **p3.3personnel.xlsx** worksheets and paste link them to the appropriate locations in the income statement. Create a hyperlink from the text labels to the appropriate source worksheet.

4. To complete the income statement, calculate the following:
   - Row 12: Total Cost of Sales
   - Row 14: Gross Profit (Gross Revenues – Total Cost of Sales)
   - Row 36: Total General and Admin. Expenses
   - Row 37: Income Before Taxes (Gross Profit – General and Admin. Expenses)
   - Row 39: Net Income (Income Before Taxes – Corporate Income Taxes)

5. Bold the Cost of Goods Sold and General and Admin. Expenses titles. Bold and use fill color to highlight the rows for Gross Revenues, Income Before Taxes, and Net Income.

6. Apply borders and fill color where appropriate and format the final values in Accounting Number format with no decimals.

7. Save the worksheet and name it **p3.3is**. Close the file.

E. Balance Sheet

This statement shows the projected assets, liabilities, and shareholders' equity for three years.

Follow these guidelines:

1. In Excel, open the draft of the balance sheet in data file **dp3.3balsheet.xlsx**.

2. Format the worksheet so that it is consistent with the other reports you just created, including the logo, color scheme, and text formats.

3. To complete the balance sheet, calculate the following:
   - Row 13: Total Current Assets
   - Row 18: Total Fixed Assets
   - Row 20: Net Fixed Assets
   - Row 22: Total Assets (Total Current Assets + Net Fixed Assets)
   - Row 27: Total Liabilities
   - Row 33: Total Shareholders' Equity
   - Row 35: Total Liabilities & Shareholders' Equity

4. Bold the Assets and Liabilities & Shareholders' Equity headings. Bold and use fill color to highlight the rows for Total Assets and for Total Liabilities & Shareholders' Equity. Format the values in Accounting Number format with no decimals.

5. Apply borders where appropriate.

6. Save the worksheet and name it **p3.3balsheet**. Close the file.

IV. FORMAT A BUSINESS PLAN AND COVER PAGE

Leigh Hill and Oliver Geary need a business plan for themselves, their bankers, and/or other investors. The business plan will help create a road map for the new business and will demonstrate how their start-up funds will be used. They have written a simple plan and want you to format it for them. You will insert the financial reports you prepared earlier into the business plan.

Follow these guidelines:

A. Open the data file **dp3.4busplantext.docx**.

B. Format the document as a report.

    1. Use the following settings:

Margins	1.25" left and right
Line spacing	Single
Paragraph spacing	
Before	0
After	0
Font	Times New Roman
Font size	12 pt

    2. Apply styles where appropriate. Add a header and/or footer that include the name of the document and page numbers. You might want to include the logo or a design in the header and/or footer to give the document a consistent, professional look. A sample page is shown in Figure 3.4.

C. Insert any predesigned cover page, and then modify it to include the following:

- Complementary design colors (red/black, gray/white)
- The company name (using the same font used for other documents)
- A relevant photograph
- The title of the document
- Today's date
- A tag line that reads: **For the Ride of Your Life!**
- The company contact information

D. Insert the financial data where indicated by a yellow highlight. If the files are not available to you, you can find them in the data folder **dp3.4busplandata**.

    1. Open the file to be copied in Excel, and select and copy the portion of the worksheet to be pasted.

    2. Switch to Word, and place your cursor in the location to insert the data. Click the Paste button arrow, and then click Paste Special. In the Paste Special dialog box, click Paste and Microsoft Office Excel Worksheet Object, and then click OK to embed the data.

    3. Apply the In Line with Text wrap and center or right-align the worksheet or chart as appropriate.

    4. Size the worksheet appropriately to present the data clearly.

    5. Delete the highlighted notations for inserting files into the document.

E. Make any necessary adjustments to best present the data.

F. Print one copy.

G. Save the file as **p3.4busplan**, and close it.

Ollie's Cycles

Business Plan

1.0 Executive Summary

At Ollie's Cycles, our goal is to provide quality bicycles and accessories at the lowest price. Our goal is to limit costs so that we can be a price leader in the county and draw customers from a large geographic area. We will also service and customize bicycles and accessories. Our low pricing, large selection, and technical service are the aspects that make our store different.

The sport of cycling is in a full growth mode in San Diego County. There are many shops, cycling clubs, and wonderful trails for bikers. The preponderance of bicycle stores is in San Diego proper. There are a limited numbers of shops and no full-service outlets in the suburb area of Vista, California. Our location in Vista represents an opportunity because of its proximity to San Diego and the low rents that will facilitate our pricing policy.

Our goal is to borrow $25,000 for five (5) years. The loan will be repaid in 60 equal payments, including interest and principal. Our present plan is to utilize the borrowed money with our investment of $75,000 to assist us in growing our business. The cash will allow us to reach a larger audience with our advertising and help with operating costs and salaries. Upon receiving our loan, we would like to incorporate, as this will protect our company, investors, lenders, products, and stockholders. We expect revenues to reach $218,500 the first year, $420,176 the second year, and $581,664 the third year.

1.1 Objectives

- ✓ To fill the demand for bicycles with top-quality products at the lowest price.
- ✓ To fill the bicycle accessory demand with top-quality products at the lowest price.
- ✓ To provide customer support and maintenance with a trained technical staff.
- ✓ To develop cycling tours by spring, 2010.
- ✓ To reach sales of $400,000 by the end of our second year in business and reach sales of $33,000 monthly.
- ✓ To encourage our customers to live healthy lives by making bicycling more fun and convenient for them.
- ✓ To offer cyclists support through our Web page, such as interviews with health professionals to answer specific health issues of bikers.

Figure 3.4

V. PRESS RELEASE

To announce the grand opening of the business, you will prepare a press release for the local newspapers.

Follow these guidelines:

A. Open the data file **dp3.5prtext.docx**, and add the company logo and address, as shown in Figure 3.5.

B. Format the text as shown, including the Contact information (Oliver Geary) and the Press Release header. *Note: Since Oliver and Leigh would like to link this release to their Website, you will need to format the text using a table and merge cells where necessary.* Use Vista, California, September 16, 2010, as the location and date information.

C. Print one copy.

D. Save the file and name it **p3.5pr**. Close the file.

980 Central Street
Vista, CA 92084-1234
P: (760) 555-5800 F: (760) 555-5801
E-mail: ollies@net.net

Contact: Oliver Geary

Press Release
For Immediate Release

**Ollie's Cycles Announces Grand Opening
in Vista, California**

Vista, California, September 16, 2010

Ollie's Cycles today announces the grand opening of their new shop, which is a full-service bike shop targeted to the cycling enthusiast. "Our goal is to become the cycling enthusiast's resource for quality products and services at competitive values." The foundation of our commitment will be to provide our customers with bicycles, accessories, and clothing for those who love to ride.

Ollie's Cycles will also be a source of information for professional bicycle racing, bike training, and bike-related fitness.

Spin to the coffee shop, the beach, or over beautiful mountains – we've got just the bike, the accessories, and the clothing to match your journey.

Ollie's cycles will open on September 16. Owners Leigh Hill and Oliver Geary, bike enthusiasts since they were very young, will be on hand to welcome you to the world of cycling.

###

Figure 3.5

VI. ADVERTISEMENT

Oliver and Leigh want to advertise the grand opening of their new company in the local newspapers. You will need to create an advertisement. They are planning their grand opening for September 16. The newspaper will accept ads in either portrait or landscape orientation.

Follow these guidelines:

A. Create an advertisement using any combination of design elements. Include the company logo and contact information as well as the following text: `There Is Nothing Better than Riding. We at Ollie's Cycles are passionate about our products. We don't just sell and rent bicycles, we set you on the path to freedom and fun. We carry a full line of bicycles and products for the cyclist. We hope to see you at our Grand Opening on September 16. The 50th visitor will win a downhill Super T Pro! Come Visit Us for the Ride of Your Life.`

B. You may use Publisher, Word, or PowerPoint to create the advertisement. A sample color ad is shown in Figure 3.6.

C. Save the file and name it **p3.6ad**. Close the file.

Figure 3.6

VII. BROCHURE

Oliver needs a trifold brochure that indicates the bicycle lines, accessories, and services provided by Ollie's Cycles.

Follow these guidelines:

A. Design the brochure using any combination of design elements.

B. Use an 8.5" by 11" page set to landscape or you can use a brochure template from Word or Publisher. You can also download a brochure template from www.microsoft.com.

C. Import the text for the brochure into Panel 1 (the outside page), which can be found on the data file under the filename **dp3.7brochuretext.docx**. Use the Column Break feature to force text into the next column where necessary.

D. If you are using Word, set three columns and apply a top and bottom border using the Header/Footer feature, as shown in Figure 3.7. *Note: Figure 3.7 shows only the outside page. You need to create the inside page as well.*

E. Apply character and paragraph spacing to make the text more engaging.

F. Insert clip art or photos where you feel they will enhance the text, and apply picture effects.

G. Create a mailer on the outside middle panel.

H. Include the logo on the outside page.

I. Print one copy of each page.

J. Save the file and name it **p3.7brochure**. Close the file.

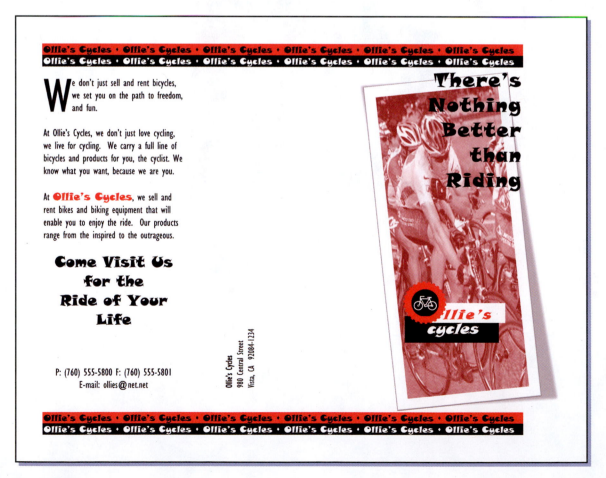

Figure 3.7

VIII. DATABASE

Lists of potential customers have been obtained from cycling clubs in the San Diego area. You will import database and spreadsheet data, as well as create cyclist and club tables, mailing labels, and other database objects.

Follow these guidelines:

A. Find the Access data file **dp3.8ollies.accdb**, and copy and paste it into your Solutions folder. Name it **p3.8ollies**, and open the file.

B. In the Excel data file **dp3.8clubs.xlsx**, there is a list of bicycle clubs in the San Diego area. Import the worksheet into the database as a table named **Clubs**. The first row contains column headings; let Access create the primary key.

C. You have obtained a list of cyclists that you can use for mailings from the various cycling clubs in the area. Import the entire **dp3.8cyclists.accdb** database into the **p3.8ollies.accdb** database and name the table **Cyclists**.

D. Create and save a relationship between the Cyclists and Clubs tables using the ClubID field from the Cyclists table and the ID field from the Clubs table. Show the new tables and create the relationship.

E. In the Cyclists table, use the Sort/Filter feature in the Bicycle column header to select Mountain. Print a list of cyclists who currently own mountain bicycles. Toggle to remove the filter.

F. Create a query using the Cyclists and Club tables to create a list of first and last names of cyclists, their phone numbers, their bicycle types, and the names of their clubs. Save the query as **Cyclists Query**.

G. Use the Cyclists Query to create a crosstab query that uses Club Name as the row heading and Bicycle as the column heading, and use the Count function for each row/column intersection. You will find out how many customers are on the list from each club and the types of bicycles they use. Save the query as **Cyclists Query_Crosstab**, and print a copy of the query.

H. In the Cyclists table, in Design view, add a **Title** field after the First Name field. Use a Lookup data type and enter **Mr.** and **Ms.** as the values. Save the design, switch to the Datasheet view and add the appropriate title, Mr. or Ms., to each record in the table.

I. Create mailing labels from the Cyclists table, and name it **Labels Cyclists**. Use a standard label size and sort the labels by ZIP Code.

J. Use the Report Wizard and the Clubs and Cyclists tables to create a report titled **Cyclist Clubs Customer List**.
1. Use the Club Name, Telephone, and Website address from the Clubs table and the Last Name, First Name, Bicycle, and Phone fields from the Cyclists table.
2. View by Clubs and sort by Last Name.
3. Use the Stepped layout and Landscape orientation.
4. Use the Apex style.

Figure 3.8

5. In Layout view, add the Ollie's Cycles logo, **dp3ollielogo.bmp** or your own, to the report and adjust column widths so that all data is visible. *Note: you may have to reduce the font size of the Website Address field to fit the report to a single page.*

6. Print one copy, as shown in Figure 3.8 on the previous page.

K. Close and save the file.

IX. INVITATION

An invitation to the grand opening will be sent to a select database of potential customers. You must create an attractive invitation for this event. The labels created in Access will be used for the envelopes.

Follow these guidelines:

A. The invitations will be printed on cards measuring 5.5" wide by 7" high, as shown in Figure 3.9.

B. Create the invitation using any combination of design elements. The invitation should include the company logo and contact information, as well as the following text:

```
There Is Nothing
Better than Riding
Join Us for the
Ride of Your Life
    Leigh Hill and
    Oliver Geary
    cordially invite
    you to the
    Grand Opening
    Celebration of
    Ollie's Cycles.
    The 50th visitor
    will win a
    downhill Super T
    Pro!
Date: Saturday,
September 16
Address: 980
Central Street
Time: 12 noon
```

C. Save the file and name it **p3.9invite**. Print one copy, and close the file.

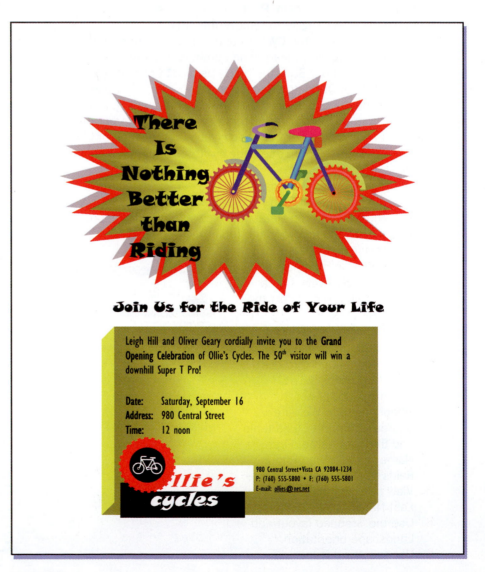

Figure 3.9

X. BUSINESS PLAN PRESENTATION

While Oliver and Leigh have enough money to open their shop, they need additional financing to grow the business. To get financing, Oliver and Leigh will be presenting their business plan to local bankers.

Follow these guidelines:

A. Open **dp3.10bpoutline.pptx**, unformatted slides containing the slide titles.

B. Open **p3.4busplan.docx**, the business plan you completed earlier, in Word. If this file is not available to you, open the data file **dp3.10busplan.docx**. You can print a copy and work from a printout, if you want.
   - Use the information in the business plan to create the slide text.
   - Use layouts that are appropriate for the information.

C. Apply any design theme, selecting a color scheme that will complement the logo's colors.

D. On the Slide Master:
   1. Include the logo on all slides layouts you use.
   2. Include the slide numbers.

E. On the title slide, insert a cycling-related photo as the background. Enter the title **Business Plan** on the slide. A sample is shown in Figure 3.10.

F. On the Objectives and Mission slides, use information from the business plan to create the slide text.

G. On the Management Team slide:
   1. Use a Two Content slide layout, and include information from the business plan in one content section.
   2. In the other content section, use a SmartArt graphic for an organization chart to show the two-member "team." Apply any desired effect. *Note: You will have to delete boxes to reduce the number of boxes to two.*

H. On the Company Location, Demographics, & Facilities slide, include the Population by Age pie chart as a graphic to reinforce your bulleted text.

I. Use a graphic on the Competition slide for visual interest.

J. On the Financial Projections slide:
   1. Apply a different background color.
   2. Summarize the introductory paragraph of the Financial Projections section of the business plan as bulleted text on the slide.

K. On the remaining financial-related slides:
   1. Copy the appropriate Excel worksheets from your solution files or from the files found in the data folder **dp3.4busplandata**, and paste them as embedded objects on the appropriate slide. Open the Excel File and select your data, right-click and then click Copy. Switch to the PowerPoint slide, and on the Home tab, click the Paste button arrow. Click Paste Special, and in the Paste Special dialog box, choose the type of file you are pasting, and then click OK.
   2. Apply a different background color to these slides to help group them.

L. On the Business Concept Summary slide, summarize information from the written business plan that you feel gives important reasons why the business is worthy of a loan from the bank.

Figure 3.10

M. On the We Serve the Cycling Enthusiast slide, use a Smart Art design and effect that best presents the following text:

    `Tours and Fitness`
    `Quality Accessories`
    `Quality Bicycles`

N. Apply any slide animations and transitions to text and objects to enhance their effect.

O. Prepare handouts that include today's date, the title of the presentation, and an attractive background.

P. Make any adjustments necessary to better present the data.

Q. Print one copy of the presentation as handouts with six slides per page.

R. Save the file and name it **p3.10bppresentation.pptx**. Close the file.

XI. WEBSITE

Oliver Geary and Leigh Hill want to develop a Website as another way to market their products. They would like you to create the site in two phases. In this first phase, you will create only the Home page. Eventually, four other pages will be created, and the home page will link to each of them.

Follow these guidelines:

A. Use the Business E-mail newsletter template, which can be found on the data under the filename **dp3.11template. docx**. *Note: This template can also be downloaded from the Microsoft Website at* www.microsoft.com.

B. Modify the template to look like Figure 3.11. *Note: You may need to merge some cells to achieve the desired effect*.

   1. Change the color of the cells to complement the colors theme used in other documents (red, gray, black, yellow, white). Use the Snap ITC font, or a font that relates to your logo, in 30 point for the page heading to maintain consistency with other documents.

   2. Include a photograph or clip art that supports the page heading. Center it below the heading and apply an In Line with Text wrap. You may apply a picture effect, if you want.

   3. Include the logo somewhere on the page.

   4. Apply any background color or effect.

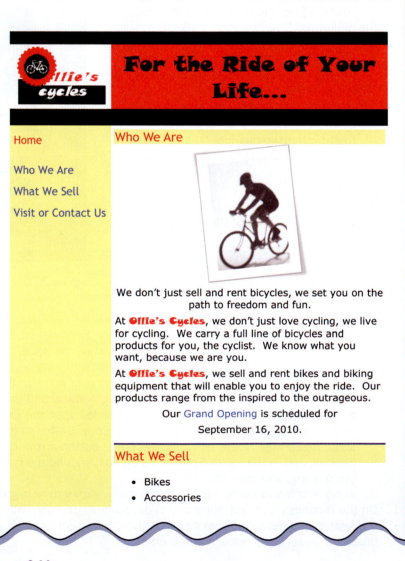

Figure 3.11

5. Set the three paragraph headings in the right column to a sans serif font in 18 point, bold, in a red font color. Apply a light yellow paragraph shading to the text.
6. Set the paragraph text to 14 point.
7. Set the text in the left column to 16 point. Apply a light yellow fill color and use red and blue font colors as shown.

C. Enter the text in the left column as shown. Enter the following text in the main paragraph sections in the right column:

```
WHO WE ARE
    We don't just sell and rent bicycles, we set you on
the path to freedom and fun.
    At Ollie's Cycles, we don't just love cycling, we
live for cycling. We carry a full line of bicycles and
products for you, the cyclist. We know what you want,
because we are you.
    At Ollie's Cycles, we sell and rent bikes and
equipment that will enable you to enjoy the ride. Our
products range from the inspired to the outrageous.
    Our Grand Opening is scheduled for September 16, 2010.


WHAT WE SELL
• Bikes
• Accessories
• Clothing
    We are also your resource for biking tours, biking
lessons, and cycling-related fitness training.


VISIT OR CONTACT US
980 Central Street
Vista, CA 92084-1234
P: (760) 555-5800 F: (760) 555-5801
E-mail: ollies@net.net
```

D. Create hyperlinks:
  1. Link the headings in the left column to the headings in the right column.
  2. Link the words "Grand Opening" to the press release you created earlier.
  3. Link the word "E-mail" to: ollies@net.net.
E. Save the file as a Single File Web Page, and name it **p3.11web**.
F. Preview the file in your browser and test the links. If the font size is too small to read, change the font size for the page text to 16 point.
G. Make any necessary adjustments to your Word file, preview the changes in your browser, and save the file again.
H. Close the file.

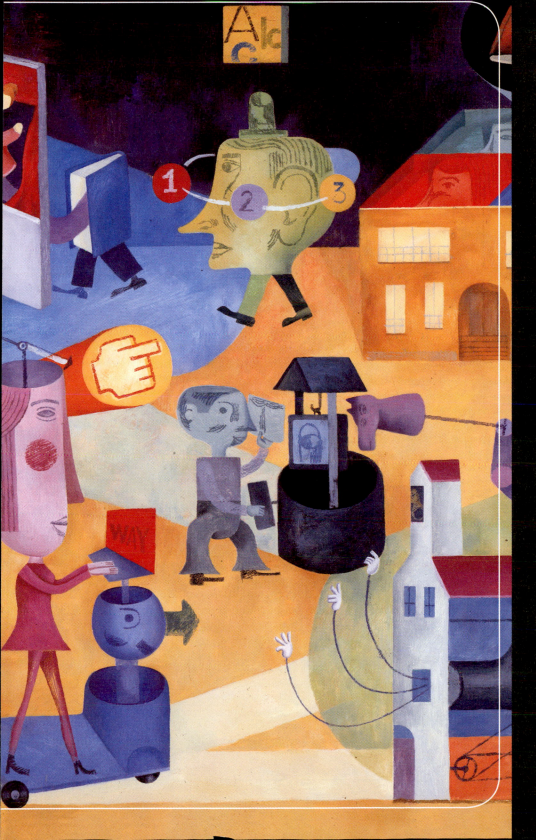

APPENDIX A
Portfolio Basics

APPENDIX B
Proofreader's Marks

APPENDIX C
Ways to Cite from
Source Material

APPENDIX D
Rubric for an
Oral Report
and PowerPoint
Presentation
Developed from
Scratch

APPENDIX A

Portfolio Basics

What Is a Portfolio?

A portfolio is a collection of evidence that showcases your skills, abilities, and accomplishments. A portfolio is a way to market yourself to college admissions committees or prospective employers.

Portfolio items may be maintained in a traditional folder or they may be prepared in digital format and burned to a CD. A portfolio may also be created as an electronic portfolio, which is a personal Website with links to all the required documents. An electronic portfolio will highlight your technical skills and competencies with Website development and design. Digital or electronic formats enable you to include presentations, animations, and graphics that demonstrate your skills in those areas.

What Should a Portfolio Include?

A portfolio should contain your best work samples, a résumé, awards, a letter of introduction, certificates (including evidence of MOS certification), and letters of recommendation. It may also include works-in-progress that illustrate the ongoing development of a project through various stages of conception and revision.

How to Use Projects for the Entrepreneur as Portfolio Materials

You may select several projects from Part I of this text as portfolio projects and tailor the selection to present your abilities or skills. For example, if you want to demonstrate your mastery of desktop publishing skills, you might group projects that involve brochures, flyers, newsletters, invitations, and reports into one portfolio. If you want to show your expertise in accounting and spreadsheets, you may group projects that involve accounting records and financial report projects into your portfolio. It is important to select the projects that demonstrate your area or areas of expertise.

Any of the Integrated Simulation Projects in Part II of this text are also ideal for portfolio presentation. Each project integrates many skills into a culminating practical activity that demonstrates a mastery of software proficiency, an understanding of business concepts, and the ability to think critically and employ problem-solving techniques.

How to Organize a Portfolio

A portfolio should be organized in a logical format. It should include a cover page (or home page, if it is a Website), which may include graphics or photographs that reflect your personal expression. A suggested portfolio organization follows:

1. Cover (home page)

2. Table of Contents

3. Letter of Introduction

4. Work or Project Sample Cover Sheet (see Figure 1)

5. Work or Project Samples

6. Résumé

7. Awards, Certificates

8. Letters of Recommendation

Guidelines for Developing Electronic Portfolios

If you are publishing a portfolio to the Web, be aware of the following:

1. Avoid including your address, phone number, and Social Security number. Use only your e-mail address as contact information.

2. Do not include information or ideas you do not want the world to see.

3. Avoid continuous animations.

4. Avoid color, background, and font formats that make pages difficult to read.

5. Avoid using large graphic files that might be difficult to download.

Letter of Introduction
A letter of introduction demonstrates your writing ability and provides a framework for what is to follow. It should include the following information:

1. A description of yourself, including your college and career goals, your important achievements, and your strengths.

2. A description of your portfolio's contents.

3. A explanation of what insights you have gained from preparing the portfolio.

Work or Project Sample Cover Sheet

A cover sheet, as shown in Figure 1, should precede each work or project sample.

Name:
Today's date:
Work sample ☐   **Project sample** ☐
Description of work or project sample included:
If this was a group project, list team members:
1.
2.
3.
Date item was completed:
What was the goal of the project or work sample?
What special skills did you use in completing this work sample?
Explain what you learned by completing this work sample.
Teacher assessment
Teacher's signature
Date reviewed
Comments

Figure 1

APPENDIX B

Proofreader's Marks

Symbol	Meaning	Illustration
(bf) ∿∿∿	Boldface	(bf) Excellent job!
≡	Capitalize	John l. smith
◡	Close up space	pres entation
℘	Delete	pagee
ds [	Double-space	ds [This is the first time I have heard about it.
∧	Insert	*it* Where will be?
∨̇	Insert apostrophe	It was Johns hat.
—	Insert italic	Time Magazine was ordered last week.
∧	Insert punctuation	If you are going I am going too.
#	Insert space	I think it will beuseful.

Symbol	Meaning	Illustration
stet or	Let the original stand (ignore correction)	The ~~main~~ building was damaged.
lc or /	Make lowercase	Her title was V̸ice P̸resident.
⟲↗	Move as indicated	This table will be omitted. Be sure to remove it from all documents.
[	Move left	[Let's go tomorrow.
]	Move right	] Everything you need is located on the CD.
¶	New paragraph	It's cold outside. ¶ The forecast for next week…
—	Replace word	*can* The mouse ~~may~~ be used to access many features.
ss[	Single-space	ss[Please be advised that there will be no delivery service next week.
◯	Spell out	③ years ago
∿	Transpose	This is intresting material.

APPENDIX C

Ways to Cite from Source Material

Citations are references made by a writer to indicate whether he/she has paraphrased or quoted material from another source (for example, a book, newspaper, magazine, encyclopedia, the Internet). It is necessary to cite someone else's ideas, words, statistics, artwork, or lab results. Failing to do so is called plagiarism, which can have serious legal consequences.

Citations that appear at the bottom of a page are called *footnotes*, those located at the end of a document are called *endnotes*, and those that immediately follow the quoted or paraphrased sentence or paragraph are known as *internal citations*. In an internal citation, the quoted material is cited within the report using the author's last name and the year of publication, for example, "In the end, the person who decides what is right is the customer." (Smith, 2010).

When a footnote or endnote cites the same source as the one that immediately precedes it, use the abbreviation Ibid., meaning "in the same place." If the reference source is the same but the page number differs, use the abbreviation Ibid. with the appropriate page number.

A bibliography identifies all sources used, quoted, or paraphrased within the report and is typically the last page of the report. Word's Citation feature automatically formats the citation information and the bibliography based on the writing style you choose. Examples of footnotes and endnotes cited from various sources follow:

BOOK
Author's name, *title*. (city where published: publishing company, year published), page number.

Charles Kupchan, *The End of an American Era: U.S. Foreign Policy and the Geopolitics of the 21st Century*. (New York: Kindle Publishing, 2007), p. 23.

MAGAZINE ARTICLE
Author's name, "title of article," *name of magazine*, date of magazine issue, page number.

P. M. Dunleavey, "Another Way of Giving," *Town and Country*, November 2007, p.184.

NEWSPAPER ARTICLE
Author's name, "title of article," *name of newspaper*, date, section, page number.

Jesse Winters, "Brooklyn Schools Get Facelift," *The New York Times*, June 3, 2003, sec. A, p. 23.

WORLD WIDE WEB SOURCE
Author's name, "title of document or article/Website," <Web address>, date posted on Internet.

Matthew Schwartz, "Something Indescribable: Foreign Direct Investment in Vietnam," <http://www.clas.ufl.edu/jur/200711/profiles/schwarz.html>, February 2008.

E-MAIL MESSAGE
Author's name, <e-mail address of sender>, "subject of e-mail," to whom message was sent, date message was sent.

Marie D'Angelo, <mdangelo@ecosystem.com>, "Warning: Depletion of the Ozone Layer," e-mail to Mark Binda, September 5, 2010.

Rubric for an Oral Report and PowerPoint Presentation Developed from Scratch

ELEMENTS	OUTSTANDING	SATISFACTORY	UNSATISFACTORY
CONTENT	Demonstrates thorough knowledge of content; information is completely accurate; topic is well developed; information is relevant; presentation is engaging and encourages active learning. Critical thinking is evident. Research is evident. **20 POINTS**	Some inaccurate information presented. Demonstrates some knowledge of content. Parts of the project are well developed. Some critical thinking is evident. Research is partially evident. **14 POINTS**	Inaccurate information presented. Project is not well-developed. Critical thinking is not evident. Little or no research is evident. **6 POINTS**
ORGANIZATION	Logical and consistent presentation process; easy to follow and understand. **20 POINTS**	Flow of presentation somewhat difficult to follow and understand. **14 POINTS**	Presentation not logical; format hard to follow. **6 POINTS**
DELIVERY	Correct pronunciation, punctuation, grammar; superior voice projection. **20 POINTS**	Includes one to three errors in pronunciation, spelling, punctuation, or grammar. **14 POINTS**	Includes four or more errors in pronunciation, spelling, punctuation, or grammar. **6 POINTS**
SUPPORTING ELEMENTS	Includes at least three of the following: charts, tables, graphs, and supplementary data. **20 POINTS**	Includes two or fewer of the following: charts, tables, graphs, and supplementary data. **14 POINTS**	Includes only one of the following: charts, tables, graphs, or other supplementary data. **6 POINTS**
SPECIAL EFFECTS	Includes many engaging and relevant graphics, pictures, sounds; includes transitions and animations. **20 POINTS**	Uses minimal or irrelevant graphics, pictures, and sounds; uses minimal transitions and animations. **14 POINTS**	No graphics, pictures, or sounds included; no transitions and/or animations used. **6 POINTS**
TOTAL POINTS	100	70	30

INDEX

3-D references, entering, Excel 102

A

absolute and relative references, Excel 74–75

Access 2007
See also databases, datasheets, queries
exporting tables, queries to Word, Access 104–105
exporting tables to Excel, Access 102–103
fields. See fields
forms. See forms
program described, Access 4
reports. See reports
saving files for earlier versions, Access 108

accessing
font collections, Word 13
Web page templates, Word 192

account statements, creating, Excel 46

accounting number format, Excel 22

accounting worksheets, completing, Excel 98–99

accounting worksheets, hyperlinking, Excel 100–101

accounts payable ledger accounts, Excel 44–45

accounts receivable
creating aging reports, Excel 60–61
ledger accounts, Excel 42–43

action buttons, using, PowerPoint 32

actions, undoing series of, PowerPoint 7, Word 8

activities schedules, creating, Word 72–73

adding
backgrounds to worksheets, Excel 78–79
borders to worksheets, Excel 16–17, Excel 82
calculated controls to reports, Access 86–87

calculated fields to queries, Access 68–69
columns to tables, Word 61–62
comments to documents, Word 170
comments to presentations, PowerPoint 79–80
controls to forms, Access 44–45
fields, controls to forms, Access 46
input masks to tables, Access 28–31
labels, titles, legends to charts, Excel 116–117
labels to reports, Access 84–85
media clips to slides, PowerPoint 52–55
pictures into worksheets, Excel 128–131
postmarks, Word 121, Word 124
presentation annotations, PowerPoint 74
property information to files, Word 185
records to database tables, Access 38–39
slide transitions, PowerPoint 18–19
slides to presentations, PowerPoint 23
sound effects to animations, PowerPoint 66–67
special effects to images, Word 90
text to slides, PowerPoint 9
total rows to tables, Excel 70
watermarks, Word 128

AddressBlock merge code, Word 50

addresses
on envelopes, Word 25
for foreign mail, Word 74
and hyperlinks, Word 188
worksheet cell, and inputting formulas, Excel 42

advertisements
creating, Integration 37, Word 97–99
creating direct-mail, Word 100–101

designing, Word 18–19
flyers. See flyers
formatting, Word 102–103

agendas
creating, Word 56–63
creating calendars, Word 83

aggregate functions, adding, Access 68

aging reports, creating accounts receivable, Excel 60–61

aligning
charts on pages, Excel 139
graphics, Word 88, Word 90
labels, Excel 4
objects on slides, PowerPoint 32
tables on pages, Word 62
text, Word 13
text in tables, Word 61

alphabetic sorts, Word 59

analysis tables
creating billings, Excel 70–71
creating listings, Excel 72–73

animating charts, PowerPoint 66–67

animations, creating for presentations, PowerPoint 19

annotations, adding to presentations, PowerPoint 73–75

annual reports
formatting, Word 176–180
linking charts and worksheets in, Excel 142–146

append queries, creating, Access 98–99

applications
See also specific application
copying and pasting data between, Excel 136

arithmetic functions and AutoCalc feature, Excel 58

arranging
layers, Word 93
objects on slides, PowerPoint 32
workbooks on screen, Excel 90

arrowheads on lines, Word 95
articles, creating, Word 170–173
ascending sorts, Access 56, Word 59
assets
   creating accounts receivable aging
      reports, Excel 60–61
   creating asset records, Excel 60–61
asterisks (*), wildcard character,
   Access 42, Access 54
attachments, e-mail, Word 47–48
attention line in letters, Word 27
audience for presentations,
   PowerPoint 21, PowerPoint 24
audio. *See* sound
autobiography, composing your, Word 10
AutoCalc feature, Excel 58
AutoComplete feature, Excel 22
AutoCorrect features, Word 4
AutoFill feature
   filling formulas horizontally, Excel 48
   using, Excel 28, Excel 94
AutoFilter feature, Excel 71
AutoFit feature, table formatting with,
   Word 61, Word 76
AutoFormat As You Type feature, Word 6
AutoFormat, using on forms,
   Access 42–44
AutoNumber data type, Access 16,
   Access 24
AutoSum feature, Excel 10, Excel 16,
   Excel 48–49
Average function, Excel 48–49, Excel 58
averaging
   ROUNDUP, ROUNDDOWN
      functions, Excel 96
   values in database records, Access 62–63

B

background colors, adding to pages,
   Word 125
Background Styles button,
   PowerPoint 18
backgrounds
   adding to Web pages, Word 190
   adding to worksheets, Excel 78–79
   formatting slide, PowerPoint 31
backing up databases, Access 106–107
balance sheets
   analyzing data, Excel 112–113
   creating, formatting, Excel 98,
      Excel 106–109
bar charts, Excel 117, Excel 119,
   Excel 122, Excel 126
bibliographies, styles, Word 157–158,
   Word 161

billings analysis tables, creating,
   Excel 70–71
billings and revenue analyses, creating,
   Excel 82–83
Blank Form button, Access 46
block letter format, Word 25, Word 151
bolding text, Excel 4
borders
   adding effects to images, Word 90
   adding to placeholders, PowerPoint 9
   adding to shapes, Word 92
   adding to worksheets, Excel 16–17,
      Excel 82
   applying to tables, Word 64
Borders and Shading dialog box,
   Word 125
bound controls, Access 46
brackets ([ ]) in expressions, Access 48,
   Access 68
breaks
   inserting section, Word 67–68,
      Word 171–172
   inserting text column, Word 128
   using section, Word 118
Bring to Front button, Word 93
brochures
   creating for cycle shop, Integration 38
   creating for events, Word 128–131
   creating product, Word 132–134
browsers, opening Web pages in,
   Word 189
budgets, creating, Integration 10,
   Excel 66–69
bulleted lists, creating, Word 56–57
bulletins, embedding charts and
   worksheets in, Excel 139–140
bullets, formatting, PowerPoint 31,
   Word 59
business forms. *See specific form*
business letters
   composing and e-mailing,
      Word 45–46
   creating, formatting, Word 24–34
   creating from templates, Word 36–37
   formatting and formatting multi-page,
      Word 147–152
   formatting two-page, Word 144–146
   formatting with special notations,
      Word 27–28
business plans, Excel 10
   creating presentation,
      Integration 41–42
   embedding worksheets into,
      Excel 136–138

formatting, Integration 34–35,
   Word 174–175
business, starting new, Integration 27–43
business trips, organizing,
   Integration 3–13

C

calculated controls
   adding to forms, Access 51–52
   creating forms with, Access 48–50
calculated fields
   adding to queries, Access 68–69
   creating using Expression Builder,
      Access 90, Access 94
calculating
   AutoCalc feature, Excel 58
   data in reports, Access 86–87
   depreciation, Excel 60–61
   numeric data in tables, Word 74–75
   percentages, Excel 66
   using dates, Excel 86
Calendar Wizard, Word 83
calendars, creating, Word 79–82
capitalization, Word 6
captions
   See also labels
   changing text box control,
      Access 51–52
   inserting, Word 132
catalogs, creating, Word 136–140
CDs, burning presentations to,
   PowerPoint 81–82
Cell Styles gallery, Excel 24
cells, table
   See also rows, columns
   calculating numeric data in,
      Word 74–75
   formatting and editing, Word 61–62
   splitting, merging, Word 72
   tabs within, Word 108–110
cells, worksheet
   adding comments, Excel 54
   clearing formula data, Excel 32
   copying formats between, Excel 48
   customizing styles, Excel 28
   editing and clearing data, Excel 24
   formatting, Excel 10
   formula error triangle, Excel 52
   formulas using addresses, Excel 44
   indenting text in, Excel 66
centering
   labels, Excel 18–19
   text, Word 13
   worksheets, Excel 28

changes, tracking in documents,
    Word 170–171
changing
    animation order, PowerPoint 67
    case of letters, Word 6
    fields to lookup fields, Access 56
    fonts, font styles, Word 12–13
    between list styles, Word 59
    section breaks, Word 118
    slide masters, PowerPoint 31
    table formatting, text, Word 61–62
    views, Access 10
character spacing, Word 106
characters
    counting, Word 154
    drop caps, Word 118
    small caps, Word 114
    wildcard, Access 42
charting
    expense data, Excel 120–126
    mutual fund data, Excel 128–131
    sales data, Excel 116–119
    stock prices, Excel 132–133
charts
    animating, PowerPoint 66–67
    creating and formatting,
        Excel 116–119
    creating stock, Excel 132–133
    importing as linked objects,
        PowerPoint 89
    using in presentations, PowerPoint 43,
        PowerPoint 62
check registers, creating, Excel 56–57
citations, report, Word 154–161
clearing
    cell data, Excel 24
    formats, Excel 42
    formula data, Excel 32
clip art
    See also media
    described, inserting, Word 88–89
    editing, PowerPoint 21
    inserting in presentations,
        PowerPoint 18
Clipboard, copying and pasting using,
    Excel 46, Word 8
clips, using media, PowerPoint 52–55
colors
    adding background to Web pages,
        Word 190
    adding page background, Word 125
    adding sheet tab, Excel 102
    changing border, Excel 82
    changing font, Word 12–13

changing in slide shows, PowerPoint 14
changing tones, Excel 24
filling rows with, Excel 10
filling shapes with, Word 95
filling worksheet columns, Excel 98–99
text highlight, Word 14–15
using in magazine articles, Word 20–21
using in slide shows, PowerPoint 39
using in tables, Word 62
using in text boxes, Word 101
columns, datasheet
    displaying overflow text, Excel 58
    freezing headings, Excel 56
    inserting, Excel 66
    selecting for reports, Access 78
    widening, Access 32
columns, text
    creating tabular, Word 85
    creating, using, formatting, Word 64–65
    inserting breaks, Word 128–131
    in Word tables, Word 62
columns, worksheet, hiding, Excel 84
comma (,), and number format, Excel 22
comments
    adding to documents, Word 170
    adding to presentations,
        PowerPoint 79–80
    adding to worksheet cells, Excel 54
commissions, and sales reports,
    Excel 94–95
compacting databases, Access 106–107
composing
    at the computer, Word 10, Word 31
    and formatting résumés, Word 44–46
conference programs, creating,
    Word 79–82
continuous section breaks, inserting,
    Word 67–68, Word 137,
    Word 171–172
controls
    adding to reports, Access 86–87
    creating forms with calculated,
        Access 48–52
    described, adding to forms,
        Access 44–46
    label. See label controls
    using on forms, Access 46
converting
    text to upper- or lowercase, Excel 58
    Word documents into Web pages,
        Word 189
copy notation in letters, Word 27
copying
    See also backing up

data for import, Access 96–97
data using Clipboard, Excel 46
formatting, Word 14–15, Word 20
objects, Word 92
objects for import, PowerPoint 89
and pasting data between applications,
    Excel 136
and pasting formulas, Excel 10
and pasting text, Word 8–9
presentations to CDs,
    PowerPoint 81–82
slides in presentations, PowerPoint 7
corporate dining menus, creating,
    Word 106–107
corporate identity materials,
    Integration 28–29
correspondence described, Word 25
Count function, Excel 48, Excel 58
counting
    values in database records, Access 62–63
    words in documents, Word 154
cover letters, Word 47
cover pages for reports, Word 157,
    Word 159
creating
    account statements, Excel 46–47
    articles, Word 170–173
    asset records, Excel 60–61
    balance sheets, Excel 106–109
    bibliographies, Word 157–158,
        Word 161
    billings and revenue analyses,
        Excel 82–83
    billings, listings analysis tables,
        Excel 70–73
    brochures, Word 132–136
    budgets, Excel 66–69
    business letters, Word 24–34
    catalogs, Word 136–140
    charts, Excel 116–119
    composing at the computer, Word 10,
        Word 31
    database files, Access 16–18
    document headers and footers,
        Word 144
    documents from templates,
        Word 36–41
    drop caps, Word 118
    event programs, Word 79
    financial reports, Integration 30–33
    flyers, Word 88–96
    forms, Access 38–47, Word 87–88
    handbooks, Word 166–169
    hyperlinks, Excel 90, Word 188

income analysis statements,
     Excel 102–105
income statement analyses,
     Excel 78–79
income statements, Excel 74–75
investment analyses, Excel 86–87
invitations, Word 114–115
invoices, Excel 4–5, Excel 8–9
ledger accounts, Excel 42–45
lists, Word 56–66
mailing labels, Word 29–30, Access 80
mass mailings, Word 49–53
meeting agendas, minutes,
     Word 56–66
memos, Word 185–187
newsletters, Word 118–126
payments journals, Excel 56–57
personal business letters, Word 33–34
personnel plans, Excel 10–15
petty cash registers, Excel 58–59
photo albums, PowerPoint 68–69
presentations. *See* presentations
programs, Word 79
project schedules, Word 78
projected cash flow statements,
     Excel 16–19
purchase journals, Excel 54–55
purchase orders, Excel 22–27
queries. *See* queries
Quick Parts entries, Word 29
rate schedules, Word 74–75
records lists, Word 76–77
relationships between tables,
     Access 70–71
relationships in open databases,
     Access 34–36
reports. *See* reports
résumés, Word 40–41
revenue forecasts and analyses,
     Excel 84–85
sales analyses, Excel 80–81
sales and commissions report,
     Excel 94–95
sales invoices, Excel 28–33,
     Excel 36–37
sales journals, Excel 52–53
schedules, Word 72–75
section breaks, Word 118
SmartArt graphics, PowerPoint 44
stock charts, Excel 132–133
styles, Word 167
tables. *See* tables
tables of content, Word 85–86
text boxes, Word 100–101

text columns, Word 64–65, Word 119
time cards, Excel 34–35
watermarks, Word 128
Web pages from templates,
     Word 192–193
Websites, Word 194–197
credits, in ledger accounts, Excel 44
Crosstab Query Wizard, Access 60,
     Access 62
cue marks, adding to presentations,
     PowerPoint 74
currency number format, Excel 22
current date
     See also dates
     entering, Excel 86
     inserting, Word 24
custom templates, creating, Word 42–43
customer form, creating, Access 40–41
customizing
     animations, PowerPoint 19
     presentation handouts, notes,
          PowerPoint 72–75
     queries, Access 66–67
     report headers, footers, Access 84
     shapes, Word 92
     slide shows, PowerPoint 39–40
     tabs, Word 85

D

data
     appending to existing tables,
          Access 98–99
     calculating in reports, Access 86–87
     changing orientation, Excel 120
     copying and pasting with Clipboard,
          Excel 46
     editing, clearing cell data, Excel 24
     entering in series, Excel 28
     entering in tables, Access 17
     exporting, Access 104–105
     finding and replacing in tables,
          Access 54–55
     finding and replacing in worksheets,
          Excel 108
     formatting as tables, Excel 70
     importing as linked objects,
          PowerPoint 89
     importing Excel, into tables,
          Access 98–99
     importing from other databases,
          Access 96–97
     integrating between applications,
          Excel 136
     referencing between workbooks,
          Excel 90

data entry
     controlling with input masks,
          Access 28–31
     using AutoComplete feature, Excel 22
     using AutoFill feature, Excel 28
data source documents, Word 49–50,
     Word 51
data types, Access 16, Access 22,
     Access 24
database objects, dependencies between,
     Access 108
database records, doing calculations
     with, Access 62–63
databases
     backing up, defragmenting,
          compacting, Access 106–107
     creating files from templates,
          Access 16–18
     creating relationships between tables,
          Access 34–36
     creating suppliers, Integration 6
     customer, Integration 39–40
     described, using, Access 4–5
     importing objects from other,
          Access 96–97
     importing Word table data into,
          Access 100–101
     new employee, Integration 16–17
     queries and reports, Access 7–8
     relationships in, Access 10–11
Datasheet view, Access 10
     creating tables in, Access 22–23
     sorting tables in, Access 56–57
datasheets
     See also worksheets
     printing, Access 32
     viewing new data in, Access 38
Date & Time button, Controls group,
     Access 46
Date and Time feature, using, Word 24
dates
     adding to forms, Access 46
     entering into fields with input masks,
          Access 32
     placeholder, Word 38
     setting date format, Excel 4
     updating in documents, Word 24
     using in calculations, Excel 86
debts, in ledger accounts, Excel 44
defragmenting databases,
     Access 106–107
deleting
     See also removing
     database fields, Access 16

database records, Access 17,
  Access 42–43
slides from presentations, PowerPoint 7
table rows, columns, Excel 72
worksheet cell comments, Excel 54
worksheet columns, rows, Excel 66
delimited text, Access 100
dependencies, viewing object, Access 108
depreciation, calculating, Excel 60–61
descending sorts, Access 56, Word 59
Design view
  creating queries in, Access 60
  creating tables in, Access 24
  query, report, Access 13–14, Access 82
  table, Access 10–11
designing
  advertisements, Word 18–19
  invitations, Word 115–116
  menus, Word 112–113
  slide shows, PowerPoint 8
  Web pages, Word 190
destination
  files and linked objects,
    PowerPoint 89–90
  files described, Word 182
diagrams, using SmartArt, Word 112–113
Dictionary, accessing, Word 165
direct-mail advertisements, creating,
  Word 100–101
discounts, calculating, Access 102
displaying
  control properties, Access 86
  grouped data in reports, Access 88–89
  hidden worksheet columns, Excel 84
  nonprinting codes, Word 6
documents
  See also specific document type
  agendas, creating, Word 56–63
  bibliographies, Word 157–158,
    Word 161
  columns in, Word 166
  comments, adding, Word 170
  creating from templates, Word 36–43
  data source, Word 49–50, Word 51
  e-mailing, Word 45–46
  embedding portion of file in,
    Excel 136
  headers and footers, Word 144
  inserting clip art into, Word 88–89
  inserting continuous section breaks,
    Word 67–68
  inserting date and/or time, Word 24
  inserting files into, Word 106
  inserting page numbers, Word 144

inserting Quick Parts into, Word 29
magnifying (zooming), Word 6
merging, Word 49
opening, Word 4–5
paragraph indents, Word 147–152
reports. See reports
saving as templates, Word 42
saving as Web pages, Word 188–195
searching with Find feature, Word 170
tables in, Word 61–62
thank you letters, composing,
  Word 11–12
tracking changes in, Word 170–171
Word Count feature, Word 154
zooming, Word 6
dollar sign ($) and absolute references,
  Excel 74
dot leaders, Word 85
downloading
  template presentations, PowerPoint 56
  templates, Excel 36, Word 135
  Web page templates, Word 192
drafts, Word 10
drawing
  lines, Word 95
  shapes, Word 92
drop caps, creating, Word 118
duplicate queries, Access 64–65

E

e-mail
  attachments, Word 47
  described, Word 45
e-mailing
  business letters, Word 45–46
  presentations, PowerPoint 92–93
  worksheets, Excel 30
editing
  business letters, Word 29–30
  charts, PowerPoint 44
  database records, Access 42–43
  document text, Word 147
  embedded worksheets, Excel 136
  field names, data types in Design view,
    Access 22
  formatting, Word 16–19
  formulas, Excel 52
  hyperlinks, Excel 90
  imported objects, Word 182
  lists, Word 56–57
  presentation comments,
    PowerPoint 79
  presentations, PowerPoint 21–22
  relationships, Access 73–75

report layouts, designs, Access 78
templates, Word 42
text box placeholders, PowerPoint 9
WordArt, Word 89
effects
  See also special effects
  animation, PowerPoint 19
  embedded fonts, PowerPoint 82
  embedded, vs. linked objects,
    PowerPoint 89
embedding
  charts in worksheets, Excel 117,
    Excel 125
  tables in reports, Word 182–184
  worksheets into business plans,
    Excel 136–138
employee benefits summaries, creating,
  Integration 19–20
employee newsletters, creating,
  Integration 22
employee orientation, creating,
  Integration 15–26
Encarta Dictionary, Word 165
enclosure/attachment notation in letters,
  Word 27
Encyclopedia, accessing, Word 165
[End] key, Word 6
ending presentations, PowerPoint 5
endnotes, Word 155, Word 164
envelopes
  creating with Mail Merge, Word 51
  formatting, Word 24–26
equal sign (=)
  in 3-D references, Excel 102
  in expressions, Access 48
  in formulas, Excel 10
errors, formula, Excel 52, Excel 110
Euros, Word 74
evaluating slide shows, PowerPoint 8
event brochures, creating, Word 128–131
event programs, creating, Word 79
Excel 2007
  charts. See charts
  creating folder for files, Excel 4
  exporting Access tables to,
    Access 102–103
  importing into Access tables,
    Access 98–99
  reports. See reports
  worksheets. See worksheets
expense data, charting and analyzing,
  Excel 120–126
expense reports, creating,
  Integration 12–13

exporting
  Access tables to Excel, Access 102–103
  queries to Word, Access 104–105
  slides, presentations to Word,
    PowerPoint 87–88
express movement keys, Word 6
Expression Builder, Access 90, Access 92,
  Access 94
expressions
  in calculated controls, Access 48
  creating using Expression Builder,
    Access 90–94
  specifying field criteria in queries,
    Access 66–67

F

fax covers, creating, Integration 8,
  Word 42–43
fields
  adding to forms, Access 44–45
  changing to lookup, Access 56
  creating tables with lookup,
    Access 26–27
  and data types, Access 16
  performing calculations with,
    Access 62–63
  and table relationships, Access 10–11
  text, sizing, Access 19–20
  unique identifier, Access 5
  using calculated, Access 8, Access 68–69
file formats
  See also saving
  MHTML format, saving documents in,
    Word 189
  PDF (Portable Document Format),
    Excel 30
  Rich Text Format (.rtf), Access 104
files
  adding property information to,
    Word 185
  attaching to e-mails, Word 47
  burning presentations to CD,
    PowerPoint 81–82
  database. *See* database files
  embedding, Excel 136
  inserting into documents, Word 106
  linking, Excel 141
  saving in PDF format, Excel 30
  saving to earlier versions of Access,
    Access 108
filling
  formulas horizontally, Excel 48
  shapes with color, Word 95
filtering
  data using AutoFilter, Excel 70–71

records, Access 58–59
financial reports, creating,
  Integration 30–33
Find and Replace feature
  using in worksheets, Excel 108
  using on table, Access 54–55
Find Duplicates Query Wizard,
  Access 60, Access 64–65
Find feature, using, Word 170
Find Unmatched Query Wizard,
  Access 60
finding
  See also searching
  data, records, Access 42
  and replacing data in tables,
    Access 54–55
first-line indents, Word 151
flipping objects, PowerPoint 35
flyers
  creating, Word 88–89
  creating with special effects,
    Word 90–91
  creating with tear-off, Word 92–94
  formatting, Word 95–96
folders, creating for Excel files, Excel 4
fonts
  changing, Word 12–13
  changing size in template, Word 38
  formatting, Excel 22–23
  for headers, Word 145
  increasing, decreasing size, Excel 24
  limiting number of, Word 16
  small caps, using, Word 114
  when to use embedded, PowerPoint 82
footers
  adding slide numbers,
    PowerPoint 30–33
  customizing report, Access 84
  expanding, contracting form,
    Access 48
  in multi-page reports, Excel 102
  using in documents, Word 144
  using in worksheets, Excel 74–75
  viewing form, Access 46
footnotes, inserting, Word 155, Word 162,
  Word 164
Form object, creating, Access 38
Form view, Access 10
Form Wizard, Access 40, Access 44,
  Access 51, Access 90
Format Painter
  copying formats using, Excel 48–49
  copying formatting using, Word 14,
    Word 20

formatting
  See also specific document type
  advertisements, Word 102–103
  agendas, Word 56–57
  annual reports, Word 176–180
  AutoFormat As You Type feature,
    Word 6
  balance sheets, Excel 108–109
  budgets, Excel 68–69
  business letters, Word 24–34,
    Word 144–152
  business plans, Integration 34–35,
    Word 174–175
  cells, Excel 10
  chart legends, Excel 123
  charts, PowerPoint 44, Excel 120–121
  copying, Word 14–15
  editing, Word 16–19
  footnotes, endnotes, Word 164
  forms, Access 42
  handbooks, Word 166–169
  letters with special notations,
    Word 27–28
  mailing labels, Access 80
  negative numbers, Excel 66
  newsletters, Word 125–127
  numbers as numeric labels,
    Excel 74–75
  personal business letters, Word 33–34
  presentation notes masters,
    PowerPoint 73
  programs, Word 81–82
  reports, Access 78–79, Word 154–165
  results of calculations, Access 68
  section breaks, Word 166
  slides with slide masters,
    PowerPoint 30–31
  SmartArt graphics, PowerPoint 44
  styles, Word 166
  tables, Word 61–62
  text, Word 12–13
  text columns, Word 64–65,
    Word 118–119, Word 128–131,
    Word 166
  text fonts, styles, colors, Excel 22–23
forms
  See also specific form
  adding calculated controls to,
    Access 51–52
  adding controls to, Access 44–45
  creating with calculated controls,
    Access 48–50
  described, creating, Word 87–88
  described, using, Access 4–5

filtering data in, Access 58–59
and subforms, Access 90
views of, Access 10–11
formulas
See also expressions
copying and pasting, Excel 10
editing, Excel 52
entering by selection, Excel 12
error triangle, managing, Excel 110
inputting with symbols and cell
addresses, Excel 44
inserting functions in, Excel 48
relative and absolute references,
Excel 74–75
using in spreadsheets, Access 102–103
using mathematical operators, Excel 52
using parentheses to prioritize,
Excel 60–61
fractions, formatting, Excel 86
Freeform line style, Word 95
freezing column headings, row labels,
Excel 56
Full Screen button, View tab, Excel 6–7
functions
See also specific function
date, Excel 86
frequently used, Excel 48
using aggregate, Access 68

G

.gif files, PowerPoint 52
grammar, correcting with AutoCorrect,
Word 4
graphics
See also images, pictures
charts. *See* charts
clip art. *See* clip art
inserting into worksheets, Excel 106,
Excel 128–131
inserting on Web pages, Word 190
layering, grouping, Word 92–93
SmartArt. *See* SmartArt
graphs, importing, embedding in reports,
Word 182
grayscale
printing in, PowerPoint 14
viewing presentations in,
PowerPoint 15
greater than (>), in expressions, Access 66
Greeting Line merge code, Word 50
Grid and Guides feature, PowerPoint 40
gridlines, adding to worksheets,
Excel 76–77
grids, snapping objects to,
PowerPoint 40

grouping
objects, graphics, Word 92–93
records for calculations, Access 68
records in reports, Access 82–83
and upgrouping objects, PowerPoint 35
worksheets, Excel 80

H

handbooks, creating and formatting,
Word 166–169
handouts
enhancing presentations with,
PowerPoint 72–75
printing presentations as,
PowerPoint 15
headers
customizing report, Access 84
expanding, contracting form, Access 48
in multi-page reports, Excel 102
using in documents, Word 144–145
using in worksheets, Excel 74–75
viewing form, Access 46
headings, freezing column, Excel 56
hiding
slides in presentations, PowerPoint 21
worksheet columns, Excel 84
highlighting text, Word 14–15
[Home] key, Word 6
home pages, Word 190, Word 194
horizontal alignment ob tables, Word 62
HTML (Hypertext Markup Language)
and Web documents, Word 188
hyperlinks
See also linking
activating, PowerPoint 23
adding to worksheets, Excel 100–101
linking documents with, Word 188
in templates, Word 192
using, inserting, Excel 90

I

icons, and objects, Access 4
ID numbers, sorting by, Access 56
IF statements in formulas, Excel 94–95
illustrations
See also graphics, images, pictures
adding to worksheets, Excel 128
using SmartArt, Word 112
images
See also clip art, graphics, pictures
adding captions, Word 132
changing with special effects, Word 90
rotating, Word 89
Import Excel spreadsheet button,
Access 98

importing
Excel data into Access tables,
Access 98–99
objects from other databases,
Access 96–97
tables as embedded objects, Word 182
Word contact lists, Access 100–101
income analysis statements
creating, Excel 102–103
creating quarterly, Excel 104–105
income statements
analyses, Excel 78–79, Excel 112–113
creating, Excel 74–75
indenting
paragraphs, Word 147–152
tables in cells, Excel 66
Input Mask Wizard, Access 28
input masks
adding to tables, Access 28–31
using, Access 19
Insert text from File feature, Word 106
inserting
breaks in text columns, Word 128–131
captions, Word 132
clip art into documents, Word 88–89
clip art into presentations,
PowerPoint 18
columns in tables, Word 61–62
continuous section breaks,
Word 67–68, Word 137
cue marks to presentations,
PowerPoint 74
current date and time, Excel 86
date and/or time into documents,
Word 24
files into documents, Word 106
footnotes, endnotes, Word 162
functions in formulas, Excel 48
graphics into worksheets, Excel 106,
Excel 128–131
nonbreaking spaces, Word 6
page numbers, Word 144,
Word 162–163
Quick Parts into documents, Word 29
section breaks, Word 171–172
slides from other presentations,
PowerPoint 84–86
spaces, Word 4
symbols, Word 16–17
table rows, columns, Excel 72
tables or charts in presentations,
PowerPoint 43
WordArt, Word 89
worksheet columns or rows, Excel 66

insertion point, moving around document, Word 6

integration
  of charts into Word documents, Excel 139–140
  of data between applications, Excel 136
  described, Word 182
  projects. *See* Projects

IntelliMouse, using, Word 6

internal citations, Word 155, Word 157–160, Word 162, Word 165

Internet Explorer, opening Web pages in, Word 189

inventory form, creating, Access 44–45

investment analyses, charting mutual fund data, Excel 128–131

invitations, creating, Word 114–116, Integration 40

invoices
  creating for professional services, Excel 4–5
  creating, proofing from existing file, Excel 8–9
  creating sales, Excel 28–33
  previewing and printing, Excel 6–7

italicizing text, Excel 4

itineraries, creating, Integration 9, Word 70–71

J

job application letters, Word 47

job interview follow-up letters, Word 11

journals
  creating payment, Excel 56–57
  creating purchase, Excel 54–55
  creating sales, Excel 52–53

K

kerning characters, Word 106

kiosks
  preparing presentations for, PowerPoint 76–78
  showing slides in, PowerPoint 8

L

label controls
  adding titles, captions to forms with, Access 46
  modifying, Access 84

Label Wizard, creating reports using, Access 80–81

labels
  See also captions
  adding to charts, Excel 116–117

aligning, Excel 4

centering over cell range, Excel 18–19

changing alignment, Excel 4

creating mailing, Word 29–30

creating with Mail Merge, Word 51

formatting numbers as numeric, Excel 74–75

and printing large worksheets, Excel 100–101

worksheet rows, freezing, Excel 56

Labels feature, Word 29

landscape orientation, Word 128

layering objects, graphics, Word 92–93

Layout view, Access 10, Access 42–43, Access 82

layouts
  of forms, Access 40
  presentation, PowerPoint 9–10, PowerPoint 62
  slide, PowerPoint 16
  using worksheet backgrounds, Excel 78

ledger accounts
  creating, Excel 42–45
  linking trial balance and schedules, Excel 90–91

legends, chart, Excel 116, Excel 123

less than (<), in expressions, Access 66

letterhead, creating, Word 24–26, Word 42–43

letters
  business. *See* business letters
  changing case, Word 6
  characters. *See* characters
  cover, Word 47
  creating personal business, Word 33–34
  format, Word 25
  new hire congratulations, Integration 18–19
  salutations in, Integration 7, Word 38
  thank you, Word 11–12

liabilities, in ledger accounts, Excel 44

line spacing
  changing, Word 24
  in reports, Word 154
  setting, Word 20
  in templates, Word 38

lines, counting with Word Count feature, Word 154

linked objects
  described, creating, Word 182
  memo with linked table, Word 185–187
  vs. embedded objects, PowerPoint 89

linking
  custom shows, PowerPoint 40
  files, Excel 141
  schedule data to trial balance, Excel 90–91

listings analysis tables, creating, Excel 72–73

lists
  creating bulleted, numbered, multilevel, Word 56–66
  creating records, Word 76–77
  sorting, Word 59–60

logos, inserting, Excel 128

lookup fields
  changing fields to, Access 56
  controlling data input using, Access 30–31
  creating tables with, Access 26–27

Lookup Wizard, Access 26–27, Access 31

looping clips in slide shows, PowerPoint 53

lowercase, changing letters to, Word 6

Ltd, Word 74

M

magnifying (zooming) documents, Word 6

Mail Merge feature, using, Word 49, Word 51

Mail Merge Wizard, Word 49–52

mailers, creating newsletters with, Word 121–124

mailing labels, creating, Access 80, Word 29–30

mailing notations, Word 27

many-to-many relationships, Access 70

margins
  changing, Word 24
  report, Word 154

mass mailings, creating, Word 49, Word 51–53

masthead of newsletters, Word 119

mathematical operators, using, Excel 52

Max function, Excel 48–49

media, using in slide shows, PowerPoint 52–53

MEDIAN function, Excel 48–49

meeting agendas, creating, Word 56–63

meeting minutes, creating, Word 64–66

memos
  creating, Word 36–37
  creating from templates, Integration 5
  creating with linked tables, Word 185–187
  pasting worksheets into, Excel 134–135

menus
  creating corporate dining,
    Word 106–107
  creating restaurant, Word 108–111
  designing, Word 112–113
merging
  documents, Word 51
  and sorting, Word 76–77
  table rows, Word 72
MHTML format, saving documents in,
  Word 189
Microsoft Clip Art and Media Web
  page, Excel 128
Microsoft Office Online, downloading
  templates, Excel 36, Word 135
Min function, Excel 48
Mini toolbar, formatting options with,
  Excel 22
minus sign (−), calculating differences,
  Excel 16–17
minutes, creating, Word 64–66
mixed numbers, formatting, Excel 86
modifying
  See also changing
  table design, Access 34–36
  templates, Word 42
money values, formatting for commas,
  Excel 96
movie collection form, creating,
  Access 38–39
movies, playing in slide shows,
  PowerPoint 53
moving
  chart legends, Excel 123
  within forms, Access 38
  placeholders in slide shows,
    PowerPoint 9
  presentation comments, PowerPoint 79
  range of cells, Excel 16
  slides in presentations, PowerPoint 7
  text, Word 8–9
  between workbooks, Excel 46
multi-table queries, creating,
  Access 70–71, Access 92
multilevel lists, creating, Word 56–57
mutual fund data, charting,
  Excel 128–131

N

names of icons and objects, Access 4
navigating
  within forms, Access 38
  presentations, PowerPoint 4–6
  using form toolbar, Access 38–39
navigation bar, Website, Word 194

Navigation Pane, Access 4–5
negative numbers, formatting, Excel 66
new employee orientation, creating,
  Integration 15–26
new hires Web page, creating,
  Integration 23
newsletters
  creating, Word 121–124
  creating employee, Integration 22
  formatting, Word 125–127
  masthead of, Word 119
nonbreaking spaces, inserting, Word 6
nonprinting codes, displaying, Word 6
notations, formatting letters with,
  Word 27–28
notes, speaker, PowerPoint 72
nudging objects, PowerPoint 21
number formats
  for ledger accounts, Excel 42
  setting with Mini toolbar, Excel 22
  worksheet, Excel 22
number sign (#) and overflow values,
  Excel 28
numbered lists, creating, Word 56–57
numbers
  adding page, Word 144
  adding slide, PowerPoint 30–33
  formatting as numeric labels,
    Excel 74–75
  formatting mixed, Excel 86
  formatting negative, Excel 66
  and money values, Excel 96
numeric data, calculating in tables,
  Word 74–75
numeric labels, Excel 74–75

O

objects
  See also specific object
  creating animations with,
    PowerPoint 19
  database, Access 4
  dependencies, Access 108
  embedding, Excel 136
  formatting in PowerPoint,
    PowerPoint 32
  grouping and ungrouping,
    PowerPoint 35
  importing as embedded vs. linked,
    PowerPoint 89
  importing, embedding in reports,
    Word 182
  linked, Word 182
  nudging, PowerPoint 21
  positioning, PowerPoint 40

rotating, flipping, PowerPoint 35
Office Online, downloading templates,
  Excel 36, Word 135
one-to-many relationships, Access 70
one-to-one relationships, Access 70
opening
  database files, Access 4
  documents, Word 4–5
  presentations, PowerPoint 4–5
  templates, Excel 32
  Web pages in browsers, Word 189
operators, mathematical, Excel 52
organizing a business trip (Project 1),
  Integration 3–13
orientation
  of chart data, Excel 120
  new employee, creating,
    Integration 15–26
  page, Word 128
outlines
  around text boxes, Word 101
  formatting, printing presentations as,
    PowerPoint 23–26

P

Page Break Preview button, View tab,
  Excel 68
Page Layout View, Excel 6–7
page numbers, inserting, Word 144,
  Word 162–163
pages
  adding borders around, Word 125
  cover, Word 157, Word 159
  ending, Word 144
  fitting large worksheet on, Excel 56
  orienting, changing size, Word 100,
    Word 128
  Web. *See* Web pages
paragraphs
  counting, Word 154
  creating, Word 36
  drop caps, creating, Word 118
  indenting, Word 147–152
parallel columns, creating documents
  with, Word 64
paraphrased text, Word 155
parentheses (( )), prioritizing formula
  calculations, Excel 60–61
paste link feature, Excel 141
Paste Special feature, Excel 78,
  PowerPoint 89, Excel 139–140
pasting
  and copying text, Word 8–9
  data between applications, Excel 136
  importing. *See* importing

worksheets into memos, Excel 134–135

payments journals, creating, Excel 56–57

payrolls

creating, Integration 25–26,
Excel 48–51

using Internet paycheck calculator,
Excel 50

PDF (Portable Document Format),
Excel 30

pen tool, annotations presentations with,
PowerPoint 73–75

percentages

in balance sheet analyses, Excel 112

calculating, Excel 66

personal business letters, creating,
Word 33–34

personnel plans

arranging, formatting, Excel 14–15

creating and formatting, Excel 10–13

photo albums, creating,
PowerPoint 68–69

photos

See also graphics, images, pictures

including on résumés, Word 40–41

picture styles, Word 90

pictures

See also clip art, graphics, images

inserting onto slides, PowerPoint 21–22

watermarks, Word 128

pie charts, Excel 117, Excel 121

PivotChart view, Access 10

PivotTable view, Access 10

placeholders

adding animations to, PowerPoint 67

notes, PowerPoint 72

in slides, PowerPoint 9, PowerPoint 18

template, Word 36, Word 38

planning presentations, PowerPoint 5–6

points (character spacing), Word 106

positioning

graphics on worksheets, Excel 130

objects with guides, PowerPoint 40

postcards, direct-mail, Word 101

postmarks, adding, Word 121, Word 124

pound sign (#) and overflow values,
Excel 28

PowerPoint 2007

See also *presentations, slide shows*

starting, PowerPoint 4

.pptx files, PowerPoint 10

presentations

See also slide shows

adding, printing comments,
PowerPoint 79–80

adding slides to, PowerPoint 9

business plan, Integration 41–42

copying to CDs, PowerPoint 81–82

creating, PowerPoint 9–11,
Integration 11–12

creating and printing,
PowerPoint 14–17

creating from templates,
PowerPoint 56–61

creating photo albums,
PowerPoint 68–69

creating slide masters, PowerPoint 39

creating to sell products,
PowerPoint 35–38

creating to sell services,
PowerPoint 39–42

creating with charts, SmartArt
and media, PowerPoint 52–55,
PowerPoint 62–65

delivering persuasive, PowerPoint 53

developing from scratch, PowerPoint 24

e-mailing, PowerPoint 92–93

editing, PowerPoint 21–22

employee orientation, Integration 24

enhancing, PowerPoint 18–22,
PowerPoint 30–38

enhancing with animated charts,
SmartArt, PowerPoint 66–67

enhancing with handouts,
PowerPoint 72–75

exporting to Word, PowerPoint 87–88

inserting slides from other,
PowerPoint 84–86

opening, navigating, PowerPoint 4–6

page setup, orientation, PowerPoint 7

preparing for kiosk, PowerPoint 76–78

printing as outlines, PowerPoint 23–26

saving as templates, PowerPoint 48

saving as Web pages, PowerPoint 92–93

using charts, SmartArt in,
PowerPoint 43, PowerPoint 62

press release, preparing, Integration 36

previewing

formatting changes, Word 16

invoices prior to printing, Excel 6–7

presentations as Web pages,
PowerPoint 93

price quotation templates, Excel 38–39

primary keys

changing or removing, Access 24

in databases, Access 16

setting in Design view, Access 22

Print Preview for reports, Access 82

printing

chart sheets, Excel 118

datasheets, Access 32

forms, Access 38

invoices, Excel 6–7

large worksheets, Excel 100

presentations, PowerPoint 14–15

presentations as outlines,
PowerPoint 23–26

sizing worksheets for, Excel 68

sorted tables, Access 56

table relationships, Access 34

workbooks, Excel 80

product brochures, creating,
Word 132–134

product catalogs, creating, Word 137–138

products, presentations that sell,
PowerPoint 35–38

programs

formatting, Word 81–82

workshop, creating, Integration 20–21

project schedules, creating, Word 78

projected cash flow statements, creating,
Excel 16–19

Projects

#1 organizing a business trip,
Integration 3–13

#2 New Employee Orientation,
Integration 15–26

#3 Starting a New Business,
Integration 27–43

proofreader's marks, Word 4–8

properties

displaying control, Access 86

form control's, Access 46

setting field, Access 22

Properties feature, Word 185

publishing

income statement analyses, Excel 78–79

presentations to the Web,
PowerPoint 93

workbooks to the Web, Excel 76–77

pull quotes, Word 171

purchase journals, creating, Excel 54–55

purchase orders, creating and formatting,
Excel 22–27

Q

quarterly income analysis statements,
creating, Excel 104–105

queries

adding calculated fields to,
Access 68–69

creating, Access 106

creating append, Access 98–99

creating multi-table, Access 70–71

creating using wizards, Access 60–65

crosstab, Access 60, Access 62–63
described, using, Access 7–8
duplicates, unmatched, Access 64–65
exporting to Word, Access 104–105
specifying field criteria, Access 66–67
using for reports, Access 84–85
viewing from two, Access 90–91
views of, Access 13–14
Query Design view, Access 13–14,
   Access 66–67, Access 75
Query Wizards, Access 60–67
Quick Parts feature, Word 29
Quick Styles, Word, Word 167
Quick Table feature, Word 83
quotation marks ("")
   and IF statements, Excel 94
   text data values containing,
      Access 66–67
quotations
   formatting, Word 155
   pull quotes, Word 171

R

rate schedules, creating, Word 74–75
"Re:" in memos, Word 37
read-only files, copying presentations as,
   PowerPoint 81–82
real estate commissions, Excel 95
Recent Documents list, PowerPoint 4
records, asset, Excel 60–61
records, database
   calculations with, Access 62
   and database objects, Access 4
   deleting, Access 17
   entering, editing, deleting,
      Access 42–43
   grouping in reports, Access 82–83
   sorting, filtering, Access 56–59
   unique identifier fields, Access 4,
      Access 10
records lists, creating, Word 76–77
references, relative and absolute,
   Excel 74–75
registers
   creating check, Excel 56–57
   creating petty cash, Excel 58–59
   payroll, Excel 48
Rehearse Timings button,
   PowerPoint 76
relationships (database)
   correlating table data with, printing,
      Access 34
   between database tables, Access 11
   editing, Access 73–75

types of, Access 70–71
relative and absolute references,
   Excel 74–75
removing
   See also deleting
   primary keys, Access 24
   section breaks, Word 166
   table borders, Word 64
renaming worksheets, Excel 80
replacing, and finding, PowerPoint 35,
   Word 170
report Design view, Access 13–14
Report View, Access 82
Report Wizard, Access 82–83
reports
   adding calculated controls to,
      Access 86–87
   with citations, Word 154–161
   creating accounts receivable aging,
      Excel 60–61
   creating expense, Integration 12–13
   creating financial, Integration 30–33
   creating from queries, Access 84–85
   creating using Label Wizard,
      Access 80–81
   creating using Report button,
      Access 78–79
   creating using Report Wizard,
      Access 82–83
   creating with embedded tables,
      Word 182–184
   described, Access 78, Word 154
   described, using, Access 7–11
   formatting annual, Word 176–180
   formatting, with foot- and endnotes,
      Word 162–164
   formatting, with internal citations,
      Word 154–161
   headers and footers in multi-page,
      Excel 102
   linking charts, worksheets in annual,
      Excel 141–146
   printing relationships, Access 34
   researching, writing, formatting,
      Word 165
   using summary options in,
      Access 88–89
   views of, Access 13–14
Research feature, Word 165, Word 170
researching
   business trips, Integration 4
   new businesses, Integration 29–30
   writing, formatting reports, Word 165
resizing
   See also sizing

charts, Excel 117
columns and rows in tables,
   Word 61–62
form sections, Access 48
text boxes, Word 100–101
text in database tables, Access 19–20
restaurant menus, creating,
   Word 108–111
restricting data input with input masks,
   Access 28
résumés
   composing and formatting,
      Word 47–48
   creating from templates, Word 40–41
   submitting electronically, Word 44
revenue forecasts and analyses, creating,
   Excel 84–85
reviewing slide shows, PowerPoint 8
Ribbon
   See also specific tabs
   Table Tools Design and Layout tabs,
      Word 61
Rich Text Format, Access 104–105
rotating
   images, Word 89
   objects, PowerPoint 35
   text, Word 72
   text within text boxes, Word 100
rotation handles
   on graphics, Word 88
   on shapes, Word 92
ROUNDUP, ROUNDDOWN
   functions, Excel 96
row labels, freezing, Excel 56
rows, datasheet
   filling with color, Excel 10
   freezing, Excel 56
   inserting, deleting, Excel 72
rows, table
   calculating numeric data in,
      Word 74–75
   changing height, Word 85
   formatting, resizing, Word 61–62
   merging, Word 72
R.S.V.P., Word 116
.rtf files, Access 104
ruler, displaying, Word 24

S

salaries, creating analyses of increases,
   Excel 96–97
sales analyses, creating, Excel 80–81
sales and commissions reports, creating,
   Excel 94–95

sales data, charting and analyzing, Excel 116–119

sales invoices, creating, Excel 28–33, Excel 36–37

sales journals, creating, Excel 52–53

salutations in letters, Integration 7–8, Word 38

sans serif fonts, Word 12, Word 14, Word 17

Save As option
saving documents as Web pages, Word 189
saving file under different name, Word 5
saving queries, Access 66, Access 84
saving to earlier versions, Access 108

saving
documents as templates, Word 42
documents as Web pages, Word 189
files as templates, Excel 32
files in PDF format, Excel 30
files under different names, Word 5
presentations, PowerPoint 10
presentations as Web pages, PowerPoint 92–93
presentations to CDs, PowerPoint 81–82
queries, Access 7, Access 66–67
slide masters as templates, PowerPoint 48
workbooks as Web pages, Excel 76–77
worksheets as templates, Excel 50

scaling text, Word 106

schedules
creating activities, Word 72–73
creating event programs, Word 79
creating project, Word 78
creating rate, Word 74–75
trial balance and, Excel 90–91

Scribble line style, Word 95

script fonts, Word 12

searching
See also finding
for clip art, PowerPoint 18, Word 88
databases, Access 42
with Find feature, Word 170
for online templates, Word 36, Excel 38–39
using Find and Replace feature, Excel 108

section breaks
continuous, Word 67–68, Word 137, Word 171–172
formatting, Word 166

inserting, Word 67–68
using, Word 118

section headings, formatting, Excel 12–13

sections, report, Access 84

Send to Back button, Word 93

sending documents through e-mail, Word 45–46

separators, footnote, Word 162

serif fonts, Word 12, Word 17

services, presentations that sell, PowerPoint 39–42

setting
custom tabs, Word 85
indents, Word 147–152
margins, Word 24
primary keys, Access 22

shading
paragraph, Word 166
using in tables, Word 62, Word 64

shapes
drawing, inserting text into, Word 92
filling with color, Word 95

Shapes gallery, Word 95, Excel 128

Show/Hide button, Word 6

signatures, adding to e-mails, Word 45

Simple Query Wizard, Access 60–63

single file Web pages, Excel 76, PowerPoint 92

sizing
See also resizing
page, paper size, Word 100
worksheet columns, Excel 28
worksheet to one page, Excel 56
worksheets for printing, Excel 68

sizing handles
on graphics, Word 88, Excel 106
on text boxes, Word 100

Slide Master feature, using, PowerPoint 30–31

slide masters
saving presentations as, PowerPoint 48
using, PowerPoint 67

slide shows
See also presentations, slides
adding slide transitions, PowerPoint 18–19
creating self-running, PowerPoint 76–78
customizing, PowerPoint 39–40
evaluating, PowerPoint 8
formatting with slide masters, PowerPoint 30–31
using media clips in, PowerPoint 52–53

slide transitions, adding, PowerPoint 18–19

slides
See also slide shows
adding annotations, PowerPoint 74
adding media clips to, PowerPoint 52–55
adding to presentations, PowerPoint 23
exporting to Word, PowerPoint 87–88
inserting from other presentations, PowerPoint 84–86
inserting Word tables on, PowerPoint 90
moving, copying, deleting, PowerPoint 7
numbering, PowerPoint 30–33
in photo albums, PowerPoint 68
placeholders in, PowerPoint 9
printing, PowerPoint 15
and template presentations, PowerPoint 56

small caps, using, Word 114

Smart Tag triangle, Excel 52

SmartArt
adding to worksheets, reports, Excel 130
using in documents, Word 112
using in presentations, PowerPoint 43–44, PowerPoint 62

Snap objects to grid option, PowerPoint 40

sorting
data, Excel 70
data in tables, Word 76–77
database records, Access 56–57
lists, Word 59–60

sound
See also media
adding clips to slide shows, PowerPoint 52
adding to animations, PowerPoint 66–67

source files
described, Word 182
and linked objects, PowerPoint 89–90

sources
bibliographies, Word 157–158
report citations, Word 155

spaces, inserting, Word 4

spacing
between characters, changing, Word 106
line. See line spacing
paragraph indents, Word 147–152

speaker notes, PowerPoint 72, PowerPoint 74

speaking style in presentations, PowerPoint 5

special effects
  See also specific effect
  adding to presentations, PowerPoint 21
  animations. *See* animations
  changing images with, Word 90–91

spelling
  correcting with AutoCorrect, Word 4
  spell-checking worksheets, Excel 8

split forms, using, Access 40

splitting
  and sorting, Word 76–77
  table cells, Word 72

spreadsheets
  See also worksheets
  exporting database tables into, Access 102–103
  importing into databases, Access 98–99

Statistics tab, Advanced Properties, Word 185

Step-by-Step Mail Merge Wizard, Word 49–50, Word 51

stock prices, charting, Excel 132–133

Stock quotes, Word 165

styles
  See also specific style
  background, for presentations, PowerPoint 18
  bibliographical, Word 157–158
  described, using, Word 166–167
  form, Access 40
  formatting, Excel 22–23
  line, Word 95
  page border, Word 125
  picture, Word 90
  PowerPoint, PowerPoint 32
  table, Word 62
  Table Styles Gallery, Word 62
  template, Word 36
  text box, Word 101
  worksheet cell, Excel 24, Excel 28

subforms, using, Access 90–91

subject line in letters, Word 27

subtotaling columns, Excel 10

Sum function, Excel 48, Excel 58

summary expressions, Access 68–69

summary information, saving for document files, Word 185

summary options, using in reports, Access 88–89

summing

in tables, Excel 94

values in database records, Access 62–63

Switch Windows button, View tab, Excel 46

symbols, inserting, Word 12–13, Word 16–17

T

Table Design view, Access 16–18

tables
  adding captions, Word 132
  adding input masks to, Access 28–31
  borders, Word 64
  calculating numeric data in, Word 74–75
  creating calendars, Word 79–82
  creating from templates, Access 16–18
  creating in Datasheet view, Access 22–23
  creating in Design view, Access 24
  creating relationships between, Access 70–71
  creating tables of content, Word 85–86
  creating, using, Excel 70
  creating with lookup fields, Access 26–27
  described, using in documents, Word 61–62
  and designing Web pages, Word 190
  embedding in reports, Word 182–184
  entering data in, Access 17
  exported from Access to Word, Access 104
  exporting to Excel, Access 102–103
  formatting, resizing, Word 85
  importing database objects into, Access 96–97
  importing Excel data into, Access 98–99
  importing Word data into, Access 100–101
  linked, Word 185–187
  locating and replacing data in, Access 54–55
  modifying design of, Access 34–36
  Quick Table feature, Word 83
  relating in Relationships window, Access 90–91
  resizing text in, Access 19–20
  sorting, Access 56–57
  sorting data in, Word 76–77
  splitting, merging cells, Word 72
  tabs within cells, Word 108–110
  using for product catalogs, Word 137

using in presentations, PowerPoint 43

using on Web pages, Word 103

views of, Access 10–11

Word, inserting on slides, PowerPoint 90

tables of content
  creating, Word 85–86
  for reports, Word 158
  using as outlines, PowerPoint 23

tabs
  coloring, Excel 102
  creating in presentations, PowerPoint 24
  setting with leaders, Word 85
  within table cells, Word 108–110

tabular columns, creating, Word 85

taxes
  calculating withholding, Excel 48
  Internet tax calculators, Integration 25, Excel 50
  and investment analyses, Excel 86

tear-offs, creating flyers with, Word 92–94

template presentations, PowerPoint 56

templates
  creating brochures from, Word 128–131
  creating business letters from, Word 36–37
  creating custom, Word 42–43
  creating databases files from, Access 16–18
  creating memos from, Word 36–37
  creating payrolls from, Excel 50–51
  creating presentations from, PowerPoint 56–61
  creating reports from, Word 182
  creating résumés from, Word 40–41
  creating sales invoices from, Excel 32–33
  creating tables from, Access 16–18
  creating Web pages using, Word 192–193
  described, Word 36
  downloading Office, Word 135
  price quotation, Excel 38–39
  saving documents as, Word 42
  saving presentation designs or slide masters as, PowerPoint 48
  saving worksheets as, Excel 50
  viewing installed, Excel 34

text
  See also documents, pages
  adding to slides, PowerPoint 9
  aligning, centering, Word 13

aligning vertically, rotating, Word 72
bolding, italicizing, Excel 4
changing case of letters, Word 6
column formatting, Word 64–65,
   Word 118–119, Word 128–131,
   Word 166
converting to upper- or lowercase,
   Excel 58
correcting with AutoCorrect, Word 4
creating hyperlinks on, Word 188
creating WordArt, Word 89
delimited, importing, Access 100
drop caps, Word 118
editing, Word 147
entering in labels, Access 80
entering into speaker notes,
   PowerPoint 72
indenting, Excel 66
inserting in table cells, Word 61–62
moving, copying, moving, Word 8–9
Quick Parts feature, using, Word 29
resizing in database tables,
   Access 19–20
rotating within text boxes, Word 100
small caps, Word 114
spell-checking, Excel 8
tracking changes in, Word 170–171
using in IF statements, Excel 94
watermarks, Word 128
WordArt. *See* WordArt
wrapping around graphics, Word 88,
   Word 90
text box controls, Access 4, Access 51–52
text boxes, creating and using,
   Word 100–104
Text Highlight Color feature,
   Word 14–15
Text Wrapping button, Word 88
thank you letters, composing,
   Word 11–12
themes
   and colors, Excel 24
   template, Word 36
   using in presentations, PowerPoint 14,
      PowerPoint 18
Thesaurus, Word 165, Word 170
time cards, creating, Excel 34–35
time sheets, creating, Word 87–88
timetables
   creating calendars, Word 79–82
   schedules. *See* schedules
titles
   adding to charts, Excel 116–117
   creating two-line, Excel 118

togging between open workbooks,
   Excel 90
toolbars, form navigation, Access 38–39
Track Changes feature, Word 170–171
transitions, slide, PowerPoint 18–19
trial balance and schedules, Excel 90–91
typeface. *See* fonts

U

Undo button, Word 8, Excel 42
undoing actions, PowerPoint 7
ungrouping objects, PowerPoint 35
unique identifier field in tables, forms,
   Access 5, Access 10
unmatched queries, Access 64–65
updating
   data in forms, Access 48–50
   dates in documents, Word 24
   fields with Find and Replace, Access 54
uppercase, changing letters to, Word 6

V

values
   formatting for two decimal places,
      Excel 4–5
   overflow, and number signs (#),
      Excel 28
   relative and absolute references,
      Excel 74–75
values lists and lookup fields, Access 26
viewing
   all open workbooks, Excel 46
   data from two tables, queries,
      Access 90–91
   database objects, Access 10–11
   installed templates, Excel 34
   object dependencies, Access 108
   presentation notes masters,
      PowerPoint 73
   presentations, PowerPoint 5
   presentations in grayscale,
      PowerPoint 15
   relationships between tables,
      Access 70–71
   selected records by filtering,
      Access 58–59
   slide shows as outlines, PowerPoint 23
   table relationships, Access 70–73
views
   See also specific view
   form, Access 44
   report, Access 82
   using query and report, Access 13–14
   using table and form, Access 10–11

visual aids, using with presentations,
   PowerPoint 5

W

watermarks, creating, Word 128
Web pages
   creating from templates, Word 192–193
   creating new hires, Integration 23
   HTML and, Word 188
   navigating, Word 194
   saving documents as, Word 189
   saving presentations to,
      PowerPoint 92–93
   saving workbooks as, Excel 76–77
Web, publishing presentations to,
   PowerPoint 93
Websites
   See also specific site name
   creating, Integration 42–43
   creating hyperlinks to slides,
      PowerPoint 23–24
   described, creating, Word 194–197
   home pages, Word 190
   Microsoft Office Online, Word 135
   paycheck calculator, Excel 50
   using in internal citations, Word 165
wildcards, using in queries, Access 54
wizards
   See also specific wizard
   described, Word 49
Word 2007
   documents. *See* documents *or specific*
      document type
   importing Access tables, queries to,
      Access 104–105
   importing slides, presentations,
      PowerPoint 87–88
   integration with other applications.
      See integration
   tables. *See* tables
Word Count feature, Word 185
Word Quick Styles, Word 167
WordArt
   creating, editing, Word 89
   using in slides, PowerPoint 30–32
words
   counting, Word 154
   finding and replacing, PowerPoint 35
wordwrap, presenting words splitting,
   Word 6
workbooks
   adding worksheets to, Excel 84
   printing, Excel 80
   saving as Web pages, Excel 76–77

togging between open, Excel 90

viewing all open, Excel 46

worksheet cells

adding comments, Excel 54

clearing formula data, Excel 32

copying formats between, Excel 48

customizing styles, Excel 28

editing and clearing data, Excel 24

formatting, Excel 10

formula error triangle, Excel 52

indenting text in, Excel 66

inputting formulas with symbols and, Excel 44

worksheet columns, filling with color, Excel 98–99

worksheets

See also datasheets, worksheet cells

adding borders, Excel 16–17, Excel 82

adding hyperlinks, Excel 100–101

adding illustrations, shapes to, Excel 128–131

adding SmartArt, Excel 130

adding to workbooks, Excel 84

adding to worksheets, Excel 76–77

centering, Excel 28

completing accounting, Excel 98–99

creating using existing format, Excel 8–9

customizing cell styles, Excel 28

editing, clearing cell data, Excel 24

embedding charts in, Excel 117

embedding data, Excel 136

embedding into business plans, Excel 136–138

fitting on single page, Excel 56

grouping, Excel 80

hiding columns, Excel 84

importing as linked objects, PowerPoint 89

inserting, deleting rows or columns, Excel 72

inserting graphics, pictures into, Excel 106

linking summary totals between, Excel 90

pasting into memos, Excel 134–135

saving as templates, Excel 50

sizing for printing, Excel 68

spell-checking, Excel 8

viewing prior to printing, Excel 6–7

workshop programs, creating, Integration 20–21

Y

YEARFRAC calculations, Excel 86

Z

Zoom button, View tab, Excel 6–7

zooming (magnifying) documents, Word 6

PHOTO CREDITS